architectural drafting and design

architectural drafting and design

third edition

Ernest R. Weidhaas
The Pennsylvania State University

Allyn and Bacon, Inc.
Boston, London, Sydney, Toronto

Portions of this book first appeared in *Architectural Drafting and Construction,* by Ernest R. Weidhaas, copyright © 1974 by Allyn and Bacon, Inc.

Library of Congress Cataloging in Publication Data

Weidhaas, Ernest R
    Architectural drafting and design.

    Bibliography: p.
    Includes index.
    1. Architectural drawing.   2. Architecture—Designs and plans.   I. Title.
NA2700.W4   1977   720'.28   76-16077
ISBN 0-205-05624-5

ILLUSTRATION ACKNOWLEDGMENTS

Chapter 1: Figures 1–4, 6, 8, 9, 13, Frederick Post Company; 5, 11, 12, Gramercy Instruments; 7, Eagle Pencil Company; 10, 16–19, Rapidesign; 14, 15, 20, Keuffel & Esser Company; 21, International Business Machines Corporation; 22, The Rand Corporation. *Chapter 2:* Figure 2, G. E. Kidder Smith; 14, 18, 20, 21, 23, 25, Photo Alinari, Florence, Italy; 24, The British Travel and Holidays Association; 26, 27, Ewing Galloway; 43, Rolscreen Company; 44, 50, 51, Bethlehem Steel Corporation; 45, American Iron and Steel Institute (E. S. Preston & Associates, consulting engineers; General American Transportation Corporation, fabricators); 46, American Iron and Steel Institute (Edward Durell Stone and Associates, architects; Chicago Bridge and Iron Company, fabricators); 47, Gruen Associates, Architects-Engineers-Planners; 48, 52, 55, photos by Bill Hedrich, Hedrich-Blessing; 49, Bill Engdahl, Hedrich-Blessing; 56, Balthazar Korab, photographer. *Chapter 9:* Figures 1–3, Paratone, Inc.; 10, Jack W Risheberger, William L. Cunningham, James E. Black, and Richard I. Whidet; 13, 14, Letraset, Ltd. *Chapter 10:* Figure 15, The Construction Specifications Institute. *Chapter 11:* Figure 1, Andersen Corporation, Rolscreen Company, Bill Hedrich of Hedrich-Blessing; 2–4, 7, 13–16, Andersen Corporation; 5, Rolscreen Company (Bayview Terrace Apartments, Milwaukee, Wisc.: Rasche-Schroeder-Spransy and Associates, architects; Joseph P. Jensen Construction Company, builder); 6, Rolscreen Company (Irving Robinson, architect; Avery Construction Company, builder); 10, 12, Rolscreen Company. *Chapter 12:* Figures 6, 12, 16–18, Morgan Company; 7, Rolscreen Company; 8, Rolscreen Company (Starlite Village Restaurant and Lounge, Fort Dodge, Iowa: Eugene Haire, designer; Ackerman Company, builder); 9, Rolscreen Company (Penninsula Golf Club, San Mateo, Calif.); 14, 15, Educational Facilities Laboratories (Photo Rondal Partridge). 20, Mr. and Mrs. M. C. Mateer (Philip F. Hallock, architect); 22, Frantz Manufacturing Company. *Chapter 14:* Figures 2–9, Chambers Corporation; 10, Mr. and Mrs. M. C. Mateer (Philip F. Hallock, architect); 11, Rolscreen Company; 15, 20, 24, Mr. and Mrs. Donald W. Hamer; 17, National Forest Products Association; 18, 26, California Redwood Association. *Chapter 15:* Figure 3, Weyerhaeuser Company; 13, International Business Machines Corporation. *Chapter 17:* Figure 3, Mr. and Mrs. M. C. Mateer (Philip F. Hallock, architect). *Chapter 18:* Figures 4, 5, 6, 7, Bethlehem Steel Corporation; 10, Callaway Gardens, Pine Mountain, Ga.; 8, 9, Forest Products Promotion Council; 11, California Redwood Association (Thomas Babbitt, architect); 12, Eliot Noyes & Associates, architects; 13, Perkins & Will, architects (photo by Bill Hedrich, Hedrich-Blessing); 14–17, American Iron and Steel Institute (Walker O. Cain & Associates, architects; R. L. Stinard & Associates and Severud-Perrone-Sturn-Conlin-Bandel, consulting engineers); 19, Rolscreen Company (Good Shepherd Methodist Church, Park Ridge, Ill.: Stade-Dolan & Associates, architects; Vern Bengston, builder; Hedrich-Blessing, photo); 21, 22, PPG Industries, Inc.; 26, Ventarama Skylight Corporation, *Chapter 19:* Figure 1, Rolscreen Company (G. C. Hann residence, Minneapolis, Minn.: Newt Griffith, Peterson, Clark & Griffin, Inc., architects; Johnson & Jasper, builder); 6, Bethlehem Steel Corporation; 30–32, Mr. and Mrs. Donald W. Hamer. *Chapter 20:* Figure 6, 7, Armstrong Cork Company; 12, Bilco Stairguide; 13, 15, 19, 21, Julius Blum & Co., Inc. (The Colorail ® System in Figure 15 covered by U.S. patents and pending patent applications; patterns in Figure 21 are covered by U.S. patents); 14, 16, 20, Blumcraft of Pittsburgh (Copyrights for Figures 14, 16 are registered; the stock treillage designs in Figure 20 are covered by U.S. patents and pending patent applications) *Chapter 21:* Figure 2, Mr. and Mrs. M. C. Mateer (Philip F. Hallock, architect); 9, 10, Vega Industries, Inc.; 12, 14, 15, Condon-King Division of The Majestic Company; 13, Acorn Fireplaces, Inc.; 17, Mr. and Mrs. Donald W. Hamer. *Chapter 22:* Figure 1, the Cairo Museum (photograph by the Egyptian Expedition, The Metropolitan Museum of Art); 15, 16, Department of Architecture, The Pennsylvania State University; 17, Artesano, Inc., San Francisco; 18, Bethlehem Steel Corporation; 19, Perkins & Will, architects (photo by Bill Hedrich of Hedrich-Blessing); 20, Balthazar Korab, photographer *Chapter 23:* Figure 25, Timber Engineering Company; 32, 33, California Redwood Association; 40, Rolscreen Company, 42–44, American Iron and Steel Institute (Ziegelman & Ziegelman, architects; Samuel V. Tavernit, structural engineers). *Chapter 25:* Figure 1, Armstrong Cork Company. *Chapter 26:* Figure 7, Sunwater Company, San Diego, Calif. *Chapter 27:* Figure 22–24, American Iron and Steel Institute (Vincent G. Kling, architect; Oliver & Smith, associated architects; Fraioli-Blum-Yesselman, structural engineers; Kling-Leopold, Inc., mechanical-electrical engineers). *Chapter 28:* Figure 4, Mr. and Mrs. M. C. Mateer (Philip F. Hallock, architect). *Chapter 30:* Figures 1–8, The Construction Specifications Institute. *Chapter 33:* Figures 5, 7, 17, Dr. Milton S. Osborne, Professor Emeritus of Architecture, The Pennsylvania State University; 8, Rolscreen Company; 15, 20, 26, Gruen Associates, Architects-Engineers-Planners, 16, 22, Department of Architecture, The Pennsylvania State University; 18, 19, Masonite Corporation (George A. Parenti, designer), 24, 25 Artesano, Inc. *Chapter 35:* All illustrations and drawings of South Hills Office Building courtesy of Jack W. Risheberger & Associates, Registered Architects and Engineers. Figures 53–56, First Church of Christ, Scientist, State College, Pa., designed by Roy D. Murphy & Associates, architects, Urbana, Ill. *Appendix A:* Figure 23, Dr. Milton S. Osborne, Professor Emeritus of Architecture, The Pennsylvania State University. *Appendix B:* Figures 1–7, Andersen Corporation; 8, Rolscreen Company. *Appendix C:* Figures 1–4, Morgan Company; 5, Frantz Manufacturing Company.

contents

to the instructor

To the instructor, a textbook can be a valuable assistant, relieving him of much repetitive explanation; to the student, it can be an inspiration, offering him encouragement in addition to facts and methods. The value of a textbook is determined by the extent to which these principles are recognized. *Architectural Drafting and Design* is designed as a comprehensive reference for the new teacher and a dependable tool for the experienced professor; it will challenge the advanced student as well as guide the inexperienced. It is hoped that students will enjoy studying the book as much as the author has enjoyed preparing it.

This is a book on architectural *drafting*. However, when an architectural draftsman draws a line not previously supplied him in the form of a sketch, he is also engaged in *design*. Therefore this book puts equal emphasis on architectural design. The majority of the material included here is concerned with *residential* drawing and design. Because the student is more familiar with houses than with any other structures, their design seems the proper introduction to such a vast field. To provide continuity, a contemporary home for Mr. A is designed from preliminary program to finished rendering. The plans for this house are included in the relevant chapters. The plans for a split level modular home for Mr. M and a two story traditional home for Mr. Z are in appendix a.

Also included are the plans for a five story commercial building of bolted and welded steel construction. Photographs of this building being erected are in Chapter 35. A chapter on fire protection has been added to this third edition, for everyone should become more aware of fire safety.

Each chapter is self-sufficient, so that the chapters may be arranged or omitted according to the available class time. For example, the chapters on drafting and projections added to this third edition can be omitted by students who understand drafting practice to the degree learned in basic mechanical drawing courses. The introduction to each chapter shows the relative importance of that chapter and how it fits into the overall process of drafting and design. A conscious attempt has been made to arrange the descriptive material into an interesting, easy-to-read format using step-by-step illustration whenever applicable. Color has been used to distinguish each step from the previous one, and the illustrations have been drawn for maximum clarity and accuracy. For greater realism, pictorials have been drawn in perspective.

Lumber sizes conform to the new *American Softwood Lumber Standard* PS 20-70, and structural steel designations conform to the latest revisions recommended by the American Institute of Steel Construction. Specifications follow the CSI Format.

Each chapter will provide helpful material for a range of students from beginner to advanced. The beginner should appreciate having the *reasons* behind the *rules*; the advanced creative student should enjoy taking a look into probable future developments. Many topics have a prophetic flavor and are directly related to the sciences which are shaping this age of technology. These advanced areas, which can be used in enrichment programs, are reinforced by end-of-chapter questions and exercises.

The author would be most grateful to receive suggestions and correspond with readers interested in this book.

to the student

You are about to be introduced to architectural drafting, a satisfying and creative profession: a profession of ideas and planning; of intelligent design, detailing, and specification writing, and finally, actual construction—when all will see the product of your talent and imagination.

Are you wondering if this should be your life's work? It is sincerely hoped that this book will answer that question for you. If your answer is "yes," you can look forward to an interesting life of constant and increasing challenges with full payment in the satisfaction of a job—a big job—well done.

Although the primary aim of this book is to present information vital to the profession of architectural drafting, it may also lead you into one of the many allied fields of work. But remember that neither this book nor any other can provide all the extensive information you will need to become a registered architect or architectural engineer. Most states require graduation from an approved university (usually a five-year program), plus three years of practical experience under the direction of a professional, plus a comprehensive written examination, as the minimum requirements for professional registration as an architect or engineer.

If, on the other hand, you decide that your interests lie in another direction, your time and effort will not be wasted. What you learn will be useful in many ways. You will have learned the value of creative imagination, the importance of careful investigation before making a final decision, the need for a knowledge of construction materials and methods, and an awareness of safety. All this will be helpful to you as a citizen—and especially as a home owner.

The design and drafting of a building are not easy. Even the experienced architect must work hard and long; even he will have moments of doubt. When you arrive at this point, remember: The greater the demands upon you, the greater the rewards.

Ernest R. Weidhaas

architectural drafting and design

PART ONE

introduction to architectural design

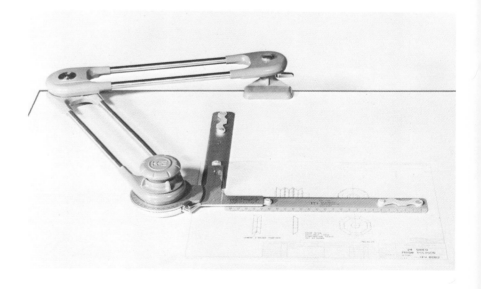

1 architectural drafting tools

To do any job properly and efficiently, you must have the proper tools. This is true of all trades and professions—whether carpentry or drafting, surgery or architecture. Keep this in mind when you select your basic drawing tools or add more advanced and special equipment. Purchase tools of good quality, since they represent an investment that you can carry with you into your career as an architectural draftsman.*

BASIC EQUIPMENT

You should be thoroughly familiar with the following basic tools of the draftsman:

Drawing board. Although the majority of architectural drafting work is mounted with tape directly to the drafting table, the drawing board (Figure 1) does have the advantage of portability. Select a smooth-surfaced board without any warpage. The ends should be true and square. Either solid basswood, hollow basswood, or metal-edged basswood is satisfactory.

T-square. Make certain that the blade of the T-square (Figure 2) is perfectly straight (except for a desirable bow away from the drawing surface) and free of nicks. For accurate work, the blade must be securely

*The term "draftsman" is derived from the earlier "draughtsman." Many years ago this was exclusively a male occupation, but today both men and women work in this field, and the term *draftsman* is applied to both.

Figure 1   Drawing board.

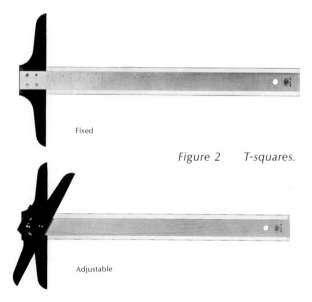

Fixed

Figure 2   T-squares.

Adjustable

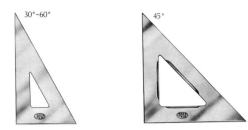

Figure 3   Triangles.

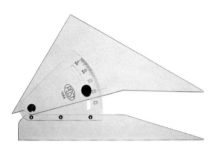

Figure 4   Adjustable triangles.

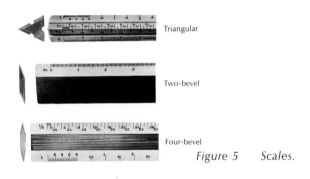

Triangular

Two-bevel

Four-bevel

Figure 5   Scales.

Figure 6   Drawing instrument set.

Figure 7   Mechanical drafting pencil.

fastened to the head (fixed T-square) or capable of being securely fastened (adjustable T-square).

Triangles. Clear plastic triangles (Figure 3) are used in sets of two: 30°–60° triangle and 45° triangle. As with the T-square blade, the outer edges should be flat and nick-free. Some draftsmen prefer an adjustable triangle (Figure 4) which permits lines to be drawn at any angle.

Scales. The architectural draftsman normally uses an architect's scale, although on occasion he may need an engineer's or mechanical engineer's scale. Either triangular, two-bevel, or four-bevel scales are used according to preference (Figure 5). The architectural scales are:

$12'' = 1'$ (full scale)

$6'' = 1'$

$3'' = 1'$

$1\frac{1}{2}'' = 1'$

$\frac{3}{4}'' = 1'$

$\frac{3}{8}'' = 1'$

$\frac{3}{16}'' = 1'$

$\frac{3}{32}'' = 1'$

$1'' = 1'$

$\frac{1}{2}'' = 1'$

$\frac{1}{4}'' = 1'$

$\frac{1}{8}'' = 1'$

$\frac{1}{16}'' = 1'$

Notice that there are really *two* architectural scale systems. One is based on the full scale and proceeds to smaller scales; the other is based on a $\frac{1}{16}'' = 1'$ scale and proceeds to larger scales. Combined, these two architectural scale systems offer a wide range of scale choice.

Drawing sets. A satisfactory drawing set (Figure 6) should contain as a minimum: dividers, pencil compass, pen compass, and drafting pen or technical fountain pen. Many sets also contain mechanical drafting pencils. The instruments in the better sets are constructed of stainless steel or nickel silver; cheaper sets are of chrome-plated brass.

Drafting pencils. One refillable drafting pencil (Figure 7) with an assortment of different grade leads is sufficient for the classroom. A professional draftsman, however, has a number of refillable pencils—each color-coded to one lead grade so that no time will be lost in switching leads. Drafting pencil leads are graded from 9H (hard) to F (firm) to 6B (black), as shown in Table 1.

Lead pointers. A mechanical lead pointer (Figure 8) provides an easy method to obtain perfectly formed conical points. The abrasive liners can be replaced quickly and easily.

Erasers. A wide variety of pencil erasers (Figure 9) is available. A satisfactory eraser should be capable of completely removing pencil and ink lines without roughing the surface of the paper or leaving colored marks. The artgum eraser is designed to remove smudges rather than lines. Electric erasing machines are helpful when a great amount of erasing is needed.

Lettering guides. A number of devices are available to assist in drawing guide lines for lettering. The Rapidesign Guide illustrated in Figure 10 is operated by placing the pencil point through the proper hole and moving the guide and pencil along the T-square. The Ames Lettering Instrument or Braddock-Rowe Lettering Triangle is preferred by some draftsmen.

Technical fountain pen. Some draftsmen prefer the technical fountain pen (Figure 11) to the standard ruling pen, since a variation in line weight may be obtained by changing the speed of the stroke. This is most useful in preparing presentation drawings.

ADVANCED AND SPECIAL EQUIPMENT

The following equipment, although not normally found in a school drafting room, is often used in a professional drafting office.

Proportional dividers. This is a very useful instrument for enlarging or reducing a drawing. Proportional dividers (Figure 12) are usually calibrated to obtain ratios from 1:1 up to 10:1.

Parallel rule drawing board. A parallel rule drawing board (Figure 13) may be used in place of the standard drawing board and T-square. The straightedge may be moved up and down, but it is designed to remain perfectly horizontal—thus allowing accurate work.

Figure 8
Pencil pointer.

Artgum

Ruby

Figure 9   Erasers.

Figure 10   Lettering guide.

Figure 11   Technical fountain pen and set. Available line widths are shown at the right.

Figure 12   Proportional dividers.

TABLE 1
Grades of Pencil Leads

9H
8H
7H
6H
5H
4H
3H
2H ⎤ used for most
H   ⎥ architectural
F   ⎦ work
HB
B
2B
3B
4B
5B
6B

Figure 13   *Parallel rule drawing board.*

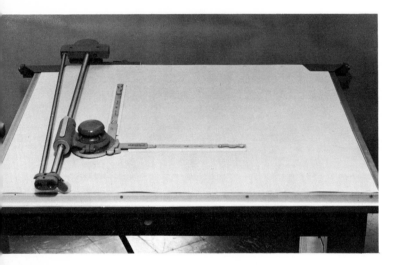

Figure 14   *Drafting machine, X-Y plotter type.*

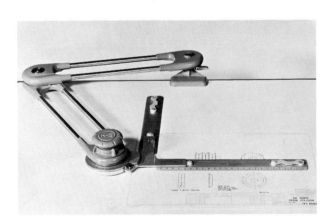

Figure 15   *Drafting machine, arm type.*

Drafting machines. Drafting machines may be used in place of the standard drawing board, T-square, triangles, scales, and protractor. As with the parallel rule drawing board, a straightedge remains horizontal. In addition, though, there is a vertical edge. Both edges are graduated to act as scales and may be rotated to any desired position by pressing a release button. The X-Y plotter (Figure 14) and arm type (Figure 15) perform similar functions.

Templates. The architectural draftsman uses a large variety of templates to speed his work. A circle template (Figure 16) may be used to supplement the compass. The architectural template (Figure 17) simplifies the drawing of kitchen and bathroom fixtures, and the furniture template (Figure 18) helps in the preliminary design stage to draw furniture the proper size. Many other specialized templates are available, such as the structural template (Figure 19), which gives the cross-sectional shapes of beams, channels, and angles.

Lettering sets. Although pencil lettering is best drawn freehand, ink lettering may be improved by the use of lettering stencils. These stencils can provide a variety of sizes and styles of letters. Figure 12 of Chapter 9 shows an architectural alphabet formed with the aid of a lettering stencil.

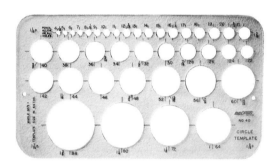

Figure 16   *Circle template.*

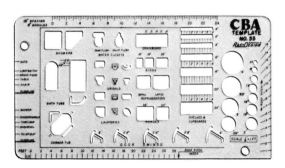

Figure 17   *Architectural template.*

FUTURE TRENDS

The present-day drafting tools described have been used for many hundreds of years. For example, the use of paper can be traced to 105 A.D., vellum to 1400 B.C., and papyrus to 3500 B.C. Tools for drawing lines and circles on this material have not changed greatly in all this time, and many of our "newer" tools also have a long history. In fact, stencils were used by Greek builders in 400 B.C.; a compass for drawing ovals and spirals was invented in 1565, a parallel ruler in 1713, and a technical fountain pen in 1864. In all likelihood, these same tools will be used for many more years. However, there are many new types of drafting machines being designed—and produced—which indicate the shape of the drafting room of the future: data plotters relieving tedious drafting chores, visual image storage and retrieval systems to record and display pictorial records, and analog devices which show trends by drawing mathematical curves on a screen. The following description of a computer-assisted drafting room shows what is now commercially available.

The draftsman sits at a console consisting of an oscilloscope screen and a panel of control switches and buttons. The oscilloscope can display an image in the conventional manner (like a television screen). Also it can receive information by means of a photoelectric device known as a light pen. See Figure 21. The light pen, when pointed at any portion of the screen, causes an internal response of the oscilloscope, thereby producing a point of light. The draftsman therefore can draw, write, or letter on the face of the scope. When the proper button is pressed, lines can be automatically leveled or revolved, and circular arcs can be drawn. Lines may be "erased" and moved to new positions by "picking them up" with the light pen. Upon command, the machine will store a finished drawing electronically and provide a "fresh sheet" (clear scope) to work on. It can also recall any stored drawing, superimposing it, if desired, upon the drawing on the screen. Drawings can be enlarged

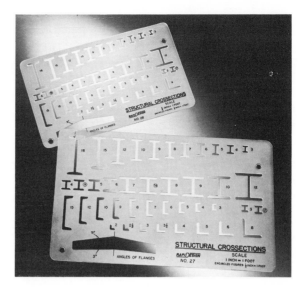

Figure 19   Structural templates.

Figure 20   Lettering set.

Figure 21   Light pen and oscilloscope.

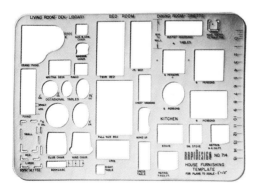

Figure 18   Furniture template.

or reduced to any desired scale permitting versatility beyond conventional means.

Hand-held electronic pens and tablets are available from the Grafcon, Rand, and Sylvania companies. Moved across the flat surface of the tablet, the pen can pick up X-Y coordinate information. The *Stanford Mouse* (so called because it has a small, round, white "body" with a connecting wire "tail") can be moved over any flat surface. This causes its two right-angled wheels to rotate and record an X-Y position change. The coordinates are then sent through the tail to be displayed on the face of a connected oscilloscope screen.

A sonic pen called the *Lincoln Wand* is available to provide all three coordinate dimensions; X, Y, and Z. For example, the Wand held at any position in front of its screen will record the X and Y coordinates together with the distance from the screen (the Z coordinate).

Draftsmen who dislike careful lettering can use a system called GRAIL developed by the Rand Corporation. This system (Figure 22) combines a computer, a scope, the Rand pen and tablet, and "software" (programming) to transcribe hand-written notes into printed lettering. For example, when the electronic pen is used to write a letter (or other symbol) on the tablet, a switch on the tip of the pen is automatically closed which causes the letter to appear as drawn on the scope screen. When the pen is slightly lifted, the computer checks and identifies the letter and replaces it with a standardized letter. If the letter is not identified, it simply disappears. To erase a word, the draftsman draws a zig-zag line through the word. This is recognized by the computer to mean "erase," and the word disappears. When all is completed to the draftsman's satisfaction, a button is pressed to store the sentences for future use or obtain an immediate print-out.

Accurately-drawn perspectives of any building are easily obtained. The draftsman must feed in the X, Y, and Z coordinate of each corner of a building and indicate what corners are to be connected by lines. A perspective is then plotted as seen by an observer located at any desired position. Programs are available which will identify hidden lines and draw them lighter or omit them entirely. Also, lines can be selectively removed. That is, walls of a building can be removed to view the interior. Correct shadows for any time or location can be added. Devices such as the M.I.T. *3-D Ball* are available which are used to rotate the perspective to permit viewing from various angles. As the Ball is turned or tilted, the perspective moves accordingly.

All of the above applications are now available. The extent of their usefulness and acceptance will depend to a large degree upon hardware costs. Although a small company cannot afford to own or even lease a large computer, it can have access to a large central computer by the use of connected typewriter-like branch terminals. This is accomplished through the concept of *time sharing.* As the name implies, time sharing is the sharing of time on a central computer by a number of branch users. Thus during periods in which a user at one terminal is preparing his next problem, the central computer can be handling problems submitted through other terminals rather than idling.

Figure 22   The GRAIL system.

STUDY QUESTIONS

1. Distinguish between:
   a. Lettering guide and lettering stencil
   b. Dividers and proportional dividers
   c. Adjustable T-square and fixed T-square
   d. Adjustable triangle and 45° triangle
   e. Two-bevel scales and four-bevel scales
   f. Ruling pen and technical fountain pen
2. Prepare a list of:
   a. Architectural scales from $\frac{1}{16}'' = 1'$ to full size
   b. Pencil grades from 6H to 2B
3. (For the advanced student) After a thorough study of drafting tools used in the past few decades, give your prediction of the kind of "drafting room" which will be used:
   a. 25 years hence
   b. 100 years hence

2 architectural history

In this age of new styles, new materials, and new building methods, we are apt to think of the contemporary house as having no ancestry—no history. Actually, the house we live in today is not a completely original design, but the outgrowth of many centuries of architectural development. No significant architectural style stands alone; rather it is the result of evolution. Every building that has ever been built is a composite idea of all the centuries of ideas that have preceded. It is thus with our present "modern" house, and the trends today will dictate the architecture of the future. We study the history of architecture, therefore, not only to enable us to appreciate the many public buildings previously built in classic styles, but also to aid in the design of present-day buildings.

In the following discussion, architectural history has been divided into separate chronological groups. But it should be remembered that architectural development is a steady and continuous process. Each age has made its contribution. Then we will see this century in true perspective and realize that no age is an ultimate—but merely one step in this continuing process.

The principal historical styles of architecture are shown below. Each is an evolution of, or influenced by, earlier styles.

Egyptian, Assyrian, Persian
Greek
Roman
Byzantine, Romanesque
Gothic
Renaissance
Classic Revival, Eclecticism
International, Contemporary

PREVIEW

If a beginning must be found, the architecture of the Egyptians will serve well. The Greeks drew on Egyptian, Assyrian, Persian, and Phoenician ideas. The Romans borrowed the ideas of the Greeks and added to them. History has approved the architecture of the Greeks and Romans to such an extent that many modern public buildings have been built in imitation of their work. Later, the acceptance of domed and arched construction permitted the new styles of Byzantine and Romanesque. The Gothic style further developed vaulting, keeping many of the forms of its predecessors. During the Renaissance, the classic civilizations were studied and revived. But this return to ancient styles led eventually into a period called Eclecticism which virtually stopped any real architectural development. In reaction to Eclecticism, architects searched for a new and true form of shelter. This was found in the Contemporary.

STRUCTURAL SYSTEMS

The history of architecture is closely tied to the development of methods of spanning the open space between two columns. To accomplish this, five fundamental structural systems (Figure 1) have been used:

1. Lintel
2. Corbel
3. Arch
4. Cohesive construction
5. Truss

The *lintel* is simply a horizontal member spanning an opening to carry the weight above. The weight of the lintel and any weight above it cause a vertical downward thrust to the columns. The Egyptians and Assyrians used the lintel almost exclusively. The Greeks developed the column and lintel, in an aesthetic sense, to perfection.

A *corbel* is a block projecting from a wall and supporting a weight. The cantilever is based upon the same principle. The Persians used corbeling extensively.

The *arch* is composed of wedge-shaped blocks, each supporting a share of the load by wedging the adjoining blocks. The weight of the blocks and any weight above cause not only a downward

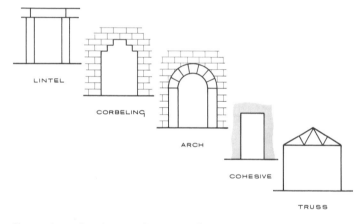

LINTEL

CORBELING

ARCH

COHESIVE

TRUSS

Figure 1   Fundamental structural systems.

Figure 2   The Sphinx and the Great Pyramid at Ghizeh.

thrust but outward thrusts also. The Assyrians built a few arched structures, but the Romans are credited with much further development. The application of the principle of the arch to the dome is credited to the Roman and Byzantine periods, while the vault reached its height in the Gothic period.

Cohesive construction employs materials which are shaped while plastic and allowed to harden into a homogeneous structure. The Romans used a kind of cohesive construction in their domes. Reinforced concrete is a modern application of this system.

A *truss* is a rigid arrangement of comparatively short members spanning a wide space.

EGYPTIAN ARCHITECTURE

It is a tribute to Egypt that her works dating back to 3500 B.C. are still standing today. The surviving architecture, however, does not represent homes or even palaces, but rather tombs and monuments to the dead. In earliest history, graves were marked by piles of stones called "cairns." The most noted outgrowth of these cairns are the pyramids built of stone or brick. There are over a hundred pyramids, varying in size and design, each containing intricate passageways designed to confuse anyone entering. Actually, no entrance can be found easily, since the tunnel is blocked once the mummy is in place. It is known that some pyramids were completed on a smaller scale, and successive outer layers were then added on. The pyramid was thus complete in case of the king's early death, but was enlarged as time permitted.

The actual construction method of the Egyptians is one of the mysteries of the past. It is true that hundreds of thousands of workers were employed in these huge monuments, but even so it is not clear how stones weighing up to 30 tons were raised. It has been suggested that a temporary sand ramp was erected, and the stone blocks were rolled up this ramp into position. The Egyptian temples of later periods could have been constructed in the same manner; the interior of the temple being filled with sand as the walls and columns were erected, and then dug out at completion. Another theory is that the stones were rocked in place using wooden rockers which have been unearthed. It has been suggested that the stone was rocked enough for a shim to be inserted under one side, and then rocked again to insert a shim on the other side. This process could continue until the stone reached any required height.

The three largest pyramids are at Ghizeh (Figure 2), the most famous being the Great Pyramid of Cheops (Figure 3). The dimensions of the Great Pyramid were originally 764' square by 482' high. Its present dimensions are 746' square by 450' high. It was built of limestone blocks upon a leveled rock plateau and was coated with smooth bands of colored granites. The king's marble sarcophagus is located in the upper chamber reached by low tunnels and bridged by stone lintels topped by a sort of lintel-arch. A large gallery, 5' wide by 28' high, is connected to this chamber. Two additional burial chambers were prepared earlier. The first was cut into solid rock 102' below ground level. The second was built below the king's chamber and formerly was thought to be the queen's chamber.

A small temple for the worship of the king was connected to each pyramid. These have been mostly destroyed, but a few ground plans have been discovered, and one called the "Temple of the Sphinx" (Figure 4) is nearly complete. It contains square columns supporting massive square lintels which in turn support the roof slabs: a very simple forefather to the elaborate columns of later periods.

While only kings built pyramids, lesser rulers built "mastabas" (Figure 5). These were long, rectangular tombs of stone or brick with only a slightly sloping exterior wall and flat roof of stone slabs. They always faced east, as did one of the four sides of the pyramids. The interior was divided into three chambers, the first being the chapel where offerings were made to sustain the "Ka" or the double of the deceased. Secondly, there was a sealed and secret inner chamber containing statues and colored reliefs of the Ka. These were meant to entertain the Ka until the soul, or "Ba," could arrive before the tribunal of Osiris. The last chamber, the "well," was deep underground, leading to the mummy chamber.

As time passed these mastabas evolved into tremendous temples (ca. 1500 B.C.) for the deification of the kings. These temples were built on a diminishing plan (see Figure 6); that is, the chambers were smaller, darker, and more mysterious the farther they were penetrated. Also, the floors became higher and the roofs lower as the chambers receded. The exteriors of the temples were windowless oblong boxes fronted by two pylons, somewhat reminiscent of the pyramids, flanking the entrance. Two rows of facing Sphinxes might border the approach.

The most noteworthy of these structures is the Karnak Temple, which was built and added to for 700 years, finally reaching dimensions of 376' wide by 1215' long. The first chambers entered, called "hypostyle halls," were entered at times by the Egyptian upper class for solemn worship. A clerestory allowed light to enter this chamber. In later periods a screen wall (Figure 7) was built between the front columns. The wall extended only half the column height, to allow light to penetrate to the hieroglyphics on the inner walls and columns. Behind the hypostyle were countless darkened inner chambers accessible only to the priests (Figure 8).

With few exceptions, Egyptian construction was based on the column and lintel. The columns were richly carved and painted; lintels were square,

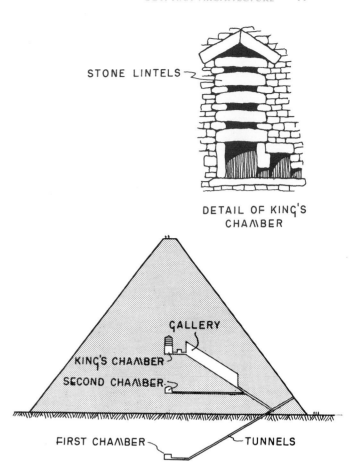

Figure 3   The Great Pyramid of Cheops.

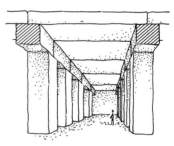

Figure 4   The Temple of the Sphinx.

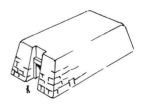

Figure 5   A typical mastaba.

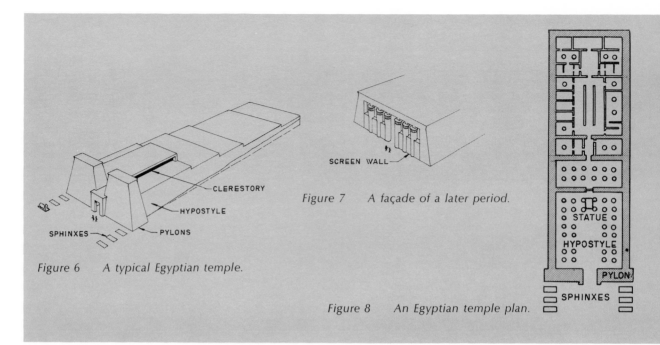

Figure 6   A typical Egyptian temple.

Figure 7   A façade of a later period.

Figure 8   An Egyptian temple plan.

plain, and massive. The entire structure was heavy—much heavier than was actually required for strength. The earliest example of an Egyptian arch dates back to 500 B.C. The principle of the 3-4-5 triangle was also known to the Egyptians and used in laying out floor plans. A cord tied in a circle with twelve equally spaced knots was pegged in the earth to produce walls perpendicular to each other. This was a priestly ritual called the "cording of the temple."

ASSYRIAN ARCHITECTURE

Though we have no Assyrian architectural remains as old as the pyramids of Egypt, these civilizations were nearly chronologically parallel. The surviving structures are not too similar, for the Egyptians have given us their tombs to study, while the Assyrians have given us palaces and fortifications. Moreover, although the Egyptian stone monuments have withstood the years, the Assyrian clay brick structures have crumbled.

Looking at the plan of an Assyrian palace (Figure 9), you will first notice the lack of symmetry which is so different from the Egyptian temple plan. The palace was laid out with open courtyards surrounded by many small rooms and hallways, all arranged in a haphazard fashion. Probably one group of rooms and courtyards housed the ruler, another his harem, and others the soldiers and servants. Large rooms are not found. Since the Assyrians did not use columns, the room width was limited to the length of its ceiling beam. The arch was known to them: arched drainage systems have been found. An in-

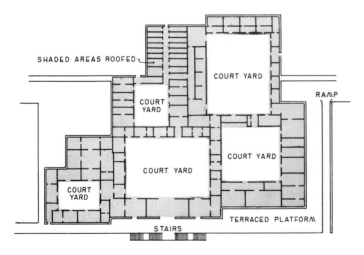

Figure 9   An Assyrian palace.

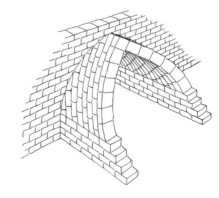

Figure 10   The Assyrian vaulting system.

clined vaulting system (Figure 10) was used to hold the blocks in place as they were laid. (The vertical keystone system requires supports until the top block is in place.) Long, narrow, horizontal openings directly beneath the roof served as the only kind of window.

Throughout history, fortifications have been built on elevated land. In the case of the Assyrians, this was impossible, since the land was perfectly flat. They solved this problem by constructing an artificial mountain, or platform, to raise the palace above the plains. This terraced platform was ascended by stairs and ramps.

Although the structures themselves were simple, there was much "applied" ornament—that is, ornament added after the structure was built. Bold colors were used—often the seven planetary colors: gold, silver, white, black, red, yellow, and blue.

PERSIAN ARCHITECTURE

The architecture of any country is influenced by the architecture of countries it knew or conquered. For example, the raised platform of the Assyrians appears in Persian architecture also. The Assyrians built entirely of brick, but the Persians built solid stone gateways and pilasters with brick filling between. The centuries have destroyed the brick, but the stone remains.

Extensive use was made of a kind of corbeled arch (Figure 11). The Persians used columns, but of more slender proportions and spaced farther apart than the Egyptians'. The Great Hall of Xerxes is a memorable work. It was twice the size of the Great Hypostyle Hall at Karnak, but the columns were spaced so much further apart that the same roof area was supported by only one-fourth the number of columns. The capitals were composed of the heads of two monsters, the space between the heads supporting the beam (Figure 12).

GREEK ARCHITECTURE

The Grecian period (500 B.C.–100 B.C.) has produced some of the most remarkable works of art and architecture known to man. The Greeks were a highly civilized and intelligent race, and they produced temples of the finest proportion and detail. Their work was influenced by Egyptian, Assyrian, Persian, Phoenician, and Lycian architecture. The Greeks developed an architecture of columned monuments and temples, but the column was used in a manner different from that used in the Egyptian temples. The Egyptians used columns for internal support, the exteriors being for the most part completely blank walls, while the Greeks surrounded their temples with columns, making them the primary elements of

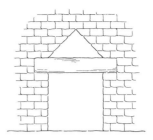

Figure 11   The Persian corbeled arch.

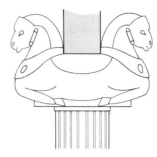

*Figure 12
A Persian column.*

Figure 13   The Greek orders.

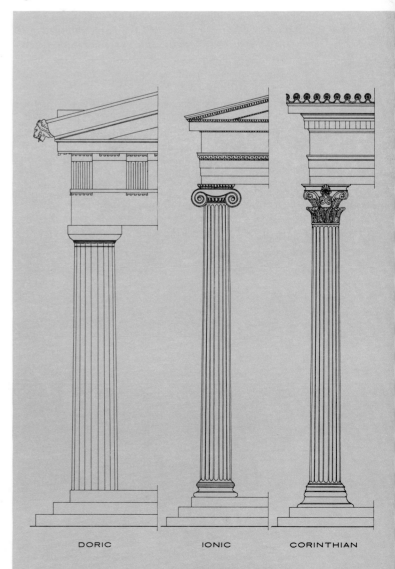

DORIC   IONIC   CORINTHIAN

exterior design. The number and arrangement of these columns varied greatly, but the plan was the same. The enclosed building itself, called the "cella," was long, narrow, and windowless. The cella housed the statue of a deity and was open to the public. A small temple might have a single chamber in the cella which would be entered from one end. Columns might be only at that end or on both ends. A larger temple, like the Parthenon, might be divided into two chambers and completely surrounded by one or more rows of columns. Interior columns might also be used. Walls and columns were of marble, and the low-pitched roof was wood, covered with marble or terra cotta tiles. Color was used on the interior and exterior reliefs, blue and gold being most popular. Moldings like the "egg-and-dart" carvings were simple but refined.

There are three styles of Greek columns, each with its own base, shaft, capital, and entablature constituting what is called an "order" (Figure 13). These three orders have been called the "Doric," "Ionic," and "Corinthian." The tribes of Dorians and Ionians have given the name to the two styles traditionally Greek, while the Romans must be credited with fully developing the Corinthian order.

The Doric column was $4\frac{1}{3}$ to 7 diameters high with 16 to 20 elliptical flutes. It had a simple capital, but no base, resting directly on the stepped platform. The finest example of Doric architecture is the Parthenon (Figures 14 and 15) on the Acropolis of Athens. It was built in 440 B.C. to enshrine the goddess Athena Parthenos and to commemorate the victory of the Athenians over the Persians. The marble blocks were cut to fit together with amazing accuracy and laid without mortar. The details were executed with exquisite refinement, giving rise to the comment that the Greeks "built like Titans and finished like jewelers." Many lines on the Parthenon

that look perfectly straight were actually slightly curved to counteract the optical illusion of curvature. Columns have a slight convex curve (only 1" in their 32' height) so that they do not appear concave. Also, the axes of the columns lean a bit inward to prevent

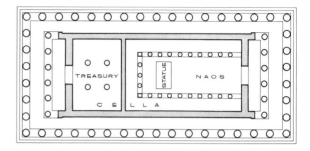

Figure 15   A plan view of the Parthenon at Athens.

Figure 16

a top-heavy look. The steps and eaves curve gently down at the ends—also for visual effect. This can be explained by referring to Figure 16. Notice that the horizontal line, which is drawn straight, appears to sag because of the effect of the inclined lines above it. The Greeks took even such details into consideration.

The Ionic column was slender in comparison, being eight to ten diameters in height with 24 flutes cut deeper than the Doric. It stood on a molded base and was finished by a capital with volutes. The only defect with this capital was that it did not readily lend itself to use as a corner column. To correct this problem, the corner volute was set at 45° so that it could be faced on both sides. The gables on Ionic

Figure 14   The Parthenon as it appears today.

buildings were frequently sculptured in relief, as were the Doric. Two examples of Ionic buildings are outstanding. One is the Erechtheion, also on the Acropolis, which is noted for its unsymmetrical plan. It enshrined many deities and heroes. Perhaps the most well-known feature of this temple is the Caryatid Porch, which uses robed female figures (caryatids) for columns. An Ionic tomb, the Mausoleum at Halicarnassus, was built by the widow of King Mausolus in 354 B.C. It had a pyramidal roof reminiscent of Egyptian architecture.

The Corinthian order was similar to the Ionic except that the capitals had smaller volutes entwined with rows of acanthus leaves. The most celebrated example of Greek Corinthian is the circular Monument of Lysicrates in Athens.

ROMAN ARCHITECTURE

Roman architecture was influenced by the Dorians, Phoenicians, Etruscans, and, most of all, the Greeks. The Romans never reached the Greek perfection of design, but they extended the services of architecture to theaters, baths, basilicas, bridges, aqueducts, and monuments—all well-engineered structures.

The three Greek orders were adopted as a direct consequence of the Roman conquest of Greece. Not only did the Romans bring home artistic wealth as part of the spoils of war, but they also brought home the desire to make Rome as magnificent as the Greek cities they had destroyed. The Greek orders were modified into what are called the five Roman orders: Tuscan, Doric, Ionic, Corinthian, and Composite. The Tuscan was a simplified Etruscan Doric, with a column seven diameters high. The Doric was similar to the Greek Doric, with a column eight diameters high and often devoid of any fluting. The Ionic was almost identical with the Greek Ionic, with a column nine diameters high. The Corinthian had a column ten diameters high. As previously stated, this order was perfected by the Romans, and became the most characteristic order, probably because its ornateness appealed to the Romans. The Composite can be described as a Corinthian column, with the volutes enlarged giving it an Ionic look.

The Romans established sets of rules to simplify the orders which, many feel, were to their detriment. For example, fine elliptical moldings and flutes were cut circular to simplify the construction. However, their tremendous output of architecture could probably not have been accomplished if this kind of standardization had not been introduced. The columns, incidentally, were often cut in one piece (called "monolithic"), instead of being built up from smaller sections, as were the Greek columns.

The Romans are credited with the development of the vault and arch. The Etruscans first used vaults; the vaulted great sewer of Rome (500 B.C.)

Figure 17   The arch order.

still remains. Roman vaults were basically of three types: barrel, groined, and dome. The barrel vault is a semi-cylinder, the groined is formed from two intersecting barrel vaults, and the dome is a hemisphere supported on a wall of circular plan. The hemisphere supported on a wall of square plan was later developed as the typical Byzantine dome. The vaults were cast over a wooden form, unlike the inclined vault which required no forms. When hardened, the vault formed a cohesive curved lintel which did not extend the outward thrust of the stone block construction.

The Romans outdid themselves in the use of the arch, combining it with the column and lintel. This combination has been called the "arch order" (Figure 17) and is a characteristic feature of Roman architecture. It is also the poorest feature, because of its inherent inconsistency; either the arch or the lintel has to be redundant. The Romans considered ornateness above function, however, and this sham did not bother them. Lintels were even scored with false joints to make them look like smaller blocks. Much Roman work, especially theaters, used the arch order. False columns were applied to the exterior, a different order for each level.

Many Roman public buildings were built around the basilica located in the Forum. The Forum was to Rome what the Acropolis was to Athens, the basilica being a meeting place and court house. The buildings were large and partially or completely roofed, the higher center portion affording a clerestory. Constantine built the first vaulted basilica; previous ones had wooden roofs.

Among the most remarkable Roman structures was the Colosseum in Rome (Figure 18) which seated 80,000. Erected to house the bloody battles between men and beasts, it could even be flooded to create sea fights. Titus finished the Colosseum in 80 A.D. The plan was a 600' × 500' ellipse; the walls were 153' high arranged in four levels. The three lower levels were based on the arch orders, using Doric half-columns at the lower level, then Ionic, and then

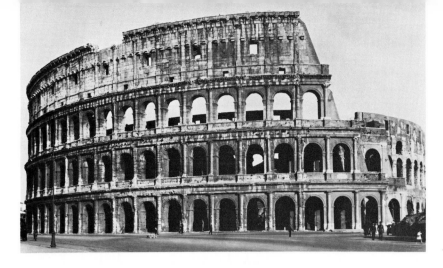

Figure 18
The Colosseum
as it appears today.

Corinthian. The upper level was composed of Corinthian columns with windows between them. A huge silk awning was stretched from this height over the galleries. The arena itself was uncovered. Ramps led to subterranean vaults which were used to house beasts and machinery.

The Circus Maximus outdid the Colosseum in that it measured 400' × 2,100' and seated 260,000. It was used for chariot races.

The Pantheon of Rome (Figure 19), built in 138 A.D., has been described as the noblest of all circular temples. It was roofed with a dome admitting light through a round opening at the top called the "eye." Rich paneling and statues covered the interior walls (Figure 20).

The Roman Thermae or baths, constructed about 300 A.D., illustrate the luxury in which the Romans loved to indulge. These tremendous structures contained rooms for gymnastic exercises and games, gardens, and usually three pools: the hot baths (Caldarium), warm baths (Tepidarium), and cold baths (Frigidarium).

Less ornamentation was lavished on the Roman aqueducts and bridges; instead the arch was used in its pure form. As a consequence, these are perhaps the Romans' best works. They were built in layers of arches, the greater arches at the bottom.

The smaller topmost arches were adjusted to the exact height required.

Due to Vesuvius' eruption in 79 A.D., we have a very good picture of the Roman house—at least the house in the provinces. A small vestibule led to the atrium, open to the sky and containing a pool to catch rain water. A second vestibule led from the atrium to the inner court, the peristyle. The peristyle (Figure 21) was also open, but was a bit larger with a garden and statues. Both courts, the front "living" room and the rear "family" room, were surrounded by smaller chambers, in a manner similar to the Assyrian plan.

BYZANTINE ARCHITECTURE

Byzantine architecture is characterized by a dome rising from a square base using transitional curved surfaces called "pendentives." Windows were pierced into the dome allowing a crown of light to enter. Later, the dome was set upon a cylindrical tower, the windows being cut in the tower instead of in the dome. Brick and stone were used for domes instead of the Roman concrete. The extra support needed was supplied by buttresses. The Hagia Sophia at Constantinople (538 A.D.) is the most renowned example of the architecture of this period (Figure 22).

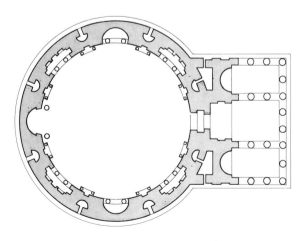

Figure 19   A plan view of the Pantheon at Rome.

Figure 20   The interior of the Pantheon at Rome

ROMANESQUE ARCHITECTURE

The transitional period from Roman and Byzantine to Gothic (ninth to twelfth centuries) has been termed "Romanesque." The foremost examples of Romanesque architecture are churches which appear with variations in many different countries. The square Byzantine plan was replaced by a rectangular plan, quite long and narrow, the interior divided by rows of arches called "arcades." The round arch and stone vault (usually a kind of groined vault) were still used, but no longer singly. The column was moved inside again and, in fact, was built in a compound form called a "pier."

GOTHIC ARCHITECTURE

The Gothic style developed in Western Europe between 1150 and 1450 as an outgrowth of the Romanesque. The Gothic was still an architecture of cathedrals, but it attacked some of the structural problems of vaulting in a different way. First, the groined vaults were supported entirely by comparatively few piers. The wall between the piers was filled in with marvelous pointed arch windows of stained glass and tracery. Secondly, the outward thrust of the vaults was countered by an exterior combination of arches and buttresses called "flying buttresses." These flying buttresses were capped with gables or small steeple-like pinnacles. The third distinguishing Gothic feature was the use of the pointed arch. This was first developed to facilitate the construction of groined vaults on a rectangular plan. The stone vaulted roofs of the cathedrals were covered with a wooden gable roof to protect them from the elements. There are innumerable fine examples of Gothic architecture in use. Outstanding are the Cathedral of Notre Dame at Paris (Figure 23), Cologne Cathedral, the Cathedral of Seville, and Westminster Abbey (Figure 24).

Figure 22   The Hagia Sophia at Istanbul (Constantinople).

Figure 23   Notre Dame.
Figure 24   Westminster Abbey, London.

Figure 21   The peristyle of a house at Pompeii.

Figure 25   The Louvre.

RENAISSANCE ARCHITECTURE

The decline of feudalism and a new freedom of expression in art, literature, and architecture characterized the period known as the Renaissance (1420–1700). The classic civilizations were rediscovered, studied, and imitated. The objection to the architecture of the Renaissance is that the structural framework was hidden beneath a false classical facade. Also, the classical orders were applied in many instances where they did not fit. Knowledge of the Roman orders was the chief stock-in-trade of the architect of this period.

The first example of this new style was the Cathedral of Florence (1420). The Pantheon in Paris is noted for its strict adherence to classical detail. The largest church in existence today is a Renaissance church: St. Peter's in Rome is 600' long and 405' high. Other notable examples are the Louvre in Paris (Figure 25), St. Paul's Cathedral in London, and the Doge's Palace in Venice.

DOMESTIC ARCHITECTURE

Throughout the previous discussion, private dwellings have not often been used as examples. The reason is that only monumental buildings were of sufficiently durable construction to survive time and the elements. However, we do have examples of comparatively recent private dwellings in all countries. For simplicity, let us look only at North American architecture.

The first shelters of the English colonists in the New World (Plymouth and Jamestown) were lean-tos called "English wigwams." They were not like Indian tents, however, but were framed with poles and covered with woven twigs called "wattle," brush, and mud or clay. Sod huts partially buried in the ground with staked walls were also built.

The log cabin was introduced by the Swedes in Delaware. This was the type of dwelling the poorer classes had used in the mother country and was unknown to the Indians. Log construction was adopted by other colonists for use in stockades and prisons. In fact, "log house" meant, at first, a jail. Later, the log house and overhanging block house moved west with the frontier.

It should be noted here that traditional American architecture has its roots in the architecture of the mother countries, particularly England. There was no Indian influence, nor was it the intention of the colonists to found a new architectural style. All they desired was to build a civilization similar to the one they had left. However, available materials and the North American climate soon dictated certain modifications of the European methods.

Around 1600, the typical English middleclass house was of half-timbered construction. That is, a heavy wooden frame was pegged together and filled in with clay-covered wattle or rolls of clay and straw called "cat and clay." In the severe New England climate, however, this construction had to be covered with a horizontal sheathing called "weather boards" (also known in England). Due to the abundance of timber, the clay or brick filling was gradually omitted, being replaced by the hollow frame construction known today. Of course in areas where there was a supply of good building stone (Pennsylvania) or clay for brickmaking (Maryland), these materials were used.

For the roof covering, thatch was replaced by shingles split from the forests of cedar. In fact, the Americans abandoned thatched roofs almost two hundred years before the English.

Classic revival. During the first half of the nineteenth century, the "Classic Revival" held sway. Even the United States turned from its wooden version of the English Georgian (called "Colonial") to Classic Revival in stone and concrete. Examples of Classic Revival in the United States were the White House (Figure 26), the national Capitol (Figure 27), several state Capitols, and many churches. This artificial return to the past slowed down any real architectural progress.

Eclecticism. The Classic Revival was shortly replaced by a conglomeration of various historical styles, any number of which might be used in a single structure, called "Eclecticism." This searching for ancient methods of enclosing modern structures brought architectural progress to a complete halt. At first, even the advent of structural steel framing did not change the Egyptian, Classical, Byzantine, and Renaissance coverings. Only when the simple structural lines of the American skyscraper were left undisguised did architecture move on. Today, Eclecticism is synonymous with all that is false in architecture.

International style. Although the United States led the way in nontraditional design for commercial building, Europe quickly applied this new "functionalism" (the doctrine that a feature should have a *function* and should not be applied for decoration only) to private dwellings. Led by Gropius of Germany and Le Corbusier of France, a type of architecture called the "International Style" developed which was characterized by simple, block-like exteriors, concrete walls with no roof overhang, and windows located at the corners rather than the sides of walls. Unfortunately, the skillful block proportions used to advantage on American commercial structures, culminating in buildings like the Empire State Building (1931) and Rockefeller Center (1930–1950), gave these smaller buildings a boxy, factorylike appearance. When the International Style of domestic architecture spread to England and then to the United States, it was not readily accepted. The lack of eaves, corner windows, and other features of the style were rejected as not being truly functional, but false, applied styling. However, the major premise of the International Style, that of planning the exterior around the interior, was quickly adopted, even though revolutionary. This idea of "form follows function" is the guiding spirit of architecture today—made possible, in reality, by the free use of a combination of old and new building methods.

With this general background of the development of domestic architecture in North America, let us look in more detail at some common examples of residential architecture. The characteristics of these buildings make up what is called "architectural styling."

ARCHITECTURAL STYLING

A working knowledge of architectural styling is important for two reasons:

1. The first decision to be made when planning to build a house is its styling. Will it be traditional or modern? Ranch house or split level? The choice will be affected by the fact that the style, or exterior appearance, influences the interior layout. Some styles, for example, require a one floor house, others one and a half or two floors. Certain styles call for a symmetrical design with a central hall.

2. Even if you have definitely decided upon the styling for a particular house, you should be able to understand and appreciate the advantages of other types.

We shall first discuss the styles and types in more common use, and then later show how to pick the style which will best suit a set of requirements. There are two general classifications of popular architectural styles: traditional and contemporary. Let us take each in turn.

TRADITIONAL

A house built in the traditional style today is a copy, with certain modifications, of a kind of house built previously. There are many dwellings built in the traditional style, but the trend has been towards contemporary. Many people feel that some traditional styles overly limit freedom of layout. Also, many traditional styles are of European, not truly American, origin. However, the traditional house has stood the test of years and will always have a place in the hearts of those who put tradition before expediency.

Figure 26   A view of the south side of the White House (executive mansion).

Figure 27   The Senate wing of the Capitol Building.

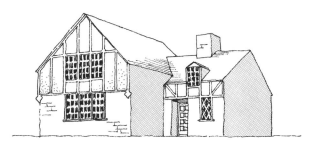

Figure 28   English styling.

Figure 29   Georgian styling.

Figure 30   Regency styling.

Figure 31   A contemporary home with a classic heritage.

English. English houses (Figure 28) are fashioned after the type built in England before the eighteenth century. Historical subdivisions of English architecture are Old English, Tudor, and Elizabethan. Each has its own particular characteristics, but all have common features as well. For example, the interior layout is informal and unsymmetrical due to the lack of exterior symmetry. Walls are of stone, brick, or stucco, and are sometimes half-timbered. The gable ends may be of dark-stained, hand-hewn beams. If the second floor overhangs the first, carved drops may be used at the corners. Fenestration (the arrangement of windows in a wall) is completely random; occasionally a window may appear to be built right through a chimney. The windows are casements (side hinged) and are made of small, diamond panes after the prototype, a style which developed because large sheets of glass were not manufactured at the time. Roofs are steeply pitched, the eaves and ridges being at various levels.

The fireplace used to have a more important function in the home than it does today, since it furnished all cooking and heating facilities. Massive chimneys were usually topped off with chimney pots (vertical extensions of tile or brick). Although some features of the English house may be used in constructing small homes, the style is at its best in larger houses.

Although you will find many examples of English homes in the United States today, most of them were built more than 25 years ago. The English style is not popular for new homes (although occasionally individual features are copied), because builders today cannot build in stone, brick, or stucco at a reasonable price. Moreover, the trend in this country is away from continental ideas and toward American Colonial and modern styles.

Georgian. As we have seen in the section on architectural history, the period of the Renaissance was

Courtesy of Scholz Homes, Inc.

characterized by the rebirth of the architecture of the classical civilizations. Georgian architecture (1714–1760) was also developed from classical principles of formality and symmetry (Figure 29). Many classical details were used, such as pedimented doorways (triangular areas above the doorways), elaborate cornices, and pilasters (bas-relief columns).

The Georgian house (so called for the kings under whom it flourished) is a large one, two or more floors high, with a gently sloping hip roof. The front of the house must be kept religiously symmetrical. The front entrance is at dead center with windows equally spaced on either side, the second floor windows directly above the first floor windows. Symmetry is carried through even to the chimneys—one at either end. If only one chimney is required, a false one is included so that symmetry will be preserved. We often find pilasters, side lights, and columned porches two stories high. The interior plan is, of course, a center hall one, with bedrooms on the second floor. These restrictions of symmetry do not affect the design of the rear of the house, however.

We shall soon see how the Georgian house served as the inspiration for the various American Colonial styles—becoming adapted to wood instead of stucco and stone.

Regency. The king of England at the time of the American Revolution was George III. His son was appointed regent by the English Parliament to reign in his father's place when George III became too old to rule. This period in English history, known as the "Regency," gave birth to a particular architectural style.

A Regency style house (Figure 30) is similar to the Georgian but has cleaner lines and finer details. Exterior walls are usually brick, often painted white. The Georgian formality and hip roof still prevail. Other typical Regency details are long shutters at the first floor level, curved copper bay or porch roofs, curved side wall extensions, and fancy iron work tracery around porches.

Colonial. The term "colonial" is loosely applied to any style developed by colonizers. Colonial architecture, or—to be more specific—English Colonial architecture, consists of Early American (before 1720) and American Colonial (after 1720). American Colonial is a modification of Georgian and consists of various regional types, such as New England, Southern, and Dutch.

Even though there were no trained architects in America before the Revolution, many well-designed houses were built. The reason is that a workable knowledge of architecture was part of every gentleman's training. Each landowner designed his own house (Jefferson designed his own and several others) with the aid of English architectural handbooks which simplified the use of the Renais-

Figure 32   New England Colonial styling.

Figure 33   Garrison styling.

sance orders. If they followed these handbooks, the landowners could not go wrong. For materials, wood was plentiful in all the colonies, although brick was often used in the South and stone in the middle colonies.

New England Colonial. The New England house (Figure 32) was simple and unpretentious, but of such good design and proportion that it has been copied through the years. Since this style is modeled after the Georgian, the front elevation is symmetrical. Wood was plentiful in the North and was used even for classical columns and pilasters. Exterior finish was a narrow clapboard with vertical boards covering the corners so that the clapboards did not have to be mitered. The roof pitch was steep to shed the heavy snows, and sometimes the eaves at the rear dropped a floor lower than the eaves at the front of the house. In early houses, one chimney was located at the center to serve as many rooms as possible, while in later work there were two chimneys, one at either end. The first windows were glassless and closed by wooden shutters. These were replaced by diamond-paned casements imported from England, and eventually by the double hung (nicknamed "guillotine") rectangular paned window. This house was called a "Salt Box" because it looked like the salt boxes sold in early general stores.

Garrison. Like all colonists, the new arrivals in America tried to duplicate the type of house they had known at home. One of the first breaks with this tradition was the garrison house (Figure 33), modeled after the blockhouses the colonists used to fight off Indian raids. These blockhouses had overhanging second stories making them difficult to

Figure 34   Cape Cod styling.

Figure 35   Southern Colonial styling.

Figure 36   Dutch Colonial styling.

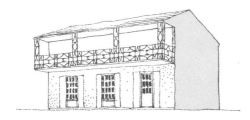

Figure 37   French Colonial styling.

Figure 38   Spanish styling.

scale and easier to defend. In imitation of these forts, some houses were built with an overhanging second floor, although they were otherwise similar to the New England Colonial. The ends of the heavy timbers projecting down below the overhang were frequently carved in some fashion.

Cape Cod. The Cape Cod section of Massachusetts has become known for its charming small homes. Although a true Cape Cod house (Figure 34) has very definite characteristics, nearly any small house having a steeply pitched gable roof with the eave line at the top of the first story may be called "Cape Cod." Actually, a true reproduction will have the following details: double hung, small paned windows with shutters, shingle or clapboard walls, a wood shingle roof (or an imitation), a main entrance in the center of the front elevation, and a massive center chimney. Small dormers at the front or a shed dormer (jokingly called a "dustpan") at the rear adds greatly to the usability of the second floor. An American architect associated with the Cape Cod house is Royal Barry Wills.

Southern Colonial. It is true that better examples of architecture can be found in the larger, more expensive houses than in the small ones. This is natural, since only the wealthy could afford the expense of the details of styling. This distinction was particularly true in the South where some very lovely plantation houses were built (Figure 35). They differed from the New England Colonial mainly in that a flat porch, two stories high and supported by columns, was used to shade the front windows. Brick was the usual material. Today the Southern Colonial style is not as popular as its Northern neighbors because the high porch looks ungainly on any but a very large house.

Dutch Colonial. Dutch and German settlers in New Amsterdam (New York), New Jersey, and Pennsylvania built houses with steeply pitched roofs, called "gambrel" (Figure 36). This type of roof was invented by a French architect named Mansard, who designed a double-pitched roof permitting the attic to be used as another floor. The tale goes that this was done originally to evade the heavier tax on two story houses. When this roof runs on four sides, it is called "Mansard" after the originator; when it is on only two sides, "gambrel" or "Dutch Colonial." The more authentic example of Dutch Colonial has a slightly curved projecting eave with a continuous shed dormer window. Stone construction should be used.

French Colonial. The best examples of authentic French Colonial architecture (Figure 37) can be found in the old French Quarter of New Orleans. Here, buildings are crowded together, each with common characteristics but each different. The hallmark of this style is a flat facade relieved only by wrought iron balconies. The balconies contain fancy scroll work and may be supported by delicate iron columns or trellises. The plastered fronts are tinted pink, yellow, or green.

Spanish. A Spanish house (Figure 38) should appear to have adobe walls in keeping with the material originally available. Roofs are tiled and low-pitched. A close reproduction should be built around a patio and have open-timbered ceilings of rough-hewn logs.

CONTEMPORARY ARCHITECTURE

Many terms such as "modernistic," "futuristic," and "functional" have been used to distinguish nontraditional architecture from traditional. The two terms most widely accepted are "contemporary" and "modern." To be perfectly correct, "contemporary" indicates any building erected at the present time regardless of style. However, since present-day construction consists mainly of ranch, split level, and modern, we will restrict this term to these three types. Occasionally, "contemporary" is used synonymously with "modern."

Ranch. The popularity of the ranch house (Figure 40) today is partly due to its blend of past and present. Most contemporary conveniences can be incorporated into a ranch house design without appearing too extreme. Also, the demand for light construction and low, land-hugging designs has increased, as has the desire for one-floor plans with no stairs to climb.

Nearly any one story house is called a ranch house today, although it should be rambling, have

Figure 40   Ranch styling.

Figure 41   Split level styling.

Figure 42   Modern styling.

an informal plan and a low-pitched roof, preferably hipped. The ranch is well suited to large, flat lots and may be built in the high, medium, and even low price ranges.

Figure 39   A contemporary home in the style of a French chateau.

Split level. A split level house (Figure 41) is arranged so that floor climbing is limited to half-flights of stairs. It is a kind of combination of ranch and two story construction. It might be laid out with bedrooms and bath on the highest level; living, dining, and kitchen half a floor lower (and to one side, of course); and garage and "free room" half a floor lower still (under the bedroom level). A free room is usually a recreation or family room built in "found" or "free" basement areas. The levels may be split between ends or between front and back depending on the terrain. Although the majority of split levels are built on a more or less stock plan, infinite variations are possible. These should offer a real challenge to the designer.

Modern. A truly modern building (Figure 42) should be "honest." That is, it should have a fresh approach to requirements such as shelter, light, and circulation. The modern architect feels that drawing on the styles of the past to any great extent is "dishonest." He designs each house to suit the requirements of those living in it without being fettered by historical styling, symmetry, or useless decoration.

A key word used in modern architecture is "functional." This means that every element of the house should have a reason—a function—for existing. The expression "form follows function" is a simplification of the idea that exterior appearance or form should be subordinated to the functional and structural aspects.

But the modern house should not be merely

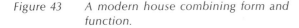

Figure 43   A modern house combining form and function.

Figure 44   A strong statement for a contemporary bank.

a "machine for living," since it also has the function of meeting the family's aesthetic needs. This one factor—a sensitivity to aesthetic need—distinguishes the truly great modern design from the mediocre. Even a mundane structure such as a water tank, when designed by an inspired architect-engineer, can be a community asset rather than a visual pollutant. The 10-million-gallon tank in Figure 45 is braced by star-shaped steel members and illuminated indirectly at night. The slender steel tower shown in Figure 46 encloses a 320,000-gallon water tank which is set in a reflecting pool. A 16-bell carillon is installed in the cage at the top of the spire.

Since sensitivity and originality are objectives of the modern architect, there can be no typical example of modern. However, the style is often marked by a simple (but interesting) design; both native and machine-produced materials; low structures with flat, shed, or clerestory roofs; provision for indoor-outdoor living; and great expanses of glass. Some architects who stand out in modern architecture are Alvar Aalto, Le Corbusier, Walter Gropius, Victor Gruen (Figure 47), Philip Johnson, Louis Kahn, Ludwig Mies van der Rohe (Figures 48 and 49), Pier Luigi Nervi, Richard Neutra, Oscar Niemeyer, Ioh Ming Pei, Eero Saarinen (Figures 50 and 51), Edward Durell Stone (Figure 46), Louis Sullivan, Frank Lloyd Wright (Figures 52–54) and Minoru Yamasaki (Figures 55 and 56).

STUDY QUESTIONS

1. Sketch and name the five fundamental structural systems. Give the civilization responsible for introducing each system.
2. Prepare an outline naming the major civilizations responsible for architectural development.
   a. Include the approximate dates of each.
   b. Indicate the structural systems used.
   c. Give examples of well-known buildings in each period.
3. Discuss the contribution to architectural development

Figure 45   A water tank in Columbus, Ohio.

made by the following civilizations:
a. Egyptian
b. Assyrian
c. Greek
d. Roman
e. Gothic
Give the methods of construction of each and examples.

4. Trace the development of architecture in North America from simple huts to contemporary buildings.
5. (For the advanced student) After a thorough study of building trends over the past 100 years, give your estimate of architectural styles:
   a. 25 years hence
   b. 100 years hence
6. (For the advanced student) Prepare a report on the life and accomplishments of one or more of the following:
   a. Frank Lloyd Wright
   b. Walter Gropius
   c. Le Corbusier
   d. Mies van der Rohe
   e. Eero Saarinen
   Include examples of structures built and proposed by each. Show how his work was influenced by his predecessors.

Figure 46   A water tank on the campus of the State University of New York at Albany. Edward Durell Stone and Associates, architects.

Figure 47   Model of the proposed United Nations Organizations Headquarters for Vienna, Austria. Gruen Associates, architects.

Figure 48   Farnsworth House at Plano, Illinois. Mies Van der Rohe, architect.

Figure 49   Architecture Hall at the Illinois Institute of Technology. Mies Van der Rohe, architect.

7. Classify the residences built today into major categories.
   a. Give a brief description of each.
   b. Include a sketch of a typical example of each.
   c. Give your estimation of its future popularity.

LABORATORY PROBLEMS

1. Prepare a chart showing the five fundamental structural systems.
2. Build a model of each of the five fundamental structural systems.

Figure 50   Yale University hockey rink, New Haven, Connecticut. Eero Saarinen & Associates, architects.

Figure 51   Dulles International Airport terminal near Washington, D.C. Eero Saarinen & Associates, architects.

Figure 52   Fallingwater; a private residence at Bear Run, Pennsylvania. Frank Lloyd Wright, architect.

The Solomon R. Guggenheim Museum, New York.

The Solomon R. Guggenheim Museum, New York.

Figure 53   Above, the exterior of the Solomon R. Guggenheim Museum, New York City. Frank Lloyd Wright, architect.

Figure 54   Above right, the interior of the Guggenheim Museum.

3. Prepare a chart of the major civilizations responsible for architectural development.
4. Build a model of one or more of the following (*for advanced students only):
   a. Pyramid of Cheops (cut away to show interior passages)
   b. Assyrian palace
   c. Parthenon
   *d. Acropolis
   *e. Pantheon
   *f. Cathedral of Notre Dame
   *g. St. Peter's
   h. White House
   i. U.S. Capitol building
   *j. Fallingwater
   k. Farnsworth House
5. Build a model of a typical residence of one or more of the following types:
   a. Egyptian
   b. Greek
   c. Roman
   d. English
   e. Georgian
   f. Colonial
   g. Ranch
   h. Split level
   i. Modern
6. Arrange for a practicing architect to visit the class and discuss contemporary architectural design.

Figure 55   Manufacturers and Traders Trust Building, Buffalo, New York. Minoru Yamasaki and Associates, architects.

Figure 56   Eastern Airlines terminal, Boston, Massachusetts. Minoru Yamasaki and Associates, architects.

3 primary considerations

Talk to persons who have recently designed a home. Ask them if they would do it again, and you'll get a variety of replies. Some will tell you that this was a most satisfying and rewarding experience; others will say it was entirely frustrating. After further questioning, you'll find that those who were most successful have an important characteristic: *sensitivity*. The successful designer has the ability to be sensitive to many factors. Some of these factors are aesthetic (such as feeling the potentials of the site), some are empathic (such as understanding the desires of his client), and some are practical (such as keeping within the budget). The designer must be sensitive to many such factors throughout the entire design process. But some factors should be considered before starting to sketch a preliminary layout (Chapter 15) or even listing program requirements (Chapter 5). These are called *primary considerations* and are discussed in this chapter:

1. The site
2. Architectural styling
3. Basic structure
     Size
     Number of floors
     Shape of plan
     Foundation
     Roof
     Expansion
4. Building codes and zoning
5. Cost

THE SITE

To the sensitive designer, each site has an individual character which suggests the most appropriate structure and style of home. The contour of the land, shape of the plot, kind of trees, surrounding views, and type of community all give broad hints toward a satisfactory solution. For example, a *sloping* contour suggests a split level or modern house. A *narrow* plot restricts the choice of styles and requires special planning to prevent a cramped appearance. A *wide* plot offers more freedom of planning, permitting a low, rambling design or several connected modules. Try to keep excavation to a minimum, for the less the natural contour of the site is disturbed, the less Nature will try to disturb the occupants of that site (Figure 1).

Take advantage of existing trees, especially if they are large; it will take many years for newly-planted trees to mature. Evergreen trees to the windward are excellent natural windbreaks, and deciduous trees located on the southern side of the site are natural "automatic" solar screens. They shade a building from the undesirable summer sun (reducing the interior temperature by about 10°) and, by shedding their leaves in the winter, permit the desirable winter sunlight to filter through.

It has always been an architectural goal to provide a building which shields the occupant from a sometimes-hostile environment. In so doing, how-

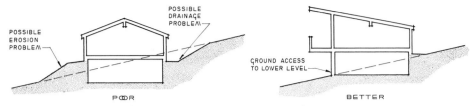

Choose appropriate structure for site.

Choose appropriate site for structure.

Figure 1

ever, the occupant does not wish to lose contact with the friendly parts of the environment. Thus exterior living space adjacent to interior living space should be provided. Also glass window walls can face the best views while unpleasant views or noisy streets can be shielded. Be sensitive to the nature of the surrounding community and avoid building in a style which is incompatible with nearby architectural styles.

The plot belonging to Mr. A* is narrow and relatively flat with an excellent view to the rear. The views to the front and left are undesirable.
Decision: Clerestory windows or atrium.

ARCHITECTURAL STYLING

As indicated in Chapter 2, the architectural styling should be considered before preliminary sketches are drawn. Although many factors influence the choice of style, the owner's personal preference will be the outstanding consideration.

The need to eliminate all front windows prevents traditional styling.
Decision: Contemporary.

*In this book, a house will be designed for Mr. A from beginning to end. He is not necessarily an average person, and his home is not to be considered a model for your future designs.

BASIC STRUCTURE

The nature of the site and architectural styling desired provide important clues to the type of basic structure required. Now is the time to make tentative decisions on the size and type of structure, number of floors, and general plan shape.

Size. The number of rooms and their special requirements are primary considerations since they determine the size of the structure. Usually a balance must be reached between the number of rooms desired and the number that can be afforded.

Careful thought should be given to the number of bedrooms. A common error on the part of young couples with no children or only a single child is building a one- or two-bedroom house with the thought that they can sell or add on if another bedroom is needed. A house with less than three bedrooms is difficult to sell, and actually adding a room (not finishing an existing one) is more costly than including it in the original plans, not to mention the sacrifice in exterior appearance.

Even minor rooms like bathrooms should be carefully planned to answer questions of: how many? what size? simple or with contemporary sectioned areas? a powder room near the front entrance? These questions, and many others, must be answered before the plans are begun.

Mr. and Mrs. A have two children, ages 3 and 9.
Decision: Three bedrooms: a master bedroom with shower

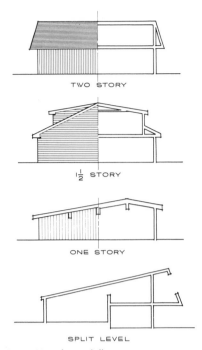

Figure 2   *Number of floors.*

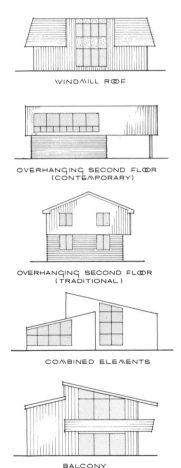

Figure 3   *Methods of relieving vertical appearance.*

and two additional bedrooms served by one main bathroom.

The A family does much entertaining (parties of 4 to 50).
Decision: Provision for living area overflow to family area, basement recreation room, and patio.

Mr. A has built a 12' power boat which he stores on the property.
Decision: Oversize or double garage, provision for future shop.

Mrs. A desires more storage space than she has had in previous kitchens.
Decision: Utility room with shelves adjacent to kitchen.

Number of floors. The number of floors is a basic decision (Figure 2). Should there be two floors, one and a half floors, one floor, or one of the combinations afforded by split level designs?

The two floor home, with sleeping areas on one floor, and living-dining-cooking areas on another, usually provides more "gracious living." Areas are definitely separated, making it easier to clean (or not to clean), to entertain, and to get all the privacy wanted. A special effort is needed to relieve the vertical appearance (Figure 3).

The one and a half story house is an attempt to capture the advantages of the two story house, but to reduce the cost by reducing the outside wall area. (Of course, portions of the bedrooms must have sloping ceilings.) Remember that the use of too many dormers will reduce any cost advantage.

For those who dislike stair climbing and want a low-cost home (two bedrooms, no dining room), the one floor house is the answer. Remember, however, that a moderately large number of rooms (six or seven) will cost more in a one floor plan, since larger roof and foundation areas are required. In general: one floor for four or five rooms, two floors for six or more.*

EXAMPLE

The A residence will require five and one half rooms; an atrium is desired.
Decision: Group rooms to create atrium; all rooms on one floor for more light into atrium.

Shape of plan. Since the shape of the floor plan affects house styling and cost, it should be given special consideration (Figure 4). In general, it is best to create a plan that is irregular enough to be interesting and to supply the needed wall area for lighting all rooms. But keep in mind that each extraneous corner adds to the total cost. If low cost is a primary objective, a square plan is the best choice,

*Living room, dining room, kitchen, bedroom, den, playroom, and enclosed heated porch are each considered one room. Attached rooms such as dining ell or kitchenette are considered as half rooms. Bath, porch, breezeway, basement, and attic are not considered rooms.

Figure 4   Plan shapes.

since it encloses a given volume with a minimum of wall area. In practice, a rectangular plan is more often used because of its appearance and planning advantages. The addition of ells (L-shaped, T-shaped, or C-shaped) is costly and should be weighed against their advantages.

EXAMPLE

To illustrate the effect of the number of floors and plan shape on the total house cost, compare the two houses in Figure 5. Each has identical floor area, the differences being the plan shape and the number of floors.

House A is a two floor house with 30 × 30 = 900 sq. ft. of floor area on each floor, giving a total of 1800 sq. ft. Its plan is square. House B is a one floor house with 60 × 30 = 1800 sq. ft. of floor area. Its plan is rectangular.

The total area of walls, roof, and slab floor needed to enclose house A is 3871 sq. ft. The total area needed to enclose house B is 5583 sq. ft. Although there are some discrepancies in any comparison such as this (house A must have an additional interior floor and heavier foundation), the increase in outside area needed to enclose this one floor, rectangular house over the two floor, square house is:

$$\frac{5583 - 3871}{3871} \times 100 = 44\%$$

	House A	House B
Front and rear elevations	1080 sq. ft.	1440 sq. ft.
End elevations	960 sq. ft.	480 sq. ft.
Roof	931 sq. ft.	1863 sq. ft.
Slab	900 sq. ft.	1800 sq. ft.
Total	3871 sq. ft.	5583 sq. ft.

Foundation. There is continuing controversy over whether or not to provide a basement in new house construction.

The advantages of a basementless house are:

1. Room for the furnace, water heater, laundry, workshop, storage area, and playroom is more convenient if located on the first floor.
2. A slight saving may be realized due to the omission of floor joists and basement stairway.
3. The house can be kept just as warm and dry as if a basement were built.

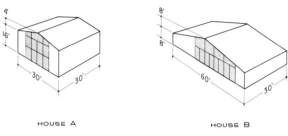

HOUSE A   HOUSE B

Figure 5

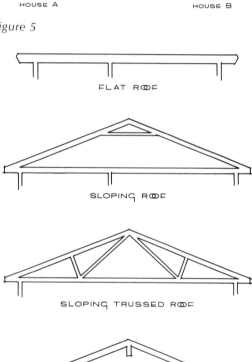

FLAT ROOF

SLOPING ROOF

SLOPING TRUSSED ROOF

SLOPING ROOF & CEILING WITH EXPOSED BEAMS

CLERESTORY ROOF FOR INTERIOR LIGHTING

Figure 6   Common roof types.

4. This is the ideal construction if a ledge is encountered on the land.
5. This may be preferred in areas having a high water table (water level in the ground).

The advantages of a basement are:

1. The total cubage enclosed by a basement cannot be provided above ground at comparable cost.
2. Due to drainage problems, a basement should be provided when building on a steeply sloping plot.
3. There is little or no saving in omitting the basement from a house built in a cold climate, since footings must go 4'-6" or more in depth.
4. There is little or no saving in omitting a basement from a house of two or more floors.
5. In some localities, zoning laws prohibit basementless construction.
6. Prevailing public opinion is in favor of basements. For this reason, banks and loan agencies will favor a house with a basement.

As you can see, there is no one simple answer for all conditions, because plot contour, climate, house size, zoning, and cost must be considered. The major advantage of a basementless house is elimination of stair climbing. Rooms above ground level are warmer and lighter, but unfortunately houses without basements are seldom designed with suitable space for all the functions a basement provides.

Studies have been conducted to determine actual savings in eliminating the basement. It has been found that slab construction reduces the cost of the foundation by 25 percent. But if space is added at the first floor level for the functions of a basement, no saving is realized, since additional foundation walls and roof must be provided. A large, rambling, one floor house will produce the greatest saving if the basement is omitted. This is not true of a house with two or more floors, since it requires a more substantial foundation and because in such a house the basement takes up a smaller proportion of the total house cubage.

In your decision, various combinations should also be considered. Many houses are built today with a basement under one portion, and slab construction or a crawl space under another. The split level house is a good example of this solution. It may have the garage under the sleeping area and the basement under the living-eating area.

EXAMPLE

The A residence will include an emergency shelter and provision for a future recreation room. Also, Mr. A wants a shop for his hobby of woodworking.
Decision: Full or partial basement.

Roof. The choice of a pitched or flat roof is somewhat dependent upon house styling (Figure 6). Although the final choice will probably depend upon

personal taste, both possibilities have advantages.
The advantages of a flat roof are:

1. Storage space such as is provided by an attic is more convenient if located on the ground floor.
2. A saving can be realized due to the reduction of framing and omission of the stairway.
3. A complicated floor plan is more easily covered with a flat roof.
4. A properly installed flat roof gives satisfactory service. Snow can accumulate on the roof serving as insulation in the winter, while a "water film roof" serves as insulation (reflector) against summer heat.

The advantages of a pitched roof are:

1. A pitched roof with attic provides cheap storage, play, and expansion area. A pitched roof with sloping ceilings provides a major design feature.
2. Certain architectural styles demand the use of a pitched roof.
3. In some localities, zoning laws prohibit flat roof construction.
4. Prevailing public opinion is in favor of a pitched roof.

Again, there is no one answer, and many factors must influence the decision. However, if low cost is a primary objective, the flat roof will offer a saving. This will, of course, restrict the style of the house. As far as function is concerned, flat roofs have been used satisfactorily on urban buildings for centuries.

EXAMPLE

A cathedral ceiling is desired in the living room. Undesirable views suggest windows above eye level to permit light without view.
Decision: Gable or clerestory roof.

Expansion. If low original cost is an object, a house can be very carefully designed so that a room or garage can be added later without a loss to the exterior appearance either before or after the addition (Figure 7). The simplest forms of expansion are the expansion attic and unfinished basement. The expansion attic will cost the owner only as much as a shed dormer, an unfinished stairway, and some electrical and heating extensions, certainly an economical provision for several additional rooms.

EXAMPLE

Mr. and Mrs. A would like to provide for the possibility of a third child, increased recreational area, and a woodworking shop.
Decision: 1) One child's bedroom to be oversized for possible future use by two children. 2) A full (or partial) basement to be finished into a recreation room and shop at a later date.

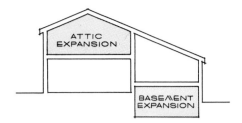

Figure 7   Plan for future expansion.

BUILDING CODES AND ZONING

Local zoning laws may be quite restrictive as to the position of a house, its cubage in relation to surrounding dwellings, and even its style. A copy of the local zoning ordinances can be obtained from any town hall. These should be studied carefully before planning is begun.

EXAMPLE

The most important zoning limitations which apply to the location of the A residence were found to be:

30' minimum front yard setback
8' minimum side yard setback
25' maximum building height

COST

Although we list cost last, it should certainly be a major consideration, influencing nearly every other factor. To be enjoyed, a home must be within the owner's means. No one wants a house that will be impossible to keep up, and might finally be lost. The following chapter on financing relates the house cost to income.

STUDY QUESTIONS

1. Indicate the most suitable style of house to build on the following type of land:
   a. A wide, flat plot
   b. A narrow, flat plot
   c. A steeply sloping plot
2. A friend tells you he has purchased a small, five-and-a-half-room house. What kinds of rooms does that house probably contain?
3. Most families live in three-bedroom houses. If no more than two children are to occupy a single bedroom, show how the three bedrooms should be utilized by the following families:
   a. One son
   b. One son and one daughter
   c. One son and two daughters

d. Three daughters

e. Two sons and two daughters

4. List the advantages of:

  a. The two floor house

  b. The one-and-a-half floor house

  c. The one floor house

5. Low-cost housing containing 1500 sq. ft. of floor area is to be built with a flat roof and full basement. Which of the following alternatives would cost the least to construct? Which would cost the most? Why?

  a. A rectangular, one floor plan

  b. A rectangular, two floor plan

  c. An L-shaped, one floor plan

  d. An L-shaped, two floor plan

6. Should a basement or slab be specified under each of the following conditions?

  a. Low-cost housing on flat land, southern states

  b. Moderate-priced housing, New England states

  c. Known ledge, 2'-6" below surface

  d. Steeply sloping land

7. Should a flat roof or pitched roof with attic be specified for:

a. A Cape Cod house

b. A modern house with a floor plan containing several ells

c. A retirement cottage for a couple unwilling to climb stairs

LABORATORY PROBLEMS

1. Complete the skeleton outline of primary considerations for your original house design:

Type of plot: _____

House style desired: _____

Number of rooms needed: _____

Number of floors desired: _____

Plan shape desired: _____

Basement or no basement: _____

Flat or sloping roof: _____

Expansion requirements: _____

Zoning limitations: _____

Tentative cost: _____

4 financing

The planning and building of a home is an important step in the life of every family. A house is usually the largest single purchase a family will make. There are a number of "rules of thumb" which will aid in deciding if this purchase can be afforded—and how large a purchase. However, none of these rules can take into consideration the "sacrifice factor"— that is, that some persons with moderate incomes want their own homes so badly that they are willing to make many sacrifices. Others will never be able to make ends meet no matter how high a salary level they reach. The following rules and information should help with these financial decisions. In the final analysis, though, only each individual knows all the details of his present financial status and earning potential.

MORTGAGE CALCULATIONS

Yearly income. The total amount invested in a house should not exceed two and one-half times the yearly income.

EXAMPLE

Mr. A earns $18,000 a year. This would justify his spending $45,000 on a house.

Down payment. A down payment of 20 percent of the total house cost is advisable, although some lending agencies accept 10 percent or less. Of course, the larger the down payment, the less mortgage interest charges.

EXAMPLE

Mr. A decides to make a down payment of 33 percent of the $45,000 total cost. This requires a down payment of $15,000, leaving $30,000 to be borrowed.

Weekly income. The monthly shelter expenses (mortgage payments, taxes, insurance) should not exceed the weekly income.

TABLE 1

Monthly Payments on Various Mortgages (figured at $8\frac{1}{2}$ percent)

Amount of Mortgage	Length of Mortgage			
	15 yrs	20 yrs	25 yrs	30 yrs
$10,000	$98.48	$86.79	$80.53	$76.90
$15,000	$147.72	$130.18	$120.79	$115.34
$20,000	$196.95	$173.57	$161.05	$153.79
$25,000	$246.19	$216.96	$201.31	$192.23
$30,000	$295.43	$260.36	$241.58	$230.68

Taxes and insurance are normally added to above payments.

Mr. A earns $18,000 a year or $346 a week. This would justify his spending $346 a month on a house. Table I shows that a 15-year mortgage on $30,000 ($45,000 total cost minus the $15,000 down payment) would be about $295 a month. This allows only $51 leeway for taxes and insurance. A 20-year mortgage would be about $260 a month allowing $86 for taxes and insurance.

Construction loan. A mortgage can be obtained only on a finished house. During building a construction loan is obtained, usually at the same interest rate as the mortgage.

Mortgage. Nearly every home bought today is financed by means of a mortgage. Most of these mortgages provide for uniform monthly payments consisting of interest, amortization, and taxes. As time passes, the proportion of the monthly payments going toward amortization (that is, payment of the principal) increases, and the amount going toward interest decreases. Thus the early payments are nearly all interest payments, while the last payments are nearly all amortization payments. If the property tax is increased, the amount of the monthly payment will be increased proportionately. A good mortgage should include these features:

1. Monthly payments which include taxes and sometimes insurance
2. Little or no charge for items like appraisal, title search, and mortgage tax
3. Prepayment of part or all of the mortgage before the end of the period if the borrower wishes
4. An open-end clause allowing the borrower to reborrow a sum equal to the amount amortized for the purpose of expanding or finishing

Mortgage interest rate. A home mortgage interest rate varies from place to place and year to year. Bank interest rates now range from 8 to 10 percent; an FHA (Federal Housing Administration) insured mortgage is lower, but added charges raise the total to approximately the same cost. For example, *mortgage insurance* (to protect the *bank* against loss on the mortgage) may add a 1 percent insurance premium.

Length of mortgage. In normal times, mortgage payments should be made over as short a term as possible.

Mr. A calculated he would have to pay a total of $83,000 on a 30-year mortgage ($30,000 amortization and $53,000 interest) at eight and one half percent. He decided on the 15-year mortgage, since he would pay only $53,000 total ($30,000 amortization and $23,000 interest).

Satisfaction piece. When the last payment is made, the bank will send a document stating that the mortgage has been paid in full. This is called a "satisfaction piece." Also, the mortgage will be returned. The satisfaction piece should be recorded; the mortgage can be burned.

COST ESTIMATION

In nearly every case, the owner will want to build as large a house as his salary will afford. There are two commonly used methods of estimating house cost. One method is based on the volume or cubage of the building, the other on the floor area.

Cubage: $1.50–$2.00 per cu. ft.
Area: $15.00–$20.00 per sq. ft. inexpensive, unfinished
$20.00–$25.00 per sq. ft. moderate
$25.00–$30.00 per sq. ft. good materials and workmanship

The unit cost of a house (by cubage or area) will vary considerably from one location to another and even from one year to another. Also, a small house will have a greater unit cost than a large one, since some expenses (such as the heating plant) remain almost the same regardless of the size of the house.

Calculation by cubage. Calculations for volume include all enclosed areas, such as the garage, basement, attic, dormers, chimneys, and enclosed porches. Outside dimensions are used (from the outside of walls, roof, and floor slab). Open porches and areaways are included at half volume.

Calculation by area. All enclosed areas are included in the area calculations, but some are reduced in the following proportions:

Garage	$\frac{2}{3}$
Enclosed porch	$\frac{2}{3}$
Open porch	$\frac{1}{2}$
Unfinished basement	$\frac{1}{2}$
(finished basement:	full area)
Carport	$\frac{1}{2}$

REDUCING COST

Many persons cut building costs by doing some of the construction themselves. Figure 1 shows the areas which will produce the greatest savings. The percentages on this pie chart represent percentages of total cost of a wood-framed house. Each category can be further split 50-50; half of each category representing labor, half material. Several thousand dollars should be added to cover miscellaneous building equipment, landscaping, and other expenses.

Warning. Anyone who has recently built a home will tell you that they have spent 10 to 25 percent more than they originally intended. Indeed, ex-apartment dwellers will sometimes spend over 50 percent more than their estimated cost when they are furnishing and buying tools and equipment.

STUDY QUESTIONS

1. The *total cost* of a house should not exceed _____.
2. The *monthly cost* of a house should not exceed _____.
3. When obtaining a house mortgage, an advisable down payment is _____.
4. Distinguish between:
   a. The construction loan and the house mortgage
   b. Mortgage interest and mortgage amortization
   c. Area cost estimation and volume cost estimation

LABORATORY PROBLEMS

1. Obtain the mortgage interest rate and an interest table from your local bank. Prepare a table of monthly mortgage payments similar to that shown in Table 1.
2. Mr. B has a yearly salary of $20,000. Prepare a list of financial considerations for him as follows:
   a. Yearly income: _____
   b. Weekly income: _____
   c. House cost: _____
   d. House area: _____ (Use average construction cost)
3. Prepare a list of financial considerations as indicated in Problem 2 to meet the requirements of a client as assigned by your instructor.

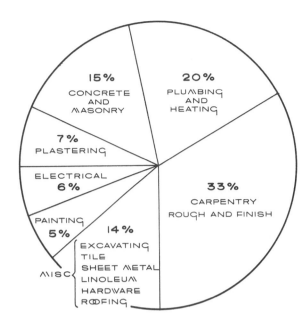

Figure 1   Where your building dollar goes.

4. Prepare a list of financial considerations for your original house design as follows:

   a. Estimated yearly income: _____
   b. Weekly income: _____
   c. House cost: _____
   d. Amount of mortgage: _____
   e. Length of mortgage: _____
   f. Interest rate of mortgage: _____
   g. Amount of down payment: _____
   h. Amount of monthly payments: _____
   i. House area: _____

5 the program

The first problem confronting an architect engaged to design a home is to find the type of house which will best suit the family's requirements and budget. To prevent items from being forgotten, a list of requirements is drawn up at the first meeting between the owner and architect. This list is called the *program*.

In studying architectural drafting, you are probably planning your own home, and thus you are taking the parts of both owner and architect. However, you will find that you should still prepare a program to help you keep your goals clearly in mind.

Your program should look somewhat like the program for the A residence.

GENERAL REQUIREMENTS

Size: 2,000 to 2,500 sq. ft.
Cost: Lot: $8,000. House: $45,000
Style: Contemporary.
Exterior finish: Vertical board and batten siding, brick or stone.
Roof: No preference.
Second floor: No.
Basement: Full or partial basement to be finished into recreation room later.

ORIENTATION

Living: West (to view).
Dining: No preference.
Kitchen: No preference.

Master bedroom: West (to view).
Other bedrooms: Not west.

ROOM REQUIREMENTS

Living area: Conversational area (fireplace with raised hearth), bridge area, and music area. Cathedral ceiling desired.
Dining area: Informal (combine with kitchen or family room).
Kitchen: U-type kitchen with baking island, built-in wall ovens, burners, dishwasher, and garbage disposer. Allow for refrigerator-freezer and breakfast bar. Connect to garage.
Utility room: For storage of canned foods and miscellaneous items.
Family area: Include if possible without exceeding cost limitations. Provide fireplace if possible.
Bedrooms: Master bedroom with double bed, separate closets for Mr. and Mrs. A, large picture window view of Mount Nittany, and attached bathroom with shower. Separate bedrooms for two children: Mark, age 9; and Beth, age 3. Beth's bedroom adjacent to master bedroom, if possible.
Hobby room: Use family room or basement.
Entertainment: Much entertaining (parties of 4 to 50).
Bathrooms: Main bathroom with toilet, lavatory, bathtub, and shower; master bathroom with toilet, lavatory, and stall shower; and powder room with toilet and lavatory (or use main bathroom).
Laundry: Locate on first floor. Provide for electric washer and dryer.
Storage: Two closets in master bedroom, one in other bedrooms, linen closets, large front entrance guest coat

closet, broom closet, garden tools.

Basement: Unfinished. Future use will be general recreation, ping-pong, snack bar and workshop. Provide outside entrance to future workshop.

Garage: One car attached, 12' power boat.

Porch: None.

Emergency shelter: For four persons.

Terrace: To rear of plot next to living area.

Garden: Flowers, not vegetables.

Fireplaces: Living area, family area, and recreation room.

Miscellaneous: Front entrance vestibule preferred. Atrium or clerestory required due to narrow lot and unpleasant views.

ROOM SIZES *

Living area: 15' × 25'
Dining and family area: 15' × 20'
Kitchen: 12' × 15'
Master bedrooms: 12' × 15'
Other bedrooms: 10' × 12', 12' × 15'
Bathrooms: Average size.
Hall width: 3' to 3½'
Stair width: 3' to 3½'
Closets: Large.
Garage: 14' × 21'

MECHANICAL REQUIREMENTS

Plumbing: Copper tubing, several outside bibbs.
Heating: No exposed radiators.
Air conditioning: Omit, but plan for future addition.
Electrical: Outside convenience outlets, silent switches.
Special equipment: Telephone wiring to each room. Television conduits to living room, family room, and master bedroom.

SITE

Location: West side of Outer Drive.
Size: 75' × 140' deep.
Zoning limitations: 30' minimum front yard setback. 8' minimum side yard setback, 25' maximum height.
Best view: West to Mount Nittany.
Trees: Eight birch, five sumac, one cherry—remove as few as possible.
Garden wanted: As extensive as possible.

After studying the program given above, it might be well to turn to the final plans (Chapter 16) and elevations (Chapter 19) to discover how the final product compares with the program. You will notice that nearly every requirement has been satisfied.

LABORATORY PROBLEMS

1. Complete the program for your original house design using the skeleton outline at right:

*Note: Room sizes should be determined only after careful comparison with familiar rooms of known size.

General requirements

Size: _____
Cost: _____
Style: _____
Exterior finish: _____
Roof: _____
Second floor: _____
Basement: _____

Orientation

Living: _____
Dining: _____
Kitchen: _____
Master bedroom: _____
Other bedrooms: _____

Room requirements

Living room or living area: _____
Dining room or dining area: _____
Kitchen: _____
Utility room: _____
Family room: _____
Master bedroom: _____
Other bedrooms: _____
Den or study: _____
Bathrooms: _____
Laundry: _____
Storage: _____
Basement: _____
Garage: _____
Porch: _____
Terrace: _____
Fireplace: _____
Miscellaneous: (Special preferences or provisions for pets, hobbies, etc.) _____

Room sizes

Living room: _____
Dining room: _____
Kitchen: _____
Master bedroom: _____
Other bedrooms: _____
Bathrooms: _____
Hall width: _____
Stair width: _____
Closets: _____
Garage: _____

Mechanical requirements

Plumbing: _____
Heating: _____
Air conditioning: _____
Electrical: _____
Special equipment: _____

Site

Location: _____
Size: _____
Zoning limitations: _____
Best views: _____
Trees: _____
Garden: _____

PART TWO

drawing conventions

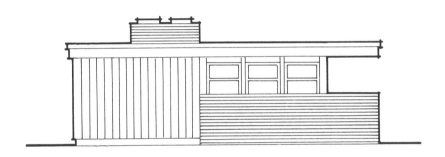

6 sketching and drafting

Each profession has a symbol which has been generally accepted as the hallmark of the field. Often the symbol is an instrument or device commonly used by the members of that profession: a palette for art, a baton for music, a transit for surveying, a stethoscope for medicine. For architects, the pencil has been their symbol, and for draftsmen, the T-square. A pencil represents freehand sketching at the initial design stage, and the T-square represents the accurate drafting of the final plans. A successful architectural draftsman certainly must be proficient in using the tools of his trade: a pencil and T-square. This chapter, then, shares with you the sketching and drafting methods which other architectural draftsmen are now using to do their jobs quickly and accurately.

SKETCHING

Freehand sketching is *not* difficult! An extremely steady hand or other special skill is not necessary. All that is needed is an understanding of what *is* required and what is *not* required to produce an excellent sketch. Just remember that you control your hand; your hand does not control you.

Lines. A freehand sketch is not intended to look like an instrumental drawing with perfectly straight and accurate lines. In fact, the unevenness of a properly sketched line is more attractive and interesting than a mechanically perfect line. The weight, direction,

and proportions of sketched lines *are* important however, and the following rules should help. But please remember to concentrate on the desired *results* rather than on the rules.

1. A soft pencil (such as an F grade) is best for sketching. The point should be shaped to a long, tapered point as shown in Figure 1. The point is slightly rounded rather than needle-sharp. After sketching each line, twist your pencil slightly to avoid developing a flat portion. This will reduce the number of necessary sharpenings.

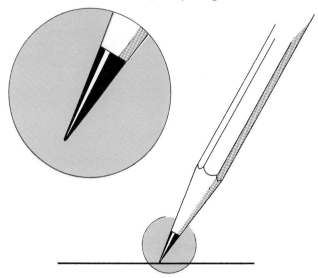

Figure 1   Lead point for sketching.

2. As you might expect, a right-handed person sketches short horizontal lines from left to right* and short vertical and inclined lines from top to bottom as shown in Figure 2. If the angle of a line seems awkward for you, your paper can be turned to a more comfortable position. This is the reason that draftsmen don't tape sketches to a drawing board as they do when drafting with instruments.

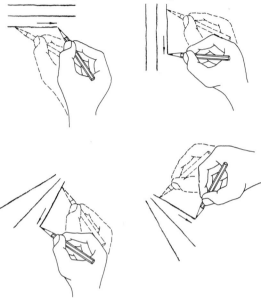

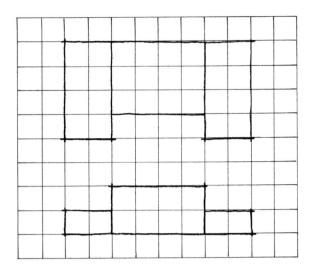

Figure 2   Sketching short lines.

3. To sketch a line, rest your hand on the drawing surface and pivot only your fingers. Most persons cannot sketch a line longer than 1″ without sliding their hand. Therefore lines longer than 1″ are sketched in short intervals leaving a small gap between each interval as shown in Figure 3. Do not omit these gaps, for they add a professional touch to a sketch.

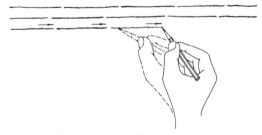

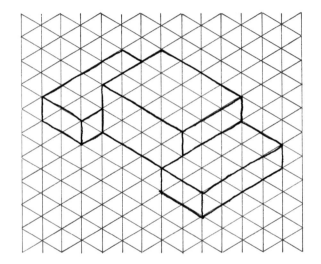

Figure 3   Sketching long lines.

4. The correct *direction* of a sketched line is most important. Horizontal lines should be horizontal and not inclined. Vertical lines should be vertical and not leaning. The easiest way to accomplish this is to sketch on graph paper or on tracing paper placed over graph paper. Graph paper with $\frac{1}{4}$″ grids is commonly used (Figure 4, top). Special tracing vellum with grid lines that disappear when

*A left-handed person sketches from right to left.

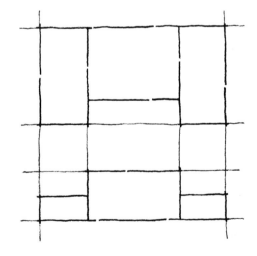

Figure 4   Top: Sketching on 1/4″ graph paper. Center: Sketching on isometric graph paper. Bottom: Blocking lines to aid direction and proportion.

reproduced is also available. Isometric paper may be used for pictorial sketching (Figure 4, center).

Another advantage of tracing paper is that alternate schemes can be sketched and studied. Details which are to remain unchanged can be easily traced from the initial scheme. Often an architectural draftsman will find it easier to correct mistakes by retracing than by erasing.

5. When graph paper is not used, the sketch is blocked in using very light construction lines (Figure 4, bottom). Before darkening with the final outlines, these construction lines give you a chance to study your sketch for the proper line direction and proportion.

6. Good *proportion* is important to all design and immediately distinguishes an excellent sketch from a mediocre one. Proportion is simply a matter of relating one length or area to another—for example, the relation of the width of an object to its height (is the width twice the height or $2\frac{1}{2}$ times the height?), or the relation of one portion of an object to another portion. The over-all proportions of an object are especially important, for they will determine the proportions of all smaller elements.

Often areas can be compared with a simple geometric form such as a square, triangle, or circle. Rectangles can be divided easily by eye into several squares. Examples are shown in Figure 5.

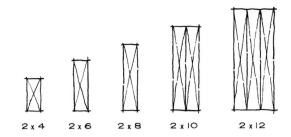

Figure 6   Lumber proportions.

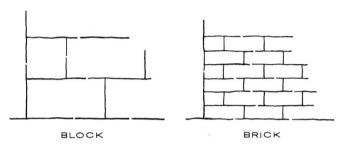

Figure 7   Masonry proportions.

BLOCK   BRICK

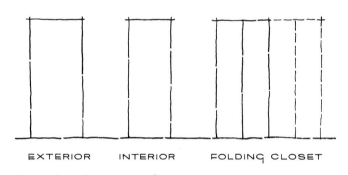

EXTERIOR   INTERIOR   FOLDING CLOSET

Figure 8   Door proportions.

Many building components occur so often that it is worth an effort to study and sketch them to become familiar with their proportions: 2″ lumber, 8″ × 16″ concrete block modules, $2\frac{2}{3}$″ × 4″ × 8″ brick modules as shown in Figures 6 and 7. In Figure 8, notice how only a slight change in the proportion of an object—a door—will change the type of door. With such basic materials properly proportioned, other elements will more easily fall into place.

Circles and arcs. Large circles are best sketched by inscribing them inside a square of light construction lines as shown in Figure 9. The center lines determine the tangent points. Small circles can be sketched using only the center lines.

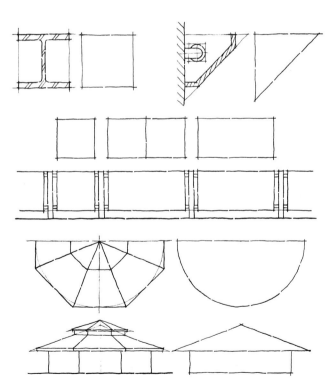

Figure 5   Proportioning by comparison with geometric forms.

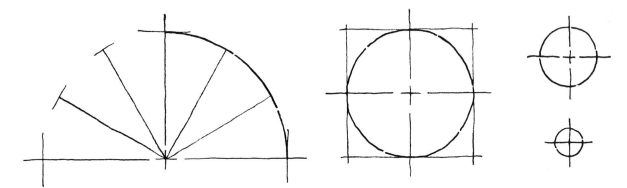

Figure 9   Sketching circles.

Ellipses. When a circle is inclined to the picture plane, it will appear as an ellipse. Consequently, ellipses often must be drawn in pictorial sketches. As with circles, the best method is to sketch first the center lines with light lines and then the enclosing rectangle with very light construction lines. Then draw tangent arcs at the ends of the major and minor axes, and complete the ellipse by connecting these tangent arcs. See Figure 10.

These sketching techniques are shown in Figure 11.

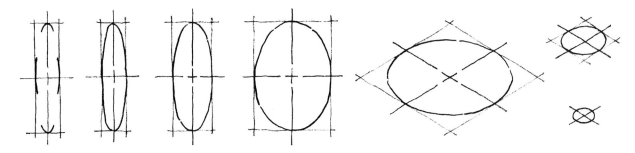

Figure 10   Sketching ellipses.

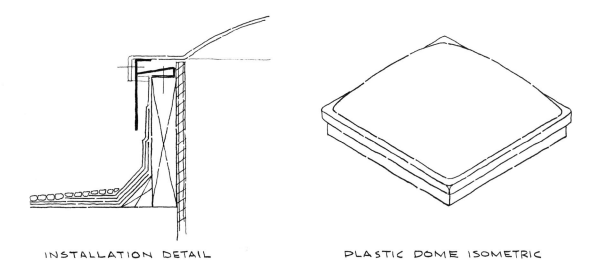

INSTALLATION DETAIL   PLASTIC DOME ISOMETRIC

Figure 11   Pencil sketching technique.

DRAFTING

Drafting usually refers to drawing with the aid of drafting instruments such as the T-square and triangles discussed in Chapter 1. With the help of these drafting instruments, drawings can be produced quickly and accurately. In some instances, they are even used as patterns for finished products.

Lines. Straight lines are drawn with the aid of a straightedge and circular lines with the aid of a compass. Here are some techniques used by experienced draftsmen:

1. The point of your drafting pencil should be long and tapered, as shown in Figure 12, and slightly sharper than the pencil point used for sketching. There is another difference between sketching and drafting. The pencil is rotated slightly *during* the drawing of each line (rather than *after* the line is drawn). This keeps the point uniform so you can produce lines of constant weight.

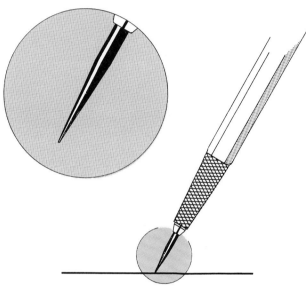

Figure 12   Lead point for drafting.

2. A right-handed person draws horizontal lines from left to right* using the top edge of the T-square, parallel rule, or drafting machine as a guide (Figure 13). When using a T-square, you first press its head firmly against the working edge of the drawing board or table with your left hand. Then you move your left hand to the middle of the blade of the T-square to hold it down. Your left hand is now in a position to also hold a triangle pressed against the top of the blade, if you wish to draw vertical lines.

*Left-handers: In general, reverse these rules. Draw horizontal lines from right to left holding your T-square with your right hand with the head of the T-square at the right. Draw vertical lines upward but using the right edge of the triangle. Draw most inclined lines from right to left.

3. A right-handed person draws vertical lines upward using the left edge of a triangle (Figure 14).*
4. Most inclined lines are drawn from left to right using the top edge of a triangle (Figure 15).*
5. Wedge points rather than conical points are used for compass leads. This is needed to keep the compass sharp, for it is not possible to rotate the compass lead (with respect to the direction of the line being drawn) as with drafting pencils. A wedge point is formed by sanding just one flat surface. That flat surface may be facing inward or outward depending on the design of the compass and the radius to be drawn. As shown in Figure 16, the lead should be perpendicular rather than inclined to the surface of the paper. Also, the needlepoint should extend slightly farther than the lead point.

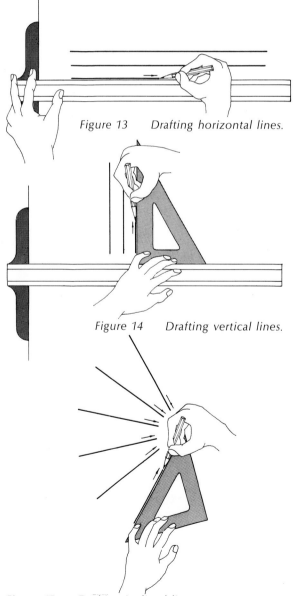

Figure 13   Drafting horizontal lines.

Figure 14   Drafting vertical lines.

Figure 15   Drafting inclined lines.

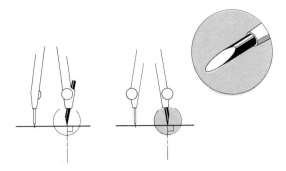

Figure 16   Lead point for compasses.

GEOMETRIC CONSTRUCTIONS

Inclined lines (Figure 17). Lines inclined 30°, 45°, and 60° to the horizontal can be drawn using the 30°–60° and 45° triangles. Lines inclined 15° and 75° can be drawn using both triangles in combination. Any angle can be measured or drawn using the adjustable triangle or protractor.
Applications: Pictorial drawings, auxiliary views, section symbols.

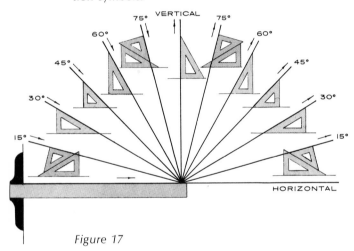

Figure 17

Parallel lines (Figure 18). A line parallel to a given line can be drawn by aligning any one edge of a triangle with the given line, and then sliding another edge of the triangle along a second triangle (or along the T-square) to the desired position. Or use an adjustable triangle.
Application: A basic construction used in all forms of projection.

Perpendicular lines (Figure 19). A line perpendicular to a given line can be drawn by aligning one leg of a triangle with the given line, and then sliding the hypotenuse of the triangle along a second triangle (or along the T-square) to the desired position. Or use an adjustable triangle.
Application: A basic construction used in all forms of projection.

Line tangent to arc (Figure 20). A line can be drawn through a point tangent to an arc by aligning one leg of a triangle to the arc and through the point. Slide the hypotenuse of the triangle along a second triangle (or along the T-square) so that the second leg is aligned with the center of the arc. The intersection of the second leg and the arc locates the point of tangency. Slide the triangle back to its original position, and draw the required tangent line. Or use an adjustable triangle.
Application: Accurate location of tangent points.

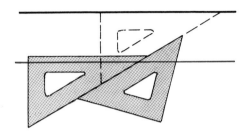

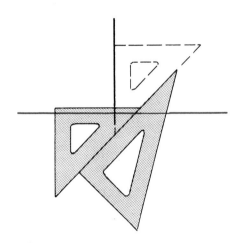

Figure 18

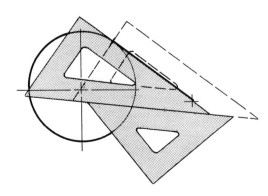

Figure 19

Figure 20

Dividing a line (Figure 21). A line can be divided into any number of equal or proportional parts by the principle of proportional triangles.

Construct a triangle with the given line as one leg and an easily divisible construction line as a second leg. Project the divisions, parallel to the third leg, back to the given line.
Application: Layout of repetitive elements such as stairs.

Arc tangent to perpendicular lines (Figure 22). An arc of desired radius can be drawn tangent to two perpendicular lines by striking an arc of the desired radius from the intersection of the perpendicular lines to locate the points of tangency. Strike arcs from the points of tangency to locate the center of the desired arc.
Application: Rounded corners.

Arc tangent to two lines (Figure 23). An arc of desired radius can be drawn tangent to any two lines by drawing construction lines parallel to the given lines, and at a distance equal to the radius to locate the center of the arc. Drop perpendiculars from the center to the given lines to locate the points of tangency.
Application: Straight forms having fillets or rounds.

Arc tangent to arcs (Figure 24). An arc of desired radius can be drawn tangent to any two arcs by striking construction arcs from the centers of the given arcs using a radius equal to the given arc radii plus (or minus, if desired) the desired radius. This locates the center of the desired arc. Draw construction lines from the center of the desired arc to the center of each given arc to locate the points of tangency.
Application: Curved forms having fillets or rounds.

Arc tangent to line and arc (Figure 25). An arc of desired radius can be drawn tangent to any line and any arc by combining the principles of the two previous geometric constructions.
Application: Combined straight and curved forms.

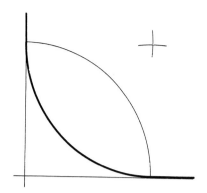

Figure 22

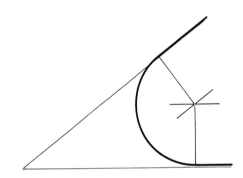

Figure 23

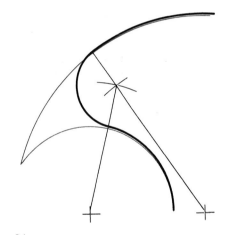

Figure 24

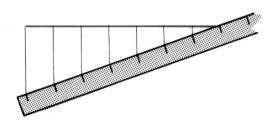

Figure 21

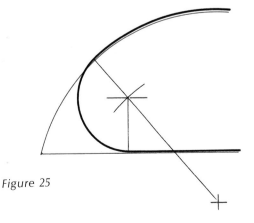

Figure 25

Equilateral triangle (Figure 26). Given a side, an equilateral triangle can be constructed by drawing 60° lines inward through the ends of the side.
Application: A basic proportional element.

Square (Figure 27). Given a side, a square can be constructed by drawing 45° construction lines inward through the ends of the side. Draw adjacent sides at 90° to the given side.
Application: A basic proportional element.

Pentagon (Figure 28). Given a side, a pentagon can be constructed by drawing 54° construction lines inward to the ends of the side to locate the center of the circumscribing circle. Draw this circle and step off the remaining sides.*
Applications: Plan shapes, polyhedra.

Hexagon (Figure 29). Given a side, a hexagon can be constructed by drawing 60° construction lines in both directions through the ends of the side to locate the center of the hexagon. Draw a construction line through the center of the hexagon and parallel to the given side to locate adjacent corners. Draw 60° lines inward through these corners to locate the remaining corners.
Applications: Plan shapes, polyhedra.

Octagon (Figure 30). Given a side, an octagon can be constructed by drawing 45° sides outwardly. Construct a square through the given side and the far ends of the 45° sides. Swing arcs with centers at the corners of the square, and radii equal to half the length of the diagonal of the square. Add the remaining sides to complete the octagon.
Applications: Plan shapes, polyhedra.

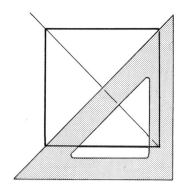

Figure 27

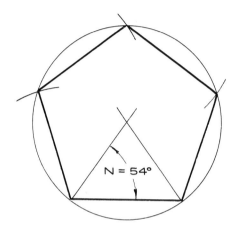

Figure 28

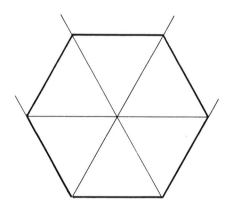

Figure 29

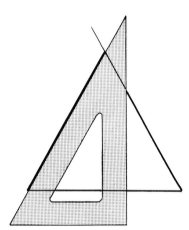

Figure 26

*This construction can be used for *any* regular polygon by using an angle of

$$90° - \frac{180°}{N}$$

where N equals the required number of sides.

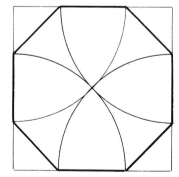

Figure 30

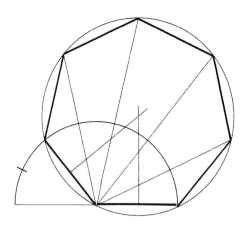

Figure 31

Ellipse (trammel method) (Figure 33). Given the major and minor axes, an ellipse can be constructed by using a trammel (a paper straightedge). On the trammel, mark off half of the major axis and half of the minor axis from a common origin. Then place the trammel in any convenient direction so that the major axis mark falls on the minor axis and the minor axis mark falls on the major axis. The origin mark locates one point on the ellipse. Rotate the trammel to obtain as many points as desired. Using an irregular curve, complete the ellipse by drawing a smooth curve through the origin marks. Two methods are illustrated.

Regular polygon (Figure 31). Given a side, a regular polygon of any number of sides (*N*) can be constructed by drawing a semicircle on the given side as illustrated. Divide the semicircle into *N* number of equal parts, and draw an adjacent side through the second outermost division. Draw perpendicular bisectors of these sides to locate the circumscribing circle. Draw radial construction lines through the divisions of the semicircle to locate the remaining corners of the polygon.
Applications: Plan shapes, polyhedra.

Conic sections (Figure 32). When a right circular cone is cut by a plane surface, the intersection is called an *ellipse* when the plane is inclined at an angle smaller than the base angle of the cone; a *parabola* when inclined at the same angle; and a *hyperbola* when inclined at a greater angle.

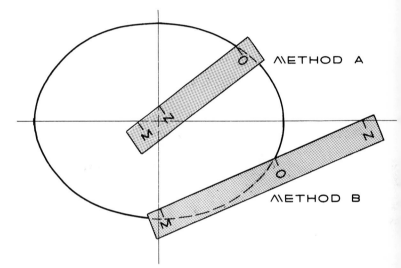

Figure 33

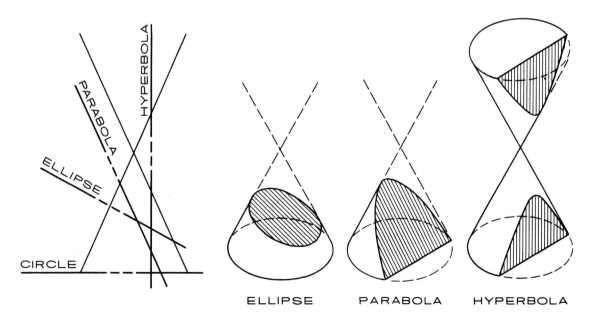

Figure 32

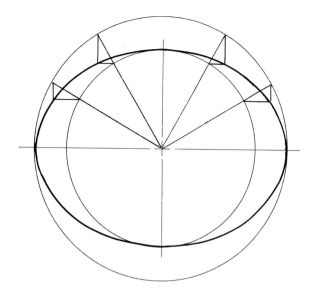

Figure 34

Often only one quadrant of the ellipse need be plotted, for you can mark your irregular curve and use it for the remaining three quadrants.
Application: Circles which project as ellipses.

Ellipse (concentric circular method) (Figure 34). Given the major and minor axes, an ellipse can be constructed by drawing two concentric circles having diameters equal to the major and minor axes. Draw any convenient number of radial construction lines. Draw construction lines parallel to the major axis through the intersection of the radial lines and the inner circle. Draw construction lines parallel to the minor axis through the intersection of the radial lines and the outer circle. Using an irregular curve, complete the ellipse by drawing a smooth curve through the intersections of the construction lines.

Often only one quadrant of the ellipse need be plotted, for you can mark your irregular curve and use it for the remaining three quadrants.
Application: Circles which project as ellipses.

Parabola of given rise and span (Figure 35). Given the rise and span, a parabola can be constructed by drawing a rectangle having the span as a base and an altitude equal to the rise. Divide the altitude and half the base into the same number of equal parts. The intersections of the construction lines locate points on the parabola as illustrated.
Applications: Approximate catenary curve, sound- and light-reflecting surfaces, bending moment at any point of a uniformly loaded beam.

Parabola tangent to two lines (Figure 36). Given two lines, a tangent parabola can be constructed by extending the lines to their intersection. Divide the line extensions into the same number of equal parts.

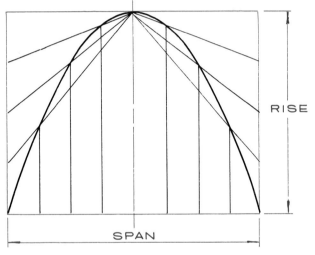

Figure 35

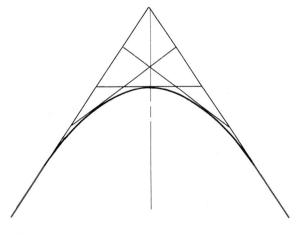

Figure 36

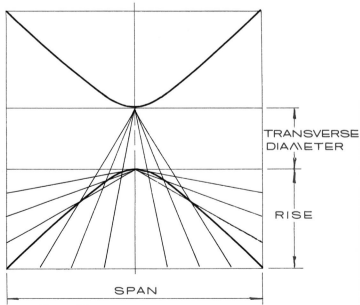

Figure 37

Draw construction lines as illustrated. The parabola will be tangent to these construction lines.
Applications: Arch forms, warped roof surfaces.

Hyperbola of given diameter, rise, and span (Figure 37). Given the transverse diameter, rise, and span, the hyperbola can be constructed by drawing a rectangle having the span as a base and an altitude equal to the rise. Divide the altitude and half the base into the same number of equal parts. Intersections of the construction lines locate points on the hyperbola as illustrated.
Application: Warped roof surfaces.

Catenary (Figure 38). Given any three points, a catenary curve can be drawn by hanging a fine chain through the three points marked on a vertical drawing board. Prick the desired number of guide points through the links of the chain. A catenary is not a conic section but can be approximated by a parabola as illustrated. For accurate results, use formulas or tables found in standard references such as *Marks' Handbook.*
Application: Cable-supported roofs, uniform cross-sectional arches.

Cylindrical helix (Figure 39). Given the cylindrical diameter and lead, a helix can be generated by dividing the circumference of the cylinder and the lead into the same number of equal parts. Project the circumference marks to the adjacent view until they intersect the lead lines. Draw the helix through these intersections as illustrated.
Applications: Spiral stairways and ramps.

Conical helix (Figure 40). Given the conic diameter, conic altitude, and lead, a helix can be generated by dividing the base of the cone and the lead into the same number of equal parts. Project the base marks to the edge view of the base in the adjacent view, and then to the vertex of the cone until they intersect the lead lines. Draw the helix through these intersections as illustrated. The plan view of the conical helix is called the *Spiral of Archimedes.*

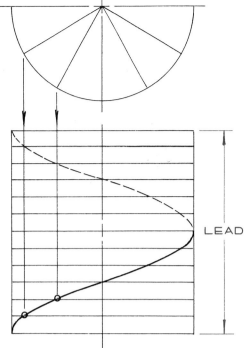

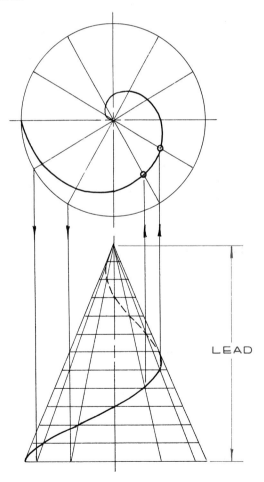

Figure 39

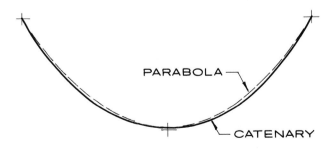

Figure 38

Figure 40

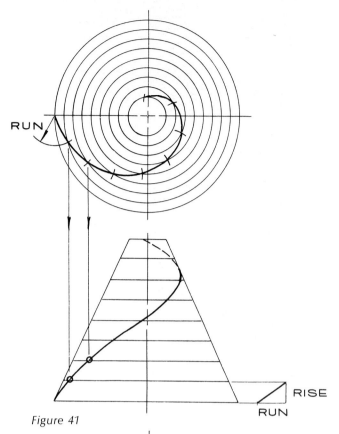

Conical helix of uniform slope (Figure 41). Given the conic diameter, conic altitude, rise and run, a helix can be generated by dividing the cone vertically into sections equal to the desired rise, and by projecting these sections to the plan view as concentric circles. Strike arcs equal to the desired run. Draw the helix as illustrated.

Applications: Conical stairways and ramps.

Spherical helix (Figure 42). Given the spherical diameter and lead, a helix can be generated by dividing the circumference of the sphere and the lead into the same number of equal parts. Project the circumference marks to the adjacent view until they intersect the lead lines. Draw the helix through these intersections as illustrated.

Application: Ornamental space curve.

Spherical helix of uniform slope (Figure 43). Given the spherical diameter, rise and run, a helix can be generated by dividing the sphere vertically into sections equal to the desired rise, and by projecting these sections to the plan view as concentric circles. Strike arcs equal to the desired run and draw the helix as illustrated. Notice that the desired slope cannot be maintained beyond the tangent point of the slope line on the spherical surface.

Applications: Spherical stairways and ramps.

Figure 41

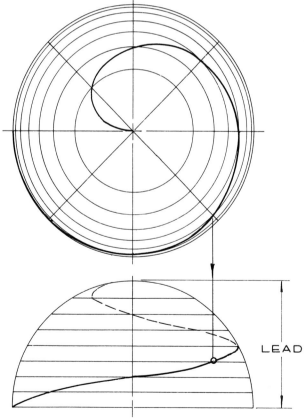

Figure 42

STUDY QUESTIONS

1. Give the reason for:
   a. Leaving gaps in sketched lines
   b. Twisting the pencil between each sketched line
   c. Rotating the pencil while drafting
2. Give the direction of stroking for the following lines sketched by a right-handed person:
   a. Horizontal lines
   b. Vertical lines
   c. Lines inclined down to the right
   d. Lines inclined down to the left
3. Give the direction of stroking for the following instrumental lines drawn by a right-handed draftsman:
   a. Horizontal lines
   b. Vertical lines
   c. Lines inclined down to the right
   d. Lines inclined down to the left
4. Give a technique for:
   a. Obtaining proper line direction when graph paper is not used
   b. Obtaining proper proportions when graph paper is not used
   c. Sketching circles and arcs
   d. Sketching ellipses
5. Give the reason for:
   a. Sharpening a compass lead to a wedge point
   b. Adjusting the needlepoint of a compass beyond the lead
   c. Changing the direction of a compass lead's flat surface

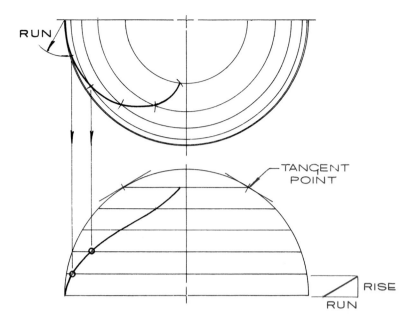

Figure 43

LABORATORY PROBLEMS

1. On $8\frac{1}{2}''$ × 11″ drawing paper, lay out twelve $2\frac{1}{4}''$ square areas. Using correct sketching technique, draw the patterns as shown in Figure 44.

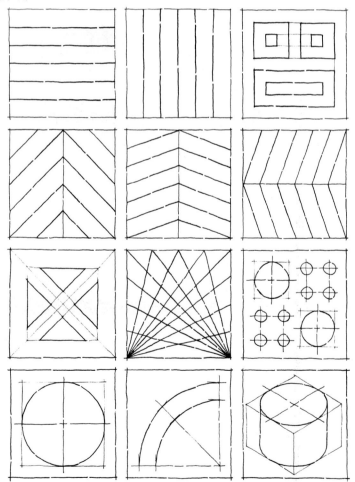

Figure 44

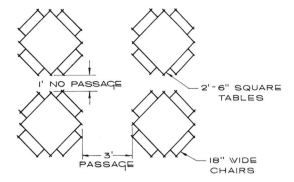

Figure 45

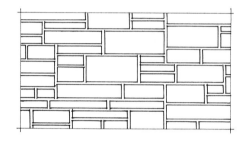

Figure 46

Figure 47

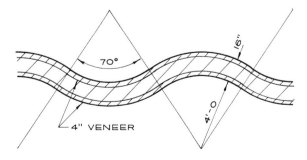

Figure 48

2. Sketch cross sections of the following structural steel members:
   a. W 12 × 40
   b. W 8 × 31
   c. W 8 × 20
   d. S 8 × 18.4
   e. C 8 × 11.5
   f. L 4 × 4 × $\frac{1}{4}$
   g. HP 8 × 36
3. Prepare sketches as assigned by your instructor.
4. On 8$\frac{1}{2}$″ × 11″ drawing paper, lay out twelve 2$\frac{1}{4}$″ square areas. Using drafting instruments, draw the patterns as shown in Figure 44. Estimate all dimensions to obtain similar proportions.
5. Using the table placement and dimensions in Figure 45, lay out a 21′ × 23′ dining room to contain the maximum number of tables. Scale: $\frac{1}{2}$″ = 1′-0.
   a. Sketch on graph paper.
   b. Draw with drafting instruments.
6. Draw a random, broken course and range, stone wall as illustrated in Figure 46. Include an area 18″ high by 3″-0 wide to a scale of 1$\frac{1}{2}$″ = 1′-0.
   a. Sketch.
   b. Draft with instruments.
7. Draw a low wall (2′ high by 6′ long) constructed of 12″ square concrete screen blocks patterned as shown in Figure 47. Use $\frac{1}{2}$″ mortar joints. Scale: 1″ = 1′-0.
   a. Sketch.
   b. Draft with instruments.
8. Draw the plan of a 33′ long serpentine wall using the dimensions given in Figure 48. Scale: $\frac{1}{4}$″ = 1′-0.
   a. Sketch.
   b. Draft with instruments.
9. Prepare instrumental drawings as assigned by your instructor.
10. Using drafting instruments, prepare a display sheet illustrating how these geometric constructions may be obtained:
    a. Lines inclined 0°, 15°, 30°, 45°, 60°, 75°, and 90° with the horizontal
    b. Arcs tangent to 2 lines, 2 circles, and a line and a circle
    c. Equilateral triangle, square, pentagon, hexagon, octagon, and any polygon
    d. Ellipse, parabola, and hyperbola
    e. Cylindrical, conical, and spherical helices
    f. Cylindrical, conical and spherical helices of uniform slope
11. Prepare geometric constructions as assigned by your instructor.

7   projections

Since early days, the ability to communicate complex ideas was one of the talents which distinguished humans from other forms of life. The first methods of communication were spoken languages and picture languages. The picture languages have developed through the years into a great number of written languages and one *universally accepted* graphic language. This universal graphic language is based upon a theory of *projections.* That is, it is assumed that imaginary sight lines, called *projectors,* extend from the eye of the observer to the object being described. The projectors transmit an image of the object onto an intervening transparent surface called the *picture plane.* This image is called a *projection* of the object.

Perspective projection. When the projectors all converge at a point (the observer's eye) as shown in Figure 1, the resulting projection of the object on the picture plane is called a *perspective projection.* Perspective projections are often used by architects to present a realistic picture of a proposed building.

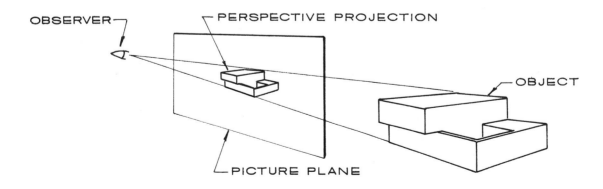

Figure 1   Perspective projection.

Parallel projection. When the projectors are all parallel to each other (as if the observer had moved to infinity), the resulting projection is called a *parallel projection*. For most architectural drafting, the projectors are also assumed to be perpendicular to the picture plane resulting in an *orthographic projection*.[1] There are two kinds of orthographic projection depending upon the relation of the object to the picture plane. These are called *multiview projection* (Figure 2a) and *axonometric projection* (Figure 2b).

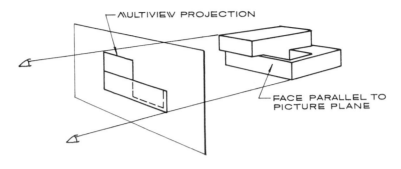

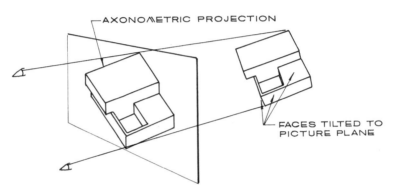

Figure 2   Orthographic projection.

Multiview projection.[2] In multiview projection, the object is positioned so that its principal faces are parallel to the picture planes. This is the type of projection most useful to architects because principal lines and faces appear true size and shape on the picture plane. It is called *multiview* projection because more than one view is required to show all three principal faces.

Axonometric projection.[3] In axonometric projection, the object is tilted in respect to the picture plane so that all faces and axes are visible but not in true shape. Axonometric projections are easier to draw than perspectives and, consequently, are often used.

Figure 3 and Table I illustrate the different features of each type of projection.

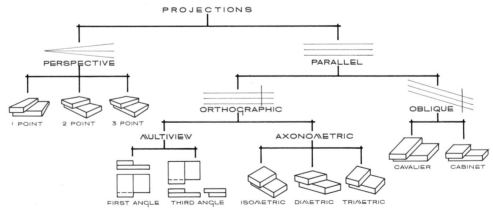

Figure 3   Types of projections.

[1] *Ortho* is a Greek prefix meaning "at a right angle."
[2] *Multi* is a Latin prefix meaning "many."

[3] *Axono* is a Greek prefix meaning "axis."

MULTIVIEW PROJECTIONS

The Glass Box. The easiest way to understand multiview projection is to imagine the object placed inside a "glass box" so that all six faces (front, rear, plan, bottom, and both ends) are parallel to the faces of the glass box. This is illustrated in Figure 4 where an object (a clay model of a building) has been surrounded by imaginary, transparent planes. Now, if projectors were dropped perpendicularly from the object to each face of the glass box, a number of projection points would be obtained which could then be connected to give a true size and shape projection of the six principal faces of the object. If the glass box is then unfolded, as shown in Figure 5, all six faces can be illustrated upon a single sheet of paper as shown in Figure 6. Note the terms *height, width,* and *depth. Height* is a vertical distance, *width* is an end-to-end distance, and *depth* is a front-to-rear distance.

Study Figure 6 and notice that all adjacent views must be in projection. For example:

1. The front view must be in projection with the rear and end views. These four views all have the same *height* and are often called *elevations* (such as front elevation, rear elevation, right end elevation, and left end elevation). In drafting, the projection between elevations is accomplished by aligning these views horizontally using a T-square.
2. The front view must be in projection with the plan and bottom views, since these views all have the same *width.* In drafting, this projection is accomplished by aligning these views vertically by using a drafting triangle.[4]
3. Also notice that four views (plan, bottom, and both ends) have a common element of *depth.* In drafting, depth measurements may be transferred by dividers, by scale, by using a 45° miter line, or by drawing 90° circular arcs (Figure 7).

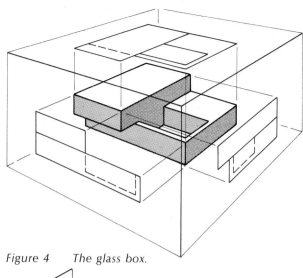

Figure 4   *The glass box.*

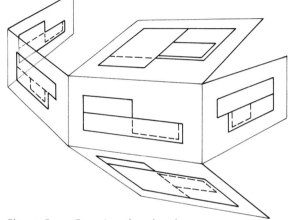

Figure 5   *Opening the glass box.*

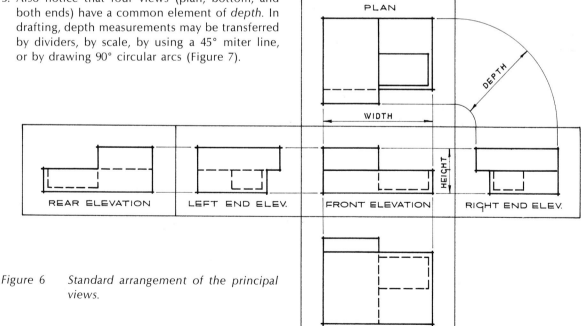

PLAN

WIDTH

DEPTH

HEIGHT

REAR ELEVATION   LEFT END ELEV.   FRONT ELEVATION   RIGHT END ELEV.

BOTTOM

Figure 6   *Standard arrangement of the principal views.*

[4]Width dimensions can be projected to the rear view using dividers.

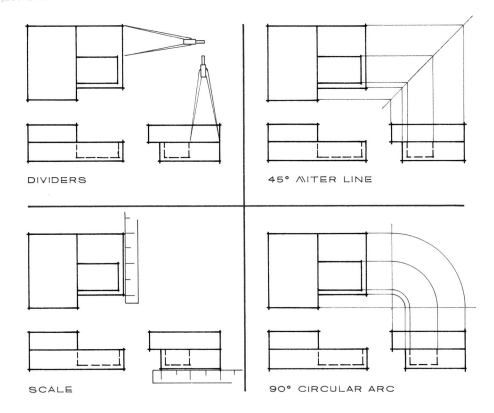

Figure 7   Methods of transferring measurements.

TABLE I

Types of Projections

Type			Relation of Projectors to:		Relation of Object Faces to Picture Plane
			Each Other	Picture Plane	
Perspective		One-point	Converging	Many angles	One face parallel
		Two-point	"	" "	Vertical faces oblique
		Three-point	"	" "	All faces oblique
Parallel	Orthographic	Multiview	First angle	Parallel	Perpendicular	Parallel
			Third angle	"	"	"
		Axonometric	Isometric	Parallel	"	Three equally oblique
			Dimetric	"	"	Two equally oblique
			Trimetric	"	"	Three unequally oblique
	Oblique		Cavalier	Parallel	Oblique	45°
			Cabinet	"	"	Arc tan 2

In architectural drafting, views of an entire building are often so large that each view requires an entire sheet of paper. In such cases, titles or other identifications are used to clarify the relationships between views.

Number of views. Six views are seldom drawn. A simple, architectural detail usually requires only two or three views, but a complex building might require a great number of views in addition to sections and details. *Partial* views may also be drawn. The governing rule is to draw as many views as necessary to describe the object clearly and accurately: no more and certainly no less.

Third and first angle projection. The frontal and horizontal planes of the glass box in Figure 4 can be extended to divide space into four sectors known in geometry as *quadrants* (Figure 8). The object can be placed in any quadrant and projected to the projection planes. The horizontal plane is folded clock-wise into the frontal plane as shown by the arrows in Figure 8. This results in four alternate arrangements of views called First, Second, Third, and Fourth angle projection.

Third angle projection produces the relationship between views previously described in the glass box paragraph in which the plan view is *above* the front elevation.

First angle projection produces a slightly different relationship between views, in that the plan is *below* the front elevation. In first angle projection, the picture plane is *beyond* the object rather than *between* the object and observer.

Second and fourth angle projection produces overlapping views and is not used.

Third angle projection is used for most architectural and technical drafting in this country. Occasionally, however, first angle projection is used in architectural drafting when it is more convenient to place a plan below an elevation. In Figure 5 of Chapter 21, notice that the plan and front elevation of each fireplace is in first angle projection, while the front and end elevations are in third angle projection.

Language of lines. Nine types of lines constitute the basic "alphabet" of drafting. They are all illustrated in Figure 9. Notice that these lines are drawn using five different line "weights." Line weight refers to the blackness and thickness of a line and ranges from an extremely heavy cutting plane line to barely visible construction lines and guide lines. A heavy line is obtained by using a soft pencil (such as an F grade), a slightly rounded point, and some hand pressure. A light line is obtained by using a hard pencil (such as a 6H grade), a sharp point, and less pressure.

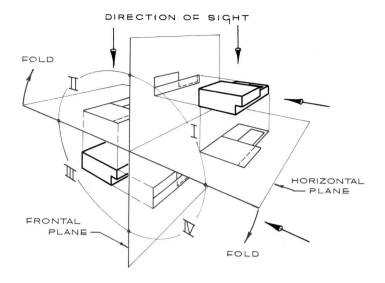

Figure 8   The four quadrants.

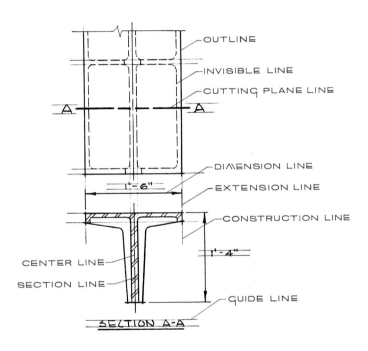

Figure 9   The language of lines.

Outline. Outlines (also called *visible* lines) are heavy lines used to describe the visible shape of an object including edges, edge views of planes, and contours of curved surfaces.

Invisible line. Invisible lines (also called hidden lines) are outlines that cannot be seen by the observer because they are covered by portions of the object closer to the observer. The location of such invisible edges are indicated when necessary to accurately describe the object. The dashes of invisible lines are about $\frac{1}{8}$" in length and $\frac{1}{32}$" apart. Invisible lines are medium weight lines.

Cutting plane line. The cutting plane line represents the edge view of a cutting plane sliced through the object to reveal inner features. It is drawn as the heaviest weight line so that the location of a section can be easily identified.

Section line. Section lines are used to crosshatch any cut portion of an object. A number of sectioning symbols are shown in Figure 5 of Chapter 8. Section, center, dimension, and extension lines are all drawn the same light weight.

Center line. Center lines indicate axes of symmetry. Most center lines consist of alternating $\frac{1}{8}''$ short dashes and 1″ long dashes spaced about $\frac{1}{32}''$ apart. In small scale drawings, spaces may be omitted.

Dimension line. Dimension lines are used to indicate the direction and limits of a linear dimension. Some types of arrowheads used with dimension lines are illustrated in Figure 4 of Chapter 10.

Extension line. Extension lines serve as an extension of a feature on the object so that dimensions can be placed *next* to a projection rather than crowding *on* the projection.

Construction line. Construction lines are extremely light lines barely visible to the eye. They are used to lay out a view or to project between views.

Guide line. Horizontal and vertical guide lines are construction lines used to guide hand lettering. See Figure 5 in Chapter 9.

Reading a drawing. In addition to drawing the projections of an object from a picture formed in his mind, an architectural draftsman must be able to "read" drawings. That is, given a projection of an object, he must be able to visualize its shape and features. The following rules may help:

1. The same features must always be in projection in adjacent views. Consequently, a point or line in one view may be projected to and read in an adjacent view to help understand what it represents.
2. Read views simultaneously rather than one at a time. Staring at a single view usually will not be particularly helpful. Your eyes should project a feature back and forth between views until you are able to visualize the feature and eventually the entire object.
3. There is a rule called the *rule of configuration* which states that the configuration (shape) of a plane remains about the same in all views, unless the plane appears in its edge view. For example, a five-sided surface will always have five sides —and not four or six—unless it appears on edge.

Sectioning. Architectural components are seldom solid objects as discussed in the preceding sections. Rather, they consist of complex assemblies which require sectional views to adequately describe them. A section is an imaginary cut through a component (part) or assembly of components. All the material on one side of the cut is removed so that the interior can be studied. Sections are often drawn through entire structures, walls, floors, roofs, foundations, structural assemblies, stairs, and fireplaces. The scale of sectional views is often increased to further clarify the details. Cutting plane lines are used only when needed to show where the cut was taken. Sight direction arrows are added to the ends of cutting plane lines only when needed to show the direction of sight.

Full section. A full section is a cut through the entire building or component as shown in Drawing No. 11 of Chapter 35. A vertical cut through the long dimension of a building is called a *longitudinal section,* and through the short dimension of a building is called a *transverse section.* Both are helpful in analyzing the building's structure and detailing.

Half section. A half section is a cut to remove only *one quarter* of a symmetrical component. Thus both the exterior and interior can be shown in one view as indicated in Figure 10.

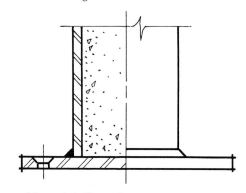

Figure 10   A half section.

Offset section. The cutting plane can be *offset* (bent) to permit it to cut through all necessary features. For example, although a horizontal cutting plane through an entire building is usually assumed to be at a height about 4 ft. above floor level, it would be offset *upward* to cut through a high strip window, and offset *downward* to cut through a lower level of a split level house. Usually such offsets need not be indicated by a cutting plane line.

Broken-out section. A broken-out section has the advantage of permitting the draftsman to select the most critical area for sectioning and still present the exterior appearance of the component—all in one view. See Figure 11.

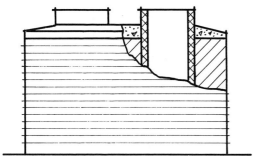

Figure 11   A broken-out section.

Revolved section. A revolved section is a section that has been revolved 90° and drawn on the exterior view of a component. Like a broken-out section this permits the showing of a greater amount of information in a small space. See Figure 12.

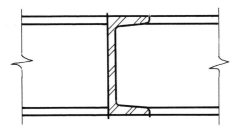

Figure 12   A revolved section.

Revolved partial sections are also used to indicate the sectional profile of a special column, jamb, or molding. See Figure 13.

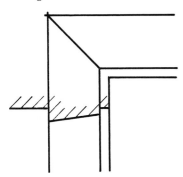

Figure 13   A revolved partial section.

Removed section. A removed section is simply a revolved section that has been removed to another location and often drawn to a larger scale. A cutting plane should be used to indicate where this sectional cut was taken.

AUXILIARY VIEWS

Occasionally in architectural drafting, a view is required which is not a principal view. Such views are called *auxiliary views* and may show the true size and shape of an inclined or oblique surface or the true length of an inclined or oblique edge. Auxiliary views are classified as *primary* auxiliary views and *secondary* auxiliary views. A *primary auxiliary view* is a view that is perpendicular to only one of the three principal planes of projection and is inclined to the other two. A *secondary auxiliary view* is an auxiliary view that is obtained by projection from a primary auxiliary view.

Primary auxiliary views. A primary auxiliary view is obtained by projection from a principal view. Common examples in architectural drafting are the auxiliary views needed to show the true size and shape of each face of a building having walls or wings that are not at a 90° angle to each other. An example is shown in Figure 14. The procedure used to draw a true size and shape elevation of the inclined wall 1-2-3-4 is as follows:

Step 1. Draw the edge view of a projection plane parallel to the edge view of plane 1-2-3-4. This is usually called a *reference line.* Since the auxiliary view is to be projected from the plan, label the reference line *P/A* (*P* for plan and *A* for auxiliary elevation).

Step 2. All points on the inclined face are projected from the adjacent view (the plan view in this example) to the auxiliary elevation view. Projection lines are *always* drawn perpendicular to their reference line. In this example, points 1 and 4 both happen to project along the same projector. Also, points 2 and 3 project along the same projector.

Step 3. Locate points 1, 2, 3, and 4 in the auxiliary elevation view by transferring distances from a *related view* (the front elevation in this example). Related views are two views which are both adjacent to the same view. Dividers are often helpful in transferring these measurements. Connect the points in the auxiliary view in the proper order.

Secondary auxiliary views. Secondary auxiliary views are auxiliary views projected from a primary auxiliary view. Although not commonly used in architectural drafting, they are occasionally required for accurate shape description or to solve structural problems. An example is shown in Figure 15 which illustrates the procedure to find the true size and shape of face 1-2-3 of the geodesic dome so that a pattern can be made. Two auxiliary views are required, because an edge view of face 1-2-3 must be drawn before the true size and shape view can be found.

Step 1. Analyze the problem. Before the true size and shape of face 1-2-3 can be found, the edge view must be drawn. To find the edge view of any plane, the procedure is to find the point view of a line in

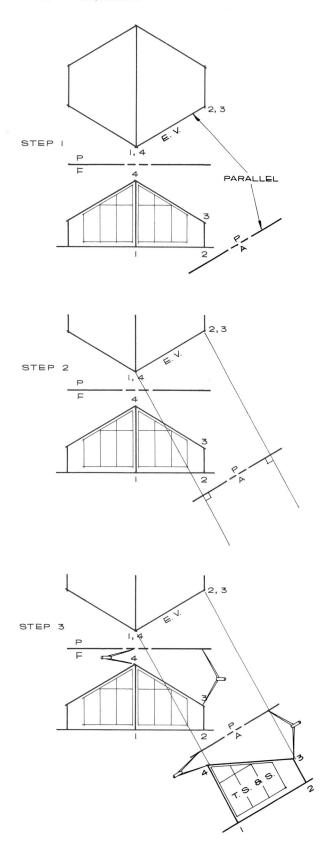

STEP 1

STEP 2

STEP 3

Figure 14   Drawing a primary auxiliary view.

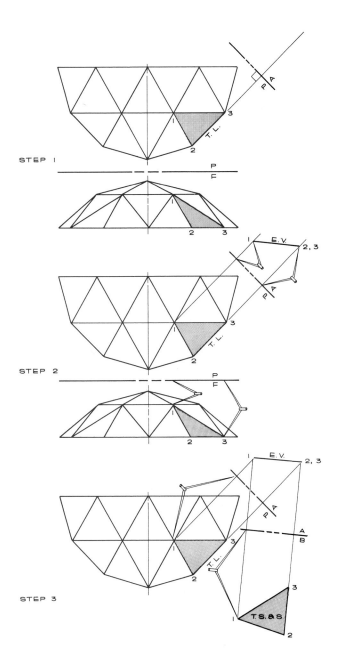

STEP 1

STEP 2

STEP 3

Figure 15   Drawing a secondary auxiliary view.

that plane. The point view of any line can be found by projecting parallel to the true length view of that line. Since line 2-3 is true length in the plan view, project parallel to it by drawing a perpendicular *P/A* reference line.

Step 2. Project face 1-2-3 to the primary auxiliary view so that it appears as an edge view.

Step 3. Draw an *A/B* reference line parallel to the edge view of face 1-2-3. Project face 1-2-3 to the secondary auxiliary view so that it appears true size and shape.

PICTORIAL PROJECTIONS

In addition to multiview projections, pictorials are often used by architects because they better describe the actual appearance of an object. All three principal faces of an object can be shown in one view, and such pictures are easily understood by people not trained in reading multiview projections.

Pictorial projections can be classified as perspective and parallel. Perspective projections are more realistic, but parallel projections are easier to draw. Perspective drawings are described in Chapter 31. Parallel pictorial projections are classified as axonometric and oblique as follows.

Axonometric projection. Like orthographic projection, the projectors in axonometric projection are parallel to each other and perpendicular to the picture plane. But the object has been tilted in respect to the picture plane so that all three principal faces are seen in one view, but not in true size or true shape. When the object is tilted so that all three principal faces are equally inclined to the picture plane, the axonometric projection is called an *isometric projection*. When only two faces are equally inclined to the picture plane, a *dimetric projection* results. When *no* two faces are equally inclined, a *trimetric projection* results. A form of isometric projection, called *isometric drawing*, is by far the most popular pictorial method.

Isometric projection. An isometric projection can be obtained by revolving an object 45° about a vertical axis as shown in Figure 16. Then the object is tilted forward so that all principal edges form equal angles with the picture plane. This angle is approximately 35°-16'. Dimetric and trimetric projections can be obtained by similar methods, but this is a cumbersome procedure and, consequently, is seldom used.

Isometric drawing. Isometric drawing differs from isometric projection in that the principal edges are drawn true length rather than foreshortened. Therefore, isometric drawings can be drawn directly and quite quickly. The principal edges appear as vertical lines or as lines making an angle of 30° to the horizontal.

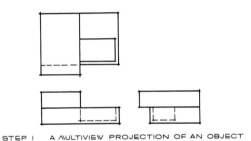

STEP 1   A MULTIVIEW PROJECTION OF AN OBJECT

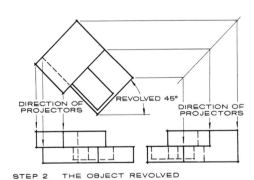

STEP 2   THE OBJECT REVOLVED

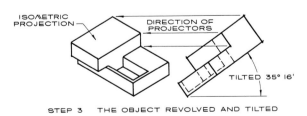

STEP 3   THE OBJECT REVOLVED AND TILTED

Figure 16   The theory of isometric projection.

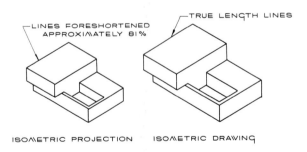

ISOMETRIC PROJECTION   ISOMETRIC DRAWING

Figure 17   Comparison of isometric projection and isometric drawing.

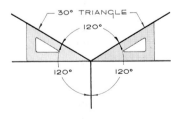

Figure 18   The isometric axes.

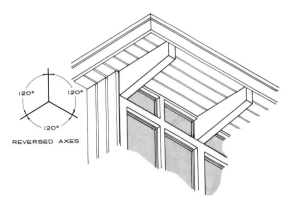

Figure 19   A reversed isometric drawing.

It is important to realize that in isometric drawing, only isometric lines (principal edges) are drawn true length. Consequently, non-isometric lines cannot be obtained by direct measurement but by *offset measurement*. Offset measurement is simply the procedure of boxing in a shape so that the position of any point can be measured along isometric lines as shown in Figure 20.

Circles in isometric drawing will appear as ellipses. But rather than plotting these ellipses by offset measurement, an elliptical template can be used. For large ellipses, a four-center approximation can also be used. An example of an approximation for a semicircle is shown in Figure 21.

Step 1. A square is assumed to be placed tangent to the semicircle at the three intersections with its center lines (points 1, 2, 3).

Step 2. The tangent square and center lines of the circle are drawn in the isometric drawing.

Step 3. Perpendiculars are erected to the sides of the isometric square at points 1, 2, and 3. The intersections of these perpendiculars are the centers of two arcs tangent to the isometric square at 1, 2, and 3.

Step 4. Using a compass, draw two arcs tangent to the isometric square.

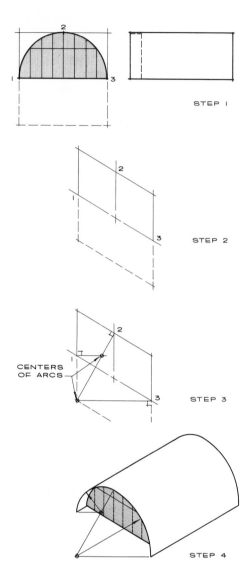

Figure 21   Plotting a semicircle in isometric drawing by the approximation method.

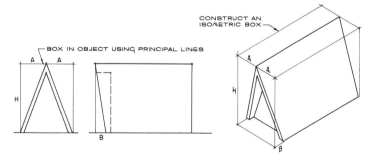

Figure 20   Drawing non-isometric lines by offset measurement.

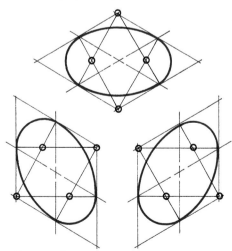

Figure 22   A four-center ellipse can be drawn in all principal planes.

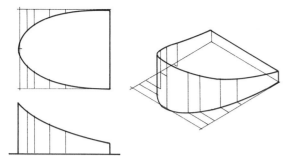

Figure 23   Plotting irregular curves using offset measurements.

Oblique projection. An oblique projection (Figure 24) is obtained by parallel projectors which are oblique rather than perpendicular to the picture plane. The projectors can be assumed to be at any angle to the picture plane, but it is most common to project them to produce receding lines which will appear at an angle of 45° to the horizontal. Usually these 45° lines are drawn to the right.

The angle of the projectors also determines the amount of foreshortening of the receding lines. For example, the receding lines can be reduced to half size (called a *cabinet* drawing) or drawn to full scale (called a *cavalier* drawing, Figure 25). The proportions of $\frac{2}{3}$ and $\frac{3}{4}$ are also used.

A major advantage of oblique drawing is that one face of the object is parallel to the picture plane and therefore remains in its true size and shape. Consequently, it is common sense to position the object so that the most irregular outline is the face parallel to the picture plane. Other faces not parallel to the picture plane are distorted and must be constructed using offset measurements. For example, circles in the parallel face can be drawn as circles (Figure 26), but circles in the receding faces must be plotted by offsets or by the four-center ellipse method.

A disadvantage of oblique drawing is that receding lines do not converge and, consequently, appear to the eye to be distorted. The distortion can be minimized by positioning the object, when possible, so that the largest dimensions are parallel to the picture plane rather than receding.

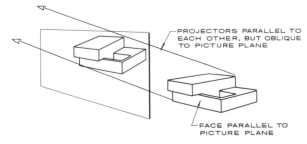

Figure 24   Oblique projection.

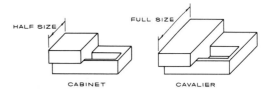

Figure 25   Comparison of cabinet and cavalier drawings.

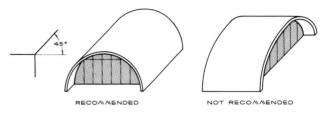

Figure 26   Positioning curved faces parallel to the picture plane.

STUDY QUESTIONS

1. Distinguish between:
   a. Perspective and parallel projection
   b. Orthographic projection and oblique projection
   c. Multiview projection and axonometric projection
   d. First angle projection and third angle projection
   e. Isometric drawing and isometric projection
   f. Dimetric projection and trimetric projection
   g. Cavalier drawing and cabinet drawing
2. Give the relationship of the projectors to each other and to the picture plane in the following types of projection:
   a. Multiview
   b. Axonometric
   c. Oblique
   d. Perspective
3. Distinguish between height, width, and depth.
4. Describe four methods of transferring depth measurements between the plan and end elevations.
5. Using a line weight scale of 5 (very heavy) to 1 (very light), give the weight of each type of line:
   a. Outline
   b. Invisible line
   c. Center line
   d. Cutting plane line
   e. Section line
   f. Dimension and extension lines
   g. Guide lines and construction lines
6. Distinguish between:
   a. Full section and half section
   b. Longitudinal section and transverse section
   c. Revolved section and removed section
7. What is the advantage of:
   a. Half sections
   b. Offset sections
   c. Broken-out sections
   d. Revolved sections
   e. Partial sections
   f. Removed sections
8. Distinguish between a primary auxiliary view and a secondary auxiliary view.

9. Why are offset measurements used to draw non-isometric lines?
10. Why is the most irregular face of an object positioned parallel to the picture plane in oblique drawing?
11. Hidden lines are usually omitted from pictorial drawings: Why?

LABORATORY PROBLEMS

1. Draw multiview projections of the mass models shown in Figure 27 as assigned:
   a. Sufficient views to describe model
   b. Front elevation, end elevation, and plan
   c. Plan and all elevations

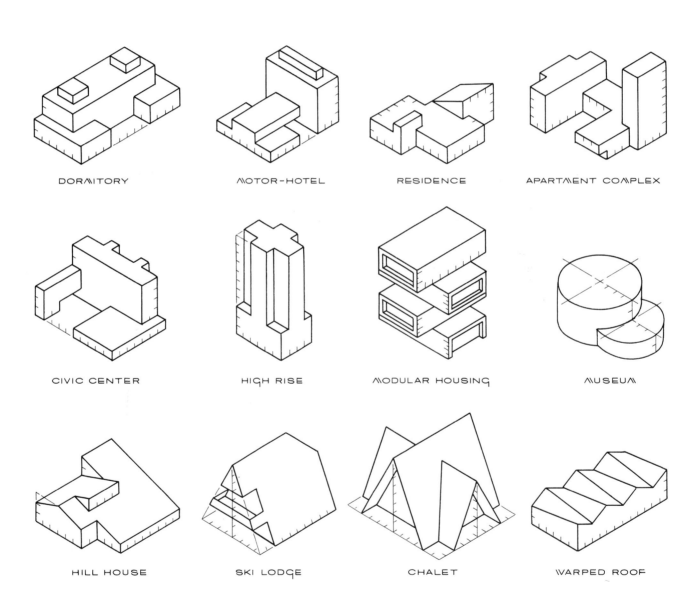

DORMITORY   MOTOR-HOTEL   RESIDENCE   APARTMENT COMPLEX

CIVIC CENTER   HIGH RISE   MODULAR HOUSING   MUSEUM

HILL HOUSE   SKI LODGE   CHALET   WARPED ROOF

Figure 27

2. Draw the multiview projections as assigned by your instructor.
3. Draw a full section of an 8″ × 16″ reinforced concrete footing for an 8″ concrete block foundation wall.
4. Draw half sections of a 3½″ concrete-filled steel pipe column at its base and cap.
5. Draw an elevation and a revolved section of a:
   a. W 8 × 31 steel beam
   b. C 8 × 13.75 steel channel
   c. L 6 × 4 × ½ steel angle
6. Using primary auxiliary views, find the true size and shape of each roof section of the residence shown in Figure 28. Compute the number of squares of roofing required (1 square = 100 sq. ft.).
7. Using a secondary auxiliary view, find the true size and shape of a typical roof section of the pavilion shown in Figure 29. Compute the number of squares of roofing required for the entire roof.
8. Using a secondary auxiliary view, find the true size and shape of a typical wall of the pavilion shown in Figure 29. Compute the square feet of insulation required for one wall section.
9. (For the advanced student) Using the required auxiliary views, find the following data for the cable-supported roof shown in Figure 30 so that proper angle brackets can be specified:
   a. The angle between each cable and the mast
   b. The angle between each cable and the roof
10. Draw pictorials of the 2″ × 4″ wood joints shown in Figure 31 as assigned:
    a. Assembled isometric drawings
    b. Exploded isometric drawings
    c. Exploded cavalier drawings
11. Draw pictorials of the buildings shown on page 317 as assigned:
    a. Isometric drawing
    b. Dimetric drawing
    c. Trimetric drawing
    d. Cavalier drawing
    e. Cabinet drawing
12. Draw the pictorial projections as assigned by your instructor.

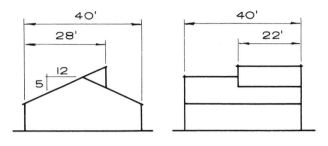

RESIDENCE

Figure 28

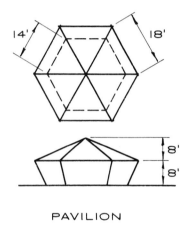

PAVILION

Figure 29

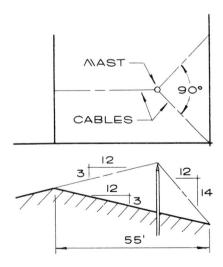

CABLE-SUPPORTED ROOF

Figure 30

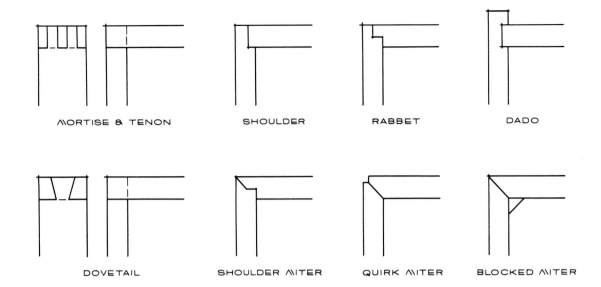

Figure 31

8 architectural technique

The technique of linework on architectural drawings is of a completely different nature from that used on other forms of mechanical drawing. In fact the difference is so great that it is difficult for a draftsman trained in another field—engineering drafting, for example—to make the switch to architectural drafting, since he must "unlearn" many accepted rules and practices. The reason for this dissimilarity is the difference in the aims or goals of the two fields. Whereas the engineer must turn out a perfectly exact and cold-blooded indication of his needs, to be used by persons trained in his own field, the architect wants to produce an artistically complete picture to be read by trained workers and laymen alike. Basically, the architect must sell his product. And to do this, his plans must be infinitely more appealing and warm.

LINE CHARACTER

The first point to be remembered is that you are not only a draftsman, but an artist as well. Don't be afraid to let your lines run past each other at their intersections (Figure 1). A better end result will be obtained if the mind and hand are not cramped by trying to stop at a given point.

Use a soft pencil. Many architects will never touch a pencil harder than 2H grade. It is impossible to obtain line quality in a drawing done with a hard

pencil. The two skills to be mastered with a soft pencil are the slight twisting to keep the point sharp

POOR   GOOD   BEST

Figure 1   Line technique at corners.

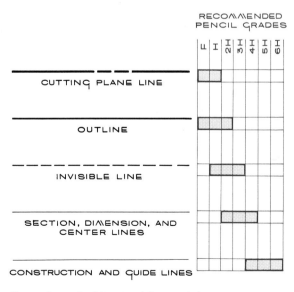

Figure 2   Architectural line weights.

71

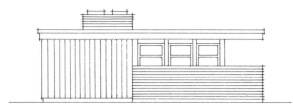

LINES TOO LIGHT FOR PROPER REPRODUCTION

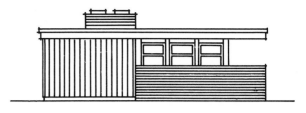

LINES HEAVY, BUT NO CONTRAST

Figure 3 Poor techniques.

and the extra care required to keep the paper clean. Recommended grades are shown in Figure 2.

Lines (other than dimension lines and a few others) are often *not* drawn uniform in weight. Indeed they may nearly fade out in the middle. The ends of the lines are accentuated and should come to a distinct stop rather than just fade away.

All instruments and materials should be kept in perfect condition. A violinist might as well try to play with boxing gloves on as a draftsman try to draw with a blunt pencil point. If a good draftsman is forced to use poor materials and produces an acceptable drawing, he does so in spite of them, not because of them. No good artistic work is sloppy.

Keep your drawings clean and smudge-free. These suggestions will help:

1. All your drafting equipment should be cleaned frequently. Soap and water, if thoroughly dried off, will not injure triangles and T-squares. Use a clean cloth or paper towel to clean your desk top before beginning work.
2. Wash your hands. Try to keep your hands off the face of your drawing. Never allow anyone else to touch your drawing. When lettering, place a clean paper shield under your hand.
3. Do not sharpen your pencil over the desk top. Be certain that all graphite particles fall only on the floor. Blow or wipe off your pencil point immediately after sharpening. Wipe off each drafting instrument regularly.
4. Cover the unworked-on portion of your drawing with a clean paper shield so that it is not smudged and dirty before you start to draw. Cover any completed portion of your drawing with a clean paper shield also.
5. Do not slide your triangles and T-square across your drawing; lift them slightly.
6. Keep all lines (especially construction lines) sharp and accurate to reduce the amount of erasing to a minimum.
7. Either blow or brush off any excess graphite from your drawing after drawing each line.
8. Some draftsmen find that a special cleaning powder (known under various trade names such as "Dry-Clean Pad," "Draft-Clean Powder," "Dust-it,"

"Scumex") will aid in keeping their drawings smudge-free.
9. As a last resort, change pencil grades. A harder pencil grade will not smudge as readily as a soft pencil grade.

LINE TECHNIQUE

Architectural draftsmen develop their own styles of linework just as they develop their own styles of lettering. Some of the most commonly used styles of line *techniques* are illustrated in Figure 4.

Cutting plane technique. This technique is used for section views. The lines formed by the cutting plane are darkened.

Distance technique. It is possible to show depth in an architectural drawing by emphasizing the lines closest to the observer. Even if the plan in Figure 4 had been omitted, you would be able to visualize the shape of the building by this technique.

Silhouette technique. The silhouette is emphasized by darkening the outline. One of the oldest techniques, it is still used today.

Shadow technique. Recessions and extensions can be shown by darkening the edges away from the light source. The light is usually assumed to be coming from the upper left.

Major feature technique. This is a commonly used technique. The major elements are outlined, while the elements of lesser importance are drawn in with finer lines. The diagrams in this text are drawn using this technique.

Obviously, all of the above techniques cannot be used simultaneously. You will develop your own favored style, but remember to remain flexible enough to be able to adapt your personal technique to the standards set up by a particular office.

ARCHITECTURAL SYMBOLS

A system of architectural symbols to indicate certain materials and features has developed through the years. Properly used, these symbols complement the architectural linework and form an attractive and useful language.

Figure 5 shows the symbols most often used on architectural sections and Figure 6 shows those used on architectural elevations. Notice that most materials have different symbols for section and elevation views. Also remember that all section and elevation symbols should be drawn lighter than the outlines.

Figure 7 shows some common structural shapes used in architectural design. Either the W shape or S shape beam may be specified for house girders. The W shape is often used as a column in industrial buildings, but pipe columns are used in residences. The angle sections may be used to sup-

port masonry over wall openings; they may be obtained with equal or unequal legs. Both angle and channel sections are generally used as elements of built-up sections for commercial structures. Steel is also obtainable in round bar shapes, square bar shapes, and rectangular plates.

Wall symbols are shown in Figure 8, together with the accepted dimensioning practices: to the outside face of the studs for frame walls, and to the outside of the masonry for masonry walls. Notice that no section symbol is specified for the frame wall. A wood symbol or poché (darkening of wall by shading or light lines) may be used.

All fixed equipment supplied by the builder should be included in the plans, while equipment furnished by the owner is omitted. Figure 9 shows an assortment of symbols that may be used. An invisible line may represent an invisible object (like the dishwasher shown built in under the counter) or a high object (like the wall cabinets that are *above*

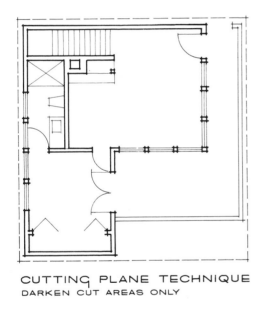

CUTTING PLANE TECHNIQUE
DARKEN CUT AREAS ONLY

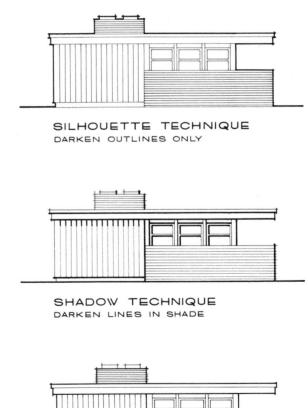

SILHOUETTE TECHNIQUE
DARKEN OUTLINES ONLY

SHADOW TECHNIQUE
DARKEN LINES IN SHADE

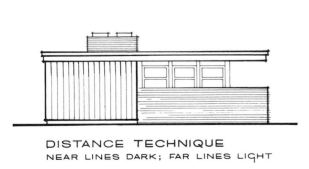

DISTANCE TECHNIQUE
NEAR LINES DARK; FAR LINES LIGHT

MAJOR FEATURE TECHNIQUE
DARKEN MAJOR ELEMENTS ONLY

Figure 4   Good techniques.

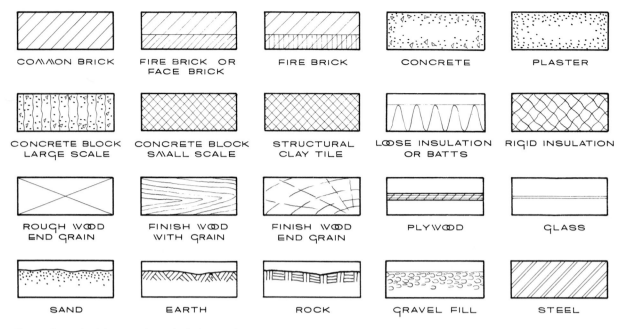

Figure 5   Architectural symbols in section.

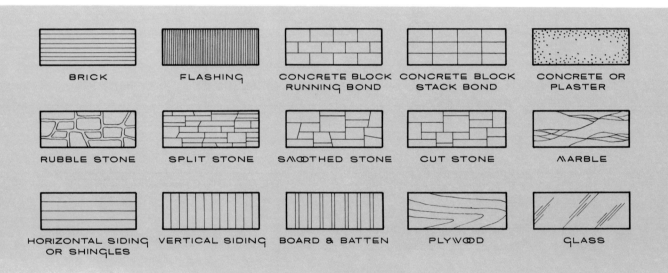

Figure 6   Architectural symbols in elevation.

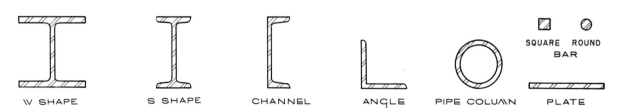

Figure 7   Structural steel shapes.

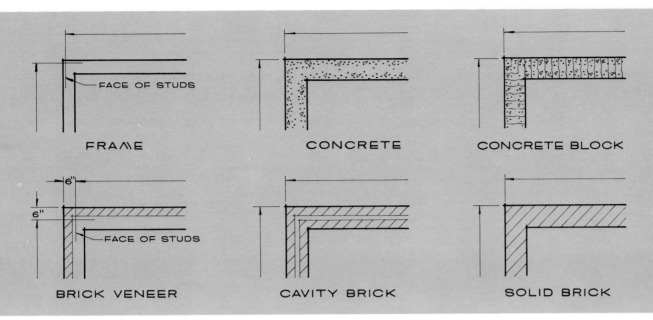

Figure 8   Wall symbols.

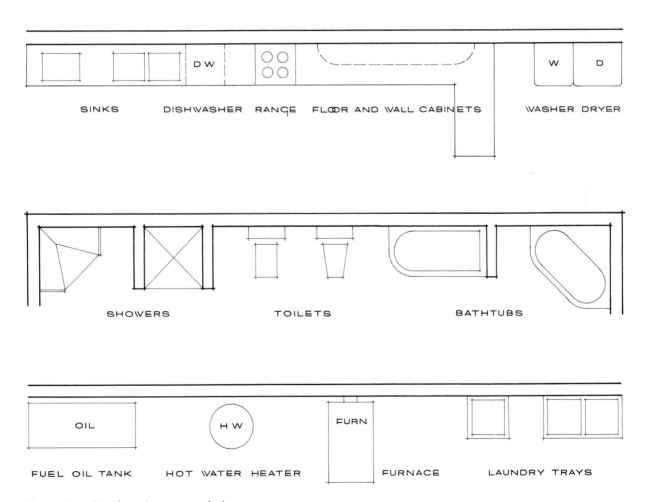

Figure 9   Fixed equipment symbols.

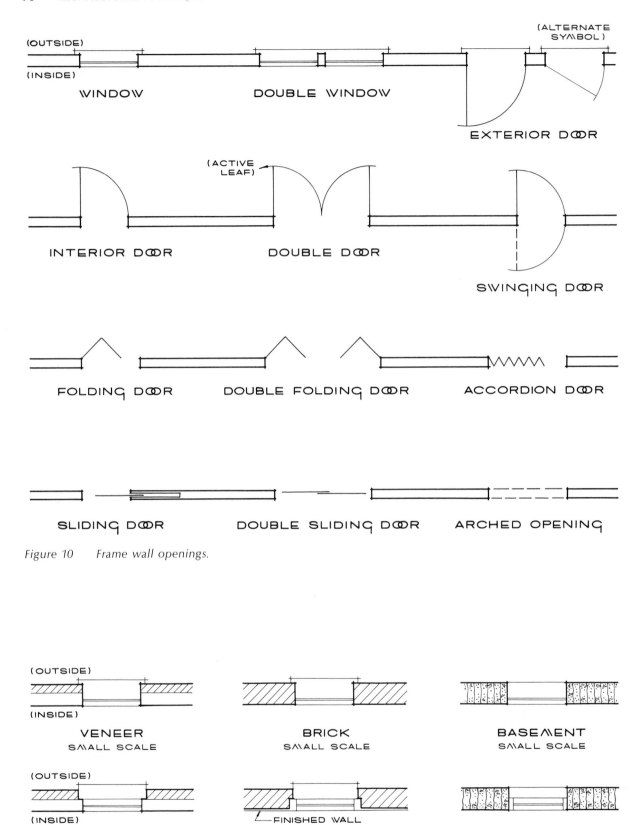

Figure 10   Frame wall openings.

Figure 11   Masonry wall openings.

the plane of the section).

The conventions used to indicate windows and doors in a frame wall are shown in Figure 10. Although the doors are shown opened a full 90°, an angle of 30° may also be used. These same window and door conventions may be adapted to other kinds of walls, as shown in Figure 11. Notice the definite contrast in line weight between the walls and conventions.

STUDY QUESTIONS

1. What is the difference between linework used on engineering drawings and architectural drawings?
2. Suggest several methods to keep architectural drawings free of smudges.
3. What is the advantage of using:
   a. Hard pencil grades
   b. Soft pencil grades
4. List five different types of line techniques used by architectural draftsmen.

LABORATORY PROBLEMS

1. Prepare a legend which lists and illustrates:
   a. Architectural section symbols
   b. Architectural elevation symbols
   c. Structural steel shapes
   d. Wall symbols
   e. Window and door symbols
   f. Fixed equipment symbols
2. Prepare classroom illustrations showing the five types of architectural line techniques.
3. Lay out the 10'-6" × 8'-0 awning window wall as shown in Figure 12. Use appropriate pencil technique. Scale: $\frac{1}{4}'' = 1'$-0.
4. Draw the elevation of a stacked bond wall containing a 2'-8" × 8'-0 door and transom as indicated in Figure 13. Masonry units are 8" × 8" × 16". Use appropriate pencil technique. Scale: $\frac{1}{4}'' = 1'$-0.
5. Draw an elevation of the helicoidal concrete stairway as shown in Figure 14. Use appropriate pencil technique. Scale: $\frac{1}{4}'' = 1'$-0.
6. Draw the cross section of a small theater using the dimensions indicated in Figure 15. Use appropriate pencil technique. Scale: $\frac{1}{8}'' = 1'$-0.

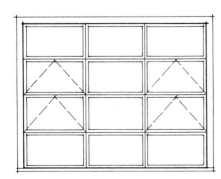

Figure 12

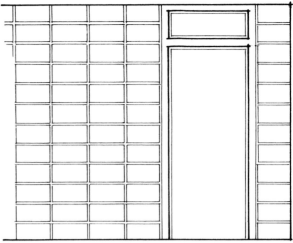

Figure 13

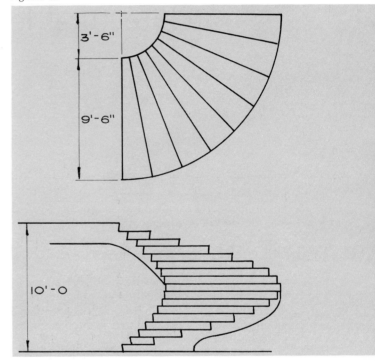

Figure 14

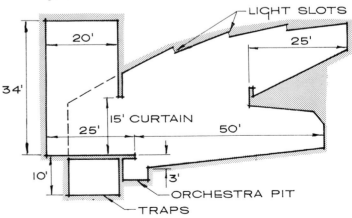

Figure 15

9 architectural lettering

The ability to letter is as important to a draftsman as the ability to paint is to an artist. An artist who has an idea for a painting must be able to put that idea on canvas in a neat, orderly fashion using a definite technique. Similarly, an architectural draftsman who has ideas for a building must be able to put these ideas on vellum in a clear, orderly manner using a definite system of notation. The ability to do a professional job of lettering is considered so important by most employers that they require a lettering sample to be submitted at the time of application for employment.

LETTERING STYLES

Of the many styles of lettering, *Old English, Roman,* and *Gothic* are best known.

Old English lettering (or "Text") is shown in Figure 1. Although it is attractive, it is not widely used today because it is difficult to letter and read. Most high school and university diplomas use Old English lettering because of its elegant appearance.

Roman letters have strokes of different widths. Notice in Figure 2 that the horizontal lines are thin and the verticals thick. This is because the early pen points (quills) were flat and made lines which varied in width depending upon the direction of stroke.

Also notice the small lines at the ends of every stroke: these are called "serifs." Roman lettering is used extensively by book and magazine publishers, but not by engineers or architects. You may find Roman lettering on monumental structures cut into stone or metal plaques.

Figure 1   Old English lettering.

Figure 2   Roman lettering.

Figure 3   Gothic lettering.

*United States of America Standards Institute (formerly American Standards Association) USA Standard Drafting Manual: Section 2 Y14.2-1957.

ABCDEFGHIJKLMNOPQRSTUVWXYZ

(14)   FLOOR   PLAN

$\frac{1}{4}$" LETTERING FOR TITLES AND DRAWING NUMBERS

ABCDEFGHIJKLMNOPQRSTUVWXYZ   0123456789

JAMB   DETAIL

$\frac{1}{8}$" LETTERING FOR HEADINGS

ABCDEFGHIJKLMNOPQRSTUVWXYZ   0123456789

2" × 8" JOIST

$\frac{3}{32}$" LETTERING FOR DIMENSIONS AND NOTES

Figure 4   USASI Commercial Gothic lettering.

Gothic lettering, Figure 3, differs from Roman lettering in two important aspects: (1) all strokes are exactly the same width, and (2) no serifs are used. Of the many types of Gothic lettering, only *one* type has been approved by USASI * for use on engineering and architectural drawings. This one approved type of Gothic lettering, called *Commercial Gothic,* is used on *all* engineering drawings. On architectural drawings, it is often altered slightly to suit the taste of the draftsman or the style of a particular office. Let us first study the standard Commercial Gothic lettering and then look at the usual methods by which it can be altered to better suit architectural needs.

Commercial gothic. Figure 4 shows the American Standard Commercial Gothic lettering in the three sizes used on architectural drawings: $\frac{1}{4}$" for important titles and drawing numbers, $\frac{1}{8}$" for lesser headings, and $\frac{3}{32}$" for dimensioning and notes. The form and proportion of each letter should be studied carefully, since this alphabet is universally used.

LETTERING SECRETS

There are six lettering "secrets" which have been collected by professional draftsmen who use Com-

mercial Gothic lettering. Practice your lettering with these secrets in mind:

Guide lines. *A professional draftsman always uses guide lines* when lettering. Guide lines are very light lines (usually drawn with a 4H pencil) that aid in forming uniformly sized letters. Guide lines are *not* erased, since they are drawn so lightly that they are not objectionable. They should be visible to you when lettering, but invisible when you hold the drawing at arm's length.

The horizontal guide lines used for capital letters (like *ABC*) are a base line and a cap line. The horizontal guide lines used for lower case letters (like *abc*) include also a waist line and a drop line (Figure 5). Lower case lettering, however, is seldom used in architectural work. If you wish to simplify the task of measuring and drawing guide lines, the Rapidesign Guide, Ames lettering device, or Braddock-Rowe lettering triangle may be used.

Figure 5   Guide lines.

G I J P R S M W   2 4

RIGHT

G I J P R S M W   2 4

WRONG

Figure 6   Common lettering errors.

B C E G H K S X Z 2 3 5 8

RIGHT (STABLE)

B C E G H K S X Z 2 3 5 8

WRONG (UNSTABLE)

Figure 7   Stability of letters.

BLDG FELT   BLDG FELT

EQUAL SPACING
WRONG   RIGHT
(EQUAL SPACING WILL GIVE   (SPACE BY EYE TO GIVE
UNEQUAL AREAS)   EQUAL AREAS)

Figure 8   Spacing of letters.

IMAGINARY "O"

Figure 9   Spacing of words.

Either vertical or inclined guide lines are also used. These are spaced at random and are used to aid in keeping all letters vertical or slanting at a uniform slope of $67\frac{1}{2}°$.

Form. The exact form of every Commercial Gothic letter should be memorized and used. This task is much simplified if you notice that all capital letters (except "S") are based upon *straight and circular lines*. The numerals (and the letter "S") are based upon *straight* and *elliptical lines*. Some of the common mistakes made in forming letters are shown in Figure 6.

Stability. You must also remember that *letters and numerals should appear stable* whenever possible. Stability means that the letters and numerals should be able to stand on their own two feet. To prevent any possibility of appearing *unstable* or topheavy, the letters B, C, E, G, H, K, S, X, and Z and the numerals 2, 3, 5, and 8 are drawn with lower portions slightly larger in area than their upper portions. Examples of stability in lettering are shown in Figure 7.

Proportion. Of all the lettering "secrets," this is the most important one to the beginner: *Make your letters much wider* than you think they should be. Notice in Figure 4 that nearly all letters are as wide as they are high. Thus the O and Q are perfect circles. The M and W are even wider than they are high. Also notice that the letters are somewhat wider than the numerals.

Letters that are narrower than standard are called "condensed," and letters wider than standard are called "extended." Condensed lettering is used only when it is absolutely necessary to fit many letters into a small space. Slightly extended lettering, on the other hand, is often used, since it is more readable and better looking than standard lettering. All of the notes on the illustrations in this book are lettered in extended lettering.

Density. *Black lines should be used for lettering.* This is necessary for two reasons: to improve the appearance of the lettering and to improve its readability so that it will show up well when reproduced. If your lettering is not black enough, simply use a softer pencil (such as H or F) and *bear down* harder on the paper. Of course you must still remember to keep a sharp point. A professional draftsman sharpens his pencil after every two or three words.

Spacing. Proper spacing of letters to form words, and words to form sentences is a "must." The best lettering has the *letters close together* to form words but the *words far apart* to form sentences. The spacing of letters cannot be measured, but is done by the eye so that the areas between letters are all equal. Notice at the left of Figure 8 that the spaces between the letters in the words "BLDG FELT" were carefully measured, with the result that the space between the L and T appears too large. The second part of the figure shows proper optical spacing, all letters having the same *area* between them.

Figure 9 shows a simple method of spacing words: Imagine the letter O (a circle) between each word.

Remember when you practice your lettering, use the six lettering secrets:

1. Guide lines
2. Straight lines and circular lines
3. Stable lettering
4. Fat lettering
5. Black lettering
6. Close spacing

ARCHITECTURAL LETTERING

Unless a beginning architectural draftsman has training in letter design, he should use the Commer-

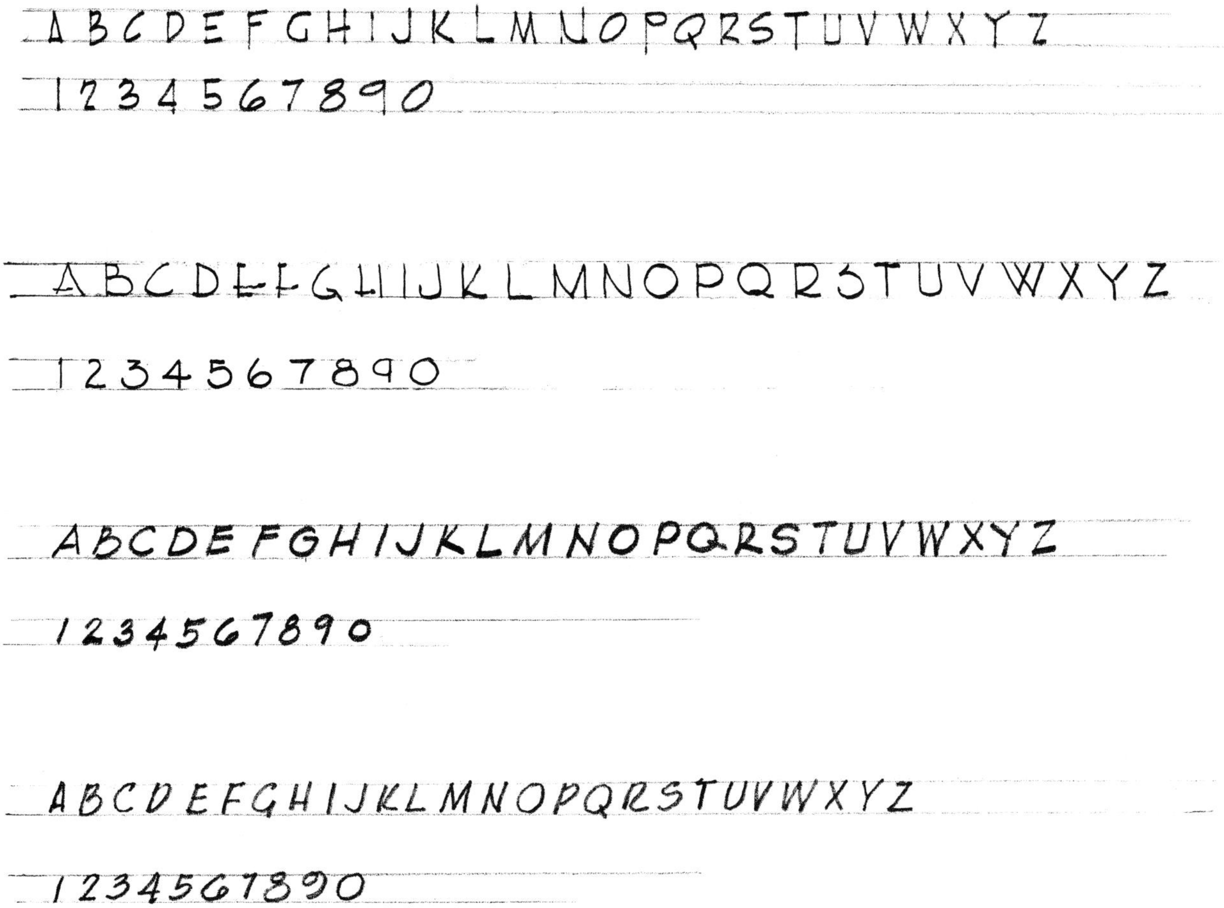

ABCDEFGHIJKLMNOPQRSTUVWXYZ
1234567890

ABCDEFGHIJKLMNOPQRSTUVWXYZ
1234567890

ABCDEFGHIJKLMNOPQRSTUVWXYZ
1234567890

ABCDEFGHIJKLMNOPQRSTUVWXYZ
1234567890

Figure 10   Examples of architectural lettering by practicing architects.

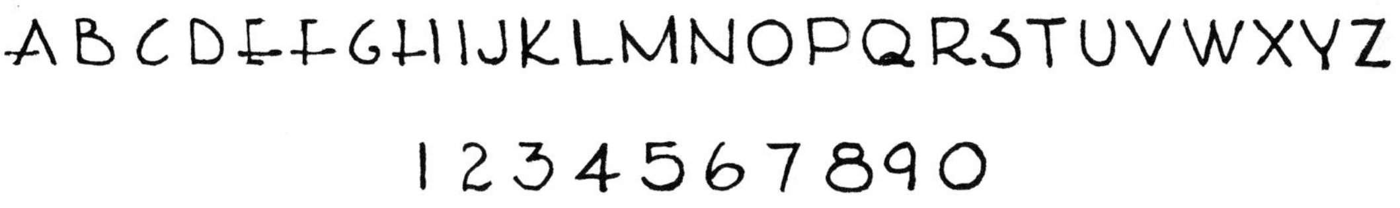

ABCDEFGHIJKLMNOPQRSTUVWXYZ
1234567890

Figure 11   Architectural lettering.

cial Gothic letter forms without change. Indeed, even some draftsmen with many years experience feel that these forms cannot be improved. However, most architectural draftsmen are not content to use Commercial Gothic lettering because it is, after all, the standard for *engineering* rather than *architectural* drawing. Since there exists no standard architectural alphabet, most architects take great pride in developing their own style (see Figure 10). It has been said that there are as many styles of lettering as there are architects! An architect will, of course, stick to his own particular style, and that style will appear uniformly on all of his drawings. If one keeps in mind

that a prime function of the architect is to *sell* his work, then it seems natural that the lettering used be as attractive as possible. However, no matter how fanciful his style in lettering titles and headings, he will always use straight-forward Commercial Gothic numerals when it comes to dimensioning.

Figure 11 shows a legible and attractive alphabet. You may wish to practice these letters first and then revise some letters until you find a type of lettering that feels right to you. During this test period, keep these rules in mind:

1. Rapidity of execution is an important factor. Time

ABCDEFGHIJKLMNOPQRSTUVWXYZ

DINING ROOM

Figure 12   The architectural alphabet, obtained from a standard lettering stencil.

is money; do not get in the habit of drawing excessively time-consuming letters. This means that the letters should be single stroke, and that stylized portions of individual letters should be drawn in a free and natural fashion. (For example, the elliptical "C" and "D" in Figure 11 should not be used if it does not seem natural to you.)

2. Accentuate the ends of the strokes. This detail comes naturally to some, and very hard to others. If you find that you cannot easily produce attractive results with these accents after a fair trial, then do not attempt them further.

3. In most cases, only vertical capitals are used. An upper and lower drop line is useful in uniformly ending those lines that drop below or above the normal guides. Each drop line is one third the capital height. The capital letters G, Q, R, T, and Y may drop down, while the capital letter L may extend upward.

4. Lettering should be legible. It can be safely stated that architectural lettering can be as fanciful as you please—as long as it is easily read.

1. Transfer of letters is effected by registering guide lines on type sheet with guide on artwork. With a very soft pencil or ballpoint pen rub down letter with light pressure.

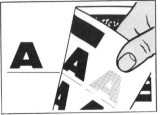

2. Carefully lift away type sheet — letter is now transferred — repeat procedure until setting is complete. Finally place backing sheet over setting and burnish for maximum adhesion.

Figure 13   How to use appliqué.

PRESENTATION DRAWING

The large majority of architectural working drawings are drawn in pencil, and therefore freehand pencil lettering is used. Occasionally, though, ink drawings are used for special requirements. A presentation drawing (a display drawing to show the prospective client) may be done in ink or even a combination of pencil and ink. Also, drawings to be printed in newspapers, magazines, or books are best reproduced when drawn in ink.

Lettering stencils. The ink lettering on presentation drawings may be drawn freehand, but a lettering stencil is usually used. Some of the popular trade names are *LeRoy, Wrico,* and *Varigraph.* These stencils may be obtained in a variety of stock sizes and styles, or they may be ordered in custom-made styles. Often the stock Commercial Gothic stencil is adjusted slightly to obtain lettering with an architectural flavor. Figure 12 shows an architectural alphabet obtained by using a standard LeRoy extended lettering stencil. A similar alphabet was used for the illustrations in this book.

Appliqué (pressure sensitive transfer). Prepared lettering sheets may be obtained from which the draftsman can transfer individual letters to his drawing merely by rubbing the letter as shown in Figure 13. Figure 14 shows only a few of the hundreds of lettering styles available. Some popular trade names are *ACS Instant Lettering, Paratone Alphabets,* and *Mico/Type.*

Instrumental lettering. Drafting instruments are seldom used for lettering because they are too slow. Occasionally a large presentation drawing may require a special title, however. Figure 15 shows one of the many possible styles of single-line lettering, and Figure 16 one style of double-line (boxed) lettering. The boxed letters may be filled in if desired.

Title box. Professional offices use vellum with printed border lines and title boxes to save drafting time. A sample 2″ × 4″ title box is shown in Figure 17. There are many other sizes and types of title boxes, but all should contain this information as a minimum:

1. Name and location of structure
2. Name and address of owner
3. Name and address of architect
4. Name of sheet (such as "First Floor Plan")
5. Number of sheet
6. Date
7. Scale
8. Draftsman's initials

STUDY QUESTIONS

1. Name and show an example of three styles of lettering.
2. What sizes of Commercial Gothic lettering are used on architectural drawings?
3. List the six "secrets" of good lettering.
4. Are guide lines erased? Why?
5. Show the difference between a drop line, base line, waist line, and cap line.
6. What is meant by "stability" in lettering? Give examples.
7. What is the difference between:
   a. Vertical and inclined guide lines
   b. Condensed and extended lettering
8. Why is it important for architectural lettering to be dense black?
9. What is the proper method for spacing letters and words?
10. When is ink lettering used in architectural work?
11. List the minimum information contained in every title box.

LABORATORY PROBLEMS

1. Four sample alphabets incorporating common architectural lettering practices are shown in Figure 10. Repeat the alphabets on drawing paper. This lettering should be $\frac{1}{4}$″ high—a common title height. Remember to use guide lines. If you are not satisfied with your results, try again on a second line.
2. Figure 11 shows an architectural alphabet. Repeat this alphabet on drawing paper using letters $\frac{1}{8}$″ high. Repeat until you are satisfied with the results.
3. On drawing paper, design a style of lettering that feels right to you. Take great care that each letter is just what you want, since you will be required to adhere to this style on all drawings. Your instructor will indicate his approval of each letter type. Use the sizes assigned:
   a. $\frac{1}{4}$″
   b. $\frac{1}{8}$″
   c. $\frac{3}{32}$″

Figure 14   Styles of appliqué lettering.

Figure 15   Single-line instrumental lettering.

Figure 16   Double-line instrumental lettering.

Figure 17   Appliqué title box used by professional architects.

10 architectural dimensioning

To read architectural plans, you must become familiar with the graphic language used in two different professions: architecture and surveying. The architect uses architectural drawing to provide the instructions for constructing a building, and the surveyor uses topographical drawing to describe the plot of land occupied by the building. The dimensioning practice in each of these fields differs slightly. Let's look at both.

ARCHITECTURAL PLAN DIMENSIONS

Architectural dimensioning practices depend entirely upon the method used to construct the building. The masonry portion of a building, therefore, is dimensioned quite differently from the frame or veneered portion. For example, in masonry construction the widths of window and door openings are shown, since these dimensions are needed to lay up the wall. Openings in a frame wall, however, are often dimensioned to their centerlines to simplify locating the window and door frames. In masonry construction, dimensions are given to the faces of the walls. In frame construction, over-all dimensions are given to the outside faces of studs because these dimensions are needed first. Masonry partitions are dimensioned to their faces, while frame partitions are usually dimensioned to their centerlines. The

thickness of masonry walls and partitions are indicated on the plan, but frame wall thicknesses are indicated on the detail drawings where construction details may be shown to a larger scale.

Masonry veneer on a wood frame wall is dimensioned as a frame wall would be (to the outside faces of the studs), since the wood frame is constructed before the veneer is laid up. Figures 1–3 illustrate these differences.

Some additional rules of architectural dimensioning follow.

1. Dimension lines are spaced about $\frac{3}{8}$" apart. Often three lines of dimensions are needed on each wall: a line of dimensions close to the wall locating windows and doors, a second line locating wall offsets, and finally an over-all dimension.
2. Dots, small circles, triangles, perpendicular lines, or diagonal lines (as shown in Figure 4) may be used in place of arrowheads. Dots should always be used when dimensioning small distances in tight spaces.
3. Extension lines may or may not touch the plan, but be consistent. Avoid crossing extension and dimension lines by placing the longer dimensions farther away from the plan, as in Figures 1–3.
4. Dimension lines are continuous with the numerals lettered above them. Numerals are placed

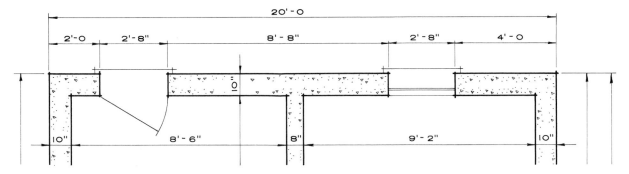

Figure 1   Dimensioning masonry construction (concrete, concrete block, solid brick, and cavity brick).

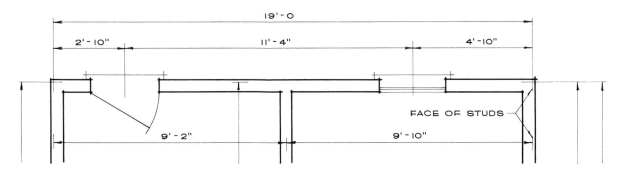

Figure 2   Dimensioning frame construction.

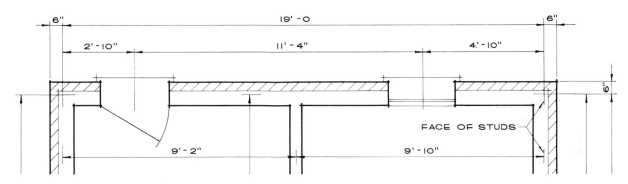

Figure 3   Dimensioning veneer construction.

to read from the bottom and right-hand side of the drawing.

5. Dimensions may be placed on the views but avoid dimensioning over other features. Several complete lines of dimensions in both directions are ordinarily needed to locate interior features.

6. Dimension numerals and notes are lettered $\frac{3}{32}''$ high.

7. Give all dimensions over twelve inches in feet and inches (to the nearest sixteenth of an inch). The symbols for feet (') and inches (") are used except for zero inches. For example:

6" not 0'-6"
1'-0 not 1'-0"
1'-6" not 1'-6

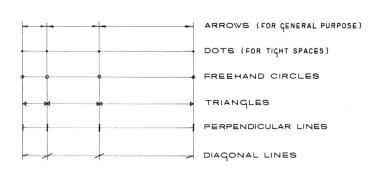

Figure 4   Arrowhead types.

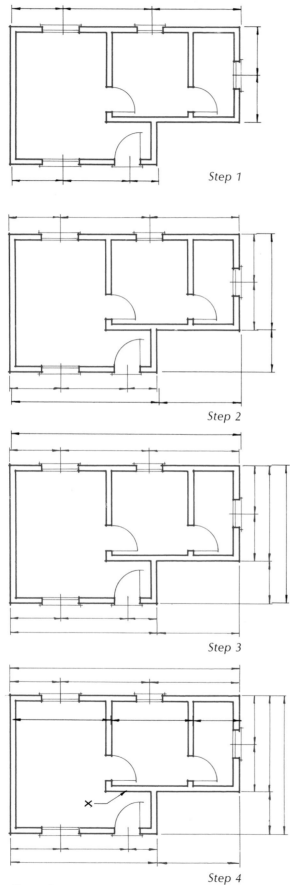

Step 1

Step 2

Step 3

Step 4

Figure 5

8. Do not try to "fancy up" dimensions with artistic numerals. *Legibility* is the only concern.

9. Never crowd dimensions.

10. No *usable* dimension is omitted even though the dimension could be obtained by addition or subtraction of other dimensions. Be sure to include over-all dimensions, any change in shape of outside walls, all rooms, halls, window locations, and exterior door locations. A common mistake is failing to check cumulative dimensions with over-all dimensions. Incorrect dimensions can cause the builder much delay and added expense.

11. All obvious dimensions *are* omitted. For example:
    a. Interior doors at the corner of a room need not be located.
    b. Interior doors centered at the end of a hall need not be located.
    c. The widths of identical side-by-side closets need not be dimensioned.

12. Columns and beams are located by dimensions to their centerlines.

13. To free the plan from excessive dimensions, the sizes of windows and doors are given in window and door schedules.

14. House drawings are usually made to a scale of $\frac{1}{4}'' = 1'\text{-}0$. Larger buildings are usually drawn to a scale of $\frac{1}{8}'' = 1'\text{-}0$. Details are drawn to larger architectural scales. *Always* indicate the scale used near the drawing or in the title block.

EXAMPLE

Show the dimensions needed on the plan of the simple frame cottage shown in Figure 5.

Step 1: Window and door locations. A line of dimensions is placed on every outside wall containing a window or door to locate them for the builder. This dimension line is positioned about $\frac{3}{8}''$ beyond the farthest projection (such as a chimney, window, or door sill). Dimension lines are spaced by eye rather than actually measured.

Step 2: Wall locations. A second line of dimensions is placed on every wall containing offsets to provide the builder with the subtotal of dimensions for each wall.

Step 3: Over-all dimensions. Both over-all dimensions are placed. Check that all cumulative dimensions equal the subtotal dimensions and that the subtotal dimensions equal the over-all dimensions.

Step 4: Partition locations. Lines of interior dimensions are placed to locate partitions and interior features. In this example only one line of dimensions is required since partition "X" is located by alignment with the exterior wall. Note that location dimensions for interior doors are not necessary, since their positions are obvious. Additional required notes and schedules will complete the dimensioning. See the drawings of the A residence in Chapter 16 for the dimensioning required on a larger plan.

ELEVATION DIMENSIONS

Of the many different methods of indicating elevation dimensions, the two following are most often used.

1. Finish dimensions. This method indicates the actual dimension of the inside of the room when completely finished. Thus the *finished floor* to the *finished ceiling* distance is specified. This method is often used by the designer, since he can quickly specify a desired room height. 8'-0 is often used for the first floor and 7'-6'' for the second floor.

2. Construction dimensions. This method indicates the dimensions actually needed by the contractor when framing a building. Thus, in platform framing, the *top of subflooring* to the *top of plate* distance indicates the exact height to construct the sections of walls and partitions. This method is preferred by builders. The National Lumber Manufacturers Association recommends a first floor height of 8'-1½'' and a second floor height of 7'-7½''. These dimensions will result in 8'-0 and 7'-6'' room heights after the finished floor and ceiling have been added.

When in doubt as to the correct method of dimensioning an architectural drawing, there is one simple rule to follow: put yourself in the place of the builder and give the dimensions that will help him build with a minimum amount of calculation. Refer to the elevation dimensions of the A residence in Chapter 19 for a complete example.

SECTIONAL DIMENSIONS

The sectional view provides an opportunity to specify the materials and sizes not shown on the plans and elevations. Since sectional views are drawn to a larger scale, more detailed dimensions may be shown. The dimensions, material, and location of all members are specified, leaving nothing to the imagination of the builder. Nominal ("name") sizes are used for rough material, but actual sizes are used for finish material, as in:

1'' × 8'' Subflooring (Use nominal dimensions)
¾'' × 7'' Fascia   (Use actual dimensions)

Some offices attempt to show rough material by omitting the inch marks from nominal dimensions. Thus 2'' × 4'' would indicate finished lumber, measuring 2'' × 4'', but 2 × 4 would indicate rough lumber measuring 1½'' × 3½''. See the A residence sections in Chapter 19 for examples of the dimensions required on sectional views.

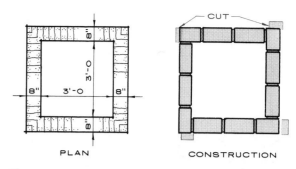

Figure 6   Nonmodular barbecue pit design.

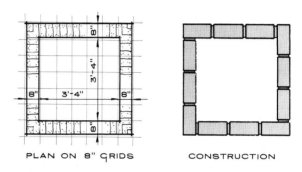

Figure 7   Modular barbecue pit design.

TOPOGRAPHICAL DIMENSIONS

A complete study of topographical drawing would be quite lengthy. Fortunately, the architectural draftsman is usually interested only in the areas of topography related to the plot plan.

The boundaries of a plot are described by dimensions given in 100ths of a foot (two places beyond the decimal point), such as 151.67'. However the surveyor will, whenever possible, lay out plots using even lengths (like 100'). When this is done, the dimension is given simply as 100' rather than 100.00'. Bearings (such as N 5° 10' 15'' E) are also given to show the compass direction of the boundaries. The bearings are given starting at one corner of the plot and proceeding around the perimeter until the starting point is again reached. Thus two opposite and parallel sides of a plot have opposite bearings (such as N 30° E and S 30° W).

Contour lines are dimensioned by indicating their elevation above sea level or some other datum plane like a street or the floor of a nearby house. The elevations of the land at the corners of the plot and the house are also shown. An engineer's scale is used rather than an architect's scale, 1'' = 20' being quite common. The plot plan of the A residence in Chapter 17 shows these required dimensions.

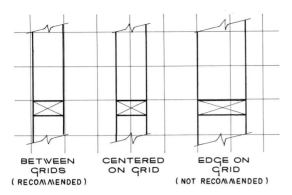

Figure 8   Relation of a stud wall to a grid line.

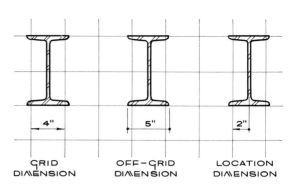

Figure 10   Modular grid dimensions, off-grid dimensions, and location dimensions.

MODULAR COORDINATION

"Module" (from the Greek "measure") means a standard unit of measurement. A modular system, then, is a system of design in which most materials are equal in size to an established module or a multiple of that module. Such a system is called *modular coordination* because the materials will fit together—or "coordinate"—without cutting. For example, let us plan an open barbecue pit to be built of 8″ × 8″ × 16″* concrete blocks with inside dimensions approximately 3′ square. If we designed this pit without giving thought to the size of the blocks, we would find that the four corner blocks in each course must be cut from 16″ to 12″ (Figure 6).

If, however, we planned on an 8″ module as shown in Figure 7, there would be no cutting required and we would obtain a larger barbecue pit without using additional blocks.

---

*The actual size of an 8″ × 8″ × 16″ block is $7\frac{5}{8}$″ × $7\frac{5}{8}$″ × $15\frac{5}{8}$″. When laid up with a $\frac{3}{8}$″ mortar joint, however, the blocks fit in an 8″ module.

Advantages. From this simple example, it is evident that modular coordination has some definite advantages:

1. It reduces cutting and fitting.
2. It reduces building costs.
3. It standardizes sizes of building materials.
4. It reduces drafting errors by reducing fractional dimensions.

At present about 20 percent of American architectural firms use modular dimensioning. These are the firms that specialize in masonry or precut lumber buildings.

Size of module. Any convenient size module may be used. An 8″ module was used in the above example. A 4′ planning module is useful in layout work. A 20′ structural module is often used in steel factory construction. The most useful module, however, is 4″, since brick, block, structural tile, window frames, and door bucks are all available in multiples of 4″. Countries with metric rather than English measurements use a 100 mm module (4″ = 101.6 mm).

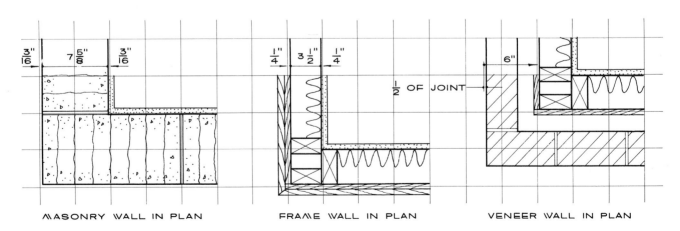

Figure 9   Dimensioning typical walls using modular coordination.

Rules of modular dimensioning

1. Show light 4 *inch* grids on all plans, elevations, and sections drawn to a scale of $\frac{3}{4}'' = 1'$ or larger. For smaller scales, only a 4 *foot* planning grid is shown, since it is impractical to show 4″ grids.

2. Whenever possible, fit the building parts *between* grid lines or *centered* on grid lines. Occasionally an edge arrangement is necessary (Figure 8). Typical walls in plan are shown in Figure 9.

3. To indicate location of building parts, use grid dimensions (dimensions from grid line to grid line). Use *arrows* for grid dimensions as shown in Figure 10. These arrows are used to indicate grid dimensions even when the grid lines do not appear on the drawing (as on the 4′ planning module).

4. To indicate any position *not* on a grid line, use a dot.

5. The plans and elevations will contain mostly grid dimensions. But since many materials are not sized in 4″ modules ($3\frac{1}{2}''$ studs, for example), these materials are related to the nearest grid line by means of location dimensions in the section views. Location dimensions will have an arrow on the grid end and a dot on the off-grid end.

6. The 4″ module is three-dimensional, applying to both horizontal and vertical dimensions. Elevation grids are established as follows (Figure 11):

a. The top of the subfloor in wood frame construction coincides with a grid line.
b. The top of a slab-on-ground coincides with a grid line.
c. The actual finished floor in all other types of construction is located $\frac{1}{8}''$ below a grid line.

For a complete set of plans dimensioned according to the modular system, see the split level house in Appendix A.

Unicom system. The National Lumber Manufacturers Association recommends a modular system of house construction called "unicom" (for *uniform components*). In the unicom system, components such as wall, window, and door sections are all based upon a 16″ or 24″ module, thus requiring suppliers to stock a smaller number of different sized components. Houses may be erected using only these prefabricated components, or framed in the conventional manner.

Unicom grid. The unicom grid is based upon the 4″ modular grid but with several variations. Figure 12 shows a unicom grid containing three weights of grid lines and a hidden line. The lightweight grids indi-

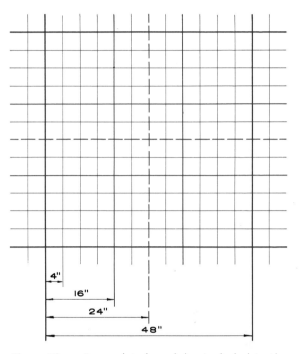

Figure 12   *Four related modules included in the unicom grid system.*

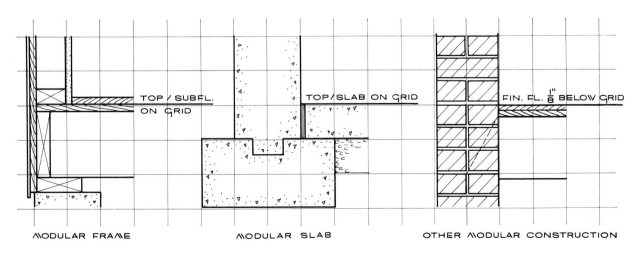

Figure 11   *Vertical positioning in modular coordination.*

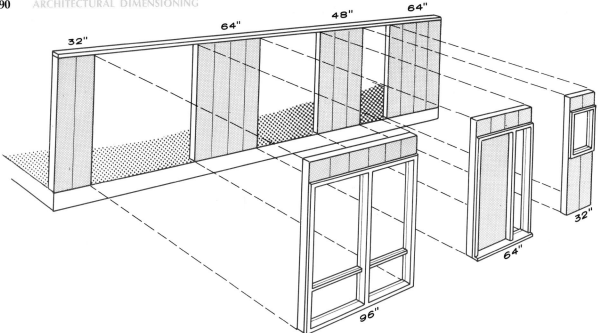

Figure 13   Unicom wall, window, and door components.

cate 4″ modules, the medium weight 16″ modules, and the heavy weight 48″ modules. The hidden line indicates 24″ modules.

Unicom panels. Some typical wall, window, and door panels are shown in Figure 13. These panels are multiples of the 16″ module and can be combined without cutting into the desired modular design. Floor panels, roof panels, partitions, roof truss components, and stairs are also available to unicom specifications.

TABLE I
Metric Prefixes

Prefix	SI Symbol	Multiplication Factor	
tera	T	10^{12}	(1 000 000 000 000)
giga	G	10^{9}	(1 000 000 000)
mega	M	10^{6}	(1 000 000)
kilo	k	10^{3}	(1 000)
hecto	h	10^{2}	(100)
deka	da	10^{1}	(10)
deci	d	10^{-1}	(0.1)
centi	c	10^{-2}	(0.01)
milli	m	10^{-3}	(0.001)
micro	μ	10^{-6}	(0.000 001)
nano	n	10^{-9}	(0.000 000 001)
pico	p	10^{-12}	(0.000 000 000 001)
femto	f	10^{-15}	(0.000 000 000 000 001)
atto	a	10^{-18}	(0.000 000 000 000 000 001)

METRIC UNITS

The metric system was conceived over 300 years ago by Gabriel Mouton, a Frenchman, who designed a decimal system based upon the circumference of the earth. The unit of length was called the meter, from the Greek "metron" (measure). In 1960 the meter was redefined internationally in terms of the wavelength of a specific color of light. Most industrialized countries have adopted this system, known as the SI (Système International) Metric System. The British adopted metric units in 1975, and the United States is following on a voluntary—but steady—basis.

SI Metric System. The SI System is based upon the following seven units which are of interest to the architect and builder. Multiples and submultiples are expressed in a decimal system.

1. Length: meter (m)
2. Time: second (s)
3. Mass: kilogram (kg)
4. Temperature: kelvin (K)
5. Electric current: ampere (A)
6. Luminous intensity: candela (cd)
7. Amount of substance: mole (mol)

Prefixes are used to eliminate insignificant digits and decimals. For example, 3 mm (3 millimeters) is preferred to 0.003 m (0.003 meters). Metric prefixes are shown in Table I.

Wherever possible, use multiple and submultiple prefixes representing steps of 1000. For example, express length in mm, m, and km. Avoid using the

This section courtesy *The Construction Specifications Institute.*

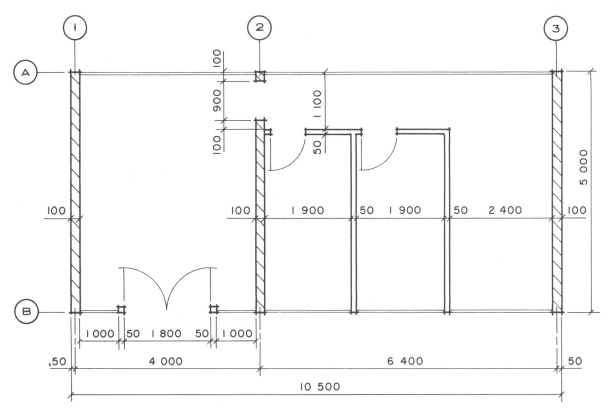

Figure 14   A plan dimensioned in metric units (mm).

centimeter and the decimeter. Do not use a period after an SI symbol except when it occurs at the end of a sentence (e.g., 2 mm not 2 mm.). To assist in reading numbers with four or more digits, and to eliminate confusion by the European use of commas to express decimal points, place digits in groups of three separated by a space, without commas, starting both to the left and right of the decimal point (e.g., 12 625 not 12,625). Figure 14 shows an example of an architectural plan dimensioned in metric units.

Dual dimensioning. Architectural offices with practice limited to work in the United States do not normally use metric units. However, when a component that has been manufactured to metric sizes is required to mate with a component manufactured to English sizes, dual dimensioning may be used. Dual dimensioning is simply the placing of the metric counterpart after the English dimension, e.g., 1″ (25.4 mm). Dual dimensioning or metric dimensioning is also used by architectural offices with practice in foreign countries. Dual dimensioning may be shown by any of the methods illustrated in Figure 15.

A number of countries are now using a metric system that varies slightly from the SI metric system. For projects in such countries, determine what metric system is used, and then give dual dimensioning with those of that country's metric units and those of the SI metric units. Particularly involved are building components or prefabricated assemblies that are

manufactured under one dimensioning system mated with those manufactured under another system (whether of English units, SI metric units, or other metric units).

English-Metric conversions. Conversions from the English to the SI Metric System can be made with the help of Table II. Retain in all conversions the number of significant digits so that accuracy is neither sacrificed nor exaggerated. Conversion is

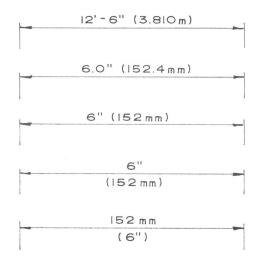

Figure 15   Dual dimensioning systems.

TABLE II

**English-Metric Conversions
(accurate to parts per million)**

```
        1 inch = 25.4 millimeters
        1 foot = 0.304 8 meters
        1 yard = 0.914 4 meters
        1 mile = 1.609 34 kilometers
        1 quart (liquid) = 0.946 353 liters
        1 gallon = 0.003 785 41 cubic meters
        1 ounce (avdp) = 28.349 5 grams
        1 pound (avdp) = 0.453 592 kilograms
        1 horsepower = 0.745 700 kilowatts

        1 millimeter = 0.039 370 1 inches
        1 meter = 3.280 84 feet
        1 meter = 1.093 61 yards
        1 kilometer = 0.621 371 miles
        1 liter = 1.056 69 quarts (liquid)
        1 cubic meter = 264.172 gallons
        1 gram = 0.035 274 0 ounces (avdp)
        1 kilogram = 2.204 62 pounds (avdp)
        1 kilowatt = 1.341 02 horsepower
```

quite easy using a pocket calculator: $1\frac{1}{16}'' = 1.0625 \times 25.4 = 27$ mm. Building site or plot plans are generally dimensioned in decimals such as 101.24'. Conversion of these dimensions is simple: $101.24' = 101.24 \times 0.3048 = 30.858$ m.

Indicating scales. When showing scales on the architectural plans, it is suggested that the inch-foot scales not be converted (1" = 1'-0 would have to be shown as 25.4 mm = 304.8 mm, which would be extremely impractical). Should any reference to scale be required, a ratio should be used such as 1 : 12.

Nominal sizes. In the construction industry, many products are referred to by nominal sizes such as 2 × 4, 12 gage, or 1" pipe. The nominal size is a value assigned for the purpose of convenient designation, existing in name only. For example, the nomenclature "8 penny nail" is still used even though they can no longer be purchased for 8¢ per hundred. There are no SI equivalents required for nominal dimensions; therefore no attempt should be made at this time to assign a new metric name for a "2 × 4." However, many products will be slightly changed in size to coordinate with a 100 mm module. For example, 4' × 8' plywood will probably be changed to 1 200 × 2 400 mm.

STUDY QUESTIONS

1. Compare the methods of dimensioning a window in a masonry wall and a window in a wood frame wall.

2. Give the proper method of indicating the following dimensions on an architectural drawing:
   a. Four inches
   b. Fourteen inches
   c. Four feet
   d. Four feet, four inches.
3. Give the recommended:
   a. Distance between dimension lines
   b. Height of dimension numerals
   c. Height of architectural notes
4. Give examples of some dimensions which may be omitted from an architectural drawing.
5. What is the purpose of window and door schedules?
6. What would be the probable scale of the architectural drawings of:
   a. A residence
   b. A 20' × 40' store
   c. A church (capacity = 200)
7. Give two methods of indicating elevation dimensions. When is each method used?
8. When are nominal sizes and actual sizes used to dimension materials?
9. On a plot plan of a rectangular lot, why do parallel lot lines have different bearings?
10. What is meant by:
    a. Modular coordination
    b. The unicom system
11. List four advantages of the unicom system.
12. What module size is most commonly used?
13. In modular dimensioning:
    a. When are 4 *inch* and 4 *foot* grids shown?
    b. When are an arrow and a dot used?
14. In modular elevation dimensioning, what is the position of the floor in respect to a grid line in:
    a. Wood frame construction
    b. Slab-on-ground construction
    c. Other types of construction
15. Give the SI metric units for:
    a. Length
    b. Mass
    c. Temperature
    d. Electric current

LABORATORY PROBLEMS

1. Using $\frac{1}{4}''$ cross-section paper, sketch a typical exterior corner of a residence constructed of:
   a. Frame
   b. Brick veneer
   c. 10" cavity brick
   d. 8" concrete block
   Indicate the method of dimensioning and completely note all materials.
2. Complete the dimensioning on your plans of the A residence.
3. Complete the dimensioning of the building assigned by your instructor.
4. Complete the dimensioning of your original house design.
5. Dimension your building using:
   a. English System
   b. SI Metric System
   c. Dual Dimensioning

11 windows

The architectural draftsman should be thoroughly familiar with *all* the building components he must specify and detail. However, the window is probably the most important single component in the design of a successful building. The proper selection and placement of windows is necessary for aesthetic as well as functional reasons. In addition to providing light and air, windows can change the interior of a room by providing framed views or window walls, and can change the exterior of a building by the fenestration.

TYPES

There are many different types of windows now on the market. Some of the most commonly used are:

Casement	Projected	Pivoted
Awning	Sliding	Jalousie
Hopper	Double hung	Fixed

These windows can be obtained in wood and in many metals in nearly any size ranging from small lavatory windows to entire window walls. Let us look at each in turn.

Casement. A casement window (Figure 1) is hinged at the side and usually swings outward so that the inside drapes are not disturbed. Screens, then, are hung on the inside. When more than two casement windows are installed side by side, it is often the practice to specify fixed sash for the middle windows, and a hinged sash at each end.

When the sash is hinged at the top, it is called an *awning* window; when the sash is hinged at the bottom, it is called a *hopper* window. To prevent rain from entering the open windows, awning windows swing outward while hopper windows swing inward.

Figure 1   Casement windows.

93

Figure 1   continued.

CASEMENT
SASH LOCK

CASEMENT
HINGES

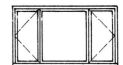

Projected. A projected window (Figure 2) is somewhat different from a casement window in that some form of linkage other than the hinge is used. A projected window will swing open and slide at the same time. Projected windows may also be classified as casement, awning, and hopper according to the direction of swing. Metal projected windows are commonly used on commercial buildings, while wooden casement (nonprojected) windows are commonly used on residences.

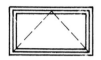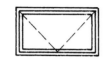

Figure 2   Projected windows.

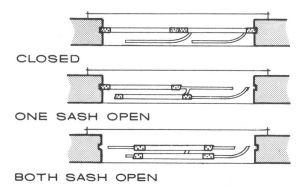

CLOSED

ONE SASH OPEN

BOTH SASH OPEN

Sliding. Sliding or gliding windows (Figure 3) are designed to run on horizontal tracks in pairs. The tracks are curved so that the sash are in line when closed but will move past each other when opened. Most sliding windows contain sash which can be removed from the frame for easy cleaning. The screen is installed on the outside of the window.

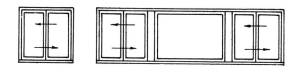

Figure 3   Sliding windows.

Double hung. The double hung window (Figure 4) is usually specified for Colonial-type houses. This window contains two sash which slide in vertical tracks. A spring-balance arrangement is used to counterbalance the weight of the sash and hold them in any desired position. The sash are easily removed for window cleaning. Double hung windows may be obtained with self-storing screens and storm windows.

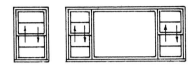

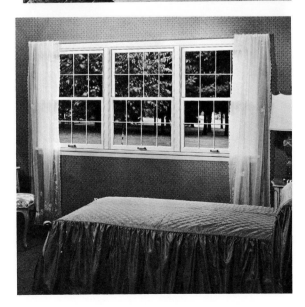

Figure 4   Double hung windows.

Figure 5 *Double hung windows combined to form curved bays. Sash pivots for ease in cleaning.*

Pivoted. This window revolves on two pivots—one at the center of the top of the sash, and the other at the center of the bottom of the sash. Not often specified for houses, the pivoted window is common in taller buildings because of the ease of cleaning.

Jalousie. The jalousie window is a series of small awning panes all operated together. It has not become very popular because the view through it is interrupted by the many intersections.

Fixed. When views and light are desired without ventilation (as is often true of air conditioned buildings), fixed windows are specified. Large fixed windows are sometimes called "picture windows." Some fixed windows are designed so that they can be opened only by window washers for cleaning. Fixed windows are stocked in both rectangular and trapezoidal shapes (Figure 6 and Appendix B).

Basement windows. The most often specified basement window is a reversible awning-hopper window (Figure 7). The sash is designed so that it can be easily removed from the frame and installed to swing up (awning) or down (hopper). In both cases the swing is toward the inside. Since a basement window is installed at the inner side of the foundation wall, there is no danger of rain entering. The screen is installed on the outside of the frame.

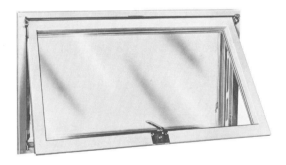

Figure 6 *Trapezoidal fixed window units.*

Figure 7 *Basement windows.*

INSTALLATION

Before studying specifications and the detailing of windows, it is necessary to understand how a window is installed in a building wall (Figure 8). The glass and its immediate framing members are called the *sash*. Except in fixed windows, the sash is designed to be opened for ventilation or entirely removed for easy cleaning. The sash is surrounded by the *window frame*, which is permanently fastened to the rough wall (studs). The window frame has an L-shaped cross-section, the outer portion of which is called the *blind stop*. The blind stop helps to properly position the frame in the rough opening. Stock windows are obtained with the sash already installed in the frame so that the entire window unit can be set into the rough opening. The rough opening is constructed several inches larger than the window frame to allow for leveling the window. After the window is in place, exterior and interior trim is used to close the cracks between the frame and the rough opening.

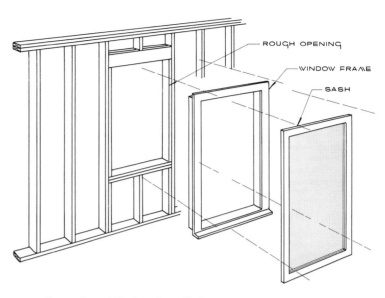

Figure 8   Window installation.

TERMINOLOGY

Many special terms are used to describe the various parts of a window. Figure 9 shows a cutaway pictorial of a double hung window and the corresponding sectional details. The terms "head," "jamb," "rail," and "sill" indicate that the sectional cuts were taken through the head (the upper horizontal members), jamb (side vertical members), meeting rail (middle horizontal members), and sill (lower horizontal members).

Sash. The members of the upper sash are called *top rail, meeting rail,* and *side rails.* The lower sash members are called *meeting rail, bottom rail,* and *side rails.*

Window frame. The members of the window frame are called *top jamb, side jamb, sill,* and *blind stop* (or "windbreaker").

Interior trim. The interior trim and *apron* cover the crack between the window frame and the interior finished wall.

Exterior casing. The exterior casing (which may be called "trim") also covers wall cracks. In addition, it serves as the frame around the *storm sash* or *screens.*

Drip cap. The drip cap prevents water from seeping into the window head. Note the *drip groove* on the underside which prevents water from seeping inward underneath the drip cap. *Flashing* can be used in place of the wooden drip cap.

Double glazing. A second glass pane may be installed on the sash creating a dead air space to provide insulation and prevent condensation on the inside pane.

Mullions and muntins are shown in Figure 10. Mullions are members (usually vertical) that separate adjacent windows. Muntins are smaller members used to subdivide large glass areas. Many manufacturers offer removable muntins so that the windows may be subdivided to any taste. Also, these muntins may be removed for easy cleaning.

SPECIFYING WINDOWS

The type of window to be specified for a building will be determined by the building style and the client's desire. Once the style is decided, the size must be determined from the many sizes available in each style. As an example, let us study the Andersen casement windows. Five window heights are obtainable, each height recommended for a different condition. Figure 11 shows how these different window sizes will fit into different types of rooms.

Manufacturers do not offer a wide variety of window widths, since wide windows are obtained by specifying a number of individual units side by side. Andersen casements may be obtained in two widths, Series N and Series W.

Each manufacturer has its own set of window

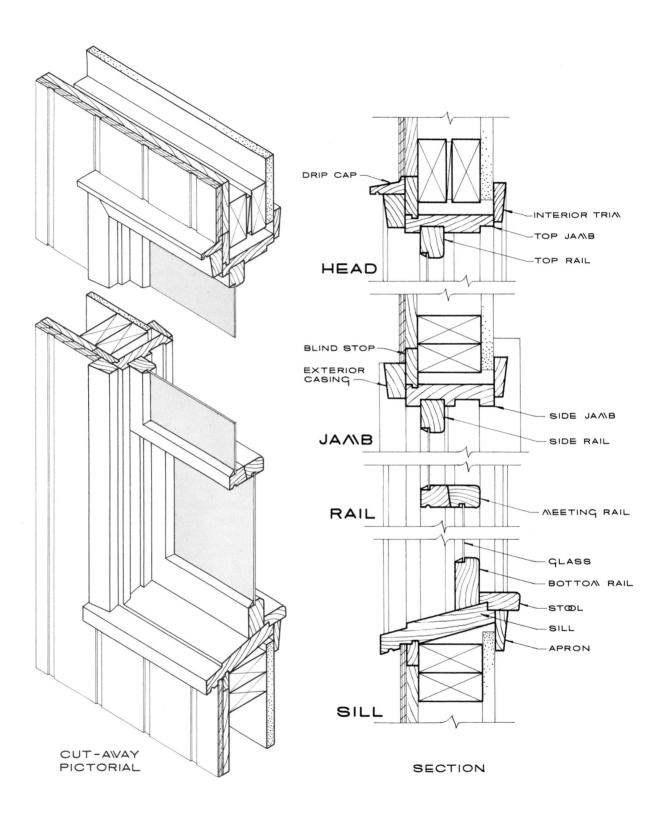

Figure 9   Double hung window in a wood frame wall.

sizes and catalog numbers. To simplify window specifications, tables showing the size and numbers may be obtained from the manufacturers. Tables for Andersen casement, sliding, double hung, and basement windows and a table for Pella fixed trapezoidal windows (much used in contemporary design) are shown in Appendix A.

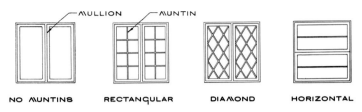

Figure 10   Removable muntins.

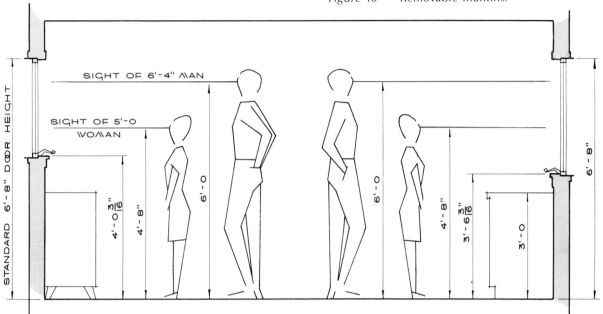

NO. 30 ANDERSEN CASEMENT WINDOW
USED IN BEDROOM

NO. 3 ANDERSEN CASEMENT WINDOW
USED IN KITCHEN

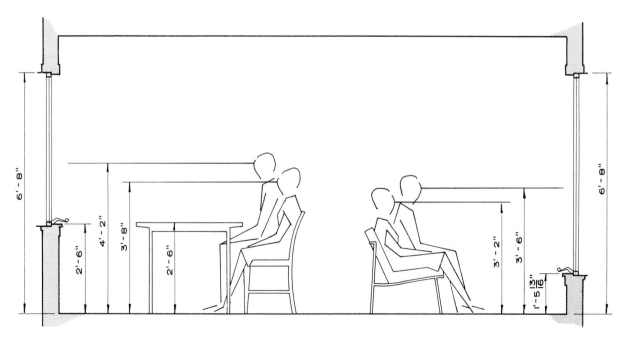

NO. 4 ANDERSEN CASEMENT WINDOW
USED IN DINING AREA

NO. 5 ANDERSEN CASEMENT WINDOW
USED IN LIVING AREA

Figure 11   Selection of window height.

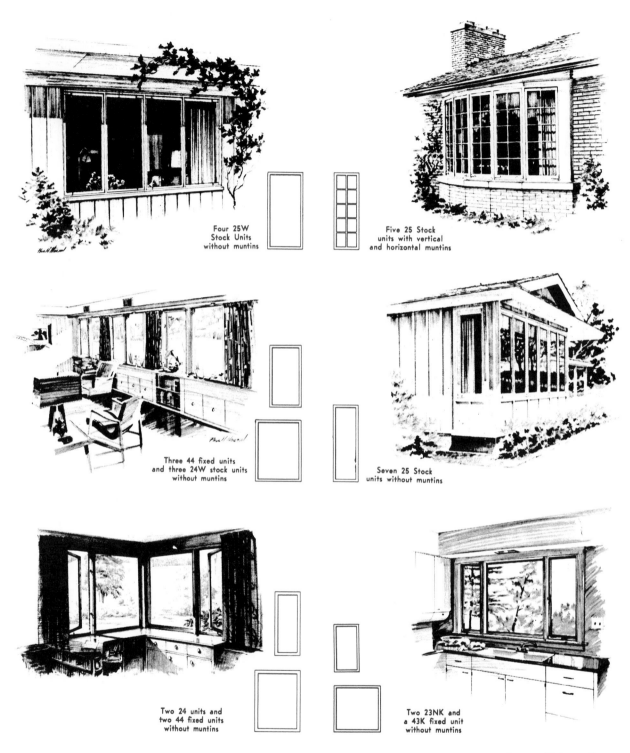

Four 25W
Stock Units
without muntins

Five 25 Stock
units with vertical
and horizontal muntins

Three 44 fixed units
and three 24W stock units
without muntins

Seven 25 Stock
units without muntins

Two 24 units and
two 44 fixed units
without muntins

Two 23NK and
a 43K fixed unit
without muntins

Courtesy of Rolscreen Company

Figure 12   Arrangements of casement and fixed window combinations.

Andersen Catalog Number	Sash Height	Recommended for
2	2'-2"	Lavatory
30	2'-8$\frac{3}{16}$"	Bedroom
3	3'-2$\frac{3}{16}$"	Kitchen
4	4'-2$\frac{3}{8}$"	Dining area
5	5'-2$\frac{9}{16}$"	Living area

Andersen Catalog Number	Sash Width	Preferred for
Series N	1'-6"	emphasis on vertical lines
Series W	1'-10$\frac{1}{2}$"	wider uninterrupted view

DETAILING

In addition to supplying size tables, manufacturers also supply *tracing details* for the convenience of architectural draftsmen. These tracing details may be slipped under tracing vellum and all applicable details copied. Although the manufacturer attempts to supply tracing details for nearly all possible types of construction, some modification is often necessary to fit the window into a particular type of wall. Tracing details for Andersen casement, sliding, double hung, and basement windows are shown in Appendix A.

WINDOW ARRANGEMENTS

Stock windows may be stacked horizontally or vertically to obtain countless distinctive arrangements. Figure 12 shows various combinations of Pella case-

Figure 14   A window wall for a select view.

Figure 15   Fixed and projected units combined.

Figure 13   Gliding units combined to form a patio window wall.

Figure 16   A dramatic window arrangement of fixed and awning units.

Figure 17   A window wall composed of adjacent casement units.

ment and fixed windows. Figures 13–17 show some
arrangements of Andersen windows.

3. What is the difference between these window terms?
   a. Head, jamb, and sill
   b. Top rail, bottom rail, and meeting rail
   c. Storm sash and double glazing
   d. Drip cap and drip groove
   e. Mullion and muntin

STUDY QUESTIONS

1. List the types of windows and indicate how each is
   opened.
2. Define these window terms:
   a. Sash
   b. Window frame
   c. Rough opening
   d. Blind stop
   e. Apron
   f. Casing

LABORATORY PROBLEMS

1. Prepare a classroom illustration showing:
   a. Types of windows
   b. Window terminology
2. (For the advanced student) Design a type of window
   entirely different from those commonly used.
3. Complete the design of the windows for the building
   assigned by your instructor.
4. Complete the design of the windows for your original
   building design.

12 doors

Doors, like windows, are important components in the design of a successful building. The main entrance door is particularly important, since it will be the first detail experienced by visitors. The other doors should also be carefully chosen; a building can be no better than its details.

TYPES

Doors are available in a wide range of types and materials. Residential doors most commonly used are:

Hinged   Sliding   Folding   Accordion

These doors may be obtained in single and double units. Wood is usually used, but metal and glass doors are also popular.

Hinged. Hinged doors (Figure 1) may be flush, paneled, or louvered. The flush door (Figure 6) is most

Figure 1   Hinged doors.

Figure 2   Sliding doors.

Figure 3   Folding doors.

Figure 4   Accordion doors.

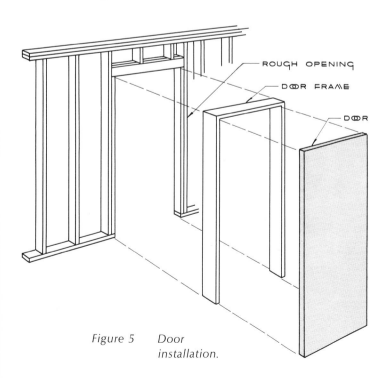

Figure 5   Door installation.

popular due to its perfectly clean lines and low cost. It may be either *solid core* or *hollow core*. The solid core flush door is constructed of solid wood covered with wood veneer and is preferred for exterior doors. The hollow core flush door has an interior of honey-combed wood strips also covered by veneer. The most popular veneers are mahogany and birch.

Paneled doors consist of ponderosa pine members framing wood or glass panels. The framing members are called *top rail, bottom rail,* and *side rails.* The mid-height rail is called a *lock rail.*

Louvered doors are constructed like paneled doors, but with louvers replacing the panels. They are often used as closet doors to permit circulation of air.

Hinged doors may be installed as a *double* unit (two doors, one hung on the right jamb, the other on the left) to allow a larger and more dramatic passageway. Hinged double doors with glass panels are called *French doors.* A *Dutch door,* on the other hand, is a single door which has been cut in halves so that the top half can be opened for light and air without opening the bottom half. Simulated Dutch doors which open like ordinary doors are specified to give the appearance of a Dutch door without the function. A door hung on special hinges which permit it to swing in both directions is called a *swinging door* and is often used between kitchen and dining area to permit operation by a simple push.

Sliding. Sliding doors (Figure 2) are used to save the floor space that is required for hinged doors. They are especially useful in small rooms. Sliding doors are hung from a metal track screwed into the door frame head. A single sliding door slides into a pocket built into the wall. Double sliding doors are usually installed so that one door slides in front of the other. This has the disadvantage of opening up only one half of the doorway space at a time. Exterior sliding doors of glass (Figure 7) serve the double purpose of a doorway and window wall.

Folding. A folding door (Figure 3) is partially a hinged and partially a sliding door. Two leaves are hinged together, one being also hinged to the door jamb. The other leaf has a single hanger sliding in a track. Although some floor space is required for the folding door, it has the advantage of completely opening up the doorway space. Single (total of two leaves) and double (total of four leaves) units are available.

Accordion. A door that operates on the principle of the folding door, but contains many narrow leaves, is called an "accordion door" (Figure 4). These leaves may be made of hinged wood or a flexible plastic material. Accordion or folding partitions are used to provide an entire movable wall between rooms. The folds of the retracted partition may be left exposed or hidden by a wall pocket (Figures 8 and 9).

MATERIALS

In addition to wood doors, metal-clad wood doors (called "kalamein" doors) or hollow metal doors are used for fireproofing and strength. Metal door frames (called door "bucks") are also available. Even all-glass doors are used. Bronze, aluminum, and glass doors are commonly used for public buildings, but wood remains the popular choice for residential construction. Figure 5 shows how a door frame fits into the rough opening in the same way a window is installed. The door, in turn, fits into the door frame.

TERMINOLOGY

Figure 10 shows a cut-away pictorial of a hinged exterior door, and the corresponding sectional details. Figure 11 shows the pictorial and details of a sliding interior door. Notice that a saddle is used to weatherproof the exterior door, but such protection is not necessary for the interior door.

SPECIFYING DOORS

The type of door to be specified for each. location will be determined by functional and aesthetic con-

Figure 7　A window wall of sliding glass doors.

Figure 8　Folding doors offer maximum flexibility and efficiency (Pella 558 series for $5\frac{5}{8}$" panels).

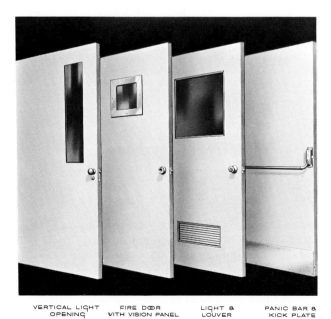

VERTICAL LIGHT OPENING　　FIRE DOOR WITH VISION PANEL　　LIGHT & LOUVER　　PANIC BAR & KICK PLATE

Figure 6　Typical light and louver openings in flush doors.

Figure 9　Heavier folding partitions can fill openings of any width (Pella 1058 series for $10\frac{5}{8}$" panels).

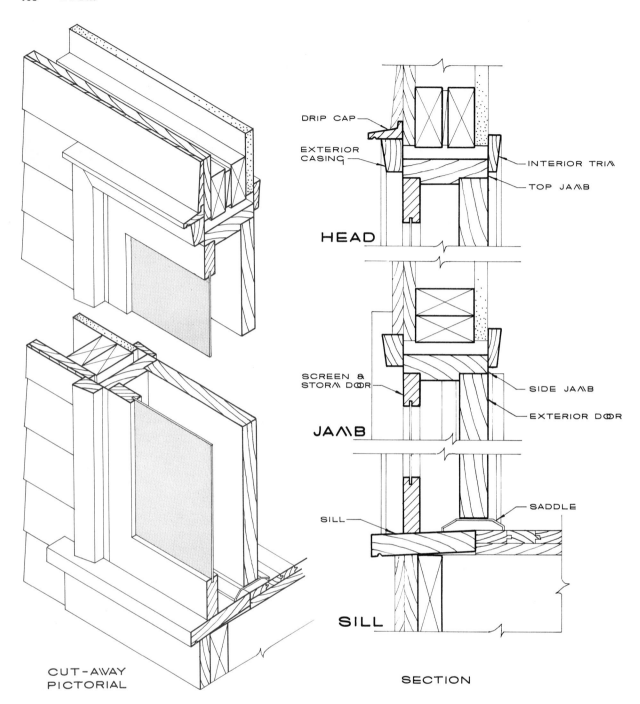

CUT-AWAY PICTORIAL

SECTION

- DRIP CAP
- EXTERIOR CASING
- INTERIOR TRIM
- TOP JAMB

HEAD

- SCREEN & STORM DOOR
- SIDE JAMB
- EXTERIOR DOOR

JAMB

- SILL
- SADDLE

SILL

Figure 10   An exterior door in a wood frame wall.

siderations. Manufacturers' catalogs should be consulted for available styles and sizes. In general, exterior doors are $1\frac{3}{4}''$ thick and interior doors are $1\frac{3}{8}''$ thick. Widths from 2'-0 to 3'-0 in even inches are available, although some manufacturers offer doors as narrow as 1'-6'' and as wide as 4'-0. Residential doors are obtainable in 6'-6'' to 7'-0 heights in even inches. 6'-8'' is the most popular height. See Appendix C.

Interior doors	$2'\text{-}6'' \times 6'\text{-}8'' \times 1\frac{3}{8}''$
Front entrance door	$3'\text{-}0 \ \times 6'\text{-}8'' \times 1\frac{3}{4}''$
Other entrance doors	$2'\text{-}8'' \times 6'\text{-}8'' \times 1\frac{3}{4}''$

The rough opening must be considerably larger than the door sizes. The frame for a 3'-0 × 6'-8'' door, for instance, would require a $3'\text{-}2\frac{3}{4}'' \times 6'\text{-}11''$ (top of subfloor to bottom of header) rough opening.

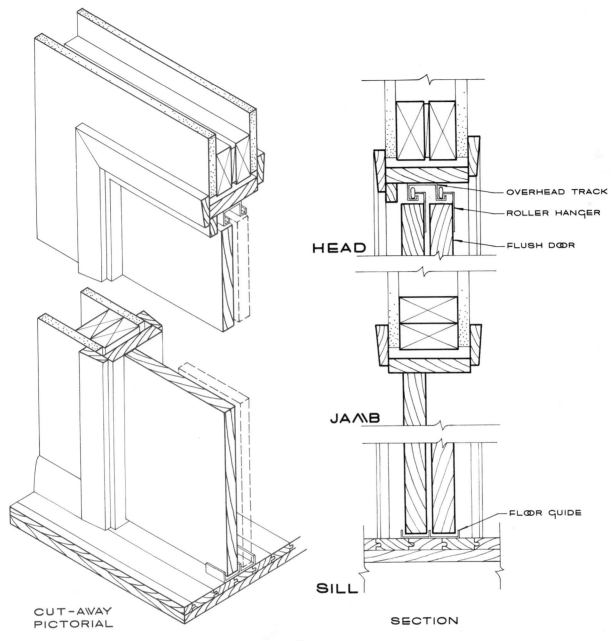

HEAD

—— OVERHEAD TRACK

—— ROLLER HANGER

—— FLUSH DOOR

JAMB

SILL

—— FLOOR GUIDE

CUT-AWAY
PICTORIAL

SECTION

Figure 11   A double sliding door in an interior wall.

ENTRANCES

The entrance provides the first close introduction to a building and therefore should be attractive and representative as well as functional (Figures 12 to 15). A completely designed entrance may be obtained from stock. One style is shown in Figure 16. Details and sizes are shown in Appendix B. Side lights are obtainable as separate units in a variety of sizes, colors, and patterns (Figure 17). A selection of contemporary and traditional entranceways is shown in Figure 18.

HARDWARE

The hardware for doors is specified by indicating the desired manufacturer and catalog number in a hardware schedule. Some of the many hardware items are:

Door butts (hinges)
Lock sets
Door stops
Door checks (for public buildings)
Cabinet hinges, handles, and catches

Figure 12   A simple double door entranceway.

Courtesy of Scholz Homes, Inc.

Figure 13   An ornamental double door entranceway.

Figure 14   An office building entranceway with
glass doors.

GARAGE DOORS

Most residential garage doors are of the overhead type (Figures 19 to 21). An overhead door is composed of several hinged sections that roll up to the ceiling on tracks. Adjustable springs are used to counterbalance the weight of the door. A range of 3″ to 13½″ of headroom (depending on the hardware type and door size) is required above the bottom of the header. Garage doors may be operated by means of remote-controlled motors.

Figure 15   Interior view of Figure 14.

Figure 16   Stock entrance.

Residential garage doors are usually stocked in 6'-6" and 7'-0 heights by 1⅜" thick. Common widths for single doors are 8'-0 and 9'-0; double doors are 16'-0 wide. See Appendix C for more detail.

In addition to wood, garage doors may be obtained in aluminum and fiberglass in the same range of sizes. Fiberglass doors are also available in 18'-0 widths.

CABINETS

A wide range of cabinets for the kitchen, laundry, and bathroom are available from stock. They include storage, china, corner, all-purpose, and ironing board cabinets.

CLEAR   GREEN DIAMOND PATTERN   AMBER RONDEL PATTERN

Figure 17   Sidelights.

Figure 18   Suggestions for contemporary and traditional entranceways.

Figure 19   Single width garage door.   *Figure 20   Single width garage doors used for a double garage.*

STUDY QUESTIONS

1. List the types of doors and indicate how each is opened.
2. Define these door terms:
   a. Door saddle
   b. Side light
   c. Kalamein door
   d. Sectional overhead door
   e. Tilt-up overhead door
3. What is the difference between these door terms:

a. Solid core and hollow core door
b. Flush, paneled, and louvered door
c. Top rail, bottom rail, side rail, and lock rail
d. French door and Dutch door
e. Door butt and door buck
f. Door stop and door check
4. Give the common sizes of the following doors:
   a. Interior door
   b. Front entrance door
   c. Rear entrance door

Courtesy of Scholz Homes, Inc.

Figure 21   Double width garage door.

RESIDENTIAL GARAGE DOOR
AVAILABLE FROM 8'-0" x 6'-6" TO 18' x 7'

Figure 22   Garage door sizes.

COMMERCIAL GARAGE DOOR
AVAILABLE TO 20' x 16'

LABORATORY PROBLEMS

1. Prepare a classroom illustration showing:
   a. Types of doors
   b. Door terminology
2. (For the advanced student) Design a type of door entirely different from those now commonly used.
3. Complete the design of the doors for the building assigned by your instructor.
4. Complete the design of the doors for your original house design.

INDUSTRIAL GARAGE DOOR
AVAILABLE TO 24' x 20'

13   schedules

A building is composed of a tremendous number of parts. In fact, if all of these parts were indicated on the plans, the plans would become so crowded that they would not be readable. Therefore the designer includes much of this information in *schedules* on the working drawings or in the written *specifications*

DOOR SCHEDULE

MK	NO.	SIZE	DESCRIPTION	REMARKS
1	1	3'-0 x 6'-8" x $1\frac{3}{4}$"	14 PANEL WP, 4 LTS	
2	1	2'-8"x6'-8" x $1\frac{3}{4}$"	FLUSH WP, 1 LT	
3	2	2'-8"x6'-8" x $1\frac{3}{4}$"	2 PANEL WP, 3 LTS	
4	10	2'-6" x 6'-8" x $1\frac{3}{8}$"	FLUSH BIRCH	
5				
6				

Figure 1

WINDOW SCHEDULE

MK	NO.	SIZE	DESCRIPTION	REMARKS
A	1	58064	ANDERSEN GLIDING	DOUBLE GLAZED
B	1	W5N5	" CASEMENT	" "
C	3	W4N4	" "	" "
D				
E				

Figure 2

(see Chapter 30 for a discussion of specifications writing).

DOOR AND WINDOW SCHEDULES

Figures 1 and 2 show minimum layouts for door and window schedules. Although this information may be included on the drawings in the form of notes, it is usually considered better practice to use schedules and keep the actual plans and elevations uncluttered. Of course, a reference mark or symbol must be placed upon each door in the plan and each window in the elevations. These marks are repeated in the door and window schedules, the schedules then giving all the necessary sizes and information. A numeral is used for doors and most other scheduled items, but a letter is used for windows. The usual place for the door schedule is near the plan, and the window schedule should be placed near the elevations. Use a different mark for different sizes or types of doors and windows, but use the same mark for similar doors and windows. Such marks should be enclosed in circles, which are drawn about $\frac{1}{4}$" in diameter.

ADDITIONAL SCHEDULES

In addition to doors and windows, other materials may be specified by the use of schedules. Figures

3-7 show the outlines of some other commonly used schedules. The plans for a large, well-detailed building might contain many other types of schedules in addition to those illustrated.

Some of the customs and rules of writing schedules follow.

1. Rather than take the time to letter the same words many times over, use the ditto mark (as in Figure 2) or the note "DO" (short for "ditto," as in Figures 6 and 7).

2. Abbreviations are often used to reduce the size of the schedule. Standard abbreviations should be used and listed in a table of abbreviations on the drawings. The abbreviations used on Figures 1–7 are: *

CL	closet
ELEV	elevation
FIN	finish
S	American Standard I beam
LAV	lavatory
LT	light (window glass)
MK	mark
NO.	number
REINF	reinforce
T & G	tongue and groove
WP	white pine
W/	with
L	angle
#	pounds or number

3. When spaces on the schedule do not apply to a material, they may be left blank (as in the Figure 1 remarks column) or filled with a strike line (as in the Figure 6 ceiling finish column).

4. The desired manufacturer of a product may be specified (as in Figure 2, Andersen windows) or merely given as an example of an acceptable product (as in Figure 7, Pass & Seymour electric fixtures).

STUDY QUESTIONS

1. Why are schedules used in preference to notes or dimensions?
2. List several building components which may be specified by means of schedules.
3. When using schedules, a _____ mark is used to indicate windows, and a _____ mark is used to indicate doors.
4. In a schedule, what is the meaning of "DO"?

LABORATORY PROBLEMS

1. Prepare the schedules of the building assigned by your instructor.
2. Prepare the schedules for your original house design.

*For a more extensive list of commonly used abbreviations, see Appendix E.

COLUMN AND BEAM SCHEDULE

MK	NO.	DESCRIPTION	LENGTH	REMARKS
1	4	3½" STEEL PIPE COLUMN W/PLATES	7'-0	
2	1	S 7 x 15.3 FLOOR GIRDER	42'-0	
3				
4				

Figure 3

LINTEL SCHEDULE

MK	NO.	DESCRIPTION	LENGTH	REMARKS
1	6	L 5 x 3½ x ⅜	4'-8"	
2				
3				

Figure 4

FOOTING SCHEDULE

MK	A	B	C	ELEV	REINF	REMARKS
1	8"	1'-4"	8"	93.4'	2 #4	
2	10"	1'-6"	8"	93.4'	2 #4	
3	8"	1'-4"	8"	97.4'	NONE	
4						

Figure 5

FINISH SCHEDULE

MK	ROOM	FLOOR	FIN	WALL	FIN	CEILING	FIN	TRIM	FIN
1	LIVING ROOM	T&G OAK	VARN-ISH	SHEET ROCK	PAINT	ACOUST TILE	—	PINE	PAINT
2	LAV	ASPHALT TILE	—	CERAMIC TILE	—	SAND PLASTER		DO	DO
2A	LAV CL	DO	—	SAND PLASTER	—	DO	—	DO	DO
3									
4									

Figure 6

ELECTRICAL SCHEDULE

LOCATION	SYMBOL	NO.	WATT	DESIGNATION	EXAMPLE
GARAGE	⊕ / O_A	2 / 2	100 / 100	DUPLEX OUTLET / CEILING MOUNT	PASS & SEYMOUR #41
LIVING ROOM	⊕ / O_B / O_C	6 / 12 / 1	100 / 60 / 100	DUPLEX OUTLET / WALL VALANCE / WALL MOUNT	DO / GENERAL #1606
KITCHEN	⊕ / O_D / O_E	4 / 1 / 1	100 / 100 / 100	DUPLEX OUTLET / FLUSH CEILING / DO	HOLOPHANE #RL-732 / DO #RL-796
BEDROOM					

Figure 7

PART THREE

plans

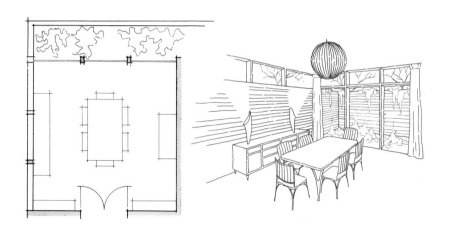

14   room design

There are two major considerations in the design of the floor plan of a house. First, each room must be designed so that it is pleasant, functional, and economical; and second, the rooms must be placed in the correct relationship to each other. This second consideration may be likened to working out a jigsaw puzzle in which the pieces may change in shape and size, giving various solutions. Some of these solutions will be better than others, but in the design of a house, the over-all plan can be no better than the design of the individual rooms.

To give some starting point, minimum and average room sizes are given in the accompanying table. Notice that the rooms are not long and narrow

Room	Minimum (inside size)	Average
Living room	12′ × 16′	14′ × 20′
Dining room	10′ × 12′	12′ × 13′
Dining area	7′ × 9′	9′ × 9′
Bedroom (master)	11½′ × 12½′	12′ × 14′
Bedroom (other)	9′ × 11′	10′ × 12′
Kitchen	7′ × 10′	8′ × 12′
Bathroom	5′ × 7′	5½′ × 8′
Utility (no basement)	7′ × 8′	8′ × 11′
Hall width	3′	3½′
Closet	2′ × 2′	2′ × 4′
Garage (single)	9½′ × 19′	12′ × 20′
Garage (double)	18′ × 19′	20′ × 20′
Garage door (single)	8′ × 6½′	9′ × 7′
Garage door (double)	15′ × 6½′	16′ × 7′

(which makes them too hall-like) nor square (which makes furniture placement difficult). Actually there is no such thing as an average, or standard, or even ideal, size or shape for a room. Design a size and shape that will best meet the requirements of function, esthetics, and economy.

The desired furniture arrangement will have a considerable effect on the design of each room. Professional designers find that furniture templates or underlays greatly simplify the design process. The furniture underlay (Figure 1) may be used when drawing floor plans to a $\frac{1}{4}$″ = 1′-0 scale. Simply slip it into position under your paper and trace off the desired elements.

KITCHEN DESIGN

When a builder puts up a low-priced house, there are a number of ways to cut corners and reduce cost. However, you have probably noticed that even the smallest house has a carefully designed and well-equipped kitchen. The reason is that builders realize the prospective woman buyer demands an efficient and cheerful kitchen. As a matter of fact, this is the first room a woman will want to see. The average housewife walks 200 miles a year in the performance of household tasks—half of this in the kitchen. Consequently, in designing any house for yourself or others, you cannot spend too much time in perfecting the kitchen design.

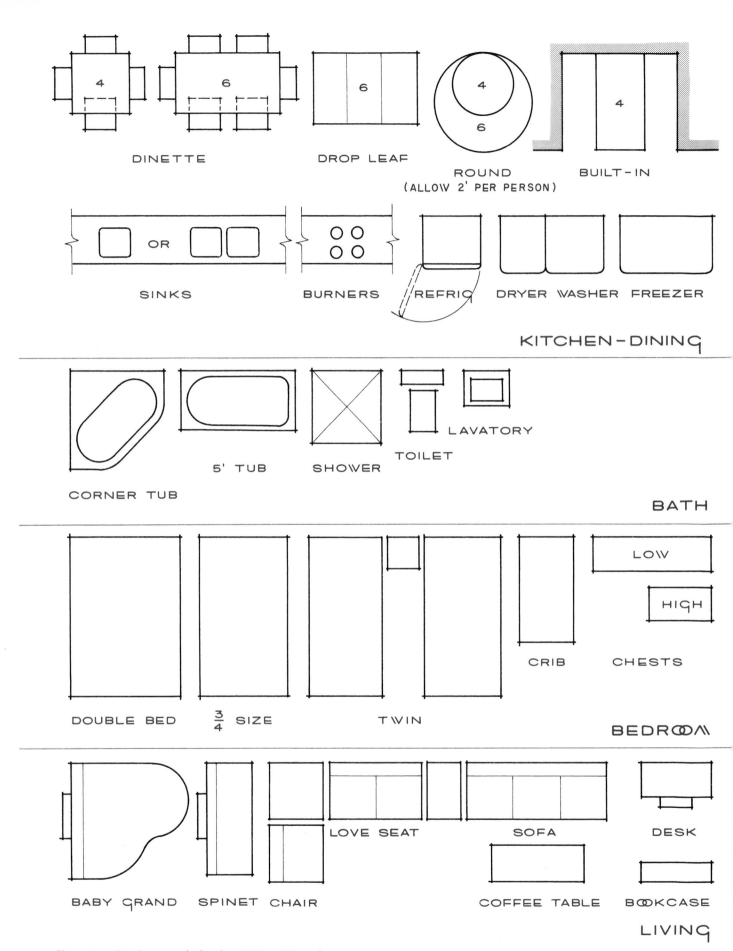

DINETTE DROP LEAF ROUND
(ALLOW 2' PER PERSON) BUILT-IN

SINKS BURNERS REFRIG DRYER WASHER FREEZER

KITCHEN-DINING

CORNER TUB 5' TUB SHOWER TOILET LAVATORY

BATH

DOUBLE BED $\frac{3}{4}$ SIZE TWIN CRIB CHESTS LOW HIGH

BEDROOM

BABY GRAND SPINET CHAIR LOVE SEAT SOFA DESK COFFEE TABLE BOOKCASE

LIVING

Figure 1   Furniture underlay for 1/4" = 1'-0 scale.

Figure 2   Over and under refrigerator-freezer.
Figure 3   Side-by-side refrigerator-freezer.

Figure 4   Electric console range.

A kitchen should be thought of as a group of three activity centers:

1. Storage
2. Preparation and cleaning
3. Cooking and serving

Storage. The focal point of the storage center is the refrigerator, although many cabinets for non-refrigerated food, dishes, and utensils must be provided. To save steps, the refrigerator may be located near the delivery door, or nearest the door to the living-dining area. Also consider a freezer or refrigerator-freezer (Figures 2 and 3), although a freezer is often removed from the kitchen itself to another area.

Preparation and cleaning. This center is built around the sink and its adjoining counter space. Do you want to include an automatic dishwasher or garbage

Kitchen Equipment

	Width	Depth	Height
Base cabinets		2'-0	3'-0
Wall cabinets		1'-0	2'-6''
Range, oven below	1'-8''	2'-1''	3'-0
Range, oven at side	3'-6''	2'-1''	3'-0
Range, built-in	2'-8''	1'-8''	
Oven	2'-0	2'-0	2'-4''
Sink	2'-0	2'-0	3'-0
Sink and drainboard	3'-6''	2'-0	3'-0
Refrigerator, 7 cu. ft.	2'-1''	2'-3''	4'-6''
Refrigerator, 14 cu. ft.	2'-8''	2'-3''	5'-4''
Washer	2'-0	2'-3''	3'-1''
Dryer	2'-6''	2'-3''	3'-1''

Figure 5   Electric surface range.

Figure 6   Gas surface range.

*Figure 7
Built-in self-cleaning electric oven.*

*Figure 8   Built-in electric self-
cleaning double oven.*

Figure 9   Electric barbecue.

disposal unit? Most women want their sink by a window.

Cooking and serving. The cooking center is grouped around the range (Figures 4 to 6). A built-in oven, being less used, may be located at a more isolated position than the range. Range-oven combinations are standardized at 36″ high, so counters should be designed at the same height. If a house is designed for especially tall or short persons, these major appliances may be built in at a convenient height. Consider an exhaust fan or hood and fan above the range burners.

A planning center consisting of a desk or table and a telephone is included in many modern kitchens. Allow space for cookbooks, recipe index, and so forth.

As a rule, the laundry (automatic clothes washer, dryer, and ironing board) is best placed in its own utility room. If it must be placed in the kitchen, it should have its own separate area.

These activity centers may be combined in a number of ways in various shaped rooms designed so that work progresses from right (storage) to left (serving). Often used combinations shown in Figure 14 are:

Figure 10   Kitchen-dining area separated by a folding door.

Figure 11   *An exposed kitchen in a dramatic design.*

1. Pullman or corridor or two-wall
2. U-shaped
3. L-shaped
4. Peninsula or island
5. One-wall

Pullman. This kitchen, consisting of a long corridor with utilities on either side, is often used where space is at a premium. Doors may be at either end or at one end only. Although this design is somewhat factory-like, it is efficient in saving space and steps.

U-shaped. The U-shaped kitchen places cabinets on three walls, the sink usually in the middle, and the refrigerator and stove on opposite sides. Space for dining may be allowed near the fourth wall. This plan is adaptable to both large and small rooms.

L-shaped. This is probably the most commonly used arrangement, since it is efficient, allows two doors without any interruption of counter top area, and may be nicely used with a breakfast table.

Peninsula. This kind of layout may be used only with large rooms. It is called "peninsula" when the counter or "breakfast bar" runs perpendicular to a wall,

Courtesy of Scholz Homes, Inc.

Figure 12   *A peninsula kitchen.*

Figure 13   An exciting kitchen design.

Courtesy of Scholz Homes, Inc.

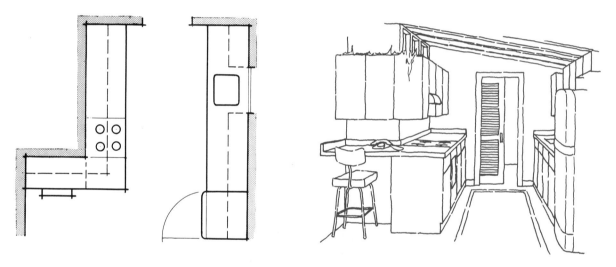

PULLMAN

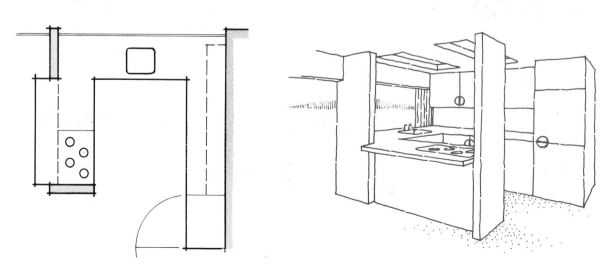

U - SHAPED

Figure 14   Kitchen design.

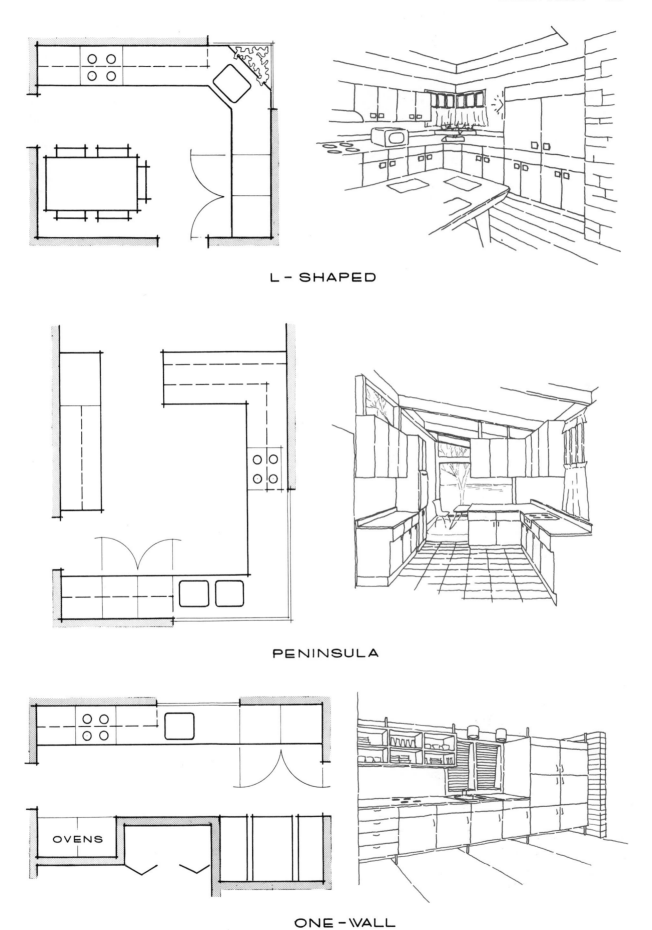

L - SHAPED

PENINSULA

OVENS

ONE - WALL

Figure 14   continued.

Figure 15   Living room of the A residence, looking toward the atrium.

Figure 16   A window wall is the major feature of this living area.

and "island" when it is freestanding.

One-wall. This layout is used when a kitchen must be fitted into a long narrow space. It is not an ideal arrangement.

Although it may seem from the previous discussion that the kitchen is greatly standardized, this is not the case. The kitchen should be original and pleasant. Avoid the monotony of the "factory" look. Consider built-in ranges, ovens, and refrigerators. Materials like brick and copper; color in appliances; and careful floor, window, and lighting design will all add to a kitchen's attractiveness. Working areas should be continuous; they may turn corners but should not be interrupted by doors. Remember that the cabinet space in an inside corner cannot be *fully* utilized.

The minimum area recommended by the Public Housing Authority for a kitchen and eating space is 105 sq. ft.

Figure 17   Pool integrates atrium with living area.

Figure 18   A sunken conversational area.

LIVING AREA DESIGN

Most people feel that since guests are entertained in the living room, it should be as large and gracious a room as can be afforded. The minimum area recommended by the Public Housing Authority is 160 sq. ft. The shape of the living area is often rectangular, the length $\frac{1}{3}$ longer than the width.

Two factors should be given careful consideration in the design of the living area: circulation and furniture grouping.

Circulation. Movement within a room and from one room to another is called "circulation." Most persons feel the "center hall" house arrangement is ideal, because circulation to all rooms is easily accomplished without using the living room as a hallway

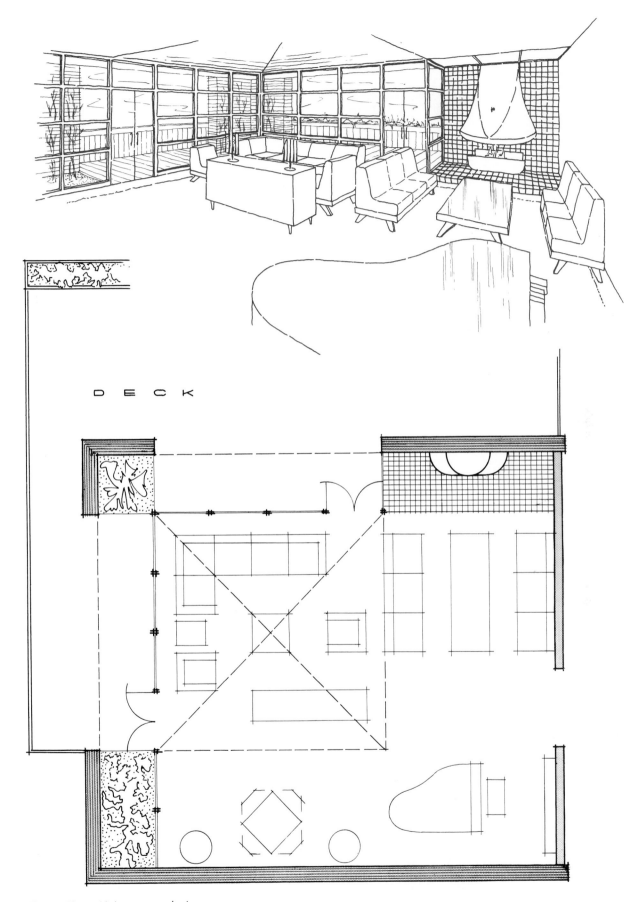

DECK

Figure 19   Living room design.

Figure 20   *Dining area of the A residence showing the breakfast bar and kitchen.*

Figure 21   *A combined dining-family room.*

Figure 22   *A kitchen area reserved for dining.*

or vestibule. When a room is not used as a throughway, it is called a "dead-end" room. There is much merit in dead-end rooms, but remember that they are not as interesting as a room that "goes somewhere." At any rate, a living room should never have to be used for trips between bedroom and bath.

Furniture grouping. The major furniture grouping should be arranged so that the circle of chairs falls within a twelve foot diameter. A living room which has a fireplace as the focal point of this major furniture grouping is at a disadvantage when the fireplace is not in use. Rather than place furniture facing a black hole, a picture window or television set might be better choices. Consider also any special living room areas for music, reading, study, or cards.

Figure 19 shows a living room designed for a contemporary executive mansion. The client required an area which could be used for large, formal receptions as well as small, intimate parties. The design requirements included provision for indoor and outdoor gatherings in the day or evening. Notice that this design met these various requirements by the use of areas which could be used individually or combined. The room itself, for example, is separated into four major furniture groupings: (1) the major formal conversational grouping, emphasized by the ceiling design; (2) a secondary conversational grouping in front of the fireplace; (3) a music area; (4) an area for card playing. For large gatherings, the outside deck could be added by opening the French doors at the two locations. To provide contrast with the long distance view through the window walls, plantings were specified immediately outside these windows. These plantings, backed by brick piers, could be illuminated in various ways depending upon the mood desired.

Undoubtedly, you will want to design a much smaller living room than this example. Please notice, though, that the plan by itself does not tell the entire story. An interior perspective of the room was needed to verify that the design requirements were met satisfactorily.

DINING AREA DESIGN

Following World War II, the dining room was usually dropped from new house plans in an attempt to reduce costs. Many families used this room seldom, eating most meals in the kitchen or breakfast nook. One of the outstanding results of a recent government survey was the discovery of the demand on the part of homemakers for the return of the separate dining room.

The size of a dining room depends entirely on the size of the table and amount of accessory furniture. A good compromise between the dining room and breakfast nook is the living-dining area or

Figure 23   Dining room design.

kitchen-dining area. The living-dining combination is economical and tends to increase the apparent size of the living room. Kitchen eating space may also be provided if desired.

The dining room shown in Figure 23 was planned for a small city lot which allowed no pleasant views. The windows were arranged high on the walls to block the view without preventing natural lighting. On the rear wall, the window was combined with an enclosed courtyard designed to be landscaped. The double entry doors, centered on the wall opposite the courtyard, provide a dramatic entrance.

BEDROOM DESIGN

The minimum area recommended by the Public Housing Authority is 110 sq. ft. for a single bedroom, and 125 sq. ft. for a master bedroom. As a general rule of thumb, bedrooms are often designed with a length two feet longer than the width. The rooms should be large enough so that the beds can be "free-standing" (that is, with only the head of the bed touching the wall), to make them easier to make. In a small bedroom, combine areas used for dressing, circulation, and closet access into one larger area

Figure 24   The master bedroom of the A residence.

Figure 25   An open bedroom.

Figure 26   Dining area under balcony, bedrooms overhead.

rather than three small ones.

Small high windows allow greater freedom of furniture arrangement and provide privacy. However, windows should not be so small and high that escape in case of fire is impossible.

The master bedroom shown in Figure 27 has been planned to include an element of symmetry in an oriental motif. The designer has located all the major items of furniture so that there will be enough room for each. This is particularly important when unusually large or irregularly shaped furniture is to be used.

Closets

	Width	Depth	Height
Clothes closet	4'-0	2'-0	
Walk-in clothes closet	6'-0	4'-0	
Linen closet	2'-0	1'-6"	1'-0 between shelves
Suits, trousers, jackets, shirts, skirts		2'-0	3'-9"
Dresses, overcoats		2'-0	5'-3"
Evening gowns		2'-0	6'-0
Children, 6 to 12 years		1'-8"	3'-9"
Children, 3 to 5 years		1'-4"	2'-6"

Closets that are carefully designed to provide room efficiently for all sorts of clothing are becoming popular. These "storage walls" may have drawers, replacing bureaus and chests. The table gives sizes which might be of help in closet design.

BATHROOM DESIGN

A bathroom may be designed to be as small and compact or as large and compartmented as you wish. The trend is toward a compartmented room— keeping the toilet and tub or shower in separate, enclosed areas.

For economy in plumbing, keep the bathrooms near the kitchen. If possible, avoid specifying a window behind a bathroom fixture. A window behind a tub or toilet is awkward, and one behind a lavatory interferes with the mirror.

The economy bathroom shown in Figure 28 has been provided with a wall hung toilet and lavatory. These will give the effect, visually, of enlarging the room. In addition, the floor will be easier to clean.

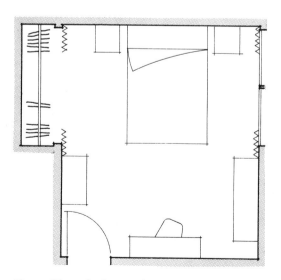

Figure 27   Bedroom design.

Bathroom Equipment

	Width	Depth	Height
Lavatory (washstand)	1'-10"	1'-7"	2'-9"
Built-in lavatory	2'-0 min.	1'-10"	2'-9"
Bathtub	5', 5'-6", 6'	2'-6"	1'-4"
Shower	3'-0	3'-0	7'-0
Toilet	1'-8"	2'-4"	2'-4"
Medicine cabinet	1'-2"	4"	1'-6"

Minimum clearance between	
Front of toilet and wall	1'-6"
Side of toilet and wall	6"
Front of lavatory and wall	2'-0
Front of lavatory and lower fixture	1'-6"
Edge of tub and wall	2'-0
Edge of tub and other fixture	1'-6"

The compartmented bathroom shown in Figure 28 has been provided with two lavatories (for a larger family), a built-in tiled vanity, a corner bathtub, and a stall toilet with swinging doors for privacy.

LAUNDRY DESIGN

The housewife of today spends less time in the laundry than she did years ago. However, she still spends more time on laundry chores than any other work with the exception of food preparation. The laundry, then, should be carefully planned. There is a sequence of laundry work just as there is a sequence

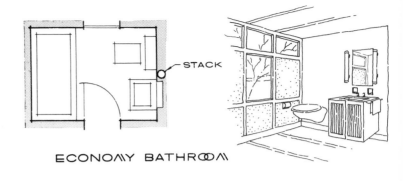

ECONOMY BATHROOM

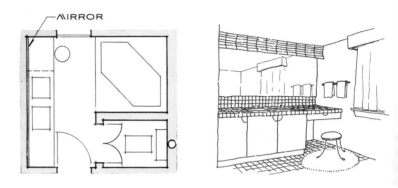

COMPARTMENTED BATHROOM

Figure 28   Bathroom design.

Courtesy of Scholz Homes, Inc.

Figure 29   A dressing room with private solarium.

Courtesy of Scholz Homes, Inc.

Figure 30   A lavish bathroom design.

of kitchen work. Proper planning should provide for each of the following steps.

1. Collection of laundry (hampers, laundry chute)
2. Treating spots (a sink for pretreating spots and stains)
3. Washing and drying (the core of the laundry)
4. Finishing (a table or counter for folding and ironing; may be away from the area where the washing is done)

A storage area for soap and supplies must be specified also.

There are a number of possible locations for a laundry (Figure 31).

Bathroom. The most efficient location for a laundry is near the bedrooms and bath where most soiled clothes originate. Additional advantages of a bathroom location are economy of plumbing and suitable interior finish. A disadvantage to be considered is the sacrifice of privacy. A combination bathroom and laundry should be a good-sized room which is well vented to remove excess moisture. Figure 31 shows a possible arrangement. The hamper is filled from the hall and emptied from the laundry. The shower doubles for drip-dry fabrics.

Kitchen. This is the most obvious laundry location, since it simplifies plumbing connections. However, a well-planned kitchen-laundry combination provides for separate areas or rooms so that clothes and cooking are not competing for the same space. Notice that the residence for Mrs. M has a small utility room containing the laundry adjacent to the kitchen.

Family room. The family room is an ideal laundry location for the large family; the wife can watch the children while doing the laundry chores. Although some might object to the appearance of laundry equipment here, this can be overcome by the use of folding, sliding, or accordion partitions.

Entry. A rear hall or area may be the perfect solution in some cases, especially if a rear mud room is specified which already requires plumbing connections.

Basement. Basement locations are often desired, since the "free" basement area is used instead of prime first-floor area. Also, a washer which accidentally overflows will cause less damage in the basement. The major disadvantage of the basement location is the additional stair-climbing required.

STORAGE DESIGN

Any wife will tell you that no house can have too much storage room. As a minimum, a well-designed house will have one closet per bedroom, two closets

Closet Sizes

Each bedroom closet	2' × 4'
Master bedroom closets	two 2' × 4'
Linen closet	1'-6" to 2' × 2'
Utility closet	2' × 4'
Guest closet	2' × 2'
Family coat closet	2' × 4'
Exterior storage	2' × 10'

in the master bedroom, a linen closet, a utility closet, coat closets, and provision for exterior storage. The most economical way to build storage space into a residence is by use of "closet walls": a double wall containing closets serving rooms on opposite sides. Closets should be designed 2' deep and wide enough to serve their function.

A small house should have approximately the sizes of closets shown in the accompanying table.

In addition, it is advisable to plan for storage walls for special activities: a bridge table, photographic equipment, hobbies, toys, musical instruments, records, shop tools, and seldom-used equipment.

PORCH DESIGN

If a porch is desired, it is usually located at the rear of the house for maximum privacy. Also, it should be conveniently near the kitchen if outdoor meals are to be served. Consider screening the porch for comfort in the summer and glazing it for winter use.

GARAGE DESIGN

A garage is usually attached to the house in some manner to provide a sheltered entry. This may be done by an attached first-floor garage, a breezeway, or a garage built into the basement. A basement garage will fit well in a split level house; it is economical and offers heat as well as shelter. An attached garage or breezeway fits well in a small house design, since it lengthens the house exterior. The breezeway may double as an open or closed porch. When completely enclosed, this space may be more efficiently used for living.

Consider a carport if you do not wish an enclosed garage. The carport is economical, but it does not offer the same protection from snow and rain. The deciding factor between garage and carport is usually climate. Whatever method is used to house the automobile, remember to include a sizeable storage wall for automotive equipment, gardening tools, and toys.

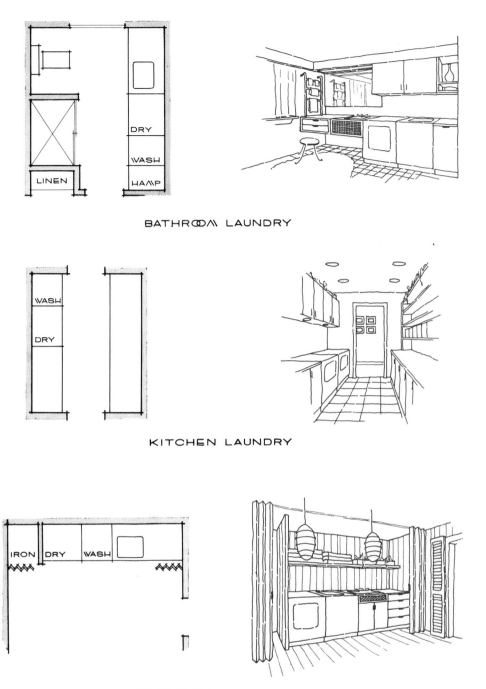

Figure 31   Laundry design.

FUTURE TRENDS

In this chapter, we have concentrated upon the design of the types of rooms found in the average house today. To get a picture of the house interior of the future, we need only look at the more advanced designs of contemporary architects. Using these contemporary designs as a guide, it is possible to predict the features likely to be found in future houses.

1. Rooms will be of all shapes—from circular or free-form to completely plastic surfaces, blending floor, wall, and ceiling into one uninterrupted flowing surface.

2. The trend will be away from the individual room concept toward multipurpose rooms and flexible areas which may be quickly rearranged by folding doors or retractable walls.

3. Multilevel floors and varying ceiling heights will become more common.

4. Furniture will often be an integral part of the architecture. (One example is the sunken living area surrounded by a carpeted lounge).

5. The outdoors will be brought indoors through the greater use of glass walls and interior planting.

6. New materials will make an appearance. Wood, stone, brick, and plaster will be gradually replaced by materials manufactured by yet-to-be-discovered methods.

7. Assembly line housing will become popular: packaged rooms which can be assembled in various combinations, and completely packaged houses. Conversely, there will also be a greater demand for custom-designed homes.

8. Revolutionary appliances will appear. Many will be built in—dust repellent surfaces, completely concealed heating, cooling, and lighting elements, communication systems, and improved systems of food storage and preparation. Cleaning facilities as we know them may become unnecessary because of the use of disposable utensils and clothing.

Figure 32   This concourse between two old buildings uses the "air rights" for maximum land use, San Francisco.

9. New systems of building will be developed so that less desirable land (and water) can be used. Refer to Figure 32 for one example.

STUDY QUESTIONS

1. Name the three activity centers included in a kitchen. What appliances are associated with each?
2. Name five kinds of kitchen layouts. Include the advantages and disadvantages of each.
3. What is meant by "room circulation"?
4. Give the advantages and disadvantages of a dining-living combination as opposed to a separate dining room and living room.
5. How many bathrooms should be specified for the following houses? List the fixtures required in each.
   a. Economy, one-bedroom summer house
   b. Moderate-priced, three-bedroom ranch house
   c. Higher priced, four-bedroom, two story Colonial house
6. Name the four activity centers included in a laundry. What appliances are associated with each?
7. (For the advanced student) After a thorough library search, prepare an illustrated paper on the history of the development of house interiors to date. Include changes in the number of rooms, room sizes, and the number and types of windows and doors.
8. (For the advanced student) After a thorough search of contemporary architectural periodicals, give your prediction of the type of house interior:
   a. Twenty-five years hence
   b. One hundred years hence

LABORATORY PROBLEMS

1. Sketch to scale or draw (as assigned) individual room layouts for the following rooms. Show the placement of major furniture.
   a. 15' × 22' living room with fireplace
   b. 12' × 14' dining room with alcove for a serving table
   c. 14' × 18' family room with fireplace and pass-through counter from kitchen
   d. 10' × 12' U-shaped kitchen
   e. 12' × 14' master bedroom with "his" and "hers" closets
2. In preparation for the layout of the rooms for your original house design, list the rooms familiar to you (your own home, neighbors' homes, and relatives' homes), their exact sizes (do not guess but actually measure or pace off), and your impression of their size (too small, satisfactory, or too large).
3. Using the information obtained from Problem 2, prepare a list of the rooms of your original house design showing the sizes you wish.
4. Using the sizes drawn up for Problem 3, sketch to scale or draw (as assigned) individual room layouts for your original house design.

15 preliminary layout

The preparation of a satisfactory preliminary layout is undoubtedly the most difficult but yet most satisfying phase of architectural design. As mentioned in Chapter 14, the placing of all the rooms in the correct relationship to each other may be likened to completing an unusual jigsaw puzzle composed of flexible pieces which must fit together in a workable pattern. This puzzle is further complicated by some considerations in addition to those of the individual room designs and their relationships:

1. The program requirements
2. Orientation
3. Circulation
4. Efficiency
5. Elevations

Each of these will be considered in turn.

THE PROGRAM

The designer must meet *all* the requirements set up in the program. The program, you recall, reflects the decisions previously made on the primary considerations of type of plot, styling, number of rooms and floors, shape of plan, inclusion of basement or attic, expansion, zoning, and cost.

ORIENTATION

The term "orientation" refers to the compass location of the various rooms of the house to make best use of views, breezes, sun, and topography.

View orientation. Major rooms such as the living room and master bedroom should be oriented to obtain the best possible view of the interesting features of the surrounding countryside. Minor rooms such as the utility room, laundry, and garage can face the less desirable views. In fact some city dwellings have been built with no windows at all in the outside walls; all windows open upon landscaped interior courts.

Wind orientation. Major living areas should be located to obtain prevailing summer breezes, while the minor areas may serve to block off the winter winds.

Solar orientation. Major living areas should face south for winter solar heat and the minor areas should face north. The breakfast room should face east to get the morning sun. Children's bedrooms should *not* face west if the occupants are expected to go to bed early.

Topographical orientation. This refers to orientation designed to take full advantage of the land contour. For example, a house on a sharply sloping plot might be designed so that lower level rooms would open directly to the low portion of the plot, and the upper level rooms would open to the high portion of the plot. In general it is well to keep excavation to a minimum for the less the natural contour of the site is disturbed, the less Nature will try to disturb the occupants of that site.

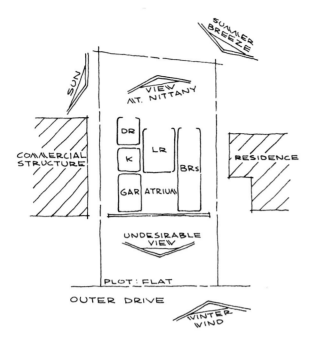

Figure 1   Orientation sketch for the A residence.

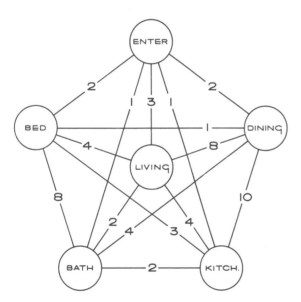

Figure 2   House circulation guide. The numbers indicate the average number of daily trips between rooms.

Designing for orientation. The best method to design for optimum orientation is to sketch the plot showing the direction of the best views, wind, sun, and slope of land. Figure 1 shows an orientation sketch for the plot of the A residence. A study of this sketch together with the program requirements will indicate the best location of many of the rooms.

CIRCULATION

The designer must carefully consider the patterns of traffic among rooms to ensure convenient and, at the same time, efficient circulation. Circulation areas are halls, stairs, and the lanes of travel through rooms. Successful circulation means that there are convenient pathways between the rooms or areas which have most connecting traffic. Usually this is accomplished by planning these rooms adjacent to each other with a common doorway. When halls are used, they should be kept as short as possible; when rooms are used for circulation, they should be planned so that the most direct route is across a corner or along one side of the room. With this arrangement, traffic will be less likely to disturb those using the room.

Probably the best way to ensure satisfactory circulation is to group all the individual rooms into three main zones:

1. Living (living room, front entrance foyer, powder room)
2. Sleeping (bedrooms and bathrooms)
3. Dining (dining areas, kitchen, service door)

Rooms of the same zone must be planned to have excellent circulation. For example: 1. the living room should be adjacent to the entrance foyer; 2. it should be easy to reach a bathroom from any bedroom; 3. the kitchen and dining room should not be separated by a hall.

In addition, the most often used rooms of different zones should be planned to have good circulation. The dining areas should be easily reached from the living area, for instance. Figure 2 shows the relative circulation between the areas of an average home. The numbers in the lines connecting the rooms are the number of trips made each day between those rooms by the average occupant. Compare circulation between *entrance* and *living* (three trips) and *entrance* and *kitchen* (one trip). This shows that it is more important to have the living room near the front entrance.

EFFICIENCY

Halls serve a very definite purpose, but should be kept at a minimum. They should not occupy more than 10 percent of the total area. The "efficiency" or "tare" of a house shows the percentage of area actually occupied by rooms. As you know, the first floor area may be taken up by stairs, heating unit, halls, walls, closets, and vestibules. Although these are all necessary items, they must be kept to a minimum in the efficient—or low cost—house. Seventy-five percent is considered excellent efficiency. Under 70 percent is considered poor efficiency.

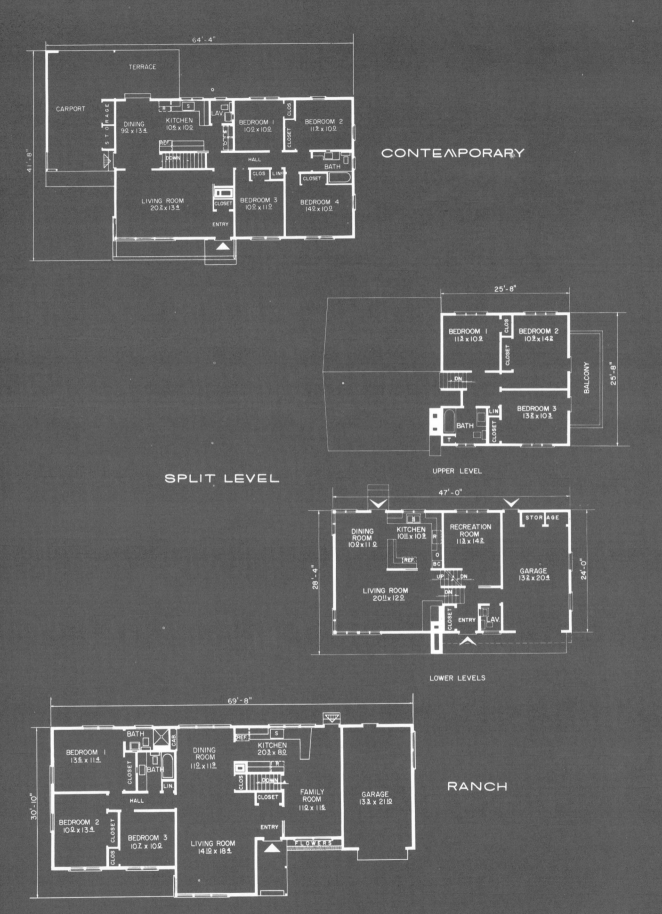

CONTEMPORARY

SPLIT LEVEL

UPPER LEVEL

LOWER LEVELS

RANCH

Figure 3   Source books provide many prototypes.

ELEVATIONS

The plans of the house should not be developed too far before elevations and framing are considered. Actually, the good architect will not completely finish one drawing at a time, but will jump from one to another until all the major plans are finished simultaneously.

PLANNING PROCEDURE

Designers do not all have the same approach to obtaining a satisfactory preliminary layout. There are, however, four methods which are widely used:

1. Prototype
2. Templates
3. Interior planning
4. Over-all planning

Let us look at each of these methods from the simple to the sophisticated. Then you can decide on the method you will want to use.

Prototype. The method of planning recommended for inexperienced persons is that of the prototype. A prototype is an example that you wish to copy fully or partially. The prototype may be an actual house you have seen and admired or a set of plans which

appears to meet your requirements. Plans may be found in a variety of sources: popular home magazines, books on residential design, and newspapers. These sources publish houses that have been designed by architects, and they are able to furnish a complete set of drawings and specifications at comparatively low cost. Figure 3 shows three typical layouts from booklets published by Weyerhaeuser. Some other sources are listed at the end of this chapter. Building material suppliers also have sets of "stock" plans that may be borrowed or purchased.

Probably you will not be fortunate enough to find a good plan which meets all the requirements of your program, but you may find a plan which will be satisfactory after some modifications and alterations are made. If major alterations are necessary (such as moving the location of a stairway), you will find that you will need to redesign the entire plan.

Excellent results have been obtained using the prototype method, but remember that this is not original designing; it is merely copying someone else's design!

Templates. A second method of planning is by use of templates: first a set of furniture templates to obtain the individual room design, and then a set of individual room templates to obtain the preliminary layout.

A furniture template should be made for each existing or proposed piece of furniture. The templates may be cut from graph paper or cardboard using a reasonable scale. The furniture underlay in the previous chapter was drawn to a scale of $\frac{1}{4}'' = 1'$, which has proved to be a satisfactory working scale. Obviously much measuring will be saved if $\frac{1}{4}'$ grid paper is used.

The furniture templates can be moved to various positions until a satisfactory grouping is obtained. Then draw the outline of the furniture templates together with lines showing the size and shape of the entire room. Remember to allow for circulation areas, doors, windows, and closets.

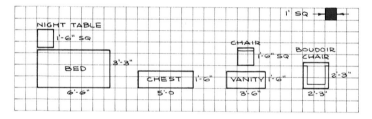

Figure 4 Furniture templates.

To design one of the bedrooms for the A residence, templates (Figure 4) are made for the principal pieces of furniture: the bed, night table, chest, vanity and its chair, and boudoir chair. These templates are shown in Figure 5 arranged in two groupings. When you study Figure 5, you will notice an inherent disadvantage in the template method of design: the furniture will have to be rearranged if the doors and windows must be placed at another location. And any change in furniture arrangement usually means a change in room dimensions also.

After the dimensions of each room are determined by use of furniture templates, room templates may be made and used in a similar manner to deter-

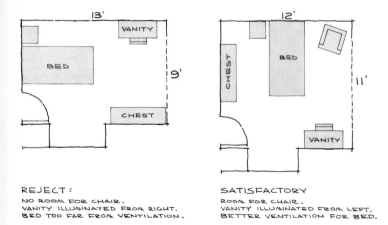

REJECT:
NO ROOM FOR CHAIR.
VANITY ILLUMINATED FROM RIGHT.
BED TOO FAR FROM VENTILATION.

SATISFACTORY
ROOM FOR CHAIR.
VANITY ILLUMINATED FROM LEFT.
BETTER VENTILATION FOR BED.

Figure 5 Room layout using method of templates.

mine alternate floor plan layouts. However, you must remember to leave spaces between the room templates—small 6″ spaces for the wall thickness and large 3′ or 4′ spaces for closets, stairs, and halls.

EXAMPLE

To design the first floor layout for the A residence templates are made for the living area, dining area, kitchen, garage, and bedrooms as shown in Figure 6. Since the sizes of the atrium and lavatories are not considered to be critical, no templates are made for them. These areas are kept in mind, however, just as are halls, closets, walls, and a stairway. The first trial proved unsatisfactory for the reasons noted in Figure 7. A later scheme shows improvement, but the last scheme shown in Figure 7 meets all established requirements. It is important that a record be made of all acceptable schemes so that they may be compared to arrive at the very best solution.

Interior planning. A widely used system of architectural planning is called interior planning. Neither prototype drawings nor templates are used, but rather a series of sketches is made to develop the house plan. The architect first shows only basic concepts by use of "thumbnail" sketches, and then works up through a series of larger and more detailed sketches until a satisfactory finished sketch is obtained. The order of procedure is shown by an example from the A residence.

Thumbnail sketches. Figure 8 shows several thumbnail sketches made to show the general location of various areas. These are purposely drawn very small or "thumbnail" so that there is no possibility of getting bogged down with detail at this early stage. Thus the designer is forced to consider only the essential elements.

Preliminary sketches. Using the thumbnail sketch as a guide, a preliminary sketch as shown in Figure 9 is prepared. This will normally be done to $\frac{1}{8}'' = 1'$ scale on graph paper, since many beautiful ideas are seen to be obviously impossible when sketched to scale. Main attention is directed to room layout, circulation, and orientation with no attention yet given to details such as door swings and exact window locations. The dwelling front will face the bottom of the sheet regardless of compass direction. Compass direction is indicated, however. Notice that the walls have been "pochéd" or darkened so that the plan will be easier to read. This is standard practice in preliminary and finished sketching.

Finished sketches. The finished sketch may be a carefully drawn freehand sketch or a drawing done with drafting instruments. The scale is usually $\frac{1}{4}'' = 1'$ for a small residence or $\frac{1}{8}'' = 1'$ for larger buildings. Rough outside dimensions and approximate inside room dimensions are indicated.

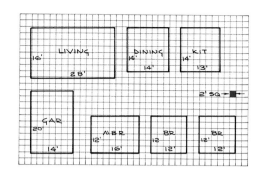

Figure 6   Room templates.

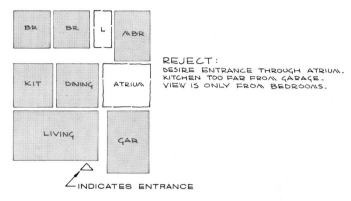

REJECT:
DESIRE ENTRANCE THROUGH ATRIUM.
KITCHEN TOO FAR FROM GARAGE.
VIEW IS ONLY FROM BEDROOMS.

INDICATES ENTRANCE

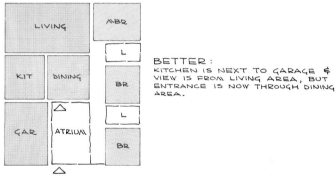

BETTER:
KITCHEN IS NEXT TO GARAGE &
VIEW IS FROM LIVING AREA, BUT
ENTRANCE IS NOW THROUGH DINING
AREA.

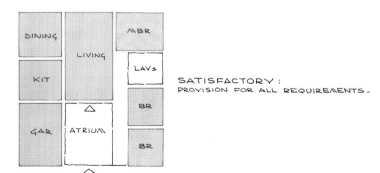

SATISFACTORY:
PROVISION FOR ALL REQUIREMENTS.

Figure 7   House layout using method of templates.

Figure 10 shows a finished sketch of the A residence made using the preliminary sketch as a model. Notice that all the requirements of the program have now been met and that considerably more

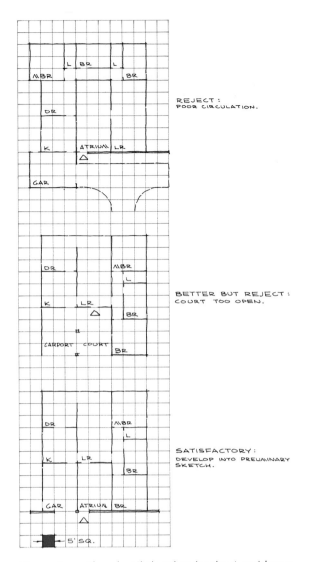

Figure 8   Thumbnail sketches for the A residence.

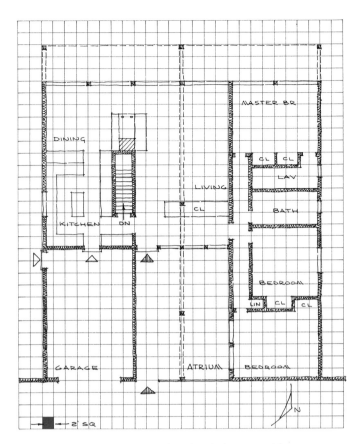

Figure 9   Preliminary sketch of the A residence.

nate front elevations of the A residence which were sketched when the plan was developed. Notice that the side elevations were not sketched, allowing the windows and doors to fall at random. The front elevation, then, represents over-all planning; the side elevations represent interior planning only.

PLAN ANALYSIS

The ability to critically analyze a plan—whether designed by you or by someone else—is a talent you must develop. The entire design process is really a series of these analyses, but the most comprehensive analysis should be made of the finished sketch, since it will serve as the basis for the working drawings.

Procedure. Each planning item that has been discussed should be studied for possible flaws or omissions:

1. *Program.* Each program requirement must be satisfied. Do not trust to memory; go through the program item by item.

2. *Orientation.* Check each room for the orientation of views, wind, and sun desired. Has best use been made of topography?

3. *Circulation.* Do not trust a visual check. Rather, take a pencil and actually trace the path of

detail has been added. Some additional minor changes will be made and details added when the finished sketch is eventually redrawn as the final plan.

Over-all planning. Experienced designers and architects use the concept of over-all planning, since it is likely to produce the best results. The actual procedure for over-all planning is identical to the procedure for interior planning except that other elements in addition to the floor plan are considered. Thus, preliminary elevations are sketched along with preliminary floor plan, plot plan, and details.

The choice of house styling may affect the type of planning. A ranch house or modern house might be planned from the inside out (interior planning), but a symmetrical, traditional structure would be planned somewhat from outside in (over-all planning). For example, Figure 11 shows two alter-

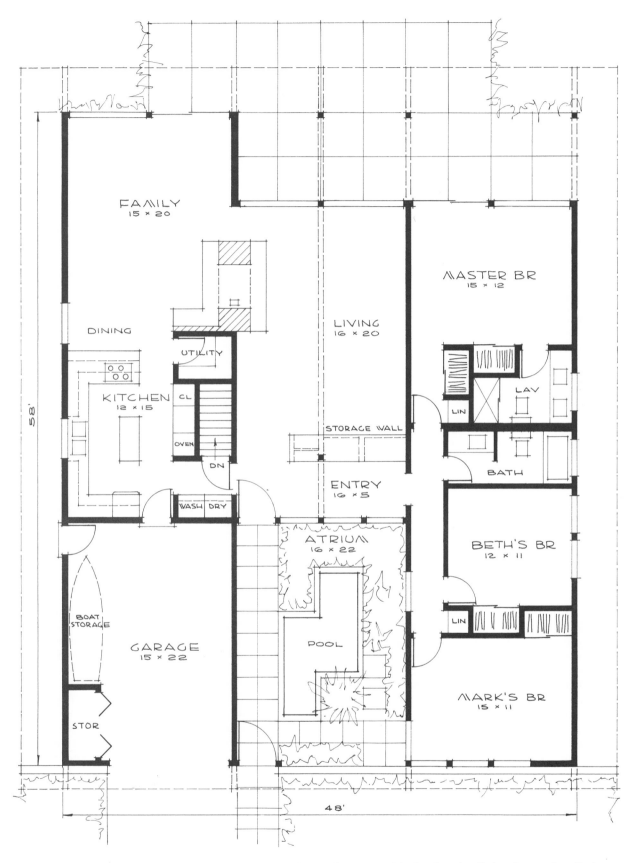

Figure 10   *Finished floor plan sketch of the A residence. Compare with the thumbnail sketches and preliminary sketches, and with the finished drawings.*

VERTICAL EMPHASIS
CENTRAL WINDOW-WALL
STACK-BONDED BLOCK
OVERHEAD GARAGE DOOR
INTERIOR BEAMS ONLY

HORIZONTAL EMPHASIS
DISTRIBUTED TRANSOM WINDOWS
HORIZONTAL JOINTS RAKED
SECTIONAL GARAGE DOOR
EXPOSE BEAM ENDS

Figure 11   Preliminary front elevation sketches of the A residence.

common circulation patterns. They should be simple and uncomplicated.

EXAMPLE

A typical early morning pattern would be:

bedroom → bathroom → bedroom → kitchen → dining area → kitchen → coat closet → garage.

4. *Efficiency.* Calculate hall area percentage (should be less than 10 percent) and house efficiency (should be greater than 70 percent).

EXAMPLE

Check hall area percentage and house efficiency of the A residence (see Figure 10).

Approximate total area: 2200 sq. ft.
Approximate hall area: 150 sq. ft.
Approximate room area: 1600 sq. ft.

Hall area percentage $= \dfrac{150}{2200} \times 100 = 7\%$ *OK*

House efficiency (tare) $= \dfrac{1600}{2200} \times 100 = 73\%$ *OK*

5. *Elevations.* Carefully consider how the floor plan will coordinate with the exterior elevations. Also consider details and construction. The framing method may affect the maximum room size.

6. *Utilities.* Has space been allowed for utilities such as plumbing walls, heating, and chimney? Are the kitchen and bathroom plumbing adjacent for economy? Are bearing partitions on different floors directly over one another?

7. *Individual room design.* Study each room separately to see if it meets its requirements of function, aesthetics, and economy. Compare the proposed room sizes with your list of familiar rooms and their sizes. Are the rooms too commonplace and ordinary? Or have you planned extreme features which will be costly and eventually embarrassing? Figure 12 shows some common planning errors.

Computer-aided design. As in most fields, the computer (Figure 13) is rapidly becoming a useful tool in architectural design. For example, the architectural firm of William W. Bond, Jr. and Associates uses an IBM 1130 computer to design *Holiday Inn* motels. Their system is named CARDS (Computerized ARchitectural Drafting System) and consists of approximately 250 programs stored on magnetic discs. Each program contains instructions which can cause a numerically-controlled drafting machine to draw one item or component such as a wall, window, door frame, stairway, or bathtub. The programs are in variable format, that is, are not dimensioned so that the designer can specify the desired size. Items which do not change in size, such as a double bed, are already dimensioned.

The sequence of the entire design system is as follows. The designer prepares dimensioned free-hand sketches of the building desired. The computer programmer uses these sketches to assemble the appropriate programs and to write instructions to connect them in their desired locations. When all steps are completed, the drafting machine can produce an inked plan at a speed of 200 inches per minute to an accuracy of .002". A standard technical fountain pen is used but with a tungsten carbide tip.

Computer programs are also presently in use for help in architectural engineering, specification writing, cost estimating, and accounting. Structural engineers can obtain aid from programs such as STRUDL (STRUctural Design Language) for structural analysis, SEPOL (SEttlement Problem Oriented Language) for soil settlement computations, ROADS (ROadway Analysis and Design System) for the location and alignment of roads, TRANSET (TRANSportation Evaluation Techniques) for the analysis of entire transportation networks, and BRIDGE for bridge design. Mechanical engineers can obtain aid in heat loss and gain computations and elevator layouts. The electrical engineer uses computer programs to calculate room illumination requirements. Specification writers and cost estimators now have master specification libraries and cost data to speed their tasks, and computers are used in many companies to provide prompt and accurate recording of the day-to-day business transactions and as an aid in management decisions.

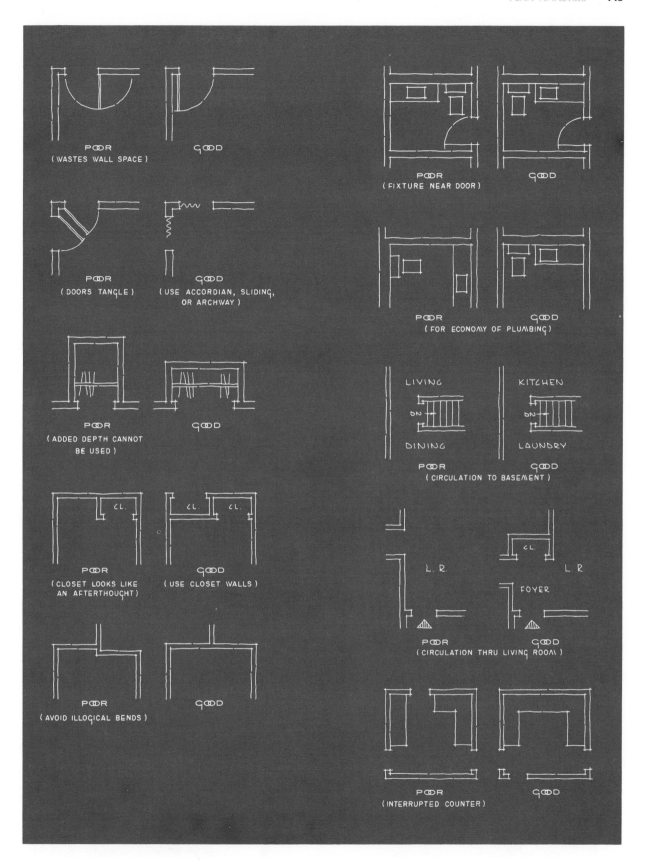

Figure 12   Correction of common planning errors.

The firm of Skidmore, Owings and Merrill has developed BOP (Building Optimization Program) to help in the efficient design of commercial office buildings. This program was used to design the one-hundred story John Hancock building in Chicago integrating the various systems such as structural, mechanical, electrical, and elevator. A number of possible solutions were printed together with basic data for each: various dimensions, the gross area, the rentable floor space, the building cost, cost per square foot, and return on investment. Several solutions were then investigated in more detail to find the number of mechanical floors required, the structural floor depth and span required, mechanical clearances and lighting clearances. Additional costs for underfloor duct and perimeter air system were provided.

FUTURE TRENDS

Methods change so quickly that it is possible that some will be outmoded by the time you enter practice. For many years, buildings have been designed in essentially the same manner: a trial-and-error procedure based upon the experience and intuition of the designer. To make more reliable information available to the architectural designer, an integrated system called MODCON (Man-machine system for the Optimum Design and CONstruction of buildings) is being developed at the Pennsylvania State University. A brief description of this concept might be interesting, since it represents one possible view of the future.

MODCON system. A preliminary layout of the proposed building is prepared in the conventional manner. The layout is taken to a MODCON service branch which is served by a large computer center within the state. The layout is scanned and read by a coordinate reader giving the central computer a "mental picture" of the building. The architect feeds in additional information such as the building category (elementary school, senior high school, or whatever). At this early stage, the computer checks against building code violations. For instance, the room area requirements for schools would be checked; also the number of toilets, minimum ceiling heights, window area, number of exits, door sizes, and location of boiler room with regard to fire hazards. Column spacing and heating duct layout are checked for the most economical design. If the architect wants to change the layout, he simply points a light pen at a partition on the plan and moves it to another position. He can also make additions and deletions. The selection of materials is made by pointing a light pen at a location on the plan and pressing a button. The computer lists all materials

Figure 13   An IBM 2250 Graphic Display Center.

suited for that location and displays images of the building finished in these materials on a screen for the architect's final selection. Accurate interior and exterior perspective drawings are displayed which are controlled by head and eye movements. This gives the designer "pre-experience" with the building since he sees the building differently as he moves his eyes. For example, he can "walk" down a long shopping mall looking right and left, up and down, or he can "ride" past a proposed store building to determine the effect on a passing prospective customer.

After this stage, the computer computes material quantities and provides a preliminary cost estimate. Finally, a set of working drawings is drawn by a data plotter, and specifications are printed by a high-speed printer. Several sets of working drawings and specifications are printed, each designed for specific building trades. For example, the print-out for the client would include a rendered perspective drawing, while the mason would receive construction plans with detailed information on the locations and quantity of bricks and blocks.

REFERENCE PLAN SOURCES

Architectural Plan Service, 69–19 178th Street, Fresh Meadows, N.Y. 11365

Better Homes and Gardens, 1716 Locust Street, Des Moines, Iowa 50303

Garlinghouse Home Plans Co., Box 299, Topeka, Kansas 66601

Good Housekeeping, 959 Eighth Avenue, New York, N.Y. 10019

Homes for Living, Inc. 107–40 Queens Blvd., Forest Hills, N.Y. 11375

Homes for Today, Designers, 16 Maple Avenue, Inwood, N.Y. 11696

Home Planners, Inc., 16310 Grand River Avenue, Detroit, Michigan 48227

Master Plan Service, Inc., 89 E. Jericho Tpke., Mineola, N.Y. 11501

National Lumber Manufacturers Association, 1619 Massachusetts Avenue N.W., Washington, D.C. 20036

National Home Planning Service, 37 Mountain Avenue, Springfield, N.J. 07801

National Plan Service, 1700 W. Hubbard Street, Chicago, Ill. 60622

Portland Cement Association, Suite 602, 1211 Connecticut Avenue N.W., Washington, D.C. 20036

Structural Clay Products Institute, 1520 18th Street N.W., Washington, D.C. 20036

Sunset, The Magazine of Western Living, Lane Publishing Co., Menlo Park, California 94025

STUDY QUESTIONS

1. In architecture, what is meant by the term "orientation"? Name four different kinds of architectural orientation.
2. In architecture, what is meant by the terms:
   a. Circulation
   b. Prototype
   c. Poché
3. Indicate which sets of rooms should be planned adjacent to one another in residential design:
   a. Kitchen and dining room
   b. Kitchen and bedrooms
   c. Bath and bedrooms
   d. Bath and dining room
   e. Living and dining room
4. What is the main advantage in planning the kitchen, laundry, and bathrooms close to one another?
5. A house of 1500 sq. ft. total floor area contains 1150 sq. ft. of area actually occupied by rooms and 100 sq. ft. of hall area. Is this an efficient house?
6. What is the difference between:
   a. Furniture templates and room templates
   b. Interior planning and over-all planning
   c. Thumbnail sketches and preliminary sketches

LABORATORY PROBLEMS

1. Using a scale of $\frac{1}{8}'' = 1'$, prepare a preliminary layout of the A residence making any improvements you feel are desirable.
2. A one floor summer cottage is to be planned to have a living area, kitchen, bedroom, bathroom, and garage. Make a thumbnail sketch showing the location of each room if the plot has the following features: level, best view to the west, winter wind from the north, summer breezes from the southwest.
3. Using the method of templates, design a master bedroom to contain 3'-3" × 6'-6" twin beds, 2'-0 × 4'-0 chest of drawers, 1'-6" × 3'-0 cedar chest, 1'-6" × 3'-0 kidney-shaped dressing table, 2'-2" × 2'-2" chair, and a 1'-6" × 1'-6" night table.
4. Using the method of templates, lay out a residence having the following rooms: 13' × 19' living area, 9' × 9' dining area, 9' × 12' kitchen, 11' × 13' master bedroom, 9' × 11' bedroom, small bathroom, and full basement.
5. Make a preliminary layout for a house meeting the requirements as assigned by your instructor.
6. Make the preliminary layout for your original house design using the planning procedure assigned by your instructor:
   a. Prototype
   b. Templates
   c. Interior planning
   d. Over-all planning
7. Make a critical plan analysis for your original house design by listing its strong and weak features.

16   floor plans

WORKING DRAWINGS

The finished drawings made by the architect and used by the contractor are called working drawings. The working drawings, together with the specifications and the general conditions, form the legal contract between the owner and contractor. Since the working drawings are a major portion of the contract documents, they should be very carefully drawn.

A complete set of working drawings includes the following sheets in this order:

1. Title page and index (a perspective is often included)
2. Plot plan
3. Foundation plan
4. First floor plan
5. Second floor plan
6. Elevations
7. Sections
8. Typical details
9. Schedules
E1. Electrical requirements
H1. Heating and air conditioning
P1. Plumbing
V1. Ventilation
S1. Floor framing plan
S2. Roof framing plan
S3. Column schedule
S4. Structural details

Usually all of the working drawings are drawn to the same scale ($\frac{1}{8}'' = 1'$ or $\frac{1}{4}'' = 1'$) with the exception of details, which are drawn to a larger scale, and the plot plan, which is drawn to an engineer's scale.

FLOOR PLANS

Of all the different kinds of working drawings, the floor plan is the most important, since it includes the greatest amount of information. The floor plan is the first drawing started by the designer, but it may be the last finished because he will transfer his attention to the sections, elevations, and details required to complete the floor plan design.

A floor plan is actually a sectional drawing obtained by passing an imaginary cutting plane through the walls about four feet above the floor (midway between floor and ceiling). The cutting plane may be offset to a higher or lower level so that it cuts through all desired features (such as a high strip window). In the case of a split level house, the cutting plane must be considerably offset.

If the finished sketch has been carefully made, the floor plan can be drawn without much trouble. Notice in the accompanying floor plan of the A residence (Figure 1), the similarity with the finished

DOOR SCHEDULE

MK	NO	SIZE	DESCRIPTION
1	1	4'-0 x 7'-0 x 1"	CEDAR GATE
2	1	3'-8" x 6'-8" x 1 3/4"	3 PANEL WP
3	3	2'-8" x 6'-8" x 1 3/4"	FLUSH-SOLID WP
4	5	2'-6" x 6'-8" x 1 3/8"	FLUSH-HOLLOW BIRCH
5	2	2'-4" x 6'-8" x 1 3/8"	" " "
6	2	3'-6" x 6'-8" x 1 3/8"	LOUVER BI-SWING WP
7	1	2'-4" x 3'-4" x 1 3/8"	LOUVER BI-SWING WP
8	2	2'-0 x 3'-4" x 1 3/8"	" " "
9	4	7'-6" x 7'-0 x 1"	BI-SLIDE ALUMINUM
10	4	4'-0 x 6'-8" x 1 3/8"	FLUSH BI-SLIDE BIRCH
11	2	3'-0 x 6'-8" x 1 3/8"	FLUSH SLIDE WP
12	1	6'-0 x 6'-8" x 1 3/8"	FLUSH BI-FOLD WP
13	1	11'-6" x 7'-0 x 1 3/8"	4 PANEL OVERHD GAR WP

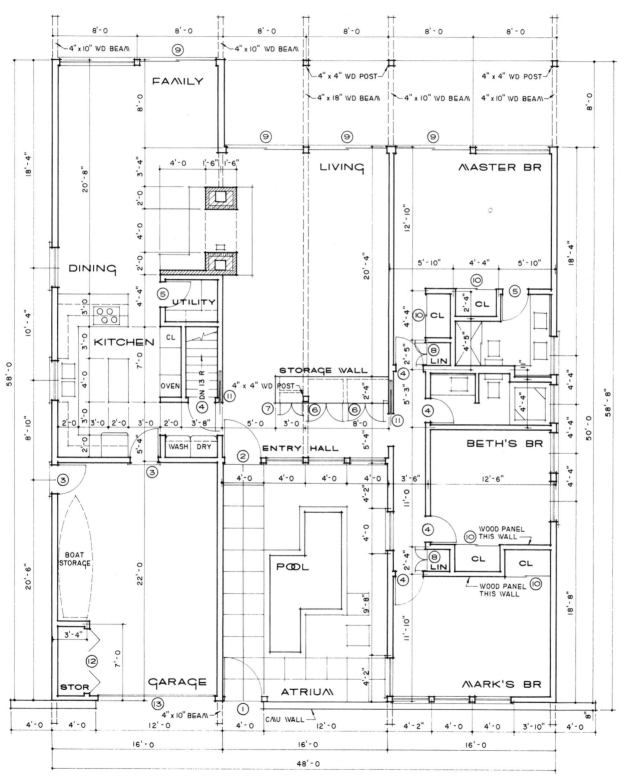

Figure 1   Floor plan of the A residence.

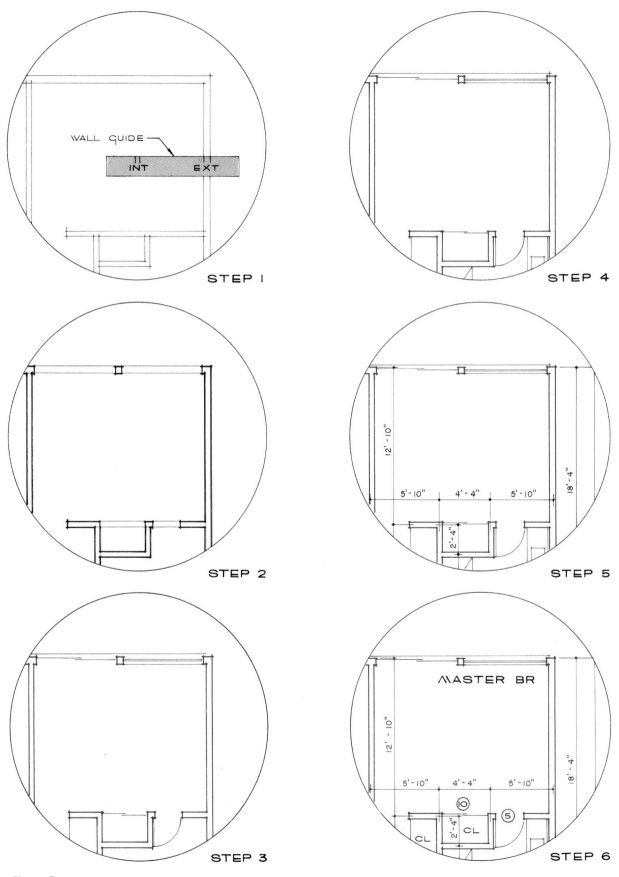

Figure 2

sketch of Figure 10 in Chapter 15. Of course, if the designer feels he can improve upon his sketch, he does so.

The steps used in drawing a floor plan are illustrated in Figure 2. A portion of the first floor plan of the A residence is used as an example.

FIRST FLOOR PLAN

Step 1: wall layout. Lay out the exterior and interior walls very lightly on tracing vellum using a hard, sharp pencil. A scale of $\frac{1}{4}'' = 1'$ should be used for a residence; $\frac{1}{8}'' = 1'$ for a larger structure. Always indicate the scale in the title block or on the drawing. To save time measuring the thickness of exterior and interior walls, a wall guide may be made by marking the wall thickness on a strip of paper. The wall sizes shown in the accompanying table may be used.

Wall Sizes

	Thickness
Wood frame walls	
exterior walls	6″
interior partitions	5″
Brick veneered walls	10″
Brick walls	
with two courses of brick	8″
with two courses of brick and air space	10″
with three courses of brick	12″
Concrete block walls	
light	8″
medium	10″
heavy	12″

Step 2: wall completion. Still using a hard, sharp pencil, the windows and doors are located on the wall layout.

Windows. The final placement of windows is determined, keeping fenestration, compass direction, pleasantness of view, and amount of light and air required in mind. Window selection depends on the style, design, and appearance of the building. See Chapter 11 for more detail.

The width of the windows given on the plan is that of the sash opening. Remember to allow room for the surrounding framing in close conditions.

Doors. The final door placement should take into consideration the door swing and furniture placement. Plan for unbroken wall spaces where they are needed, making sure no unnecessary doors are specified. Remember that every swinging door takes up valuable floor space (the area through which it swings) and two wall areas (the area containing the door and the area the door swings against). Do not

Interior doors:	2′-6″ × 6′-8″ × $1\frac{3}{8}$″
Allow for approximately 2′-9″ rough opening	
Front door:	3′-0 × 6′-8″ × $1\frac{3}{4}$″
Allow for approximately 3′-3″ rough opening	
Rear door:	2′-8″ × 6′-8″ × $1\frac{3}{4}$″
Allow for approximately 2′-11″ rough opening	

discount sliding and accordion doors for closets, and especially for little-used openings.

Doors opening into rooms from a hall should swing into the room against the wall. Use sliding, folding, or accordion doors if space is at a premium, but remember that these should not be specified for often-used bedroom and bath doors, since they require more time and energy to operate. As a rule, swinging doors should be used on all but closets.

Occasionally, it is better to use archways in place of doors for the sake of economy, appearance, and spaciousness. They should be shown on the plan by two dashed lines.

After all windows and doors have been located, the wall lines are darkened using a soft pencil. The wood frame wall convention is shown in the illustration of Step 2.

Step 3: details. Using a sharp, but black, line weight, add the floor plan details.

Windows. Show the sill and glass as indicated in Chapter 8.

Doors. Show the doors and their swings. Show the sill on exterior doors.

Stairs. A preliminary cross-sectional layout must be first drawn to determine the total run and the number and size of treads and risers. This layout is saved and used later as the basis for the finished stair details. Draw about half of the full stair run and letter a small "UP" at the stair foot, and "DN" (down) at the stair head. Indicate the number of risers. (For example: UP–14R.) See Chapter 20 for more detail.

Fireplace. Show the over-all width and depth of brickwork, location of basement flue, ash drop, and the outline of the fireplace opening and hearth. Cross sectioning is used to indicate the brickwork. See Chapter 21 for more detail.

Step 4: equipment. Show all built-in equipment, such as bathroom fixtures (bathtub, toilet, lavatory, and medicine cabinet), kitchen fixtures (cabinets, sink, built-in wall ovens, counter-top burners, and built-in refrigerator or freezer), and closet fixtures (shelves and clothes rod). The location of a movable stove or refrigerator is shown even if it is not included in the contract. Notice that the wall cabinets are shown as hidden lines. A hidden line on an architectural plan may refer to a feature (cabinet, archway, or beam) *above* the level of the imaginary cutting plane. The locations of lighting and heating devices are included only when they will not make the floor plan crowded. Occasionally, all furniture placement is shown.

Step 5: dimensioning. Dimension all walls and partitions using dimension lines spaced approximately $\frac{3}{8}''$ apart. The dimension lines are continuous with the $\frac{3}{32}''$ high figures lettered above them. The dimension figures should be in feet and inches (to the nearest sixteenth of an inch), and should read from the bottom or right-hand side of the drawing. In frame construction, the dimensions are given from the outside faces of the studs in exterior walls and to the centerlines of interior partitions. Cumulative dimensions should lie in one line if possible, but try to avoid dimensioning over other features. Also remember to allow some open spaces for lettering the room names later on. Dots or small circles may be used in place of arrowheads. Check carefully that no *necessary* dimension is omitted, but some *minor* dimensions can be omitted for the sake of clarity. For example, the width of some closets may have to be scaled from the drawing. This is accepted practice, since the exact location of these partitions is not critical. See Chapter 10.

Step 6: lettering. Letter room names in the center or lower left-hand corner of each room without lettering over other features. Room lettering should be approximately $\frac{3}{16}''$ high. Special explanatory notes on materials and construction are added using $\frac{3}{32}''$ high lettering. See Appendix F for the proper spelling of words often misspelled on architectural drawings.

A $\frac{1}{8}''$ high schedule mark (a number for doors and a letter for windows) is assigned to each door or window of the same size and type. The door numbers are placed within $\frac{1}{4}''$ diameter circles in a convenient location near the doors. The door schedule is added as shown in Chapter 13. Window marks and the window schedule may be included also, although they usually appear on the elevations.

Any additional information necessary for proper construction should be added at this point. Include such details as concrete porches, window areaways, hose bibbs, and electrical fixtures if they do not appear elsewhere.

Step 7: checking. In a professional drafting room, the checker has a most responsible position. He must certify that he has checked and approved every line and dimension on the drawings. If done correctly, this procedure should guarantee that nothing has been omitted and that nothing is in error.

In a classroom, however, there is no professional checker, and you must check your own work. This is very difficult to do properly since you will,

in all likelihood, repeat any drawing errors in your checking. If possible, it is a good idea to trade the responsibility of checking with another student. If this is not possible, you should check the drawing only after it has been put aside for several days to assure a fresh outlook.

SECOND FLOOR PLAN

After the first floor plan is completed, related plans such as those for the basement and second floor are started by tracing common features from the first floor plan. The exterior walls may usually be traced, together with bearing partitions, plumbing walls, stairways, and chimney location. Principal walls should be over one another from foundation to roof insofar as possible, to assure a stiffer frame and facilitate plumbing and heating installations. Also, the fenestration may require that first and second floor windows be directly over one another.

BASEMENT PLAN

The basement plan or foundation plan (Figure 3) is begun by tracing common features from the first floor plan: the outside lines of exterior walls, the stairway, and the chimney location. The foundation wall sizes shown in the accompanying table may be used.

A hidden line is used to indicate the size of foundation footings and column footings.

Dimensioning practice is somewhat different from that used for the floor plans, in that dimensions will run from the faces of all masonry walls or partitions rather than from their centerlines. Also the openings for windows and doors in masonry walls are dimensioned to faces rather than centerlines.

Some special considerations in designing basements must be remembered:

1. The size and location of columns and girders.

Foundation Wall Sizes

	Thickness
Under wood frame house	
concrete block	8", with pilasters 16' oc
poured concrete	10"
Under veneered construction	
concrete block	10"
poured concrete	10"
Under solid masonry construction	
concrete block	12"
poured concrete	12"

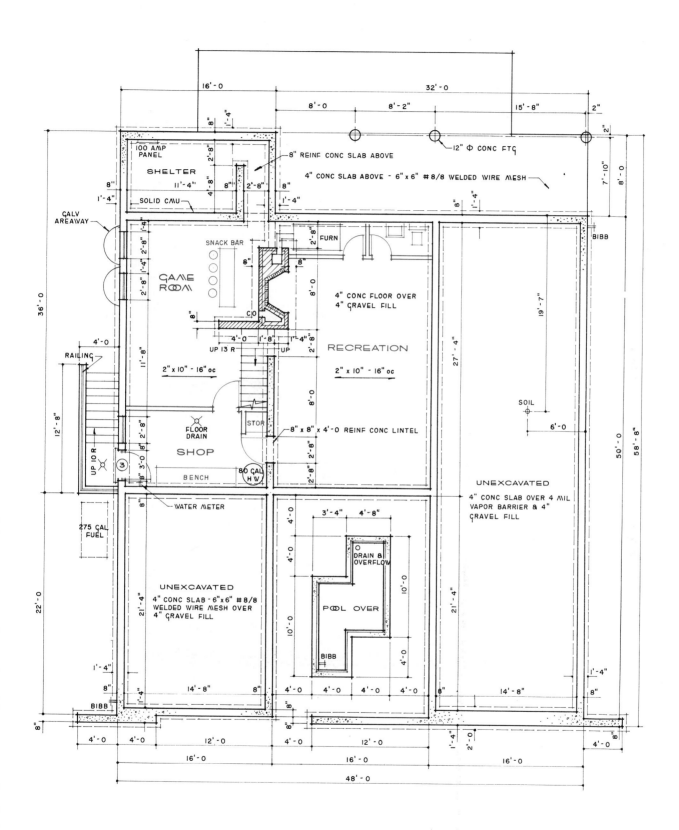

Figure 3   *Basement plan of the A residence (future construction shown in red).*

2. The size, spacing, and direction of joists (double headed arrow indicates joist direction).

3. Stiffening pilasters, needed on long, straight runs of wall.

4. The furnace, located near chimney flue (within 10').

5. Provision for fuel storage, near the driveway but removed from the furnace (beyond 10').

6. The hot water heater.

7. The water meter, located near water line entrance.

8. Floor drains.

9. Electrical entrance panel, located near entrance pole.

10. Labeling of unexcavated areas, crawl spaces, and concrete floors, together with any additional helpful information. For example, the thickness of a basement floor is usually noted on the basement plan. Specify 3" minimum concrete for a basement floor and 4" minimum concrete for a garage floor or finished slab floor.

Notice that the basement of the A residence has been designed for the future construction of a recreation room, game room, shop, and lavatory. This allows better planning in locating necessary utilities.

STUDY QUESTIONS

1. List the drawings normally included in a set of residential working drawings.
2. Sketch a section of each of the following walls, showing the actual size of materials to illustrate the total wall thickness normally used on a plan:
   a. Exterior wood frame wall
   b. Interior wood frame partition
   c. Exterior brick veneered wall
3. List the most commonly used size (width, height, and thickness) of the following doors:
   a. Front entrance door
   b. Rear entrance door
   c. Interior doors
4. What other drawings must be considered before the floor plan is completed?
5. What does a hidden line on an architectural plan represent? Give three examples.
6. When drawing a second floor plan, what features may be traced from the first floor plan?
7. When drawing a basement plan, what features may be traced from the first floor plan?
8. In the layout of a basement plan, what special considerations must be made in the location of:
   a. Furnace
   b. Fuel storage
   c. Water meter
   d. Electrical entrance panel

9. Should bedroom doors swing into the bedroom or hall? Why?

LABORATORY PROBLEMS

1. Prepare a title page and index for your set of working drawings to include:
   a. Title information (name of project, location, name of designer, date)
   b. Index listing number and title of each sheet
   c. Legend of symbols used
   d. List of abbreviations used
   e. Modular dimensioning note
   f. Interior perspective
   g. Exterior perspective
2. Using a scale of $\frac{1}{4}'' = 1'$, draw the following plans of the A residence:
   a. First floor plan
   b. Basement plan
3. Draw the plans of the building assigned by your instructor:
   a. First floor plan
   b. Second floor plan
   c. Basement plan
4. Draw the plans of a residence for the family assigned:
   a. Bank president and wife; no children; income, $50,000; wide musical interests; large art collection; two cars
   b. Physics professor and wife; two children; income, $30,000; large library and research laboratory in home; two cars
   c. Architectural draftsman and wife; three children; income, $25,000; office for additional work done at home; two cars
   d. Bachelor airplane navigator; income, $20,000; hobby: large model railroad layout; one car
   e. High school physical education director and wife; four children; income, $15,000; wife conducts dancing studio and piano lessons at home; one car
   f. Assistant manager of chain store; one child; income, $10,000; hobby, carpentry and boat building; one car
5. Draw a plan showing your concept of a dwelling to be built under one of the following conditions:
   a. Flexible plan required (must be used equally well by families with one to four children)
   b. Low cost, mass produced
   c. Unpleasant view in all directions
   d. Physically handicapped couple
6. (For the advanced student) Draw a plan showing your concept of a dwelling of the future to be built:
   a. In a desert area
   b. On extremely mountainous terrain
   c. Entirely over water
   d. Completely underground
   e. Occupying a minimum amount of land
7. Complete the plans of your original house design:
   a. First floor plan
   b. Second floor plan
   c. Basement plan

17 the plot plan

The plot plan shows the location of the house on the plot together with information on terraces, walks, driveways, contours, elevations, and utilities. A roof plan or landscaping plan may be included.

The steps used in drawing a plot plan are illustrated in Figure 1. We will use the plot plan of the A residence as an example.

STEP 1: PROPERTY LINES

Lay out and dimension the property lines using a medium weight centerline. The information is obtained from the site survey (Figure 1 of Chapter 23). The plot plan is usually drawn to an engineer's scale (such as $1'' = 20'$), rather than to an architect's scale (such as $\frac{1}{16}'' = 1'$). Show the north arrow.

STEP 2: CONTOUR LINES

A contour line is an imaginary line representing a constant elevation on the lot. The vertical distance between adjacent contour lines is called the "contour interval," and is usually one foot for a residential lot. The contour lines are drawn freehand and dimensioned by indicating their elevation above sea level or some other datum plane such as a nearby street or house. This information is also obtained from the site survey. On the plot plan of the A residence, notice that the contour lines indicate gently sloping ground with the lowest point being the south-west corner. The elevations of any permanent markers at the plot corners should also be transferred from the site survey.

STEP 3: ZONING

The first known zoning law was passed in ancient Rome to prevent industries from locating too near the central forum of the city. This established the principle that private property can be restricted in favor of the general welfare. The first comprehensive zoning ordinance in the United States was passed in New York City in 1916 as a consequence of a tragic fire at the Triangle Shirtwaist factory. Over 100 dressmakers, mostly young girls, died in that building, which was higher than the reach of fire-fighting equipment, had no sprinklers, and had an uncompleted fire escape.

Most communities now have zoning ordinances which restrict the size and location of buildings to prevent crowding and encourage the most appropriate use of the land. It is imperative that the designer be familiar with, and adhere to, all zoning regulations and building codes. Several regulations of one community's zoning ordinance are given in Table 1. Using these regulations, the following calculations are made for the A residence:

Check on lot area: $75 \times 141.6 = 10,620$ sq. ft. *O.K.* (greater than required 10,000 sq. ft.)

Check on lot width: 75' *O.K.* (equal to required minimum of 75')

Minimum front yard depth: 30'

Minimum side yard width: 8'

Minimum rear yard depth: $.20 (137.9 - 30) = 21.6'$ *O.K.* (greater than required 15')

Check on dwelling height: 14' *O.K.* (less than 26' maximum)

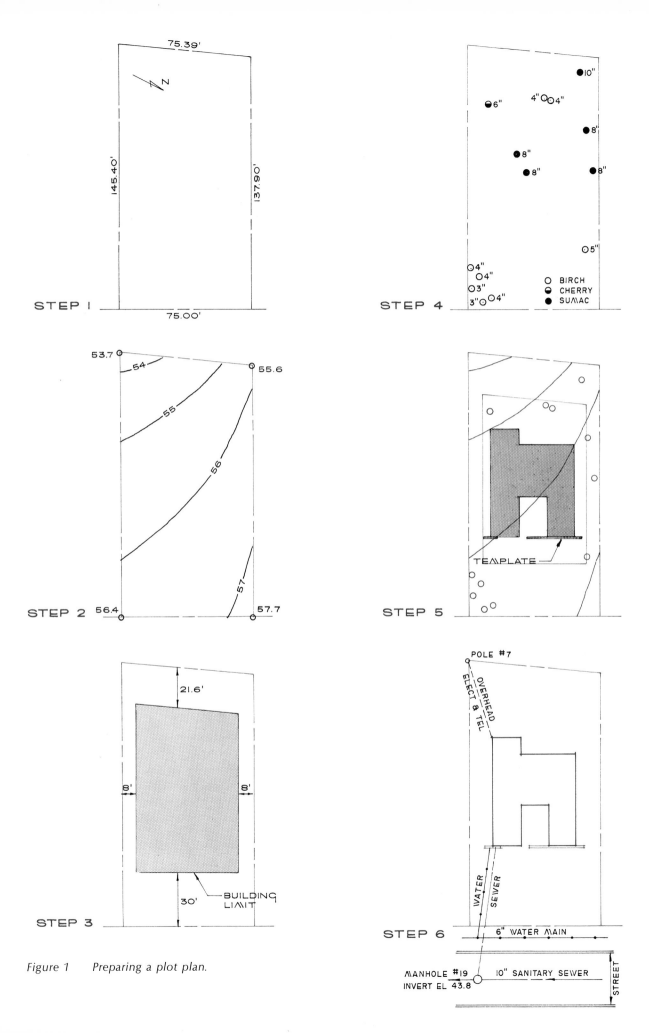

Figure 1   Preparing a plot plan.

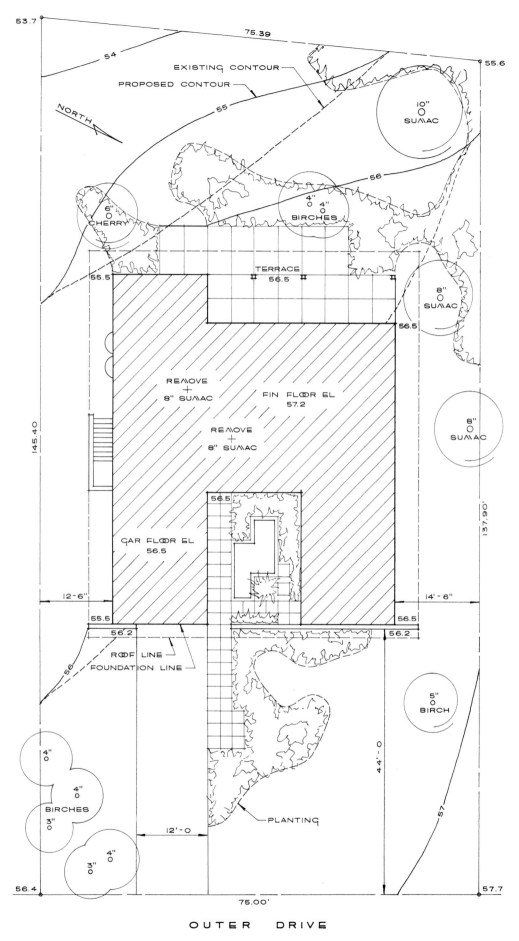

Figure 2   Plot plan of the A residence.

Using light construction lines, show the front, side, and rear yard limits calculated on page 153 so that you know exactly where you are permitted to place your house.

STEP 4: TREES

The lot of the A residence contains birch, sumac, and cherry trees. These are plotted so that the house and driveway may be located without removing many of them. The type and diameter of each tree should be noted on the plot plan to aid in identification. No tree should remain within five feet of the foundation, because the excavation will disturb the roots so much that it will eventually die.

STEP 5: LOCATION OF HOUSE

The house may now be located in the position which will satisfy all requirements of solar orientation, wind orientation, topography, landscaping, zoning, and utilities. A paper template in the shape of the basement plan is useful, since it can be shifted to various locations. When the final position is determined, draw in the plan with heavy lines using the outside basement dimensions. The plan may be sectioned if desired. Hidden lines are used to indicate roof overhang. On structures with fairly involved roof intersections, a roof plan is shown in place of a section to indicate ridges, valleys, and hips.

TABLE 1

Sample of Zoning Regulations

Article V—Residence District

Section 501. Each lot in this district shall comply with the following minimum requirements:

501-1)	Lot area per:	
	One-family dwelling	10,000 sq. ft.
	Two-family dwelling	12,000 sq. ft.
501-2)	Lot width:	
	One-family dwelling	75'
	Two-family dwelling	100'
501-3)	Front yard depth:	
	Dwelling	30'
	Non-dwelling	40'
501-4)	Side yard width:	
	Dwelling and accessory building	8'
	Non-dwelling	20'
501-5)	Rear yard depth:	

The rear yard depth shall be at least 20 percent of the depth of the lot measured from the front building line to the nearest point of rear lot line but in no case shall this be less than 15'.

Section 502. The maximum height of structures in this district shall be:

502-1)	Dwellings	26' (not exceeding two stories)
502-2)	Accessory building	16' (not exceeding one story)
502-3)	Non-dwelling	40'

Figure 3   *Plan landscaping to provide both planting groups and uninterrupted lawn.*

Courtesy of Scholz Homes, Inc.

Figure 4   A terrace well integrated with the interior plan.

Show the elevation of the finished first floor and complete all details such as walks, drives, street names, notes, and scale.

STEP 6: UTILITIES

Existing utilities—such as electric, telephone, sewer, water, and gas lines—are often noted or actually located, since they may affect the house location. For example, some of the factors to be considered in the location of the branch drain from the house to the street manhole connection are:

1. A minimum downward grade of $\frac{1}{4}''$ per foot must be maintained to the invert elevation (the bottom inside) of the sewer line.
2. The branch line must remain below the frost line to prevent damage from freezing.
3. The line must be straight, since changes in direction or grade, which collect sediment, should occur only at manholes.
4. If there are trees, cast iron drains with poured lead joints must be used instead of vitreous tile to prevent the roots growing into and blocking the drain.

STEP 7: ADJUSTMENT OF CONTOUR LINES

When the existing land contour is not satisfactory, it must be adjusted by cutting away or filling in. This is indicated on the plot plan by showing the proposed position of the contour lines with a solid line; the existing contours are still indicated, but as broken lines. Figure 2 shows how all of these steps are finished into the plot plan. It was decided to show the utilities on later mechanical plans to prevent overcrowding the plot plan.

STUDY QUESTIONS

1. Distinguish between a contour line and a contour interval.
2. List the utilities to be considered when drawing a plot plan.
3. Why is it necessary to be familiar with the local zoning ordinance when drawing a plot plan?

LABORATORY PROBLEMS

1. Draw the plot plan of the A residence.
2. Draw the plot plan of the building assigned by your instructor.
3. Complete the plot plan for your original house design.

PART FOUR

elevations

18 roofs

The type of roof specified for a house is a very important factor in exterior design. It also affects the interior. In a traditional house, the type of roof is pretty well determined by the house style. When the building is in a contemporary style, however, a wide variety of roof types may be used. The shape of the plan may also affect the roof choice. While a rectangular plan could be roofed in nearly any manner, a rambling plan would be most economically covered by a flat roof. A hip roof, in such a case, would require much additional cutting and fitting.

The various types of roofs may be classified very broadly into two categories: roofs used mostly on traditional houses and roofs used mostly on contemporary houses. Let us look at each in turn.

TRADITIONAL ROOF TYPES

Gable. To be perfectly correct, the gable is the triangular portion of the end of the house, and this type of roof is a *gabled* roof. The gable roof is the most common form of roof, since it is easy to construct, is pitched for drainage, and is universally accepted. This roof should be pitched high enough so that louvers can be installed to allow warm air and moisture to escape. This roof may also be used in contemporary design.

Hip. A hip roof is more difficult to construct than a gable, but is still used with a low pitch on ranch houses. However, every hip or valley increases chances for leakage.

Gambrel. The gambrel roof is used on Dutch Colonial designs to increase head room on the second floor. Since the framing is complicated, it is not widely used today.

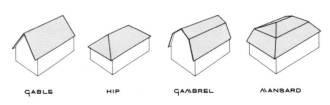

Figure 1   Traditional roofs.

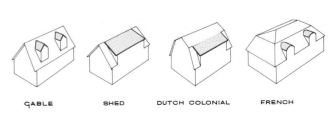

Figure 2   Dormers.

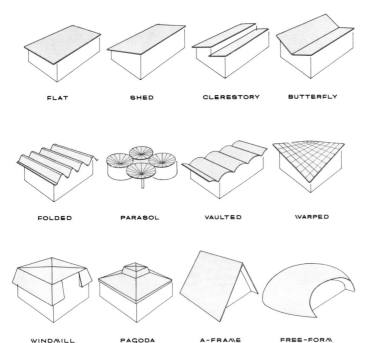

Figure 3   Contemporary roofs.

Mansard. This type was named after the French architect who originated it. The Mansard roof is not built today but it was extensively used on French-styled houses at one time.

DORMER TYPES

Gable. A dormer is used to let light into an otherwise dark area. The designer must weigh the expense of dormers against the expense of an additional story.

Shed. A shed dormer will give nearly all the advantages of a full story, without disturbing the one floor look of the house. This dormer type is sometimes called a "dustpan."

Figure 4   A flat roof on a residential design.

Dutch Colonial. A Dutch Colonial dormer might be termed a shed dormer on a gambrel roof. The second floor wall may be set back from the first floor wall.

French. Rounded dormer tops indicate French influence.

CONTEMPORARY ROOF TYPES

Flat. The flat roof is the most common commercial roof. Most roofs which appear flat actually have a slight slope of $\frac{1}{8}$" per foot to $\frac{1}{2}$" per foot for drainage. Roofing is laid in layers (called "plies") of tar and gravel. The "water film roof" is perfectly flat, allowing water to remain. This serves as insulation from cold in winter and insulation from heat (by reflection and evaporation) in summer. A generous overhang should be provided for shade and aesthetic effect.

Shed. The shed roof is ideally suited to the solar house if the high wall faces south. It will also give interesting interior effects if the beams are left exposed. Beams measuring 4" × 10" spaced 4' oc might be used. This roof takes standard roofing material.

Clerestory. This roof solves the problem of introducing light into the center of a house. The clerestory may be used with a sawtooth roof as shown or with other roof types.

Butterfly. The pitch and length of each side of the butterfly roof need not be equal. This roof "opens up" the house, providing plenty of light and air. Drains may be at the end of the valley or in the middle—running down through the center of the house.

Folded. Some roofs are so new that some imagination must be used to find descriptive names. As the name implies, the folded or pleated roof looks as though it were folded from a sheet of paper, and is quite popular in office and motel design. Roofing

Figure 5   A flat roof on a commercial design.

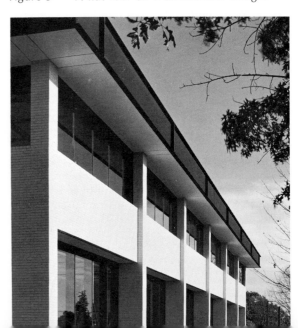

*Figure 6   A warped cable roof for the North Caro-
lina State Fair Arena.*

*Figure 7   An exterior view of the North Carolina
State Fair Arena.*

*Figure 8   A wood shingled roof of unique design
for a hillside plot.*

*Figure 9   Another view of the residence shown in
Figure 8.*

Figure 10   A beach pavilion with parasol roofs.

Figure 11   A metal roof on an A-frame.

Figure 12   *Hobe Sound Bubble House, construc-*
ted by spraying concrete on an inflated
plastic balloon.

Figure 13   *A contemporary library with a petal-*
shaped roof.

material may be exterior grade plywood or metal.

Parasol. The parasol roof has become popular since the success of Wright's Johnson's Wax Building. Round and square variations are possible. Often the material used is reinforced concrete.

Vaults and domes. Vaults and domes have staged a comeback from the Byzantine days. More often used on commercial than residential buildings, they limit considerably the possible shapes of the floor plan.

Warped. Beginnings have been made in the development of warped surfaces for roofs. In most cases this warped surface is a hyperbolic paraboloid; that is, a surface generated by a line moving so that its ends are in contact with two skew lines. This produces a superior roof due to its high resistance to

Figure 14   *A striking roof for the gymnasium at*
Princeton.

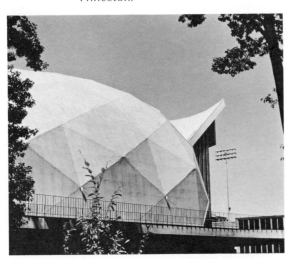

Figure 15   *Close-up of the geodesic shaping of*
the Princeton gymnasium.

Figure 16   *Construction details of the Princeton*
gymnasium.

bending. Warped roofs have been constructed of molded plywood, reinforced concrete, and sprayed plastic.

Windmill. The windmill roof is often used on two-story townhouses to lend interest to an otherwise simple design. This roof looks best when wood-shingled.

Pagoda. The pagoda roof provides an interesting interior, as well as exterior, design. The Oriental flavor should be extended to other elements of the building. Connected clusters of pagoda-roofed rooms have been successfully designed.

A-frame. Originally specified for low-cost summer cabins, larger structures such as churches have adopted this roof form.

Free-form. The shape of free-form roofs may depend upon the method of construction. Urethane foam can be sprayed on a "knit jersey" material stretched over a pipe frame. It has proved to be strong, weather-resistant, and self-insulating, but some foamed plastics are dangerously flammable and toxic.

ROOFING MATERIALS

Although several new roofing materials and methods have been mentioned, the large majority of residential roofs are constructed of built-up tar and gravel when the roof is flat and of shingle when the roof slopes more than three inches per foot.

Built-up roofing. Built-up tar and gravel roofing is used on flat and slightly sloping roofs. It is constructed of alternate layers of roofing felt and mopped-on hot tar or asphalt. Three to five layers (called "plies") are used and topped by crushed gravel

Figure 18   *A wood shingled hip roof.*

Figure 19   *A wood shingled conical roof.*

Courtesy of Scholz Homes, Inc.

Figure 20   *A tile roof used with a contemporary design.*

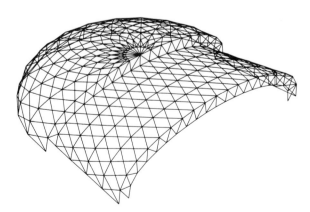

Figure 17   *Schematic of the cone and dome framing for the Princeton gymnasium.*

Figure 21   Wrecking ball used to dismantle Disneyland house.

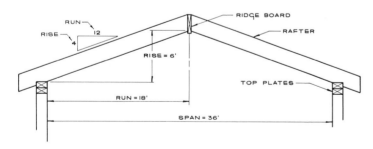

Figure 22   Clam shovel needed to complete the wrecking job.

Figure 23   Roof pitch terms.

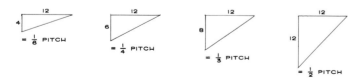

Figure 24   Alternate method of specifying pitch.

or marble chips imbedded in the tar. Roofing contractors will bond a 3-ply economy roof for ten years, and a 5-ply roof for twenty years.

Shingles. Asphalt shingles are very commonly used in house construction because their cost is low and they are fire resistant. Asbestos shingles offer even greater fire protection but they are somewhat brittle. Wood shingles and shakes are often of cedar or redwood and present a handsome appearance. Unfortunately, the fire hazard is great. Roofing shingles are sold by "squares." A square is the amount of shingling needed to roof 100 sq. ft.

Slate and tile are occasionally used for roofing materials. Both are relatively heavy and expensive, however. Metal roofs of tin, copper, zinc, aluminum, and lead are often used on commercial buildings.

Plastic foam. Sprayed urethane foam roofs offer exciting possibilities for new architectural concepts. All free-form shapes are possible, construction is economical, and it has three times the insulating value of common insulating materials. These roofs are formed by spraying on large balloons, inflatable forms, or fabric stretched over light-weight tubing. Spraying is continued until a thickness of 5″ is obtained.

Urethane foam is an organic polymer formed by chemical reaction between two liquids (isocyanate and polyol). These liquids are pumped from separate tanks to a mixing spray gun where it begins to foam immediately, expanding to 30 times its original volume. Within a few minutes, the foam has hardened. It will adhere to most surfaces. Final density is about 3 pounds per cubic foot. A serious disadvantage is that some forms of urethane foam are very flammable. Consequently it should be covered by a fireproof material rather than installed exposed. Sprayed urethane foam should always be protected against any possible source of combustion.

Another type of plastic home was built of fiber glass-reinforced polyester resin at Disneyland in 1957. When the time came to remove it ten years later, it proved almost indestructible. Chain saw blades broke, an acetylene torch wouldn't cut it, a huge wrecking ball only bounced, and a clam shovel upset (Figures 21 and 22). The wrecking job, estimated at one day, was finished two weeks later.

ROOF PITCH

Some roof pitch terms are shown in Figure 23. The terms *rise* and *run* are used in two ways:

1. To describe the rise per unit of run. For example, the roof shown in Figure 23 has a rise of 4″ in a run of 1′.

TABLE I

Recommended Roof Pitch

Type of Roofing	Recommended Roof Pitch
Built-up	under 3-12
Asphalt shingles	
Interlocking*	2-12 or more
Self-sealing*	2-12 or more
Cemented*	2-12 or more
Heavy-weight*	2-12 or more
Heavy-weight	3-12 or more
Regular	4-12 or more
Wood shingles	4-12 or more
Asbestos shingles	5-12 or more
Slate shingles	6-12 or more

*Double layer of roofing felt underlay must be used.

2. To describe the *actual* dimensions of a roof. For example, the roof in Figure 23 has a rise of 6', run of 18', and span of 36'.

The roof pitch is also described in two ways:

1. By a pitch triangle on the elevations showing the rise in whole inches per 12" of run. For example, the 4-12 pitch triangle shown in Figure 23 indicates a rise of 4" for a run of 12".

2. By a fraction whose numerator is the rise and denominator is the span. For example, a roof with a rise of 6' and a span of 36' has a $\frac{6}{36}$ pitch, which would be reduced and called a $\frac{1}{6}$ pitch.

In general, the steeper roofs are found in areas where there are heavy snowfalls, since snow is naturally shed from a steep roof.

Special steps must be taken with low pitched, asphalt shingled roofs to prevent wind from lifting the tabs and allowing water to seep under them. Several solutions are possible as indicated in Table I:

1. Use interlocking tab shingles.
2. Use self-sealing shingles which have factory-applied adhesive on the underside.
3. Cement each tab with a spot of quick-setting adhesive during installation.
4. Use heavy-weight shingles (300#, 15" × 36") which are stiffer than regular shingles (210#, 12" × 36") and are sized for triple overlap.

FLASHING

Thin sheets of soft metal are used to prevent leakage at critical points on roofs and walls. These sheets are called "flashing" and are usually of lead, zinc, copper, or aluminum. Areas which must be flashed are:

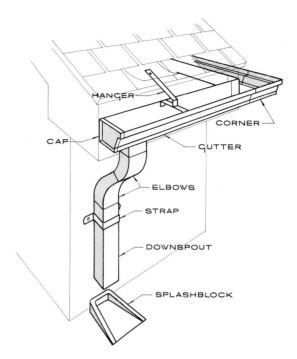

Figure 25   Guttering terms.

Intersections of roof with chimney, soil pipe, and dormer (see Figure 7, Chapter 21)
Roof valleys

GUTTERING

Gutters are used when the soil is likely to be eroded by rain dripping from the roof, or when roof overhangs are less than 12" (in a one-story structure) or 24" (in a two-story structure). Down-spouts conduct the water down the wall to a storm sewer (*not* a sanitary sewer), dry well, or splashblock (a concrete pad placed to prevent soil erosion) as shown in Figure 25. When gutters are omitted, a diverter is used to protect the entrances to the house from rain water. Guttering is made of galvanized iron, copper, aluminum, zinc alloy, or wood, or it may be built into the roof as shown in Figure 28 of Chapter 23.

SKYLIGHTS

Plastic domes are often used to light the interior of industrial buildings. Recently, skylights have been used in residences to obtain specific effects. Both fixed and ventilation types are available in sizes ranging from 24" square to 48" square (see Figure 26).

Figure 26   Plastic skylight.

CONSTRUCTION

Roof framing is described in Chapter 23. Tables for the selection of rafters are given in Chapter 24. Figure 27 shows some common terms used in roof construction.

Framing plan. When unusual or difficult roof construction is necessary, a roof framing plan is included in the working drawings. Figure 28 shows the roof framing plan for the roof shown in Figure 27. Notice that a single, heavy line is used to indicate each rafter. Floor framing plans and ceiling joist framing plans are also included when necessary.

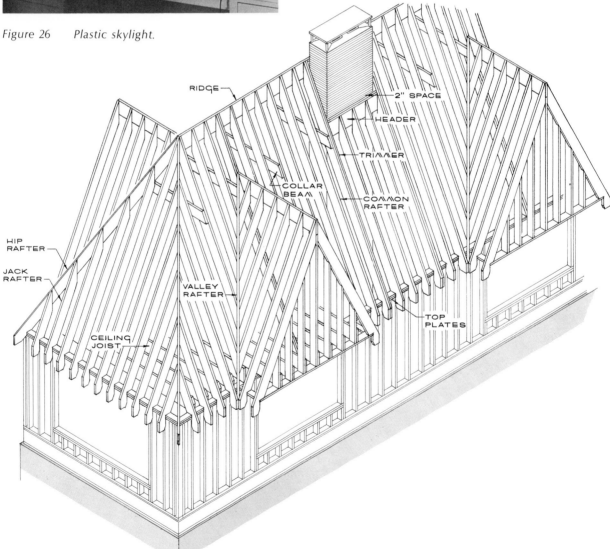

Figure 27   Roof framing terms.

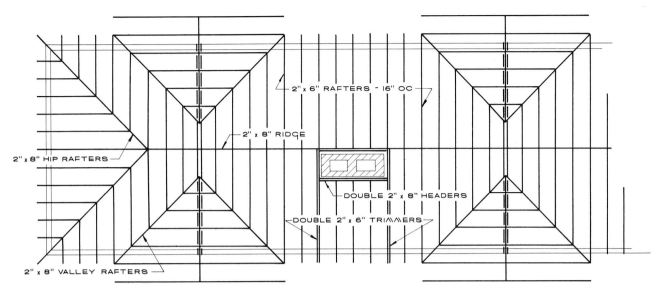

Figure 28   Roof framing plan.

STUDY QUESTIONS

1. List four types of traditional roofs.
2. Sketch four types of traditional roofs.
3. List twelve types of contemporary roofs.
4. Sketch twelve types of contemporary roofs.
5. List four types of dormer windows.
6. Sketch four types of dormer windows.
7. Should a roof sloping 3″ per foot be covered by ordinary asphalt shingles? Why?
8. Name four types of roof shingles and give the advantages of each.
9. Sketch and label the pitch triangle for a $\frac{1}{4}$ pitch roof.
10. Give two methods of indicating the pitch of a roof having an 8′ rise in a 32′ span.
11. What is the purpose of flashing? Give several examples.
12. Describe in words or by sketches the following terms:
    a. Common rafter
    b. Jack rafter
    c. Hip rafter
    d. Valley rafter
    e. Ridge board
    f. Collar beam
    g. Header
    h. Trimmer
    i. Span
    j. Run
    k. Rise
    l. Roofing square
    m. Roofing ply
13. List four methods to prevent wind from lifting roof shingles.
14. Give your estimation of the future of plastic roofing materials.

LABORATORY PROBLEMS

1. Prepare a classroom illustration showing:
    a. Traditional roofs
    b. Contemporary roofs
    c. Dormer windows
    d. Roof construction terminology
2. Construct a series of study models to illustrate various types of contemporary roofs.
3. (For the advanced student) Design a type of roof that is entirely different from those now commonly used.
4. Complete the roof framing plan for the A residence.
5. Complete the roof framing plan for the building assigned by your instructor.
6. Complete the roof design for your original house design.
7. Complete the roof framing plan for your original house design.

19   elevations and sections

An architectural elevation is a view of a building containing a height dimension. When elevations show the inside of a building, they are called *interior elevations;* when they show the outside they are called simply *elevations.*

INTERIOR ELEVATIONS

Interior elevations are included in a set of working drawings only when there is some special interior construction to be illustrated. This is quite often the case in kitchen design. Figure 2 shows the interior elevations of the kitchen of the A residence. Notice that the arrangement of the elevations is in relation to the floor plan—as though the four walls had fallen backward. To prevent this awkward appearance, the interior elevations may be removed to an upright position and even placed on a separate drawing sheet. The relation of each elevation to the plan is then shown by sight arrows as indicated in Figure 3. A sight arrow shows the drawing number on which the detail appears. Sight arrows $\frac{1}{7}$, $\frac{2}{7}$, etc., are interpreted as detail #1 on drawing #7, detail #2 on drawing #7, and so on.

ELEVATIONS

The exterior elevations are as necessary to the satisfactory appearance of a building as the floor plan is to its satisfactory functioning. Normally, the elevations of the four sides of a building are sufficient to describe it. In some cases, however, more than the four elevations are needed. For example, a structure built around an open court would require additional exterior elevations to illustrate the building as seen from the court.

ELEVATION DESIGN

The procedure used in the design of elevations is similar to the procedure used in the design of floor plans.

Figure 1   A front elevation provides the first indication of the character of a building.

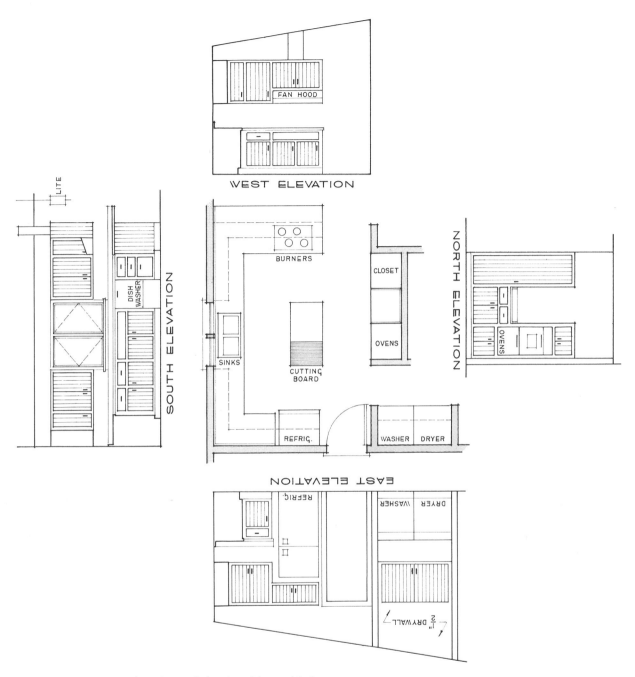

Figure 2   Interior elevations of the A residence kitchen.

Thumbnail sketches. Thumbnail sketches of elevations are somewhat simpler to draw than the thumbnail sketches of a floor plan, since overall dimensions, window locations, and door locations may be transferred from the plan. The prime purpose of the elevation thumbnail is to help decide the general exterior styling. In Figure 4, compare the thumbnail sketches for the A residence. Although they appear to be different buildings, actually they are different ways of styling the same building.

The final choice may be influenced by the character of the neighborhood. Although it is not necessary or desirable to have a neighborhood composed entirely of the same style and size houses, the surroundings will influence the appropriateness of a particular design to some extent. For example, it would not be appropriate to place a charming Cape Cod house in the midst of a section of highly experimental modern houses.

Preliminary sketches. Using the thumbnail sketch as a guide to the general styling, prepare a preliminary

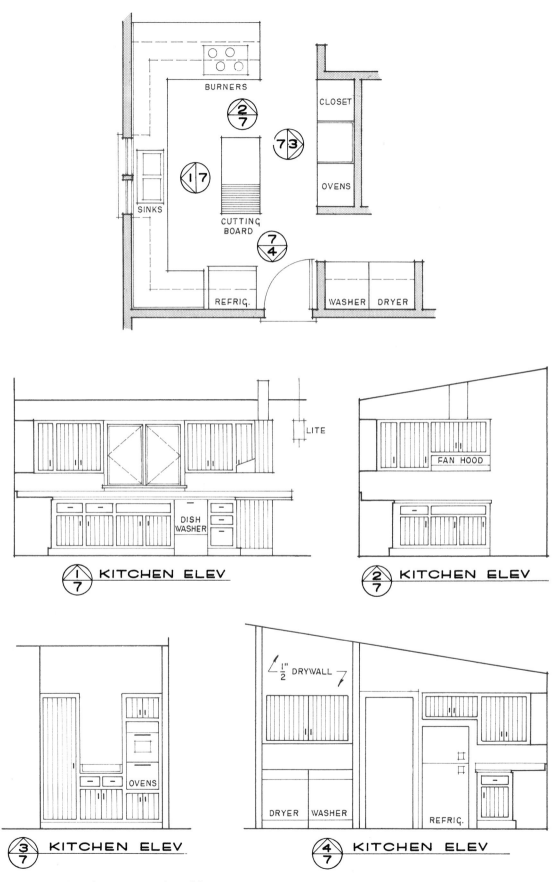

Figure 3   Interior elevations, preferred layout.

sketch. This will normally be done to $\frac{1}{8}'' = 1'$ scale on graph paper, because the location and proportion of features is very important at this stage. Main attention is given to the proportions of walls and openings and the fenestration of the window and door openings. Also consider the harmony of materials and features and the effects of orientation and shadows.

Proportion. Most people can look at a finished building and decide if it is well proportioned (Figure 5). However, designing a building so that it will have good proportion requires talent and training. In general, the term "proportion" deals with the size and shape of areas and their relation to one another. Some of the most important rules of good proportion are:

1. Avoid square areas or multiples of squares, since a rectangular area that cannot be visually divided into squares is more interesting and pleasing (Figure 7).
2. Balance areas so that they do not appear unstable. Thus the lightest appearing material or area should be above the heaviest or darkest (Figure 8).
3. Areas should be either completely symmetrical or obviously unsymmetrical (Figure 9).
4. One leading area should dominate the entire design with the other areas subordinate (Figure 10).
5. Repetition of elements may be used to advantage or disadvantage depending upon the circumstances. The repeated window arrangement shown in Figure 11 is superior, but the repeated drawer arrangement in Figure 12 is not.

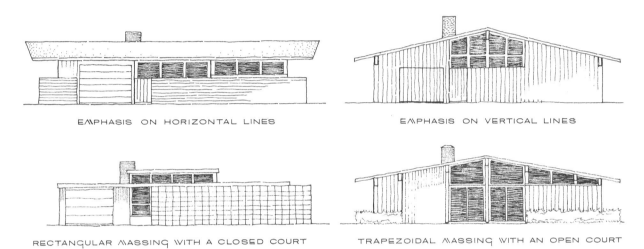

EMPHASIS ON HORIZONTAL LINES   EMPHASIS ON VERTICAL LINES

RECTANGULAR MASSING WITH A CLOSED COURT   TRAPEZOIDAL MASSING WITH AN OPEN COURT

Figure 4   Thumbnail sketches of the A residence.

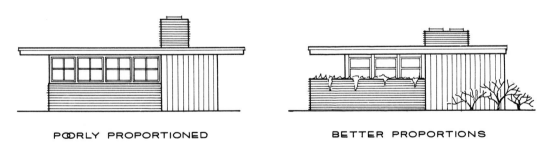

POORLY PROPORTIONED   BETTER PROPORTIONS

Figure 5   Effect of proper proportions.

Figure 6   Proportional massing lends interest to this factory warehouse.

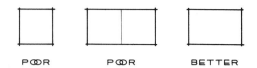

POOR   POOR   BETTER

Figure 7   Shape.

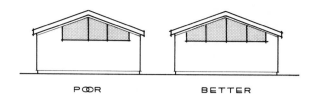

POOR   BETTER

Figure 13   Symmetrical fenestration.

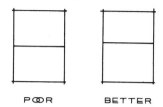

POOR   BETTER

Figure 8   Stability.

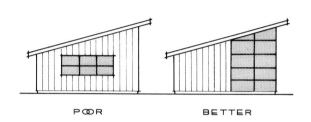

POOR   BETTER

Figure 14   Unsymmetrical fenestration.

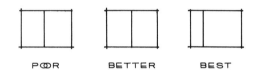

POOR   BETTER   BEST

Figure 9   Symmetry.

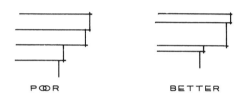

POOR   BETTER

Figure 10   Domination.

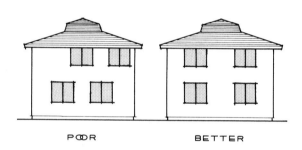

POOR   BETTER

Figure 15   Vertical alignment of windows.

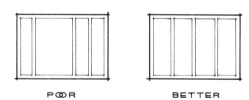

POOR   BETTER

Figure 11   Horizontal repetition.

VERY POOR

Figure 16   Disorderly fenestration.

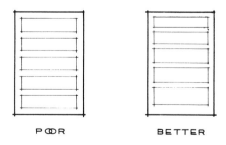

POOR   BETTER

Figure 12   Vertical repetition.

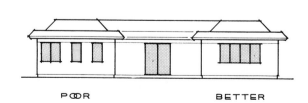

POOR   BETTER

Figure 17   Orderly fenestration.

Courtesy of Scholz Homes, Inc.

Figure 18   A symmetrical entranceway.

Courtesy of Scholz Homes, Inc.

Figure 19   An unsymmetrical entrance design.

Fenestration. The term "fenestration" deals with the arrangements of windows (and doors) in a wall. Some of the rules for satisfactory fenestration are:

1. Arrange windows symmetrically in a symmetrical elevation (Figure 13), but off center in an unsymmetrical elevation (Figure 14).
2. Line up windows on different floors. This is important for both aesthetic and structural reasons (Figure 15).
3. Do not use a variety of types and sizes of windows (Figure 16).
4. Arrange windows in groupings when possible (Figure 17).

Harmony. All features should harmonize to present a uniform elevation. Materials also should be selected to harmonize with one another. In general, it is wise to use no more than two different types of materials on one building (Figure 20).

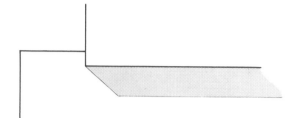

Figure 21   Shadow too simple.

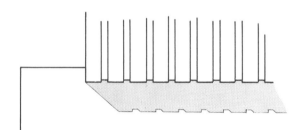

Figure 22   Shadow made more interesting by use of boards and battens.

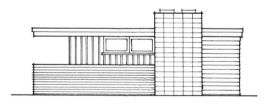

Figure 20   Lack of harmony: too many materials used.

Shadows. Consider the effect of solar orientation upon each elevation. A very simple elevation may become more interesting when designed to take full advantage of shadows. Figure 21 shows a house designed with a second floor slightly overhanging the first floor. The simple shadow lines are made more interesting by a variation in the surface casting the shadow (Figure 22), or by varying the surface receiving the shadow (Figure 23).

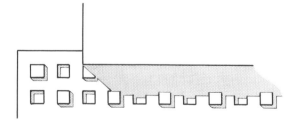

Figure 23   Shadow made more interesting by use of extended and recessed concrete blocks.

Figure 24   Actual representation (not used).

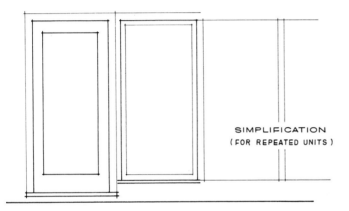

Figure 25   Standard representation.

Figure 26   Representation of hinged windows.

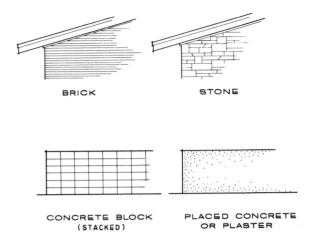

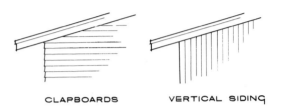

Figure 27   Representation of exterior materials.

Finished sketches. The finished sketch may be a carefully drawn freehand sketch or a drawing done with drafting instruments. If the preliminary sketch was very carefully drawn, the designer may omit the finished sketch and proceed directly to the finished elevation drawing. The scale of both is usually $\frac{1}{4}'' = 1'$ for a small residence or $\frac{1}{8}'' = 1'$ for larger buildings. Occasionally, one or two major elevations are drawn to the large $\frac{1}{4}'' = 1'$ scale, and the less important elevations are drawn to the smaller $\frac{1}{8}'' = 1'$ scale. Since these are fairly large-scale drawings, the exact size of all features must be considered together with their correct representation.

Window and door sizes. As a general rule, it is a good idea to align the tops of all exterior doors and windows. This simplifies construction by allowing the builder to use one size header for all normal wall openings and, incidentally, simplifies the drawing of the elevations. A front door will usually be 3'-0 by 6'-8'' (actual size of the door), and a rear door will be 2'-8'' by 6'-8''. A single garage door averages 9'-0 by 7'-0 high, and a double garage door 16'-0 by 7'-0 high. Window sizes must be chosen from manufacturers' catalogs, which offer a great variety of sizes and types. Windows fall into the following general types:

Fixed
Double hung (slides vertically)
Sliding (slides horizontally)
Awning (hinged at top and swings outward)
Hopper (hinged at bottom and swings inward)
Casement (hinged at side and usually swings outward)
Pivoted (hinged at center, half swings outward and half inward)
Jalousie (many individually hinged panes)

Only one or two types of windows should be specified for a house, although their sizes can be varied to suit the need.

Window and door representation. Since most architectural features are too complicated to draw in detail, certain simplifications and conventions have been established to lessen the work of the draftsman. For example, windows and doors are shown considerably simplified. Figure 24 shows how a door and window would appear if drawn completely. Fortunately, this type of representation is never used. Figure 25 shows standard representations—with lines only for the opening, the trim, and panels. Notice that even the door knob should be omitted.

A further simplification is often used: one window on an elevation is detailed as in Figure 25 and all other similar windows are merely outlined by a rectangle. The hidden lines in Figure 26 indicate a hinged window. The hinge is located where the hidden lines meet.

Material representation. Like windows and doors, materials are also represented by drawing only a few lines. Brick, for example, is indicated by several horizontal lines spaced about 3″ apart (to the proper scale) rather than showing each brick and mortar joint. When bricks are laid on edge for window sills or window and door heads, they should be shown also. Figure 27 shows the usual representation of brick, stone, concrete block, placed (poured) concrete, clapboards, and vertical siding. Roofs may be left blank.

Footings and areawalls. Hidden lines are used to indicate the location of footings, below-grade windows, and their areawalls. An areawall is a retaining wall which holds the earth back from a below-grade opening. Common materials used for areawalls are concrete, masonry, and corrugated sheets of galvanized iron. Take particular note of the hidden foundation and footing lines. Notice that the footing and the outside wall of the foundation *are* shown, but the basement floor and inside wall of the foundation are *not* shown. It is easy to remember which lines to include in an elevation view: just imagine that the ground has been removed and show only those lines that you would then see.

Labeling views. Two methods are used to label elevation views:

1. Front elevation	2. North elevation
Rear elevation	East elevation
Right end elevation	South elevation
Left end elevation	West elevation

In the second method, the north elevation is the elevation which faces generally northward, but it does not have to face exactly north. When an interior elevation is designated as a north elevation, this means the *outside* of the wall faces north, and the *inside* of the wall faces south.

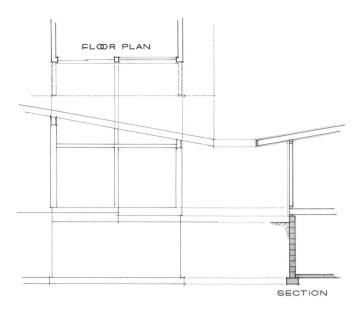

Figure 28   Step 1: layout.

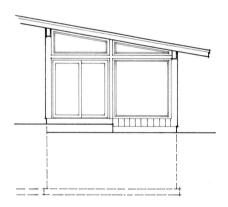

Figure 29   Step 2: details.

Dimensioning. Elevation dimensions are limited to vertical dimensions, since horizontal dimensions have already been shown on the plan. Show the depth of the footing below grade, the finished floor to finished floor heights (or finished floor to finished ceiling height for the topmost story), the roof height, and the height of the chimney above the roof. The following inside room heights (finished floor to finished ceiling) are the minimum allowable:

Basement	6′-2″ *(clear of all low beams, ducts, or pipes)*
First floor	7′-10″
Second floor	7′-4″
Garage	8′-0

Of course, when you give finished floor to finished floor heights, you must allow for the thickness of

Figure 30   Front elevation of the A residence.

Figure 31   Rear elevation of the A residence.

Figure 32   Atrium of the A residence.

the floor (finished flooring, subflooring, joists, and ceiling). This will amount to about one foot; the exact amount can be calculated by adding the actual sizes of these members as indicated on the typical section. Chimneys should extend at least 2′ above a nearby ridge line. The window schedule may be placed in any convenient location.

Changes. Remember that it is quite probable that some changes and additions in the elevations will be necessary after all the other drawings are completed.

Elevation drawing. After the elevations have been designed by use of thumbnail, preliminary, and finished sketches, the final drawing may be started. The steps used in drawing elevations are illustrated below. We will use the rear elevation of the A residence as an example:

Step 1: layout. Lay out the elevation very lightly on tracing vellum using a hard, sharp pencil (Figure 28). Using dividers or a scale, transfer horizontal dimensions from the floor plan and vertical dimensions from the sectional drawing. A scale of $\frac{1}{4}'' = 1'$ or $\frac{1}{8}'' = 1'$ is used and indicated in the title block or near the drawing. If the plan and section are drawn to the same scale as the required elevation, they may be taped in position and dimensions projected directly using a triangle and T-square. (If the plan and section have not been drawn yet, they should be drawn in rough form at this point. Save these rough drawings since they will help finish the final plan and section.)

Windows and doors are located horizontally by projecting from the plan; they are located vertically by projecting from the window and door details or simply by aligning the tops of the windows with the tops of the doors.

Step 2: details. The elevation details to be included will vary depending upon the style of the house. In the case of the A residence the following details are added (Figure 29):

1. Roof fascia
2. Roof beams
3. Chimney, saddle, and flashing
4. Window representation (if you wish, only one window is detailed)
5. Grade lines
6. Footings
7. Material representation
8. Darkened building outline

Step 3: dimensioning. Elevation dimensions and notes are added (Figures 33–37):

1. Height of roof (in this example, the roof beam height determines the roof height)

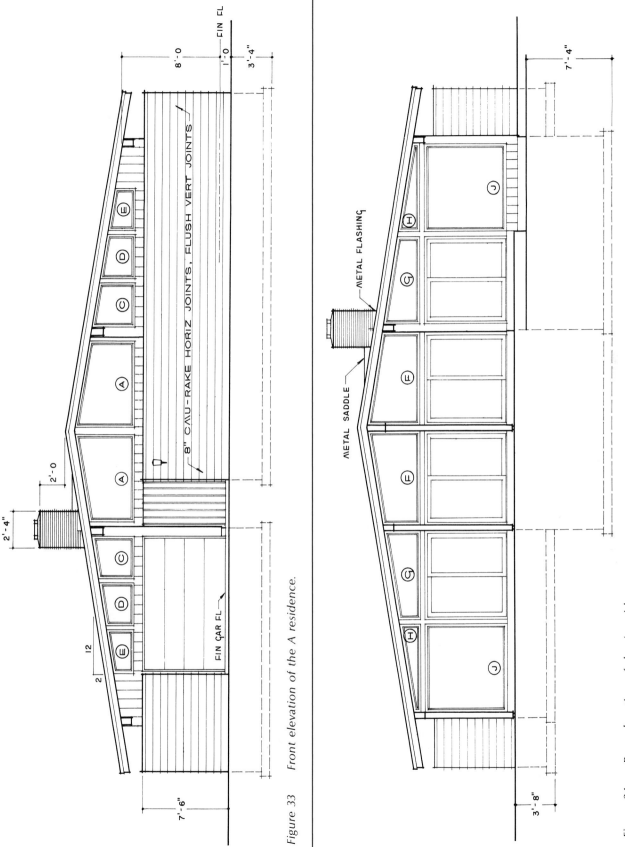

Figure 33   Front elevation of the A residence.

Figure 34   Rear elevation of the A residence.

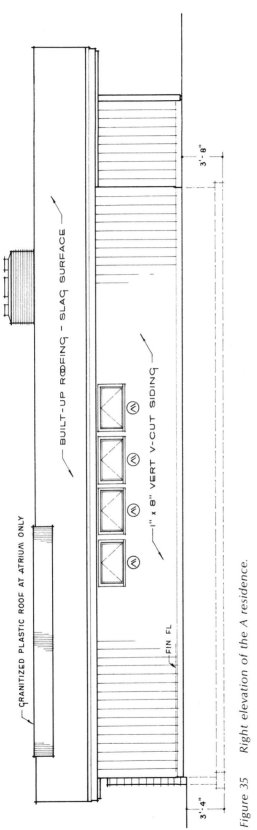

Figure 35 *Right elevation of the A residence.*

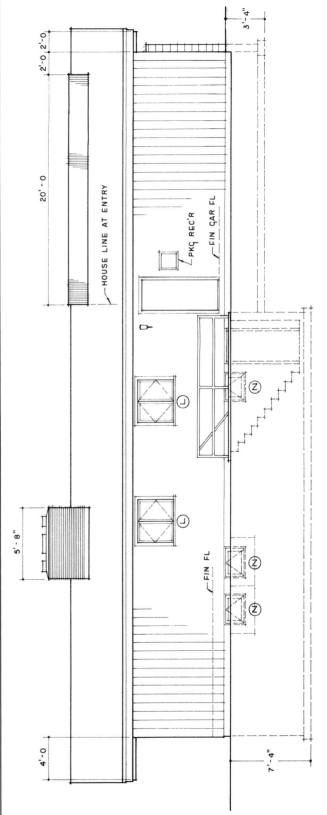

Figure 36 *Left elevation of the A residence.*

WINDOW SCHEDULE

MK	NO	SIZE	DESCRIPTION
A	2	90" x 42" x 57"	1/4" FIXED PLATE GLASS
B	3	44" x 80"	"
C	2	44" x 34" x 41"	"
D	2	44" x 26" x 33"	"
E	2	44" x 18" x 25"	"
F	2	90" x 38" x 53"	"
G	2	90" x 22" x 37"	"
H	2	90" x 6" x 21"	"
J	2	90" x 84"	"
K	2	AP421	ANDERSEN AWNING-FIXED
L	2	W2N3	CASEMENT
M	4	A41	AWNING
N	3	2820	BASEMENT

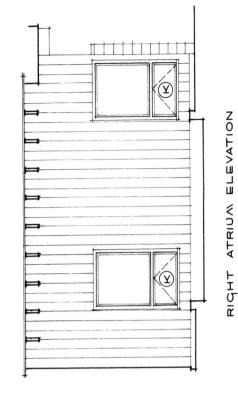

RIGHT ATRIUM ELEVATION

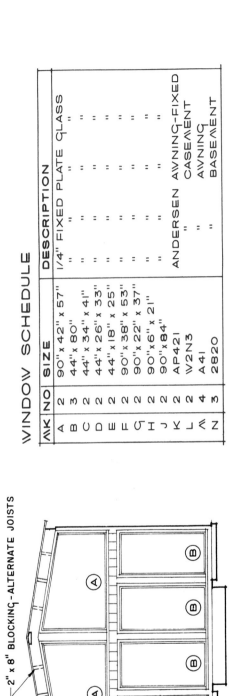

FRONT ATRIUM ELEVATION

LEFT ATRIUM ELEVATION

Figure 37   Atrium elevations of the A residence.

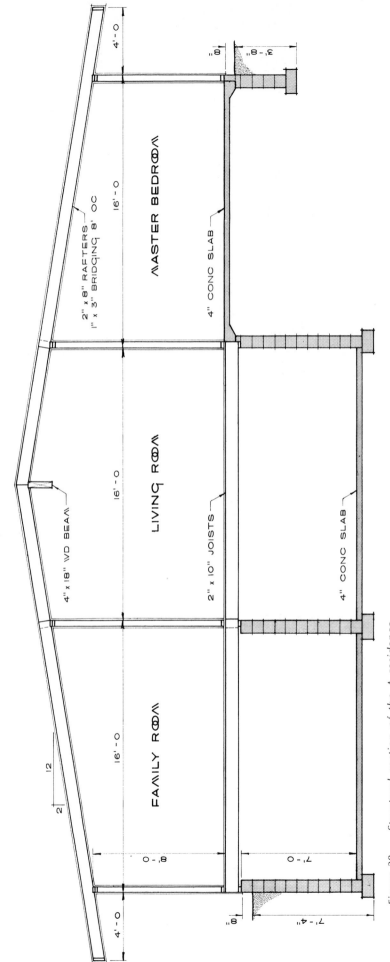

Figure 38   Structural section of the A residence.

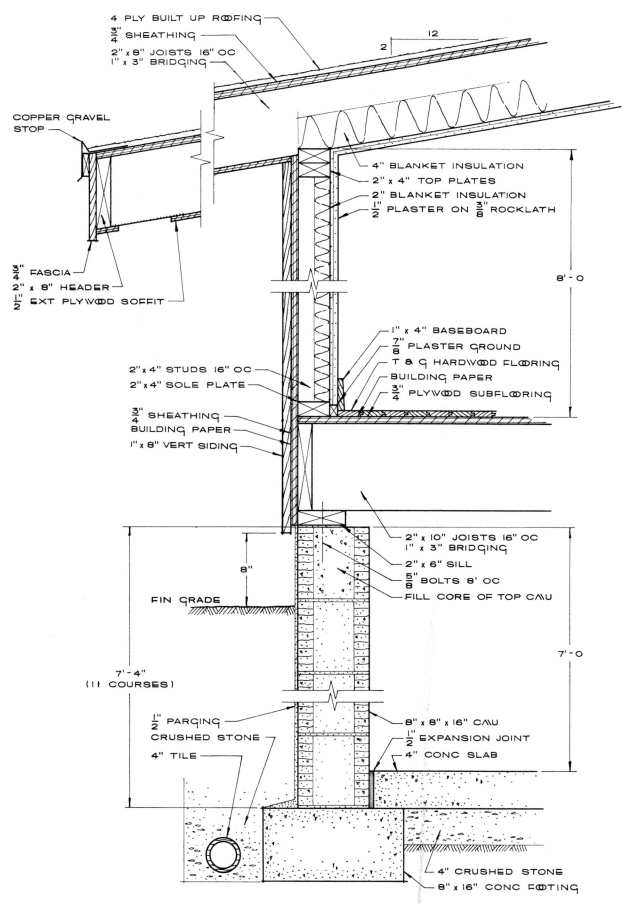

4 PLY BUILT UP ROOFING
$\frac{3}{4}$" SHEATHING
2" x 8" JOISTS 16" OC
1" x 3" BRIDGING

12
2

COPPER GRAVEL
STOP

4" BLANKET INSULATION
2" x 4" TOP PLATES
2" BLANKET INSULATION
$\frac{1}{2}$" PLASTER ON $\frac{3}{8}$" ROCKLATH

$\frac{3}{4}$" FASCIA
2" x 8" HEADER
$\frac{1}{2}$" EXT PLYWOOD SOFFIT

8'-0

1" x 4" BASEBOARD
$\frac{7}{8}$" PLASTER GROUND
T & G HARDWOOD FLOORING
BUILDING PAPER
$\frac{3}{4}$" PLYWOOD SUBFLOORING

2" x 4" STUDS 16" OC
2" x 4" SOLE PLATE

$\frac{3}{4}$" SHEATHING
BUILDING PAPER
1" x 8" VERT SIDING

2" x 10" JOISTS 16" OC
1" x 3" BRIDGING
2" x 6" SILL
$\frac{5}{8}$" BOLTS 8' OC
FILL CORE OF TOP CMU

8"

FIN GRADE

7'-0

7'-4"
(11 COURSES)

$\frac{1}{2}$" PARGING
CRUSHED STONE
4" TILE

8" x 8" x 16" CMU
$\frac{1}{2}$" EXPANSION JOINT
4" CONC SLAB

4" CRUSHED STONE
8" x 16" CONC FOOTING

Figure 39   Typical section of the A residence.

2. Depth of footings
3. Height of other features such as masonry wall and chimney
4. Height of windows (in this example, the windows fit directly under the roof and roof beams)
5. Roof slope indication
6. Window schedules
7. Titles and notes indicating materials and special details

SECTIONS

The designer shows the entire building construction by means of a few drawings called "sections." He lays out the sections in much the same order that the workmen will use in actual construction. A complete set of construction drawings would contain one or more of each of the following types of sections:

1. Structural section. A structural section shows the entire building construction. A $\frac{1}{4}'' = 1'$ scale is often used. Figure 38 shows a structural section for the A residence. This would be useful in planning for structural strength and rigidity, determining the length of members, and specifying sizes.

2. Wall section. A wall section shows the construction of a typical wall to a larger scale than the structural section ($1\frac{1}{2}'' = 1'$ is often used). Figure 39 shows a wall section for the A residence. Notice that floor to ceiling heights are shown, together with sizes and material specifications for all rough and finished members.

3. Detail section. Any deviations from the typical wall sections may be shown in detail sections. Also any special or unusual construction must be detailed, as shown in Figure 40. These sections may be drawn to a large scale (up to full size).

STUDY QUESTIONS

1. How many exterior elevations are needed to describe a building having:
   a. A rectangular floor plan
   b. An L-shaped floor plan
   c. A U-shaped floor plan
   d. An S-shaped floor plan
2. What is the purpose of:
   a. Thumbnail elevation sketches
   b. Preliminary elevation sketches
   c. Finished elevation sketches
   d. Finished elevation drawings
   Give the probable scale of each.
3. Explain how each of the following words is associated with the rules of good proportion:
   a. Squares
   b. Stability
   c. Symmetry
   d. Domination
   e. Repetition
4. Explain how each of the following words is associated with the rules of fenestration:
   a. Symmetry
   b. Alignment
   c. Variety
   d. Grouping
5. Give the most commonly used size for the following:
   a. Front door
   b. Rear door
   c. Single garage door
   d. Double garage door
6. State two methods of simplifying the representation of doors and windows.
7. How is the location of window hinges indicated on elevation drawings?
8. What is the rule for determining the below grade lines to be shown by hidden lines, and the below grade lines to be entirely omitted?
9. If an interior elevation of a room is called a *south elevation,* in what direction does the inside wall face?
10. Sketch and name three types of sectional drawings. What scale might be used for each?
11. Indicate information on wall sections:
    a. Not found on other kinds of architectural plans
    b. Repeated on other kinds of architectural plans

LABORATORY PROBLEMS

1. Using a scale of $\frac{1}{4}'' = 1'$, draw the following elevations of the A residence:
   a. Front elevation
   b. Rear elevation
   c. Right end elevation
   d. Left end elevation
   e. Atrium elevations
2. Draw the elevations of the building assigned by your instructor.
3. Complete the elevations for your original house design.
4. Draw the typical wall section of the A residence.
5. Complete the structural section for your original house design.
6. Complete the typical wall section for your original house design.
7. Complete the detail sections for your original house design.

Figure 40   Atrium pool detail for the A residence.

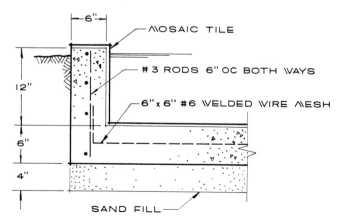

20 stairways

An important consideration in a house having more than one level is the stairway design. Often the stairway is specifically planned for its architectural effect and it can be a major design element in both traditional and contemporary house styles. In addition, the stairway must be carefully planned to conveniently perform its function of vertical circulation. Since the stairway is usually associated with the halls, it may be the key to circulation throughout the entire house.

TYPES

Straight run stairs take up the least amount of floor area and are the simplest to construct. However, some designs require a stair that turns or is shorter in length. In these cases, the designer specifies a U-type or L-type stair with a platform at the turn. The platform does have the safety feature of breaking up a long run of stairs and providing a place to pause and rest. When space is restricted, diagonal steps called

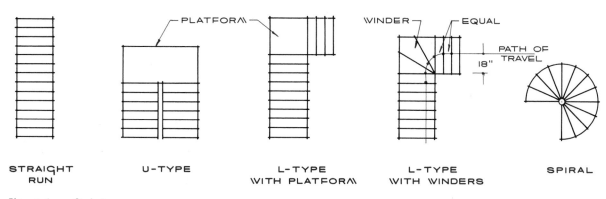

| STRAIGHT RUN | U-TYPE | L-TYPE WITH PLATFORM | L-TYPE WITH WINDERS | SPIRAL |

Figure 1   Stair types.

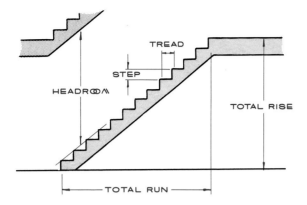

Figure 2   Stairway terminology.

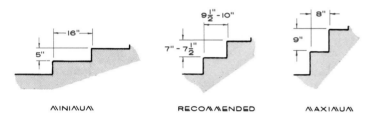

Figure 3   Stair pitch.

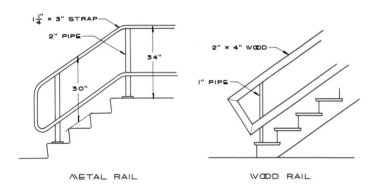

Figure 4   Contemporary handrails.

Stair Dimensions

Total Rise	Number of Risers	Riser	Tread	Total Run
8'-0	13	7.38"	9½"	9'-6"
8'-6"	14	7.29"	9¾"	10'-6¾"
9'-0	15	7.20"	9¾"	11'-4½"
9'-6"	16	7.13"	10"	12'-6"
10'-0	17	7.06"	10"	13'-4"

"winders" are used in place of the platform. Winders are designed so that the same tread depth is maintained at the normal path of travel: 18" from the inside corner. Since the tread depth is reduced inside the normal path of travel, it is obvious that winders are dangerous and should be used only as a last resort. Also avoid single steps to sunken rooms. There is less likelihood of a person tripping on two or more steps. Spiral stairs may be obtained in packaged units and will satisfy unique design requirements.

TERMS

The terms generally used in stairway design are illustrated in Figure 2.

Step or *Riser* is the vertical distance from one tread top to another.

Tread or *Run* is the horizontal distance from the face of one riser to the next. Notice that there will always be one less tread than riser.

Total Rise is the vertical distance from one finished floor to the next. This is a basic measurement in stair planning.

Total Run is the horizontal distance of the entire stairway.

Headroom is the vertical distance from the outside edge of the step to the ceiling above.

Nosing is the projection of the tread beyond the riser. It should be about 1⅛", as shown in Figure 6, and is not considered as part of the stair tread when laying out the stairway.

DESIGN

All stairways do not have the same slope or pitch. They may vary from a 5–16 pitch (that is, a 5" rise with a 16" run) to a 9–8 pitch (a 9" rise with an 8" run). A pitch less than the 5–16 limit will require a ramp; a pitch greater than 9–8 will require a step ladder or rung ladder. Figure 3 shows the minimum pitch of 5–16, which may be used for outside or monumental stairs; the recommended pitches for most stairways of 7–10 to 7½–9½; and the maximum possible pitch of 9–8. The 9–8 pitch is not recommended in a house, but may be used on board ship almost as a ladder. It is assumed that no one would use such steep stairs without holding the handrails. An 8–9 pitch (not to be confused with a 9–8 pitch) is very satisfactory for basement stairs.

In Figure 3 notice that as the run dimension decreases, the rise dimension will increase so that the over-all distance from step to step remains about the same. This fact has given us this general rule:

Rule 1   Rise + Run = 17

For example, if you decide upon a 7″ rise, the tread should be 10″. Two slightly more sophisticated rules may be used for additional checks:

Rule 2   2 × Rise + Run = 24 to 25

Notice that the 9″ rise and 8″ run would not be satisfactory according to this rule since 2 × 9 + 8 will equal 26. The 7–10 pitch, however, will equal 24, which is acceptable.

Rule 3   Rise × Run = 70 to 75

The 7–10 pitch used in the two preceding examples would equal 7 × 10 = 70, which is acceptable. None of the above rules should be used to check for monumental stairs.

Allow 7′-0 minimum headroom on a stairway, but 7′-6″ is preferred. 6′-6″ headroom may be used for basement stairs. The most comfortable handrail height is 30″ on a stair and 34″ on a landing, as shown in Figure 4. The minimum comfortable stair width is 3′-0, but 3′-6″ or 4′-0 is better for moving furniture.

LAYOUT

Tables like Table I have been devised to simplify some of the stair calculations. A stairway is best laid out using the following method.

Step 1. Draw two horizontal lines representing the finished floors to a scale of $\frac{1}{2}″ = 1′$-0. In Figure 5, the distance between finished floors (total rise) is 9′-0.

Step 2. Using Table I, we shall have 15 risers of 7.20″ each and 14 treads (treads = risers − 1) of $9\frac{3}{4}″$ each, with a total run of 11′-$4\frac{1}{2}″$. Lay out the total run to scale.

Step 3. Since there are 15 risers, divide the total rise into 15 equal parts using your scale at an angle so that the zero mark is on the other finished floor.

Step 4. Since there are 14 treads, divide the total run into 14 equal parts in the same manner using the zero mark and the 7″ mark.

Step 5. Darken in the outline of the stairway adding details like those shown in Figure 18.

A similar procedure is used for U-type, L-type, and circular stairs.

CONSTRUCTION

Figures 6–10 show different types of stairs. A 2″ × 12″ member would be used for the open stringer in Figure 11. Incidentally, the triangular pieces cut from

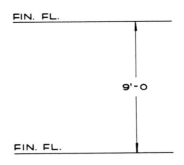

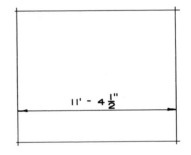

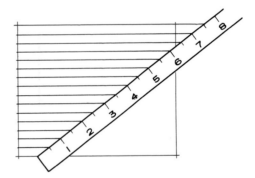

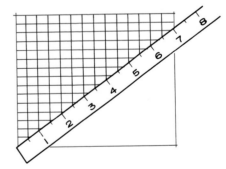

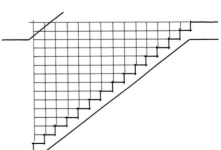

Figure 5   Stair layout (new steps shown in black).

Figure 6   A large radius spiral stairway.

Figure 7   Stair treads cantilevered from a central support.

this 2″ × 12″ are often nailed to a 2″ × 4″—serving as a middle stringer for extra support. Closed stringers are slightly different from open stringers in that no triangular pieces are cut from the stringer (Figure 11). Rather, ½″ grooves are routed to receive the treads and risers which are wedged and glued in place. This completely conceals their ends. The tongue and groove construction between riser and tread is often omitted for economy. Prefabricated stairways are becoming increasingly popular. Figure 12 shows one method of simplifying stair construction by the use of preformed metal stair guides.

Stock components are often used for stairs and railings in commercial buildings. In addition to the metal systems shown in Figures 13 to 15, a ½″ tempered glass railing is available (Figure 16).

STAIR DETAILS

A complete set of stair details includes a section or elevation together with a plan view of each stairway. Details of tread construction and handrail construction may be included. Some of these drawings may be incorporated with other plans. The stair plan, for example, may be satisfactorily shown on the floor plan. Notice in Figure 18 that arrows with the notation "UP" and "DN" are used to show stair direction. The number of risers is also included. Always use capital letters for "UP" and "DN" notations, since when viewed from the opposite direction, a lower case "up" looks like "dn" and a lower case "dn" looks like "up." When there are both "up" and "down" stairs over one another, they are separated by a break line.

Figures 17 and 18 show details of the stairs for the A residence and the Z residence.

TREILLAGE*

Treillage is used for building facing, partitions, room dividers, privacy fences, or concealment of unsightly elements. Stock components are available in many patterns (Figures 19 to 21).

*Pronounced "trail-lige" in French, with the accent on the first syllable. The last syllable is pronounced like the last syllable in the word "pillage."

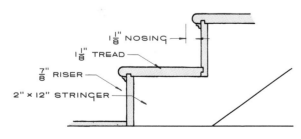

Figure 8   Closed riser stair.

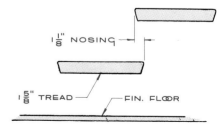

Figure 9   Open riser stair.

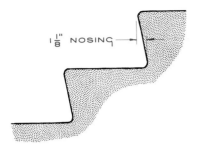

Figure 10   Concrete stair.

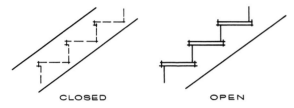

Figure 11   Stringer types.

Figure 12   Installing metal stairguides.

OPTIONS FOR MOUNTING
Connectorail® posts may be embedded in floor slab or side mounted on facia or stringer by means of facia flanges. A solid aluminum rod insert is used at the base of the post for added strength and stiffness.

ADJUSTABLE BRACKETS
An adjustable bracket may be fitted to the post by means of a simple adapter. The handrail bracket tilts to conform to stair angle. Recommended for ramps or unusual stair angles.

MECHANICAL CONNECTIONS
Non-welded connections eliminate welding discoloration and expensive grinding. Strong structural adhesive, stainless steel machine screws with lock washers, and threaded tubular rivets assure positive connections at joints.

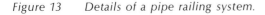

Figure 13   Details of a pipe railing system.

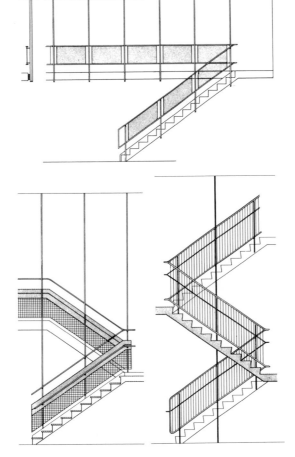

Figure 14   Some stock metal railing designs.

STUDY QUESTIONS

1. Give the main advantage and disadvantage of:
   a. Introducing a platform into a straight run of stairs
   b. Using winders in place of a platform in an L-type stairway
2. What is the difference between:
   a. Rise and total rise
   b. Run and total run
   c. 8-9 pitch and 9-8 pitch
   d. Open stringer and closed stringer
   e. Open riser and closed riser
3. Using each of the three rules of rise and run proportions, figure the tread dimensions for:
   a. a 7″ rise
   b. a 7½″ rise
   c. an 8″ rise
4. How many risers and treads should be specified for a total rise of:
   a. 8′-9″
   b. 4′-9″ (split level house)
   c. 1′-9″ (sunken room)
5. Show how to divide any line into three equal parts using:
   a. Your scale
   b. Your dividers
   Do not use trial and error solutions.
6. (For the advanced student) After a thorough library search, prepare an illustrated paper on the history of the

BRACKET AND SUPPORT SECTION
The handrail bracket can be tilted to conform to stair angle. Bracket extensions allow variation in length to conform to varying conditions. Tee-shaped support sections give **Colorail** the required stiffness.

BRACKET ASSEMBLY
The **Colorail** bracket assembly has two interlocking parts which, engaged with the bracket arm, clamp the tee-shaped handrail support bar for convenient field assembly without drilling and tapping.

FLOOR MOUNTING
Floor mounting is provided for three post sizes. An aluminum floor cover flange is used for finished appearance. Posts may be embedded in concrete or mechanically fastened under flooring.

Figure 15   Details of a metal railing system.

POST CONSTRUCTION
Post assemblies include plastic-clad aluminum post whose hollow core houses concealed fastening devices. Sleeves provide color variation in one of five colors.

development of the various methods of vertical circulation in buildings.

7. (For the advanced student) After a thorough library search, give your estimate of the status of the various methods of vertical circulation 50 years hence.

LABORATORY PROBLEMS

1. Draw the plan and sectional elevation of:
   a. Interior stairway of the A residence
   b. Exterior stairway of the A residence
   c. Main stairway of the Z residence
2. Draw the plan and sectional elevation of stairways with the following requirements:
   a. Straight run, 13 risers to the basement of a ranch house, total rise = 8'-6"
   b. Straight run, 7 risers between two levels of a split level house, total rise = 4'-3"

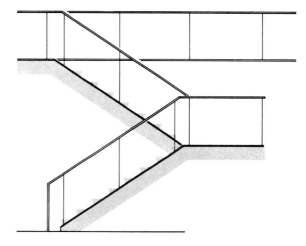

Figure 16   Structural glass railing.

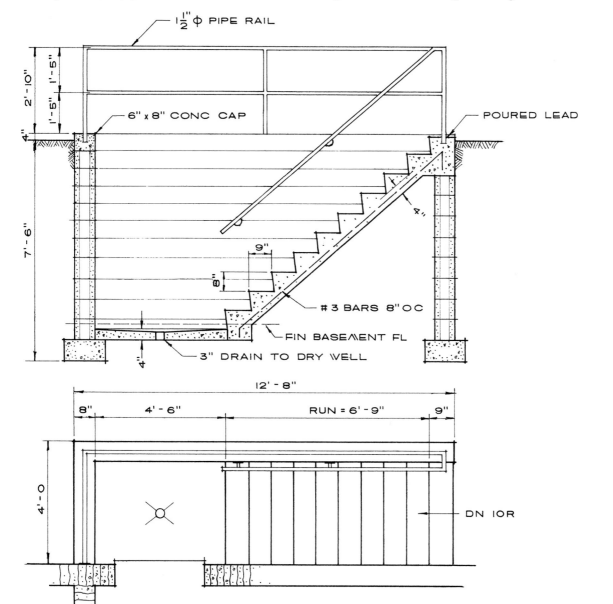

Figure 17   Exterior stairway detail of the A residence.

c. U-type, 7 risers each between three levels of a split level house, total rise = 8'-8"

d. L-type, 3 risers and 11 risers (14 risers total) to the second floor of a two story apartment, total rise = 8'-9"

3. Prepare a classroom illustration showing:
   a. Stairway terminology
   b. Stairway construction
   c. Recommended stairway dimensions for tread, rise, width, headroom, and handrail heights
4. (For the advanced student) Design a means of vertical circulation that is entirely different from those now commonly used.
5. Draw the stairway details for the building assigned by your instructor.
6. Complete the stairway details for your original house design.

Figure 19   Use of treillage for architectural effect.

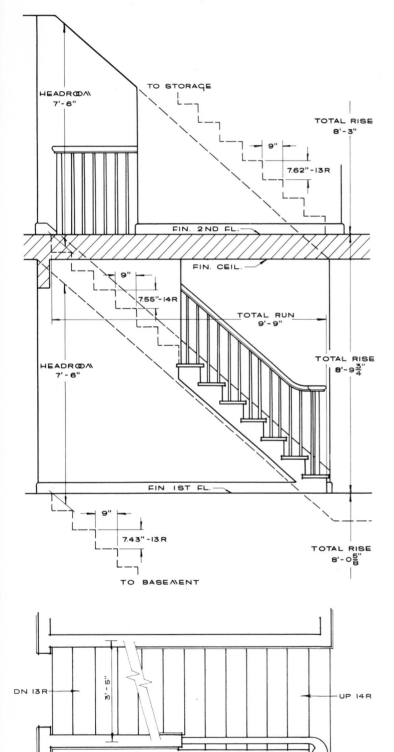

Figure 18   Stair detail of the Z residence.

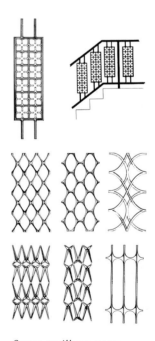

Figure 20   Some treillage patterns.

SHORT POST FOR COUNTER SCREEN

PANELS WITH SPANS OVER 4'-0" WIDTH AND 4'-6" HEIGHT MUST USE A CENTER SUPPORT

Figure 21   Some stock treillage designs.

21 fireplaces and chimneys

The fireplace, although no longer a necessity as the major heat source, is considered by many to be a "must" luxury. A blazing fire or glowing embers on a cold winter day create a mood of cheerfulness and comfort which cannot be achieved by a concealed heating system. The fireplace is usually the major element of interior design in a living room or family room. In addition, it is occasionally specified for the family-type kitchen or master bedroom. Careful planning and thoughtful design are always required to obtain proper styling, the best location in a room, and coordination with the heating plant and the other fireplaces in the house.

STYLING

Several types of fireplaces are illustrated in Figure 1. Notice that the designer may work with a great variety of sizes and styles of fireplace openings, hearths, mantels, and materials. Fireplace openings may be single faced (the basic type), double faced (with faces on adjacent or opposite sides), three-faced (serving as a peninsula partition between two areas), or even free standing (in the center of an area). Multi-faced fireplaces are associated with contemporary design, but corner fireplaces have been in use for many years. The double faced (opposite sides) and three-faced fireplaces are often used as room dividers, but they are not particularly useful for heating as the open design reduces the reflection of heat. Also large flues must be used to obtain an adequate chimney draft. Cross-drafts may cause smoke to enter the room unless glass fire screens are added.

Hearths may be flush with the floor or raised to any desired height. The back hearth serves as the base for the fire; the front hearth protects a combustible floor from sparks. The front hearth and edges of the fireplace opening may be surfaced with an ornamental material such as a ceramic tile, which is highly heat resistant. Mantels may be of various designs or omitted entirely. Brick, block, stone, tile, and metal are used for fireplace construction. When the fireplace is used as the primary element in the decorative scheme, log bins, shelves, or cabinets are often included.

FUEL

The usual fuel is wood: softwood for kindling and logs of hickory, birch, beech, ash, oak, or maple. Andirons or some form of grating may be an integral part of the fireplace design. A suspended grill might be considered for indoor charcoal grilling.

LOCATION

A fireplace may be located on a wall, in a corner, on a projecting corner, or free standing. When the

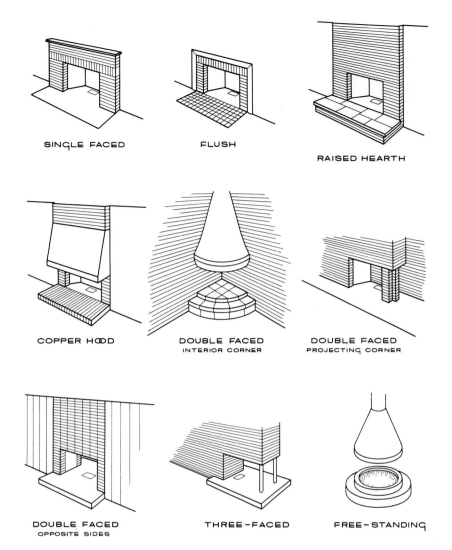

SINGLE FACED

FLUSH

RAISED HEARTH

COPPER HOOD

DOUBLE FACED
INTERIOR CORNER

DOUBLE FACED
PROJECTING CORNER

DOUBLE FACED
OPPOSITE SIDES

THREE-FACED

FREE-STANDING

Figure 1   Fireplace types.

fireplace is to be located on a wall, the designer must choose between interior and exterior walls. Most older houses located chimneys in the center of the house: they drew better and the heat could not escape directly outdoors. Newer houses tend to have exterior wall chimneys to save floor space. The exterior chimney can be a distinct feature of the exterior design; however, more flashing and finish brick is required. Remember that a frame structure is weakened by having a masonry fireplace and chimney on an exterior wall; a masonry structure is stiffened.

Split level houses pose a special problem because the chimney should not emerge at a location close to higher elevation roofs. The chimney will not draw properly unless it is extended at least 2′ higher than any portion of the roof located within 10′ (see Figure 3).

SIZE

Figures 4 and 5 give minimum and recommended dimensions for single and multi-faced fireplace designs: some of these dimensions will vary according to the size category as shown in Table I. The size category will depend upon the room size and the emphasis to be placed upon the fireplace. For example, the *medium* size fireplace might be specified for a living room of 300 sq. ft.; the *medium large* size for a living room of 350 sq. ft. Notice that the dimensions in Figure 4 are nearly all multiples of 4″. To reduce the amount of brick trimming and waste, it is important to establish a modular system such as that shown in Figure 6. Here a $2\frac{1}{6}″ \times 3\frac{1}{2}″ \times 7\frac{1}{2}″$ modular brick is laid up with $\frac{1}{2}″$ joints resulting in a 4″ module. Table III may be consulted for a quick

Figure 2   A single faced fireplace with raised hearth.

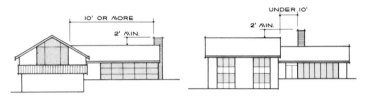

Figure 3   Minimum chimney height.

reference of modular sizes of brick, tile, and block. If you are using common brick, Norman brick, Roman brick, or some other tile or block size, it is a good idea to make up a similar table. The actual sizes of these bricks are given in Table II.

CONSTRUCTION

A chimney is a complete structure in its own right—unsupported by any wooden member of the house framing. Recall how often you have seen a house that has burned to the ground, while the chimney remained standing. It is equally improper to use the chimney as a support for girders, joists, or rafters, since a wooden member framing into a chimney may eventually settle and crack it. Actually, no framing lumber should come closer than 2″ from the chimney due to the fire hazard. The 2″ space should be filled with noncombustible material to act as a fire stop. Subflooring, flooring, and roof sheathing may come within $\frac{3}{4}$″ of the chimney.

Figure 7 shows the type of overlapping flashing used at the roof. This allows movement between the chimney and roof due to settling without damage to the flashing.

The construction of a fireplace and chimney should be entrusted only to experienced workmen, since improper construction can cause a fire hazard or a smoking fireplace. Due to its great weight, the chimney should have a sizeable footing. Each fire-

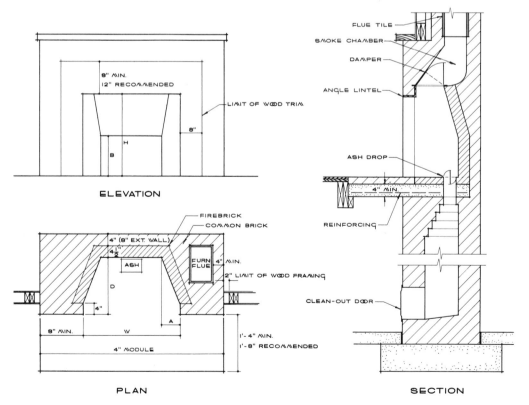

Figure 4   Fireplace dimensions.

TABLE I
Sizes for Fireplace Design

Size Category	Width of Opening W	Height of Opening H	Depth of Opening D	A*	B*	Nominal Flue Size
Single faced						
Very small	2'-0	2'-0	1'-5"	6"	1'-0	8" × 12"
Small	2'-8"	2'-3"	1'-8"	$6\frac{1}{2}$"	1'-2"	12" × 12"
Medium (most common)	3'-0	2'-5"	1'-8"	$6\frac{1}{2}$"	1'-2"	12" × 12"
Medium large	3'-4"	2'-5"	1'-8"	$6\frac{1}{2}$"	1'-2"	12" × 16"
Large	4'-0	2'-8"	2'-0	9"	1'-4"	16" × 16"
Very large	5'-0	3'-1"	2'-0	9"	1'-4"	16" × 20"
Double faced, corner						
Small	2'-8"	2'-3"	1'-8"		1'-2"	12" × 16"
Medium	3'-0	2'-5"	1'-8"		1'-2"	16" × 16"
Medium large	3'-4"	2'-5"	1'-8"		1'-2"	16" × 16"
Large	4'-0	2'-5"	2'-0		1'-2"	16" × 16"
Double faced, opposite sides						
Small	2'-8"	2'-5"	3'-0			16" × 16"
Medium	3'-0	2'-5"	3'-0			16" × 20"
Medium large	3'-4"	2'-5"	3'-0			16" × 20"
Large	4'-0	2'-8"	3'-0			20" × 20"
Three-faced						
Small	3'-4"	2'-3"	3'-0			20" × 20"
Medium	3'-8"	2'-3"	3'-0			20" × 20"
Medium large	4'-0	2'-3"	3'-0			20" × 20"
Large	4'-8"	2'-3"	3'-0			20" × 24"

*See Figure 4 or 5.

place is fitted with an ash dump (5" × 8" is a common stock size) to the ash pit which is fitted in turn with a clean-out door (12" × 12" is often used). The hearth is supported by a 4" thick concrete slab reinforced with $\frac{3}{8}$" diameter bars spaced 6" oc both ways. The opening to the fireplace is spanned by a steel angle lintel using 4" × $3\frac{1}{2}$" × $\frac{5}{16}$" stock. The back and sides of the fireplace are firebrick laid up in fire-clay mortar which is more heat resistant than ordinary brick and mortar. The sides are sloped to direct the heat toward the room and the smoke to the smoke chamber. A metal damper set below the smoke chamber is used to control the draft. The damper and the base of the smoke chamber form a smoke shelf which is important in preventing backdraft. The smoke chamber is corbeled into the flue itself, which conducts the smoke and waste gas safely outside.

Tile flue. The flue is often constructed of rectangular terra cotta tiles surrounded by 4" or 8" masonry. For proper draft, the area of the flue should not be less than $\frac{1}{10}$ the area of the fireplace opening. When computing the flue size of multi-faced fireplaces, the

TABLE II
Masonry Sizes

Modular brick	$2\frac{1}{6}$" × $3\frac{1}{2}$" × $7\frac{1}{2}$"
Common brick	$2\frac{1}{4}$" × $3\frac{3}{4}$" × 8"
Norman brick	$2\frac{1}{4}$" × $3\frac{3}{4}$" × 12"
Roman brick	$1\frac{5}{8}$" × $3\frac{3}{4}$" × 12"
Firebrick	$2\frac{1}{4}$" × $4\frac{1}{2}$" × 9"
Tile	$4\frac{5}{6}$" × $7\frac{1}{2}$" × $11\frac{1}{2}$"
Block	$7\frac{5}{8}$" × $7\frac{5}{8}$" × $15\frac{5}{8}$"

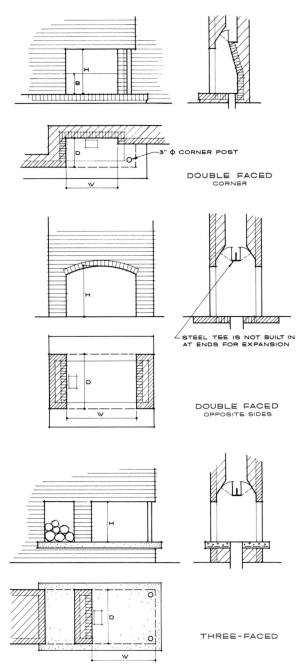

DOUBLE FACED
CORNER

3" φ CORNER POST

STEEL TEE IS NOT BUILT IN
AT ENDS FOR EXPANSION

DOUBLE FACED
OPPOSITE SIDES

THREE-FACED

Figure 5   Multi-faced fireplace designs.

areas of *all* faces must be included. The flue tile sizes given in Table I meet this requirement. A sharp chimney capping, usually obtained by extending the flue tile 4″ above the masonry, also improves draft. Remember to extend the chimney 2′ higher than any portion of a roof located within 10′. A tall chimney has a naturally better draft than a short chimney.

Each fireplace or furnace must have a separate flue to prevent the interference of drafts, although these flues may all be combined within a common chimney. This is usually stated, "a flue for every fire." For example, an average home may have two flues: one for the oil furnace and another for the living room fireplace. Both the flues should be set side by side in one chimney separated by 4″ of brick (called a "withe"). Even a house with no fireplace must have a chimney if it is heated by an oil, coal, or gas fired furnace. For the flue size, see the manufacturer's specifications; 12″ × 12″ is often used.

Prefabricated flue. The prefabricated non-masonry flue and chimney shown in Figure 8 consist of insulated and fireproof flue sections and a metal housing placed above the roof to simulate a masonry chimney. This costs considerably less than a masonry chimney and is often used for oil and gas furnace flues.

Fireplace liner. Since a skilled mason is needed for the proper construction of a masonry fireplace, metal fireplace liners are often used (Figure 11). These liners consist of the fireplace sides and back, damper, smoke shelf, and smoke chamber all in one prefabricated unit and provide a form for the mason to work to. They also contain a duct system which draws in the room-air through inlet registers, warms it, and then discharges it back to the room through outlet registers. This increases the heating capacity of the fireplace.

Metal fireplaces. Fireplaces constructed entirely of metal have been used for many years, and faithful simulations of these early models are still manufac-

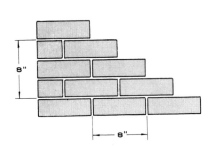

8″

8″

Figure 6   Common brick modular dimensions.

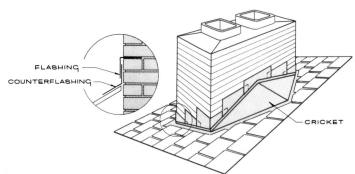

FLASHING

COUNTERFLASHING

CRICKET

Figure 7   Chimney flashing.

tured. Some contemporary types made of sheet steel are shown in Figures 12 to 15.

Since a metal fireplace is usually used with a metal chimney, the cost is quite low. In addition, a metal fireplace heats up faster and gives more heat than a masonry fireplace.

Metal fireplaces are sold in a variety of sizes, colors, and coatings. Some are made of porcelain enamel steel in a choice of colors. Others use black painted sheet steel. Others come with a factory prime coat over heavy gauge sheet steel—leaving the final choice of color to the user. Steel fireplaces can be hung from a wall or ceiling, stand on a platform on their own legs, or be recessed into the floor.

FIREPLACE AND CHIMNEY DETAILS

The architect shows the fireplace and chimney design by means of detail drawings and specifications. The detail drawings usually consist of a front elevation showing the design of the fireplace opening and trim, and sectional plans showing dimensions of the fireplace and chimney together with flue placement. A

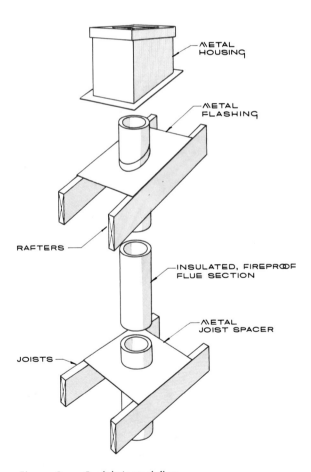

Figure 8   Prefabricated flue.

TABLE III
Masonry Sizes (3 brick + 3 joints = 8″)

Number of Courses				Number of Courses			
Modular Brick	Tile	Block	Size	Modular Brick	Tile	Block	Size
1			2⅔″	51		17	11′-4″
2	1		5⅓″	52	26		11′-6⅔″
3		1	8″	53			11′-9⅓″
4	2		10⅔″	54	27	18	12′-0
5			1′-1⅓″	55			12′-2⅔″
6	3	2	1′-4″	56	28		12′-5⅓″
7			1′-6⅔″	57		19	12′-8″
8	4		1′-9⅓″	58	29		12′-10⅔″
9		3	2′-0	59	-		13′-1⅓″
10	5		2′-2⅔″	60	30	20	13′-4″
11			2′-5⅓″	61			13′-6⅔″
12	6	4	2′-8″	62	31		13′-9⅓″
13			2′-10⅔″	63		21	14′-0
14	7		3′-1⅓″	64	32		14′-2⅔″
15		5	3′-4″	65			14′-5⅓″
16	8		3′-6⅔″	66	33	22	14′-8″
17			3′-9⅓″	67			14′-10⅔″
18	9	6	4′-0	68	34		15′-1⅓″
19			4′-2⅔″	69		23	15′-4″
20	10		4′-5⅓″	70	35		15′-6⅔″
21		7	4′-8″	71			15′-9⅓″
22	11		4′-10⅔″	72	36	24	16′-0
23			5′-1⅓″	73			16′-2⅔″
24	12	8	5′-4″	74	37		16′-5⅓″
25			5′-6⅔″	75		25	16′-8″
26	13		5′-9⅓″	76	38		16′-10⅔″
27		9	6′-0	77			17′-1⅓″
28	14		6′-2⅔″	78	39	26	17′-4″
29			6′-5⅓″	79			17′-6⅔″
30	15	10	6′-8″	80	40		17′-9⅓″
31			6′-10⅔″	81		27	18′-0
32	16		7′-1⅓″	82	41		18′-2⅔″
33		11	7′-4″	83			18′-5⅓″
34	17		7′-6⅔″	84	42	28	18′-8″
35			7′-9⅓″	85			18′-10⅔″
36	18	12	8′-0	86	43		19′-1⅓″
37			8′-2⅔″	87		29	19′-4″
38	19		8′-5⅓″	88	44		19′-6⅔″
39		13	8′-8″	89			19′-9⅓″
40	20		8′-10⅔″	90	45	30	20′-0
41			9′-1⅓″	91			20′-2⅔″
42	21	14	9′-4″	92	46		20′-5⅓″
43			9′-6⅔″	93		31	20′-8″
44	22		9′-9⅓″	94	47		20′-10⅔″
45		15	10′-0	95			21′-1⅓″
46	23		10′-2⅔″	96	48	32	21′-4″
47			10′-5⅓″	97			21′-6⅔″
48	24	16	10′-8″	98	49		21′-9⅓″
49			10′-10⅔″	99		33	22′-0
50	25		11′-1⅓″	100	50		22′-2⅔″

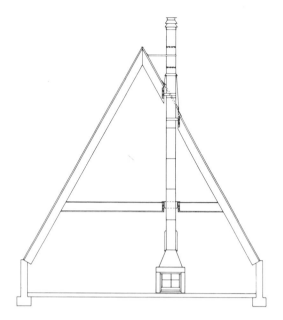

Figure 9   *Installation of a metal fireplace prefabricated flue.*

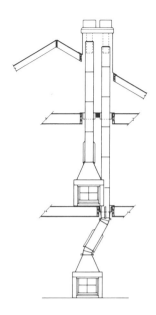

Figure 10   *Installation of metal fireplaces on two levels.*

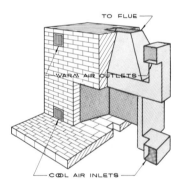

Figure 11   *Metal fireplace liner.*

Figure 12   *Wood-burning metal fireplace.*

side vertical section may be included. A $\frac{1}{2}'' = 1'-0$ scale is often used. Some dimensions, such as the height of the chimney above the roof, are shown in the house elevation views.

Figure 16 shows the detail drawings of the fireplaces for the A residence. Notice that dimensions are based upon the 4" module to reduce the amount of brick cutting.

STUDY QUESTIONS

1. Compare the advantages and disadvantages of a chimney located on an interior wall with a chimney located on an exterior wall.

Figure 13   *Wall hung steel fireplace.*

Figure 14   *Ceramic fireplace available in several colors.*

2. Why should a chimney be extended higher than any nearby construction?
3. What is the actual size of:
   a. Common brick
   b. Modular brick
   c. Firebrick
   d. Roman brick
   e. Norman brick
4. Why is it considered poor practice to frame a girder into a chimney?
5. What is the purpose of the:
   a. Ash dump
   b. Clean-out door
   c. Front hearth
   d. Damper
   e. Smoke shelf
   f. Firebrick
   g. Flue
   h. Steel lintel over fireplace opening
6. How many flues are required for an oil-heated house with two fireplaces?
7. What are the advantages of a fireplace liner?
8. What are the disadvantages of multi-faced fireplaces?

LABORATORY PROBLEMS

1. Draw the fireplace details for the A residence:
   a. First floor fireplace
   b. Basement fireplace
2. Draw the fireplace and chimney details as assigned by your instructor:

Location:	a. Interior wall	
	b. Exterior wall	
	c. Corner	
Size:	a. Small	
	b. Average	
	c. Medium large	
Styling:	a. Traditional	
	b. Contemporary	
Fireplace openings:	a. Single faced	
	b. Double faced with adjacent faces	
	c. Double faced with opposite faces	
	d. Three faced	
	e. Four faced	
Materials:	a. Modular brick	
	b. Norman brick	

Figure 15   *Metal fireplace in an office setting.*

c. Roman brick
d. Common brick with ceramic tile
e. Block
f. Stone

Hearth: a. Flush with floor
b. Raised 12″ from floor

Accessories: a. Log bin
b. Built-in bookshelves
c. Built-in record cabinet
d. Fireplace liner with air registers

3. Complete the fireplace and chimney details for your original house design.

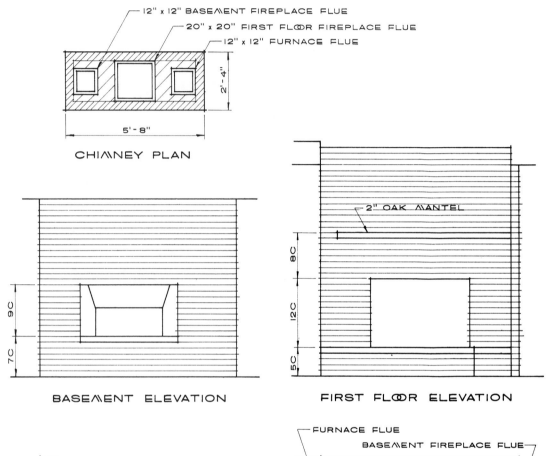

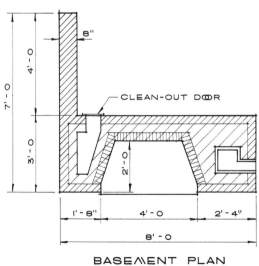

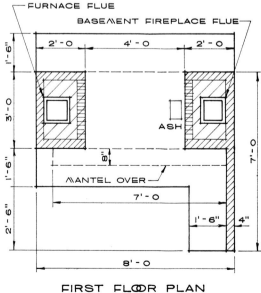

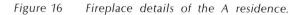

Figure 16   Fireplace details of the A residence.

Figure 17   *A finished fireplace of the A residence.*

22 architectural models

Models have always been an important tool of the architect. Before the discovery of the blueprinting process, architects used models to describe their projects to craftsmen. It was common practice to scale measurements directly from working models. Architects also used presentation models to attract new patrons, carrying models of their best works from town to town.

The model of an Egyptian residence shown in Figure 1 was taken from the XI Dynasty tomb of Meket-Re. It is one of the oldest known models, dating to 2500 B.C. It was built of carved, painted wood. Walls were mitered together and mortised to the base. Tree branches, leaves, and fruit were made of doweled wood, and the atrium pool was lined with copper sheet to hold water.

Nearly everything we use in today's living was first constructed in model form. The ground, water, and air vehicles we ride in, the commercial, industrial, and educational structures we work in, and the residences we live in were all modeled before they were actually built. The construction of architectural models, therefore, is a definite part of the services performed by the architect and is a useful skill for the architectural draftsman.

TYPES OF MODELS

Various kinds of architectural models are used for different purposes. In general, though, architectural models fall into two categories: study models and presentation models.

Figure 1   Model of an Egyptian residence. Cairo Museum. Photograph by the Egyptian Expedition. The Metropolitan Museum of Art.

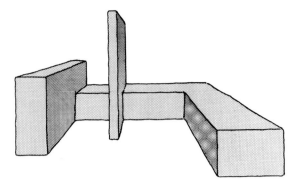

Figure 2   Mass model.

Study models. The study model, as the name implies, is constructed by the designer to help him *study* the function or appearance of a building. A study model is built during the planning stage and may be modified many times before a satisfactory solution is found. Obviously, then, a study model is not a carefully constructed finished model. In fact, very crude materials may be used. A *mass model*, for

example, is used to study the general effect of the position (or *massing*) of architectural elements (see Figure 2). Modeling clay is an excellent medium for this, although balsa wood, styrofoam, soap, and even raw potatoes are used. Other types of "thumbnail" models may be used to study plot contours, roof intersections, landscaping, interiors, and the like.

Presentation models. Presentation models are finished scale models showing *exactly* how a proposed building will appear and function. They may be built after the preliminary planning stage to help the architect explain his ideas to the clients, or they may be built after the finished plans are drawn to help the clients raise money for the actual construction. In larger offices, the presentation models are built by a special model-making department; smaller offices often contract with professional architectural model building concerns.

In the following pages we will discuss some materials and methods used in building presentation models. First, however, two important rules in architectural model building should be pointed out.

Neatness. Take great care to be accurate and neat in all phases of the building. A sloppy modeling job is completely useless because it will not serve its main function—that of selling the design to the client.

Scale. Every feature of the structure down to the smallest detail must be built to the same scale. When this is carefully done, the model will have the professional look of a scale model; when it is not, it will look like a toy. The most commonly used scales are $\frac{1}{8}'' = 1'$ and $\frac{1}{4}'' = 1'$.

MATERIALS

The most often used and versatile material for architectural modeling is heavy cardboard. Properly selected, cardboard can serve as finished walls and roofs, or as the base for the application of other finished materials. It is known as *mat board, mount board,* or *display cardboard.* Fourteen ply cardboard ($\frac{1}{8}''$ to $\frac{3}{16}''$ thick) of the best quality should be used. These boards may be obtained permanently embossed with scaled surface detail of several types (see Table I).

Another popular architectural modeling material is two or three ply *Strathmore drawing paper,* plate surface. It is often used for trims and overlays, since it has a hard, tough surface, cuts cleanly, can be bent sharply without tearing, and will take paint without wrinkling.

These cardboards are cut with a new razor or razor knife, using a steel straightedge as a guide. The first cut should be fairly light, the cuts being repeated

TABLE I
Available Mat Boards

	Surfaces	Sheet Size	Scale
	Smooth surface	30″ × 40″	
	Pebbled surface	30″ × 40″	
	Embossed surfaces		
	9″ weatherboard or shiplap	3″ × 22″	$\frac{1}{8}''$
	12″ weatherboard or shiplap	3″ × 22″	$\frac{1}{8}''$
	12″ board and batten	3″ × 22″	$\frac{1}{8}''$
	brick siding	3″ × 22″	$\frac{1}{8}''$ and $\frac{1}{4}''$
	concrete block siding	3″ × 22″	$\frac{1}{8}''$ and $\frac{1}{4}''$
	stucco siding	3″ × 22″	$\frac{1}{8}''$ and $\frac{1}{4}''$
	shake roofing	3″ × 22″	$\frac{1}{8}''$ and $\frac{1}{4}''$

until the edge cuts through. The outside corners of walls must be carefully mitered. Good work can be done only with *sharp* instruments.

Some professional model makers prefer wood to cardboard. Basswood and ponderosa pine are used for their fine, even grain, and balsa wood is used for its extreme softness. Table II shows the available sizes of these woods in sheets, strips, and structural shapes. Thin wood may also be cut by razor, but heavier stock is best cut by a razor saw.

Household cement (such as Dupont Duco) may be used for cementing cardboard, paper, and wood. After one hour setting it will make a glue joint which is stronger than the materials joined. Rubber bands, drafting tape, straight pins, and small "lills" are used as clamps to hold the materials until set. To prevent model parts from adhering to a template, waxed paper may be used over the template.

BASE

Since a structure is designed in relation to its surroundings, the model is constructed showing some of its surrounding topography. The usual procedure is to select a base which is scaled to the plot size and shape. Plywood $\frac{1}{2}$" thick is quite satisfactory for this purpose.

Flat plot. The plywood base may be finished directly with paint, flocking, or a loose material sprinkled over glue (such as dyed sawdust or sand). Sandpaper or black garnet paper may be glued face up with rubber cement to give the effect of concrete or asphalt driveways.

Contoured plot. To obtain an accurate reproduction of a contoured plot, the usual procedure is to build up successive layers of chipboard which have been cut to conform to the contour lines on the plot plan. Chipboard is an inexpensive cardboard available in thicknesses of $\frac{1}{16}$", $\frac{3}{32}$", $\frac{1}{8}$", and $\frac{5}{64}$". The thickness is selected to equal the scaled contour interval (vertical distance between contour lines). For example, the contour interval in Figure 3 is 2'. If the contour model is to be built to a $\frac{1}{8}$" = 1' scale, each layer of chipboard must be $\frac{1}{4}$" thick. Therefore, two $\frac{1}{8}$" chipboards should be used. Usually this kind of contour model is left in terraced steps for easy comparison with the plot plan rather than being smoothed to shape. It is finished in the same manner as the flat plot.

The materials in the table at right are obtainable from model suppliers such as Walthers, 1245 N. Water St., Milwaukee, Wisconsin 53202 (ask for their ARCHITECTURAL INDUSTRIAL CATALOG OF MODEL SUPPLIES) and America's Hobby Center, 146 W. 22nd St., New York, N.Y. 10011 (ask for their model train catalog; this includes architectural modeling materials).

TABLE II

Available Wood Sizes

Sheet balsa (36" × 2", 3", 4", and 6") — $\frac{1}{32}$", $\frac{1}{16}$", $\frac{3}{32}$", $\frac{1}{8}$", $\frac{3}{16}$", $\frac{1}{4}$"

Strip balsa (36" long)

	$\frac{1}{16}$"	$\frac{3}{32}$"	$\frac{1}{8}$"	$\frac{3}{16}$"	$\frac{1}{4}$"
$\frac{1}{16}$"	√		√	√	√
$\frac{3}{32}$"		√	√		
$\frac{1}{8}$"	√	√	√	√	√
$\frac{3}{16}$"	√		√	√	
$\frac{1}{4}$"	√		√		√

Sheet pine (22" × 1", 2", and 3") — $\frac{1}{32}$", $\frac{1}{16}$", $\frac{3}{32}$", $\frac{1}{8}$", $\frac{3}{16}$", $\frac{1}{4}$"

Strip basswood (24" long)

	$\frac{1}{32}$"	$\frac{1}{16}$"	$\frac{3}{32}$"	$\frac{1}{8}$"	$\frac{5}{32}$"	$\frac{3}{16}$"	$\frac{1}{4}$"
$\frac{1}{32}$"	√	√	√	√	√	√	√
$\frac{1}{16}$"	√	√	√	√	√	√	√
$\frac{3}{32}$"	√	√	√	√	√	√	√
$\frac{1}{8}$"	√	√	√	√	√	√	√
$\frac{5}{32}$"	√	√	√	√	√	√	√
$\frac{3}{16}$"	√	√	√	√	√	√	√
$\frac{1}{4}$"	√	√	√	√	√	√	√

Milled basswood ($3\frac{1}{2}$" × 24" sheets)

	$\frac{1}{32}$"	$\frac{1}{16}$"	$\frac{1}{8}$"
6" and 9" clapboard ($\frac{1}{8}$" scale)		√	
6" clapboard ($\frac{1}{4}$" scale)			√
12" board and batten ($\frac{1}{8}$" scale)		√	
9" board and batten ($\frac{1}{4}$" scale)		√	
3", 4", 6", 9", and 12" scribed planking ($\frac{1}{8}$" scale)	√	√	
3", 4", 6", and 9" scribed planking ($\frac{1}{4}$" scale)	√	√	
shingled siding ($\frac{1}{4}$" scale)			√
brick siding ($\frac{1}{8}$" and $\frac{1}{4}$" scale)		√	
concrete block siding ($\frac{1}{4}$" scale)			√
flagstone ($\frac{1}{8}$" and $\frac{1}{4}$" scale)	√	√	

Structural shapes (24" long)

	$\frac{3}{64}$"	$\frac{1}{16}$"	$\frac{5}{64}$"	$\frac{3}{32}$"	$\frac{1}{8}$"	$\frac{3}{16}$"	$\frac{1}{4}$"
angles	√	√		√	√	√	
tees	√	√		√	√	√	
channels			√	√	√	√	
WF beams				√	√	√	
I beams				√	√	√	
quarter round	√			√	√		

Hillside plot. When the plot has a very steep slope, the method described above requires too many layers of cardboard. The professional modeler then uses an alternate technique. He builds up the land model using bandsawed wood forms and covers them with wire screening as shown in Figure 4. The screening is plastered with a $\frac{1}{4}''$ thick mix of 50 percent (by volume) plaster, 50 percent asbestos fibers, dry color, and water. Asbestos fibers of the type used for insulation greatly increase the strength of the mix (like the aggregate in concrete). The dry colors are obtained from an art store, and are sometimes called "earth colors." A brown color is used so that the plaster will look like earth if it is chipped. This mix is troweled on roughly to indicate rock outcrops, and smoothed or stippled with a brush to indicate grass areas. Thin washes or oil stains are used for the final painting. The following colors are common:

Grass: color varies from pale yellow to olive green
Brown soil: burnt umber stain
Reddish soil: burnt and raw sienna stain
Brown rock: Van Dyke brown stain
Reddish rock: Van Dyke brown and burnt sienna stain
Gray rock: thin wash of black

WALLS

The selection of the method and materials used for wall construction depends upon the scale of the model. When models are built to a scale smaller than $\frac{1}{8}'' = 1'$, the walls are usually built of painted mat board. The recommended order of procedure is:

1. Accurately lay out all wall sizes in pencil on the mat board using T-square and triangles. Cut out with a *sharp* razor knife (Figure 5).

2. Paint the walls using poster paint (tempera) carefully mixed to the desired colors. When they are dry, rule on white or black lines (depending upon the color of the desired mortar mix) representing brick or stone joints and wood siding. These lines need not be completely ruled—only enough to give the impression of the surface (Figure 6).

3. Since stock windows are not available—or desirable—for such small scales, they are painted on or outlined by scaled strip wood (Figure 7). The professional model builder uses a flat black or dark grey for glass areas, since this is the actual appear-

TABLE III
Available Plastic Material

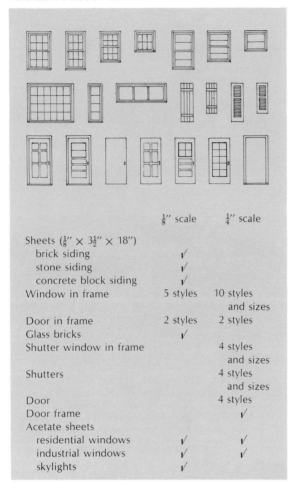

	$\frac{1}{8}''$ scale	$\frac{1}{4}''$ scale
Sheets ($\frac{1}{8}'' \times 3\frac{1}{2}'' \times 18''$)		
brick siding	✓	
stone siding	✓	
concrete block siding	✓	
Window in frame	5 styles	10 styles and sizes
Door in frame	2 styles	2 styles
Glass bricks	✓	
Shutter window in frame		4 styles and sizes
Shutters		4 styles and sizes
Door		4 styles
Door frame		✓
Acetate sheets		
residential windows	✓	✓
industrial windows	✓	✓
skylights	✓	

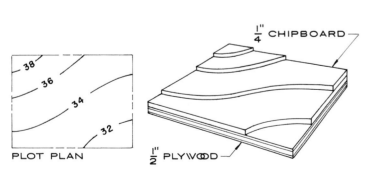

Figure 3 Modeling a contoured plot.

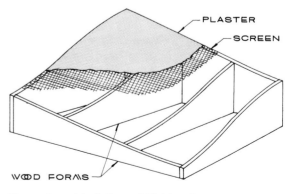

Figure 4 Modeling a hillside plot.

ance of windows. Muntins and mullions are ruled on in white ink (such as Pelikan white drawing ink) with a ruling pen or technical fountain pen.

4. Miter corners and assemble, being careful not to smudge the prepainted surfaces. All corners must be square (Figure 8).

Models built to a scale of $\frac{1}{8}''$ and $\frac{1}{4}'' = 1'$ are somewhat simpler to construct, since a great variety of stock material is available in these scales. These are common scales for residential models and probably the best ones for the beginner. The procedure is as follows:

1. Select the desired material from Tables I–IV. Milled basswood, embossed mat board, and balsa wood are all satisfactory materials. If the model is to have a removable roof so that rooms inside can be viewed, the thickness of the material should scale to the actual wall thickness. Although it requires much more work, custom siding can be constructed by cementing thin strips of Strathmore paper to sheet stock (Figure 9).

2. Accurately lay off all walls, windows, doors in pencil on the siding (Figure 10). If stock windows and doors are to be used, some adjustment may have to be made to fit the available material to your plan. Cut out walls, windows, and doors using a *sharp* razor knife.

3. Windows and doors may also be custom built (Figure 11). The construction of a sliding window is illustrated.

4. Carefully miter all corners and assemble the sides directly upon a floor plan cut from sheet stock. If this sheet stock is sufficiently thick, it can serve as the exposed portion of the foundation. Use pins or tape to hold the model until dry (Figure 12).

ROOFS

Flat built-up roofs of all scales can be made very simply of sandpaper glued face up to mat board and finished with the desired color latex paint. Marble chip roofs are simulated by sprinkling fine sand or

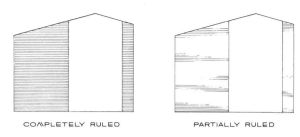

COMPLETELY RULED PARTIALLY RULED

Figure 6   A model wall.

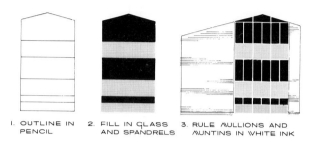

1. OUTLINE IN PENCIL 2. FILL IN GLASS AND SPANDRELS 3. RULE MULLIONS AND MUNTINS IN WHITE INK

Figure 7   A model window.

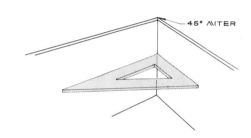

45° MITER

Figure 8   Miter and square corners.

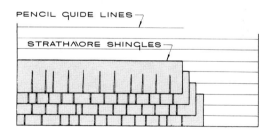

PENCIL GUIDE LINES
STRATHMORE SHINGLES

Figure 9   Modeling a shingle roof.

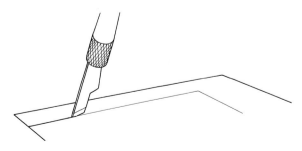

Figure 5   Use of the razor knife.

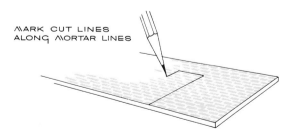

MARK CUT LINES ALONG MORTAR LINES

Figure 10   Lay out on mortar lines.

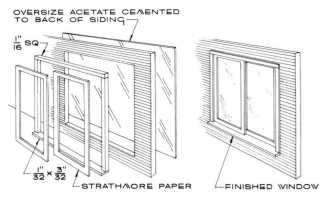

Figure 11   Custom-built window construction.

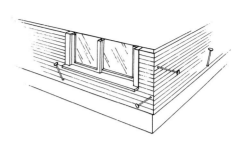

Figure 12   Pin corners until cement dries.

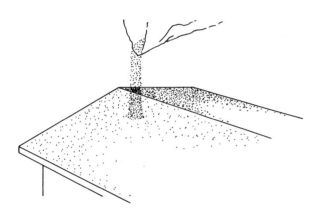

Figure 13   Built-up roofing simulation.

salt on the wet white paint to add sparkle to the surface (see Figure 13). Preformed shingle roof material is available, but roofs may be custom-built by gluing strips of notched Strathmore paper to a mat board roof base.

Sheet metal roofs and flashing are modeled with strips of drafting tape cut to shape and painted copper or silver. A properly scaled fascia of strip basswood provides a finished look to any roof. Gutters and downspouts are built of properly scaled wire or strip basswood.

Chimneys should be cut from a balsa wood block with the horizontal brick joints scribed in (Figure 14). Bricks are painted on over a white undercoat to represent mortar. Of course, any of the stock brick sheet material may be used.

ACCESSORIES

Accessories added to the structure (such as front door lamps), those added to the topography (such as shrubs and trees), and entourage (such as cars and people) may be custom built or purchased from stock. Some architectural modelers find it more convenient to obtain supplies from a model railroad supplier. For this purpose, it is necessary to know that O gauge is $\frac{1}{4}''$ scale, HO gauge is approximately $\frac{1}{8}''$ scale, and N gauge is approximately $\frac{1}{16}''$ scale. See Table V for the exact conversion size.

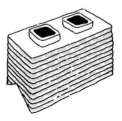

Figure 14   Modeling a chimney.

TABLE IV
Available Building Paper

		$\frac{1}{8}''$ scale, 6″ × 9″ sheets	$\frac{1}{4}''$ scale, 9″ × 12″ sheets
Red brick		√	√
Yellow brick		√	√
Brown fieldstone		√	√
Grey fieldstone		√	√
Grey flagstone		√	√
Brown ashlar stone		√	√
Grey ashlar stone		√	√
Yellow ashlar stone		√	√
Concrete block		√	√
Brown wood shingles		√	√
Grey wood shingles		√	√
Green wood shingles		√	√
Grey slate		√	√

Figure 15   *Model contemporary house, student design by William Travis, Jr. (Scale: $\frac{1}{8}$ = 1'-0.)*

Figure 16   *Another view of the model house shown in Figure 15.*

Nearly any architectural modeling element may be purchased, but often custom-built accessories are less toy-like and more professional looking. Realistic trees may be modeled from dried yarrow or culex weeds dipped in shellac to prevent deterioration, shrubs and ground cover formed from lichen obtainable in many colors, hedges from sponge rubber or styrofoam, people carved from erasers or soap, and stylized cars from balsa blocks. Care must be taken that all accessories are properly scaled.

CUT-AWAY MODELS

A cut-away model of a structure is used to show actual construction methods and materials. Such models are very popular classroom projects, since they must be built up of studs, sheathing, and finish material in much the same manner used in current building practice. For example, a wall is constructed by pinning each stud and plate over a framing drawing. The framing is glued together rather than nailed, with wax paper used to prevent it from sticking to the drawing. This is followed by wood sheathing, felt paper, and finish siding—each layer cut back so that the previous layer is left exposed for inspection.

Insulation, heating ducts, and piping may also be shown in the walls. Other procedures are similar to those already described in this chapter. Recommended scales are $\frac{3}{8}'' = 1'$ and $\frac{3}{4}'' = 1'$.

Figure 17   *Professional architectural models.*

TABLE V
Scale Conversions

Model Railroad Gauge	Equivalent Architectural Scale
O gauge	$\frac{1}{4}'' = 1'$-0
S gauge	$\frac{3}{16}'' = 1'$-0
HO gauge*	$\frac{1}{8}'' = 1'$-0
TT gauge	$\frac{1}{10}'' = 1'$-0
N gauge*	$\frac{1}{16}'' = 1'$-0

*Actually HO gauge is 3.5mm = 1', which is approximately 1/7.3'' = 1'-0, and N gauge is .075'' = 1', which is approximately 1/13.3'' = 1'-0.

Figure 18   Scale model of museum helped designers to plan aircraft placement, Air Force Museum, Dayton, Ohio.

Figure 19   Model of Madison Square Garden Sports and Entertainment Center.

Figure 20   Architectural model of the Lecture Center, University of Illinois, Chicago.

STUDY QUESTIONS

1. How does a *study model* differ from a *presentation model?*
2. Why are *neatness* and *scale* important in building presentation models?
3. Match these modeling requirements with the materials to be used:
   a. Temporary fastener   Lills
   b. Permanent fastener   Acetate sheet
   c. Window and door trim Mat board
   d. Window glass   Household cement
   e. Walls and roof   Strathmore drawing paper
4. How is the size of the base of a model determined?
5. Describe the modeling technique used to build the following bases:
   a. Flat plot
   b. Contoured plot
   c. Hillside plot
6. Describe the technique used to build model walls to a scale of:
   a. $\frac{1}{16}'' = 1'$
   b. $\frac{1}{4}'' = 1'$
7. What materials are used to model:
   a. Built-up roofs
   b. Shingle roofs
   c. Flashing
   d. Guttering

Figure 21   Architectural model of the World Trade Center, New York City. Minoru Yamasaki and Associates, architects.

8. Give the equivalent architectural scale for:
   a. O gauge
   b. S gauge
   c. HO gauge
   d. TT gauge
9. What materials are used to model these accessories:
   a. Trees
   b. Shrubs
   c. Hedges
   d. People
   e. Automobiles

LABORATORY PROBLEMS

1. Construct a study model of:
   a. The building assigned by your instructor
   b. Your original house design
2. Construct a presentation model of:
   a. The A residence
   b. The building assigned by your instructor
   c. Your original house design
3. Construct a cut-away model of a building using the specifications given by your instructor.

PART FIVE

23 building construction

It is extremely important that you, as a student of architectural drafting, be thoroughly familiar with standard construction practices. An architectural draftsman attempting to design a building without knowledge of its construction would be like a contractor trying to build without being able to read blueprints. In either case, chaos would result.

Although there are many different types of acceptable construction in use today, we shall proceed by studying in detail the most commonly used type: the *platform frame*. This will be done step by step, starting with the site survey and excavation, and working up to the roof and finish materials—as though we were actually building. Later, we will look at other kinds of construction to see how they differ from the platform frame.

SURVEY

Before starting construction, the house lot should be surveyed by a registered surveyor who will accurately locate the property lines. The property corners are marked with 30″ long galvanized iron pipes driven almost completely into the ground. The surveyor may also stake out the corners of the house, checking the local building ordinance for requirements on minimum set-back from the road, and minimum side and rear yards. The ordinance may state that the front

of the building must align with adjacent buildings.

As previously mentioned, if there are trees on the site, the house should be placed to save a maxi-

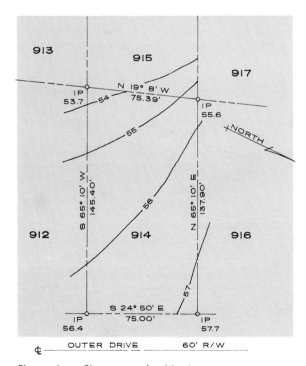

Figure 1   Site survey for Mr. A.

217

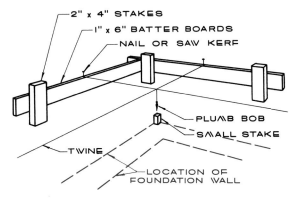

Figure 2   Staking.

mum number. As a rule, all trees within 5' of the proposed building are cut down, since the excavation will disturb their roots so much that they will die.

The surveyor will also establish correct elevations, usually using the adjoining road or house as a reference. All of this information is placed on a survey map which will be the basis of the plot plan. Figure 1 shows a survey map for the A residence.

STAKING

Although the surveyor may stake out the house foundation, this is usually done by the building contractor. He locates the future outside corners of the foundation and marks these points with tacks in small stakes. Then, since these stakes will be disturbed by the excavation, larger 2" × 4" stakes are driven 4' beyond the foundation lines, three at each corner. Figure 2 shows 1" × 6" batter boards nailed to these stakes so that their tops are of the same

elevation. Using a plumb bob, he stretches stout twine across the batter boards directly above the corner tacks. Saw kerfs (cuts) or nails are located on the batter boards where the twine touches to establish a more permanent record of the foundation lines (Figure 3). Of course, it is particularly important to check for squared corners. This may be done with surveying instruments, by measuring diagonals, or by using the principle of the 3-4-5 triangle (Figure 4).

EXCAVATION

The excavation is usually done by power equipment. First, about 1' of topsoil is removed and stored at the side of the lot to be used later in the finish grading. Then the excavation itself is made, the depth depending upon these factors:

1. On sloping land, the foundation must extend above the highest perimeter point of finished grade by:

a. 8" in wood frame construction to protect the wood from rotting due to moisture
b. 2" in brick construction to protect the first brick course from constant exposure to moisture which may eventually work into the joints

2. The footing must extend below the lowest perimeter point of finished grade by the prevailing frost line depth. This is necessary to prevent upheaval when the ground freezes. Figure 5 may be consulted for a general indication of frost line depth, but a more accurate depth for a particular area may be obtained from local architects and builders.

3. When a full foundation is to be built, allow a minimum of 6'-9" from the top of the basement floor to the bottom of the floor joist as shown in

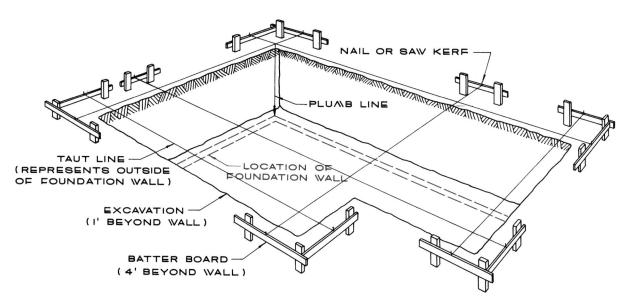

Figure 3   Excavation.

Figure 6. Remember that a girder under the joist will reduce the headroom. The minimum comfortable ceiling height for a habitable room is considered to be 7'-6"; 8' more often is used for the main living areas.

4. When a crawl space (for inspection and repair) is to be built, allow a minimum of 18" to the bottom of the joists. Specify 2'-6" for a more comfortable working height. Prevent water from accumulating in the crawl space by:

a. Locating the crawl space $1\frac{1}{2}$" above the outside finish grade
b. Providing a special drain to a lower elevation or storm sewer
c. Relying on local soil conditions which may be such that water will naturally drain from the crawl space

5. The excavation should extend down to *unfilled* ground. Because it is so important that a good bearing surface be provided, the trench for the footings should be dug shortly before pouring the concrete to prevent a possible softening of the bearing ground by exposure to rain and air.

FOOTING

Footings increase the bearing surface of the house upon the ground so that there will be less settling. The footings should be of concrete poured on undisturbed land. Average residential construction on firm land calls for footings twice as wide as the foundation wall, from 16" to 24". The depth of the footing should equal the wall thickness, ranging from 8" to 12". Side forms may be omitted if the ground permits sharply cut trenches. Reinforcing steel is used when the footing spans pipe trenches. As mentioned previously, the frost line determines the minimum depth of footing excavation, this varying from 1'-6" in Florida to 4'-6" in Maine.

The bottom of footings should always be horizontal, never inclined. Thus on sloping land, *stepped footings* such as shown in Figure 10 are used. The horizontal portion of a step footing should not be less than 32"; the vertical portion should not exceed 24". To reduce cutting when building the foundation wall, these dimensions should be in modular block units. The horizontal and vertical portions of the stepped footing should be of equal thickness, and both portions should be poured at the same time.

Footings are also required for chimneys and columns. Since column footings must support as much as one quarter of the total weight of the house, they are stepped out even farther (usually to 24" square or 30" square). By the use of the tables in Chapter 24, it is possible to calculate the required size of foundation, chimney, and column footings.

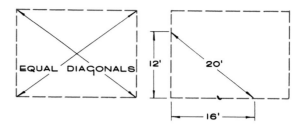

Figure 4   Methods of squaring corners.

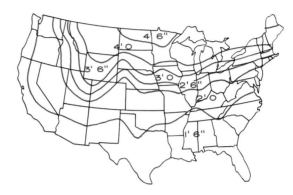

Figure 5   Footing depth.

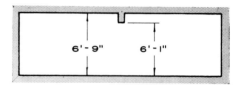

MINIMUM BASEMENT HEIGHTS

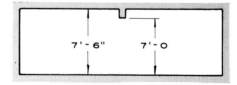

MINIMUM HABITABLE ROOM HEIGHTS

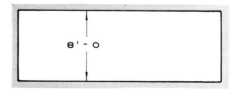

RECOMMENDED ROOM HEIGHT

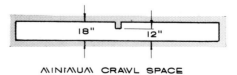

MINIMUM CRAWL SPACE

Figure 6   Minimum design heights.

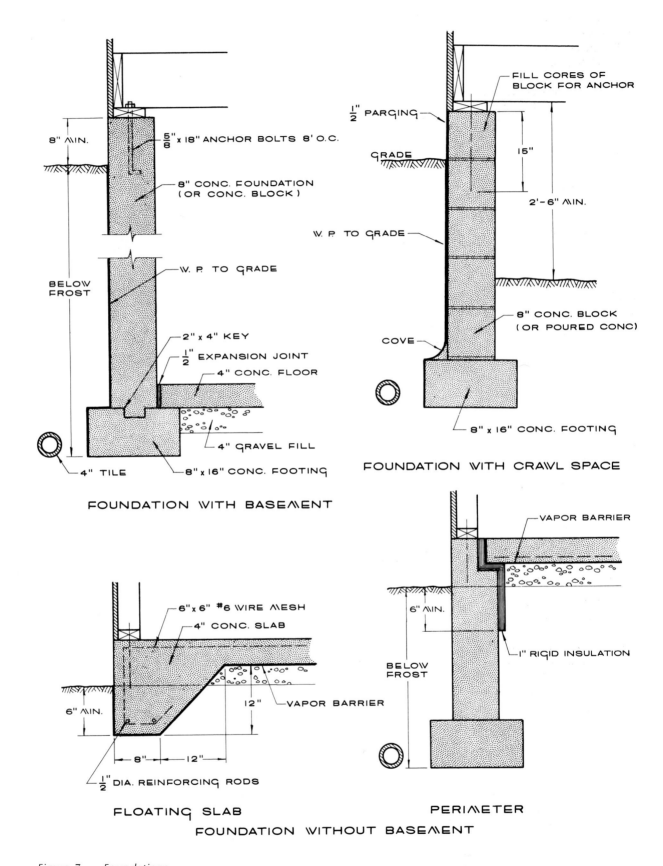

8" MIN.

$\frac{5}{8}$" x 18" ANCHOR BOLTS 8' O.C.

8" CONC. FOUNDATION
(OR CONC. BLOCK)

W. P. TO GRADE

BELOW
FROST

2" x 4" KEY

$\frac{1}{2}$" EXPANSION JOINT

4" CONC. FLOOR

4" GRAVEL FILL

8" x 16" CONC. FOOTING

4" TILE

FOUNDATION WITH BASEMENT

FILL CORES OF
BLOCK FOR ANCHOR

$\frac{1}{2}$" PARGING

GRADE

15"

2'-6" MIN.

W. P. TO GRADE

8" CONC. BLOCK
(OR POURED CONC)

COVE

8" x 16" CONC. FOOTING

FOUNDATION WITH CRAWL SPACE

6"x 6" #6 WIRE MESH

4" CONC. SLAB

6" MIN.

12"   VAPOR BARRIER

8"   12"

$\frac{1}{2}$" DIA. REINFORCING RODS

FLOATING SLAB

VAPOR BARRIER

6" MIN.

BELOW
FROST

1" RIGID INSULATION

PERIMETER

FOUNDATION WITHOUT BASEMENT

Figure 7   Foundations.

TILE DRAINAGE

To provide drainage around the foundation and ensure a dry basement, 4″ drain tiles are laid in the foundation excavation or footing excavation. The joints between the tiles are left open and covered with building paper. Gravel or cinder fill above ensures drainage to the tiles. The tile should slope slightly ($\frac{1}{16}$″ per foot minimum) to a catch basin, dry well, or sewer.

FOUNDATION

Foundations (Figure 7) may be constructed to provide a basement or crawl space. When a concrete floor is poured at ground level, it is called "slab" construction. It may be floating or perimeter. The floating slab requires reinforcing, since it is meant to "float" as an integral unit on the ground. Although this construction has been used in cold climates, it is best suited to areas where frost penetration is no problem. The perimeter foundation, on the other hand, provides a complete foundation wall for the protection of the slab from frost. The rigid insulation reduces heat loss from the house.

Materials. The two most common foundation materials are poured concrete (8″ to 12″) and concrete blocks (8″, 10″, or 12″).

Poured concrete. The poured concrete foundation is usually considered superior because it is more likely to be waterproof and termite-proof. A 1–2$\frac{1}{2}$–5 concrete mix is often used. This means 1 part cement, 2$\frac{1}{2}$ parts fine aggregate (sand), and 5 parts coarse aggregate (gravel or crushed stone). Poured concrete walls are sometimes battered (sloped) from 12″ thickness at the bottom to 8″ thickness at the top. This is to prevent any adhesion between the walls and clay ground due to freezing and to guard the wall from being lifted by frost action. The outside faces of the foundation and footing are mopped with hot tar or asphalt for additional protection against water. For this purpose, emulsified or hot tar (pitch) is superior to asphalt, since asphalt in continual contact with moisture may eventually disintegrate.

Concrete block. A $\frac{1}{2}$″ layer of cement plaster (called "parging") is applied to the outside block wall and covered with hot tar or asphalt waterproofing. It is good practice to fill the cores of the top course of concrete blocks with concrete to prevent passage of water or termites. Long stretches of wall are often stiffened with 8″ × 16″ pilasters every 16′ as shown in Figure 11. This is particularly important when using walls of only 8″ block.

Foundation height. Remember that the foundation

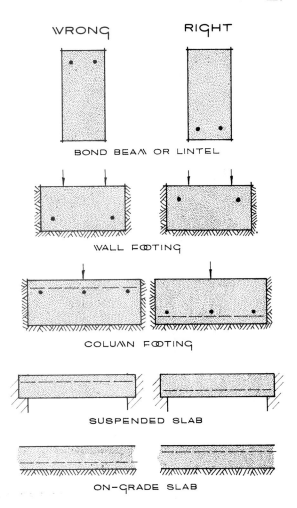

Figure 8   Placement of reinforcing steel in light construction.

must extend above the highest perimeter point of finished grade by 8″ in wood frame construction to protect lumber from ground moisture. When a brick veneer construction is used, the foundation should extend at least 2″ above the finished grade.

Reinforcing. Concrete has excellent strength in *compression,* but is weak in *tension.* Therefore when any portion of a concrete member is expected to be subjected to tension, steel rods or steel wire mesh are cast in that portion to resist the tension. This is called *reinforcing steel.* In light construction, reinforcing is used in concrete bond beams, concrete lintels, and occasionally in concrete slabs and footings. This reinforcing should be placed near the *bottom* of bond beams, lintels, column footings, and suspended slabs to best resist the tension there. It is common building practice to also place reinforcing near the bottom of wall footings and on-grade slabs upon the assumption that these members are similar to bond beams. However, many engineers now specify that reinforcing rods in wall footings be near

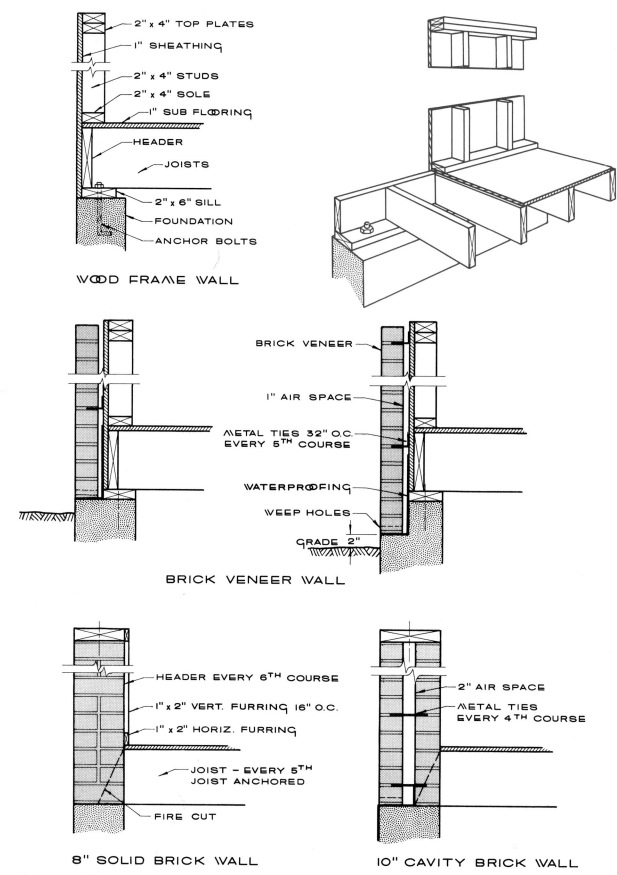

- 2" x 4" TOP PLATES
- 1" SHEATHING
- 2" x 4" STUDS
- 2" x 4" SOLE
- 1" SUB FLOORING
- HEADER
- JOISTS
- 2" x 6" SILL
- FOUNDATION
- ANCHOR BOLTS

WOOD FRAME WALL

- BRICK VENEER
- 1" AIR SPACE
- METAL TIES 32" O.C. EVERY 5TH COURSE
- WATERPROOFING
- WEEP HOLES
- GRADE 2"

BRICK VENEER WALL

- HEADER EVERY 6TH COURSE
- 1" x 2" VERT. FURRING 16" O.C.
- 1" x 2" HORIZ. FURRING
- JOIST – EVERY 5TH JOIST ANCHORED
- FIRE CUT

8" SOLID BRICK WALL

- 2" AIR SPACE
- METAL TIES EVERY 4TH COURSE

10" CAVITY BRICK WALL

Figure 9   Walls.

the *top* to better prevent cracking that could then extend up into the wall above. Reinforcing wire mesh in slabs poured on grade is also specified near the *top* of the slab to better control cracking which would affect the exposed floor surface. See Figure 8.

SILL

The sill is a 2″ × 6″ plank resting directly on top of the foundation wall. Notice in Figure 9 that the sill is set back about 1″ from the outside wall so that the sheathing, which is nailed to the sill, will be flush with the outside foundation wall. Some builders allow for irregularities in the face of the foundation wall by setting the sill flush so that the sheathing projects beyond the outside of the foundation wall. This is illustrated in Figures 8 and 9 of Appendix A. The sill should be fastened by $\frac{1}{2}$″, $\frac{5}{8}$″, or $\frac{3}{4}$″ bolts spaced 8′ apart. These extend 6″ into a poured concrete foundation and 15″ into a concrete block foundation. Holes are drilled into the sill, a bed of mortar (called "grout") is spread on the foundation and the sill is tapped into a level position. The nuts and washers are tightened by hand. Several days later they may be wrench-tightened. The grout provides a level bed for the sill and makes an airtight joint.

HEADER

Headers and joists are the same size. The header is spiked upright to the top outside edge of the sill. Where a basement window or door breaks the foundation wall, it is good practice to let the header, rather than the sill, act as the spanning member. This is best accomplished by a ledger strip spiked to the header and extending at least 6″ beyond the opening as shown in Figure 12. The joists are cut to rest on the ledger and are also spiked to the header. A steel angle lintel may also be used.

GIRDER

The dimensions of most houses are so great that joists cannot span the foundation walls. In that case a wood girder (that is, several 2″ thick members spiked together) or steel beam is used, as shown in Figure 13. Notice that the girder is also too long to span the foundation walls and must be supported by wood or steel columns as in Figure 14. Steel pipe columns (usually referred to by the trade name of "Lally columns") are capped with a steel plate to increase the bearing surface with the wood girder. A $3\frac{1}{2}$″ diameter column is large enough for ordinary requirements.

The girder is framed into the foundation wall as shown in Figure 16 so that it bears a minimum

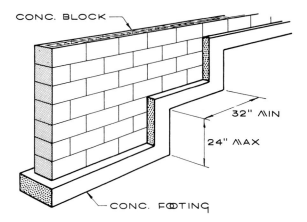

Figure 10   *Stepped footing.*

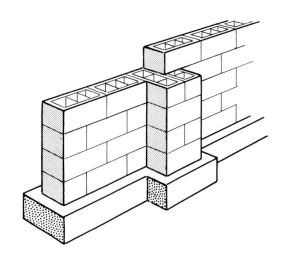

Figure 11   *Pilaster construction.*

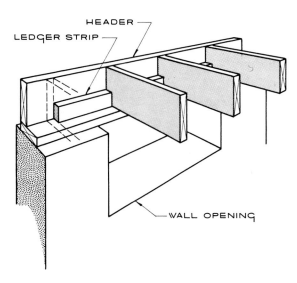

Figure 12   *Use of a ledger strip.*

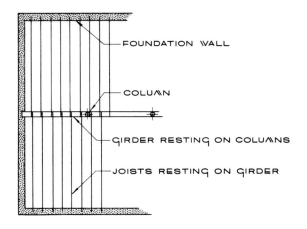

Figure 13   Use of a girder.

of 4". Incidentally, this is a good rule to remember: *always provide the greatest possible bearing surface between two members.* In the case of wood, the length of bearing surface should not be less than 4" (see Figure 15) for safest construction. However, to save headroom, joists are occasionally framed level with the girder using iron stirrups, ledger strips, or framing anchors. Joists may also be set "level" with a steel beam. (Actually such joists are installed with their upper edges an inch above the steel beam to allow for wood shrinkage and to prevent a bulge in the floor above.)

The wall pocket for a wood girder should be large enough to allow a minimum of $\frac{1}{2}$" air space at the sides and ends of the girder. This allows moisture to escape and reduces the possibility of decay.

Sizes of wood girders and steel beams may be calculated as shown in Chapter 24.

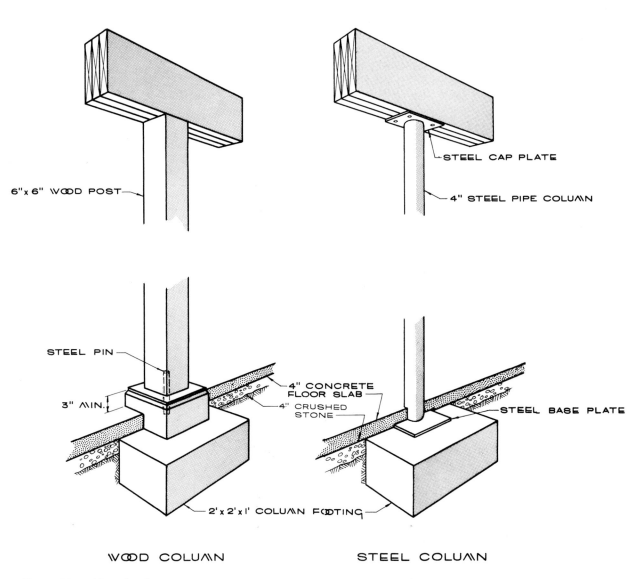

Figure 14   Use of columns.

FLOOR JOISTS

Because so much material is made in 4′ lengths
(4′ × 8′ plywood, plasterboard, rigid insulation, 4′
rock lath lengths, and so forth) it is desirable that
floor joists, wall and partition studs, and rafters be
spaced either 12″, 16″, or 24″ oc (all even divisions
of 4′) to avoid cutting. Since 24″ oc is usually too
weak and 12″ oc is wasteful, 16″ oc is normally used.
The joist sizes are determined by the tables in Chapter 24. Joist spans are often 14′ to 16′.

Joists and headers are doubled around all
openings (such as stairwells and chimneys) as shown
in Figure 17. When a partition runs parallel to a joist,
its entire weight must be supported by one (or two)
joists. Since this weight might cause excessive bending, such a joist is also stiffened by doubling. When
partitions run at right angles to joists, no extra support is necessary. Joists may be spaced 12″ oc instead
of the usual 16″ oc under bathrooms and occasionally under kitchens, to allow for weakening
caused by pipes being set into the floor.

When joists frame into masonry walls as in
Figure 9, their ends should be firecut to prevent the
walls being pushed outward if the joists should sag.

Firecutting also helps prevent cracks in the masonry
wall due to the joists settling (see Figure 18).

BRIDGING

Bridging (Figure 19) is used to keep the joists vertical
and in alignment, and to distribute a concentrated

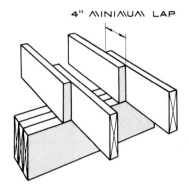

**JOISTS
OVER WOOD GIRDER**

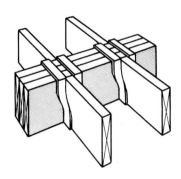

USING IRON STIRRUPS

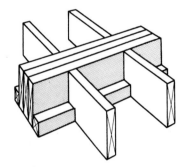

USING LEDGER STRIPS

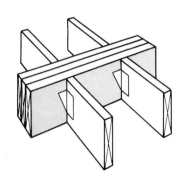

USING FRAMING ANCHORS

JOISTS LEVEL WITH WOOD GIRDER

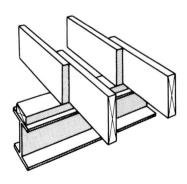

**JOISTS
OVER STEEL BEAM**

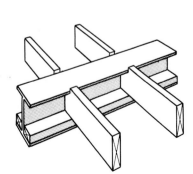

RESTING ON WOOD NAILERS

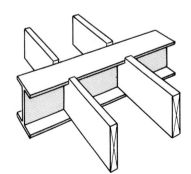

RESTING ON BEAM

JOISTS LEVEL WITH STEEL BEAM

Figure 15   Methods of framing joists.

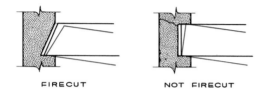

Figure 16   Girder pocket.

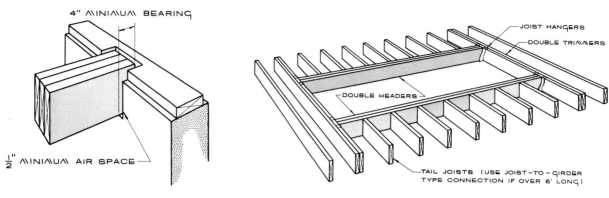

Figure 17   Stairwell framing.

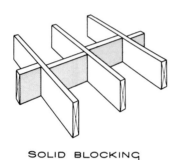

Figure 18   Use of firecutting.

load on more than one joist. Solid wood blocking, 1″ × 3″ wood bridging, or metal straps may be used. Rows of bridging should be spaced a maximum of 7′ apart. Since the subflooring has a tendency to align the joist tops, the lower end of the wood and strap bridging is not nailed until the subflooring is laid.

SUBFLOORING AND FLOORING

Subflooring is a wood floor of $\frac{5}{8}$″ plywood or 1″ boards laid over joists to serve as a base for the finished floor. The finished floor is usually of tongue and grooved hardwood; oak, maple, and birch are used. When plywood or boards laid diagonally are used for subflooring, the finished flooring is laid parallel to the long dimension of the room; when boards laid perpendicular to the joists are used for subflooring, the finished flooring must be laid perpendicular to the subflooring regardless of the room proportions. Building paper is laid between subflooring and flooring as a protection against air and moisture.

STUDS

A "wall" means an exterior wall; a "partition" means an interior wall. Partitions may be either bearing or curtain (nonbearing). A wall or partition consists of vertical members spaced 16″ oc called "studs," a lower horizontal sole plate, and doubled top plates, as shown in Figure 9. All of these members are 2″ × 4″ lumber. When a 4″ cast iron soil stack is used, however, the wall is made of 2″ × 6″ lumber, to conceal it. Often an entire wall including sole and top plates is assembled horizontally on the subflooring and then raised and braced in position while the sole is spiked to the subflooring. This method avoids toenailing the stud to the sole. Sheathing serves as an additional tie between wall, header, and sill.

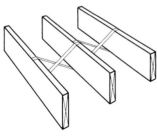

Figure 19   Bridging.

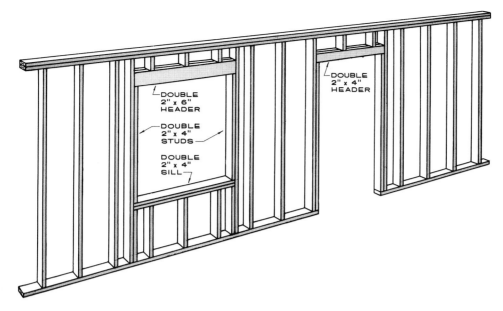

Figure 20   Rough framing of windows and doors.

WINDOW AND DOOR OPENINGS

The horizontal framing member above a window or door opening is called a "header," and the horizontal framing member below the window is called the "rough sill" (Figure 20). All members framing an opening should be doubled for greater strength and to provide a nailing surface for trim. The headers are laid with the long edge vertical to provide greater strength. They must be shimmed, however, to increase their 3″ (2 × 1½″) thickness to 3½″. The size of the headers ranges from doubled 2″ × 4″ members up to doubled 2″ × 12″ members, depending upon the span and superimposed load. The table in Chapter 24 may be used to determine the required size of headers.

CORNER POSTS

Corner posts must provide surfaces for nailing the sheathing at the corner and the lath at both interior walls. Two methods of accomplishing this are illustrated in Figure 21.

CANTILEVER FRAMING

Figure 22 shows the method of framing for cantilevered construction such as the second floor overhang of a garrison house. The length of the lookouts should be at least three times the length of the overhang.

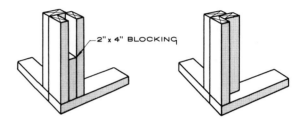

Figure 21   Methods of framing corner post.

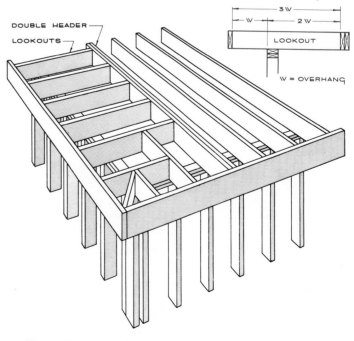

Figure 22   Cantilever framing.

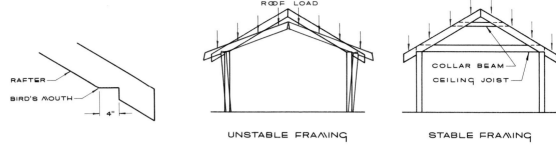

Figure 23   *Bird's mouth.*   *Figure 24*   *Framing for outward thrust.*

SHEATHING

Sheathing is nailed to the exterior of the studs in a manner similar to that used for the subflooring. Common sheathing materials are:

1. $\frac{5}{16}$″ min. × 4′ × 8′ plywood
2. $\frac{1}{2}$″ min. × 4′ × 8′ composition board. This has the advantage of providing some additional insulation but does not make a good base for exterior finish nailing nor does it provide the diagonal bracing strength of plywood. When composition board is used as outside sheathing, it should be asphalt-coated to prevent disintegration and serve as a moisture barrier.
3. 1″ × 6″ boards applied diagonally. If the boards are applied horizontally, corner braces must be let into the studs to stiffen the wall.

Plywood or 1″ boards should be used for roof sheathing.

BUILDING PAPER

Building paper is asphalt saturated felt or paper used between subflooring and finished flooring, sheathing and finished wall covering, and roofers and roof covering. It prevents wind and water from entering the building between cracks, while still allowing water vapor to escape.

RAFTERS

Rafter size and spacing may be determined by the tables in Chapter 24. A 16″ or 24″ spacing is often used. The upper end of the rafter is spiked to a 1″ or 2″ thick ridge board, the depth of which is not less than the end cut of the rafter. The lower end of the rafter is cut to obtain a full bearing on the top plate. This cut is called a "bird's mouth" (see Figure 23).

Figure 25   *Erecting trussed rafters.*

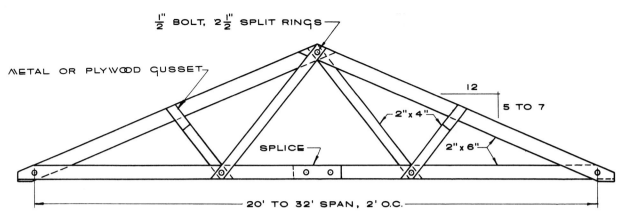

Figure 26   Typical trussed rafter.

ROOF THRUST

A sloping roof exerts not only a *downward* thrust on the exterior walls, but also an *outward* thrust which tends to push the exterior walls apart as shown in Figure 24. The result of this outward thrust may be prevented by the following measures:

1. Run the ceiling joists parallel to the rafters together with 1" × 6" or 2" × 4" collar beams spaced 4' oc.

2. Support the rafters at the ridge by a bearing partition or beam.

3. Roof trusses or trussed rafters* (Figure 25) may be used for large spans without bearing partitions, allowing great freedom in room planning. Notice, though, that a truss greatly reduces the usefulness of the attic space. Because a truss is composed of a number of small spans, the members need not be heavy. A typical trussed rafter is shown in Figure 26. The Timber Engineering Company of Washington, D.C. publishes a reference book which is very helpful to designers planning to specify trusses or trussed rafters.

FLAT ROOFS

Flat roofs may be laid level to hold water on the roof (called a "water film roof") or, more commonly, sloped slightly to prevent water from collecting. The roof joists rest directly on the top plates and serve a double purpose, as roof rafters and ceiling joists. When a wide overhang is desired, the roof joists are framed for cantilever framing, as shown in Figure 22. Although wood roof joists are used to frame flat roofs in residential construction, steel *open web joists* (also called *bar joists,* Figure 27) are normally used in commercial construction, since they can span up to 48'. Because shingles cannot be used for a flat roof

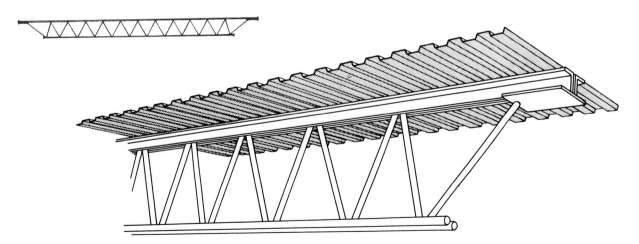

Figure 27   Open web joist.

---

*A trussed rafter is a truss spaced close enough to adjacent trusses that purlins are unnecessary.

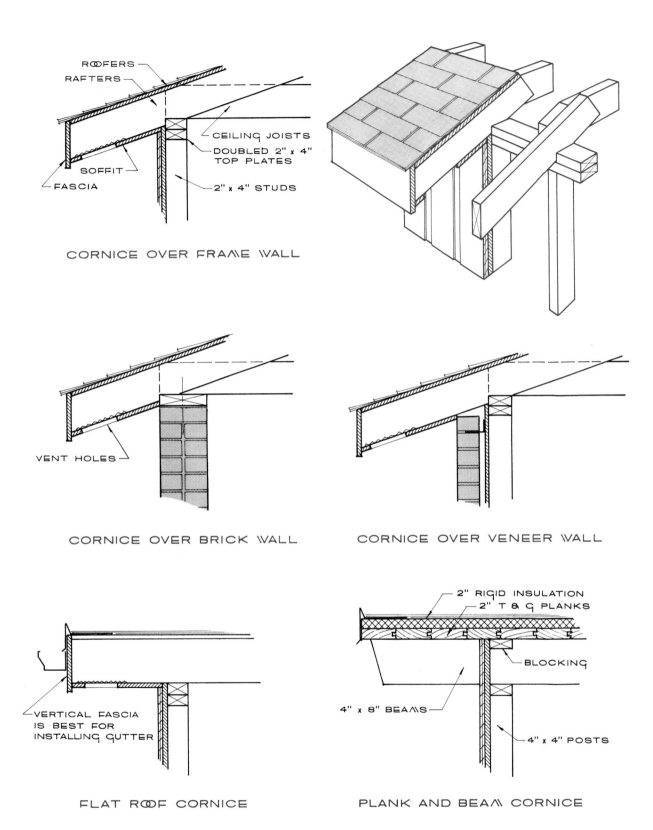

ROOFERS
RAFTERS
CEILING JOISTS
DOUBLED 2" x 4" TOP PLATES
SOFFIT
FASCIA
2" x 4" STUDS

CORNICE OVER FRAME WALL

VENT HOLES

CORNICE OVER BRICK WALL

CORNICE OVER VENEER WALL

VERTICAL FASCIA IS BEST FOR INSTALLING GUTTER

FLAT ROOF CORNICE

2" RIGID INSULATION
2" T & G PLANKS
BLOCKING
4" x 8" BEAMS
4" x 4" POSTS

PLANK AND BEAM CORNICE

Figure 28   Cornices.

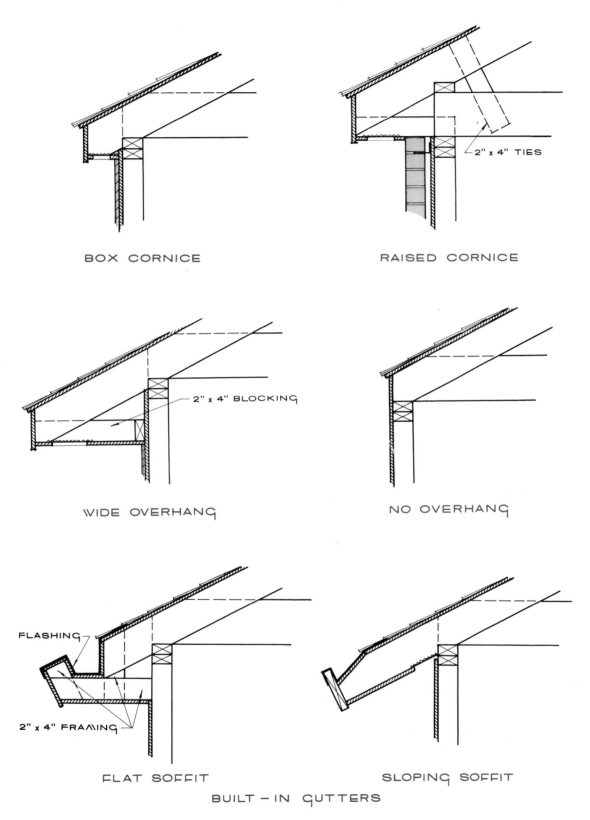

BOX CORNICE

RAISED CORNICE

2" x 4" TIES

2" x 4" BLOCKING

WIDE OVERHANG

NO OVERHANG

FLASHING

2" x 4" FRAMING

FLAT SOFFIT

SLOPING SOFFIT

BUILT — IN GUTTERS

Figure 28   continued

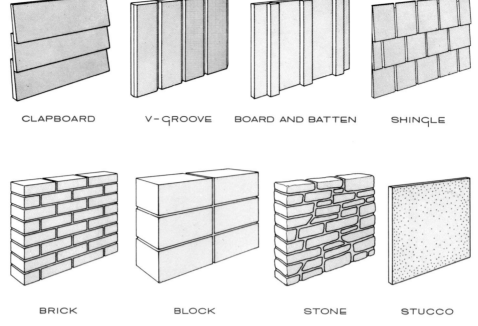

| CLAPBOARD | V-GROOVE | BOARD AND BATTEN | SHINGLE |
| BRICK | BLOCK | STONE | STUCCO |

Figure 29   Types of exterior finish.

covering, a "built-up" roof finish is used. A built-up roof is constructed by laying down successive layers of roofing felt and tar or asphalt topped with roll roofing, gravel, or marble chips.

CORNICES

Figure 28 shows cornice construction over a frame wall, brick wall, and brick veneer wall. Also the methods of framing various overhangs are shown ranging from wide overhangs to a flush cornice. The raised cornice is used to provide an additional foot of headroom in the attic space or, in the case of wide overhangs, to provide more clearance above the windows beneath the cornice. Since roof gutters are often unsightly, they may be built into the roof as shown. Obviously, built-in gutters must be very carefully flashed.

EXTERIOR FINISH

Exterior wall finish (Figure 29) covers the sheathing and building paper. Since the choice of finish will greatly influence the final appearance and upkeep of a house, the materials should be carefully selected.

Clapboards are usually of red cedar, cypress, or California redwood, because these materials have superior weather-resistance. Corners may be mitered for a neat appearance, but wood or metal corners are more durable (see Figure 30). The style of the house will also influence the corner treatment. Aluminum siding, although its initial cost is high, has the advantage of a bonded finish which lasts for years.

The vertical V-groove siding shown in Figure 29 is of tongue and grooved lumber; it is often used as an interior finish also.

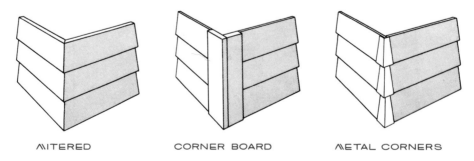

| MITERED | CORNER BOARD | METAL CORNERS |

Figure 30   Siding corner construction.

Board and batten siding is relatively inexpensive and presents a neat appearance.

Wood shingles are also of red cedar, cypress, or redwood. Hand split shakes may be used for a special effect. Shingles are often left unpainted and unstained to obtain a delightfully weathered finish. Red cedar and California redwood weather to a dark gray color; cypress weathers to a light gray with a silver sheen. Various types of composition siding—hardboard, fiberboard, asbestos, asphalt, and so forth, in imitation of wood, brick, or stone—have certain advantages. But they must be carefully specified so that they do not cheapen the appearance of the building.

Brick and stone finishes are durable, require very little upkeep, and present a fine appearance. Types of brick bonds are shown in Figure 31. The word "bond" used in reference to masonry has several meanings. *Mortar bond* is the adhesion of the mortar to the brick or block units. *Structural bond* is the method of overlapping the masonry units so that the entire wall is a single structural member. *Pattern bond* is the decorative pattern formed by the use of various units in different combinations. The pattern may result from the type of structural bond specified (as an 8″ solid brick Flemish bond wall using full brick laid as stretchers and headers), or it may be purely decorative (as a 4″ brick veneer

Flemish bond wall using full and half brick).

The *stretcher* or *running* bond is the most popular bond. Since no headers are used, this is often used in single width walls (veneer and cavity) with metal ties. The *common* bond is a variation of the running bond with a course of headers every fifth, sixth, or seventh course to tie the face wall to the backing masonry. The *English* bond is laid with alternate courses of headers and stretchers, and the *Flemish* bond is laid with stretchers and headers alternating in each course. The *stack* bond is a popular contemporary pattern. Because of the alignment of all vertical joints, reinforcing is needed in the horizontal joints. A masonry wall may be varied by diamond, basket weave, herringbone, and other patterns. Also, brick can be recessed or projected for special shadow effects. Decorative variations are endless.

Concrete block lends itself well to contemporary designs. Special effects may be obtained by the bond or by the block itself, which can be specified in many textured and sculptured surfaces.

Stucco is a cement plaster which may be used on exterior walls for special effects.

Combinations of exterior finishes. As mentioned in Chapter 19 it is not wise to mix many different kinds of exterior finishes on one house, as this will result

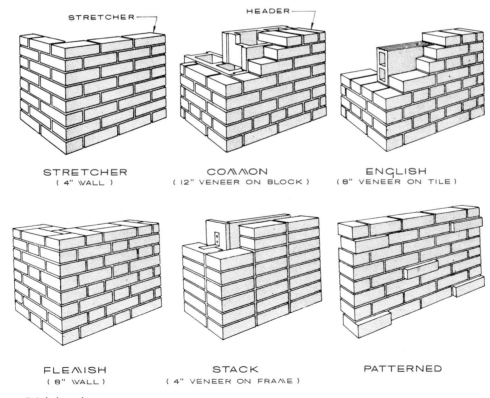

STRETCHER

HEADER

STRETCHER
(4″ WALL)

COMMON
(12″ VENEER ON BLOCK)

ENGLISH
(8″ VENEER ON TILE)

FLEMISH
(8″ WALL)

STACK
(4″ VENEER ON FRAME)

PATTERNED

Figure 31   Brick bonds.

Figure 32   Interior finished with horizontal planking.

Figure 33   Interior finished with vertical planking.

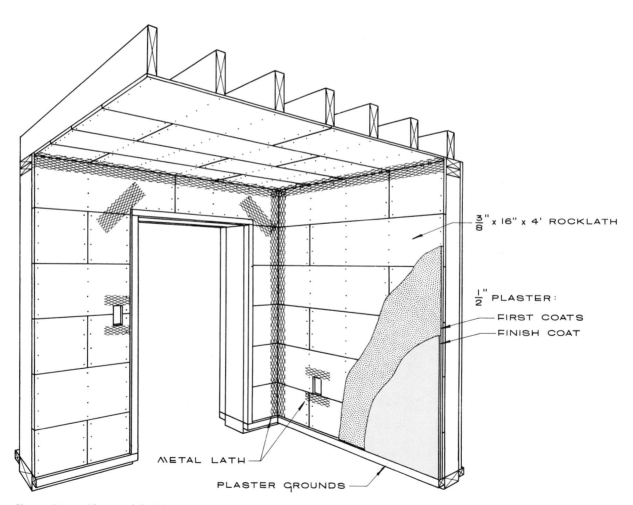

$\frac{3}{8}$" x 16" x 4' ROCKLATH

$\frac{1}{2}$" PLASTER:

FIRST COATS

FINISH COAT

METAL LATH

PLASTER GROUNDS

Figure 34   Plastered finish.

in a confusing appearance. Normally, no more than two finishes should be used, and the lighter finish should be above the heavier finish. (Notice that the M and the Z residences have wood siding stories over masonry stories.)

INTERIOR FINISH

Interior walls are often of plaster or dry wall finish. Ceilings may be of the same finish or of ceiling tile. Figures 32 and 33 illustrate contemporary interiors finished in horizontal and vertical redwood planking.

Plaster. Plaster finishing is considered superior to dry wall finish, but it has the following disadvantages:

1. It is more likely to crack.
2. Wet plaster requires many days to dry, during which all construction must be halted.
3. Wood framing is completely soaked with moisture during the drying period and may warp.

Gypsum lath measuring $\frac{3}{8}'' \times 16'' \times 4'$ (usually referred to as "rocklath") or $27'' \times 8'$ metal lath is

nailed to the studs and joists as a base for the plaster. Notice in Figure 34 that a gypsum lath base requires strips of metal lath to reinforce the areas most susceptible to cracking: wall and ceiling intersections, the upper corners of door and window openings, and other openings such as electric outlets. Wood grounds, equal in thickness to the lath and plaster, are installed around openings and near the floor. They serve as a leveling guide for the plaster, and act as a nailing base for the finished trim and the baseboard. Steel edges must be used on outside corners to protect the edges from chipping.

Three coats of plaster—a scratch coat (so called because it is scratched to provide a rough bond with the next coat), a brown coat (which is leveled), and a finish coat—are used over metal lath. Two coat "double-up" plaster (the scratch coat and brown coat combined or "doubled up") is used over rock lath. The finished coat may be a smooth, white coat which is painted or wallpapered, or it may be a textured coat (called "sand finish"), which usually has the color mixed into the plaster so that no finishing is necessary. A moisture resistant plaster (called "Keene's cement") is used in the kitchen and bathrooms. It is also possible to plaster with only

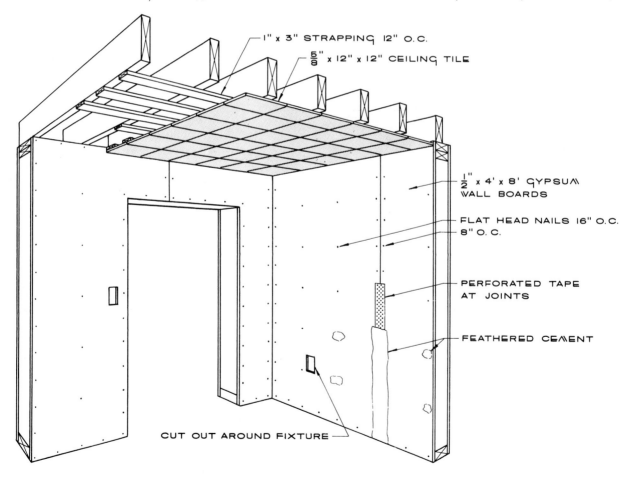

Figure 35   Dry wall finish.

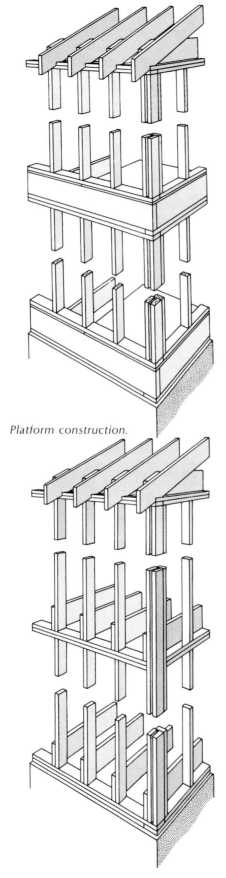

Figure 36   Platform construction.

Figure 37   Modern braced construction.

a single $\frac{1}{4}''$ coat of finish plaster when applied over a special $\frac{1}{2}'' \times 4' \times 8'$ gypsum lath.

Dry wall. The most common type of dry wall material is $\frac{3}{8}''$ or $\frac{1}{2}''$ gypsum board, as shown in Figure 35. When finished, this wall will look just like a plastered wall. Other kinds of dry wall finishes, such as $\frac{1}{4}''$ plywood panels (with a hardwood veneer) are used for special effects such as a single bedroom wall or fireplace wall. A den may be completely paneled, but take care that paneling is not overdone. For all dry wall finishes, it is important that the studs or joists be carefully aligned.

Gypsum board. Gypsum board consists of a cardboard sandwich with a gypsum filler. It is installed by nailing $4' \times 8'$ sheets directly to the studs or joists, and slightly setting the nail heads. Joint cement then covers the nail heads; joint cement over perforated paper tape is used at the joints. When the joint cement has been sanded, a smooth wall results.

OTHER CONSTRUCTION TYPES

Platform framing (Figure 36), in which framing studs only one story high rest on a complete platform, has been discussed in detail. Other construction types are *braced* framing, *balloon* framing, and *plank and beam* framing.

Braced framed construction was used in Colonial times and is still used today in modified forms (Figure 37). Braced framing utilized heavy (4″ thick) sills and corner posts. In two story construction, the corner posts ran the full height of the building, with heavy girts let into them to support the second floor. In early braced framing, the studs served only as a curtain wall, carrying no load. Recently, a type of modular construction using corner and wall posts in a manner similar to braced framing has been gaining popularity.

The **Balloon** framed house is characterized by studs resting directly on the sill and extending the full height of the stories, as shown in Figure 38. Second floor joists rest on a ledger, which is spiked to the studs. The joists are also lapped and spiked to the studs. This type of framing has been largely replaced by platform framing, but balloon framing does have the advantage of lessening vertical shrinkage, and therefore is best for two story brick veneer or stucco construction. However, additional firestopping of 2″ blocking must be provided to prevent air passage from one floor to another.

Plank and beam. A building method called *mill* construction has been used for years in factories and warehouses where the loads are heavy and the fire danger high. In mill construction, a few heavy posts and beams support a solid wood floor 3" to 6" thick—since a few large members will resist fire longer than many small members. Although mill construction has been largely replaced by steel and concrete construction methods, an adaption has been widely used in residential construction. This is called plank and beam construction.

In plank and beam construction, 2" thick tongued and grooved planks replace the 1" subflooring of conventional framing, 4" × 8" beams 4' to 7' oc replace conventional 2" joists 16" oc, and 4" × 4" posts under the beams replace the conventional 2" × 4" studs.

Plank and beam framing in residential construction developed from the trend toward picture windows and window walls, which made it necessary to frame a number of large openings in the exterior walls. Consequently, it is usually used in the construction of modern houses. Other advantages are:

1. A few large structural members replace many small members.
2. Planks and beams are left exposed, eliminating the need for additional interior finish such as plastering and cornices.
3. A saving is made on the total height of the building.
4. Fire hazard is reduced.

Some disadvantages of this type of construction are:

1. Special furring must be used to conceal pipes and electrical conduits installed on the ceiling.
2. Additional roof insulation must be used due to the elimination of dead air spaces between the roof and ceiling.
3. It is more difficult to control condensation. Exhaust fans are used to reduce moisture in the house to a minimum.

Figure 39 shows a typical plank and beam construction. Notice that the large open areas between posts may be used for window walls as shown in Figure 40 or may be enclosed with curtain walls. It should be mentioned that combinations of plank and beam and conventional construction are possible, using the advantageous features of each type.

Theory of plank and beam construction. Compare the deflection of single span planks and continuous span planks as shown in Figure 41 and notice that the continuous span will deflect less. In fact the continuous span will have about twice the stiffness of the single span. Of course, it is important that the floor be constructed so that it acts as one homogeneous unit. This is done by using tongue and groove planks with staggered end joints.

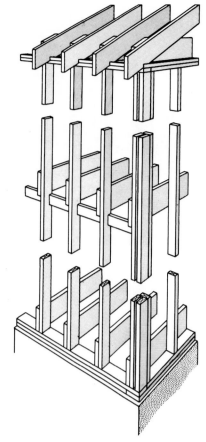

Figure 38   Balloon construction.

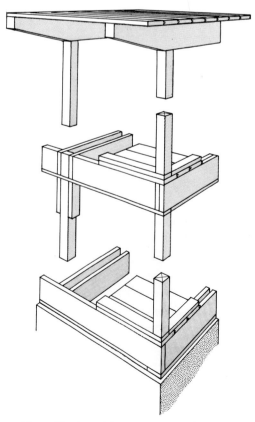

Figure 39   Plank and beam construction.

Figure 40   *A cathedral ceiling and window walls provided by plank and beam framing.*

DEFLECTION   DEFLECTION

SINGLE SPAN   CONTINUOUS SPAN

Figure 41   *Plank and beam construction theory.*

Figure 42   *Interim Branch Bank, Bank of the Commonwealth, Detroit, Michigan.*

FUTURE CONSTRUCTION METHODS AND MATERIALS

Today's methods of building construction are based mostly on lumber and nails put together in a specific way. It certainly does not take much foresight to realize that there will be revolutionary changes in building construction in the next few decades. It is quite possible that some of these changes will be evident by the time you actually begin to practice architectural drafting. Already many companies are manufacturing precut buildings (with lumber cut to the correct size), prefabricated ones (with entire wall sections already factory assembled), and even entirely mass-produced buildings. Assembly-line methods are not the only answer, however, since most people want custom-built homes. There are other companies (such as United States Steel Homes) who have made complete breaks from traditional construction, and still more who have launched full-scale research and development programs in the housing field.

Some mobile home manufacturers have departed from the traditional house trailer to build modular units which can be connected side by side, end to end, or stacked several stories high in various combinations. Figure 42 illustrates a bank which was factory-built in three sections weighing $7\frac{1}{2}$ tons each, transported to the site (Figure 43), and bolted together. The structural system is a welded three-dimensional truss made of steel tubular beams and columns. Four lift rings are provided on the roof for a crane (Figure 44) to move each unit to a flatbed train or truck. All panels, glass, and interior finishes are installed at the factory. Final erection can be completed in three days.

Although we can easily predict changes, it is impossible to predict their exact form and direction, since they will depend upon future engineering research and development. Be alert to these changes and accept them readily. For the present, though, learn all you can about current construction methods and materials.

STUDY QUESTIONS

1. In proper order, list the steps necessary for staking the excavation of a 26′ × 44′ house.
2. Indicate the factors that determine the depth of excavation under the following conditions:
   a. Wood frame construction with a full foundation in Augusta, Maine
   b. Brick veneer construction with a crawl space in San Diego, California
   c. Brick and slab construction on low land (to be filled 4′ higher) in Baltimore, Maryland
3. A heavy downpour occurs immediately after digging the footing trenches and before the concrete is poured. What must be done? Why?
4. A one story flat-roofed house with full basement has the

dimensions of 30' × 40' with three columns spaced 10' oc. Estimate:

  a. The total load to be carried by the foundation walls

  b. The load on each column

5. A residence built on firm ground has 10″ thick concrete block foundation walls. What would be the probable width and depth of its wall and column footings?

6. Under what conditions would you specify:

  a. Poured concrete foundation walls

  b. Concrete block foundation walls

  c. Concrete blocks filled solid with concrete

  d. Pilasters

  e. Reinforcing rods in footings

  f. Reinforcing rods in slabs

  g. Stepped footings

7. What is the difference between:

  a. Sill and sole

  b. Ledger and girt

  c. Girder and joist

  d. Wall and partition

  e. Flooring and subflooring

  f. Rafter and truss

  g. Precut and prefabricated

8. Describe briefly each term:

  a. Grout

  b. Lath

  c. Expansion joint

  d. Bridging

  e. Bird's mouth

  f. Built-up roof

9. Give the normal oc spacing of:

  a. Anchor bolts

  b. Joists

  c. Studs

  d. Roof trusses

10. For an average sized, one story, platform framed house, give the probable nominal size of:

  a. Poured concrete foundation wall

  b. Concrete block foundation wall

  c. Anchor bolts

  d. Sill

  e. Header

  f. Joists

  g. Cross bridging

  h. Subflooring

  i. Sole

  j. Studs

  k. Top plate

  l. Sheathing

11. What lumber size is required to span 13 feet if Ponderosa Pine is to be used spaced 16″ oc?

  a. Floor joists

  b. Ceiling joists

  c. 1 in 12 slope roof joists

  d. 6 in 12 slope rafters

12. When would floor joists be:

  a. Spaced 12″ oc

  b. Doubled

13. a. List the advantages of a built-up wood girder over a solid wood girder.

  b. What is the principal advantage of a solid wood girder (used exposed under a living area ceiling) over a built-up wood girder?

14. Sketch three methods of framing joists level with a wood girder.

Figure 43   *Trucking modular units to the site.*

Figure 44   *Crane lifting modular unit from flatbed truck.*

15. What is the reason for using:
    a. Cross bridging
    b. Building paper
    c. The "key" between footing and foundation wall
16. What length lookouts should be specified for a 1'-8" second story overhang?
17. Show three methods of counteracting the outward thrust of a gable roof upon its supporting walls.
18. When would the following types of cornice be used?
    a. Raised cornice
    b. Cornice with built-in gutter
    c. Cornice with wide overhang
    d. Flush cornice
19. What woods are normally used for clapboards? Why?
20. Compare plaster and dry wall finishes by listing the advantages of each.
21. What type plaster should be used:
    a. Over metal lath
    b. Over gypsum lath
    c. In a laundry room
22. List the advantages and disadvantages of plank and beam construction.

LABORATORY PROBLEMS

1. Draw a typical wall section of a one story house with requirements as assigned by your instructor:
   Foundation:
   a. With basement
   b. With crawl space
   c. Without basement, floating slab
   d. Without basement, perimeter foundation
   Wall:
   a. Wood frame
   b. Brick veneer
   c. Solid brick
   d. Cavity brick
   Roof:
   a. Pitched 6 in 12
   b. Pitched 4 in 12
   c. Pitched 2 in 12
   d. Flat
   Cornice:
   a. No overhang
   b. 8" overhang
   c. 4' overhang
   d. Raised
   e. Built-in gutter
2. (For the advanced student) Draw a typical wall section of a building showing your conception of a framing system that is entirely different from those now in use:
   a. Using standard materials readily obtainable
   b. Using revolutionary materials
3. Construct a cut-away model showing the method of building:
   a. Platform framed house
   b. Balloon framed house
   c. Plank and beam framed house
4. (For the advanced student) Construct a cut-away model showing your conception of a framing system that is entirely different from those now in use.
5. (For the advanced student) After a thorough library search, prepare a set of pictorial drawings or panoramas illustrating the history of the development of building methods to date.

24 structural calculations

In professional offices, architectural design is the responsibility of registered architects, and structural design is the responsibility of registered architectural engineers. However, most architects and engineers appreciate the draftsman who has the ability to make simple design and structural decisions on his own. When the principal architect or engineer is busy or away from the office, many hours can be wasted if the draftsman is not willing to make such decisions and continue working. Of course it is very important that the principal be informed of such tentative decisions at a more appropriate time for his approval or revision.

STRUCTURAL MEMBERS

The tables* in this chapter will enable the architectural draftsman to size the structural members in the average house or small building. However, for unusual framing methods or loading conditions, these tables will be inadequate. Each of the following structural members will be considered in turn:

1. Footings:
   Wall footings
   Column footings
2. Columns:
   Wood posts
   Steel columns
3. Beams:
   Wood girders
   Steel beams
4. Joists:
   Floor joists
   Ceiling joists
   Roof joists
   Rafters
5. Headers and lintels

Loads. The size and spacing required for any structural member depends upon a combination of elements—the distance spanned, the material used, and the load applied. The total applied load supported by the structural members of a house consists of a live load and a dead load. The live load is the weight supported by the house (furniture, people, wind and snow loads), while the dead load is the weight of the house itself. Although these loads may be fairly accurately calculated using the typical weights of materials given in *Architectural Graphic Standards,* a quicker method is to assume each floor has a live load of 40#/sq. ft. and a dead load of 20#/sq. ft. Attic live load may be assumed as 20#/sq. ft. if used for storage only, and a dead load of 10#/sq. ft. if not floored. When interior partitions exist, add an extra 20#/sq. ft. to the dead load of the whole floor upon which the partitions rest, remembering that

---

*For more complete tables than are given in this book, see the *AISC* (American Institute of Steel Construction) *Handbook, FHA* (Federal Housing Administration) *Bulletins,* or *Architectural Graphic Standards.* Lumber tables IV, VI, and XII are based upon the former Product Standard SPR 16-53 which assumes actual lumber sizes as $1\frac{5}{8}''$, $3\frac{5}{8}''$, $5\frac{1}{2}''$, $7\frac{1}{2}''$, $9\frac{1}{2}''$, and $11\frac{1}{2}''$. Revised tables for the new Product Standard PS 20-70 are not available at time of publication.

TABLE I
Residential Live and Dead Loads

	Live	Dead
Each floor	40#/sq ft	20#/sq ft
Attic (storage only)	20#/sq ft	20#/sq ft
Attic (not floored)	0	10#/sq ft
Roof (built up)	30#/sq ft (snow and wind load)	20#/sq ft
Roof (asphalt shingled)	30#/sq ft (snow and wind load)	10#/sq ft
Partitions	0	20#/sq ft

TABLE II
Weights of Materials

Type of Material	Pounds Per Cu. Ft.
Poured concrete	150
Concrete block (including mortar)	80
Brick (including mortar)	120

TABLE III
Safe Ground Loadings

Type of Ground	Pounds Per Sq. Ft.
Ledge rock	30,000
Hard pan	20,000
Compact gravel	12,000
Loose gravel	8,000
Coarse sand	6,000
Fine sand	4,000
Stiff clay	8,000
Medium clay	4,000
Soft clay	2,000

TABLE IV
Safe Loads for Wood Posts in Kips

Lumber	Size	Unbraced Length			
		6'	7'	8'	9'
Spruce and pine[1]	6″ × 6″ (5½″ × 5½″)	16.7^K	16.4^K	15.9^K	15.3^K
	8″ × 8″ (7½″ × 7½″)	31.5^K	31.3^K	31.0^K	30.6^K
Douglas Fir[2]	6″ × 6″ (5½″ × 5½″)	29.5^K	29.0^K	28.1^K	26.8^K
	8″ × 8″ (7½″ × 7½″)	56.2^K	55.6^K	55.0^K	54.3^K

Table IV adapted from *Light Frame House Construction*, U.S. Department of Health, Education, and Welfare.
[1] Red, White, and Sitka Spruce; the White Pines, No. 1 Common.
[2] Douglas Fir, Southern Pine, and North Carolina Pine, No. 1 Common.

these partitions also transmit any additional weight resting on them. Since roofs usually rest on exterior walls only, they should not normally add to the total girder or column load. However, if they are included, add 30#/sq. ft. (snow and wind) live load and a dead load of 10#/sq. ft. (for asphalt shingle) or 20#/sq. ft. (for built-up tar and gravel, slate, or tile).

For convenient reference, these loads are listed in Table I.

Tributary area. Each structural member supports a certain proportion of the total house weight or area, called the *tributary area*. The word "tributary" refers to the weight *contributed* to each member. Figure 1 illustrates the tributary area of a column and a beam of the Z residence. One beam running the length of the house will normally have a tributary area equal to half the total floor plan area. When columns are used, the tributary area is reduced in proportion to the reduction of the beam span. If joists run uncut across the beam, the beam supports $\frac{5}{8}$ of the weight above instead of $\frac{1}{2}$. Notice in Table I that values are given in pounds per square foot. Therefore, the live and dead loads must be multiplied by the tributary square foot area to determine the total load supported by a member.

FOOTINGS

By the use of Tables I, II and III, it is possible to calculate the required sizes of footings for foundation walls, columns, and chimneys. The procedure is to calculate the total weight to be contributed to the footing using the Live and Dead Load table (I) and the Weights of Materials table (II). When calculating tributary areas, remember it is the usual practice to support the roof by exterior walls, not interior partitions. The pressure of the footing on the ground may not be greater than the safe ground loadings given in Table III.

Calculations for the footings of the Z residence will be used as an example.

FOUNDATION FOOTING CALCULATIONS

Find the load per running foot on the foundation footing. In Figure 2 notice that the live and dead loads have been multiplied by half the joist spans to obtain the total load.

COLUMN FOOTING CALCULATIONS

Find the total load carried by a column footing. In Figure 3, notice that the average load per square foot has been multiplied by the tributary area to obtain the total load.

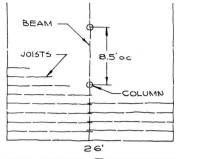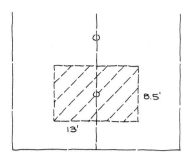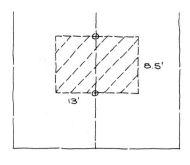

PLAN OF THE Z RESIDENCE   TRIBUTARY AREA OF COLUMN   TRIBUTARY AREA OF BEAM

Figure 1   Calculation of tributary areas.

WOOD POSTS

Structural framing of a small house might consist of wood posts (usually 6″ × 6″ or 8″ × 8″) supporting the center girder (usually 8″ × 8″ or three 2″ × 10″'s spiked together) which in turn supports the floor joists. Table IV is used to determine the post size required.

EXAMPLE

The load on each post of the Z residence was calculated in Figure 3 to be 22.1 kips.* If 7′ long Douglas Fir posts are to be used, a 6″ × 6″ size will be satisfactory, since they will safely support 29.0 kips.

*1 kip = 1000 pounds.

STEEL PIPE COLUMNS

Wood post and girder framing is not practical for larger houses, since the posts might have to be

TABLE V
Safe Loads for Heavy Weight Columns in Kips

Column Diameter	Unbraced Length			
	6′	7′	8′	9′
3½″	37.9^K	35.1^K	32.3^K	29.4^K
4″	49.2^K	46.1^K	43.1^K	40.1^K
4½″	61.8^K	58.5^K	55.3^K	52.0^K

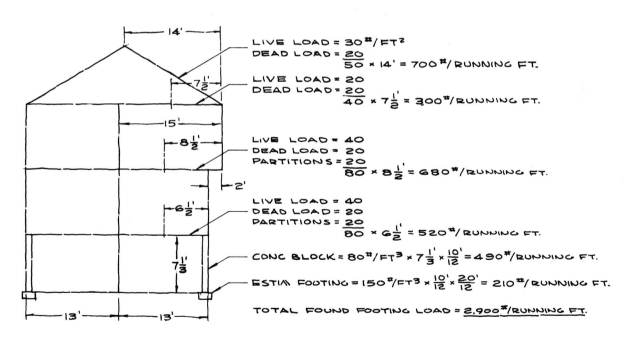

Figure 2   Foundation footing calculations.

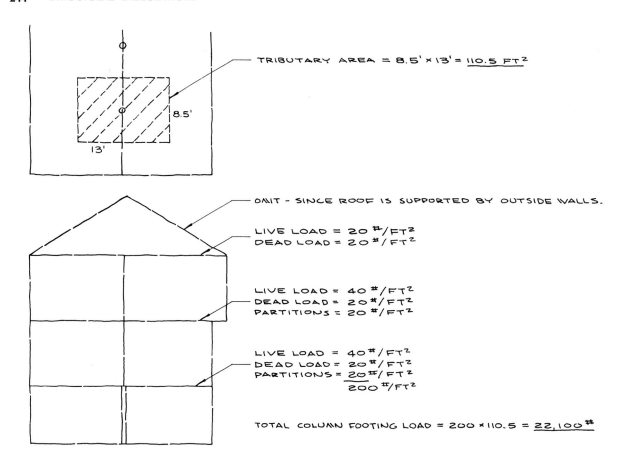

TRIBUTARY AREA = 8.5' × 13' = 110.5 FT²

OMIT - SINCE ROOF IS SUPPORTED BY OUTSIDE WALLS.

LIVE LOAD = 20 #/FT²
DEAD LOAD = 20 #/FT²

LIVE LOAD = 40 #/FT²
DEAD LOAD = 20 #/FT²
PARTITIONS = 20 #/FT²

LIVE LOAD = 40 #/FT²
DEAD LOAD = 20 #/FT²
PARTITIONS = 20 #/FT²
        200 #/FT²

TOTAL COLUMN FOOTING LOAD = 200 × 110.5 = 22,100 #

IF GROUND IS MEDIUM-STIFF CLAY, COLUMN FOOTING AREA MUST BE $\frac{22,100 \#}{6,000 \#/FT^2}$ = 3.7 FT²
∴ 20" SQ (2.8 FT²) IS TOO SMALL, BUT 24" SQ (4 FT²) IS O.K.

Figure 3   Column footing calculations.

TABLE VI
Wood Girder Sizes

		Safe Span*		
Structure Width	Girder Size (solid or built-up)	Two Story Supporting Bearing Partition	One Story Supporting Bearing Partition	Supporting Nonbearing Partition
Up to 26' wide	6" × 8"	6'-0	7'-0	9'-0
	6" × 10"	7'-6"	9'-0	11'-6"
	6" × 12"	9'-0	10'-6"	12'-0
26'-32' wide	6" × 8"	5'-6"	6'-6"	8'-6"
	6" × 10"	7'-0	8'-0	10'-6"
	6" × 12"	8'-0	10'-0	12'-6"

Tables VI–XI are adapted from FHA standards. For more complete information, see *Minimum Property Standards for One and Two Living Units*. Federal Housing Administration.
*Based upon allowable fiber stress of 1,500 psi (such as Douglas Fir or Southern Pine).

spaced so close together that use of the basement is restricted. Furthermore, deeper timbers for girders are too costly and either add to the house cubage or reduce headroom.

The solution, then, is to use steel columns and steel girders—as are specified in many building codes. Because steel is so much stronger than wood, steel columns can be spaced farther apart, giving more free basement area, and steel girders can be shallower than wood girders, saving on the cubic content or giving more basement headroom. W shapes, S shapes, and even channels are used for industrial building columns; round, hollow piping called *pipe columns* are used for houses. The hollow center of the pipe column may be filled with concrete to further increase its strength. Notice that a cap and base plate must be used (see Figure 14, Chapter 23).

The column diameter can be obtained by referring to a table published by the Lally Company, a popular manufacturer of pipe columns. A portion of this table is shown as Table V.

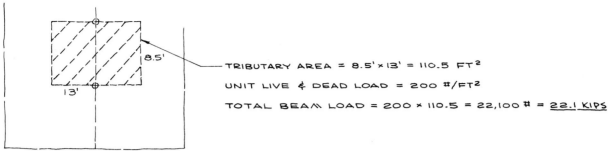

TRIBUTARY AREA = 8.5' × 13' = 110.5 FT²

UNIT LIVE & DEAD LOAD = 200 #/FT²

TOTAL BEAM LOAD = 200 × 110.5 = 22,100# = <u>22.1 KIPS</u>

Figure 4   Steel beam calculations.

EXAMPLE

In the Z residence, the previously calculated load of 22.1 kips on a 7' long column will be amply supported by a 3½" Lally column, since it will safely support 35.1 kips.

WOOD GIRDERS

Wood girders built up of 2" lumber spiked together or solid wood beams are often used in combination with steel columns. Table VI may be used to determine the safe span of various sizes of wood girders.

EXAMPLE

For the Z residence, the width is 25' 10" (under 26' wide) and the columns are two stories supporting a bearing partition. If we wish to space columns 8'-6" oc, we must use a 6" × 12" girder.

STEEL BEAMS

Steel beams of various sizes are especially useful when spanning distances greater than 10'. Steel beams are obtained cut to length (up to 60') and in various weights (an 8" W shape beam weighing 20#/ft will support more than an 8" W shape beam weighing 17#/ft). Only the more popular sizes stocked by suppliers are shown in Table VII.

EXAMPLE

For the Z residence, the desired span is 8'-6" and the load to be supported is found as shown in Figure 4 to be 22.1 kips. Reading between the 8' and 9' columns in Table VII, it will be seen that the W 8 × 17 beam will just support this weight. To be on the safe side, specify W 8 × 20 which will support approximately 26 kips.

JOISTS

The sizes of floor joists, ceiling joists, roof joists, and rafters are determined by Tables VIII to XI. Notice that you must know the span, spacing, and material.

EXAMPLE

For the Z residence, #2 Southern Pine floor joists 16" oc are to span 13'. From Table VIII we see that 2" × 8" joists will span only 12'-3", and 2" × 10" joists will span 15'-8". Therefore 2" × 10" should be used for first floor joists, but 2" × 8" will be satisfactory for second floor joists because of the slightly smaller second floor load.

Ceiling joists and rafters must span 14'. From Table IX we see that 2" × 6" joists will span only 11'-9", and 2" × 8" joists will span 15'-6". Therefore use 2" × 8" ceiling joists. From Table XI we see that 2" × 8" rafters will span 14'-7". Therefore use 2" × 8" rafters or 2" × 6" rafters of a higher grade than shown in the table.

LAMINATED DECKING

Laminated wood decking from 2" to 4" thick is often used for floors and roofs. Table XII gives the maximum allowable uniformly distributed load for floors or roofs up to 3–12 pitch.

EXAMPLE

A plank and beam building is designed on an 8' module. If the total live and dead roof load is determined to be 50 #/sq ft, a 3" thick laminated roof deck is required, as a 2" deck will span only 26' if laid in single span and only 37' if laid in continuous spans.

ROOFS

It is good practice to use the exterior walls, and not interior partitions, for roof support. If the span be-

TABLE VII
Safe Loads for Steel Beams in Kips

Size*	Span						
	8'	9'	10'	11'	12'	13'	14'
S 7 × 15.3	17.3ᴷ	15.4ᴷ	13.9ᴷ	12.6ᴷ			
W 8 × 17	24ᴷ	21ᴷ	18.8ᴷ	17.1ᴷ	15.7ᴷ		
W 8 × 20	28ᴷ	25ᴷ	22.6ᴷ	20.6ᴷ	18.9ᴷ	17.4ᴷ	
W 10 × 21	36ᴷ	32ᴷ	29ᴷ	26ᴷ	24ᴷ	22ᴷ	21ᴷ
W 10 × 25	44ᴷ	39ᴷ	35ᴷ	32ᴷ	29ᴷ	27ᴷ	25ᴷ

*Note: S 7 × 15.3 refers to an S shape I beam 7" high weighing 15.3 pounds per foot of length. W 8 × 17 refers to a W shape beam 8" high weighing 17 pounds per foot of length.

TABLE VIII
Floor Joist Sizes (40# live load)

Size	Spacing (oc)	Maximum Span		
		#1 Southern Pine	#2 Southern Pine	#3 Southern Pine
2" × 6"	16"	10'-2"	9'-4"	7'-10"
	12"	11'-2"	10'-3"	9'-1"
2" × 8"	16"	13'-4"	12'-3"	10'-5"
	12"	14'-8"	13'-6"	12'-0
2" × 10"	16"	17'-0	15'-8"	13'-2"
	12"	18'-9"	17'-3"	15'-4"
2" × 12"	16"	20'-9"	19'-1"	16'-1"
	12"	22'-10"	21'-0	18'-8"

TABLE IX
Ceiling Joist Sizes (Plaster ceiling, limited attic storage)

Size	Spacing (oc)	Maximum Span		
		#1 Southern Pine	#2 Southern Pine	#3 Southern Pine
2" × 4"	24"	7'-1"	6'-6"	5'-8"
	16"	8'-1"	7'-6"	6'-11"
2" × 6"	24"	11'-2"	10'-0	8'-4"
	16"	12'-9"	11'-9"	10'-3"
2" × 8"	24"	14'-8"	13'-2"	11'-1"
	16"	16'-10"	15'-6"	13'-5"
2" × 10"	24"	18'-9"	16'-10"	14'-0
	16"	21'-6"	19'-9"	17'-2"

TABLE X
Roof Joist Sizes (30# live load, any slope, plaster ceiling)

Size	Spacing (oc)	Maximum Span		
		#1 Southern Pine	#2 Southern Pine	#3 Southern Pine
2" × 6"	24"	9'-9"	8'-2"	6'-9"
	16"	11'-1"	10'-0	8'-3"
2" × 8"	24"	12'-10"	10'-10"	8'-11"
	16"	14'-8"	13'-3"	11'-0
2" × 10"	24"	16'-5"	13'-9"	11'-5"
	16"	18'-9"	16'-11"	13'-11"
2" × 12"	24"	20'-0	16'-9"	13'-10"
	16"	22'-9"	20'-6"	17'-0

TABLE XI
Rafter Sizes (30# live load, light roofing, slope over 3 in 12, no ceiling)

Size	Spacing (oc)	Maximum Span		
		#1 Southern Pine	#2 Southern Pine	#3 Southern Pine
2" × 4"	24"	7'-5"	6'-4"	5'-1"
	16"	8'-11"	7'-9"	6'-3"
2" × 6"	24"	10'-11"	9'-1"	7'-6"
	16"	13'-4"	11'-1"	9'-2"
2" × 8"	24"	14'-4"	11'-11"	9'-10"
	16"	17'-7"	14'-7"	12'-1"
2" × 10"	24"	18'-4"	15'-2"	12'-7"
	16"	22'-6"	18'-7"	15'-5"

Tables VIII–XI are adapted from *Technical Bulletin #2* of the *Southern Forest Products Association.*

VENEER   10" CAVITY   8" SOLID   12" SOLID

Figure 5   Use of angle lintels in brick wall openings.

tween exterior walls is so great that ordinary rafters cannot be used, either wood trusses or steel beams are used. Probably, a sloping roof would call for wood trusses, and a flat roof would call for steel open-web joists.

HEADERS

Large openings for windows and doors are spanned by wood or steel structural members. Wood members are called "headers," and steel members are called "lintels." Table XIII gives the maximum safe span for wood headers in light frame construction. For unusual loading conditions, special design is necessary.

EXAMPLE

Several 8' wide window openings in the Z residence will require two 2" × 12" headers, since two 2" × 10" headers will span only 7'-6" safely.

LINTELS

To span openings in masonry walls, wood headers are not satisfactory because wood shrinkage will cause cracks in the masonry above. Instead, steel angle lintels are used as shown in Figure 5. The $3\frac{1}{2}$" horizontal leg provides support for a $3\frac{3}{4}$" wide brick, and the vertical leg provides the resistance to bending. Table XIV may be used to find the lintel size required in a simple masonry wall. If joists or other members frame into the wall above the lintel, their contributing weight must also be supported, and a larger size lintel will be necessary.

EXAMPLE

In the Z residence, the angles needed to span the 3'-4" and 4'-0 fireplace openings are found to be 4" × $3\frac{1}{2}$" × $\frac{5}{16}$".

GENERAL EXAMPLE

Mr. X decides that he wants a full basement under his 24' × 48', flat roofed house. Design one girder running the length of the basement down its center, giving 12' floor joist spans. Find the size of the girder and the number and size of the columns.

Loads. First calculate the total live and dead load acting on the girder, remembering that in this plan the roof must be supported by interior partitions.

First floor live load	40 #/sq. ft.
First floor dead load	20 #/sq. ft.
First floor partitions	20 #/sq. ft.
Roof live load	30 #/sq. ft.
Roof dead load	20 #/sq. ft.
Unit live and dead load	130 #/sq. ft.

The tributary area is 12' × 48' = 576 sq. ft. Therefore the total live and dead load acting on the beam is 130#/sq. ft. × 576 sq. ft. = 74,880# = 75 kips.

Beam. Now determine the number of columns and size of the beam by trial and error, as shown in Figure 6 and the accompanying table.

The first three trials are no good, but the last three are possible. The final selection might be influenced by the future location of basement partitions or the difference in cost. (Since steel is sold by the pound, the lighter weight beams should be compared with the cost of extra columns.)

Column. If the four column solution is selected, the load on each column will be the tributary weight plus the weight of the girder.

Column load = 15 kips + (10 × 17#) = 15.2 kips

TABLE XII
Allowable Loads for Laminated Decking

Nominal Thickness	Span	Allowable Uniformly Distributed Load[1] (pounds per sq ft)	
		Single Span	Continuous Spans[2]
2"	6'	61	87
	7'	39	55
	8'	26	37
	9'	18	26
	10'	13	19
3"	10'	71	108
	12'	41	62
	14'	26	40
	16'	18	27
	18'	13	19
4"	14'	62	93
	16'	41	62
	18'	29	44
	20'	21	32

Table XII is adapted from *Koppers Company Design Manual*.
[1]Based upon allowable fiber stress of 1,500 psi (such as Southern Pine) and deflection limited to 1/240.
[2]For continuous random lay up over 3 or more spans.

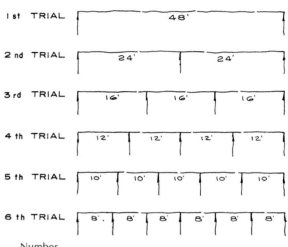

BASEMENT PLAN

Trial	Number of Columns	Span	Load in Kips	Size of Beam
1st	none	48'	75^K	No good. These large spans require
2nd	1	24'	37.5^K	deep beams, cutting down on base-
3rd	2	16'	25^K	ment headroom.
4th	3	12'	18.8^K	W 8 × 20 beam may be used (Table VII).
5th	4	10'	15^K	Use W 8 × 17 beam (Table VII).
6th	5	8'	12.5^K	Use S 7 × 15.3 beam (Table VII).

Figure 6   Calculations for Mr. X.

TABLE XIII
Safe Spans for Headers

Size	Span
Two 2" × 4"	3'-6"
Two 2" × 6"	4'-6"
Two 2" × 8"	6'-0
Two 2" × 10"	7'-6"
Two 2" × 12"	9'-0

TABLE XIV
Safe Spans for Lintels in 4" Masonry
($3\frac{1}{2}$" leg horizontal)

Size	Span
$3\frac{1}{2}$" × $3\frac{1}{2}$" × $\frac{1}{4}$"	3'
4" × $3\frac{1}{2}$" × $\frac{5}{16}$"	5'
5" × $3\frac{1}{2}$" × $\frac{5}{16}$"	6'

Using Table V, the $3\frac{1}{2}''$ diameter pipe column will be more than sufficient, and any length may be chosen ($6\frac{1}{2}'$ to $7'$ is common).

The footing, joist, and header sizes are calculated in the manner previously shown.

STUDY QUESTIONS

1. Name three factors that affect the size and spacing of structural members.
2. Distinguish between:
   a. Live load and dead load
   b. Wood beam, wood girder, and wood post
   c. Header and lintel
   d. Kip and ton
3. Give two methods used to determine dead loads.
4. What is meant by "tributary area"?
5. How much does a 20' long, W 10 × 25.4 beam weigh?
6. Why are lintels used in place of headers to support masonry construction?
7. What size of (a) steel column, and (b) Southern Pine post, would be specified to support a 40 kip tributary load if the unbraced length of column is 7'-6"?
8. What size steel beam would be specified to support a 25 kip tributary load over a 10' span?
9. What size Ponderosa Pine floor joists would be specified to span 13'-6" in a residence if the joist spacing is to be 16" oc?
10. What size header should be used for a 4' opening in a frame wall?
11. What size lintel should be used for a 4' opening in an 8' masonry wall?

LABORATORY PROBLEMS

1. Calculate the minimum safe sizes of the structural members of the Z residence assuming the following specifications:
   a. Wall footing: medium clay ground
   b. Column footing: medium clay ground
   c. Steel column: 6'-8" unbraced length
   d. Wood girder: Douglas Fir
   e. Joists: Douglas Fir
   f. Headers: 7'-6" maximum span
   g. Lintels: 4'-4" maximum span
   Use the examples given in this chapter as a guide, but note that some of the specifications have been changed.
2. Calculate the sizes of the structural members of the building assigned by your instructor.
3. Calculate the sizes of the structural members of your original building design.

25   electrical conventions

An electrical lighting system is an important part of a building, contributing both to its aesthetic effect and usefulness. The lighting system provides the major design feature during nighttime hours and, as shown in Figure 1, may affect the mood in some rooms during daytime as well. Nearly all the mechanical servants in the home—necessities and luxuries—are operated by electricity.

To design an electrical system properly, the architectural draftsman must be thoroughly familiar with the available fixtures, switches, and outlets; the symbols used for them; and how to combine these symbols properly.

FIXTURES

The symbol used for an electric fixture is either a $\frac{3}{16}''$ diameter circle for an incandescent lamp or a $\frac{1}{8}''$ wide rectangle for a fluorescent lamp on a $\frac{1}{4}' = 1'\text{-}0$ scale plan (Figure 3). These simple symbols may, however, represent a wide variety of fixture types and mountings, the exact design being further detailed to a larger scale and outlined in the specifications.

Fixture types may be either (1) direct lighting, as provided by the more commonly used fixtures, recessed lights, and spotlights, or (2) indirect lighting, as provided by valance and cove lighting. Some fixtures provide a combination of direct and indirect lighting.

Figure 1   *This library's lighting system is an important part of the building design—in both night and day.*

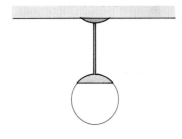

PENDANT

USED FOR GENERAL ILLUMINATION

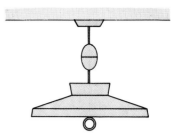

REEL

PERMITS FIXTURE TO BE ADJUSTED
TO DESIRED HEIGHT

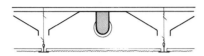

LUMINOUS CEILING

USED WITH A SUSPENDED CEILING

RECESSED

PERMITS BUILT-IN LIGHTING AT
SELECTED POSITIONS

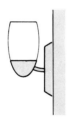

WALL

USED FOR GENERAL OR DECORATIVE
ILLUMINATION

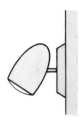

SPOT

USED FOR ACCENT ILLUMINATION

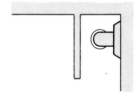

VALANCE

USED AT EDGE OF CEILING AND UNDER
KITCHEN CABINETS

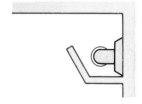

COVE

REFLECTS UP AT CEILING FOR SOFT,
INDIRECT LIGHTING

Figure 2   Fixture types.

A detailed classification of fixture types and mountings is given in Figure 2.

All of the fixture types shown in Figure 2 (except spotlighting) may be obtained with either incandescent or fluorescent lamps. Fluorescent lamps are more efficient than incandescent lamps; that is, a 40-watt fluorescent lamp will give about as much light as a 75-watt incandescent lamp. Also, the average life of the fluorescent lamp is many times longer. However some people object to their flicker, slow starting, and higher initial cost. Fluorescent lamps may be obtained in lengths between 6″ and 24″ at 3″ intervals, and also 3′, 4′, 5′, and 8′ lengths.

SWITCHES

Wall switches are often used to control the fixtures in rooms and halls. In living rooms and bedrooms, the switch may also control one or two convenience outlets. As in the case of fixtures, the symbol for a switch (the letter "S", Figure 3) may represent a wide

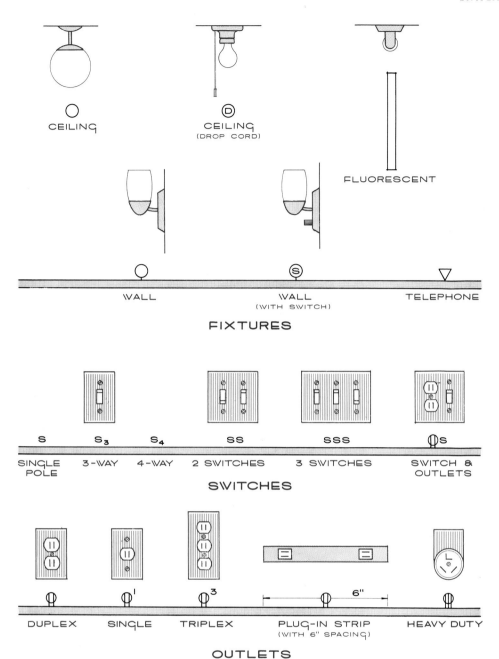

Figure 3   Electrical symbols.

variety of switch types. The most inexpensive switch is a simple on-off *toggle switch,* although most persons prefer a *quiet switch* (very faint click) or a *mercury switch* (completely silent). *Push button* types come in a wide range of button sizes ranging up to the *push plate* (in which the entire plate acts as the button). For special requirements, you may specify a *dimmer switch* (enabling a full range of light intensity to be dialed) or a *delayed action switch* (which gives light for one minute after the switch has been turned off).

Switches are usually located 4' above the floor and a few inches from the door knob side of each entrance door to a room. They are placed inside most rooms. Occasionally it may be convenient to place the switch outside the room entrance (as in a walk-in closet). Three-way switches are used when a room contains two entrances over 10' apart. Two sets of three-way switches are used at the head and foot of stairs: one set for the upstairs hall, and another set for the downstairs hall. When it is desirable to control a fixture from three or more locations, three-

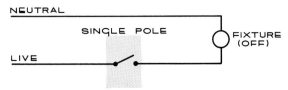

FIXTURE CONTROLLED BY ONE SWITCH

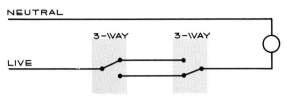

FIXTURE CONTROLLED FROM TWO LOCATIONS
(TWO 3-WAY SWITCHES)

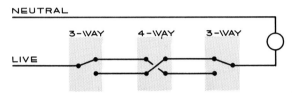

FIXTURE CONTROLLED FROM THREE LOCATIONS
(TWO 3-WAY AND ONE 4-WAY SWITCH)

Figure 4   Theory of electric switches.

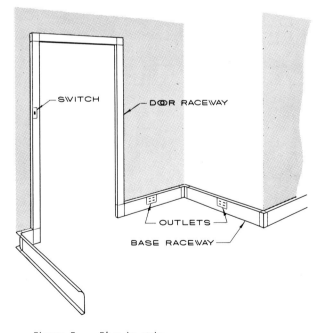

Figure 5   Plug-in strip.

way switches are used at two locations and four-way switches must be used for each additional location. (Figure 4 shows the wiring of these switches.) Pull switch fixtures in each clothes closet are useful.

OUTLETS

Room outlets should be duplex and specified no farther than 10' apart. They should be provided wherever they might be needed so that no extension cord longer than 6' need be used. Include short wall spaces, fireplace mantels, bathroom shaving, kitchen clock, and other special requirements. Consider how the outlets will serve furniture groupings; also consider possible future changes in the use of the room. Hall outlets should be specified for every 15' of hall length. Outlets are located 18" above the floor except for higher positions in the kitchen and dining areas to accommodate counter appliances. Symbols for convenience outlets are given in Figure 3. The circles are $\frac{1}{8}$" in diameter on a $\frac{1}{4}$" = 1'-0 scale plan. The two-line symbol indicates a 120-volt outlet, and the three-line symbol indicates a 240-volt, heavy duty outlet such as would be required for a range, oven, or dryer. Outdoor outlets for Christmas decorations or patio should be marked "WP" (weatherproof) on the plan.

In addition to individual outlets, *plug-in strips* are available containing outlets spaced 6", 18", 30", or 60" apart. These plug-in strips are often used behind kitchen counters when many outlets are required. They are also available as replacements for room baseboards as shown in Figure 5. Both individual outlets and plug-in strips may be wired to obtain constant electrical service on one of a set of dual outlets, and switch-controlled service on the other.

TELEPHONES

Even though only one telephone is planned in a new home, it is well to run concealed wires to all possible future telephone locations. As a minimum, one telephone should be specified on each active floor level. Also consider the kitchen planning center, master bedroom, den or study, living room, teen-ager's bedroom, guest room, recreation room, patio, and workshop. Some occasionally used rooms may be equipped for portable plug-in telephones. Most telephone companies will pre-wire residential and commercial structures while under construction upon request of the owner, unless concealed wiring can be provided after completion of construction. In either case, there is no charge for this service. At added expense, telephone lines can be run underground from the street to the house.

USE OF CONVENTIONS

After you have decided upon the number of fixtures, switches, and outlets desired, together with their locations, the completion of the electrical plan is a simple matter. A freehand, hidden line is shown connecting each fixture with its controlling switch(es). Remember this line does not represent an actual electric wire, but merely indicates that a particular switch controls a particular fixture or outlet. Examples of some typical plans are shown in Figure 6. Study them carefully.

SERVICE

Electricity is normally supplied to the home by means of an overhead three-wire service with a capacity for 150 amperes. The minimum wire size for this service is #2-gauge wire (see Figure 7). A large home (over 3000 sq. ft.) or a home with electric heat would require a larger service of 200 amperes. At extra cost, unsightly overhead wire can be eliminated by underground conductors.

CIRCUITS

To distribute electricity throughout the house, branch circuits of various capacities are installed. Several outlets or fixtures may be placed on one branch circuit for protection by a common circuit breaker in the entrance panel. Normally, house circuits are of three types:

1. *Light-duty* circuits (outlets, 2,400 watts maximum*)
   Amperage: 20
   Voltage: 120†
   Wire size: #12-gauge wire
   Description: ordinary lights
2. *Appliance* circuits (one circuit for kitchen, one circuit for laundry, and so forth)
   Amperage: 20
   Voltage: 120†
   Wire size: #12-gauge wire
   Description: refrigerator, freezer, toaster, ironer, washer, TV
3. *Heavy-duty circuits* (one individual circuit for each appliance)
   Amperage: 30
   Voltage: 240†
   Wire size: #6-gauge wire
   Description: range, oven, water heater, dryer, air conditioner

*20 amp × 120v = 2,400 watts.

† These voltages may be 120–240 volts, 115–230 volts, or 110–220 volts, depending upon the service supplied by the power company.

TABLE I
Minimum Electrical Requirements

Room	Minimum Fixtures	Minimum Outlets
Living area	Valence, cove, or accent fixtures	Outlets 10' apart plus smaller usable spaces One or several outlets controlled by switches Fireplace mantel outlet
Dining area	One reel fixture Possible valance or cove fixtures	Outlets 10' apart plus smaller usable spaces Table height appliance outlets near buffet and table
Kitchen	Ceiling fixture for general illumination Fixture over sink, controlled by switch near sink Possible under-cabinet valance fixtures	Appliance outlets 4' apart Refrigerator-freezer outlet Dishwasher outlet Kitchen clock outlet Heavy duty range outlet Heavy duty oven outlet
Laundry	Ceiling fixture at each work center	Outlets for iron Heavy duty outlets for washer and dryer
Bedroom	One ceiling fixture per 150 sq. ft. or major fraction, possibly controlled from bed location in addition to entrance door	Outlets 10' apart plus smaller usable spaces Possibly one or several outlets controlled by switch
Bathroom	One ceiling fixture if area greater than 60 sq. ft. Two wall fixtures on either side of mirror One vaporproof ceiling fixture in enclosed shower stall	One outlet for electric shaver
Hall	Ceiling fixtures 15' apart controlled from both directions	Outlets 15' apart
Stairways	One ceiling fixture on each floor or landing, controlled from both directions	None
Closets	One pull switch or automatic door switch ceiling fixture in each clothes closet	None
Front and trades entrances	One or several weatherproof fixtures per entrance Bell or chime button	Weatherproof outlet for decorative lighting
Recreation room	One flush ceiling fixture per 150 sq. ft. or major fraction Possible valance, cove, or wall fixtures	Outlets 10' apart plus smaller usable spaces
Porch, patio	One ceiling fixture per 150 sq. ft. or major fraction	Weatherproof outlets 15' apart
Utility room, basement	One ceiling fixture per 150 sq. ft. or major fraction Fixtures over work benches	Workshop outlets as required Special outlets for heating and electric hot water heater
Garage	One ceiling fixture per two cars	One weatherproof outlet per two cars
Attic	One ceiling fixture	One outlet

REQUIRED:

1 CEILING FIXTURE CONTROLLED BY
1 SWITCH, CLOSET LIGHTS

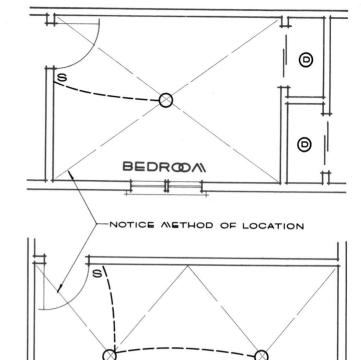

BEDROOM

NOTICE METHOD OF LOCATION

REQUIRED:

2 CEILING FIXTURES CONTROLLED BY
1 SWITCH

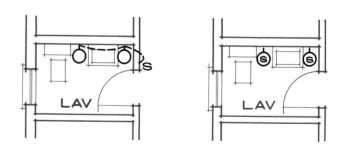

PLAYROOM

REQUIRED:

2 WALL FIXTURES CONTROLLED BY
1 SWITCH
OR
2 WALL FIXTURES WITH INTEGRAL
SWITCH

LAV   LAV

REQUIRED:

1 FLUORESCENT CEILING FIXTURE
CONTROLLED BY 2 SWITCHES

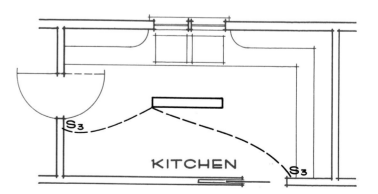

KITCHEN

Figure 6   Typical electrical plans.

REQUIRED:

I VESTIBULE CEILING FIXTURE,
I FAMILY ROOM CEILING FIXTURE,
2 OUTDOOR WALL FIXTURES,
CONTROLLED BY 3 SWITCHES IN I PLATE

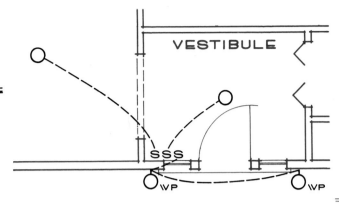

REQUIRED:

FIRST FLOOR HALL FIXTURE AND
SECOND FLOOR HALL FIXTURE
CONTROLLED BY SWITCHES ON
BOTH FLOORS

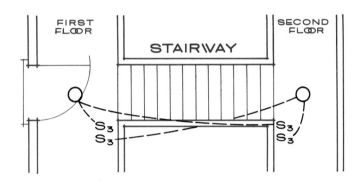

REQUIRED:

CONVENTIONAL NUMBER OF OUTLETS,
2 CONTROLLED BY SWITCH

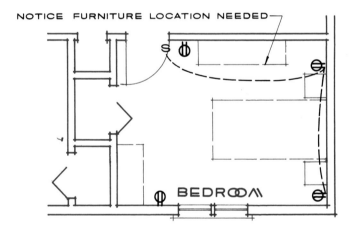

REQUIRED:

PLUG-IN STRIP WITH OUTLETS SPACED 18" APART

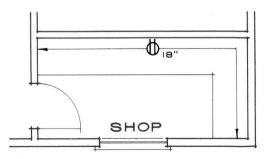

Figure 6   continued

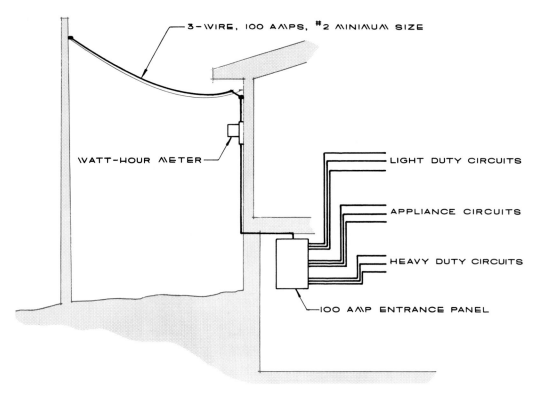

3-WIRE, 100 AMPS, #2 MINIMUM SIZE

WATT-HOUR METER

LIGHT DUTY CIRCUITS

APPLIANCE CIRCUITS

HEAVY DUTY CIRCUITS

100 AMP ENTRANCE PANEL

Figure 7   Typical electrical supply to the home.

Notice that the lower the wire gauge number, the heavier the wire. Copper wires offer resistance to the flow of electricity; the smaller the wire, the greater the resistance. Since electric energy is necessary to overcome this resistance, an underdesigned wire will heat up, causing inefficient and expensive operation (a 10 percent voltage drop reduces the light from a lamp by 30 percent), and possibly a fire hazard.

LOW-VOLTAGE SYSTEM

An electric system requiring a transformer to furnish low voltage (24 volts) has been gaining popularity recently. The major advantage of this system (also called the "remote-control system") is that a fixture may be controlled from a multitude of switch locations, the wiring being simpler than for the conventional system. Master switches may be installed that control all the house circuits. For example, all the house lights can be turned off by one master switch located in the master bedroom. Many other conveniences are possible, such as turning on the front entrance light from a kitchen location, turning off a radio or TV from the telephone locations, or controlling an attic fan from the lower house levels.

CODES

In the design of any electric system, try to meet all the special requirements of your client. Also, check that all wiring meets the requirements of the National Electric Code and existing state and municipal codes, as well as the requirements of the local utility company.

ELECTROLUMINESCENCE

It is always interesting to speculate on future developments and improvements. In the area of electric lighting, possibly the electroluminescent lamp will become popular.

This lamp can be roughly described as a thin sandwich of three sheets of material:

1. The rear sheet of metal
2. The middle sheet of plastic impregnated with zinc sulphide and purposely introduced "impurities"
3. The front sheet of transparent enamel

The front and rear sheets are electrically conductive. When alternating current is passed through them, a stream of electrons passes through

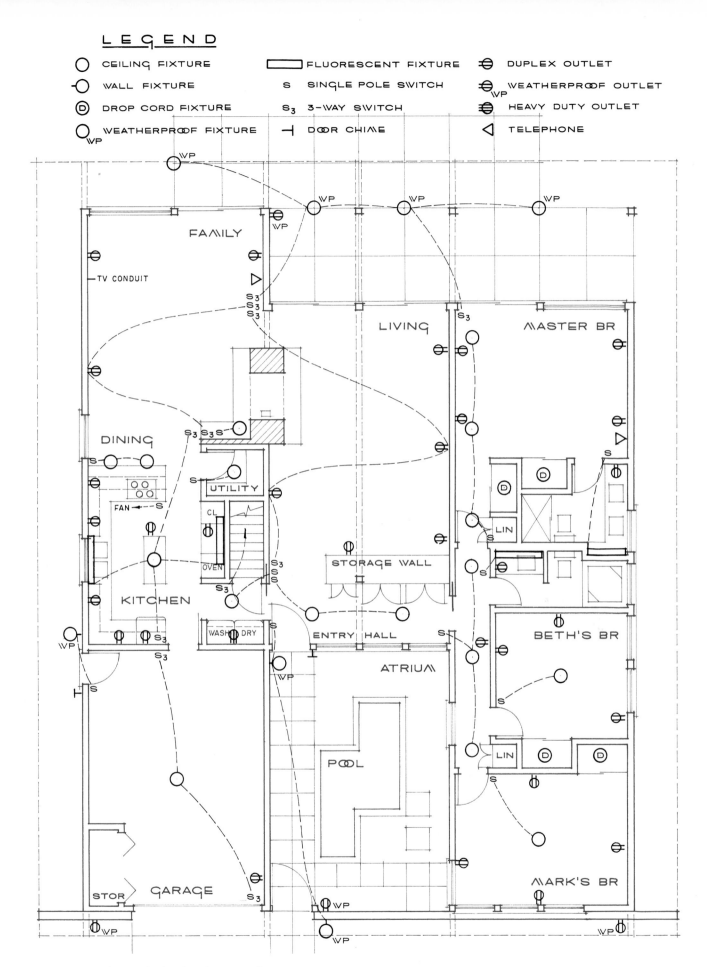

Figure 8   Electrical plan for the A residence.

the middle sheet, emitting light—thus the term *electroluminescent.*

The major advantages of this type of illumination are:

1. It provides glareless, uniform light distribution.

2. It is shockproof (eliminating periodic bulb replacement).

3. An infinite variety of sizes, shapes, and colors are possible, allowing entire walls or ceilings to be light-emitting surfaces. Experimentally produced lamps have been made in the general form of cloth and paper—suggesting drapes or wallpaper of light which may be changed in color by varying the electric frequency. It has also been suggested than an electroluminescent panel will provide the means of copying a television image—allowing flat TV screens to be hung on the walls of each room, like pictures.

A major disadvantage is that the frequencies and voltages necessary for operation are higher than are presently available in the home.

STUDY QUESTIONS

1. State the two general types of electrical fixtures and give two specific examples of each.
2. Give eight different classifications of electrical fixtures. Indicate where each type would be used.
3. List the fixtures and outlets in each major room of your home. Which of these fixtures and outlets are never used? What additional fixtures, outlets, or switches would be desirable?
4. Compare the advantages and disadvantages of incandescent and fluorescent lamps.
5. List seven types of switches giving the uses of each.
6. When are the following pieces of electrical equipment used?
   a. Three-way switches
   b. Four-way switches
   c. Heavy duty outlets
   d. Weatherproof outlets and fixtures
   e. Plug-in strips
7. List nine rooms to be considered when planning telephone installations.
8. List three types of house circuits giving the amperage, voltage, and wire size of each.
9. Will a #6 wire or a #12 wire have the greatest heat loss? Why?
10. Give two advantages of a low-voltage system.
11. (For the advanced student) After a thorough library search, prepare an illustrated paper on the history of the development of electricity to date.
12. (For the advanced student) After a thorough library search, give your estimate of the status of electricity in the home:
    a. 25 years hence
    b. 100 years hence

LABORATORY PROBLEMS

1. Prepare a legend of the commonly used electrical symbols. List each type of electrical requirement and show its conventionally used symbol.
2. (For the advanced student) Include in the legend of Problem 1 seldom used electrical symbols. (Hint: Refer to a reference such as *Architectural Graphic Standards.*)
3. Draw the electrical plan for the A residence.
4. Draw the electrical plan for rooms of your own design with the following requirements:
   a. 14' × 23' living room with fireplace
   b. 14' × 14' dining room
   c. 15' × 27' playroom
   e. $3\frac{1}{2}$' × 14' hall
   f. front entrance vestibule with an outdoor fixture and outlet
   g. stairways appearing on the first floor plan (to the second floor and basement)
5. Draw a diagram showing how electrical energy is supplied to a house lamp from the street service wire. Include changes in amperage and wire size.
6. (For the advanced student) Construct a working model of cardboard demonstrating:
   a. How a fixture is controlled from two locations
   b. How a fixture may be controlled from three locations
7. Draw the electrical plan for the building assigned by your instructor.
8. Complete the electrical plan for your original house design. To prevent cluttering the floor plan, the electrical plan is often a separate drawing—the wall, door, and window indications being *lightly* retraced with *darker* electrical symbols.

26 plumbing

An understanding of plumbing systems is important to the architectural designer and draftsman. Since the plumbing and heating systems account for one-fifth of the total house cost, the designer is interested in obtaining an economical, as well as functional, design. The draftsman often prepares mechanical plans—plumbing, heating, electrical, and structural—in addition to the architectural plans. Although plumbing plans may be omitted from the design of a small residence (leaving all decisions to the contractor), they are always included in the design of a larger building.

A plumbing system performs two major functions:

1. Water distribution
2. Sewage disposal

The water distribution system consists of the supply pipes that conduct water from the water main or other source to lavatories, bathtubs, showers, and toilets. A portion of this must be routed through a water heater to provide hot water. Most of the water piped into a building must also be drained out together with water-carried wastes. The *sewage disposal* system is composed of the waste pipes that conduct this water to the public sewer or disposal field.

WATER DISTRIBUTION

Piping. A wide variety of water supply pipes are available.

Copper tubing with soldered joints is usually used in residential work. The nominal diameter indicates the approximate inside diameter of the tubing. The designations K, L, and M indicate wall thickness from heavy to light. Compare the inside and outside diameters listed below:

1″ Cu. Tubing Type K:	0.995″I.D.	1.125″O.D.
1″ Cu. Tubing Type L:	1.025″I.D.	1.125″O.D.
1″ Cu. Tubing Type M:	1.055″I.D.	1.125″O.D.

The designation DWV (drainage, waste, and vent) indicates a still lighter tubing intended for sewage disposal only.

Brass pipe is more rigid than copper and is used with screwed fittings in large, expensive buildings.

Iron pipe is used for underground supply outside buildings, but is not used inside.

Steel pipe is inexpensive but not durable due to corrosion. Both iron and steel pipe must be galva-

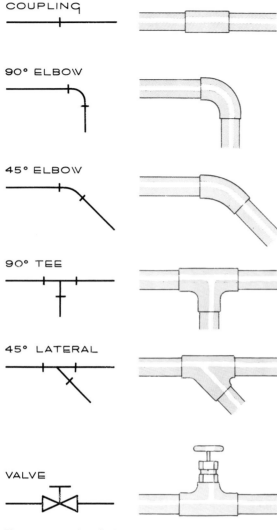

COUPLING

90° ELBOW

45° ELBOW

90° TEE

45° LATERAL

VALVE

Figure 1   Pipe fittings.

nized or coated with hot pitch to reduce this corrosion.

Plastic pipe comes in a wide range of sizes and flexibilities, but most plumbing codes will not accept it for water supply.

Fittings. Pipe is joined by *couplings* to connect straight runs, or *elbows* to connect 45° or 90° bends (Figure 1). *Tees* are used for 45° and 90° branches. *Gate valves* are used to completely shut off the water supply for repair; *globe valves* to provide a range of water regulation from off to on (like a faucet). *Check valves* permit flow in one direction only and are used when there is a possibility of back pressure. Valves are also called *cocks, bibbs,* and *faucets.*

Cold water supply. Let us trace the path of the water

from the street main to the house faucets as shown in Figure 2. Upon request, the city water department excavates the street to the public water main and installs a *tap* (pipe) to the property line. A gooseneck is included to allow for future settling of the pipe. Two cocks are installed on the tap—one close to the main, called the *corporation cock,* and another close to the property line, called the *curb cock.* The curb cock is attached to a long valve stem reaching up to the ground so that water can be disconnected without another excavation.

The contractor connects $\frac{3}{4}$″ copper tubing to the curb cock and runs it in a trench below the frost line to the building. It enters the building through a caulked pipe sleeve, and immediately the *service cock, water meter,* and *drain valve* are installed. The service cock is a gate valve which allows the owner to shut off water throughout the building. The water meter registers the quantity of water used. The drain valve is used when it is necessary to drain all water from the system. If a water softener is to be included, lines for hard water hose bibbs are first connected.

A $\frac{3}{4}$″ cold water feeder line is then installed in the basement ceiling with $\frac{1}{2}$″ risers running directly to each fixture. Each riser is extended 2′ higher than the fixture connection to provide an air chamber to reduce knocking (water hammer). Valves are installed at the bottom of each riser so that repairs can be made without shutting off the water for the entire house.

Hot water supply. A tee is installed on the $\frac{3}{4}$″ cold water supply line so that some water is routed through the water heater—entering at 70°F and leaving at 130°F. A $\frac{3}{4}$″ feeder and $\frac{1}{2}$″ risers are again installed leading to each fixture (the lavatory, tub, and shower require hot and cold water, but a toilet requires only cold). A gate valve is installed at the entrance to the water heater so that it can be shut off for repair. Water may be heated by the existing house heating system or independently by means of electric or gas heaters.

Pipe sizes. Proper pipe sizing depends upon a number of factors, such as the average water consumption, peak loads, available water pressure, and friction loss in long runs of pipe. For the average residence, however, this procedure may be simplified by the use of the minimum sizes recommended by the Federal Housing Administration as shown in Table I. Notice that waste and vent stack sizes are also included to help in sizing the sewage disposal system.

SEWAGE DISPOSAL

The water distribution system just described is roughed in a new house before the interior walls

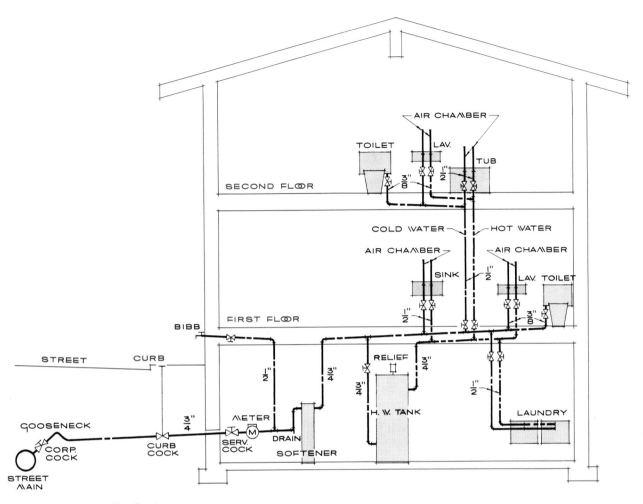

Figure 2   Water distribution.

are finished. The sewage disposal system which conducts waste water from the home is installed at the same time. The fixtures themselves are added after the interior walls are finished. Let us trace the path of the waste water from the fixtures to the public sewer (shown in Figure 3).

Fixture branches. The fixture branches are nearly horizontal pipes of cast iron, brass, copper, or galvanized steel which conduct the waste water from the fixtures to the vertical waste stacks (vertical pipes are called "stacks"). They are pitched $\frac{1}{8}$" to $\frac{1}{2}$" per foot away from the fixtures, and they should be as short as possible. Sizes are shown in Table I.

Traps. To prevent sewer gases in the fixture branches from entering the living quarters, a U-shaped fitting called a *trap* is connected close to each fixture. This trap catches and holds waste water at each discharge, thus providing a water seal. Lavatory and bathtub traps like those shown in Figure 4 are installed in

TABLE I
Minimum Pipe Sizes

	Hot Water	Cold Water	Soil or Waste Branches	Vent
Supply lines	$\frac{3}{4}$"	$\frac{3}{4}$"		
Feeder lines				
bathroom group plus one or more fixtures	$\frac{3}{4}$"	$\frac{3}{4}$"		
3 fixtures (other than bathroom group)	$\frac{3}{4}$"	$\frac{3}{4}$"		
bathroom group	$\frac{1}{2}$"	$\frac{1}{2}$"		
2 fixtures	$\frac{1}{2}$"	$\frac{1}{2}$"		
hose bibb plus one or more fixtures		$\frac{3}{4}$"		
hose bibb		$\frac{1}{2}$"		
Fixture risers				
toilet		$\frac{3}{8}$"	3"	2"
bathtub	$\frac{1}{2}$"	$\frac{1}{2}$"	$1\frac{1}{2}$"	$1\frac{1}{4}$"
shower	$\frac{1}{2}$"	$\frac{1}{2}$"	2"	$1\frac{1}{4}$"
lavatory	$\frac{3}{8}$"	$\frac{3}{8}$"	$1\frac{1}{4}$"	$1\frac{1}{4}$"
sink	$\frac{1}{2}$"	$\frac{1}{2}$"	$1\frac{1}{2}$"	$1\frac{1}{4}$"
laundry tray	$\frac{1}{2}$"	$\frac{1}{2}$"	$1\frac{1}{2}$"	$1\frac{1}{4}$"
sink and tray combination	$\frac{1}{2}$"	$\frac{1}{2}$"	$1\frac{1}{2}$"	$1\frac{1}{4}$"

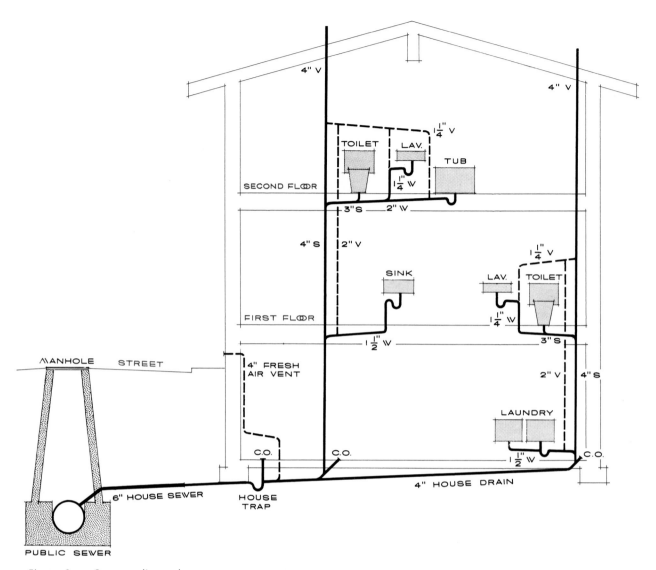

Figure 3   Sewage disposal.

the fixture branch lines; toilet traps are cast as part of the fixture.

Vent stacks. A sudden discharge of waste water causes a suction action which may empty the trap. To prevent this, vent pipes are connected beyond the trap and extended through the roof to open air. Vent stacks should be installed not less then 6″ nor more than 5′ from the trap. Vent stack sizes may be obtained from Table I. The portion extending through the roof is increased to 4″ diameter to prevent stoppage by snow or frost. The 4″ section should begin at least 1′ below the roof, extend 1′ above the roof, and be no closer than 12′ to ventilators or higher windows.

Waste and soil stacks. It would be very costly to carry each fixture branch separately to the sewer;

therefore the fixture branches are connected at each floor level to a large vertical pipe. This pipe is called a *waste stack* if it receives discharge from any fixture except a toilet. It is called a *soil stack* if it receives discharge from a toilet, with or without other fixtures. Soil stacks are often 4″ diameter, waste stacks 3″ diameter. As with vent stacks, their upper ends should be 4″ in diameter and extend 1′ above the roof to open air. This retards the decomposition of organic matter, since bacteria do not work in the presence of free oxygen. For maximum economy, fixtures should be grouped so that all fixture branches drain into only one or two stacks.

House drain and house sewer. The soil and waste stacks discharge into the *house drain*—an extra heavy cast iron pipe with lead joints under the basement floor. It is a 4″ diameter pipe running under the footing and 5' past the foundation wall. The house drain is then connected to the *house sewer* which may also be of 4" cast iron or of 6" vitrified clay. Both the house drain and house sewer are sloped ¼" per foot to the public sewer.

Cleanouts. Cleanouts are elbows projecting through the basement floor to permit cleaning the house drain and sewer. They are installed in the house drain beyond the last stack, just inside the basement wall, and in between at points not over 50' apart. It is best to include cleanouts at the foot of each waste or soil stack and at each change of direction of the horizontal run. Threaded plugs are used to close the cleanouts.

House trap. The trap installed next to the building in the house drain is called a *house trap*. It furnishes

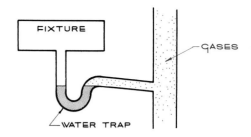

Figure 4   *Fixture trap.*

a water seal against the entrance of gas from the public sewer to the building piping. Cleanouts are located at the top of one or both sides of the trap.

Fresh air inlet. A 4" diameter air vent installed next to the house trap admits fresh air to the house drain.

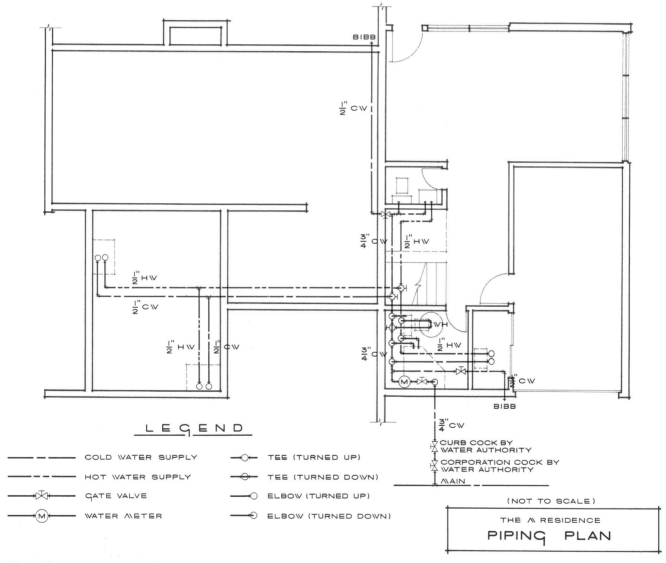

LEGEND

COLD WATER SUPPLY	TEE (TURNED UP)
HOT WATER SUPPLY	TEE (TURNED DOWN)
GATE VALVE	ELBOW (TURNED UP)
WATER METER	ELBOW (TURNED DOWN)

CURB COCK BY WATER AUTHORITY
CORPORATION COCK BY WATER AUTHORITY
MAIN

(NOT TO SCALE)

THE M RESIDENCE
PIPING PLAN

Figure 5

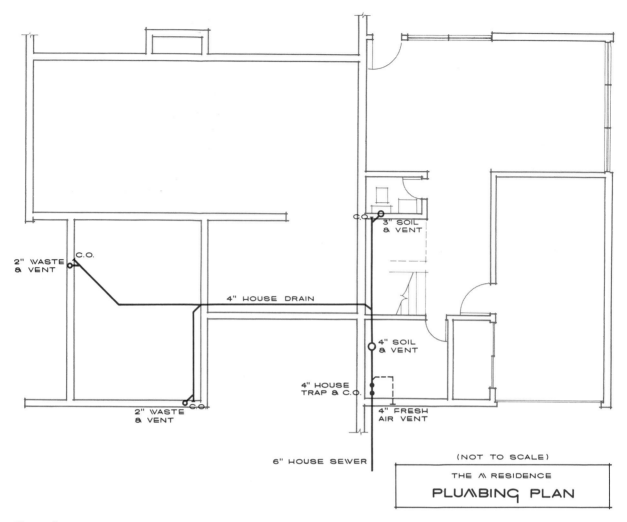

Figure 6

The fresh air inlet does not run through the roof, but rather to a place 6″ above the ground. It is finished with a gooseneck bend or grille.

PIPING AND PLUMBING PLANS

The water distribution and sewage disposal systems may be shown in an elevation (as in Figures 2 and 3) or in an isometric drawing, but it is usually shown in plan (as in Figures 5 and 6). The water distribution system is shown in the *piping plan,* and the sewage disposal system is shown in the *plumbing plan.* Notice that since these plans are schematic drawings it is not necessary to hold to scale.

Some typical instructions appearing on such plans follow.

GENERAL NOTES

1. All underground piping should be type K copper

(soft temper) with screwed pressure type joints.

2. All hot and cold water piping inside the building should be type L copper (hard temper) with soldered joints.

3. All soil and waste piping above ground should be type M copper with soldered joints.

4. All soil and waste piping under ground should be heavy cast iron with lead and oakum bell and spigot joints.

5. Furnish and install stop valves in all hot and cold water lines before fixtures; if visible, valves to have same finish as fixture trim.

6. All fixtures shown on drawings to be furnished and completely connected with approved chrome-plated brass trim, traps, and suitable supports. Furnish and install chrome-plated escutcheon plates where pipes pierce finish walls.

For more detailed information than is given in this chapter, obtain the *ASHRAE Guide* from the American Society of Heating, Refrigerating, and Air Conditioning Engineers, or the *National Plumbing Code* from the National Printing Office in Washington, D.C.

FUTURE TRENDS

Sovent plumbing. A single-stack, self-venting sewage disposal system was developed recently and holds promise for multistory buildings. The first American installation was in the model apartments (called "Habitat") at the Expo 67 World's Fair in Montreal, Canada. This system is called "sovent" indicating a combination of *soil* stacks and *vent* stacks. The key to this system is an aerator fitting which is located at the connection of each fixture branch to the soil stack. This fitting limits the sewage flow velocity in the stack, thus reducing the suction which would siphon the traps. The sovent stack extends through the roof and acts both as a soil stack and a vent stack.

Solar water heating. Solar water heaters are available in countries such as Japan, Australia, and Israel where energy costs are high, but are not yet popular in the United States where low cost electrical, gas, and oil heaters are available. If fossil fuels become scarce, it is predicted that solar domestic water heating will find a significant place.

Experimental solar heaters for swimming pools have been constructed, but they also are not economically competitive with other sources of heat.

Solar stills.* In some locations a supply of potable (drinkable) water has become a critical need. The solar still provides an effective solution. The first large solar still used to purify salt or brackish water was built in Chile a century ago (1872). In recent years, more than twenty community-size solar stills, ranging from 100 to several thousand gallons per day, operating on sea water or inland brackish water, have been built in ten different countries. This type of usage predictably will increase.

Small home stills to convert seawater to drinking water are being manufactured by the Sunwater Company of San Diego and have been installed along the coasts of California and Mexico. These stills consist of shallow pans covered by glass panels as shown in Figure 7. Installed on a flat roof, an automatic feed pump provides a constant supply of seawater. The daily output of such an installation is about $1\frac{1}{2}$ gallons of potable water.

Solar farming. The development of solar stills has been expanded to provide the means to farm in areas where only salt water is available. The process requires air-inflated plastic greenhouses in which the water transpired by vegetable plants is condensed on the plastic roof and then reused for root irrigation.

An integrated plant which can supply potable water and food as well as power is being built in the Arabian state of Abu Dhabi by the University of Arizona. Among other benefits, it is expected that the price of fresh vegetables can be lowered enough

*Courtesy Horace McCracken, Solar Equipment Consultant.

to provide a new food source for the 40,000 people of the state.

STUDY QUESTIONS

1. Distinguish between:
   a. K, L, M, and DWV copper tubing
   b. Coupling, elbow, and tee
   c. Gate valve, globe valve, and check valve
   d. Corporation cock, curb cock, and service cock
2. Give the minimum pipe sizes for:
   a. Supply lines
   b. Feeder line to a bathroom
   c. Feeder line to a hose bibb
   d. Feeder line to a powder room
   e. Fixture risers to a lavatory
3. Give the principal reasons for using:
   a. Traps
   b. Vent stacks
   c. Cleanouts
4. Distinguish between:
   a. Soil stack and waste stack
   b. House drain and house sewer
   c. Piping plan and plumbing plan

LABORATORY PROBLEMS

1. Prepare a legend of the commonly used piping and plumbing symbols. List each requirement and show its conventionally used symbol.
2. (For the advanced student) Include in the legend for Problem 1 seldom used piping and plumbing symbols. (Hint: Refer to a reference such as *Architectural Graphic Standards.*)
3. Draw (a) the piping plan and (b) the plumbing plan for the A residence.
4. Draw a diagram showing:
   a. How water is distributed from street main to fixtures
   b. How waste water is carried from fixtures to the sewer
5. Draw (a) the piping plan and (b) the plumbing plan for the building assigned by your instructor.
6. Draw (a) the piping plan and (b) the plumbing plan for your original building design. To prevent confusing the floor plan, the piping and plumbing plan is often a separate drawing—the wall, door, and window indications being *lightly* retraced with *darker* piping and plumbing symbols.

Figure 7   *A 2-gallon/day solar still installed on the roof of a San Diego home.*

27 heating and air conditioning

The earliest known central heating systems were built by the Romans to heat their bath houses. Tile hot air ducts were used to heat the buildings, and lead pipes were used to conduct hot water to the baths. Although such systems have been used in palaces for several thousand years, they were not used for small home heating until about a hundred years ago. Today we can choose from a multitude of systems which include cooling, humidity control, ventilation, and filtering, in addition to heating.

HEATING

The most expensive appliance in a building is the heating system—its initial cost amounts to about 10 percent of the total house cost and the fuel costs amount to several hundred dollars per year. A building's heating system is specified by an architectural engineer (specializing in heating) after consulting with the client. The architectural draftsman must be able to prepare heating plans from the heating engineer's calculations and sketches. Therefore the draftsman should be familiar with all heating systems, their design and layout, and how they are represented on the heating plan. We will consider heating systems of five general types:

1. Warm air   4. Electric
2. Hot water   5. Solar
3. Steam

Let us look at the operation of each, together with its advantages and disadvantages.

Warm air. In *forced warm air,* warm air is circulated through sheet metal supply ducts to the rooms, and cold air is pulled through return ducts to the furnace for reheating (usually to about 150°F). Duct-work may consist of a number of small individual ducts leading to each room (*individual duct system,* Figure 1), or a master duct which reduces in size as it branches off to feed the rooms (*trunk duct system,* Figure 2). Circular ducts are 4″ diameter tubes which slip together like stovepipe, with flexible elbows to form any angle up to 90 degrees. Rectangular ducts are custom made to fit in spaces between joists and studs.

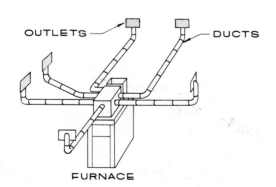

Figure 1   Individual duct system.

A fan, operating either continuously or intermittently, circulates the air. The thermostat * controls the fan in the intermittent system. The fan may be similar to a common electric fan, but more probably it will be a centrifugal type called a *blower.*

For even temperature throughout the house, the warm air should be delivered to the places that lose heat fastest—the exterior walls. The warm air is supplied through grilles with manually operated louvers located in the exterior walls or floor, preferably under windows. These grilles are called *registers* or *diffusers.* In place of registers, warm air *baseboard units* (Figure 3) may be used to distribute the heat along a wider portion of the exterior wall.

Since the heating element, air, is actually blown into the room, warm air heating has the inherent disadvantage of distributing dust throughout the house. This is somewhat checked by *filters*—pads of spun metal or glass coated with oil to catch dust. These must be replaced or cleaned often to be effective. Another method is attracting dust by a high voltage screen.

Perimeter heating. This forced warm air system was developed for a special need—to heat the basementless house. As previously described, warm air is delivered to the exterior walls, or *perimeter,* of a building. Perimeter heating, however, has an additional function—to warm the floor itself, thus replacing the heat lost through the concrete slab floor or wood floor over a crawl space.

The recommended perimeter heating system for a slab floor is the *perimeter loop,* Figure 4. This consists of a 6″ diameter tile duct imbedded in the outer edge of the slab and supplied by warm air fed through radial ducts. The ducts warm the slab, while floor registers in the ducts supply heat to the rooms.

Another perimeter heating method is called the *perimeter radial* system, Figure 5. Radial ducts run directly to the floor registers with no outer loop. This system is often used in crawl spaces.

The *crawl space plenum* system, Figure 6, utilizes the entire crawl space as a plenum (warm air reservoir). Short ducts (6′ minimum length) from the furnace heat the crawl space plenum, which then supplies heat to the rooms through perimeter floor registers. All perimeter heating requires careful insulation of the foundation to prevent excessive heat loss.

Hot water. In *forced circulation hot water,* a hot water boiler heats the circulating water to 200°–

---

*A thermostat is an instrument sensitive to changes in temperature. One type contains two metal strips having different temperature coefficients brazed together. One end of the strips is fixed, but the free end will move due to dissimilar expansion of the metals. This closes an electric contact to start a motor which controls the heating and cooling systems.

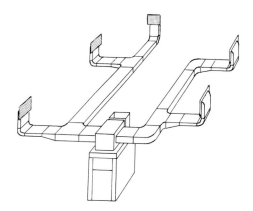

Figure 2   Trunk duct system.

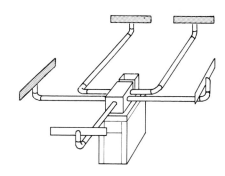

Figure 3   Warm air baseboard units.

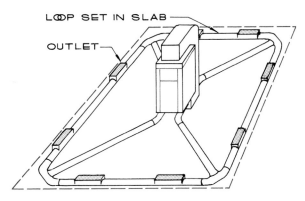

Figure 4   Perimeter loop system.

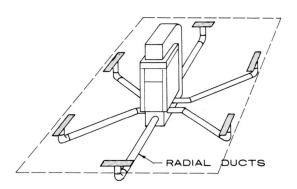

Figure 5   Perimeter radial system.

215°F.* An electric pump controlled by the thermostat circulates the water through narrow ($\frac{1}{2}''$–$\frac{3}{4}''$) flexible tubing to radiators or convectors giving up heat to the room. The temperature of the return water

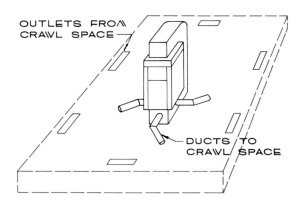

Figure 6   Crawl space plenum system.

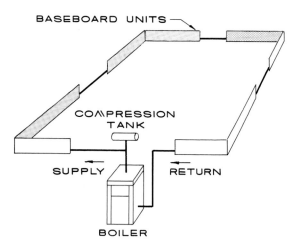

Figure 7   Series loop.

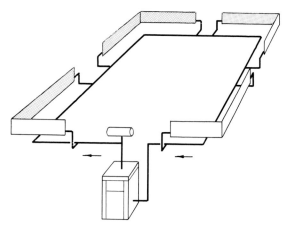

Figure 8   One-pipe system.

is about 20°F lower than the boiler delivery. The temperature of the delivery water can be automatically adjusted by a mixing valve which determines the amount of hot water required in the circulating system. Also, each radiator can be regulated by automatic or manual valves. Usually the boiler is fitted with additional heating coils to supply hot water, winter and summer, to the sinks, tubs, and laundry.

A hot water system is also called *hydronic* heating. Three hot water piping systems can be used:

1. Series loop
2. One-pipe system
3. Two-pipe system

Series loop. The series loop system (Figure 7) is, in effect, a single baseboard radiator extending around the entire house and dropping under doorways and window walls. Hot water enters the baseboard near the boiler and travels through each baseboard section and back to the boiler for reheating. It is often used in small homes because it is inexpensive to install, but there can be no individual control of the heating units. Either the entire house is heated or none of it. A compromise is the installation of *two* series loops in two zones which may be independently controlled.

One-pipe system. The one-pipe system (Figure 8) is often specified for the average size residence. Hot water is circulated through a main; special tee fittings diverting a portion of the water to each radiator. Radiators can be individually controlled by valves and located either above the main (*upfeed* system) or below it (*downfeed* system). Downfeed is less effective because it is difficult to coax the water into the branches.

Since water expands when heated, a compression tank is connected to the supply main. A cushion of air in the tank adjusts for the varying volume of water in the system as the water temperature changes.

Two-pipe system. The two-pipe system is used for large installations. The hot water is circulated by two main pipes, one for supply and one for return. The water is diverted from the supply main to a radiator, and then flows from the radiator to the return main. In this manner, all radiators receive hot water at maximum temperature. The *reversed return* system of Figure 9 is preferred to the *direct return* system of Figure 10. Piping is saved in the direct return system, but the total length of supply and return piping is the same in the reversed return system, assuring equal flow due to equal friction.

Piping in the one- and two-pipe systems needs no pitch except for drainage. All hot water systems must be drained or kept operating to prevent their freezing when the house is not occupied.

Heating units. The heating units used in hot

---

*The entire system contains water under slight pressure to prevent the formation of steam at 212°F.

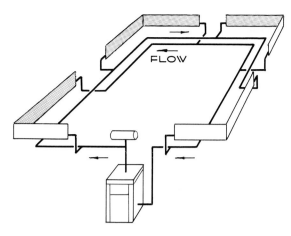

Figure 9   Two-pipe system, reversed return.

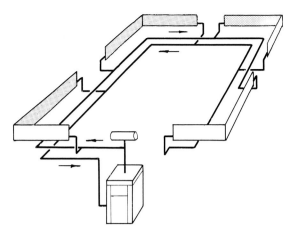

Figure 10   Two-pipe system, direct return.

water heating are either radiators, convectors, or combinations of radiator and convector. A radiator has large, exposed surfaces to allow heat to *radiate* to the room. Radiant heat does not depend upon air movement; it passes through the air directly to any object. A convector, however, draws in cool air from the room at the bottom, warms it by contact with closely spaced fins, and forces it out into the room again. Heat is therefore circulated by air movement. The major disadvantage of convection is that the heat rises to the ceiling, leaving the floor cold.

Radiators and convectors (Figure 11) may be recessed into the wall to increase floor space. Baseboard heating may be radiant or convector. The distribution system is identical for conventional and baseboard heating.

Radiant panel heating. In this system the entire floor, the ceiling, or the walls serve as radiators. The heating element may be hot water or steam in tubing, hot air, or even electricity. In the hot water system, prefabricated loops of tubing are imbedded into a concrete floor (Figure 12) or attached to the ceiling or walls before plastering (Figure 13). In dry wall construction, the tubing is installed behind the wall or ceiling panels. In the warm air system, ducts may be laid in the floor or ceiling, or the entire space above the ceiling may be heated by blowing warm air into it.

Steam heating. Steam heating is often specified in very large buildings. As in hot water heating, one-pipe and two-pipe systems are available.

In the one-pipe system (Figure 14), a steam boiler heats water to steam, which is then circulated through one main to single runouts on the radiators. The runouts are sloped so that condensate (steam cooled to water) can run back through the same runout to the main to be reheated. The main is sloped so that the steam and condensate run in the same direction. A radiator valve helps control heat and an air vent allows air to escape from the

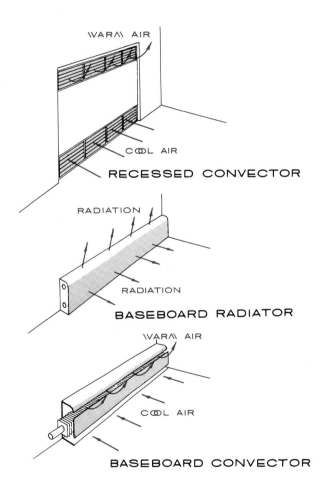

Figure 11   Types of heating units.

radiators without allowing steam to escape. The two-pipe steam heating systems are called *vapor* or *vacuum* systems. They operate under high boiler pressure in severe weather and reduced pressure in mild weather. Thus they can respond better to the demand for heat.

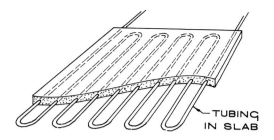

Figure 12   Radiant floor panel.

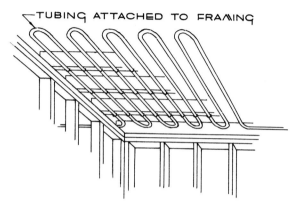

Figure 13   Radiant ceiling panel.

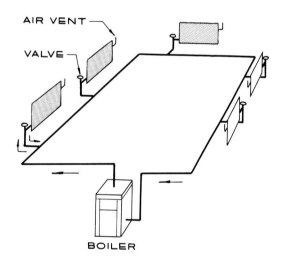

Figure 14   One-pipe steam system.

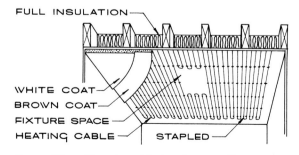

Figure 15   Electric cable in plaster ceiling.

Electric heat. Electric heating systems offer many advantages: low installation cost, no exposed heating elements, individual room control, cleanliness, and silent operation. The main disadvantage is the high cost of operation in localities not offering low electric rates. Heavy insulation is required to keep operation costs to a minimum. The most popular electric heating systems for homes are:

1. Electric resistance cable
2. Electric panels
3. Electric baseboards
4. Heat pump

Electric resistance cable. Covered wire cables are heated by electricity and concealed in the ceiling or walls. The wires are manufactured to specific lengths to provide the rated wattage. They are stapled to gypsum lath in a gridlike pattern, only a few inches apart. Then they are covered by a $\frac{1}{2}$" brown coat and finish coat of plaster (Figure 15) or gypsum board (Figure 16). The temperature of each room can be individually controlled by thermostats.

Electric panels. Prefabricated ceiling panels (Figure 17) are only $\frac{1}{4}$" thick and constructed of a layer of rubber containing conductive material and backed with asbestos board. They cover the entire ceiling, and can be painted, plastered, or papered. Smaller glass wall panels are backed with an aluminum grid for the resistance element and are available in radiant, convection, and fan-forced types. These panels are set into the outside walls under the windows and are best suited for supplemental or occasional heating.

Electric baseboard. Most electric baseboards are convection heaters (Figure 18). They consist of a heating element enclosed in a metal baseboard molding. Slots at the bottom and top of the baseboard permit the circulation of warmed air.

Heat pump. The heat pump (Figure 19) works on the same principle as the refrigerator, which takes heat out of the inside compartments and discharges it into the room. The heat pump takes heat from the outdoors and brings it into the house. It does this by further "refrigeration" of the outside air. A refrig-

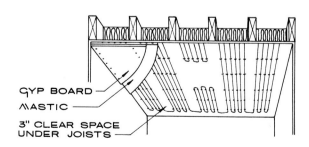

Figure 16   Electric cable in gypsum board ceiling.

erant (which acts to absorb heat) circulates between two sets of coils—the evaporator and the condenser. During cold weather the outside air is blown over the evaporator coils. Although this air is cold, the refrigerant is much colder and thus absorbs heat as it changes from liquid to gas. The warmed refrigerant is then pumped to the condenser where the room air is blown over the coils and is heated by the refrigerant as it changes back to a liquid. The still colder outside air is blown back outdoors again. During warm weather the operation is reversed so that heat is removed from the room.

Solar heat. A solar heating system uses the sun's rays as the heating source. This is a comparatively new concept and is therefore not widely used as yet. However, when we hear that the earth's deposits of coal and oil will be depleted in 150 years, it is obvious that such additional energy sources must be exploited.

The simplest of solar heating systems consists of large glass areas on the southern wall which permit the sun's rays to heat the house. As shown in Figure 20, the roof overhang is designed to permit the winter sun swinging low on the horizon to warm the house, but exclude the summer sun which is high in the sky. The exact angle of the sun by hour, date, and latitude is given in standard reference books. This is not an efficient system, however, since in the evening and on cloudy days much heat escapes through the same glass areas. Other systems permit storage of the solar energy during sunny hours so that heat will be supplied for a few hours after the sun disappears. Because long-term storage (several days, for example) is not yet economically feasible, a supplemental heating system is still needed.

The most promising solar heat system uses the *heat of fusion* to store heat. A great amount of heat is required to melt a solid into a liquid. When this melting or "fusion" occurs, the temperature does not change. For example, one Btu of heat is required to raise the temperature of one pound of water 1°F, but 144 Btu is needed to melt one pound of 32°F ice to 32°F water. In the heat of fusion system, heat is collected through glass panels mounted on the roof, as shown in Figure 21. This heat is then blown through tubing surrounded by a chemical compound having a melting point of about 90°F. As the chemical compound is melted from a solid to a liquid, it stores heat until the heat is released later by its changing back to a solid again.

The accompanying table of advantages and disadvantages may help in the selection of heating systems for an individual case. You may want to add to it.

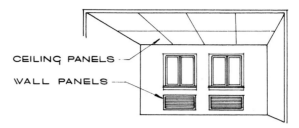

Figure 17   Electric panels.

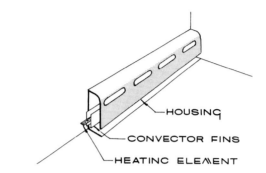

Figure 18   Electric baseboard.

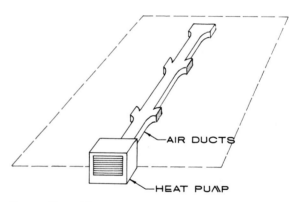

Figure 19   Heat pump.

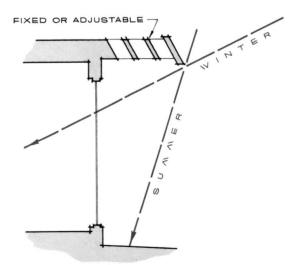

Figure 20   Design of roof overhang for solar windows.

HEAT COLLECTION PANELS

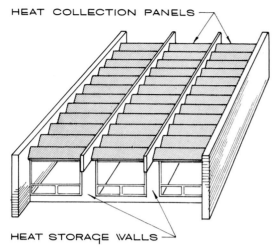

HEAT STORAGE WALLS

Figure 21   Solar heating system.

Figure 22   Norfolk City Hall.

TABLE I
Comparison of Heating Systems

	Advantages	Disadvantages
Warm air	Quick heat	Ducts take up basement headroom
	No radiators or convectors to take up floor space	Ducts convey dust and sound
	Air conditioning and humidification possible	Flue action increases fire danger
	Cannot freeze	Separate hot water heater required
	Low installation cost	
Hot water	Low temperature heat possible for mild weather	Retains heat during periods when no longer required
		Slow to heat up
		Radiators require two lines
		Must be drained to avoid freezing when not in use
Radiant	No visible heating device	Slow response to heat needs
	Economical operation	Air conditioning must be separate unit
	Good temperature distribution	Repair costly
Steam (one pipe)	Radiators require only one line	Large size pipes required
		Sloping pipes take up basement headroom
		Inefficient: time and pressure required to vent air from radiators
		Water hammer
Electric	No visible heating device	Operation cost high in many locations
	Low installation cost	Heavy insulation required
	Individual room control	
	Clean, silent operation	
Solar	Low operation cost	Supplemental heating system necessary
		System not fully developed

Insulation.* Houses should be insulated to obtain the maximum efficiency from the heating and cooling systems, and to provide the comfort of a steady temperature. Properly installed insulation can reduce heating and cooling costs by as much as 40 percent while at the same time making the house warm in winter and cool in summer.

Insulation is available in many forms. For new house construction, batts or blankets (rolls) are often specified. They are sized to fit snugly between studs and joists or rafters. A 3″ to 4″ batt or blanket is termed full-thick, and one $1\frac{1}{2}$″ to 2″ is termed semi-thick. Mineral wool batts are also available in 6″ thickness. Both rockwool and glass wool are available. Most insulation batts and blankets are made with a vapor barrier on one side, which is installed facing the inside (warm side) of the house to prevent condensation. Condensation occurs only when moisture reaches a cold surface through which it cannot readily pass, and the vapor barrier, when properly installed, does not become cold. If the insulation is improperly installed, with the vapor barrier toward the outside (cold side) of the house, moisture will condense upon contact with the cold vapor barrier, making the insulation ineffective.

Rigid insulation made of asphalt-impregnated fiberboard, and foamed plastics, such as Styrofoam and Urethane, are frequently used as insulation under built-up roofs. A common size for these materials is 24″ × 48″ in thicknesses of $\frac{1}{2}$″ to 3″ in $\frac{1}{2}$″ increments. Foamed plastics are popular as perimeter

*Courtesy B. E. Beneyfield, Moisture Control Consultant.

Figure 23   Norfolk City Hall—corner detail.

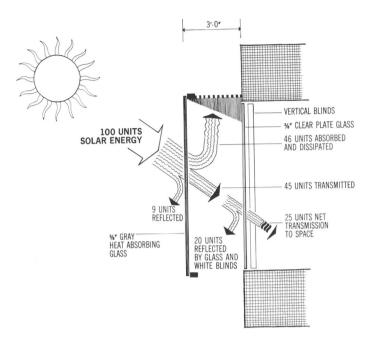

Figure 24   Norfolk City Hall—typical window section.

insulation, installed between the foundation and the floor slab. Insulation can also be sprayed on the interior of a building in thicknesses up to 2″.

To insulate existing buildings, loose fill insulation can be poured between studs and joists, or blowing wool can be blown in, filling the walls to the full depth of the studs and to the desired depth between joists.

To reduce solar heat and glare, windows can be glazed with heat-absorbing glass. Such glass, combined with an ingenious design, reduced the solar heat load by 75 percent in the Norfolk City Hall shown in Figures 22 and 23. An outer window wall is fastened three feet from the inner window wall with tubular steel trusses. This permits a cooling air flow between both layers of glass as illustrated in Figure 24. The upper grid serves as a solar screen and is also used as a walkway for window washers.

Snow removal. When building in cold climates, it is advisable to consider adding a snow removal system to the heating plant. Pipes may be imbedded in the concrete or asphalt of drives and walks to carry heat in the form of steam, hot oil, alcohol, or water. Since the pipes will be subjected to subfreezing temperatures between periods of operation, an antifreeze (to lower the freezing point) must be added when water is the circulating medium. Ethylene glycol has been the most widely used. Figure 25 illustrates the operation of a typical system. Hot water or steam from the boiler is passed through the heat exchanger to heat the mixture of water and antifreeze. This mixture is then pumped through

piping laid in the driveway to melt the snow, after which it returns to the exchanger for reheating. The 1″ iron or steel piping is laid 4″ below the surface. The pipes are spaced 15″ apart in concrete and 12″ apart in asphalt. The system may be started by a manually operated switch, a thermostat, a photoelectric device, or a scale tripped by a given weight of snow.

Heat loss calculations. A heating system should be designed by a heating engineer specializing in the field. The draftsman will prepare the heating plans, however, and should be familiar with the design process. Let us look, then, at the steps necessary to design a typical system.

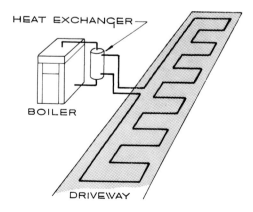

Figure 25   Snow removal system.

TABLE II

Coefficients of Transmission (U)
(Btu per hour per sq. ft. per degree)

Walls

Wood siding, plastered interior, no insulation	0.26
Wood siding, plastered interior, 2″ insulation	0.10
Brick veneer, plastered interior, no insulation	0.26
Brick veneer, plastered interior, 2″ insulation	0.10
8″ solid brick, no interior finish	0.50
8″ solid brick, furred and plastered interior	0.31
12″ solid brick, no interior finish	0.36
12″ solid brick, furred and plastered interior	0.24
10″ cavity brick, no interior finish	0.34
10″ cavity brick, furred and plastered interior	0.24

Partitions

Wood frame, plastered, no insulation	0.34
4″ solid brick, no finish	0.60
4″ solid brick, plastered one side	0.51
4″ solid brick, plastered both sides	0.44
6″ solid brick, no finish	0.53
8″ solid brick, no finish	0.48

Ceilings and Floors

Frame, plastered ceiling, no flooring, no insulation	0.61
Frame, plastered ceiling, no flooring, 2″ insulation	0.12
Frame, plastered ceiling, no flooring, 4″ insulation	0.06
Frame, no ceiling, wood flooring, no insulation	0.34
Frame, no ceiling, wood flooring, 2″ insulation	0.09
Frame, no ceiling, wood flooring, 4″ insulation	0.06
Frame, plastered ceiling, wood flooring, no insulation	0.28
Frame, plastered ceiling, wood flooring, 2″ insulation	0.09
Frame, plastered ceiling, wood flooring, 4″ insulation	0.06
3″ bare concrete slab	0.68
3″ concrete slab, parquet flooring	0.45
3″ concrete slab, wood flooring on sleepers	0.25

Roofs

Asphalt shingled pitched roof, no ceiling, no insulation	0.52
Asphalt shingled pitched roof, no ceiling, 2″ insulation	0.11
Asphalt shingled pitched roof, plastered ceiling, no insulation	0.31
Asphalt shingled pitched roof, plastered ceiling, 2″ insulation	0.10
Built-up flat roof, no ceiling, no insulation	0.49
Built-up flat roof, no ceiling, 2″ board insulation	0.12
Built-up flat roof, plastered ceiling, no insulation	0.31
Built-up flat roof, plastered ceiling, 2″ board insulation	0.11

Windows and Doors

Single glazed windows	1.13
Double glazed windows	0.45
Triple glazed windows	0.28
Glass blocks (8″ × 8″ × 4″)	0.56
1¾″ solid wood doors	0.44
1¾″ solid wood door with storm door	0.27

Although every heating system must be individually designed, there are certain elements common to all. For example, the total heat loss through the walls, ceiling, and floor of each room must be balanced by the heat delivered to each room. The first step, therefore, is to calculate the heat losses.

Heat losses. Heat escapes from a room in two ways:

1. Transmission through walls, ceiling, and floor
2. Infiltration through cracks around windows and doors

Transmission losses. Heat loss by transmission will increase in proportion to the area A of the surfaces of the room, the difference between the inside temperature and outside temperature $(t_i - t_o)$, and the coefficient of transmission U:

$$H = AU(t_i - t_o)$$

Where: H = Heat loss (Btu/hr.)
   A = Area (sq. ft.)
   U = Coefficient of transmission (see Table II)
   t_i = Inside temperature (70°F is often assumed)
   t_o = Outside temperature (assume 15°F above lowest recorded temperature; 0°F is used for New York, Boston, and Philadelphia)

The coefficient of transmission is a factor which indicates the amount of heat in Btu that will be transmitted through each square foot of surface in one hour for each degree of temperature difference. A poor insulator will have a high U value; a good insulator will have a low U value. U values have been computed by tests for a number of surfaces as shown in Table II.

Air infiltration losses. In addition to the heat which is lost directly through the room surfaces, heat will escape through the cracks between windows and window frames and doors and door frames.

$$H = 0.018LV(t_i - t_o)$$

Where: H = Heat loss (Btu/hr.)
   0.018 = 0.24×0.075 (0.24 is specific heat of air in Btu/pound; 0.075 is density of air in pounds/cu. ft.)
   L = Length of all cracks (ft.)
   V = Volume of air infiltration per foot of crack per hour (see Table III)
   t_i = Inside temperature
   t_o = Outside temperature

Values for the volume of air infiltration (V) for the average doors and windows are given in Table III.

EXAMPLE

Find the hourly heat loss from the front bedroom of the M residence (Appendix A) using the following data:

Door: Weatherstripped, $1\frac{3}{4}''$ solid wood with storm door
Windows: Weatherstripped, double glazed
Walls: Wood siding, plastered interior, 2'' insulation
Floor: 4'' insulation
Ceiling: 4'' insulation

Solution

	A	U	(t_i-t_o)	$H = AU(t_i-t_o)$
Door	20 sq. ft.	0.27	(70-0)	378 Btu/hr.
Windows	24 sq. ft.	0.45	(70-0)	756 Btu/hr.
Walls	168 sq. ft.	0.10	(70-0)	1176 Btu/hr.
Floor	137 sq. ft.	0.06	(70-20)	411 Btu/hr.
Ceiling	137 sq. ft.	0.06	(70-0)	575 Btu/hr.

Transmission losses = 3296 Btu/hr.

	L	V	(t_i-t_o)	$H = 0.018\ LV(t_i-t_o)$
Door	19'	55	(70-0)	1317 Btu/hr.
Windows	34'	24	(70-0)	1028 Btu/hr.

Infiltration losses = 2345 Btu/hr.
Total heat losses = 3296 + 2345 = 5641 Btu/hr.

System design. After the total heat loss from each room has been calculated, a system must be designed that will replace the loss. For our example, we will assume that a series loop baseboard hot water system is desired for the M residence. Two loops will be used on the main levels: one loop through the vestibule, kitchen-laundry, and dining-living areas; and a second loop through the bathroom, bedrooms, and study. The order of design is as follows.

1. Calculate the length of exterior wall avail-

TABLE III
Volume of Infiltration (V)
(cubic feet per foot of crack per hour)

Doors not weatherstripped	111
Doors weatherstripped	55
Windows not weatherstripped	39
Windows weatherstripped	24

TABLE IV
Radiant (R) and Radiant Convector (RC) Baseboard Outputs
(average water temperature = 200°F)

Type	Height	Rated Output (Btu/hr./ft. of baseboard)
R	Low (7'')	255
R	High (10'')	365
RC	Low (8'')	430
RC	High (10'')	605

able for baseboard heating units in each room and tabulate them in a form like that shown in Table V.

2. Divide the heat loss by the available length of wall to find the minimum output required.

3. Select a baseboard type from Table IV with a slightly greater output than required.

4. Divide the heat loss by the rated output of the baseboard selected to find the revised length of baseboard required.

5. Divide the radiation approximately into thirds. Increase the middle third by $7\frac{1}{2}$ percent and the last third by 15 percent to compensate for the cooling of the water as it proceeds along its run.

6. Select a boiler with a capacity equal to the

TABLE V
Baseboard Heating Design

	Room	Heat Loss (Btu/hr.)	Exterior Wall Available (ft.)	Minimum Output (Btu/hr./ft.)	Baseboard Selected	Baseboard Length (ft.)	Correction Factor	Final Baseboard Length (ft.)
Loop 1	vestibule	5,950	10	595	RC high 605	9.9	×1	10
	kitchen-laundry	6,240	13	480	RC high 605	10.3	×1.075	11
	dining-living	10,570	38	280	R high 365	29	×1.15	33
Loop 2	bathroom	2,150	4	540	RC high 605	3.6	×1	4
	bedroom	5,640	18	310	R high 365	15.5	×1	16
	master bedroom	8,000	14	570	RC high 605	13.2	×1.075	14
	study	3,670	14	260	R high 365	10	×1.15	12
Loop 3	lower level	17,500						

Total heat loss = 59,720 Btu/hr.

total heat loss (59,720 Btu/hr.). Boilers for small buildings are usually rated on the basis of the net output rather than the gross output, so that a 60,000 Btu/hr. boiler will be large enough to include all heat losses and domestic hot water demand.

7. Using manufacturers' catalogs, the sizes of the compression tank, pump, and main are determined. In this case, an eight gallon compression tank and 1″ diameter main are selected. A separate 1″ pump is installed in each of the three loops so that zone control of each loop is possible.

8. Lay out the system as shown in Figure 26.

AIR CONDITIONING

Air conditioning means different things to different people. The man on the street thinks of air conditioning as the cooling of a building on a hot day. The professional engineer, though, considers air conditioning to have a broader meaning: both heat-

ing and cooling in addition to humidity control, ventilation, filtering, and other processing. All of these elements are essential to human comfort and should be considered when planning a building.

Cooling. Heat will transfer from a warm surface to a cooler surface. Air cooling may be accomplished by withdrawing heat from the air by transferring it to the cooler surface of evaporator coils in a refrigerating unit. As described in the section on heat pumps, a *compressor* circulates a *refrigerant* between two sets of coils: *evaporator* coils and *condenser* coils. The refrigerant is a volatile liquid with such a low boiling point that it is a gas (*vapor*) under normal pressure and temperature. Common refrigerants are freon 11 (CCl_3F) and freon 12 (CCl_2F_2). As a vapor the freon is compressed in the compressor, increasing its temperature. At this high pressure and temperature, the vapor passes through the condenser coils to be cooled by the surrounding water and condensed into a liquid as shown in Figure 27. Still

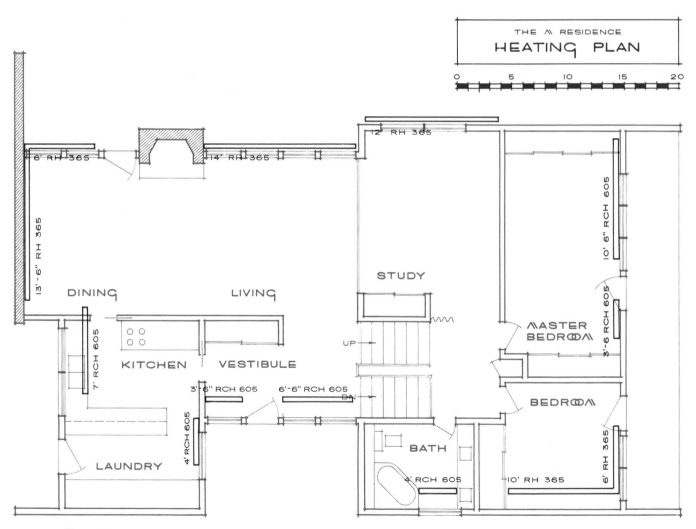

Figure 26

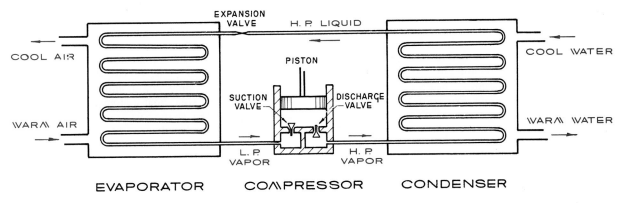

Figure 27   Mechanical air conditioner.

under pressure, the liquid refrigerant enters through the expansion valve into the evaporator where the pressure is lowered by the suction stroke of the compressor. The boiling point of the liquid refrigerant drops, and it changes into a gas (*vaporizes*). For this vaporization a great deal of heat is withdrawn from the air or water surrounding the evaporator coils. The vaporized refrigerant is drawn back into the compressor through the suction valve to be again compressed in a continuous cycle.

In large air conditioning systems, water is chilled in the evaporator and piped to the desired portion of the building. In smaller systems, such as unit air conditioners, the air to be cooled is allowed to enter the evaporator cabinet directly.

Humidity control. As far as human comfort is concerned, temperature and humidity are inseparable. In dry air (low humidity), perspiration evaporates readily and cools the skin. Consequently winter heating should be accompanied by *humidification*. In moist air (high humidity), perspiration will not evaporate, and the skin and clothing become wet and uncomfortable. Summer cooling, then, can be aided by *dehumidification*.

It is generally agreed that a comfortable winter temperature is 74° with a relative humidity * between 30 and 35 percent. Lower humidity will dry furniture and house members causing them to crack and warp. A higher humidity causes condensation on windows and possibly on walls. A summer temperature of 76° at a relative humidity under 60 percent is desirable. Indoor temperatures in the summer are not lowered more than 15° below the outdoor temperatures to prevent an unpleasant chill upon entering or the feeling of intense heat upon leaving the building.

In addition to thermostats for controlling temperature, air conditioners are provided with *hygrostats* (also called *humidistats*) which are sensi-

tive to and control the humidity of the air. Separate humidifiers and dehumidifiers in portable units are also available.

Ventilation. Temperature, humidity, and ventilation are all important to human comfort. A too-warm room having a gentle air motion may be more comfortable than a cooler room containing still, stale air. For air motion, a velocity of about 25 feet per minute is considered satisfactory. Much higher velocities cause uncomfortable drafts. Air conditioning systems in large buildings continuously introduce some fresh outdoor air and exhaust stale air containing excess carbon dioxide, reduced oxygen, and unpleasant odors. Air from toilets, kitchen, and smoking and meeting rooms is not recirculated but exhausted directly. A complete air change every 15 minutes is recommended for most activities. In uncrowded homes, natural infiltration provides a satisfactory amount of fresh outdoor air.

Filtering. Air contaminated with dust, smoke, and fumes can be purified by filters and air washers of many designs. The most commonly used air filters are dry filters, viscous filters, and electric precipitators. Dry filters are pads of fibrous material such as spun glass or porous paper or cloth which must be cleaned or replaced to remain effective. Viscous filters are screens coated with viscous oil to trap dust. They may be cleaned by air or water and recharged by dipping in oil. Electric precipitators remove particles by passing the air through a high voltage field. This charges the particles, which are then attracted to plates of opposite polarity.

Air conditioning systems. Air conditioning systems are designated *central* or *unit* systems. A *central* system may be designed as part of the heating system, using the same blower, filters, ducts or pipes, and registers. Or it may be separate from the heating system, having its own distribution method. In general a single, combined, all-season system is more

* Relative humidity is the ratio of the quantity of water vapor actually present to the greatest amount possible at that temperature.

economical than two separate ones which must duplicate equipment.

For greater accuracy of control, it is often desirable to divide a building into zones for cooling as well as for heating. Frequently the sections of a house vary in the amount of heating and cooling required due to different exposures to prevailing winds and sun, varying construction materials, and different uses. Thermostats are placed in each zone. The zones may be groups of rooms or individual rooms each with its own thermostat controlling the air conditioning.

Cooling systems may be combined with most heating systems. The warm air system can supply cooled air as well. Chilled water can be circulated through the same pipes used in hot water or steam heating systems. In this case the room convectors are equipped with blowers to circulate the warm room air over the chilled coils. The operation of the heat pump can be reversed to either supply or withdraw heat as required.

Self-contained room-sized *unit* systems are particularly effective in buildings with naturally defined zones. The units may be controlled automatically or manually as desired. Room units are built into the exterior walls in new construction and installed in window openings in existing dwellings.

Heat gain calculations. Summer heat enters a room just as winter heat escapes: by transmission through walls, ceiling, and floor and by air infiltration through cracks around windows and doors. But some additional factors, such as solar radiation, heat produced within the house, and latent heat, must also be considered.

Transmission. Heat gained by transmission is calculated in the manner previously discussed for each area having a temperature difference between the inside of the room and the outside. For example, a wall adjacent to a garage without air conditioning should be included, but a below grade wall should not.

TABLE VI
Heat Emission of Appliances

Electric oven	10,000 Btu/hr.
Electric range, no hood	4,000 Btu/hr./burner
Electric range, with hood	2,000 Btu/hr./burner
Electric warming compartment	1,000 Btu/hr.
Gas oven	10,000 Btu/hr.
Gas range, no hood	8,000 Btu/hr./burner
Gas range, with hood	4,000 Btu/hr./burner
Gas pilot	250 Btu/hr.
Electric motors	2,544 Btu/hr./horsepower

Solar radiation. In addition to the normal transmission gain through glass, there is also a sun load through unshaded glass. Glass sun load is calculated only for the wall containing the largest area of unshaded glass, because the sun can shine directly on only one wall at a time. For an approximate calculation, assume that solar heat will enter through each square foot of glass on the east, south, and west walls at the rate of 100 Btu/hr. Double this amount for horizontal windows like skylights. Windows facing north are omitted.

Infiltration. Heat gained by air infiltration is calculated in the same manner as winter infiltration losses. The air conditioning system can be designed, however, to introduce sufficient outdoor air to maintain an indoor pressure capable of eliminating infiltration.

Occupants. The human body produces heat at an average rate of 300 Btu/hr. Therefore a heat gain for occupants is included by multiplying 300 times the assumed number of occupants.

Lighting. The equivalent heat of each watt of electric lighting is 3.4 Btu/hr. Therefore multiply 3.4 times the total wattage generally in use at one time. For fluorescent lights, use 4.0 in place of 3.4.

Appliances. The heat gain due to appliances can be estimated from Table VI. A figure of 1,200 Btu/hr. is often used for the average residential kitchen.

Latent heat. Latent heat gains must be included when water vapor has been added to the inside air. If the air conditioner is designed to condense an equal amount of moisture from the room, this factor is omitted.

Sizing the system. The total of all preceding heat gains is termed the *sensible heat gain.* The required size of the unit to be installed is found by multiplying the sensible heat gain by a performance factor of 1.3. A unit having this required heat removal rate in Btu/hr. can then be selected from the manufacturers' catalogs. Cooling units may also be rated in tons of refrigeration.* A ton is equivalent to 12,000 Btu/hr. The size in tons, therefore, can be found by dividing the required size in Btu/hr. by 12,000. A small house will usually require a two or three ton unit; a large house a five ton (60,000 Btu/hr.) unit.

A large, commercial building might require several thousand tons of refrigeration. A 3500-ton chiller and its computerized control center (Figure 28) are located on a mechanical floor (the 63rd floor) of the U.S. Steel building in Pittsburgh. The com-

*A ton of refrigeration is the amount of refrigeration produced by melting a ton of ice in 24 hours.

puter center senses the solar energy being absorbed by the building and makes the required adjustments in the air conditioning.

Solar air conditioning. Research is now under way to perfect an air cooling system powered by some natural process rather than by a costly mechanical process. Recently an experimental solar air conditioned home was built in Phoenix, Arizona. This building has a flat water film roof in thermal contact with metal ceilings beneath and covered by horizontal plastic panels. During winter daylight, the panels are retracted to allow the sun to heat the water and the house. The panels are retracted during summer nights also—but for a different reason. This allows the water film to evaporate, which cools the water and the house.

Figure 28   Checking temperature readings at air conditioning control panel. U.S. Steel Building, Pittsburgh.

STUDY QUESTIONS

1. Distinguish between these forced warm air systems:
   a. Individual duct and trunk duct
   b. Perimeter loop and perimeter radial
2. Distinguish between these forced hot water systems:
   a. Series loop, one-pipe, and two-pipe
   b. Upfeed and downfeed
   c. Direct return and reversed return
   d. Radiator and convector
3. Describe the method of operation of:
   a. The electric baseboard
   b. The heat pump
   c. Solar heat (heat of fusion system)
   d. The hot water snow removal system
   e. The mechanical air conditioning system
4. List the advantages and disadvantages of these heating systems:
   a. Warm air
   b. Hot water
   c. Radiant
   d. Steam
   e. Electric
   f. Solar
5. Name the principal causes of heat gain and heat loss in a building.
6. Give the equations which describe heat loss by transmission and by infiltration.
7. Give the coefficient of transmission for:
   a. Brick veneer wall, plastered interior, without insulation
   b. Brick veneer wall, plastered interior, 2″ insulation
   c. 10′ cavity brick wall, without interior finish
   d. Wood frame floor, without ceiling below, without insulation
   e. Wood frame floor, without ceiling below, 4″ insulation
8. Distinguish between:
   a. Heat loss and heat gain
   b. Central and unit air conditioning
   c. Compressor, condenser, and evaporator
   d. Thermostat, hygrostat, and humidistat
   e. Infiltration and solar radiation

LABORATORY PROBLEMS

1. Prepare a legend of the commonly used heating and air conditioning symbols. (Hint: Refer to a reference such as *Architectural Graphic Standards.*)
2. For the A residence:
   a. Make the necessary calculations and draw the heating plan. Use the heating system of your choice.
   b. Include central air conditioning.
3. Using the following data from the living room of the Z residence:
   Windows: Weatherstripped, double glazed
   Unshaded area of east windows: 42 sq. ft.
   Unshaded area of south windows: 27 sq. ft.
   Unshaded area of west windows: 27 sq. ft.
   Walls: brick veneer, plastered interior, 2″ insulation
   Floor: no insulation
   Outside temperature: 0°
   First floor temperature: 70°
   Second floor temperature: 70°
   Basement temperature: 60°
   Number of occupants: 5
   Wattage generally in use: 1000
   a. Find the hourly heat loss.
   b. Find the hourly summer heat gain.
4. For the building assigned by your instructor:
   a. Make the necessary calculations and draw the heating plan.
   b. Include central air conditioning.
5. For your original building design:
   a. Make the necessary calculations and draw the heating plan.
   b. Include central air conditioning.

28 design for durability

MOISTURE CONTROL*

Two unseen elements play an important part in the life and livability of houses—temperature and moisture. As we have seen, temperature is relatively easy to control through the use of adequate insulation and a properly designed and functioning heating

*Courtesy B. E. Beneyfield, Moisture Control Consultant.

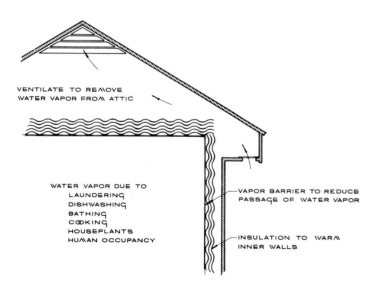

VENTILATE TO REMOVE
WATER VAPOR FROM ATTIC

WATER VAPOR DUE TO
LAUNDERING
DISHWASHING
BATHING
COOKING
HOUSEPLANTS
HUMAN OCCUPANCY

VAPOR BARRIER TO REDUCE
PASSAGE OF WATER VAPOR

INSULATION TO WARM
INNER WALLS

Figure 1   Water vapor protection.

system. Moisture also can be easily controlled through proper building design and construction. However, since the control of moisture is so little understood, moisture damage is undoubtedly the most prevalent of all problems connected with the home.

Water vapor. Water vapor, moisture, humidity, and steam are all the same. They are just different names given to water when it has evaporated to a gas state. Water vapor is invisible, but it is present to some degree in nearly all air. Two factors associated with water vapor should be clearly understood: vapor pressure and condensation.

Vapor pressure. The water vapor in wet air always tries to flow toward drier air to mix with it. This "vapor pressure" causes the water vapor in a house to seek escape to the drier air outside, traveling through walls and roof, Figure 1. Water vapor is a gas, like air, and can move wherever air can move. It is not generally understood that water vapor can travel through materials that air cannot readily penetrate, such as wood, brick, stone, concrete, and plaster. Under the vapor pressure of warm moist air, the vapor constantly tries to escape through most building materials to the cooler outside where the pressure is lower.

The extent of this problem may be realized when you consider the numerous sources of water vapor in a home: laundering, dishwashing, bathing, cooking, house plants, and human occupancy. All this may amount to 20 gallons of water per week which enter the air and must escape from the home.

Condensation. When warm moist air is cooled, as happens when it comes in contact with a cold surface, the water returns to a liquid state, or "condenses." Figure 2 shows water vapor condensing into droplets of liquid water upon contact with the cold surface of a glass of iced tea. The same condensation will occur when water vapor, under pressure to escape from a warm house, comes in contact with cooler surfaces in attics, crawl spaces, and wall interiors. This trapped condensation may cause mildewing and decay of structural members; damage to plaster, insulation, and roofing; blistering and peeling of paint; window sweating; musty odors; and many other problems.

Comfort. Although some people believe that high humidity is beneficial to health, this question is unsettled and probably academic. Florida is a health resort and has a high humidity; Arizona, too, is a health resort and has low humidity. Neither state shows superior advantages for all people. Moisture can cause more damage than its slight comfort benefits can offset. It is best to get rid of excess moisture in order to protect clothing, tools, and leather goods as well as the building itself.

Control. There are two principal ways of controlling water vapor and preventing moisture damage. One is to stop the passage of vapor through the structure so that it cannot reach a surface cold enough to cause condensation. This can be done by the use of *vapor barriers* on the inside (warm side) of walls. The second is to *ventilate* the outer walls and ceilings so that any water vapor reaching the outer surfaces of the structure can continue flowing to the colder outside air.

Vapor barriers. A vapor barrier is any material that resists the passage of water vapor. Among the commonly used vapor barriers are:

1. Membrane vapor barriers which cover the entire wall and ceiling with openings only at the windows, doors, and electric boxes
2. Blanket insulation containing a barrier on one side
3. Aluminum-foil reflective insulation
4. Aluminum primer under wall paint
5. Asphalt coating on the back of interior wall surfaces

In every case, the vapor barrier must be kept warm by installation on the warm side of the wall. If it is installed on the cold side, condensation will form immediately. Storm windows and double glazed windows operate on the same principle—condensation on the window is reduced in propor-

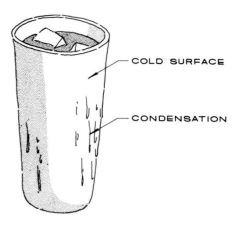

Figure 2   Condensation.

MINIMUM NET VENTILATION AREA
(RATIO TO CEILING AREA)

EAVES $\frac{1}{250}$

FLAT ROOF

PEAK VENTS $\frac{1}{300}$

GABLE ROOF

PEAK VENTS $\frac{1}{900}$

EAVES $\frac{1}{900}$

GABLE ROOF AND EAVE

PEAK VENTS $\frac{1}{900}$

EAVES $\frac{1}{900}$

HIP ROOF

Figure 3   Roof ventilation.

Figure 4   Roof ventilation disguised in gable design.

tion to the temperature of the inside glass. Also, since no vapor barrier will completely prevent the passage of all water vapor, it is important that any penetrating vapor be permitted to continue flowing through the cold side of the wall to the outside air. This is the reason that building paper is made water resistant but not vapor resistant.

Ventilation. Although little can be done to reduce the amount of water vapor poured into a house, much of this vapor can be removed by ventilation in one or more of the following areas:

1. Openings at the eave and ridge of the roof. The ratios given in Figure 3 can be used to calculate the minimum net ventilation area required. Often unsightly roof vents can be disguised by careful design as shown in Figure 4.
2. Crawl space ventilation together with a ground covering of water-proofed concrete or vapor barrier to reduce moisture entering from the ground, Figure 5

3. Exhaust fans in kitchen, bathrooms, laundry, and basement
4. Venting of gas appliances, since water vapor is a product of gas combustion
5. Outside cold air intake on hot air furnace, damper controlled

Find the size of ventilators for a 25' × 36' gable roofed home with flush cornice.

Solution

1. Calculate the ceiling area: 25' × 36' = 900 sq. ft.
2. Using Figure 3, a gable house with a flush cornice, calculate the minimum net ventilation area:

$$\frac{1}{300} \times 900 = 3 \text{ sq. ft.}$$

3. Double this area due to louvers reducing the actual opening area: 3 sq. ft. × 2 = 6 sq. ft.
4. Since two ventilators are used, each must be 3 sq. ft. minimum.

TERMITE PROTECTION

Nature has provided insects whose primary function is to accelerate the reduction to dust of dead wood on the forest floor (or on a house). These insects are of two kinds: subterranean termites located in the southern part of the United States as shown in Figure 6, and dry-wood termites located only in southern California and southern Florida.

Dry-wood termites can live in wood without having contact with moisture or the ground. Fortunately though, they are fewer in number and less of a threat than the subterranean termites. Subterranean termites breed underground and then tunnel through the earth for the wood they need for food. They will even construct tunnels *above* ground, as shown in Figure 7, to reach wood within 18" of the

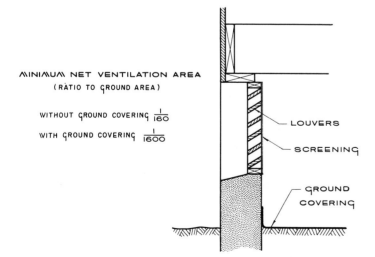

MINIMUM NET VENTILATION AREA
(RATIO TO GROUND AREA)

WITHOUT GROUND COVERING $\frac{1}{160}$

WITH GROUND COVERING $\frac{1}{1600}$

LOUVERS

SCREENING

GROUND COVERING

Figure 5   Crawl space ventilation.

ground. In areas of termite hazard, the following precautions must be taken in building:

1. Keep wood members 18″ above ground. Since this is not always possible, termite shields of 16 oz. copper (Figure 8) can be installed over the foundation walls and under the sill.

2. Solid concrete walls with reinforcing to prevent cracks are necessary, since termites are soft-bodied and able to squeeze through a paper-thin fissure. They may even tunnel through low-grade concrete.

3. If wood must be in contact with the ground (as in the case of wooden steps), use a concrete base under the wooden member, use the heartwood of redwood or cypress, and pressure-treat the lumber with coal tar creosote or zinc chloride.

4. Properly drain the area surrounding the house, since subterranean termites need moisture to live.

5. Remove all dead wood from the building vicinity and treat the ground with anti-termite chemicals.

6. Make sure that all areas such as crawl spaces are accessible for periodic inspections.

7. Screen all openings (such as attic ventilation) with 20-mesh bronze screening.

In addition to termites, *carpenter ants* also live in wood. They may colonize and expand termite nests after the termites have been exterminated. Although carpenter ants do not eat wood, they can chew such large nests in wood that the building is weakened. Prevention methods are similar to those described above. Carpenter ants can also be controlled by insecticides dusted or sprayed into their nests.

DECAY PREVENTION

Nature has also provided a low form of plant life, called fungus, which, like termites, serves to disintegrate wood. Fungus may be of a type that merely produces mold or stains (unsightly but not structurally dangerous), or of a type that produces actual decay.

Major conditions necessary for decay are:

1. Moisture in a moderate amount. Dry wood (less than 20 percent moisture content) and wood kept under water will not decay. Even so-called "dry rot" must have moisture present.

2. Moderately high temperature (70° to 85°F.). High temperature such as used in kiln-drying will kill fungus, but low temperature merely retards it.

Since the conditions necessary for the survival of fungus are similar to those needed by termites, the preventive measures are fortunately the same:

1. Protect lumber from wetting by wide cornice overhangs, proper construction and flashing,

Figure 6   Areas of termite danger.

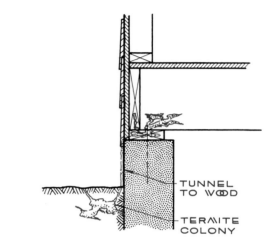

Figure 7   Termite damage.

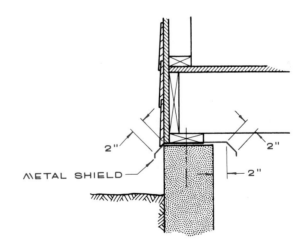

Figure 8   Termite shield.

painting, and keeping all wooden members at least 8″ above ground.

2. Use the heartwood of redwood, cedar, and cypress, pressure-treated with creosote or zinc chloride. The heartwood of all lumber is more resistant to decay than the sapwood. Heartwood of redwood, cedar, and cypress is especially resistant to decay.

TABLE I

Table of Metals Subject to Galvanic Corrosion

1. Aluminum
2. Zinc
3. Steel
4. Iron
5. Nickel
6. Tin
7. Lead
8. Stainless steel
9. Copper
10. Monel metal

3. Make sure there is proper drainage of the ground surrounding the building. A vapor barrier, water-proofed concrete, or sand spread over crawl areas reduces the ground moisture evaporation.

4. Remove all dead wood from the area of the building, since fungi spores float through the air from decayed wood.

5. Ventilate enclosed spaces.

CORROSION PREVENTION

As wood is disintegrated by termites and decay, metal is disintegrated by rusting (corrosion). Rather than attempting to remove the conditions, such as moisture, that cause corrosion, the best prevention is simply to use metals that are more corrosion resistant.

Nonferrous metals such as bronze, copper, brass, and aluminum are corrosion resistant and therefore should be used for piping, flashing, guttering, and screening.

Ferrous metals such as steel, wrought iron, and cast iron are susceptible to corrosion, but may be used for interior structural members without fear of their weakening. When they are exposed to moisture, however (as in exterior work), they must be constantly protected by painting or galvanizing (coating with zinc). Stainless steel can also be used.

Galvanic corrosion. Occurs when different metals come in contact in the presence of an electrolyte, as in an electric battery. This process will cause one of the metals to corrode. Therefore, certain combinations of metals should not be used in exterior construction, since water may act as a weak electrolyte. The lower numbered metals in Table I will be corroded by contact with a higher numbered metal; in addition, the corrosion will increase in proportion to the difference between their numbers.

1. If aluminum storm windows are installed over stainless steel casement windows, the aluminum will corrode.
2. If galvanized nails (iron and zinc) are used to fasten copper gutters, the nails will corrode.

LIGHTNING PROTECTION

In locations of frequent thunderstorms, a lightning conductor system should be installed to protect the occupants of a building and the building itself. Lightning protection consists of paths that permit lightning to enter or leave the earth without passing through a nonconducting part of the building such as wood, masonry, or concrete. These paths can be metal air terminals (often called "lightning rods") with ground conductors or grounded structures of metal. There are many advantages to including lightning protection in the initial design of a building instead of adding it later. To assure that the system will be effective, it should be designed by an architectural engineer. See the *National Fire Codes* for recommended practices.

STUDY QUESTIONS

1. Give two methods to control:
   a. Temperature
   b. Moisture
2. Give three additional names for water vapor.
3. Why does water vapor in a building tend to escape to the outside?
4. List the sources of water vapor in the home.
5. What causes water vapor to condense?
6. List five commonly used vapor barriers.
7. List five commonly used methods of ventilation.
8. Why is building paper made *water* resistant but not *vapor* resistant?
9. List the precautions to be taken:
   a. When building in high termite hazard areas
   b. For protection from decay
   c. To protect ferrous metal from rusting
10. Why would it be poor practice to use lead flashing in direct contact with aluminum fittings?

LABORATORY PROBLEMS

1. Find the size of ventilators for:
   a. A 24′ × 40′ flat roofed building
   b. A 30′ × 40′ gable roofed home with eaves
   c. A 30′ × 50′ hip roofed house
2. Calculate the ventilator sizes for:
   a. The Z residence
   b. The building assigned by your instructor
   c. Your original house design
   Also indicate the type of vapor barrier to be used.

29   fire protection

BUILDING CODES

The earliest record of an attempt to improve building safety is the Code of Hammurabi, a Babylonian king and lawmaker in 2100 B.C.:

> "In the case of collapse of a defective building the architect is to be put to death if the owner is killed, and the architect's son if the owner's son is killed."

Laws governing building construction and land use were first introduced by the ancient Romans. During the reign of Julius Caesar, Rome grew rapidly, and tall, speculative apartments were built which often collapsed. Roman laws first limited heights to 70', and later reduced them to only 60'. In the 14th century, the City of London adopted a law which prohibited the building of wooden chimneys. Building codes governing building construction methods and zoning ordinances governing land use were adopted in English, French, and Prussian Cities by the 19th century, and were accepted by all American cities and most towns in the early 20th century.

The basic concept of a building code or a zoning ordinance is that individual actions should be regulated in favor of the welfare of the general public. It has been shown many times over that such protection is necessary, and courts have supported the inherent power of the government to protect citizens from unsafe building practices. Building codes specify acceptable building materials and construction methods, allowable loads and stresses, mechanical and electrical requirements, and other specifications for health and safety. The architect has both a moral and a legal obligation to study and follow the building code requirements* of the city in which he builds. An architectural draftsman, also, is more effective when he understands some of these requirements.

Among the most important portions of any building code are the sections on fire protection. One need not experience the terror of fire to realize how necessary it is to design buildings which will not be a hazard to their occupants. In the United States, over 10,000 persons are killed each year in fires. Many of these deaths occur in buildings which are in violation of fire protection codes.

BUILDING CLASSIFICATIONS

Building code requirements vary depending upon such factors as type of occupancy, building contents, type of construction, location, and fire-extinguishing

*Building codes are minimum requirements and may be outdated. When this occurs, the architect, as a professional, is expected to design at the current state-of-the-art.

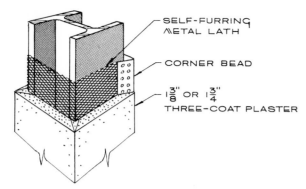

Figure 1   Plaster-on-metal-lath fire protection of columns. (See Table IV)

SELF-FURRING METAL LATH

CORNER BEAD

$1\frac{3}{8}''$ OR $1\frac{3}{4}''$ THREE-COAT PLASTER

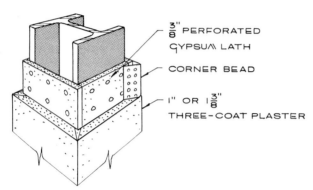

Figure 2   Plaster-on-gypsum-lath fire protection of columns. (See Table IV)

$\frac{3}{8}''$ PERFORATED GYPSUM LATH

CORNER BEAD

$1''$ OR $1\frac{3}{8}''$ THREE-COAT PLASTER

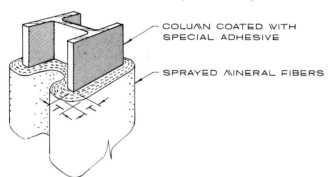

Figure 3   Sprayed fibrous fire protection of columns. (See Table IV)

COLUMN COATED WITH SPECIAL ADHESIVE

SPRAYED MINERAL FIBERS

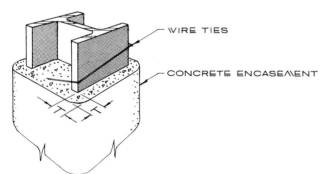

Figure 4   Concrete fire protection of columns. (See Table IV)

WIRE TIES

CONCRETE ENCASEMENT

systems. The codes permit "trade-offs" between these classifications with the goal of obtaining that degree of public safety as can be reasonably expected. For example, greater fire protection is required for a building which will be highrise, densely occupied, constructed of flammable materials or have hazardous contents. Building codes try to avoid requirements which involve unnecessary inconvenience or interference with the normal use of a building. However, the codes do set minimum standards for public safety which must be followed even though a financial hardship may be imposed upon individuals or groups.

Classification by occupancy. The Life Safety Code* developed by the *National Fire Protection Association* classifies buildings by eight types of occupancy:

1. Assembly (theatres, restaurants, churches, and museums)
2. Educational
3. Institutional (hospitals and prisons)
4. Residential (hotels, apartments, and dwellings)
5. Mercantile
6. Offices
7. Industrial
8. Storage

The code deals with the design of various types of buildings to reduce the danger from fire, panic, fumes, and smoke. It specifies the number, size, and arrangement of exits to allow prompt escape from buildings of each occupancy type. The code recognizes that safety is more than a matter of exits and therefore recommends a number of additional requirements. Following are some abstracts from the Residential and Assembly sections of this code to give you an idea of the variety of regulations which have been included. This is only a partial list of requirements, and local building codes should always be consulted for complete, updated requirements.

ONE- AND TWO-FAMILY DWELLINGS

The requirements for residences are far short of complete requirements for fire safety, but are those which can reasonably be enforced by law. Some of these requirements are:

1. In all residences, every occupied room (except storage rooms) must have at least two means of exit (such as a doorway or window). At least one exit must be a doorway. Below-grade sleeping areas must have direct access to the outside.
2. Exit doors must be at least 24" wide (30" preferred).
3. Occupied rooms must not be accessible only by folding stairs, trapdoor or ladder.

*The Life Safety Code is only one portion of the ten-volume *National Fire Codes*. These codes are purely advisory, but are widely used as a basis for establishing local or state building codes.

4. All door-locking devices must be such that they can be easily disengaged from the inside by quick-release catches. All closet door latches must be such that they can be easily opened by children from inside the closet. All bathroom door locks must be such that they can be opened from the outside without the use of a special key.

5. The path of travel from any room to an exit must not be through a room controlled by another family, nor through a bathroom or other space subject to locking.

6. Passages from sleeping rooms to exits must be at least 3'-0 wide.

7. Stairs must be at least 3'-0 wide with risers no greater than 8" and treads not under 9".

8. Every sleeping room, unless it has a direct exterior exit or two interior exits, must have a window which can be easily opened from the inside without use of tools. This window must provide a clear opening of at least 5 sq. ft. with not less than 22" in the least dimension. The bottom of the opening must not be more than 4'-0 above the floor. Awning and hopper windows must be designed to permit full opening.

9. Storm windows, screens, and burglar guards must have quick-opening devices.

10. Combustion heaters and stoves must not be so located as to block escape in case of a malfunction.

See the *National Fire Codes* or local codes for more detailed requirements.

ASSEMBLY BUILDINGS

1. An assembly area must be at least fifteen square feet per person. Seating area must be at least seven square feet per person. Standing area (such as waiting rooms) must be at least three square feet per person.

2. A satisfactory grade-level door must be provided for each 100 persons. A door to a stair or fire escape must be provided for each 75 persons.

3. Assembly buildings with a capacity of over 1,000 persons must have at least 4 exits widely separated from each other. Assembly buildings with a capacity of over 600 persons must have at least 3 widely separated exits. Smaller assembly buildings must have at least 2 widely separated exits.

4. Exits must be arranged so that the total length of travel from any point to the nearest exit does not exceed 150' for unsprinklered areas, and 200' in areas protected by automatic sprinklers.

5. Exit doors must be at least 2'-4" wide. The floor on both sides of a door must be level and at the same elevation for a distance at least equal to the width of the door; except exterior doors which may be one step ($7\frac{1}{2}$") higher inside.

6. Exit doors must swing in the direction of travel. Screen or storm doors must also swing in the direction of travel. Sliding, rolling, or folding doors must not be used.

7. Exit doors must be readily opened from the inside of the building. Latches must be simple and easily operable, even in darkness. Conventional hardware such as panic bars or doorknobs are satisfactory, but an unfamiliar method of operation (such as a blow to break glass)

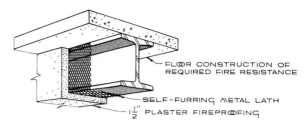

Figure 5   *Plaster fire protection of beams. (See Table V)*

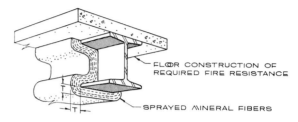

Figure 6   *Sprayed fibrous fire protection of beams. (See Table V)*

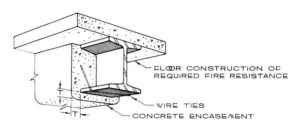

Figure 7   *Concrete fire protection of beams. (See Table V)*

is prohibited. Exit doors of assembly buildings with a capacity over 100 persons must have panic bars.

8. Locks must not require a key to operate.

9. Doors to stair enclosures and smoke stop doors must be provided with reliable self-closing mechanisms and never secured open unless provided with a reliable release device.

10. No mirrors shall be placed on exit doors. Doors must not harmonize in appearance with the rest of the wall.

11. Revolving doors must never be installed at the foot or top of stairs. They must not be considered as a portion of the required exits. No turnstiles which restrict exit are permitted.

12. Approved exit signs, lighting, and emergency lighting must be provided at all exits and approaches. Doors which lead to dead-end areas must be identified by signs indicating their character (such as "linen closet").

13. No open flames (such as candles) are permitted unless adequate precautions are made to assure that no other material is ignited.

14. Assembly buildings must be designed so the principal floor is not below grade unless protected by automatic sprinklers. Non-fire-resistive assembly buildings must have the principal floor not more than 28' above grade.

TABLE I
Construction Classifications

Type I.	Fire-resistive construction: noncombustible materials with four-hour bearing members	
Type II.	Heavy timber construction: timber interior with two-hour masonry walls	
Type III.	Noncombustible construction: unprotected steel	
Type IV.	Ordinary construction: wood interior with two-hour masonry walls	
Type V.	Wood frame construction: wood interior and walls	

15. All interior stairways must be enclosed to prevent spread of fire.
16. All interior decorations must be of fire-resistive or non-flammable materials.
17. A row of seats between aisles must not exceed 14 seats. A row of seats opening to an aisle at one end only must not exceed 7 seats.
18. Seats must be at least 18" wide, spaced at least 33" between rows, with at least 12" leg room (measured between plumb lines).
19. Aisles must be at least 3'-0 wide. Steps must not be used in aisles unless the slope exceeds 1' rise in 8' run. Ramps must not exceed 1' rise in 8' run.
20. Balcony rails must be substantial and at least 26" high, at least 30" high at the foot of an aisle, and at least 36" high at the foot of a stepped aisle.
21. Rooms containing pressure boilers, refrigerating machinery, transformers, or other service equipment subject to possible explosion must not be located adjacent to or under the exits.
22. Special regulations govern air conditioning, ventilating, and heating equipment. For example, automatic devices must be provided to prevent circulation of smoke through ductwork.
23. Areas used for painting or repair must be effectively cut off from assembly areas or protected by automatic sprinklers.
24. Fire alarm systems must be visual and coded to alert employees rather than audible to alert the entire audience. Audible devices such as gongs or sirens may create panic in conditions where fire drills are not feasible. Employees must be drilled and present when the building is occupied by the public.
25. Automatic sprinklers are required for any stage rigged for movable scenery, as well as for under-stage areas, dressing rooms, and storerooms. An approved fire-resisting curtain with an emergency closing device must be provided. The stage roof must contain an approved, operable ventilator having a free-opening area at least 5% of the stage floor area.
26. Motion picture projection apparatus must be enclosed by a fixed, fire-resistive booth.

See the *National Fire Codes* or local codes for more detailed requirements.

Classification by contents. The *Life Safety Code* also classifies buildings according to their contents by three ratings: ordinary hazard contents, extra hazard contents, and light hazard contents.

1. *Ordinary hazard contents* represents the conditions found in most buildings having contents which are moderately combustible, but which are not explosive and will not release poisonous fumes.
2. *Extra hazard contents* are liable to burn rapidly, explode (such as gasoline), or release poisonous fumes.
   All extra hazard contents buildings must have sufficient exits to allow occupants to escape with a travel distance not over 75'. It is assumed that this distance can be traveled in ten seconds, which is the time a normal individual can hold his breath.
3. *Light hazard contents* have low combustibility and consequently the primary danger will be from panic.

Classification by construction type. The *National Fire Codes* of the *National Fire Protection Association* classify buildings into five principal construction types as follows.

Type I Fire-resistive construction: Members are of noncombustible materials with fire ratings not less than:

4 hours for bearing walls
4 hours for columns and beams supporting more than 1 floor
3 hours for columns and beams supporting only 1 floor
2 hours for interior partitions

Type II Heavy timber construction: Bearing walls are of noncombustible materials (usually masonry) with a minimum two-hour fire rating, and laminated or solid wood members are not less than:

8" × 8" for columns
6" × 10" for beams
4" × 6" for trusses or arches supporting roof loads
4" for flooring
2" for roof deck

Type III Noncombustible construction: Structural members, walls, and partitions are of noncombustible construction such as unprotected steel.

When bearing walls are protected to a two-hour fire rating, and columns, floors, and roofs are protected to a one-hour fire rating; this is designated *Protected Noncombustible Construction.*

Type IV Ordinary construction: Exterior bearing walls are of noncombustible materials (usually ma-

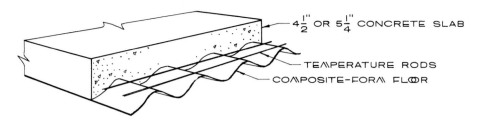

Figure 8   Unprotected floors and roofs. (See Table VI)

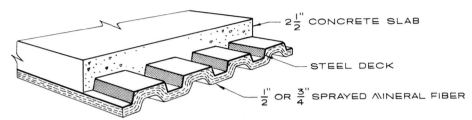

Figure 9   Sprayed fibrous fire protection of floors and roofs. (See Table VI)

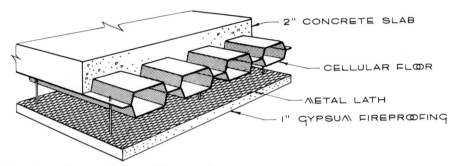

Figure 10 · Membrane fire protection of floors and roofs. (See Table VI)

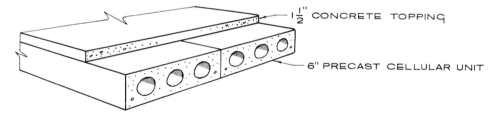

Figure 11   Unprotected cellular floors and roofs. (See Table VI)

sonry) with a minimum two-hour fire rating, and interior framing, roofs, and floors are combustible (usually wood).

When roofs, floors, and their supports have a one-hour fire rating, this is designated *Protected Ordinary Construction*.

Type V   Wood frame construction: All elements are of wood or other combustible material, but it does not qualify as heavy timber construction or ordinary construction.

When roofs, floors, and their supports have a one-hour fire rating, this is designated *Protected Wood Frame Construction*.

Table I simplifies these definitions.

Fire ratings. The fire protection sections of building codes are based upon studies made by fire protection engineers who have tested various building methods to determine the fire resistance of each. The *standard fire test* (E119-58) of the *American Society for Testing Materials* is the accepted standard for such tests. The degree of fire resistance of each building method is measured in terms of its ability to withstand fire for a time from one to four hours. For example, a two-hour fire rating would indicate that a structural member could withstand the heat of fire (or the cooling of a fire hose) for two hours before serious weakening; or that a wall, floor, or roof would not allow passage of flame and hot gasses for two hours.

The fire resistance ratings for typical walls, columns, beams, floors, and roofs are given in Tables II to VI. Notice that the fire rating of masonry and concrete walls can be improved simply by increasing their thickness. Steel members, however, must be screened by additional fire protection. Usually gypsum, perlite, vermiculite, or mineral fiber is used.

TABLE II
Fire-resistance Ratings for Masonry Walls

Type of Masonry Wall	Minimum Thickness for Ratings of:			
	4 hr.	3 hr.	2 hr.	1 hr.
Heavyweight concrete masonry units* (coarse aggregate, siliceous gravel)	6.7″	6.7″	4.5″	3″
Lightweight concrete masonry units* (coarse aggregate, unexpanded slag)	5.9″	5″	4″	2.7″
Lightweight concrete masonry units* (coarse aggregate, expanded slag)	4.7″	4″	3.2″	2.1″
Solid brick masonry†	8″	8″	8″	4″ (nonbearing)
Clay tile masonry†	16″	12″	12″	8″
Solid stone masonry*	12″	12″	12″	8″

*Abstracted from National Building Code (1955).
†Abstracted from Uniform Building Code (1958).

TABLE III
Fire-resistance Ratings for Concrete Walls

Type of Concrete Wall	Minimum Thickness for Ratings of:			
	4 hr.	3 hr.	2 hr.	1 hr.
Plain concrete	$7\frac{1}{2}″$	$6\frac{1}{2}″$	$5\frac{1}{2}″$	4″ (nonbearing)
Reinforced concrete (unplastered)	$7\frac{1}{2}″$	$6\frac{1}{2}″$	$5\frac{1}{2}″$	4″ (nonbearing)
Reinforced concrete ($\frac{3}{4}″$ portland cement or gypsum plaster, each side)	6″	5″	4″	3″

Abstracted from National Building Code (1955).

TABLE IV
Fire-resistance Ratings for Steel Columns

Type of Column Protection	Minimum Thickness for Ratings of:			
	4 hr.	3 hr.	2 hr.	1 hr.
Vermiculite or perlite-gypsum plaster on self-furring metal lath (see Figure 1)	$1\frac{3}{4}″$	$1\frac{3}{8}″$		
Perlite-gypsum plaster on $\frac{3}{8}″$ perforated gypsum lath (see Figure 2)		$1\frac{3}{8}″$	1″	
Sprayed mineral fiber (see Figure 3)	$2\frac{1}{2}″$	2″	$1\frac{1}{2}″$	
Concrete encasement (see Figure 4)	3″	$2\frac{1}{2}″$	2″	$1\frac{1}{2}″$

Abstracted from *Fire-resistant Construction in Modern Steel-Framed Buildings*, AISC (1959).

TABLE V

Fire-resistance Ratings for Steel Beams, Girders, and Trusses

Type of Beam Protection	Minimum Thickness for Ratings of:			
	4 hr.	3 hr.	2 hr.	1 hr.
Vermiculite or perlite-gypsum plaster on self-furring metal lath (see Figure 5)	1½″			
Sprayed mineral fiber (see Figure 6)	1⅞″	1 7/16″	1⅛″	
Concrete encasement (see Figure 7)	3″	2½″	2″	1½″

Abstracted from *Fire-resistant Construction in Modern Steel-framed Buildings*, AISC (1959).

TABLE VI

Fire-resistant Ratings for Floor and Roof Systems

Type of Floor and Roof Protection	Minimum Thickness for Ratings of:			
	4 hr.	3 hr.	2 hr.	1 hr.
Light-gage steel, not fireproofed (see Figure 8) sand-limestone Concrete Slab of thickness equal to:			5¼″	4½″
Light-gage steel, contact fireproofing (see Figure 9) 2½″ sand-gravel slab with sprayed mineral fiber of thickness equal to:		¾″	½″	
Light-gage steel, membrane fireproofing (see Figure 10) 2″ sand-gravel slab and 1″ vermiculite-gypsum fireproofing on metal lath installed at a distance of:	2″	15″		
Precast cellular system, not fireproofed (see Figure 11) 1½″ sand-gravel concrete topping over a limestone concrete precast unit of thickness equal to:		6″		

Abstracted from *Fire-resistant Construction in Modern Steel-framed Buildings*, AISC (1959).

Classification by location. Buildings constructed in closely packed communities are a greater threat to the general public than buildings located in an open area. Therefore building codes establish *fire limits* or *fire zones*. Within the limits of a fire zone, all buildings must be designed so that a fire will remain contained and not sweep on to adjacent building after building.

Originally, fire codes required masonry exterior walls to act as fire barriers, but present codes allow other construction methods having satisfactory wall fire ratings. Such walls must also be able to remain standing under fire conditions.

Extinguishing systems. Building codes often require automatic water sprinkler systems, for they give ex-cellent fire protection in all types of buildings. Records show that when fires occurred in sprinkler-protected buildings, 80% of those fires were extinguished by the sprinklers and another 18% held in check.

A sprinkler system consists of a network of piping placed under the ceiling and provided with a number of nozzles called *sprinklers* (Figure 12). When activated, the sprinklers spray water downward in a hemispherical pattern. The sprinkler systems are *fixed temperature* and *rate-of-rise*.

Fixed temperature sprinkler heads. These are usually designed so temperatures of 135° to 170°F will cause them to open automatically. Fixed temperature sprinkler heads are color-coded to show their

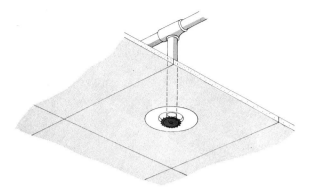

Figure 12   A flush-type ceiling sprinkler.

temperature ratings. Fixed temperature sprinkler systems are *wet pipe* with water stored in the piping and *dry pipe* with no water in the piping.

The *wet pipe system* is commonly used for most indoor conditions where temperatures will not fall below freezing. The water in the piping is kept under pressure behind each sprinkler. Sprinklers contain fusible links which are melted by heat and automatically open the sprinkler. Only sprinklers exposed to heat will open, thus preventing unnecessary water damage. A fire alarm sounds when the first sprinkler is opened. An antifreeze solution may be used in the piping for limited protection from freezing.

Buildings likely to have temperatures below freezing (such as unheated warehouses) can be protected by the *dry pipe system*. The piping contains air under pressure rather than water. When heat from a fire opens one of the sprinklers, the air is released and water flows into the piping network and through any opened sprinklers. A fire alarm also sounds.

Rate-of-rise sprinkler systems. Detectors open valves to the sprinkler piping rather than to the sprinkler heads. Rate-of-rise detectors open valves upon any abnormal increase of temperature. They are very sensitive and consequently give quicker warning of a fire hazard. Rate-of-rise sprinkler systems are *deluge* and *pre-action*.

The *deluge system* is used for extra hazard conditions. All sprinkler heads are open, but the piping is dry. When a rate-of-rise detector opens the water supply valve, water rushes into the piping and out through all heads simultaneously, giving better protection for difficult conditions such as flammable liquid fires. An alarm also sounds.

The *pre-action system* is used when it is important to reduce the possibility of accidental water damage. The principal difference between a pre-action and a standard dry pipe system is that the water supply valve operates independently of the sprinkler heads; that is, a rate-of-rise detector first opens the valve and sounds an alarm. The fixed temperature sprinkler heads do not open until their temperature ratings are reached. This gives time for small fires to be extinguished manually before the heads open.

Sprinkler layout. The layout of a sprinkler system is performed by a professional engineer using established standards as a guide. Sprinkler layout depends upon the building classifications. For example, the *National Fire Codes* specifies the following under a smooth ceiling construction:

1. *Light hazard:* The protection area per sprinkler must not exceed 200 ft². The maximum distance between lines and between sprinklers on lines is 15 ft. Sprinklers need not be staggered. See Figure 13.
2. *Ordinary hazard:* The protection area per sprinkler must not exceed 130 ft². The maximum distance between lines or between sprinklers on lines is 15 ft. Sprinklers on alternate lines must be staggered if the distance between sprinklers on lines exceeds 12 ft.
3. *Extra hazard:* The protection area per sprinkler must not exceed 90 ft². The maximum distance between lines and between sprinklers on lines is 12 ft. The sprinklers on alternate lines must be staggered.

See the *National Fire Codes* or local codes for more detailed requirements.

Standpipes. Standpipes are vertical water pipes with fire hose outlets at each floor. They can be designed for small (1½″) hose to be used by the building occupants in the event of fire or large (2½″) hose to be used by fire departments—or both. Standpipes are usually wet pipe rather than dry pipe. At ground level, branches extend outside the building and are finished with "Siamese connections." Should there be insufficient pressure in the public water system, the fire department can pump water into the standpipe through these connections to increase the pressure. Check valves relieve the pumps from back pressure.

Standpipes are located so that any fire can be reached by a stream from not more than 75' of small hose or 100' of large hose.

See the *National Fire Codes* or local codes for more detailed requirements.

Some other extinguishing systems are foam, carbon dioxide, halons and dry chemical. Foam is an aggregate of tiny gas-filled or air-filled bubbles used to smother fire by excluding air. Because foam contains water, it also has cooling properties. The principal use for foam is in fighting fires involving flammable liquids. Carbon dioxide, the halons, and dry

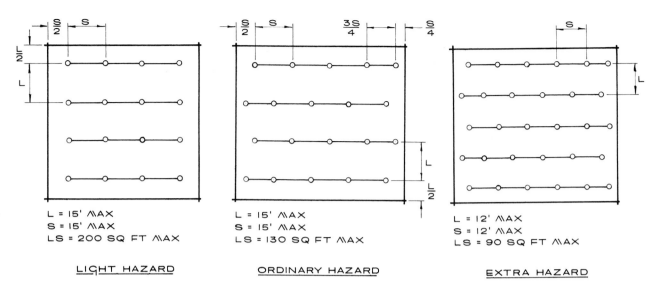

Figure 13   Sprinkler layouts for smooth ceiling.

chemical are nonconductive and therefore can be used on electrical fires in addition to flammable liquid fires.

Highrise buildings. Research is constantly being conducted to find better ways to prevent or control building fires. Special attention is being given to the problem of fire safety in highrise buildings, for their construction is increasing—some to heights of 1000 ft. and more. These buildings may contain more than 25,000 persons—equivalent to the population of a small city. Special precaution for fire protection must be taken in such buildings, for prompt evacuation is usually not possible. In addition, the building height may contribute to a stack effect, and many floors may be beyond the reach of fire department aerial equipment. Therefore, fire must be controlled and fought internally. A combination of three methods is usually used:

1. All building materials and furnishings selected to provide no potential fuel for a fire, including no potential for emitting smoke and toxic gases
2. Compartmented structures capable of resisting and containing a fire within a relatively small portion of the building
3. Automatic fire-extinguishing systems capable of prompt and effective operation

An innovative fire protection system was used in the United States Steel building of Pittsburgh, Pennsylvania (Figure 14). Conventional sprayed cementitious fire protection was used for interior columns, beams, and floors. However, exterior columns were protected by using hollow box-columns

Figure 14   U.S. Steel Building in Pittsburgh contains water-filled columns for fire protection.

of weathering steel filled with water plus antifreeze and corrosion-inhibiting additives. In the event of fire, the water will absorb heat and keep the temperature of the columns below a critical point. Any steam generated escapes through vents. To prevent excessive hydrostatic pressure, the columns are divided into four separate sections each 16 stories high.

STUDY QUESTIONS

1. List the eight building classifications by occupancy as established by the National Fire Protection Association.
2. List the three building classifications by hazard as established by the National Fire Protection Association.
3. List the five building classifications by construction type as established by the National Fire Protection Association.
4. What is the difference between:
   a. Fire-resistive and noncombustible construction
   b. Heavy timber, ordinary, and wood frame construction
   c. Wet and dry pipe sprinkler systems
5. Give the meaning of "three-hour fire rating."
6. Give the minimum thickness required to achieve a three-hour fire rating for:
   a. Lightweight CMU walls (with unexpanded slag)
   b. Solid brick masonry walls
   c. Reinforced concrete walls, unplastered
   d. Sprayed mineral fiber on steel columns
   e. Sprayed mineral fiber on steel beams
   f. Sprayed mineral fiber on $2\frac{1}{2}''$ concrete slab poured on light-gage steel decking

LABORATORY PROBLEMS

1. Check your original building design for compliance with your local exits code or the National Building Exits Code.
2. Using local codes or the National Fire Protection Association Codes, draw the fireproofing details for the building assigned by your instructor:

   a. Columns
   b. Beams or girders
   c. Trusses
   d. Floors
   e. Roof

3. Using local codes or the National Fire Protection Association Codes, draw the fireproofing details for your original building design:
   a. Columns
   b. Beams or girders
   c. Trusses
   d. Floors
   e. Roof
4. Using the National Fire Protection Association Codes, lay out the sprinkler system for the building assigned by your instructor.
5. Using the National Fire Protection Association Codes, lay out the sprinkler system for your original building design.

30   the construction documents

In addition to the working drawings, any large project also requires a number of written documents that are needed to advertise for and obtain bids, award a contract, and assure the satisfactory completion of the project. The index of a typical set of construction documents will give an idea of the many different documents required.

I INDEX

Document	Title	
I	Index	
II	Invitation to Bid	Bidding
III	Instructions to Bidders	Require-
IV	Bid Form	ments
V	Agreement	
VI	Performance Bond	Contract
VII	Labor and Material Bond	Forms
VIII	Estimate of Payment Due	
IX	General Conditions	
X	Supplementary Conditions	
XI	Specifications	
XII	Working Drawings	

Some of the sections listed are comparatively short, simple documents; others (like the specifications) may consist of many hundreds of pages. The specifications are prepared by a "specs" writer who is specially trained to do this work. To give a better idea of the makeup of the various sections of the construction documents, let us look at each in more detail.

II INVITATION TO BID

In public work, bid invitations are mailed to all contractors who might be interested in the proposed project. Also, newspaper advertisements for bids are placed. (Occasionally in private work only selected contractors are invited to bid.) The advertisements are placed three times in three weeks, and they include a brief description of the work and location, together with the requirements (time and place) of bid delivery. A sample Invitation to Bid is shown in Figure 1. A sample Advertisement for Bids is shown in Figure 2.

III INSTRUCTIONS TO BIDDERS

This section gives more detailed information that a bidder needs to intelligently prepare and submit a bid. The information includes the following:

A. Availability of construction documents
B. Examination of construction documents and site
C. Resolution of questions
D. Approval for substitution of materials
E. Basis of bids

Jones and Brown, Architects   INVITATION TO BID
5555 Main Street   STATE UNIVERSITY SCIENCE BUILDING
Smithville, Ohio   Project 3813
Phone: 888-777-6666   October __, 197_

You are invited to bid on a General Contract, including mechanical
and electrical work, for a two-story, thin-shell concrete, circular
Science Building, approximately four hundred feet in diameter. All
Bids must be on a lump sum basis; segregated Bids will not be
accepted.

The State University Board of Governors will receive Bids until 3:00
p.m. Central Standard Time on Tuesday, November 8, 197_, at 233
Uptown Street, Room 313, Smithville, Ohio. Bids received after this
time will not be accepted. All interested parties are invited to
attend; Bids will be opened publicly and read aloud.

Drawings and Specifications may be examined at the Architect's office
and at:

     The Plan Center   Associated Plan Bureau
     382 West Third Street   1177 South Barnes
     Smithville, Ohio   Smithville, Ohio

Copies of the above documents may be obtained at the office of the
Architect in accord with the Instructions to Bidders upon depositing
the sum of $100.00 for each set of documents.

Any bona-fide bidder, upon returning the documents in good condition
immediately following the public opening of said bids, shall be
returned his deposit in full. Any non-bidder returning the documents
in good condition will be returned the sum of $75.00.

Bid Security in the amount of _____ percent of the Bid must accompany
each Bid in accord with the Instructions to Bidders.

The Board of Governors reserves the right to waive irregularities and
to reject Bids.

                                    By order of the Board of Governors

                                    State University
                                    Smithville, Ohio

                                    Hirmats J. Downe, Secretary

Figure 1   Sample "Invitation to Bid."

F. Preparation of bids
G. Bid security information
H. Requirements for the Performance Bond and the Labor and Material Bond
I. Requirements for listing any subcontractors
J. Identification and submission of bid
K. Modification or withdrawal of bid
L. Disqualification of bidders
M. Governing laws and regulations
N. Opening of bids
O. Award of contract
P. Execution of contract

A sample Instructions to Bidders section is shown in Figure 3.

IV BID FORM

The Bid Form is a sample bidding letter from the bidder to the prospective owner. It contains blank spaces to be filled in by the bidder and a place for his signature (and for the seal of corporations) to indicate agreement with all provisions. The Bid Form includes the following:

A. Acknowledgment that all construction documents were received by bidder.
B. Agreement statements that bidder will hold bid open until a stated time and that bidder will abide by the "Instructions to Bidders."
C. Price of project including price of any alternatives. Alternate bids should be included in addition to the base bid as a means of keeping the project cost within the budget and as a "keep honest" feature; that is, the bid may be higher if there are no allowable substitutes for materials for competitive bidding. Some alternate bids for a large project might be the following:
   1. Asphalt tile as an alternative to rubber tile in corridors
   2. Quarry tile as an alternative to terrazzo on interior floor slabs
   3. Asphalt and slag roof as an alternative to a pitch and slag roof
   4. Cold-mixed bituminous surfacing as an alternative to hot-mixed asphaltic concrete surfacing course on driveways and service areas
D. Attachment statement that required information (such as a subcontractor listing or evidence of bidder's qualifications) is enclosed.

A sample Bid Form is shown in Figure 4.

Figure 2   Sample "Advertisement for Bids."

ADVERTISEMENT FOR BIDS

Bids: November 8, 197_
STATE UNIVERSITY
SCIENCE BUILDING
SMITHVILLE, OHIO
Project 3813
October __, 197_
Jones and Brown, Architects
5555 Main Street
Smithville, Ohio
Phone 888 777-6666

The Board of Governors, State University, Smithville, Ohio will receive sealed bids on a General Contract, including mechanical and electrical work, for a two-story thin-shell concrete circular Science Building, approximately four hundred feet in diameter.

All Bids must be on a lump sum basis; segregated Bids will not be accepted.

The State University Board of Governors will receive Bids until 3:00 p.m. Central Standard Time on Tuesday, November 8, 197_ at 233 Upton Street, Room 313, Smithville, Ohio. Bids received after this time will not be accepted. All interested parties are invited to attend. Bids will be opened and publicly read aloud.

Drawings and Specifications may be examined at the Architect's office and at:
   The Plan Center
   382 West Third Street
   Smithville, Ohio
   Associated Plan Bureau
   117 South Barnes
   Smithville, Ohio
Copies of the above documents may be obtained at the office of the Architect in accord with the Instructions to Bidders upon depositing the sum of $100.00 for each set of documents.

Any bona-fide bidder, upon returning the documents in good condition immediately following the public opening of said bids, shall be returned his deposit in full. Any non-bidder returning the documents in good condition will be returned the sum of $75.00.

Contracts for work under this bid will obligate the Contractor and subcontractors not to discriminate in employment practices. Bidders must submit a compliance report in conformity with the President's Executive Order No. 11246.

This contract is Federally assisted. The Contractor must comply with the Davis-Bacon Act, the Anti-Kickback Act, and the Contract Work Hours Standards.

Bid Security in the amount of _____ percent of the Bid must accompany each Bid in accord with the Instructions to Bidders.

The Board of Governors reserves the right to waive irregularities and to reject Bids.

By order of the Board of Governors
   STATE UNIVERSITY
   SMITHVILLE, OHIO
   October __, 197_

To be considered, Bids must be made in accord with these instructions to Bidders.

DOCUMENTS. Bonafide prime bidders may obtain _____ sets of Drawings and Specifications from the Architect upon deposit of $_____ per set. Those who submit prime bids may obtain refund of deposits by returning sets in good condition no more than _____ days after Bids have been opened. Those who do not submit prime bids will forfeit deposits unless sets are returned in good condition at least _____ days before Bids are opened. No partial sets will be issued; no sets will be issued to sub-bidders by the Architect. Prime bidders may obtain additional copies upon deposit of $_____ per set.

EXAMINATION. Bidders shall carefully examine the documents and the construction site to obtain first-hand knowledge of existing conditions. Contractors will not be given extra payments for conditions which can be determined by examining the site and documents.

QUESTIONS. Submit all questions about the Drawings and Specifications to the Architect, in writing. Replies will be issued to all prime bidders of record as Addenda to the Drawings and Specifications and will become part of the Contract. The Architect and Owner will not be responsible for oral clarification. Questions received less than _____ hours before the bid opening cannot be answered.

SUBSTITUTIONS. To obtain approval to use unspecified products, bidders shall submit written requests at least ten days before the bid date and hour. Requests received after this time will not be considered. Requests shall clearly describe the product for which approval is asked, including all data necessary to demonstrate acceptability. If the product is acceptable, the Architect will approve it in an Addendum issued to all prime bidders on record.

BASIS OF BID. The bidder must include all unit cost items and all alternatives shown on the Bid Forms; failure to comply may be cause for rejection. No segregated Bids or assignments will be considered.

PREPARATION OF BIDS. Bids shall be made on unaltered Bid Forms furnished by the Architect. Fill in all blank spaces and submit two copies. Bids shall be signed with name typed below signature. Where bidder is a corporation, Bids must be signed with the legal name of the corporation followed by the name of the State of incorporation and legal signatures of an officer authorized to bind the corporation to a contract.

BID SECURITY. Bid Security shall be made payable to the Board of Governors, State University, in the amount of _____ percent of the Bid sum. Security shall be either certified check or bid bond issued by surety licensed to conduct business in the State of Ohio. The successful bidder's security will be retained until he has signed the Contract and furnished the required payment and performance bonds. The Owner reserves the right to retain the security of the next _____ bidders until the lowest bidder enters into contract or until _____ days after bid opening, whichever is the shorter. All other bid security will be returned as soon as practicable. If any bidder refuses to enter into a Contract, the Owner will retain his Bid Security as liquidated damages, but not as a penalty. The Bid Security is to be submitted _____ day(s) prior to the Submission of Bids.

Figure 3   Sample "Instruction to Bidders."

PERFORMANCE BOND AND LABOR AND MATERIAL PAYMENT BOND. Furnish and pay for bonds covering faithful performance of the Contract and payment of all obligations arising thereunder. Furnish bonds in such form as the Owner may prescribe and with a surety company acceptable to the Owner. The bidder shall deliver said bonds to the Owner not later than the date of execution of the Contract. Failure or neglecting to deliver said bonds, as specified, shall be considered as having abandoned the Contract and the Bid Security will be retained as liquidated damages.

SUBCONTRACTORS. Names of principal subcontractors must be listed and attached to the Bid. There shall be only one subcontractor named for each classification listed.

SUBMITTAL. Submit Bid and Subcontractor Listing in an opaque, sealed envelope. Identify the envelope with: (1) project name, (2) name of bidder. Submit Bids in accord with the Invitation to Bid.

MODIFICATION AND WITHDRAWAL. Bids may not be modified after submittal. Bidders may withdraw Bids at any time before bid opening, but may not resubmit them. No Bid may be withdrawn or modified after the bid opening except where the award of Contract has been delayed for _____ days.

DISQUALIFICATION. The Owner reserves the right to disqualify Bids, before or after opening, upon evidence of collusion with intent to defraud or other illegal practices upon the part of the bidder.

GOVERNING LAWS AND REGULATIONS
NON DISCRIMINATORY PRACTICES. Contracts for work under the bid will obligate the contractor and subcontractors not to discriminate in employment practices. Bidders must submit a compliance report in conformity with the President's Executive Order No. 11246.

U.S. GOVERNMENT REQUIREMENTS. This contract is Federally assisted. The Contractor must comply with the Davis Bacon Act, the Anti-Kickback Act, and the Contract Work Hours Standards.

OHIO EXCISE TAX. Bidders should be aware of the Ohio Law (_____) as it relates to tax assessments on construction equipment.

OPENING. Bids will be opened as announced in the Invitation to Bid.

AWARD. The Contract will be awarded on the basis of low bid, including full consideration of unit prices and alternatives.

EXECUTION OF CONTRACT. The Owner reserves the right to accept any Bid, and to reject any and all Bids, or to negotiate Contract Terms with the various Bidders, when such is deemed by the Owner to be in his best interest.

Each Bidder shall be prepared, if so requested by the Owner, to present evidence of his experience, qualifications, and financial ability to carry out the terms of the Contract.

Notwithstanding any delay in the preparation and execution of the formal Contract Agreement, each Bidder shall be prepared, upon written notice of bid acceptance, to commence work within _____ days following receipt of official written order of the Owner to proceed, or on date stipulated in such order.

The accepted bidder shall assist and cooperate with the Owner in preparing the formal Contract Agreement, and within _____ days following its presentation shall execute same and return it to the Owner.

Figure 3   continued

```
TO:                                STATE UNIVERSITY SCIENCE BUILDING
The Board of Governors                           Project 3813
State University
233 Uptown Street, Room 313
Smithville, Ohio


I have received the documents titled "Specifications for State
University Science Building" and Drawings A-1 through A-27, S-1
through S-10, and M-1 through M-15. I have also received Addenda Nos.
_____, and have included their provisions in my Bid. I have
examined both the documents and the site and submit the following
Bid:

In submitting this Bid, I agree:

   1. To hold my bid open until December 8, 197_.

   2. To accept the provisions of the Instructions to Bidders
regarding disposition of Bid Security.

   3. To enter into and execute a Contract, if awarded on the basis of
this bid, and to furnish Guarantee Bonds in accord with Article 30 of
the General Conditions of this Contract.

   4. To accomplish the work in accord with the Contract Documents.

   5. To complete the work by the time stipulated in the Supplementary
Conditions.

I will construct this project for the lump-sum price of _____
_____ dollars ($_____).

I will include the following alternatives as specified substitutes
for the additional costs listed:

   1. Elevators Nos. 5 and 6                    +$_____

   2. Steam pipe system                         +$_____

If the following items, which are based on unit prices, vary more
than 10 percent from the estimates furnished by the Architect, I will
adjust the Contract Sum in accord with the following rates:

Concrete piling             +$_____    -$_____

Interior gypsum partitions,
including plaster and paint,
per square foot             +$_____    -$_____

I have attached the required Bid Security and Subcontractor Listing
to this Bid.


        Date: _____    Signed: _____
```

Figure 4   *Sample "Bid Form."*

V AGREEMENT

The Agreement is one of several forms that are pre-printed to simplify contract preparation. The contract forms supplied by the American Institute of Architects are commonly used, but many government agencies have developed standard contract forms for their own uses.

The Owner-Architect Agreement includes a statement of the architectural services ordinarily considered necessary and the owner's usual obligations. Many different forms of Agreements are used, but they differ mainly in the method by which the architect's compensation is determined. The fee can be as follows:

1. A percentage of the construction cost (usually from 5 to 15 percent)
2. A professional fee plus expenses
3. A multiple of personnel expenses

VI PERFORMANCE BOND

The Performance Bond is a guarantee to the client that the contractor will perform all the terms and conditions of the contract, and if defaulted will protect the client up to the bond penalty. The Performance Bond should be distinguished from the Labor and Material Bond, which protects the laborers and material men.

VII LABOR AND MATERIAL BOND

The Labor and Material Bond guarantees that the bills of the materials suppliers and subcontractors will be paid.

VIII ESTIMATE OF PAYMENT DUE

A first payment of 10 percent of the architect's fee is paid upon the execution of the Agreement. Additional payments of the fee are made monthly in proportion to the services performed. The total payments are increased to the following percentages at the completion of each phase:

1. Schematic design   15%
2. Design development   35%
3. Construction documents   75%
4. Receipt of bids   80%
5. Construction   100%

IX GENERAL CONDITIONS

This section is among the most important in the construction documents. The General Conditions con-tain additional contractual-legal requirements not covered by other contract forms. While some architects use A.I.A. Document A-201 without change, others write the General Conditions to satisfy their own particular requirements. It is also possible to note only those modifications of the A.I.A. Document that apply to each job. Typical subsections are the following:

A. Definitions
B. Architect's supervision
C. Architect's decision
D. Notice
E. Separate contracts
F. Intent of plans and specifications
G. Errors and discrepancies
H. Drawings and specifications furnished to contractors
I. Approved drawings
J. Patents
K. Permits, licenses, and certificates
L. Supervision and labor
M. Public safety and watchmen
N. Order of completion
O. Substitution of materials for those called for by specifications
P. Materials, equipment, and labor
Q. Inspection
R. Defective work and materials
S. Failure to comply with orders of architect
T. Use of completed parts
U. Rights of various interests
V. Suspension of work due to unfavorable conditions
W. Suspension of work due to fault of contractor
X. Suspension of work due to unforeseen causes
Y. Request for extension
Z. Stoppage of work by architect
AA. Default on part of contractor
BB. Removal of equipment
CC. Monthly estimates and payments
DD. Acceptance and final payment
EE. Deviations from contract requirements
FF. Estoppel and waiver of legal rights
GG. Approval of subcontractors and sources of material
HH. Approval of material samples requiring laboratory tests
II. Arbitration
JJ. Bonds
KK. Additional or substitute bonds
LL. Public liability and property damage insurance
MM. Workmen's Compensation Act
NN. Fire insurance and damage due to other hazards
OO. Explosives and blasting
PP. Damages to property
QQ. Mutual responsibility of contractors
RR. Contractor's liability

DIVISION 1—GENERAL REQUIREMENTS
01010 SUMMARY OF WORK
01100 ALTERNATIVES
01200 PROJECT MEETINGS
01300 SUBMITTALS
01400 QUALITY CONTROL
01500 TEMPORARY FACILITIES & CONTROLS
01600 PRODUCTS
01700 PROJECT CLOSEOUT

DIVISION 2—SITE WORK
02010 SUBSURFACE EXPLORATION
02100 CLEARING
02110 DEMOLITION
02200 EARTHWORK
02250 SOIL TREATMENT
02300 PILE FOUNDATIONS
02350 CAISSONS
02400 SHORING
02500 SITE DRAINAGE
02550 SITE UTILITIES
02600 PAVING & SURFACING
02700 SITE IMPROVEMENTS
02800 LANDSCAPING
02850 RAILROAD WORK
02900 MARINE WORK
02950 TUNNELING

DIVISION 3—CONCRETE
03100 CONCRETE FORMWORK
03150 EXPANSION & CONTRACTION JOINTS
03200 CONCRETE REINFORCEMENT
03300 CAST-IN-PLACE CONCRETE
03350 SPECIALLY FINISHED CONCRETE
03360 SPECIALLY PLACED CONCRETE
03400 PRECAST CONCRETE
03500 CEMENTITIOUS DECKS

DIVISION 4—MASONRY
04100 MORTAR
04150 MASONRY ACCESSORIES
04200 UNIT MASONRY
04400 STONE
04500 MASONRY RESTORATION & CLEANING
04550 REFRACTORIES

DIVISION 5—METALS
05100 STRUCTURAL METAL FRAMING
05200 METAL JOISTS
05300 METAL DECKING
05400 LIGHTGAGE METAL FRAMING
05500 METAL FABRICATIONS
05700 ORNAMENTAL METAL
05800 EXPANSION CONTROL

DIVISION 6—WOOD & PLASTICS
06100 ROUGH CARPENTRY
06130 HEAVY TIMBER CONSTRUCTION
06150 TRESTLES
06170 PREFABRICATED STRUCTURAL WOOD
06200 FINISH CARPENTRY
06300 WOOD TREATMENT
06400 ARCHITECTURAL WOODWORK
06500 PREFABRICATED STRUCTURAL PLASTICS
06600 PLASTIC FABRICATIONS

DIVISION 7—THERMAL & MOISTURE PROTECTION
07100 WATERPROOFING
07150 DAMPPROOFING
07200 INSULATION
07300 SHINGLES & ROOFING TILES
07400 PREFORMED ROOFING & SIDING
07500 MEMBRANE ROOFING
07570 TRAFFIC TOPPING

07600 FLASHING & SHEET METAL
07800 ROOF ACCESSORIES
07900 SEALANTS

DIVISION 8—DOORS & WINDOWS
08100 METAL DOORS & FRAMES
08200 WOOD & PLASTIC DOORS
08300 SPECIAL DOORS
08400 ENTRANCES & STOREFRONTS
08500 METAL WINDOWS
08600 WOOD & PLASTIC WINDOWS
08650 SPECIAL WINDOWS
08700 HARDWARE & SPECIALTIES
08800 GLAZING
08900 WINDOW WALLS/CURTAIN WALLS

DIVISION 9—FINISHES
09100 LATH & PLASTER
09250 GYPSUM WALLBOARD
09300 TILE
09400 TERRAZZO
09500 ACOUSTICAL TREATMENT
09540 CEILING SUSPENSION SYSTEMS
09550 WOOD FLOORING
09650 RESILIENT FLOORING
09680 CARPETING
09700 SPECIAL FLOORING
09760 FLOOR TREATMENT
09800 SPECIAL COATINGS
09900 PAINTING
09950 WALL COVERING

DIVISION 10—SPECIALTIES
10100 CHALKBOARDS & TACKBOARDS
10150 COMPARTMENTS & CUBICLES
10200 LOUVERS & VENTS
10240 GRILLES & SCREENS
10260 WALL & CORNER GUARDS
10270 ACCESS FLOORING
10280 SPECIALTY MODULES
10290 PEST CONTROL
10300 FIREPLACES
10350 FLAGPOLES
10400 IDENTIFYING DEVICES
10450 PEDESTRIAN CONTROL DEVICES
10500 LOCKERS
10530 PROTECTIVE COVERS
10550 POSTAL SPECIALTIES
10600 PARTITIONS
10650 SCALES
10670 STORAGE SHELVING
10700 SUN CONTROL DEVICES (EXTERIOR)
10750 TELEPHONE ENCLOSURES
10800 TOILET & BATH ACCESSORIES
10900 WARDROBE SPECIALTIES

DIVISION 11—EQUIPMENT
11050 BUILT-IN MAINTENANCE EQUIPMENT
11100 BANK & VAULT EQUIPMENT
11150 COMMERCIAL EQUIPMENT
11170 CHECKROOM EQUIPMENT
11180 DARKROOM EQUIPMENT
11200 ECCLESIASTICAL EQUIPMENT
11300 EDUCATIONAL EQUIPMENT
11400 FOOD SERVICE EQUIPMENT
11480 VENDING EQUIPMENT
11500 ATHLETIC EQUIPMENT
11550 INDUSTRIAL EQUIPMENT
11600 LABORATORY EQUIPMENT
11630 LAUNDRY EQUIPMENT
11650 LIBRARY EQUIPMENT
11700 MEDICAL EQUIPMENT
11800 MORTUARY EQUIPMENT

11830 MUSICAL EQUIPMENT
11850 PARKING EQUIPMENT
11860 WASTE HANDLING EQUIPMENT
11870 LOADING DOCK EQUIPMENT
11880 DETENTION EQUIPMENT
11900 RESIDENTIAL EQUIPMENT
11970 THEATER & STAGE EQUIPMENT
11990 REGISTRATION EQUIPMENT

DIVISION 12—FURNISHINGS
12100 ARTWORK
12300 CABINETS & STORAGE
12500 WINDOW TREATMENT
12550 FABRICS
12600 FURNITURE
12670 RUGS & MATS
12700 SEATING
12800 FURNISHING ACCESSORIES

DIVISION 13—SPECIAL CONSTRUCTION
13010 AIR SUPPORTED STRUCTURES
13050 INTEGRATED ASSEMBLIES
13100 AUDIOMETRIC ROOM
13250 CLEAN ROOM
13350 HYPERBARIC ROOM
13400 INCINERATORS
13440 INSTRUMENTATION
13450 INSULATED ROOM
13500 INTEGRATED CEILING
13540 NUCLEAR REACTORS
13550 OBSERVATORY
13600 PREFABRICATED BUILDINGS
13700 SPECIAL PURPOSE ROOMS & BUILDINGS
13750 RADIATION PROTECTION
13770 SOUND & VIBRATION CONTROL
13800 VAULTS
13850 SWIMMING POOLS

DIVISION 14—CONVEYING SYSTEMS
14100 DUMBWAITERS
14200 ELEVATORS
14300 HOISTS & CRANES
14400 LIFTS
14500 MATERIAL HANDLING SYSTEMS
14570 TURNTABLES
14600 MOVING STAIRS & WALKS
14700 PNEUMATIC TUBE SYSTEMS
14800 POWERED SCAFFOLDING

DIVISION 15—MECHANICAL
15010 GENERAL PROVISIONS
15050 BASIC MATERIALS & METHODS
15180 INSULATION
15200 WATER SUPPLY & TREATMENT
15300 WASTE WATER DISPOSAL & TREATMENT
15400 PLUMBING
15500 FIRE PROTECTION
15600 POWER OR HEAT GENERATION
15650 REFRIGERATION
15700 LIQUID HEAT TRANSFER
15800 AIR DISTRIBUTION
15900 CONTROLS & INSTRUMENTATION

DIVISION 16—ELECTRICAL
16010 GENERAL PROVISIONS
16100 BASIC MATERIALS & METHODS
16200 POWER GENERATION
16300 POWER TRANSMISSION
16400 SERVICE & DISTRIBUTION
16500 LIGHTING
16600 SPECIAL SYSTEMS
16700 COMMUNICATIONS
16850 HEATING & COOLING
16900 CONTROLS & INSTRUMENTATION

Figure 5   The Divisions and Broadscope Sections of the CSI Format.

SS. Familiarity with contract documents

TT. Shop drawings

UU. Guarantee of work

VV. Clean up

WW. Competent workmen (state law)

XX. Prevailing wage act (state law)

YY. Residence of employees

ZZ. Nondiscrimination in hiring employees (state law)

AAA. Preference to employment of war veterans (state law)

BBB. Hiring and conditions of employment (state law)

X SUPPLEMENTARY CONDITIONS

The Supplementary Conditions contain special modifications to the basic articles of the General Conditions, together with any additional articles of a contractual legal nature that might be needed for a particular project.

XI SPECIFICATIONS

The Specifications give detailed instructions on the required materials, finishes, and workmanship—all grouped by building trades. Each trade is included in the order of actual construction. Nearly all offices use the standardized specification system as recommended by the *Construction Specifications Institute.* This system is called the "CSI Format" and consists of 16 "Divisions" (grouped by building trades) and a number of related "Broadscope Sections" (grouped by units of work) as shown in Figure 5. The Broadscope Sections (printed in capital letters) are further refined into "Narrowscope Sections" (printed in lowercase letters). The Narrowscope Section of Divisions 6, 7, and 8 are shown in Figure 6. A specifications writer will select only those sections that apply to a particular job. Notice that a five-digit numbering system is used for the designation of all Broadscope and Narrowscope Sections. This helps offices that use automated printing and data retrieval systems.

The Construction Specifications Institute also recommends a uniform three-part approach for writing each section:

Part 1—General

  Description

  Quality Assurance

  Submittals

  Product Delivery, Storage, and Handling

  Job Conditions

  Alternatives

  Guarantee

Part 2—Products

  Materials

  Mixes

  Fabrication and Manufacture

Part 3—Execution

  Inspection

  Preparation

  Installation / Application / Performance

  Field Quality Control

  Adjust and Clean

  Schedules

Although architects still refer to "writing" specifications, actually the majority of sections are assembled from a data book of carefully worded and approved paragraphs.

Three basic sentence structures are commonly used in specifications to convey the architect's intent clearly and concisely: the indicative mood, the imperative mood, and streamlining.

The indicative mood, requiring the use of "shall" in nearly every sentence, is the traditional language of specs writing: "Two coats of paint shall be applied to each exposed surface."

The imperative mood is more concise. A verb begins the sentence and immediately defines the required action: "Apply two coats of paint to each exposed surface."

Streamlining is used to itemize products, materials, and reference standards:

Materials shall meet the following requirements:

Portland Cement: ASTM C 150, Type I.

Aggregate: ASTM C 33.

Some additional "rules of thumb" for specifications writing are the following:

1. Use short sentences and simple, declarative statements.

2. Avoid complicated sentences whose meanings are so dependent on punctuation that inadvertent omission or insertion of punctuation changes the meaning or creates ambiguity.

3. Choose words and terms that are plain and well understood to convey the information. Avoid pompous or highly embellished language. For example, use "shall" rather than "it is incumbent upon" or "it is the duty." Use "the contractor may" rather than "if the contractor so elects, he may" or "the contractor is hereby authorized to." Use "means" rather than "shall be interpreted to mean." Use "by" rather than "by means of." Use "to" rather than "in order to." Never use "herein," "hereinbefore," "hereinafter," or "wherein." Avoid using "and/or," "etc.," and "as per."

4. Use the word "shall" for the work of the Contractor. Use the word "will" for acts of the owner or architect. Do not use "must."

5. Use numerals (figures) instead of words for numbers over twelve. For example: one, six, twelve, 13,

DIVISION 6—WOOD & PLASTICS		DIVISION 7—THERMAL AND MOISTURE PROTECTION		DIVISION 8—DOORS & WINDOWS	
06100	**ROUGH CARPENTRY**	07100	**WATERPROOFING**	08100	**METAL DOORS AND FRAMES**
06110	Framing and Sheathing	07110	Membrane Waterproofing	08110	Hollow Metal Work
06111	Light Wooden Structures—Framing	07111	Elastomeric Membrane Waterproofing	08111	Stock Hollow Metal Work
06112	Preassembled Components	07120	Fluid Applied Waterproofing	08112	Custom Hollow Metal Work
06113	Sheathing	07121	Liquid Waterproofing	08120	Aluminum Doors and Frames
06114	Diaphragms	07130	Bentonite Clay Waterproofing	08130	Stainless Steel Doors and Frames
06130	**HEAVY TIMBER CONSTRUCTION**	07140	Metal Oxide Waterproofing	08140	Bronze Doors and Frames
06131	Timber Trusses	07150	**DAMPPROOFING**	08200	**WOOD AND PLASTIC DOORS**
06132	Mill-Framed Structures	07160	Bituminous Dampproofing	08210	Wood Doors
06133	Pole Construction	07170	Silicone Dampproofing	08211	Flush Wood Doors
06150	**TRESTLES**	07175	Water Repellent Coatings	08212	Panel Wood Doors
06170	**PREFABRICATED STRUCTURAL WOOD**	07180	Cementitious Dampproofing	08213	Plastic Faced Wood Doors
06180	Glued Laminated Construction	07190	Vapor Barriers/Retardants	08220	Plastic Doors
06181	Glue-Laminated Structural Units	07191	Bituminous Vapor Barrier/Retardants	08300	**SPECIAL DOORS**
06182	Glue-Laminated Decking	07192	Laminated Vapor Barrier/Retardants	08310	Sliding Metal Fire Doors
06190	Wood Trusses	07193	Plastic Vapor Barrier/Retardants	08320	Metal-Clad Doors
06191	Wood-Metal Joists	07200	**INSULATION**	08330	Coiling Doors
06200	**FINISH CARPENTRY**	07210	Building Insulation	08340	Coiling Grilles
06220	Millwork	07211	Loose Fill Insulation	08350	Folding Doors
06240	Laminated Plastic	07212	Rigid Insulation	08351	Folding Doors: Panel
06300	**WOOD TREATMENT**	07213	Fibrous and Reflective Insulation	08353	Accordion Folding Doors
06310	Pressure Treated Lumber	07214	Foamed-in-Place Insulation	08355	Flexible Doors
06311	Preservative Treated Lumber	07215	Sprayed-On Insulation	08360	Overhead Doors
06312	Fire Retardant Treated Lumber	07230	High and Low Temperature Insulation	08370	Sliding Glass Doors
06400	**ARCHITECTURAL WOODWORK**	07240	Roof and Deck Insulation	08375	Safety Glass Doors
06410	Cabinetwork	07250	Perimeter and Under-Slab Insulation	08380	Sound Retardant Doors
06411	Wood Cabinets: Unfinished	07300	**SHINGLES AND ROOFING TILES**	08390	Screen and Storm Doors
06420	Paneling	07310	Shingles	08400	**ENTRANCES & STOREFRONTS**
06421	Architectural Hardwood Plywood Paneling	07311	Asphalt Shingles	08450	Revolving Doors
06422	Softwood Plywood Paneling	07312	Asbestos-Cement Shingles	08500	**METAL WINDOWS**
06430	Stairwork	07313	Wood Shingles and Shakes	08510	Steel Windows
06431	Wood Stairs and Railings	07314	Slate Shingles	08520	Aluminum Windows
06500	**PREFABRICATED STRUCTURAL PLASTICS**	07315	Porcelain Enamel Shingles	08530	Stainless Steel Windows
06600	**PLASTIC FABRICATIONS**	07316	Metal Shingles	08540	Bronze Windows
		07320	Roofing Tiles	08600	**WOOD & PLASTIC WINDOWS**
		07321	Clay Roofing Tiles	08610	Wood Windows
		07322	Concrete Roofing Tiles	08620	Plastic Windows
		07400	**PREFORMED ROOFING AND SIDING**	08621	Reinforced Plastic Windows
		07410	Preformed Wall and Roof Panels	08650	**SPECIAL WINDOWS**
		07411	Preformed Metal Siding	08700	**HARDWARE & SPECIALTIES**
		07420	Composite Building Panels	08710	Finish Hardware
		07440	Preformed Plastic Panels	08720	Operators
		07460	Cladding/Siding	08721	Automatic Door Equipment
		07461	Wood Siding	08725	Window Operators
		07462	Composition Siding	08730	Weatherstripping & Seals
		07463	Asbestos-Cement Siding	08740	Thresholds
		07464	Plastic Siding	08800	**GLAZING**
		07500	**MEMBRANE ROOFING**	08810	Glass
		07510	Built-Up Bituminous Roofing	08811	Plate Glass
		07520	Prepared Roll Roofing	08812	Sheet Glass
		07530	Elastic Sheet Roofing	08813	Tempered Glass
		07540	Fluid Applied Roofing	08814	Wired Glass
		07570	**TRAFFIC TOPPING**	08815	Rough and Figured Glass
		07600	**FLASHING AND SHEET METAL**	08820	Processed Glass
		07610	Sheet Metal Roofing	08821	Coated Glass
		07620	Flashing and Trim	08822	Laminated Glass
		07630	Roofing Specialties	08823	Insulating Glass
		07631	Gutters and Downspouts	08830	Mirror Glass
		07660	Gravel Stops	08840	Glazing Plastics
		07800	**ROOF ACCESSORIES**	08850	Glazing Accessories
		07810	Skylights	08900	**WINDOW WALLS/CURTAIN WALLS**
		07811	Plastic Skylights	08910	Window Walls
		07812	Metal-Framed Skylights	08911	Steel Window Walls
		07830	Hatches	08912	Aluminum Window Walls
		07840	Gravity Ventilators (not connected to ductwork)	08913	Stainless Steel Window Walls
		07850	Prefabricated Curbs	08914	Bronze Window Walls
		07860	Prefabricated Expansion Joints	08915	Wood Window Walls
		07900	**SEALANTS**		
		07950	Joint Fillers and Gaskets		
		07951	·Sealants and Calking		

Figure 6   Some Narrowscope Sections of the CSI Format.

18, 100. But use numerals for all sums of money, e.g., $1.00. Give numbers preceding a numeral as words, e.g., fifteen 8-hour days.

To get a better idea of the specifications, let us look at one of the sections in more detail. We have chosen Division 8 (Doors and Windows), Broad-scope Section 08800 (Glazing) for this study.

Section 08800 Glazing

08801 STIPULATION

Applicable requirements of the "General Conditions" apply to this entire Specification, and shall have the same force and effect as if printed here in full.

08802 SCOPE OF WORK

The work covered by this Section consists of furnishing all labor, materials, equipment, and services necessary to complete all glass and glazing required for the project, in strict accordance with this Section of the Specifications and the Drawings; including, but not limited, to the following:

a. Glazing of exterior doors, sidelights, transoms, fixed metal window frames;
b. Glazing of interior doors, sidelights and frames;
c. Mirrors

08803 WORK EXCLUDED

The following items are included in other sections of the General Contract Specifications:

a. All bank equipment shall be factory glazed.

08810 GLASS

All glass shall comply with Federal Specification DD-G-45a for glass, flat, for glazing purposes.

08813 TEMPERED GLASS **(Exterior doors and sidelights at doors)**

Tempered glass for the above locations shall be "Solarbronze Twindow" with $\frac{1}{4}$" polished plate Solarbronze exterior sheet and $\frac{1}{4}$" clear tempered plate interior sheet. Glass in doors shall be $\frac{13}{16}$" thick and $\frac{1}{4}$" airspace. Other glass shall be $1\frac{1}{16}$" thick with $\frac{1}{2}$" airspace. Set in metal glazing beads.

08823 INSULATING GLASS **(Fixed exterior windows and transoms in aluminum frames)**

Insulating glass shall be $1\frac{1}{16}$" thick "Solarbronze Twindow" set in metal glazing beads. Glass shall have a $\frac{1}{4}$" polished plate Solarbronze exterior sheet, $\frac{1}{2}$" air space and $\frac{1}{4}$" clear polished plate interior sheet.

Section 08800 courtesy of Jack W Risheberger & Associates, Registered Architects and Engineers.

08830 MIRRORS

Over lavatories in toilet rooms, provide and install mirrors. Each mirror shall be of size indicated on the Drawings, equal to No. 53020, as manufactured by the Charles Parker Company, 50 Hanover Street, Meriden, Connecticut, complete with $\frac{1}{4}$" polished plate glass, moisture proof backing, removable back, narrow channel type plated brass or stainless steel frame, with concealed vandalproof mirror hangers. Mirrors shall be centered over lavatories, and set at height shown on Drawings or as directed by the Architect.

08840 GLAZING COMPOUND

Glazing compound for bedding glazing, Federal Specification TT-P-791a, Type I, elastic glazing compound. Glazing compound shall be specially prepared for the purpose, tinted to match frames, and shall remain plastic under a strong surface film similar to the product manufactured by "Tremco," "Pecora," or "Kuhls." *No putty will be accepted* (glass in doors and windows shall be set in glazing compound secured by glazing beads).

08841 SAMPLES

Samples of each type of glass and glazing compound shall be submitted for approval of the Architect.

08842 SETTING

All glass shall be properly bedded in glazing compound previously specified. Glazing compound shall not be applied in temperatures below 40°F, or during damp or rainy weather. Surfaces shall be dry and free of dust, dirt, or rust.

Glazing compound shall be used as it comes from the container without adulteration and only after thorough mixing. If thinning is required, use only such type of thinner as recommended by the manufacturer.

08843 REPLACEMENT AND CLEANING

Upon completion of the glazing, all glass shall be thoroughly cleaned, any paint spots and labels and other defacements removed, and all cracked, broken, and imperfect glass, or glass which cannot be properly cleaned, shall be replaced by perfect glass.

At the time of acceptance of the building, all glass shall be clean, whole, and in perfect condition, including glazing compound. Glazing compound applied after completion of painting shall be painted not less than two (2) coats.

08844 LABELS

Each light shall bear the manufacturer's label indicating the name of the manufacturer and the strength and quality of the glass. Labels shall remain in place until after final acceptance of the building, at which time the labels shall be removed and glass shall be given its final cleaning.

JONES AND SMITH, Architects: John Doe Bldg.
                    Washington, D.C.
First National Bank of Brownsville: Project No. 11863

ADDENDUM NO. 2: August 15, 1970

To: All prime contract bidders of record.

This addendum forms a part of the Contract Documents and modifies the
original specifications and drawings, dated July 1, 1970, and
Addendum 1, dated August 1, 1970, as noted below. Acknowledge receipt
of this Addendum in the space provided on the Bid Form. Failure to do
so may subject bidder to disqualification.

This Addendum consists of _____. (Indicate the
number of pages and any attachments or drawings forming a part of the
addendum.)

ADDENDUM NO. 1

1. Drawings, page AD 1-1. In line 3, number of the referenced Drawing
is changed from "G-1" to "G-7."

INSTRUCTIONS TO BIDDERS
2. Proposals. The first sentence is changed to read: "Proposed
substitutions must be submitted in writing at least 15 days before
the date for opening of bids."

GENERAL CONDITIONS
3. Article 13, Access to Work. The following sentence is added: "Upon
completion of work, the Contractor shall deliver to the Architect all
required Certificates of Inspection."

SUPPLEMENTARY CONDITIONS
4. Article 19, Correction of Work Before Substantial Completion. This
Article is deleted and the following is inserted in its place: "If
proceeds of sale do not cover expenses that the Contractor should
have borne, the Contractor shall pay the difference to the Owner."

SPECIFICATIONS
5. Division 7
Waterproofing: Page 4, following Paragraph 7C-02 Materials, add the
following: "(d) Option. Factory mixed waterproofing containing
metallic waterproofing, sand and cement, all meeting the above
requirements, may be used in lieu of job-mixed waterproofing."

6. Division 15
Refrigeration: Page 10, Paragraph 4—Chillers item "e" Line 4: Change
total square feet of surface from 298 to 316.

Liquid Heat Transfer: Page 17, Paragraph 10—Convectors item "b" Line
3: Delete "as selected—or owner."
Page 23, Paragraph 13—Wall Fin: Omit entirely.

DRAWINGS
7. S-9, Beam Schedule. For B-15 the following is added: "Size, 12 x
26; Straight, 3—#6; Bent, 2—#8, Top Over Columns: 3—#7."

8. M-1: At room 602 change 12 x 6 exhaust duct to 12 x 18; at room
602 add a roof ventilator. See print H-1R attached and page 16,
paragraph 13 Roof Ventilators addenda above.

Figure 7   Sample "Addendum."

```
JONES AND SMITH, Architects/Engineers John Doe Bldg.,
               Washington, D.C.
CHANGE ORDER NO. 5: September 9, 1970
JOB NO. 11863: First National Bank of Brownsville
OWNER: ABC Corp., Brownsville, Virginia
CONTRACTOR: Bildum Construction Co., Washington, D.C.
CONTRACT DATE: July 4, 1970


TO THE CONTRACTOR: You are hereby authorized, subject to Contract
provisions, to make the following changes:
Bulletin No. 1                                      ADD $ 73.24
Bulletin No. 2                                      ADD   138.07
Bulletin No. 3 No Charge,/No Credit
Bulletin No. 4                    DEDUCT $ 75.32
Bulletin No. 5                    DEDUCT   36.99
                                  _____
TOTAL                             DEDUCT $112.31    ADD $211.31
NET ADD $99.00


ORIGINAL CONTRACT AMOUNT:         $1,234,567.89
PRIOR CHANGE ORDERS (+, −):          +2,000.00
THIS CHANGE ORDER (+, −):               +99.00
                                  _____
REVISED CONTRACT AMOUNT:          $1,236,666.89


TIME EXTENSION/REDUCTION: None


OTHER CONTRACTS AFFECTED: None


SUBMITTED BY: _____ DATE: _____
                  (arch/engr's signature)


APPROVED BY: _____ DATE: _____
                  (owner's signature)


ACCEPTED BY: _____ DATE: _____
                  (contractor's signature)


DISTRIBUTION: Owner, Contractor, Architect/Engineer,
              Field Representative, Other _____.
```

Figure 8   Sample "Change Order."

XII WORKING DRAWINGS

The Working Drawings together with the Specifications are the most important parts of the documents constituting the contract. Information on the design, location, and dimensions of the elements of a building is found on working drawings, and information on the quality of materials and workmanship is found in the specifications. A good working drawing gives the contractor the exact information he needs, is clear and simple, arranged in an orderly manner, and accurately drawn so that scaled measurements will agree with dimensions. (See Chapter 16 for more information.)

ADDENDA AND CHANGE ORDERS

Addenda and Change Orders are used to correct or change the original construction documents. The main difference between an Addendum and a Change Order is the timing. An Addendum revises the original construction documents *before* the contract is awarded, but a Change Order is a revision *after* award of the contract. A sample Addendum is shown in Figure 7 and a sample Change Order is shown in Figure 8.

STUDY QUESTIONS

1. Why is it important to prepare specifications for every architectural project?
2. List the 12 documents included in a typical set of construction documents.
3. List the 16 divisions of a typical set of specifications.
4. Give the reasons for including the following documents in a set of construction documents:
   a. Specifications
   b. Working drawings
   c. Agreement
   d. Bid form
   e. Performance bond
   f. Labor and material bond

LABORATORY PROBLEMS

1. Prepare an outline of the specifications for the building assigned by your instructor.
   a. Include the broadscope section headings only.
   b. Include the broadscope and narrowscope section headings.
   c. Write a detailed specification for the section assigned by your instructor.
2. Obtain a set of specifications from a local architect for classroom study.

PART SIX

rendering

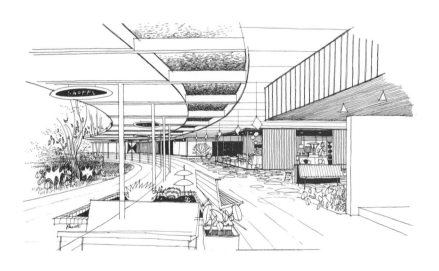

31 perspective drawing

In addition to *working drawings,* an architectural draftsman must be able to prepare *presentation drawings.* A presentation drawing is used to help describe or *present* the proposed building to the client. For this purpose, a *perspective drawing* is nearly always used, since it shows the appearance of the finished building exactly. Even persons trained in other types of drawing are able to visualize a design better in perspective. The architectural draftsman, for example, will prepare thumbnail perspectives of each alternate scheme so that he can choose the most satisfactory design.

A perspective drawing shows exactly how the building will appear to the eye or to a camera. The illustrator in Figure 1, drawing on a window with a wax pencil, will obtain the same perspective as a camera—as long as the relative positions of the observer, object, and picture plane are identical.

THREE TYPES OF PERSPECTIVE

If the picture plane is placed parallel to a face of the object, the resulting perspective is called a *one-point* perspective. If it is placed parallel to one set of lines (usually vertical lines), the resulting perspective is called a *two-point* perspective. When the picture plane is oblique to all of the object's lines and faces, a *three-point* perspective results (see Figure 3).

The two-point perspective is more commonly

used than either the one-point or three-point perspective. A one-point perspective of the exterior of a building is unsatisfactory for most purposes since it looks very much like a standard elevation drawing. Room interiors, however, may well be drawn in one-point perspective, as shown in Figure 2. A three-

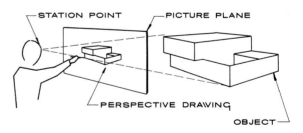

Figure 1   Perspective sketch.

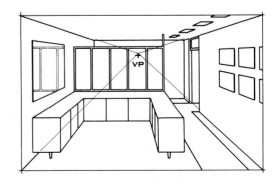

Figure 2   One-point interior perspective.

311

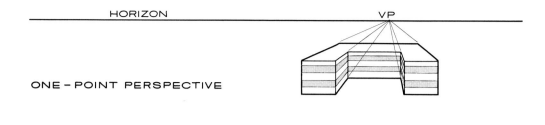

ONE – POINT PERSPECTIVE

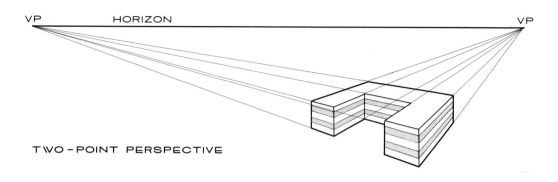

TWO – POINT PERSPECTIVE

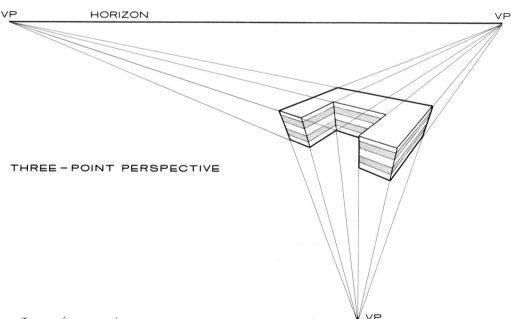

THREE – POINT PERSPECTIVE

Figure 3   Types of perspective.

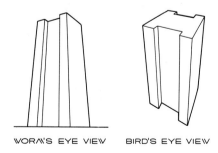

WORM'S EYE VIEW   BIRD'S EYE VIEW

Figure 4   Three-point perspective.

point perspective of a building exterior is not often used, since it means that the observer must be looking *up* at the building ("worm's eye view") or *down* on the building ("bird's eye view", Figure 4). Obviously, neither of these is considered a normal line of sight.

There are many methods of obtaining a two-point perspective, but the most often used are the *common method,* the *direct projection method,* and the *perspective grid method.* Let us look at each.

TWO-POINT PERSPECTIVE BY COMMON METHOD

Step 1. Locate the plan view behind the picture plane so that the front face is inclined 30° and the desired end face is inclined 60° to the picture plane. Actually, any set of complementary angles may be used, but the 30°–60° combination is most often used.

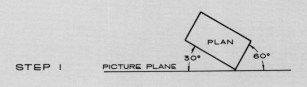

Step 2. Select any elevation view and position it on the ground line. Locate the horizon 6′ (to scale) above the ground line. This means the eye of the observer is 6′ above the ground. Other eye heights may be used if desired.

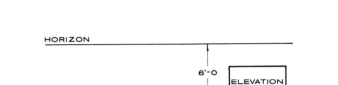

Step 3. Locate the station point (representing the location of the eye of the observer) directly in front of the plan view with a 45° maximum cone of vision. Occasionally a greater cone of vision angle is used to produce more dramatic results. The station point, however, should not be moved sideways because it will give a distorted perspective which does not represent the true proportions of the building.

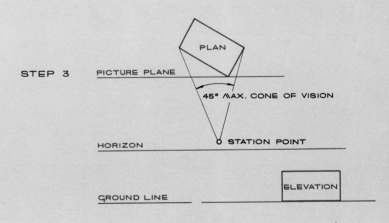

Step 4. Find both vanishing points. In two-point perspective, a vanishing point is the perspective of the far end of an infinitely long, horizontal line. The vanishing point for all horizontal lines extending 60° to the right (VPR) is found by drawing a parallel sight line 60° to the right until it intersects the picture plane. This is the plan view of the VPR. The perspective view of the VPR is found by projecting from the plan view down to the horizon. The VPL (vanishing point left) is located in a similar manner.

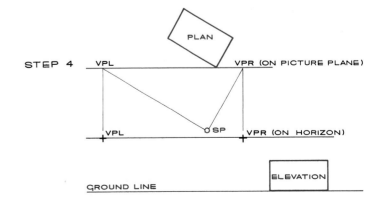

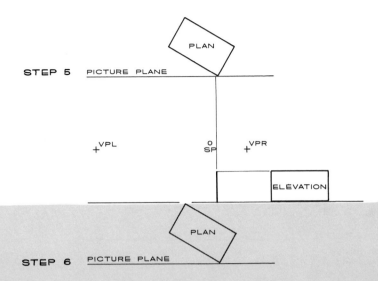

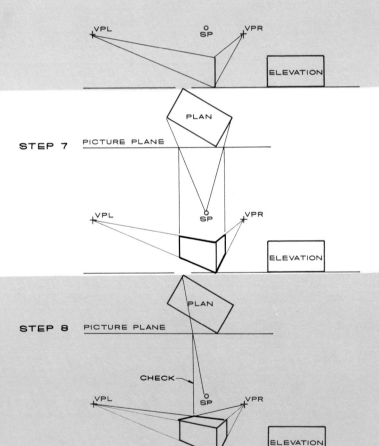

Step 5. Only lines located on the picture plane are shown true length in a perspective drawing. If a line is behind the picture plane, it will appear shorter; if it is in front, it will appear longer. Project the front corner which is located on the picture plane to the perspective view and lay off its true height by projecting from the elevation view.

Step 6. Find the perspective of horizontal lines by projecting from the vertical true length line to the vanishing points.

Step 7. Draw sight lines from the station point to the corners of the plan view. The intersections of these sight lines with the picture plane are projected to the perspective view to find the extreme corners.

Step 8. Complete the perspective by projecting from the extreme corners to the vanishing points. The far corner may be checked by projecting from the picture plane. Notice that invisible lines are omitted in a perspective drawing.

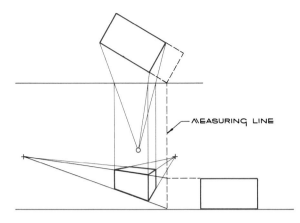

Figure 6   Use of the measuring line.

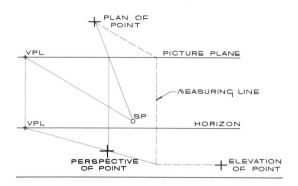

Figure 7   Perspective of a point.

Measuring line. In the preceding step-by-step illustration of the common method of drawing two-point perspective, the plan view was located so that the front corner touched the picture plane. This corner, then, was used to show the true height of the object in the perspective drawing. Occasionally *no* line in the plan view is located on the picture plane. When this occurs, as in Figure 6, a *measuring line* must be used. Simply imagine the plan view to be extended until a corner touches the picture plane. This corner is then projected to the perspective drawing for the true height measurement.

Perspective of a point. Figure 7 illustrates the method of finding the perspective of any point. This is a very useful exercise, because the perspective of the most complicated object can be constructed merely by finding the perspectives of a sufficient number of points on the object. The perspective of an oblique line, for example, is constructed by finding the perspective of both ends of the line. The perspective of a curved line can be constructed by finding the perspective of a number of points along the line.

Enlarging a perspective drawing. Often a perspective layout requires so much additional drawing space for the plan, elevation, and vanishing points, that the resulting perspective drawing is smaller than desired. A number of "tricks" may be used to correct this.

   1. Overlap the plan, elevation, and perspective drawings. Also, only an elevation *line* is needed—not an entire elevation view (Figure 8).
   2. Place the plan view *in front* of the picture plane to obtain larger perspectives (Figure 9).
   3. Allow the vanishing points to fall beyond the limits of the paper (Figure 10). The vanishing points may fall off the drawing table entirely. In this case, a curved cardboard strip is prepared so that the T-square will project non-parallel lines.

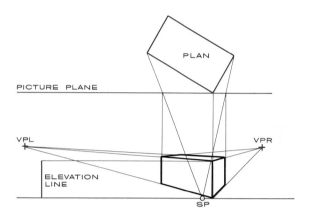

Figure 8   Overlapping views.

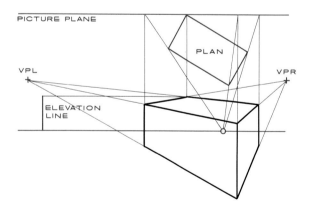

Figure 9   Plan in front of picture plane.

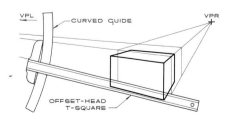

Figure 10   Use of curved guide.

4. A perspective can be enlarged by the use of radiating lines. Each radiating line shown in Figure 11 has been doubled in size. There are many other enlarging devices (such as pantographs) which may be used.

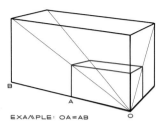

Figure 11   Use of radiating lines.

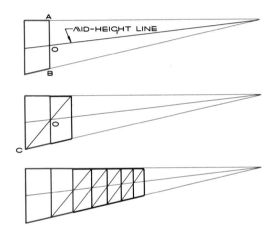

Figure 12   Spacing of lines.

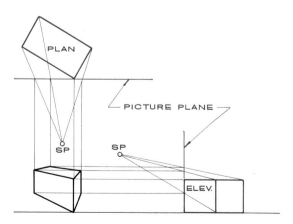

Figure 13   Direct projection method.

Spacing of lines. In perspective drawing, it is often desirable to show features which are evenly spaced without going through the trouble of projecting from the plan and elevation views. For example, a row of adjacent windows will appear smaller as they recede into the distance. If the first window is drawn in perspective, adjacent windows may be found as follows (Figure 12):

1. Draw a mid-height ($OA = OB$) line to the vanishing point.
2. Draw a diagonal (CO) and project it to locate the adjacent window.
3. Repeat as often as required to accurately locate each window.

DIRECT PROJECTION

The direct projection method of perspective drawing is similar to the common method with the exception of the addition of the end elevation view of the object, station point, and picture plane (Figure 13). Perspective widths are obtained, as previously, by projecting from the plan view, and perspective heights are obtained by projecting from the end elevation view. This system has the advantage of not requiring a measuring line. In fact, even the vanishing points may be omitted if desired. In this case, however, very accurate projection is required.

PERSPECTIVE GRIDS

Perhaps the simplest method of constructing a perspective drawing is by the use of prepared grid sheets obtainable in a number of sizes (Figure 14). The perspective may be drawn directly on these grids or on tracing overlays.

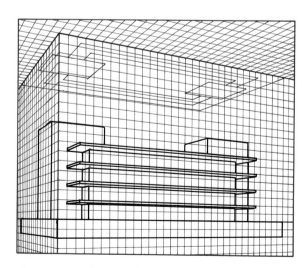

Figure 14   Perspective grid method.

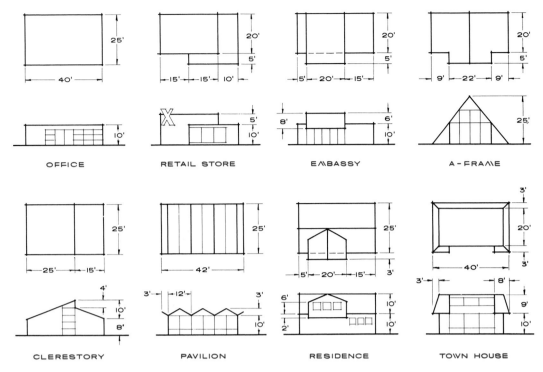

Figure 15

STUDY QUESTIONS

1. What is the principal difference between one, two, and three-point perspective? When is each used?
2. Sketch a two-point perspective layout of a simple object and label the picture plane, horizon, station point, right and left vanishing points, plan view, elevation view, and perspective view.
   a. Use the common method
   b. Use the direct method
3. Sketch a two-point perspective layout illustrating the correct method to obtain the perspective of a horizontal line making an angle of 30° with the picture plane.
   a. Use the common method
   b. Use the direct method
4. Sketch a two-point perspective layout illustrating the correct method to obtain the perspective of a point.
   a. Use the common method
   b. Use the direct method
5. Give the four methods used to enlarge a perspective drawing.

LABORATORY PROBLEMS

1. Prepare two-point perspectives of the buildings shown in Figure 15. Use the method assigned by your instructor.
2. Prepare a two-point perspective of the A residence.
3. Prepare a two-point perspective of the building assigned by your instructor.
4. Prepare a two-point perspective of your original house design.

32 shadows

A knowledge of shadows is important to both the architectural designer and the architectural draftsman. The designer will consider the effect of shadows upon his proposals. The draftsman will show these shadows on the presentation drawings to give them an extra three-dimensional quality.

Historically, shadows have greatly influenced architectural design. For example, Greek architecture evolved in a latitude where the bright sunlight exquisitely modeled the bas relief carvings and fluted columns. Gothic cathedrals would lose their mystic beauty in the same climate. Today, much emphasis is given to the sun shielding and the patterns created by overhangs. In some instances, the shadows may be a major element in the final solution.

TERMINOLOGY

In a study of shadows, these terms should be understood (Figure 1):

Shade: A surface turned away from light
Umbra: The space from which light is excluded by the shaded surface
Shadow: A surface from which light is excluded by the shaded surface

Of the three, only the umbra is never shown on a drawing. Shaded surfaces are usually shown as a light gray, and shadows are shown as a darker gray or black. It is very easy to determine the surfaces in shade, since they are merely the surfaces turned away from the direct rays of light. Shadows, though, are harder to find.

MULTIVIEW SHADOWS

Presentation drawings may include elevation views and a plot plan rendered to give a pictorial quality. Shadows are always included as shown in Figure 2 to increase the three-dimensional appearance.

In architectural renderings, it is conventional to employ a distant source of light (the sun) as the basis for establishing the shade and shadow lines. The sun's rays are parallel and are usually assumed to have the direction of the diagonal of a cube

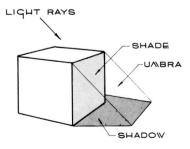

Figure 1   Terminology.

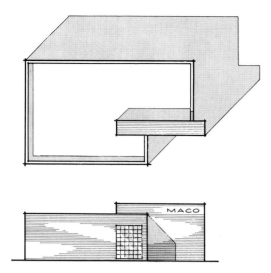

Figure 2   Multiview shadows.

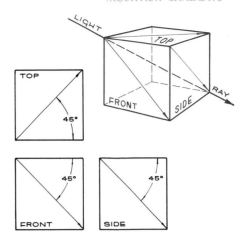

Figure 3   Conventional light direction in multi-view drawing.

extending from the upper left front to the lower right rear as shown in Figure 3. This is a convenient direction, since the orthographic views of this diagonal are 45° lines.

To find shadows in multiview projection, two rules are used:

Rule I: The shadow of a point upon a plane may be easily found in the view showing the plane as an edge.

Rule II: The shadow of a line may be found by first finding the shadows of both ends of the line and then connecting these points.

EXAMPLE

Find the shadow cast upon the ground by a flat roofed structure (see Figure 4).

Step 1: The points *A, B,* and *C* will cast shadows upon the ground. Therefore draw lines through both views of these points parallel to the light direction (45°).

Step 2: Find where these 45° lines intersect the ground plane. This is found in the front view, since the ground plane appears as an edge in the front view (*Rule I*).
Project from the front view to the top view.

Step 3: Connect the shadows of points *A, B,* and *C* (*Rule II*).

A_sB_s represents the shadow of line *AB.*
B_sC_s represents the shadow of line *BC.*

Notice that the shadow of a line upon a parallel plane will appear as a parallel line.

AA_s and CC_s represent the shadows
of vertical lines (*Rule II*).

Figures 5–16 show the multiview shadows cast by a variety of architectural shapes. Study each to find how the shadows were determined.

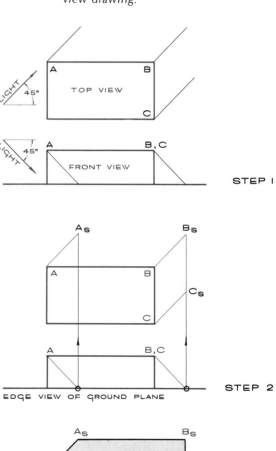

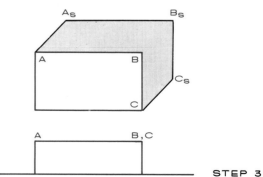

Figure 4   Finding a shadow in a multiview projection (new steps in black).

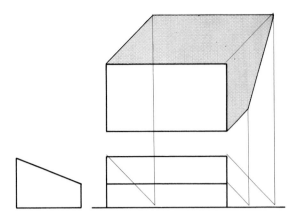

Figure 5   Shed roof.

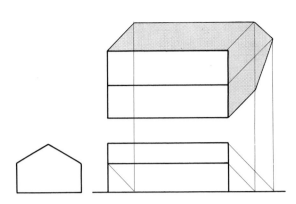

Figure 6   Gable roof.

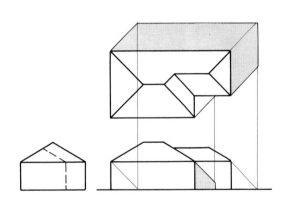

Figure 7   Hip roof.

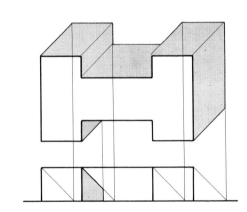

Figure 8   Irregular plan.

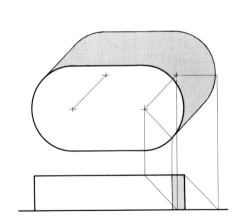

Figure 9   Rounded plan.

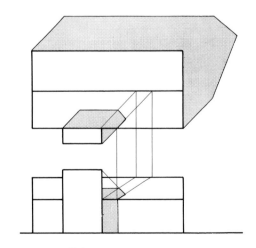

Figure 10   Chimney.

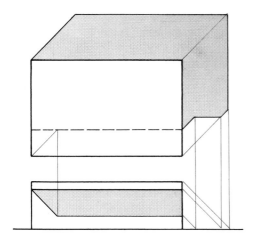

Figure 11   Flat roof overhang.

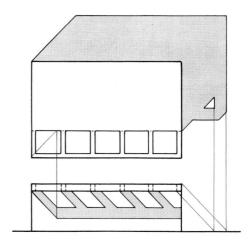

Figure 12   Open overhang.

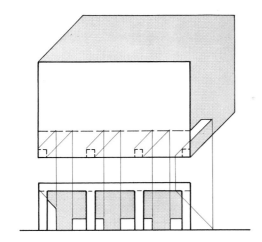

Figure 13   Colonnade.

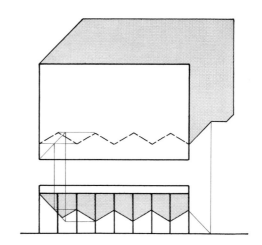

Figure 14   Accordion wall.

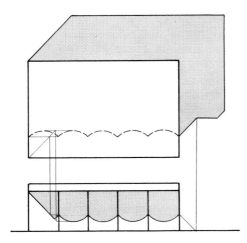

Figure 15   Fluted wall.

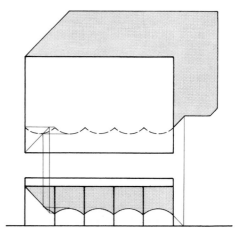

Figure 16   Beaded wall.

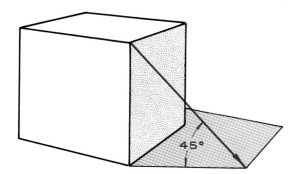

Figure 17   *Conventional light direction in perspective.*

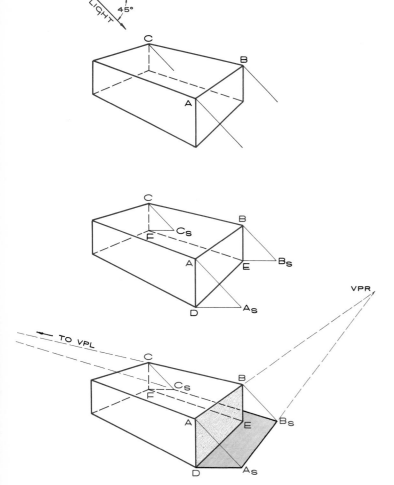

Figure 18   *Shadow in perspective (new steps in black).*

SHADOWS IN PERSPECTIVE— PARALLEL LIGHT RAYS

There are two methods of constructing the shadow of a building in a perspective drawing.

1. The shadow may be first obtained in the multiview drawings and then projected to the perspective view in the same manner as any other line. This method is easy to understand but requires more work.

2. The shadow may be constructed directly in the perspective view. This method requires a bit of explanation but is often used, since it is shorter and more direct. To further simplify this method, the direction of light rays is assumed to be parallel to the picture plane and to make an angle of 45° (or some other convenient angle) with the ground, as shown in Figure 17.

To find shadows in a perspective view, two rules are again used:

Rule I: The shadow of a vertical line upon the ground (or any horizontal plane) is a horizontal line.

Rule II: The shadow of a horizontal line upon the ground (or any horizontal plane) is parallel to the line.

EXAMPLE

Find the shadow cast upon the ground by a flat roofed structure (Figure 18).

Step 1: The points *A, B,* and *C* will cast shadows upon the ground. Therefore draw 45° lines through these points parallel to the assumed light direction.

Step 2: Find where the 45° lines intersect the ground plane by drawing horizontal lines from points *D, E,* and *F* (*Rule I*).

DA_s represents the shadow of line *DA*.
EB_s represents the shadow of line *EB*.
FC_s represents the shadow of line *FC*.

Step 3: Connect the shadows of points *A, B,* and *C*.

A_sB_s represents the shadow of line *AB*
and appears parallel to line *AB* (*Rule II*).
B_sC_s represents the shadow of line *BC*
and appears parallel to line *BC* (*Rule II*).

Notice that these lines will not be drawn exactly parallel to each other, but will be connected to their vanishing points.

Figures 19–26 show the perspective shadows cast by a variety of architectural shapes. As before, study each to learn how the shadows were determined.

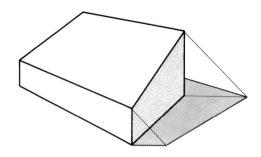

Figure 19   Shed roof.

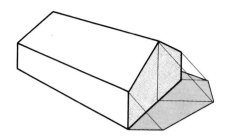

Figure 20   Gable roof.

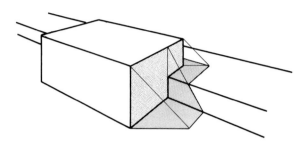

Figure 21   Offset surface.

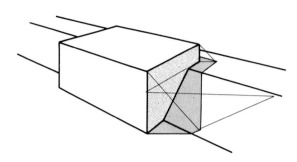

Figure 22   Sloping surface.

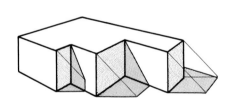

Figure 23   Irregular plan.

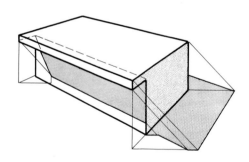

Figure 24   Flat roof overhang.

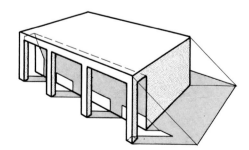

Figure 25   Colonnade.

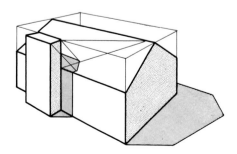

Figure 26   Chimney.

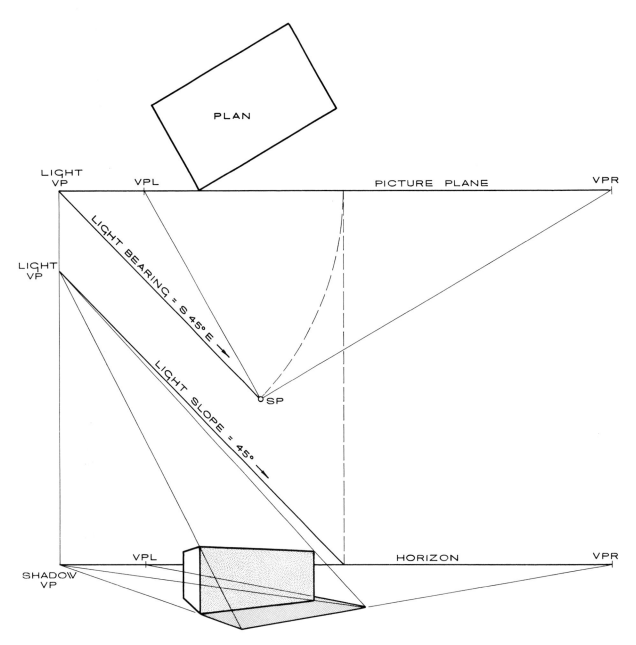

Figure 27   Shadow in perspective—oblique light rays.

SHADOWS IN PERSPECTIVE— OBLIQUE LIGHT RAYS

In perspective drawing, a shadow found by light rays parallel to the picture plane is not always entirely satisfactory. Although it is a difficult process, the shadow may be found by using light rays oblique to the picture plane. The main difference is that the light rays must be drawn from their vanishing point rather than 45° with the ground. Figure 27 illustrates how the vanishing point of the light rays is found.

In actual practice, shadows are seldom deter-mined by accurate construction, since this is a time-consuming process. Rather, the architectural drafts-man draws upon his knowledge of the general form of shadows to estimate the position and shape of the shadows. After a little experience, a fairly accu-rate estimation is possible.

SHADOW INTENSITY

In addition to determining the location of a shadow, the architectural draftsman must also make decisions concerning the intensity of the shadow, which may vary from black to a very light tone. This variation is due principally to the amount of light reflected upon the surface. This reflected light causes shadows to assume varying tones rather than one uniform tone. This variation may be useful for several purposes: to sharpen the shadow outline, to show changes in the direction of adjacent surfaces, to express changes in the depth of receding surfaces, and to show changes in surface texture. In general, the draftsman must use a great deal of imagination and "artistic license" to obtain the desired result.

STUDY QUESTIONS

1. Define each of the following:
   a. Shade
   b. Umbra
2. What is meant by "conventional light direction"? Why is it used?
3. Give two methods that may be used to find the shadow of a building in a perspective drawing.
4. Give four reasons to vary shadow intensity.

LABORATORY PROBLEMS

1. Add shadows to the two-point perspectives you drew for Problem 1 of the last chapter. Use the method assigned by your instructor.
2. Add shadows to: (a) the presentation drawing, and (b) the perspective of the A residence.
3. Add shadows to: (a) the presentation drawing, and (b) the perspective of the building assigned by your instructor.
4. Add shadows to: (a) the presentation drawing, and (b) the perspective of your original house design.

33 architectural rendering

The ability to prepare a finished rendering is a desirable goal for every architectural draftsman. Even a large architectural firm with a separate art department occasionally needs help to meet a deadline. Smaller offices must depend upon the regular staff for renderings or send the work out to companies specializing in presentation drawings. These companies produce excellent results but, of course, time and coordination must be considered.

Since a rendering shows a structure as it actually appears to the eye, it is used for presentation drawings that will be seen by laymen who, in all likelihood, cannot read ordinary blueprints. As a matter of fact, the quality of the rendering may well influence the final decision of the client to continue with the proposed building. Most clients feel (and rightly so) that the finished product will look and function no better than the drawings. In addition to finished renderings, the architectural draftsman should be able to make quick sketches of alternate solutions to a problem to show to the architect who makes the final decision.

TYPES OF RENDERING

There are many kinds of renderings. Among the most common are:

Pencil	Water color
Pen and ink	Tempera
Scratch board	Spray
Appliqué	Combination of the above

In this chapter, we will study each of these techniques—putting the emphasis upon those which will be most useful to you. *Pencil rendering* is most often used, since it requires no special equipment and is very versatile. Drawings from small, quick sketches all the way up to large, finished presentation displays can be rendered in pencil. *Ink,* however, is preferred for drawings to be reproduced in media such as newspapers, books, and brochures. *Appliqués* offer a quick and effective method of applying a professional-looking shading. *Scratch board* is occasionally used, as is *water color. Tempera* applied by *brush* or *spray* is the normal medium used by the professional artist for a colored rendering.

PENCIL RENDERING

Pencil rendering is the most popular form of rendering because it is quick, errors are easily corrected, no special equipment is needed, and it is very versatile. Pencil renderings range from rough freehand sketches to accurate drawings using a straightedge for outlines and shading.

Pencils. The softer lead grades are used in pencil rendering. Although the final choice will depend upon the paper texture and personal preference, the following selection is ordinarily satisfactory:

2H for layout
F for medium tone rendering
2B for dark tones

A sharp conical point is used for the layout work and detailing, but a flat chisel point is used to obtain the broad rendering strokes.

Paper. The paper selected should take pencil lines and erasures nicely. Bristol board, Strathmore paper, and tracing vellum meet these requirements. Fine or coarse textured paper may be used depending upon the result desired. During rendering, keep the paper clean by working with a paper shield under your hand. A fixative spray is used to protect the finished rendering from smudges.

Textures. The success of a pencil rendering depends, to a large extent, upon the ability of the draftsman to indicate the proper texture of surfaces and materials. Some of the most common materials encountered are:

Glass and mirrored surfaces (Figure 1). Small areas are quite simply rendered by blackening with a 2B pencil. Larger window areas may be toned from a dark corner to an opposite light corner. Very large expanses of glass, however, require more thought. Normally, some of the surroundings are shown reflected in the glass. Highlights are made with an eraser and erasing shield. If desired, the glass rendering may be omitted in order to show interior features.

Brick. Brick surfaces are indicated by closely spaced lines made with a flat pointed F pencil. The length of the lines does not matter, since the horizontal brick joints are more important to show than the vertical joints (see Figure 2).

Stone. Stone surfaces are rendered by drawing a few individual stones leaving large expanses of "white" space. In Figure 3, notice that the shadow line is darkest near its extremity.

Roof. Shingled roofs are shown by long, closely spaced lines—somewhat like brick. The lines may fade into light areas as in Figure 4. Built-up roofs, concrete, and plaster are stippled.

Procedure. The usual procedure for rendering in pencil follows. We will use the A residence for illustration (see Figure 6).

Figure 1   Glass renderings.

Step 1. A rough pencil sketch is made to determine the most suitable perspective angle, light direction, and shadow locations. In general, there should be a balance between white, black, and gray areas.

Step 2. Transfer the mechanically drawn perspective to the finished paper. Outline with a sharp

Figure 2   Brick rendering.

Figure 3   Stone rendering.

Figure 4   Shingled roof rendering.

Figure 5   Pencil grades indicate depth and texture.

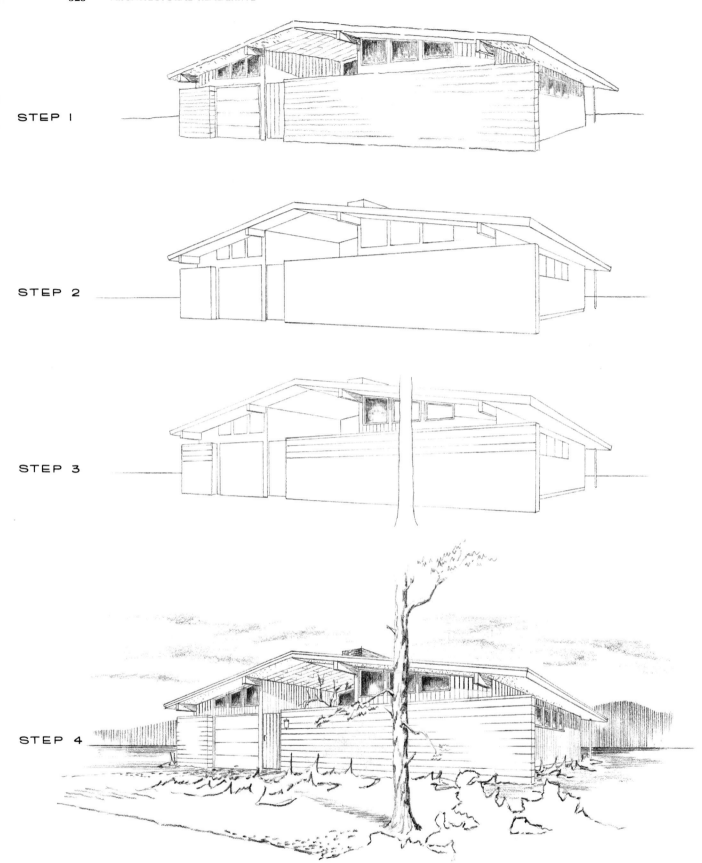

STEP 1

STEP 2

STEP 3

STEP 4

Figure 6   The procedure for pencil rendering.

2H line. Portions of these outlines may be erased later to provide highlights (bright areas).

Step 3. Render the central structure using an F or 2B pencil, depending upon the desired blackness. Windows are done first, followed by walls and roofs.

Step 4. Render the foreground details followed by the background elements. Use an eraser to provide highlights.

Color. Pencil renderings may be colored with light water color washes. Select the colors carefully to prevent disappointing results. Colored pencils are often used on colored mat boards. Monochromatic schemes (various tones and shades of one color) are particularly effective. White pencil or ink is used for highlighting.

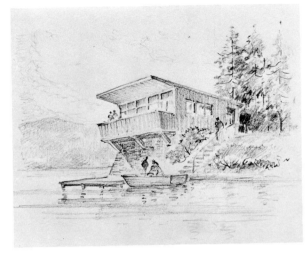

Figure 7   Pencil sketch of a summer camp. A successful sketch must blend perspective, shadows, and rendering.

Figure 8   Showing texture and shading in pencil rendering.

Courtesy of Scholz Homes, Inc.

Figure 9   Professional pencil renderings. Study these examples and start a collection of additional samples of pencil renderings.

INK RENDERING

Black ink rendering is the most suitable medium for drawings to be reproduced by any of the printing processes. Colored drawing inks are occasionally used for display drawings. Ink rendering differs from pencil rendering in that the shades of gray are more difficult to obtain. A wash of ink diluted with water may be used, but usually shading is done by varying the width of stroke or spacing between strokes as shown in Figures 11 and 12. The stippling technique, Figure 13, is also often used. Notice that the completely black shading in Figure 14 requires that the mortar joints be changed from black to white.

Paper. The paper used for ink rendering must take ink without fuzzing, allow ink erasures, and be smooth surfaced. Some satisfactory materials are:

Mat boards (available in white and colors)
Bristol boards, plate surface
Strathmore paper, plate surface
Tracing paper (use only better quality)
Tracing cloth

Pens. The technical fountain pen or ordinary pen nibs and holder may be used. A ruling pen (drafting pen), of course, is not used to draw freehand lines. Technical fountain pen points are sized:

00 fine
 0 medium fine
 1 medium
 2 medium heavy
 3 heavy

The most popular pen nibs are:

Crow quill: Hunt 102 or Gillott 659   very fine
Hawk-quill: Hunt 107 or Gillott 837   fine
Round-pointed: Hunt 99 or Gillott 170   medium
Bowl-pointed: Hunt 512 or Speedball B-6   heavy

Figure 10   Window rendering.

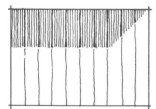

Figure 11   Vertical siding.

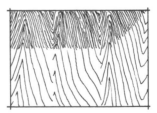

Figure 12   Plywood.

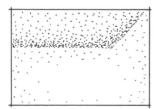

Figure 13   Concrete.

Figure 14   Stone.

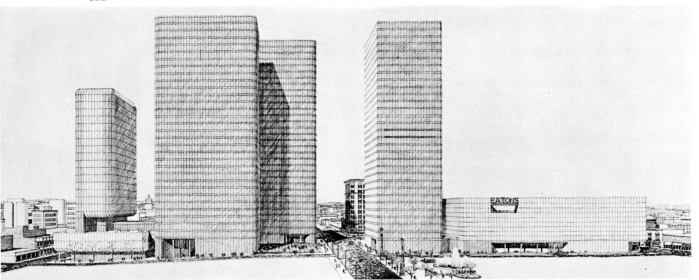

Figure 15   An ink and pencil rendering of Canada's Pacific Centre, Vancouver, B.C.

Figure 16   Ink rendering.

Figure 17   Realistic rendering obtained by rapid ink strokes.

Inks. Satisfactory drawing inks are produced by Higgins, Weber, and Pelikan. The following colored inks are available. Other shades are obtained by mixing.

Yellow	Violet	Brick red
Orange	Blue	Russet
Red orange	Turquoise	Brown
Red	Green	Indigo
Carmine red	Leaf green	White
Red violet	Neutral tint	Black

Ink erasing is done with a pencil eraser to prevent damage to the paper's surface. A sharp razor blade is used to pick off small ink portions.

Procedure. The usual procedure for an ink rendering is:

1. Make a charcoal study or rough ink sketch to determine the most suitable light direction and shadow locations. Try to obtain a balance between white, black, and gray areas.
2. Outline lightly in pencil on finished paper.
3. Ink in outlines with fine lines (unless the surfaces are to be defined by shading differences only).
4. Render each feature separately—first windows, then walls, and so on, working from foreground to background.

The student wishing to learn the technique of ink rendering would be well advised to copy a good rendering before attempting an original. Also, he should start a collection of ink renderings by various artists so that he can study the numerous methods of handling the details. In Figure 16 notice how the entourage is subordinated to direct your attention to the pavilion structure. Also notice that every shingle and blade of grass need not be drawn. Figure 18 shows ink renderings drawn with a coarser pen in a freer style.

Figure 18   Ink rendering.

Figure 19   Scratch board rendering.

FLASHING

FASCIA

JOIST

HEADER

WIRE LATH

PLATE

PLASTER   TRIM

MASONITE
SHADOWVENT

METAL
CHANNEL

ROYALCOTE
WALNUT

BUILDING PAPER

SHEATHING

INSULATION

MASONITE
SHADOWVENT

2"x 4"
STUDS

PLATE

MASONITE PRESDWOOD
1/4" STARTER STRI

ANCHOR BOLT

2"x 4" PLATE (NAILER FOR RIDGELINE

2" x 6"

5/16" MASONITE
RIDGELINE

BATTENS NAILED INTO 2"x 4"
POSTS SPACED 24" O.C.

SCRATCH BOARD

A simple method to create a rendering of white lines on a black background is provided by *scratch board*, which is a board having a white chalky surface. The surface is coated with black ink, and a rendering is obtained by drawing with a sharp pointed stylus. The stylus will scratch through the black coating leaving a white line. A knife-edged tool is used to whiten larger areas. If desired, large portions of the scratch board may be left white (not coated with black ink). In these areas, ink rendering is done in the usual manner.

      The pictorial detail at the bottom of Figure 19 was done on scratch board.

APPLIQUÉ

An appliqué (pressure-sensitive transfer) is a thin transparent plastic sheet with a printed pattern of black dots or lines. The sheet is coated on one side with a special adhesive to make it stick to the draw-

ing. A wide variety of patterns is available; some are illustrated in Figure 21. Various shades of gray can be obtained by choosing the proper transfer or by applying several transfer sheets over each other for darker shades. In addition to patterns, a number of architectural symbols for trees, shrubbery, people, automobiles, and furniture may be obtained. See Figure 22.

Procedure. The order of procedure is:

1. Outline in ink.
2. Select the desired transfer, remove its protective backing, and place it over the area to be rendered, adhesive side down. Rub gently with your fingernail to increase adherence.
3. Lightly score around the outline with a razor blade without cutting the paper underneath.
4. Peel off the excess material and rub again with your fingernail to insure permanent adherence.

      Figure 23 shows a very simple—yet effective—presentation. One sheet of appliqué is the sole rendering medium.

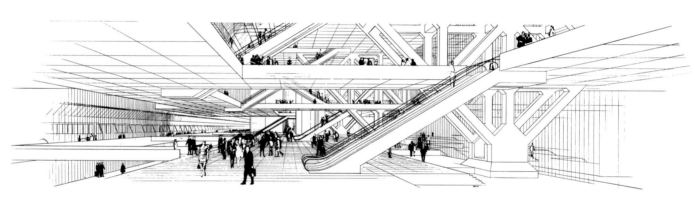

Figure 20   *Ink rendering of proposed interior, United Nations Organizations Headquarters.*

Figure 21   *Typical appliqué patterns.*

Figure 22   *Typical appliqué symbols.*

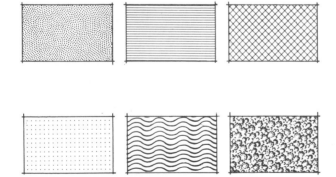

Figure 23   *Ink and appliqué rendering.*

Figure 24   *A monotone rendering.*

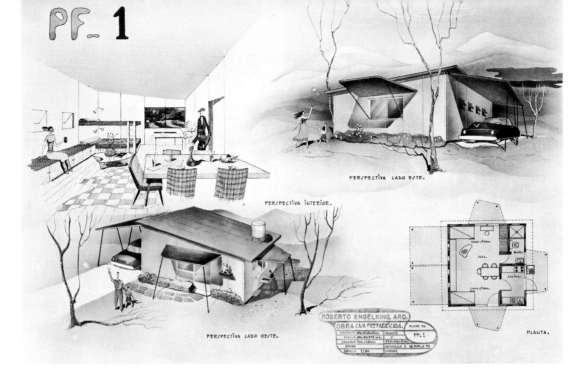

Figure 25   Combined ink, airbrush, and tempera.

Figure 26   Texture obtained by pebbled surface mat board. Notice the reflection of the building on the street.

WATER COLOR AND TEMPERA RENDERING

Water color refers to a transparent water based paint; *tempera* refers to an opaque water based paint. Both are used (separately or together) to render large presentation drawings: water color giving a refined, artistic effect, tempera giving a more vivid and striking effect.

Water color may be applied with a brush using a very thin mixture of paint and water called a *wash,* or it may be applied directly from a *palette* used for mixing the colors. The professional obtains his water colors in tubes and half-tubes rather than in dried cake form.

Tempera (known also as *poster paint, opaque water color,* and *showcard color*) is usually applied directly from the palette. Tempera is obtainable in jars and tubes. In addition to color illustration, tempera is very effective when used as a monotone medium. Black, white, and several tones of gray are often used. Figure 24 shows an example of such a rendering.

SPRAY RENDERING

The smooth gradation of tones seen in professional renderings is usually obtained by spraying with an airbrush. This technique is excellent for the indication of smooth, glassy surfaces and background sky.

An airbrush is simply a nozzle which sprays a fine mixture of paint and air. The compressed air is obtained from a compressor or tank of carbonic gas. Since this equipment is expensive and not available to the average student, other methods are often used. Hand spray guns, pressurized spray cans, and even spattered paint (tooth brush rubbed on screening) have been used successfully. Tempera paint is used due to its fast drying quality.

Procedure. The procedure for a typical spray rendering is:

1. Block in the desired illustration using a sharp pencil line. The paper must be clean and smudge-free. A spray rendering is transparent and all smudges will show.
2. Select the area to be sprayed. Usually the structure is completed first, then sky, and finally the entourage. Mask out all other areas so that they will not be painted also. Transparent *frisket* paper is used which is applied like an appliqué.
3. Make a few test sprays upon scratch paper to determine the proper distance and motion of the spraying device. A light spray is preferred, since a too-dark spray cannot be corrected. Carefully lift the frisket paper occasionally to compare relative shades and tones.
4. When the paint is dry, remove the frisket and move on to the next area.
5. Accent details with tempera using a fine brush.

STUDY QUESTIONS

1. Give the principal uses of the following types of renderings:
   a. Pencil
   b. Pen and ink
   c. Scratch board
   d. Appliqué
   e. Water color
   f. Tempera
   g. Spray
2. In pencil rendering, how are each of the following materials treated?
   a. Windows
   b. Brick walls
   c. Stone walls
   d. Concrete walls
   e. Shingled roofs
3. In ink rendering, what is meant by the following terms?
   a. Wash
   b. Stipple
   c. Crow-quill
4. How does water color differ from tempera?
5. Give four methods of producing a spray rendering.

LABORATORY PROBLEMS

1. Start a collection of renderings by various artists in the medium of your choice.

Figure 27   A professional rendering of Canada's Pacific Centre using several media. Note reflections of existing buildings in window walls.

2. Obtain a good example of a rendering in the medium of your choice and make an accurate copy.
3. Prepare a "style sheet" showing how various materials and textures may be rendered. Use the medium of your choice.
4. Render: (a) the presentation drawing, and (b) the perspective, of the A residence in the medium of your choice.
5. Render: (a) the presentation drawing, and (b) the perspective of the building assigned by your instructor. Use the medium of your choice.
6. Render: (a) the presentation drawing, and (b) the perspective of your original building design using the medium of your choice.

34 entourage

In architectural design, a structure is planned in relation to its environment. The character of the land, trees, and surrounding buildings are all considered. The quantity and location of traffic—both vehicle and pedestrian—affect the design. To present the design in its proper context, then, an architectural rendering also includes an indication of the character and quantity of these surrounding elements. If this is done well, the client will be able to identify the surroundings and visualize the proposed building in them. If it is done poorly, the client may reject the entire plan. Subconsciously, he will feel that a poorly executed drawing means a poorly designed building. In architectural drawing, the word used to describe the surroundings is "entourage."* It is used to describe objects—trees, shrubbery, background mountains, human figures, and vehicles—which are included to increase the realistic appearance or decorative effect of the drawing. In addition to their use on perspective renderings, entourage may be used on presentation plans and elevations to increase their pictorial quality.

Contrary to what you might expect, entourage is drawn in a simplified, stylized manner rather than in a detailed, photographic style. There are three good reasons for this:

*Pronounced "n-tur-ahge." This is a French word with the accent on the last syllable which is pronounced like the last three letters in the word "garage."

1. Only a trained artist can draw objects like trees, vehicles, and people to look exactly as they are.
2. There is a constant shortage of time in an architectural drafting room, so short cut techniques must be used whenever possible.
3. Entourage drawn in great detail would detract from the central structure.

The stylized forms of trees, human figures, and vehicles shown in this chapter may be traced directly or increased in size to .fit a particular requirement. The student is advised, however, to develop his own individual style by improving upon these drawings. In addition to entourage in perspective, the plan and elevation symbols are included, since a presentation drawing often contains the plan and elevations.

Nearly all of the plan view trees in Figure 1 are based upon a lightly drawn circle. Remember to change the size of the circles for variety, but do not mix many different symbols on the same drawing.

Choose trees that will fit the location. Palm trees, for example, would be appropriate in Southern states; cacti in Western states (Figure 3). The foreground in Figure 2 may be drawn across the bottom of a rendering indicating shrubbery near the observer.

Choose a style of background mountains or trees from those shown in Figure 3 which is compatible with your tree style.

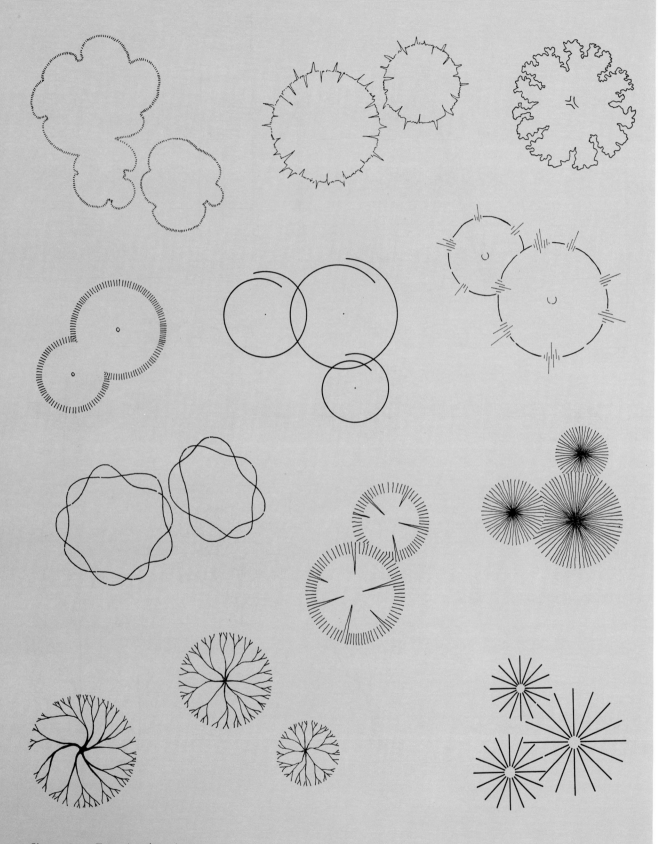

Figure 1   *Trees in plan view.*

SOFTWOOD TREES

FOREGROUND SHRUBBERY

Figure 2   Trees in elevation.

HARDWOOD TREES

BACKGROUND

EXOTIC

Figure 3   Planting.

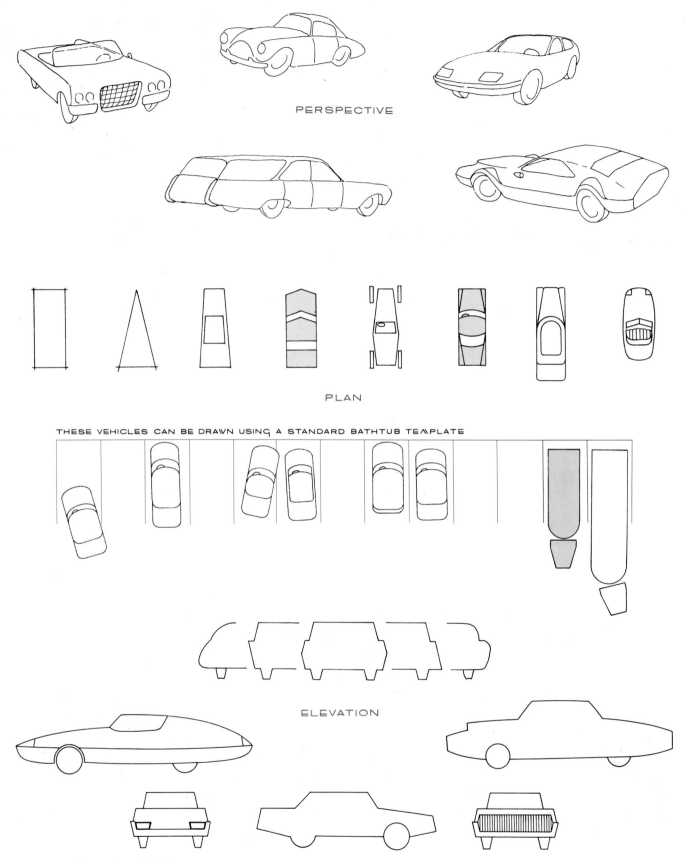

PERSPECTIVE

PLAN

THESE VEHICLES CAN BE DRAWN USING A STANDARD BATHTUB TEMPLATE

ELEVATION

Figure 4 Vehicles.

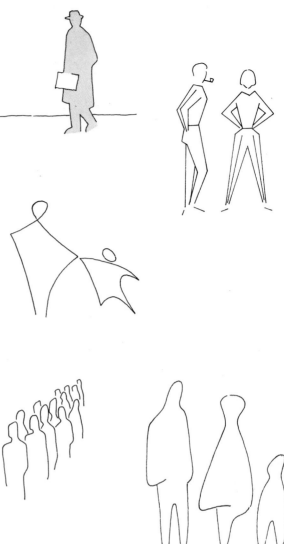

Figure 5   Human figures.

The perspective automobiles (Figure 4) are easily traced from advertisements found in magazines. The plan view autos are drawn by adapting standard templates.

Human figures are most difficult to draw realistically, and therefore the outline forms shown in Figure 5 are used.

STUDY QUESTIONS

1. What is the meaning of the word "entourage"?
2. Why is it important to include entourage on a presentation drawing?
3. Give three reasons why entourage is drawn in a simplified rather than detailed manner.

LABORATORY PROBLEMS

1. Prepare a "style sheet" of your individual treatment of the following elements:
   a. Evergreen trees in plan
   b. Evergreen trees in elevation
   c. Deciduous trees in plan
   d. Deciduous trees in elevation
   e. Foreground shrubbery
   f. Background scenery
   g. Human figures
   h. Vehicles
2. Include entourage on: (a) the presentation drawing, and (b) the perspective of the A residence.
3. Include entourage on: (a) the presentation drawing, and (b) the perspective of the building assigned by your instructor.
4. Include the entourage on: (a) the presentation drawing, and (b) the perspective of your original house design.

commercial design
and construction

35 commercial design and construction

There are important differences between the design, drafting, and construction of a residence and that of a commercial building:

1. Design. A single individual can design and draft the plans for a residence, but a number of specialists, including a registered architect and professional engineer, are needed to plan a commercial building. This involves all the consequent problems of coordination, cooperation, and human relations.

2. Drafting. More drawings are required for a commercial building due to its sheer size. But in addition, the plans must be more completely detailed to permit all interested builders to bid on a competitive basis.

3. Construction. A light wood frame construction, as described in Chapter 23, is adequate for a residence, but a commercial building is usually framed in steel or reinforced concrete and finished with masonry or prefabricated composition panels.

A small commercial structure, the South Hills Office Building recently designed and built in State College, Pennsylvania, will be used in this chapter to illustrate each of these aspects.

DESIGN

Three businessmen—the owners of a law office, a real estate firm, and an advertising agency—joined together to solve a common problem; that of finding suitable space for their offices. They formed a partnership, purchased a half-acre site, and asked a local architect to design a building to satisfy their needs. As is customary with most architects, his design procedure consisted of four major stages:

1. The program
2. Presentation drawings of several schemes
3. Preliminary drawing of the chosen scheme
4. Working drawings

At one of the early meetings, a *program* was prepared which indicated the owners' requirement of 4,000 sq. ft. of office space plus an additional 12,000 sq. ft. of rentable space for other companies. An attractive, contemporary exterior appearance was considered to be an important requirement. A preliminary study of the zoning and building code requirements showed that building height would be limited to 55' (not including mechanical features occupying less than one-tenth of the roof area). It was also determined that one off-street parking stall would have to be provided for each office for a total of 24 stalls.

The architect proceeded to develop *sketch plans* and *presentation drawings* of three alternate solutions: a two-, three-, and five-story building. The solution preferred by the owners was a five-story basementless building with the first (plaza) level open to provide adequate parking. This solution included glass window walls and a central elevator shaft.

Preliminary drawings consisting of 4′ modular plans and elevations were then prepared for this chosen solution. The framing was visualized as consisting of steel beams supported by ten steel columns. Each pair of columns would form a bent spanning 40′, and adjacent bents would be 24′ oc. Welded connections would be used where necessary to obtain a rigid frame. To provide uninterrupted glass window walls, the outer wall was cantilevered 4′ beyond the columns resulting in a rectangular floor plan of 48′ × 104′. Stair wells were placed at both ends of the floor plan and were connected by a longitudinal corridor. The elevator shaft, rest rooms, and maintenance room were placed in a central location. The remaining area was then available as clear floor space for maximum flexibility. A hydraulic piston elevator was chosen in preference to a hoist elevator to eliminate the unsightly elevator penthouse needed for the hoisting machinery. The piston elevator, however, does require that a piston shaft be drilled into the ground equal to the distance of the total lift. Piston elevators generally are not specified for lifts exceeding 60′ in height. Heating and cooling were provided by electric air conditioning space units installed in wall panels.

The preliminary drawings were approved by the owners with only one major change: the glass window walls were rejected due to the additional air conditioning capacity required. The architect replaced the window walls with vertically-aligned windows and air conditioning units set in exterior brick walls. Vertical lines were emphasized by mullions framing each stack of windows.

DRAFTING

Working drawings of the final solution were prepared as shown on Drawings No. 1 to S5. These drawings are nearly identical* to the set of working drawings used to construct the South Hills Office Building except they were redrawn in ink to assure good reproduction in this book. Study these plans until you are confident that you understand how they are used to describe this project. The following remarks may help.

Drawing No. 1. Index. This is the cover sheet for the entire set of working drawings. In addition to the index of drawings, it includes a legend of all abbreviations and symbols used on the drawings. Some architectural offices also include a sketch of the building on the cover sheet.

Drawing No. 2. Plot Plan. This plot plan positions the building on the site, shows the existing and proposed land contour, landscaping, parking, walks,

gas lines, water lines, and sanitary waste lines. The note "Swale to CB" indicates a downward slope to a catch basin. "BC 100.5" fixes the bottom of the curb (road level) at an elevation of 100.5′, and "TC 101.5" fixes the top of the curb (ground level) at an elevation of 101.5′.

Notice that two indications for north are given at the lower right corner. The large arrow enclosed in a circle is the direction of north, while "building north" shows the side of the building which is named the "north elevation." This is particularly important when a building is positioned so that two sides might both be considered north elevations.

Drawing No. 3. Foundation Plan. A 4′ modular grid system is used with coordinate identification letters and numbers. This identification system helps to locate details on the plans, in the written specifications, and in the field. Notice that this system was adapted to use arrow heads to indicate both on-grid and off-grid dimensions. The callouts "0" and "6" refer to masonry courses, each 8″ high. Thus the CMU (concrete masonry unit) wall marked "6" can be started 6 courses (48″) above the walls marked "0". Refer to Drawing No. 11 for a better understanding of these masonry course identification numbers.

A test boring was taken at each column location. Firm rock was only 6′ to 8′ deep at the three "A" locations, but was 16′ to 18′ deep at the seven "B" locations. Therefore two types of footings were designed. Notice on Drawing No. 4 that the contractor was given the option of using the reinforced footing "A" at all ten locations. He chose that alternative in preference to driving piles as required for footing "B." To support walls, either 8″ or 12″ thick CMU foundations were used depending upon the weight of the wall to be supported. This and all similar plans were originally drawn to a scale of $\frac{1}{4}'' = 1'-0$.

Drawing No. 4. Footing Details. Four details are included on this sheet to show the reinforced concrete construction of footing "A," steel pile footing "B," the column waterproofing, and the reinforced concrete footing for the CMU walls. "HP 10 × 42" refers to a 10″ × 10″ bearing pile weighing 42 pounds per foot of length. "5-#11 bars" means five reinforcing steel bars each $\frac{11}{8}''$ in diameter. See Drawing No. 1 for the meaning of all abbreviations. These and similar details were originally drawn to a scale of $\frac{1}{2}'' = 1'-0$.

Drawing No. 5. Plaza Floor Plan. Dashed lines are used to indicate overhead features such as the building line or overhead simulated beams. Each room, stairway, or corridor has an identification number (such as "P2"). Doors also have an identification number which is coded to the proper room

*Some details such as stair and elevation sections are omitted.

(such as "P2/1" and "P2/2"). See the legend on Drawing No. 1 for the meaning of all such identification numbers.

Drawing No. 6. First Floor Plan. Six air conditioning units are located on the south wall, but only four units are required for the north wall. This is because the south wall cooling requirements are greater than the north wall heating requirements.

Drawings No. 7–9. Elevations. Although 4′ horizontal modules are used on the plans, 8″ vertical modules are used on elevations to indicate courses of masonry 8″ apart (a CMU course of 8″ or three brick courses of 2-$\frac{2}{3}$″). For example, the balloon "39" means that the second floor is 39 courses or 26′ (39 × 8″ = 26′) above the top of the footing marked with a balloon "0." Control joints are formed by raking and caulking masonry joints. This directs any cracking along these joints rather than allowing it to occur at random. These elevations were originally drawn to a scale of $\frac{1}{4}$″ = 1′-0.

Drawing No. 10. Interior Elevations. Interior elevations of all specially-equipped rooms would be included in addition to these rest room elevations. The elevation identification "10/1" indicates Elevation No. 1 on Drawing No. 10.

Drawing No. 11. Longitudinal Section. This section is needed to explain the structural system and assure proper clearances and room heights. Only the more useful coordinate identification numbers are included. "AC CLG BD" is an abbreviation for acoustical ceiling boards.

Drawing No. 12. Typical Sections. Section 12/1 is a vertical section cut through a window (see Drawings No. 6 and 7). Section 12/2 is a vertical section through a simulated plaza roof beam (see Drawing No. 7). Section 12/3 is a horizontal section through a column (See Drawing No. 7). Multiple balloons such as "B" and "L" on Section 12/3 show that this section is typical of columns centered on both grid B and grid L.

Drawing No. 13. Typical Details. Plan Detail 13/1 is a horizontal section cut through the window mullions (see Drawing No. 6). The two alternate details show the installation of panels and louvers. The callout "362 DS 16 PUN @ 16″ oc" refers to 3$\frac{5}{8}$″ prefabricated metal studs as manufactured by the Keene Company: model no. 362, double stud, 16 gage, punched, 16″ on center.

Drawings No. 14 and 15. Schedules. Room finish information is contained in schedules such as shown on these two sheets. Complete schedules for all floors require many more pages. The written specifications contain even more detailed information.

Drawing No. E1. Electrical Plan. The dark rectangles represent the fluorescent ceiling fixtures and dark circles represent incandescent fixtures. The letter within each fixture symbol identifies the type of fixture (see Lighting Fixture Schedule on Drawing No. 14). The alphameric designation at the end of each home run identifies the floor level and circuit number (see Legend on Drawing No. 1). An emergency lighting circuit is indicated by the letter "E." See the legend for exit light information.

Drawing No. H1. Heating-Cooling Plan. The dark rectangles with diagonal lines represent the Remington electric heating-cooling units, and the dark hexagons indicate Electromode electric baseboard heaters. See Drawing No. 14 for more detailed information. The two hash marks on each home run indicate 208 volt circuits.

Drawings No. P1 and P2. Water Supply and Sanitary Plan. Drawing No. P1 shows the hot and cold water supply piping and the dry fire piping both in plan and pictorial projection. The plan also includes an air circulation system for the rest rooms. Drawing P2 shows the waste and soil disposal systems.

Drawing No. S1. First Floor Structural Plan. Each heavy line indicates the location of a steel member. "W 16 × 36 (-4)" refers to a 16″ wide flange beam weighing 36 pounds per foot with its upper flange 4″ below the concrete slab surface. This and all similar plans were originally drawn to a scale of $\frac{1}{8}$″ = 1′-0.

Drawing No. S2. Roof Structural Plan. "12 H5 EXT END (-2$\frac{1}{2}$)" refers to a 12″ deep H5 series open web joist with an extended end and located 2$\frac{1}{2}$″ below the roof surface. "DO" means ditto. The dashed lines show the location of cross bridging. The note "ship lone" means that elevator beam 6 B 16 should be shipped without any shop connections because this beam is to be installed by the elevator technicians rather than the structural fabricators.

Structural steel designations were revised by the American Institute of Steel Construction in 1970. Although the "new" designations are used on the plans of the South Hills Office Building and throughout this book, the "old" designations are shown on Drawing No. S2. It would be well to become familiar with these earlier designations since they will still be seen on plans for many years.

Type of Shape	"Old" Designation	"New" Designation
W shape (formerly "wide flange")	8 **WF** 31	W 8 × 31
W shape (formerly "light beam")	8 B 20	W 8 × 20
S shape (formerly "American Standard I beam")	8 I 18.4	S 8 × 18.4
American Standard channel	8 [11.5	C 8 × 11.5
Angle	∠ 4 × 4 × ¼	L 4 × 4 × ¼
HP shape (formerly "bearing pile")	8 BP 36	HP 8 × 36

Note: "8 **WF** 31" and "W 8 × 31" refers to a wide flange beam 8" high weighing 31 pounds per foot of length.

Drawing No. S3. Column Schedule. Refer to Drawing No. S1 for an explanation of the double designations S3/1 and S3/2. The column schedule shows a typical bent. Notice that the column sections are spliced between floors where the bending moment is smaller.

Drawing No. S4. Structural Details. The location of Sections S4/1 and S4/2 is indicated on Drawings No. S1 and S2. The welding symbols used on this sheet include a closed triangle for a fillet weld, an open triangle for a vee weld, a closed circle for a field weld, and an open circle for an all-around weld.

Drawing No. S5. Concrete Slab Plan. "#4 @ 9 TOP" refers to ⁴⁄₈" diameter steel reinforcing rods placed 9" apart and near the top surface of the concrete slab. "Granco" is the trade name for a decking manufacturer.

CONSTRUCTION

Careful design and detailing of the South Hills Office Building permitted the construction to be completed in three months without any major design changes or emergencies.

Although two column foundations were designed, the contractor was given the option of using the reinforced concrete foundation at all ten locations. He chose that alternative.

The main steel members (Figure 25) were erected and held in place by temporary bolting until the weldments were made. Secondary members were fastened by high-strength bolts or unfinished bolts as specified. In Figure 26, notice that steel angles were welded to the exterior I beams to form a masonry shelf at each floor level. Also notice that intermediate floor beams are required to support the

concrete floor at each level except the roof. At the roof, steel open web joists are sufficient to support the roof deck. All structural steel was fireproofed as specified by the architect (Figure 28).

Six-inch batt insulation was installed with a special attention to the plaza roof. The plaza roof beams and tapered columns were simulated by light channels wired to shape (Figure 31) and covered with a metal lath base used under the final coating of cement plaster (Figure 32). Two-inch rigid insulation was used for the exterior walls.

A specialty metal company supplied the anodized aluminum components for window mullions which are so important to the exterior design. Figure 34 shows the entire four-floor section being field fabricated before final erection. After erection, the electric heating-cooling units and window frames were placed in the mullions.

Interior partitions were framed in lightweight metal as shown in Figure 36 using the system marketed by the Keene Company. The partition members were shop welded into convenient wall sections and then field welded in the final position. The vertical metal studs are supplied with a nailing groove to facilitate fastening the finished dry wall. This groove is formed by two channels fastened together in such a way that a nail can be driven between them. The nail is held not only by friction, but is also deformed when driven to provide greater holding power. The stair wells and elevator shaft were built of concrete masonry units. Wood strapping (Figure 37) was nailed to the masonry units to provide a base for the dry wall of ½" vinyl covered gypsum board. A suspended system of steel channels was used to support the finished ceiling panels (Figure 38), and vinyl-asbestos tile flooring was laid directly over the concrete floor. The electrical and plumbing work was completed in appropriate steps during the various stages of construction. Figures 41 to 44 show the completed structure.

Study the photographs in this chapter until you are familiar with the main construction steps. Also try to visit construction sites near you at least once a week to become familiar with the latest construction techniques.

STUDY QUESTIONS

1. Name the four major steps in the design and drafting of a commercial structure.
2. List the drawings normally included in a set of commercial working drawings.
3. What is the principal reason for including details of alternate construction methods in the working drawings?
4. On the working drawings of the South Hills Office Building, the vertical modular grid system is different from the horizontal grid system. Why?
5. Are the same number of heating-cooling units used on opposite walls of the South Hills Office Building? Why?

6. Describe briefly each term:
   a. structural bent
   b. swale
   c. control joint
   d. building north
   e. roof scuttle
7. Give the meaning of these abbreviations:
   a. FTG, HTG, LTG
   b. HTR, WTR
   c. CMU, DO, GL, VAT
   d. ₵, ℔
   e. WC, WF
8. Give the meaning of:
   a. Detail 12/3
   b. Door S2/2
   c. Elevation 10/6
9. Give *two* meanings for each of the following abbreviations:
   a. E
   b. ELEV
   c. W
   d. φ
   e. #

LABORATORY PROBLEMS

1. Complete the working drawings for the South Hills Office Building as assigned:
   a. Second floor plan
   b. Roof plan
   c. Interior elevations of lobby
   d. Transverse section
   e. Stair section and details
   f. Elevator section and details
   g. Roof cornice detail section
   h. Lobby sill detail section
   i. Second floor schedules
   j. Plaza electrical plan
   k. Telephone plan
   l. Fire alarm diagram
2. Prepare working drawings of the building assigned by your instructor:
   a. Title page
   b. Plot plan
   c. Foundation plan
   d. Floor plan
   e. Elevations
   f. Sections
   g. Details
   h. Schedules
   i. Electrical plan
   j. Heating-cooling plan
   k. Plumbing plan
   l. Structural plan
3. The presentation drawings of a community church are shown in Figures 45–48. Using 6″ × 24″ laminated roof beams 8′ oc, prepare the working drawings as assigned:
   a. Floor plans
   b. Elevations
   c. Transverse section through auditorium
   d. Typical wall sections
   e. Stair details
   f. Schedules
   g. Electrical plan
   h. Heating and air circulation plan
   i. Plumbing plan
4. Design and prepare preliminary drawings for the project assigned:
   a. An innovative children's playground for a 50′ wide by 150′ deep urban site.
   b. A drive-in movie screen structure. The screen is to be 120′ wide by 50′ high and at an angle of 12° from the vertical. The bottom of the screen is 12′ above the ground level. Use timber or steel construction as assigned.
   c. An 80′ by 160′ unheated storage warehouse for a building supply distributor. Clear ceiling height should be 12′-0″. Use masonry (10″ CMU) or wood frame construction (2″ × 6″ studs 24″ oc with corrugated aluminum siding). Provide a small, heated office and lavatory, rail receiving dock, and truck shipping dock. Fire protection will include a dry sprinkler system.
   d. A single story retail candy store for a 24′ wide by 120′ deep commercial site. Use a brick bearing-wall and steel joist roof construction. Provide an attractive front elevation with display window, rear office of 200 sq. ft., and storage of 300 sq. ft. with delivery door. Show details of interior planning.
   e. A two-story community college academic building containing an auditorium seating 200 students, five classrooms each seating 40 students, a drafting room for 30 students, eight two-man faculty offices, restrooms, and maintenance. Use steel and masonry construction.
   f. (For the advanced student) A world's fair pavilion representing your state. Provide for a 4,000 sq. ft. major working attraction, 3,000 sq. ft. small products display and sales area, offices, restrooms, and maintenance. Use a progressive structural system.
5. (For the advanced student) Design and prepare presentation drawings for:
   a. A community action center
   b. An urban pedestrian mall
   c. A low-cost housing module
   d. A manufacturing plant for the production of low-cost housing modules
   e. A processing plant for the conversion of sewage into potable water
   f. A processing plant to convert scrapped automobiles into structural units
   g. A processing plant to convert residential waste into building blocks
   h. A seagoing processor to neutralize floating oil slick

CONSTRUCTION DRAWINGS
FOR THE
SOUTH HILLS OFFICE BUILDING
STATE COLLEGE, PENNSYLVANIA

INDEX OF DRAWINGS

1	INDEX
2	PLOT PLAN
3	FOUNDATION PLAN
4	FOOTING DETAILS
5	PLAZA FLOOR PLAN
6	FIRST FLOOR PLAN
7	SOUTH ELEVATION
8	NORTH ELEVATION
9	EAST & WEST ELEVATIONS
10	INTERIOR ELEVATIONS
11	LONGITUDINAL SECTION
12	TYPICAL SECTIONS
13	TYPICAL DETAILS
14	ROOM SCHEDULES
15	DOOR & WINDOW SCHEDULES
E1	ELECTRICAL PLAN
H1	HEATING-COOLING PLAN
P1	WATER SUPPLY PLAN
P2	SANITARY PLAN
S1	FIRST FLOOR STRUCTURAL PLAN
S2	ROOF STRUCTURAL PLAN
S3	COLUMN SCHEDULE
S4	STRUCTURAL DETAILS
S5	CONCRETE SLAB PLAN

LEGEND

-100- EXIST CONTOUR
-100- REVISED CONTOUR
PROPERTY LINE
BRICK
CMU
CRUSHED STONE
EARTH
STEEL
CONCRETE SECTION
"   IN PLAN
BITUMINOUS
RIGID INSULATION
BATT   "
ROUGH WOOD
GYPSUM BOARD
PLASTER
CERAMIC TILE
SHEET NO / SECTION NO
SHEET NO / ELEVATION NO
ROOM NO / DOOR NO
WINDOW SYMBOL
ROOM SYMBOL

SWITCH LEG
SWITCHED CIRCUIT
BRANCH CIRCUIT
D-1 HOME RUN w/ CIRCUIT NO
208V HOME RUN
INCANDESCENT FIXTURE, CLG
"   "   WALL
FLUORESCENT   "
CONVENIENCE OUTLET
S SWITCH
S_3 THREE WAY SWITCH
S_4 FOUR   "
E EMERGENCY CIRCUIT
"   LIGHTING
EXIT LIGHT, QTH B1412
"   "   B1414
HEATING-COOLING UNIT
BASEBOARD HEATING   "
COLD WATER
HOT WATER
SANITARY WASTE
VENT

ABBREVIATIONS

ACOUSTIC	AC	HEATING	HTG
ALUMINUM	ALUM	HEXAGONAL	HEX
AMPHERES	A	HOLLOW METAL	HM
ANGLE	L	HOT	H
AT	@	BEARING PILE	HP
BEAM	B	INSULATION	INSUL
BEARING PILE	HP	IRON PIPE	IP
BITUMINOUS	BIT	JUNCTION BOX	JB
BOARD	BD	LAVATORY	L or LAV
BOTTOM OF CURB	BC	LIGHTING	LTG
BRITISH THERMAL UNIT	BTU		
BUILDING	BLDG	MANUFACTURER	MANUF
		MATERIAL	MAT'L
CABINET	CAB	MAXIMUM	MAX
CATCH BASIN	CB	METAL	MET
CEILING	CLG	MINIMUM	MIN
CEMENT	CEM		
CENTER LINE	₵	NORTH	N
CENTER TO CENTER	CC	NUMBER	NO or #
CERAMIC TILE	CER T	ON CENTER	o c
CHANNEL	[or C		
CLEAN OUT	CO	PARTITION	PART
CLEAR	CLR	PHASE	Φ
COLD	C	PLASTER	PLAST
COLUMN	COL	PLATE	℗
CONCRETE	CONC	PORCELAIN	PORC
CONCRETE MASONRY UNIT	CMU	POUNDS PER SQUARE INCH	PSI
CONSTRUCTION	CONST	PUNCHED	PUN
CUBIC FEET PER MINUTE	CFM		
		RAIN WATER CONDUIT	RWC
DIAMETER	Φ	RECEPTACLE	REC
DITTO	DO or "	RIGHT OF WAY	R/W
DOUBLE STUDS	DS	RISER	R
DOWN	DN		
		SHOCK ABSORBER	SA
EACH	EA	SOUTH	S
EAST, EMERGENCY	E	SPECIFICATIONS	SPECS
ELEVATION, ELEVATOR	ELEV	STEEL	STL
EQUAL	EQ	SYSTEM	SYS
EXHAUST	EXH		
EXISTING	EXIST	THRESHOLD	THRESH
EXPANSION JOINT	EXP JT	TOP OF CURB	TC
EXTENDED	EXT		
		UNPUNCHED	UNP
FINISH	FIN	URINAL	U
FLASHING	FLASH		
FLOOR	FL	VINYL ASBESTOS TILE	VAT
FOOTING	FTG	VOLTS	V
FRESH AIR	FA		
FURRING	FUR	WASTE, WATTS, WEST	W
		WATER CLOSET	WC
GYPSUM	GYP	WATER HEATER	WTR HTR
GLASS	GL	WIDE FLANGE	W
		WITH	w/

Drawing No. 1   Index of the South Hills Office Building.

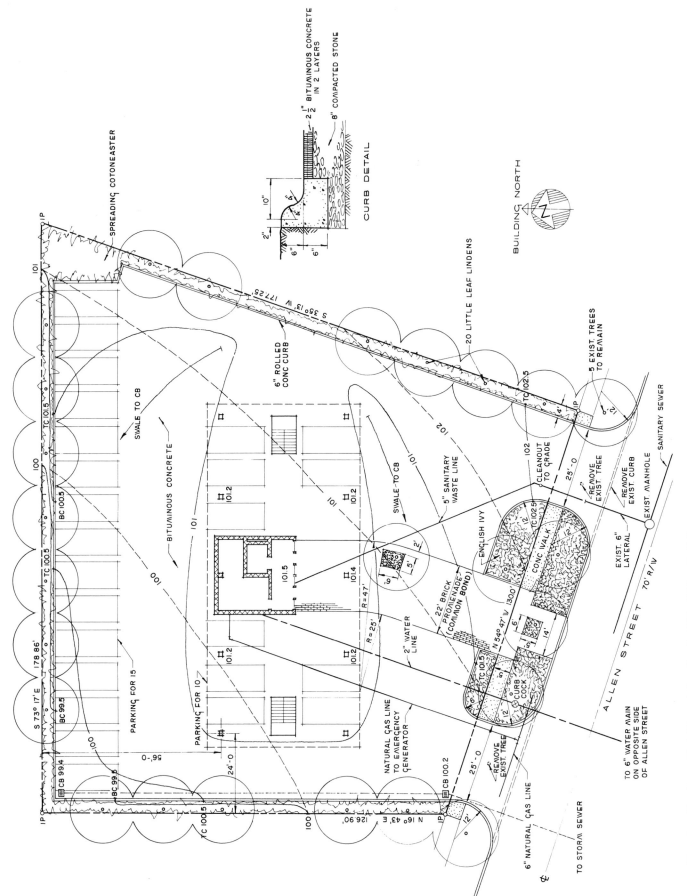

Drawing No. 2   Plot Plan of the South Hills Office Building.

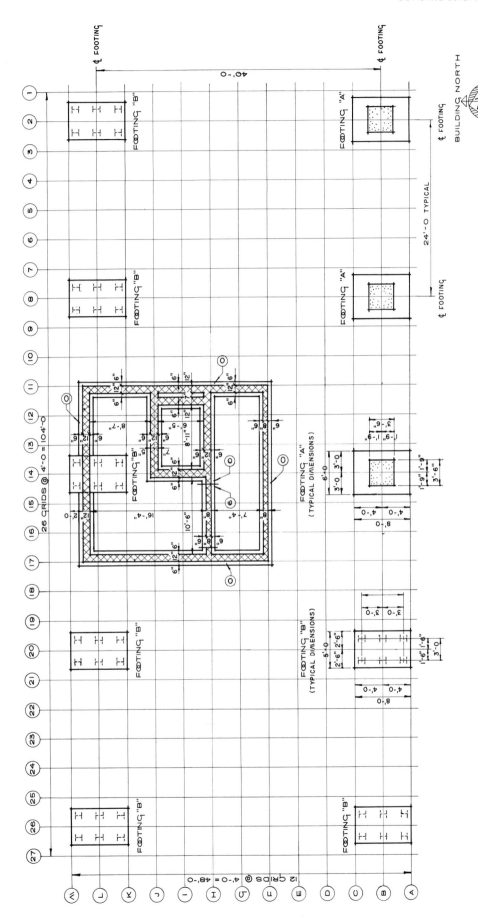

Drawing No. 3   Foundation Plan of the South Hills Office Building.

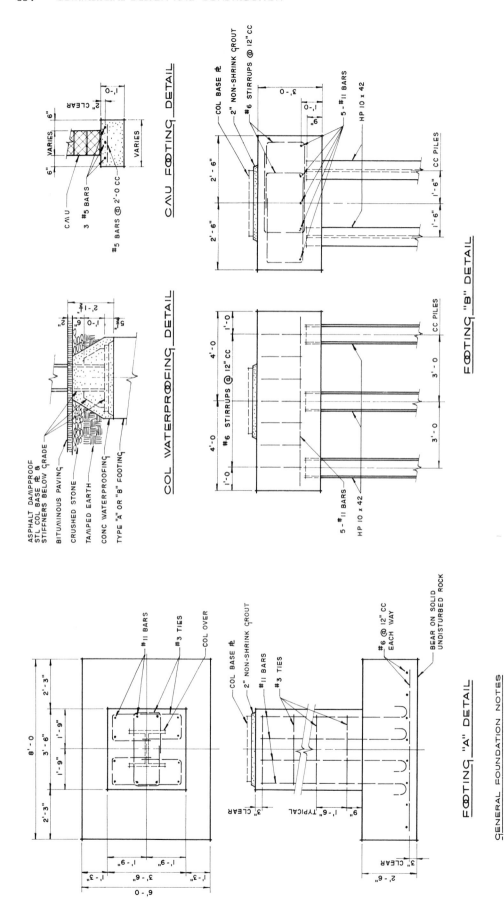

CMU FOOTING DETAIL

COL WATERPROOFING DETAIL

FOOTING "B" DETAIL

FOOTING "A" DETAIL

GENERAL FOUNDATION NOTES

1 FOOTING "A" MAY BE SUBSTITUTED FOR FOOTING "B" AT CONTRACTOR'S OPTION.

2 ALL CONCRETE SHALL HAVE AN ULTIMATE 28 DAY COMPRESSIVE STRENGTH OF 3000 PSI.

3 ALL REINFORCING STEEL SHALL BE ASTM A15 INTERMEDIATE GRADE.

4 STEEL BEARING PILES FOR FOOTING "B" SHALL BE ASTM A36. PILES SHALL BE DRIVEN TO REFUSAL ON SOLID ROCK. SEE TEST BORING RESULTS FOR APPROXIMATE DEPTH OF ROCK.

Drawing No. 4   Footing Details of the South Hills Office Building.

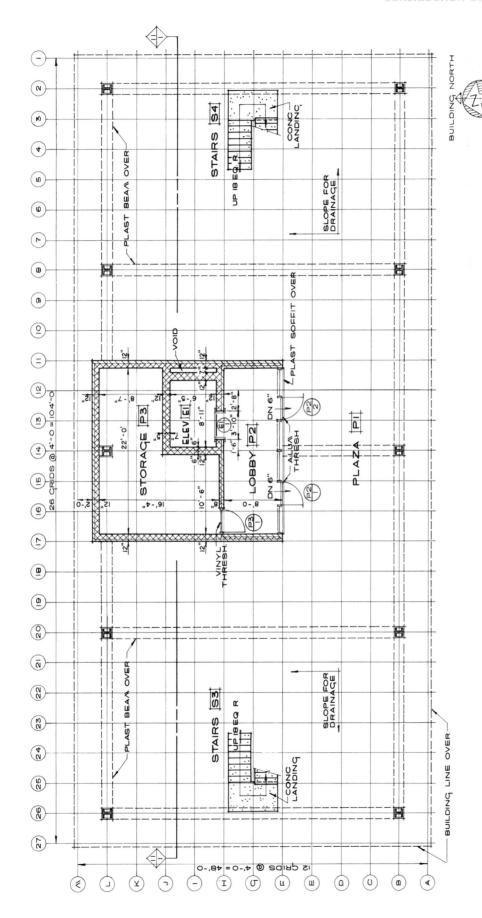

Drawing No. 5   Plaza Floor Plan of the South Hills Office Building.

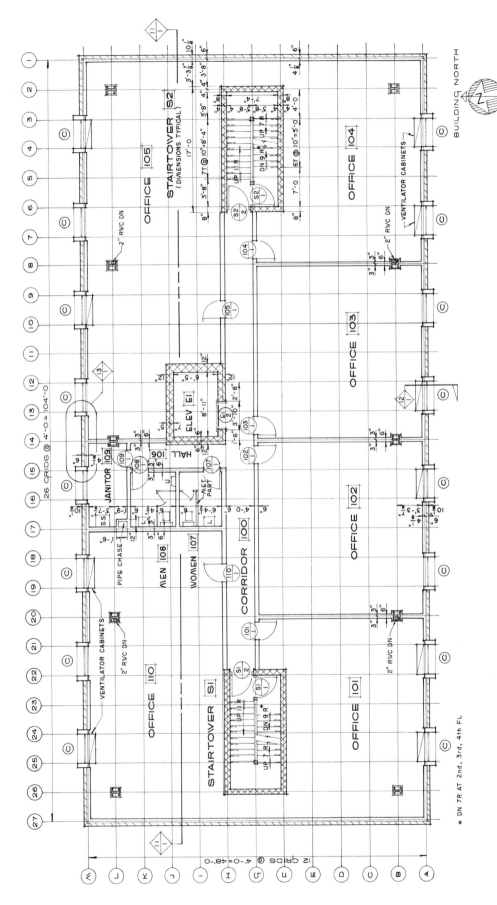

Drawing No. 6   First Floor Plan of the South Hills Office Building. (Second, third, and fourth floor plans similar.)

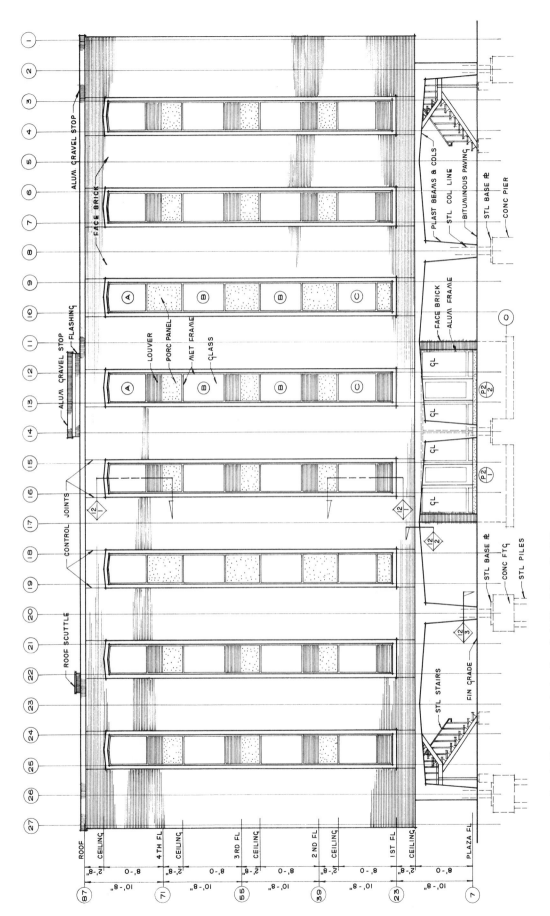

Drawing No. 7   South Elevation of the South Hills Office Building.

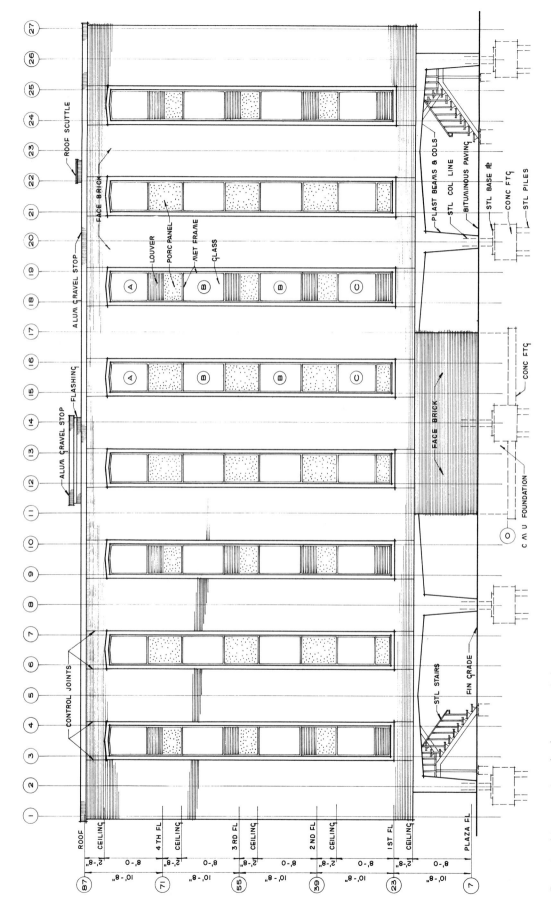

Drawing No. 8   North Elevation of the South Hills Office Building.

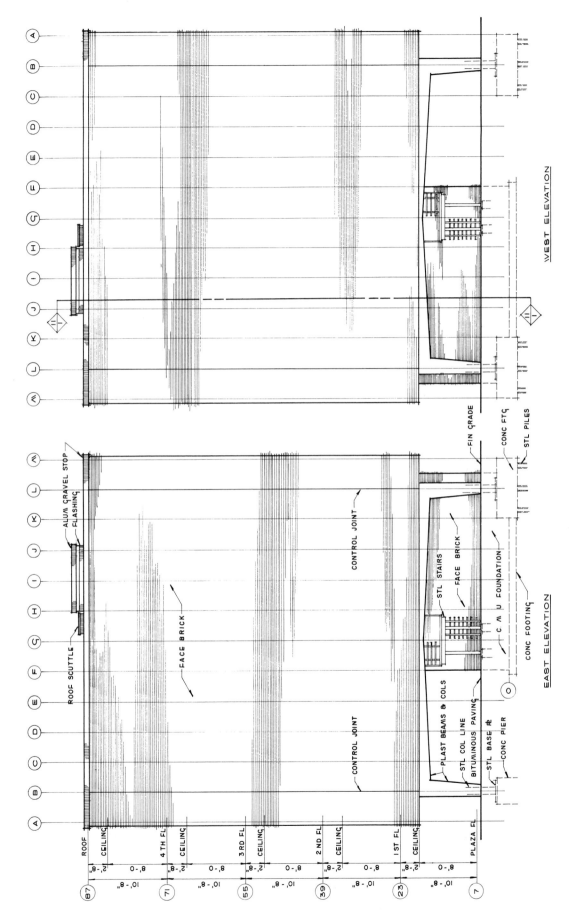

Drawing No. 9   East and West Elevations of the South Hills Office Building.

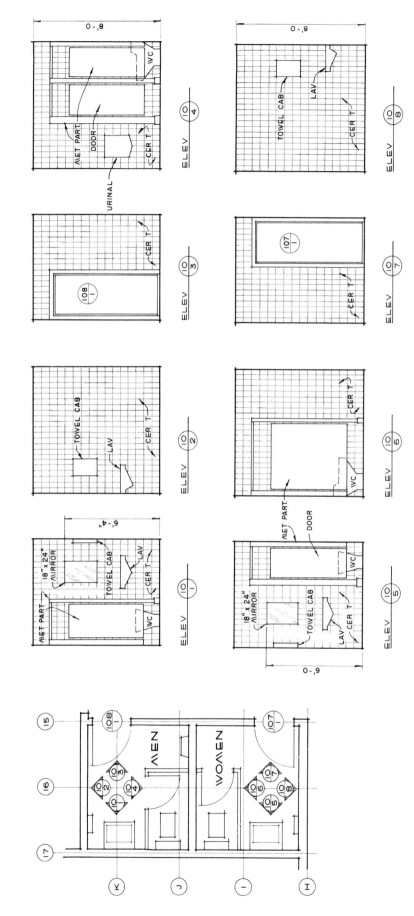

Drawing No. 10   Interior Elevations of the South Hills Office Building.

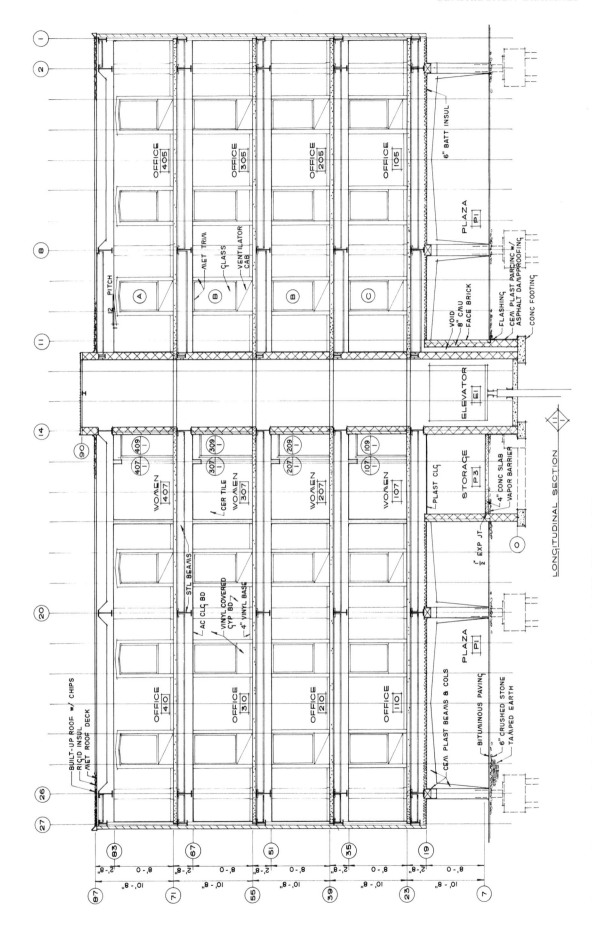

Drawing No. 11   *Longitudinal Section of the South Hills Office Building.*

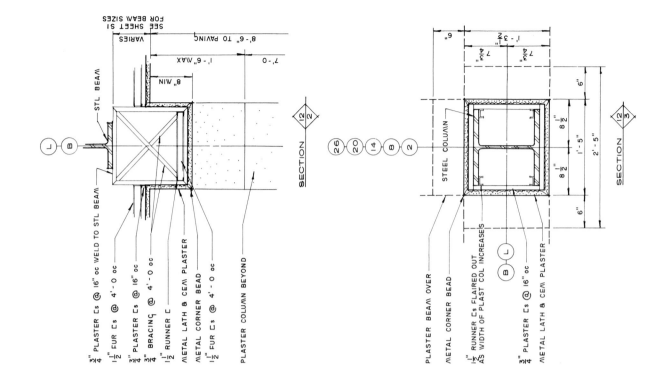

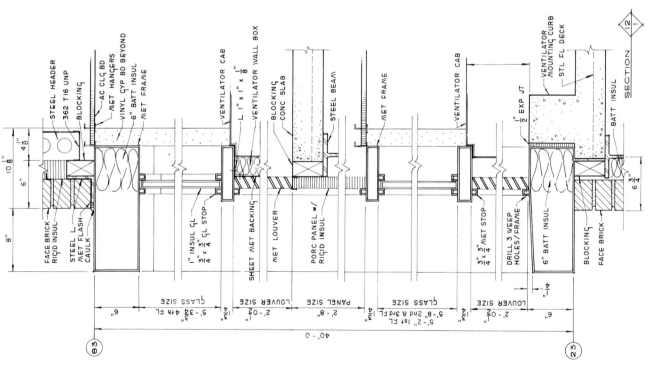

Drawing No. 12 Typical Sections of the South Hills Office Building.

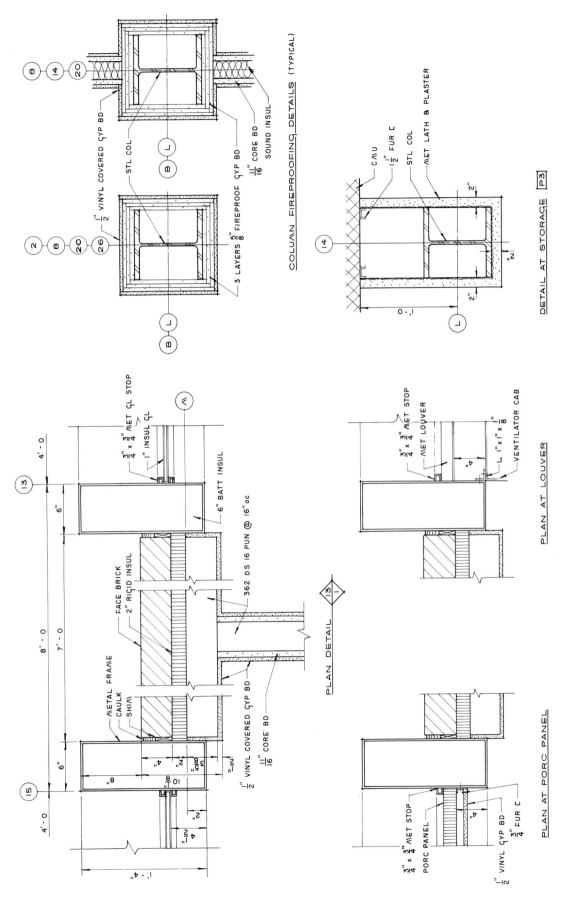

Drawing No. 13   Typical Details of the South Hills Office Building.

LIGHTING FIXTURE SCHEDULE

NO	MANUFACTURER	CATALOG NO	FINISH	WATTS
A	LIGHTOLIER	7792		300
B	"	7794		100
C	"	7827 & 7821	WHITE	150
D	"	7827 & 7822	"	150 & 25
F	PRESCOLITE	WB-28-2	ALUM	150 & 100
G	LIGHTOLIER	81675	WHITE	4L-40
H	STONCO	CD8501	ALUM	500

MAIN DISTRIBUTION PANEL

400A-3P-SW-W/3-300A-FU- PANEL A
400A-3P-SW-W/3-225A-FU- PANEL B
400A-3P-SW-W/3-225A-FU- PANEL C
400A-3P-SW-W/2-275A-FU- PANEL D
100A-2P-SW-W/2-100A-FU- PANEL E
60A-2P-SW-W/2-50A-FU- PANEL EM SW
*200A-3P-SW-W/3-200A-FU- ELEVATOR
*TIME DELAY FUSES (FUSETRON)
1200A-BUS 3Φ-4W-120/208V

ELECTRICAL PANEL SCHEDULES

PANEL D (TYPICAL)

31-20A-1P-CB-LTG, REC
9-30A-2P-CB-HTG, WTR HTR
2-20A-2P-CB-HTG
4-20A-2P-CB-SPARES
4-20A-1P-SPACE ONLY
400A-MLO 3Φ-4W-120/208V

PANEL E

9-20A-2P-CB-LTG, FA SYS EXH FAN
4-20A-1P-CB-LTG, REC
4-20A-1P-CB-SPARES
4-20A-1P-SPACE ONLY
100A-MLO 1Φ-3W-120/208V

PANEL EM

5-20A-1P-FU-LTG, ELEV JB
5-20A-1P-FU-SPARES
100A-MLO 1Φ-3W-120/208V

ELECTRIC HEATING-COOLING UNITS

NO	MANUFACTURER	HEATING		COOLING	
		BTU	WATTS	BTU	WATTS
EK-7S	REMINGTON	8400	2460	6500	1240
EK-10S	"	8400	2460	9000	1520
EK-10M	"	11330	3320	9000	1520
EK-12S	"	8470	2480	11700	1770
EK-12L	"	15300	4480	11700	1770
EK-15L	"	15370	4500	14100	2220

ELECTRIC BASEBOARD HEATING

NO	MANUFACTURER	CATALOG NO	BTU	WATTS
A	ELECTROMODE	8950-D	2560	750
B	"	8950-A	1707	500
C	"	8960-C	4439	1300

ROOM FINISH SCHEDULE

NO	NAME	FLOOR	BASE	WALL	TRIM	WINDOW STOOL	CEILING	HGT	REMARKS
P1	PLAZA	BITUM		BRICK 5	ALUM 9		PLAST 11	VARIES	CEM PLAST BEAMS & COLS
P2	LOBBY	VAT 1		" 5	" HM 9/10		" 13	8'-0	
P3	STORAGE	CONC 17		CMU 6	HM 10		" 11	8'-0	
100	CORRIDOR	VAT 1	VINYL	VINYL BRICK 7/5	HM 10		AC CLG BD 14	8'-0	NO BASE AT BRICK WALL
101	OFFICE	"	"	VINYL 7	" 10	ALUM 9	" 14	8'-0	
102	"	"	"	" 7	" 10	" 9	" 14	8'-0	
103	"	"	"	" 7	" 10	" 9	" 14	8'-0	
104	"	"	"	" 7	" 10	" 9	" 14	8'-0	
105	"	"	"	" 7	" 10	" 9	" 14	8'-0	
106	HALL	"	"	VINYL BRICK 7/5	" 10		PLAST 12	8'-0	
107	WOMEN	CER T 4	CER T	CER T 8	" 10		" 12	8'-0	PROVIDE MIRROR, TOWEL CAB, MET PART
108	MEN	CER T 4	CER T	" 8	" 10		" 12	8'-0	
109	JANITOR	VAT 1	VINYL	VINYL CMU 7/6	ALUM 10	9	AC CLG BD 14	8'-0	
110	OFFICE	"	"	VINYL 7	" 10	9	" 14	8'-0	

STAIRTOWER FINISH SCHEDULE

NO	RISER	TREAD	STRINGER	INTERMEDIATE FLOOR	FLOOR LANDING	BASE	SOFFIT	CEILING	RAILING	WALL RAILING	WALLS
S1	STL 15	VAT 1	STL	VAT 15	VINYL 3	VAT 15	PLAST 13	13	VINYL 16	VINYL 16	CMU 6
S2	" 15	" 1	"	" 15	" 3	" 15	" 13	13	" 16	" 16	" 6
S3	CONC 17	CONC 17		CONC 17			" 11	11	STL 15	STL 15	PLAST 11
S4	" 17	" 17		" 17			" 11	11	" 15	" 15	" 11

INTERIOR MATERIAL SCHEDULE

NO	MATERIAL	TYPE	SIZE	FINISH
1	VINYL ASBESTOS TILE	SEE SPECS	9"x9"x$\frac{1}{8}$"	WAX
2	CERAMIC FLOOR TILE	CERAMIC MOSAIC	1$\frac{1}{16}$"x1$\frac{1}{16}$"	FACTORY FINISH, UNGLAZED
3	VINYL COVE BASE		4" HIGH	"
4	CERAMIC BASE TILE	COVE BASE	4$\frac{1}{4}$"x 6"x$\frac{5}{16}$"	" MATTE GLAZE
5	BRICK	SEE SPECS, COMMON BOND	3 COURSES = 8"	$\frac{1}{4}$" $\frac{3}{8}$" CONCAVE JOINT
6	CONCRETE MASONRY UNIT		1 COURSE = 8"	PAINT
7	VINYL COVERED GYP BD		4'-0x8'-0x$\frac{1}{2}$" SHEETS	ALUM BATTENS
8	CERAMIC WALL TILE	WALL TILE	4$\frac{1}{4}$"x 6"x$\frac{5}{16}$"	FACTORY FINISH, MATTE GLAZE
9	ALUMINUM	SEE SPECS		FACTORY FINISH, MATTE GLAZE
10	HOLLOW METAL			PAINT
11	PLASTER	CEMENT		SPRAYED ON WHITE
12	"	KEENE CEMENT		WHITE COAT
13	"	SAND FINISH GYPSUM		PAINT
14	ACOUSTICAL CEILING BOARD	SEE SPECS, EXPOSED "T" BARS	2'-0x2'-0x$\frac{5}{8}$"	FACTORY FINISH
15	STEEL	STEEL STAIR PARTS		PAINT
16	STAIR RAILING	VINYL STAIR RAIL		FACTORY FINISH, PAINT BASE
17	CONCRETE		2"x2"x$\frac{3}{8}$" STEEL BASE PLATE	SEAL w/ LIPIDOLITH

Drawing No. 14   Room Schedules of the South Hills Office Building.

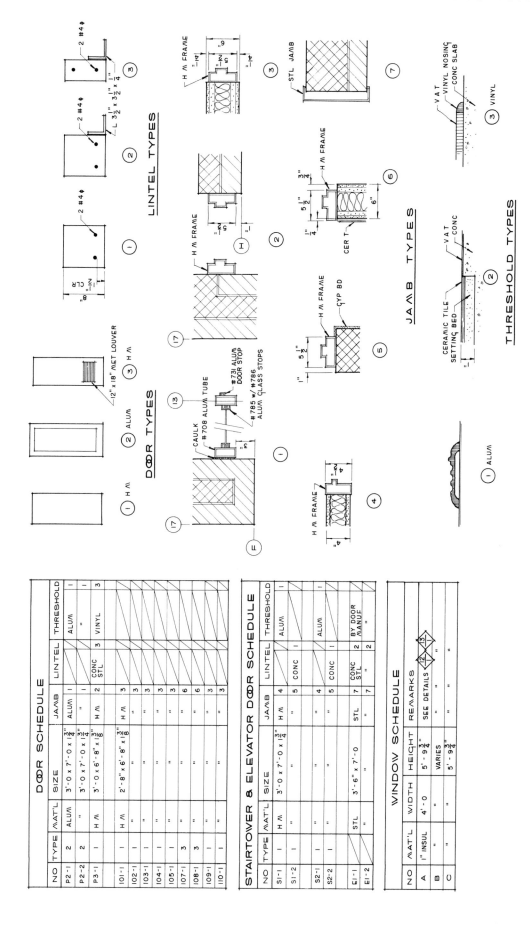

Drawing No. 15   Door and Window Schedules of the South Hills Office Building.

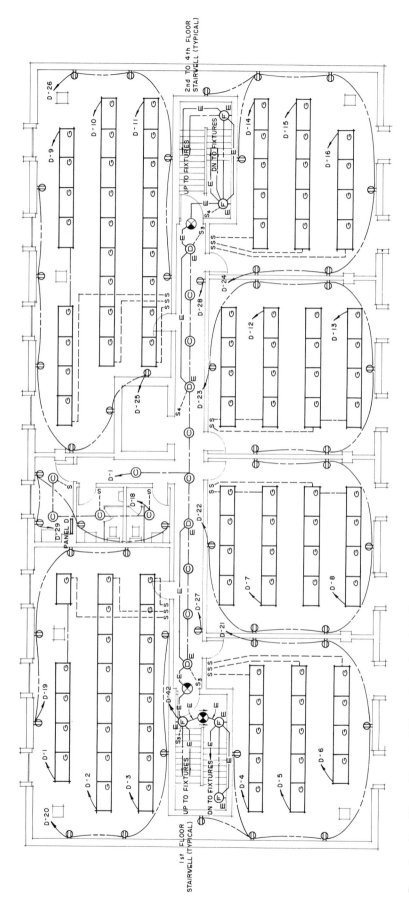

Drawing No. E1   Electrical Plan of the South Hills Office Building.

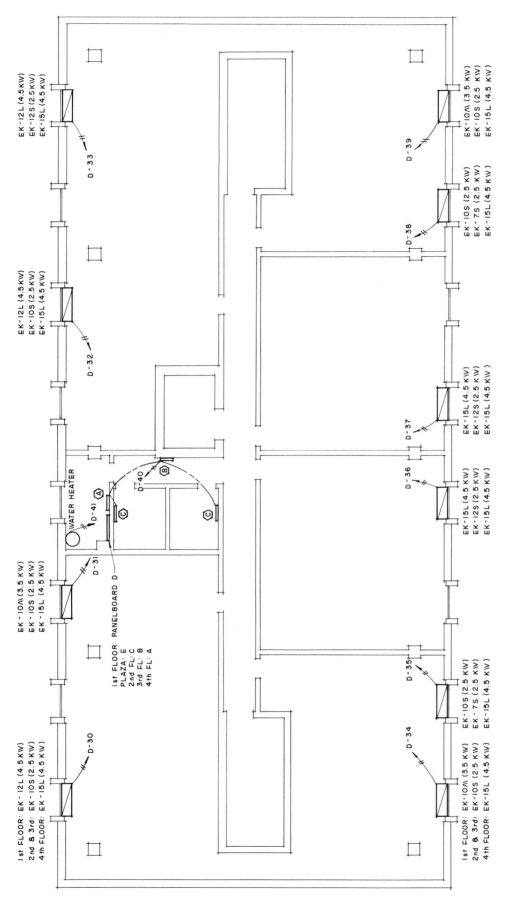

EK-12L (4.5KW)
EK-12S (2.5KW)
EK-15L (4.5KW)

D-33

EK-10M (3.5 KW)
EK-10S (2.5 KW)
EK-15L (4.5 KW)

D-39

EK-12L (4.5KW)
EK-10S (2.5KW)
EK-15L (4.5KW)

D-32

EK-10S (2.5 KW)
EK-7S (2.5 KW)
EK-15L (4.5KW)

D-38

EK-15L (4.5 KW)
EK-12S (2.5 KW)
EK-15L (4.5 KW)

D-37

WATER HEATER

D-40

B

A

D-41

C

D-31

PANELBOARD D

1st FLOOR: PANELBOARD D
PLAZA: E
2nd FL: C
3rd FL: B
4th FL: A

EK-15L (4.5 KW)
EK-12S (2.5 KW)
EK-15L (4.5 KW)

D-36

EK-10M(3.5 KW)
EK-10S (2.5 KW)
EK-15L (4.5 KW)

EK-10S (2.5 KW)
EK-7S (2.5 KW)
EK-15L (4.5 KW)

D-35

D-30

1st FLOOR: EK-12L (4.5KW)
2nd & 3rd: EK-10S (2.5KW)
4th FLOOR: EK-15L (4.5 KW)

EK-10M(3.5 KW)
EK-10S (2.5 KW)
EK-15L (4.5 KW)

1st FLOOR: EK-10M (3.5 KW)
2nd & 3rd: EK-10S (2.5 KW)
4th FLOOR: EK-15L (4.5 KW)

D-34

Drawing No. H1   Heating-Cooling Plan of the South Hills Office Building.

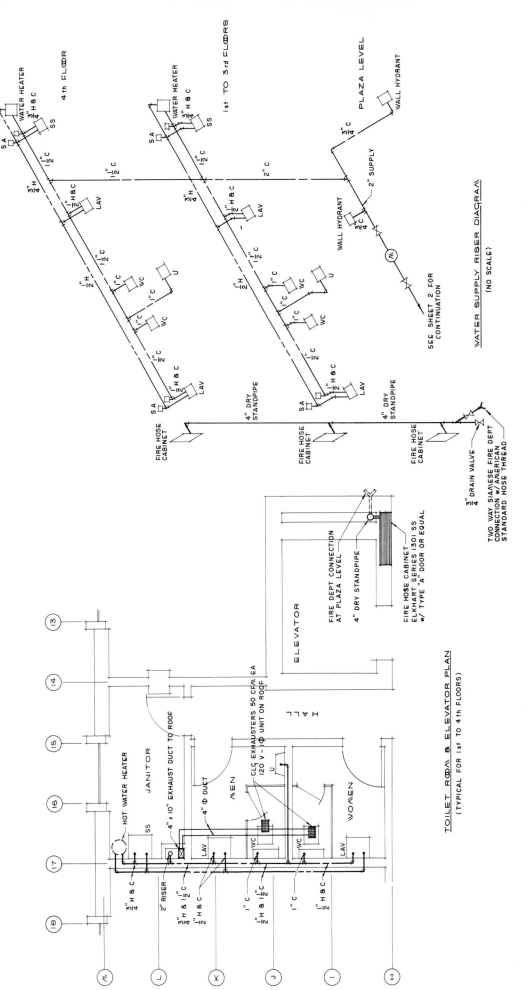

Drawing No. P1   Water Supply Plan of the South Hills Office Building.

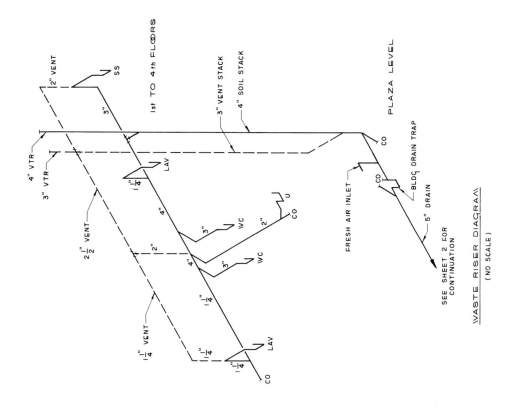

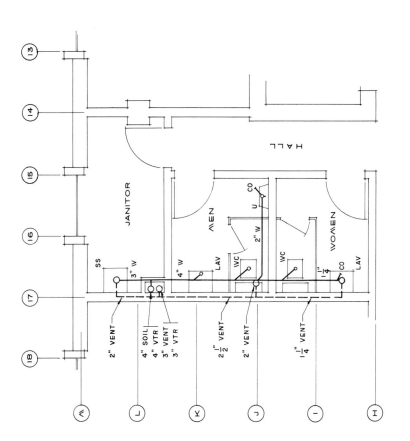

Drawing No. P2   Sanitary Plan of the South Hills Office Building.

370

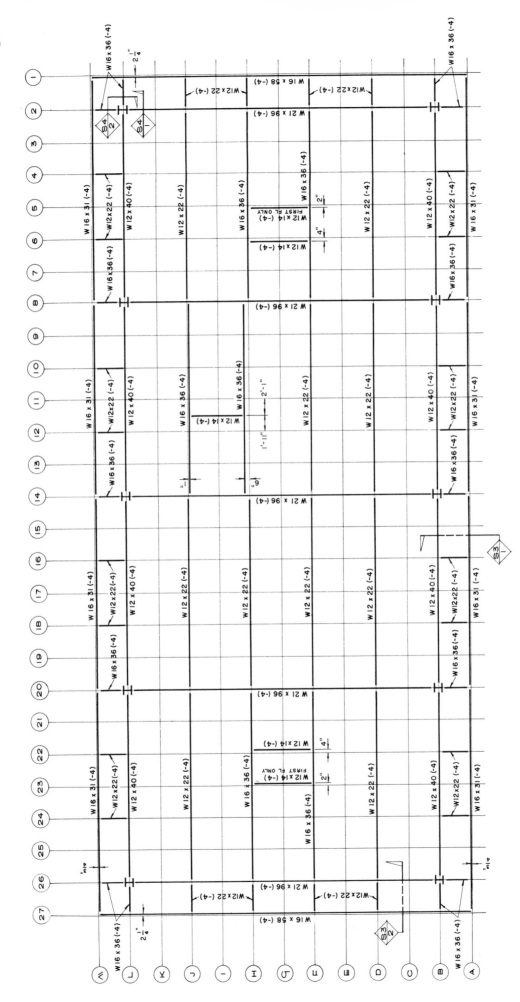

Drawing No. S1   First Floor Structural Plan of the South Hills Office Building. (Second, third, and fourth floor structural plans similar.)

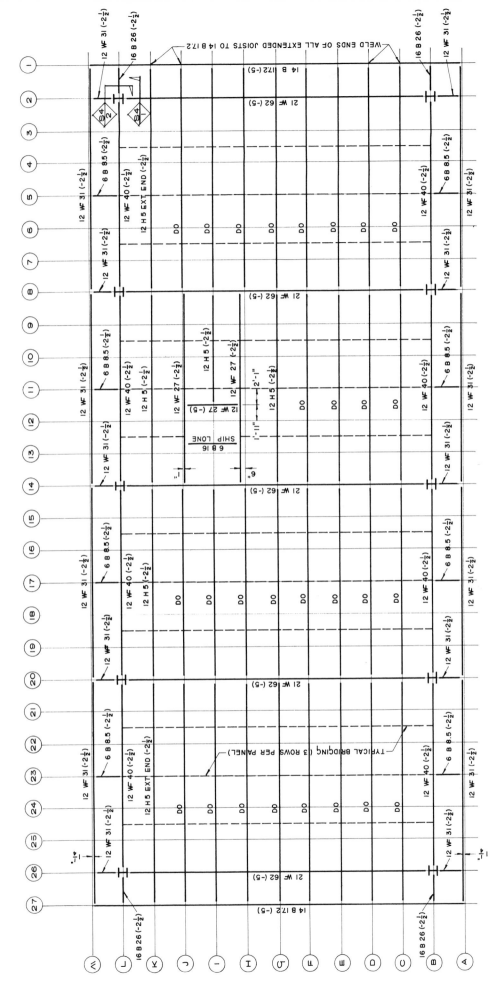

Drawing No. S2   Roof Structural Plan of the South Hills Office Building (using "old" steel designations).

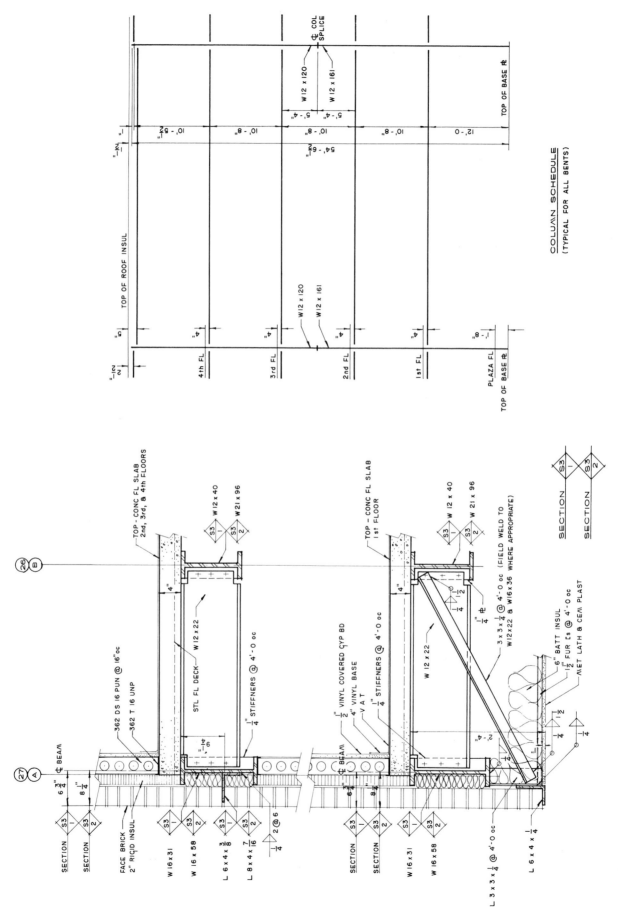

Drawing No. S3   Structural Section and Column Schedule of the South Hills Office Building.

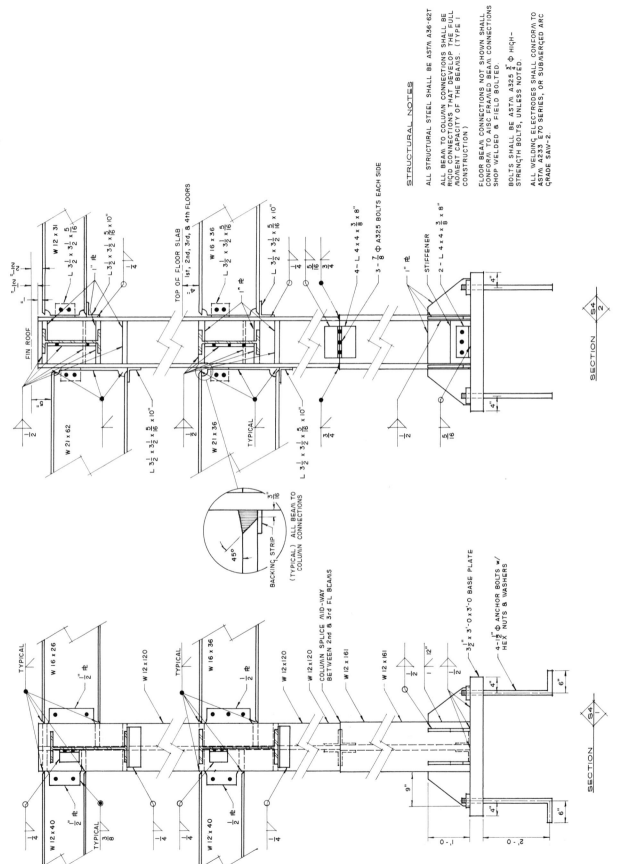

Drawing No. S4   Structural Details of the South Hills Office Building.

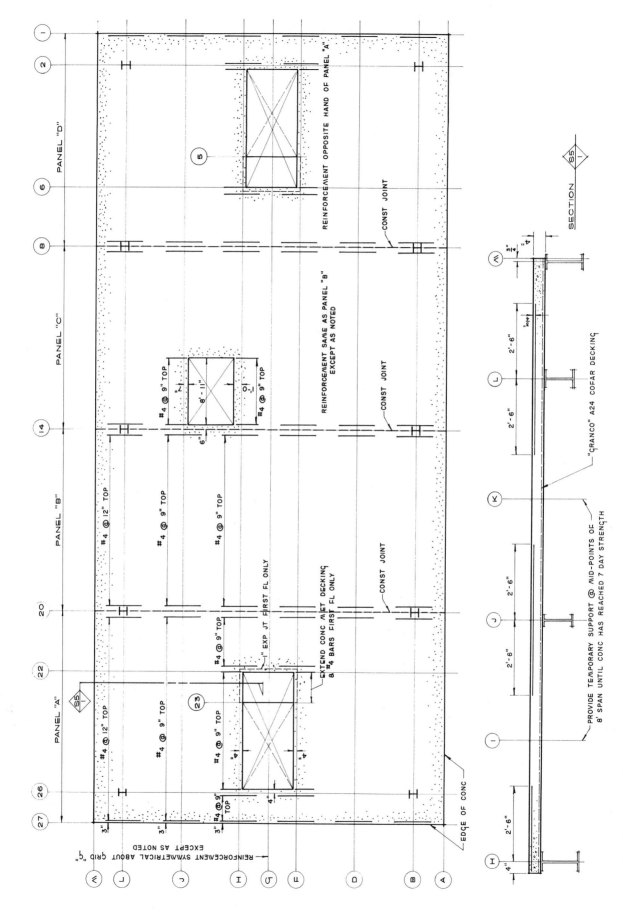

Drawing No. S5   Concrete Slab Plan of the South Hills Office Building. (First, second, third, and fourth floors.)

Figure 25   Steel framing of the South Hills Office Building.

Figure 26   Close-up of framing showing masonry shelves.

Figure 27   Detail of welded beam-to-column connection.

Figure 28   Detail of fireproofing sprayed on steel beams.

Figure 29   Corrugated forms for reinforced concrete floors.

Figure 30   Corrugated decking over open web roof joists.

Figure 31   Installing forms for simulated beams over plaza level.

Figure 32   Metal lath installed prior to plastering.

Figure 33   Outside wall detail before mullion installation.

Figure 34   Assembling aluminum window mullions before erection.

Figure 35   Outside wall detail after mullion installation.

Figure 36   Steel interior partition framing.

Figure 37   Wood strapping nailed to masonry stairwell in preparation for dry wall installation.

Figure 38   Hung metal channels will support ceiling panels.

Figure 39   Completion of masonry.

Figure 40   Mullions and simulated plaza beams in place.

Figure 41   *Exterior view of the completed South Hills Office Building.*

Figure 42   *The law office in the South Hills Office Building.*

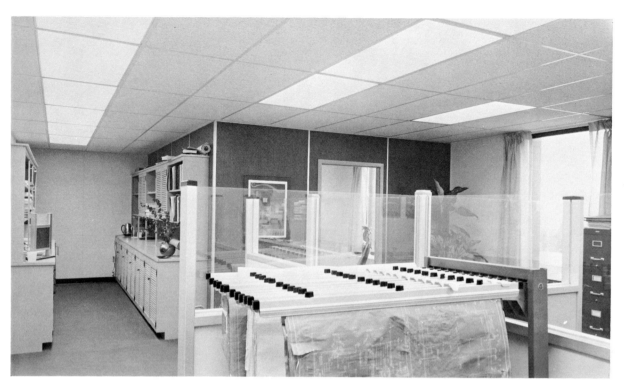

Figure 43   The real estate office in the South Hills Office Building.

Figure 44   The advertising agency's conference room in the South Hills Office Building.

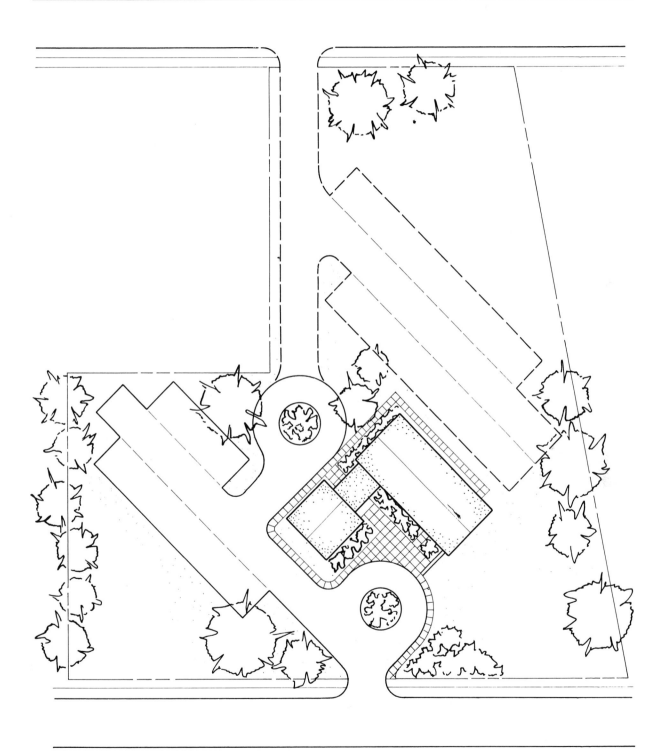

Figure 45   Plot plan of a community church.

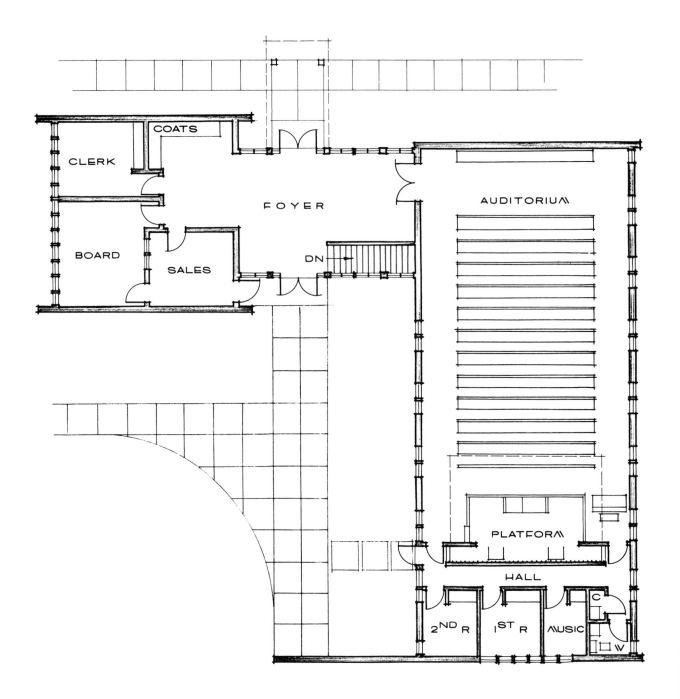

Figure 46   *Upper level plan of a community church.*

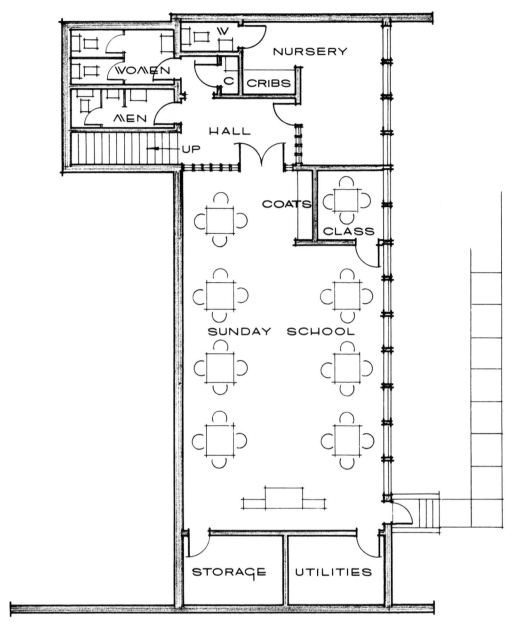

Figure 47   Lower level plan of a community church.

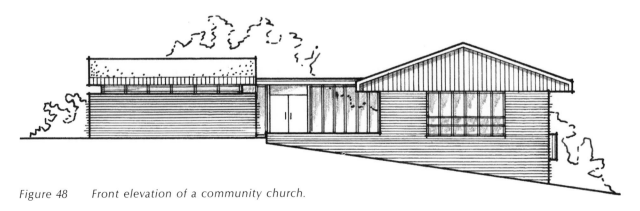

Figure 48   Front elevation of a community church.

appendix a   plans of a split level and a two story residence

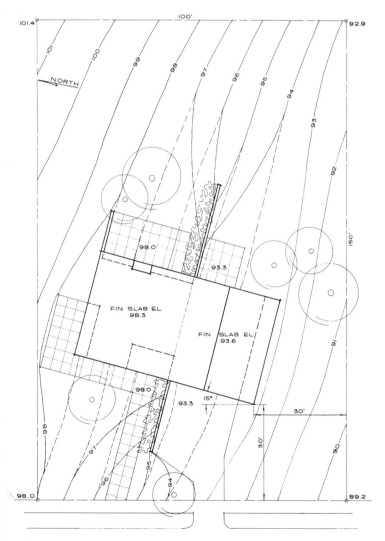

A single story contemporary house designed for Mr. A has been used as an example throughout the preceding chapters.* To provide a wider base of comparison, plans of two quite different houses for Mr. M and Mr. Z follow.

The residence for Mr. M is a split level house—also of contemporary design. The working drawings have been prepared using modular dimensioning practices.**

The residence for Mr. Z is a two story traditional house in an English garrison styling.

*Courtesy of Mr. & Mrs. Donald W. Hamer, State College, Pa.

**Courtesy of Professor M. Eisenberg, The Pennsylvania State University.

Figure 1   Plot plan of the M residence.

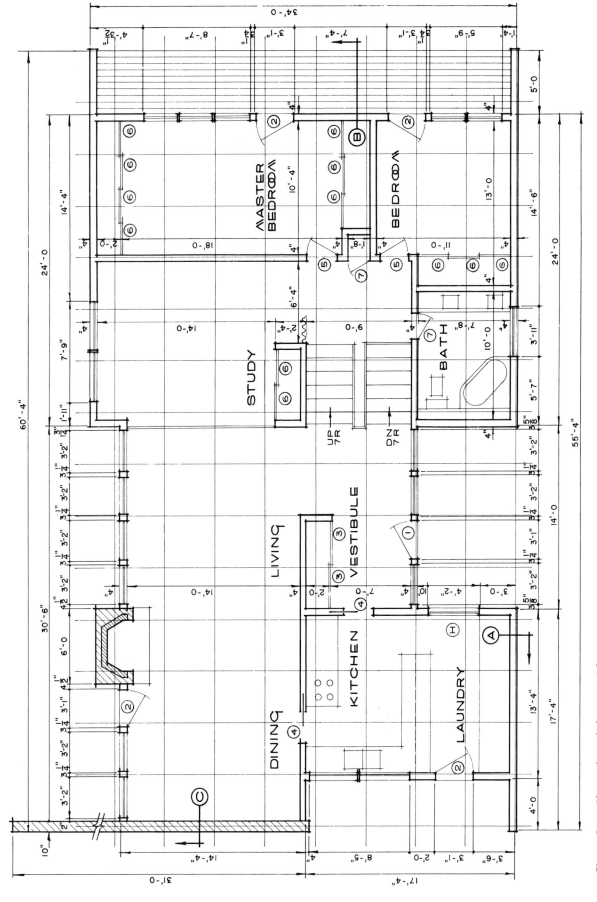

Figure 2   *Floor plan of the M residence.*

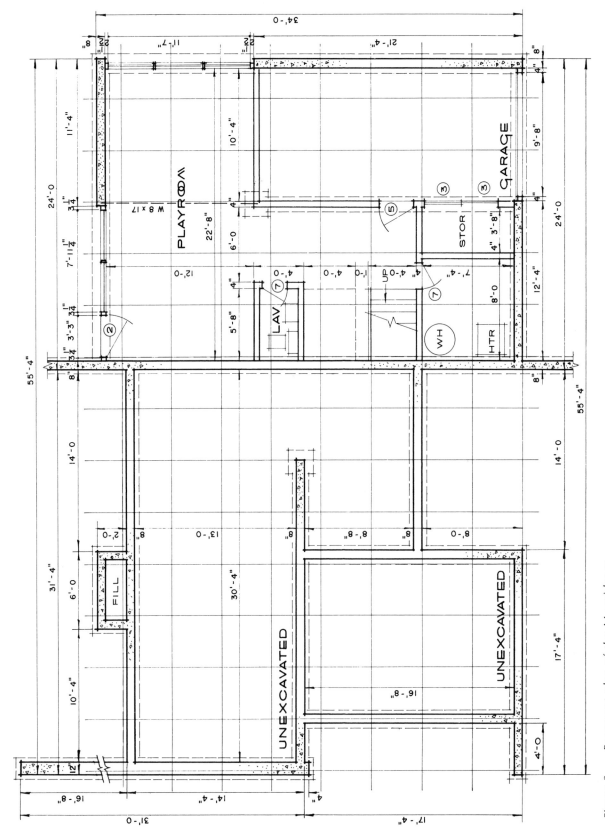

Figure 3   Basement plan of the M residence.

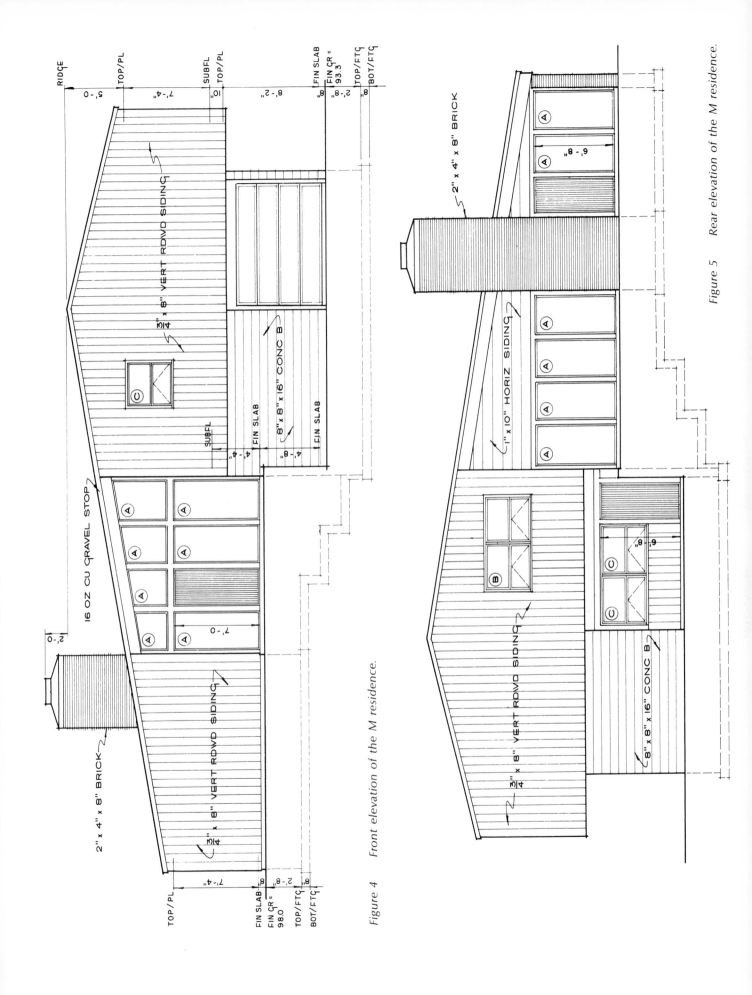

Figure 4   Front elevation of the M residence.

Figure 5   Rear elevation of the M residence.

Figure 6   Right end elevation of the M residence.

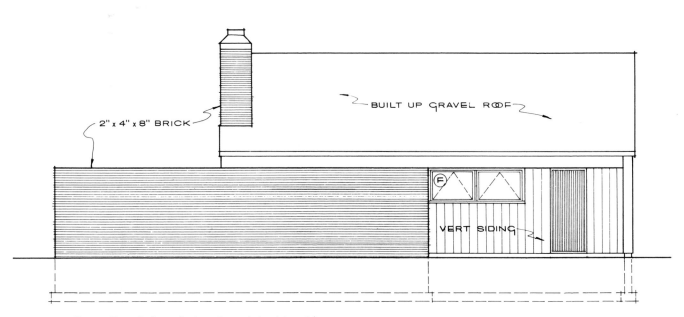

Figure 7   Left end elevation of the M residence.

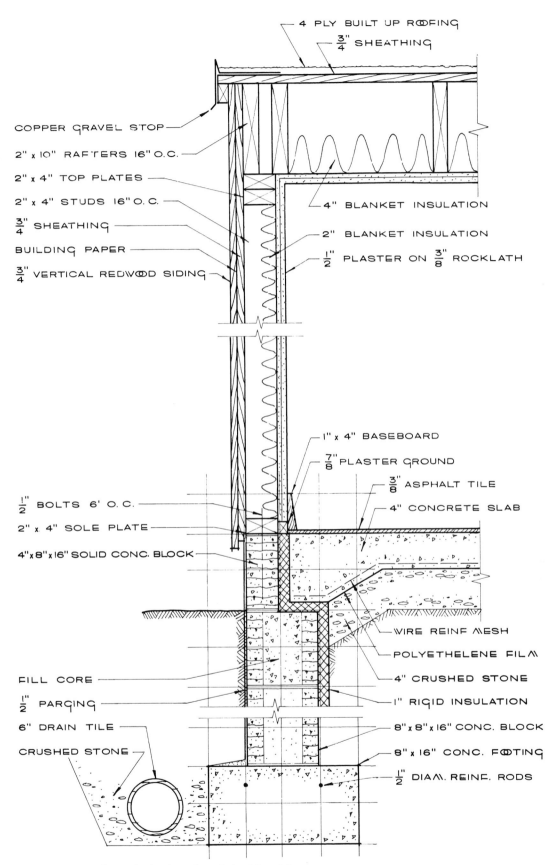

4 PLY BUILT UP ROOFING

$\frac{3}{4}$" SHEATHING

COPPER GRAVEL STOP

2" x 10" RAFTERS 16" O.C.

2" x 4" TOP PLATES

2" x 4" STUDS 16" O.C.

$\frac{3}{4}$" SHEATHING

BUILDING PAPER

$\frac{3}{4}$" VERTICAL REDWOOD SIDING

4" BLANKET INSULATION

2" BLANKET INSULATION

$\frac{1}{2}$" PLASTER ON $\frac{3}{8}$" ROCKLATH

1" x 4" BASEBOARD

$\frac{7}{8}$" PLASTER GROUND

$\frac{3}{8}$" ASPHALT TILE

4" CONCRETE SLAB

$\frac{1}{2}$" BOLTS 6' O.C.

2" x 4" SOLE PLATE

4" x 8" x 16" SOLID CONC. BLOCK

WIRE REINF MESH

POLYETHELENE FILM

4" CRUSHED STONE

1" RIGID INSULATION

FILL CORE

$\frac{1}{2}$" PARGING

6" DRAIN TILE

CRUSHED STONE

8" x 8" x 16" CONC. BLOCK

8" x 16" CONC. FOOTING

$\frac{1}{2}$" DIAM. REINF. RODS

Figure 8   Section A through the laundry of the M residence.

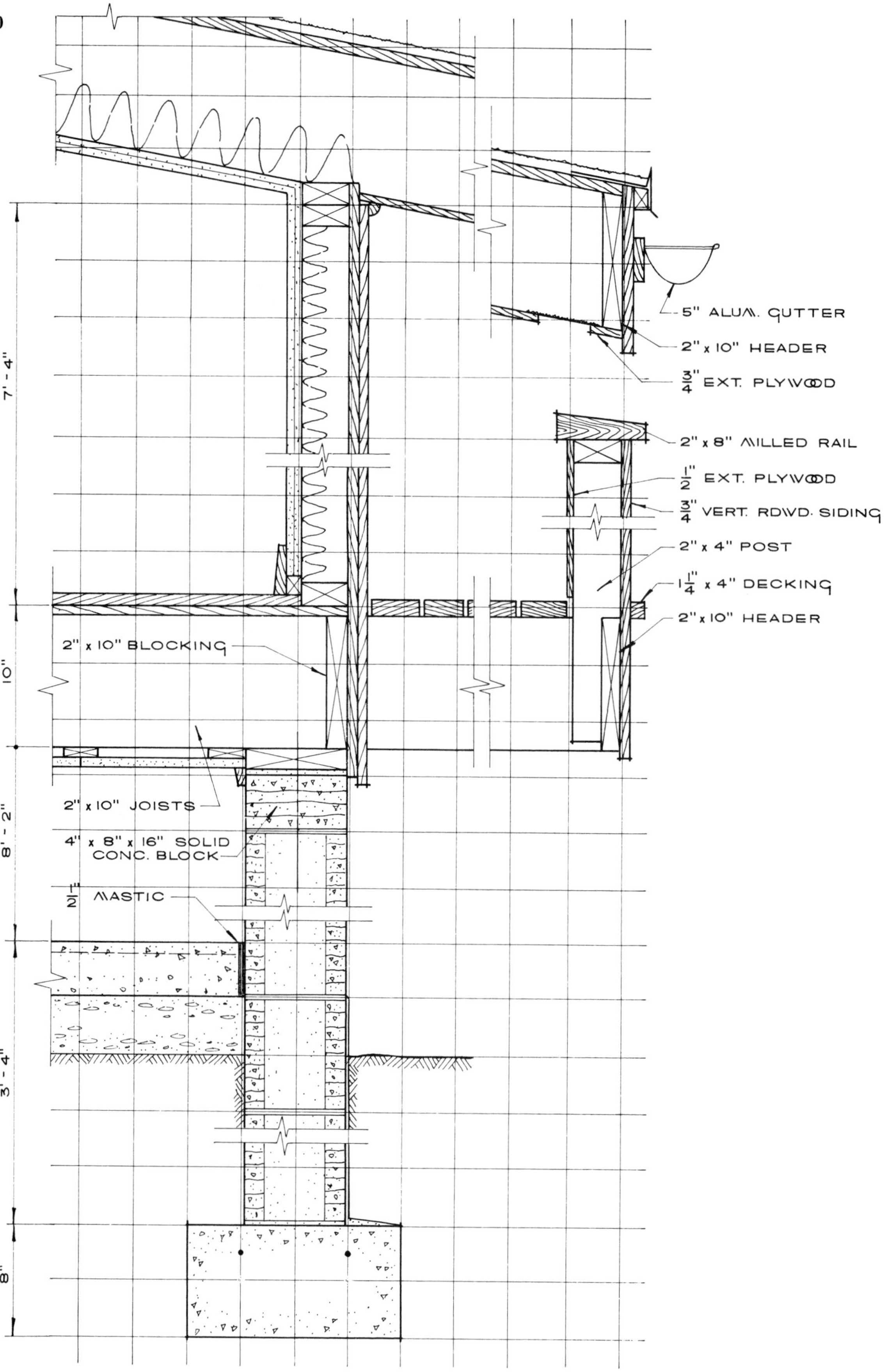

390

5" ALUM. GUTTER

2" x 10" HEADER

$\frac{3}{4}$" EXT. PLYWOOD

2" x 8" MILLED RAIL

$\frac{1}{2}$" EXT. PLYWOOD

$\frac{3}{4}$" VERT. RDWD. SIDING

2" x 4" POST

$1\frac{1}{4}$" x 4" DECKING

2" x 10" HEADER

7' - 4"

10"

2" x 10" BLOCKING

8' - 2"

2" x 10" JOISTS

4" x 8" x 16" SOLID
CONC. BLOCK

$\frac{1}{2}$" MASTIC

3' - 4"

8"

Figure 9   Section B through bedrooms of the M residence.

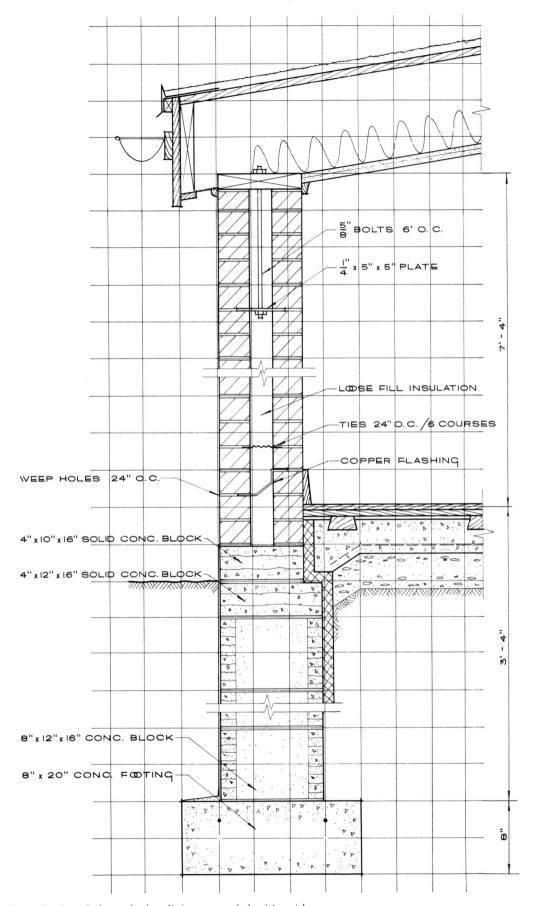

$\frac{5}{8}"$ BOLTS 6' O.C.

$\frac{1}{4}"$ x 5" x 5" PLATE

LOOSE FILL INSULATION

TIES 24" O.C. /6 COURSES

COPPER FLASHING

WEEP HOLES 24" O.C.

4" x 10" x 16" SOLID CONC. BLOCK

4" x 12" x 16" SOLID CONC. BLOCK

8" x 12" x 16" CONC. BLOCK

8" x 20" CONC. FOOTING

7'-4"

3'-4"

8"

Figure 10   Section C through the dining area of the M residence.

WINDOW SCHEDULE

MK	NO	MANUF.	STOCK	TYPE	R. O.	REMARKS
A	13			FIXED	3'-3"	$\frac{1}{4}$" PLATE
B	1	ANDERSEN	41402	BEAUTY-LINE	7'-8$\frac{1}{2}$"	
C	3	"	41401	"	3'-10$\frac{1}{2}$"	
D	1	"	29402	"	5'-8$\frac{1}{2}$"	
E	1	"	29403	"	8'-6$\frac{1}{2}$"	
F	1	"	41242	"	7'-8$\frac{1}{2}$"	
G	1	"	41403	"	11'-6$\frac{1}{2}$"	
H	1	"	41412	FLEXIVENT	4'-1$\frac{1}{2}$"	

DOOR SCHEDULE

MK	NO	SIZE	TYPE	MTL.	FINISH	RMKS.
1	1	2'-10"x 7'-0 x 1$\frac{3}{4}$"	SOLID CORE	PINE	PAINTED	
2	5	2'-10"x 6'-8"x 1$\frac{3}{4}$"	"	"	"	
3	4	3'-2"x 6'-8" x 1$\frac{3}{8}$"	HOLLOW CORE	BIRCH	NATURAL	SLIDING
4	2	2'-10"x 6'-8"x 1$\frac{3}{8}$"	"	PINE	PAINTED	"
5	3	2'-8"x 6'-8"x 1$\frac{3}{8}$"	"	BIRCH	NATURAL	
6	12	2'-6"x 6'-8" x 1$\frac{3}{8}$"	"	"	"	"
7	4	2'-8"x 6'-8" x 1$\frac{3}{8}$"	"	"	"	

MATERIAL SCHEDULE

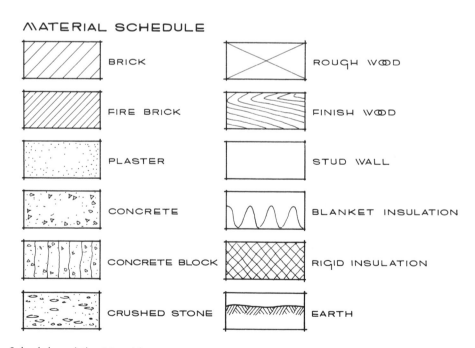

BRICK

ROUGH WOOD

FIRE BRICK

FINISH WOOD

PLASTER

STUD WALL

CONCRETE

BLANKET INSULATION

CONCRETE BLOCK

RIGID INSULATION

CRUSHED STONE

EARTH

Figure 11   Schedules of the M residence.

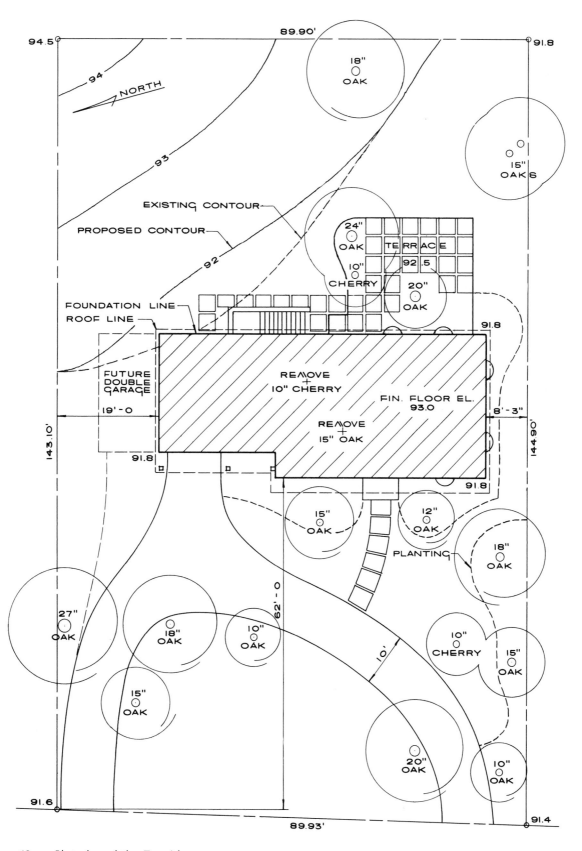

Figure 12   Plot plan of the Z residence.

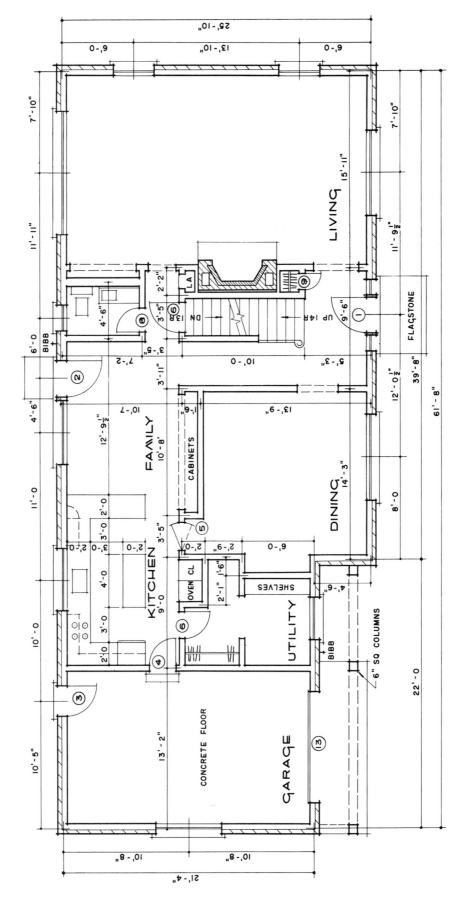

Figure 13   First floor plan of the Z residence.

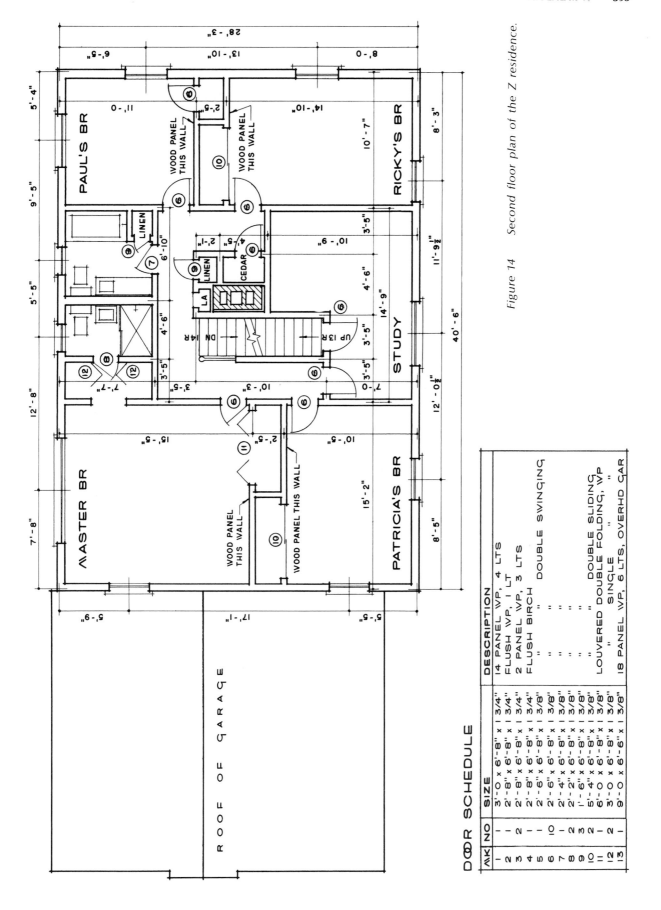

Figure 14   Second floor plan of the Z residence.

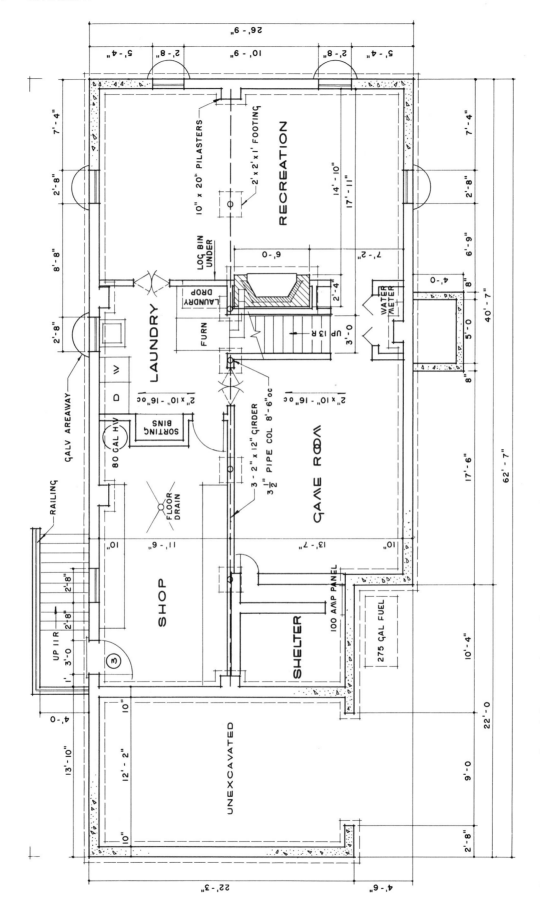

Figure 15   Basement plan of the Z residence (future construction shown in red).

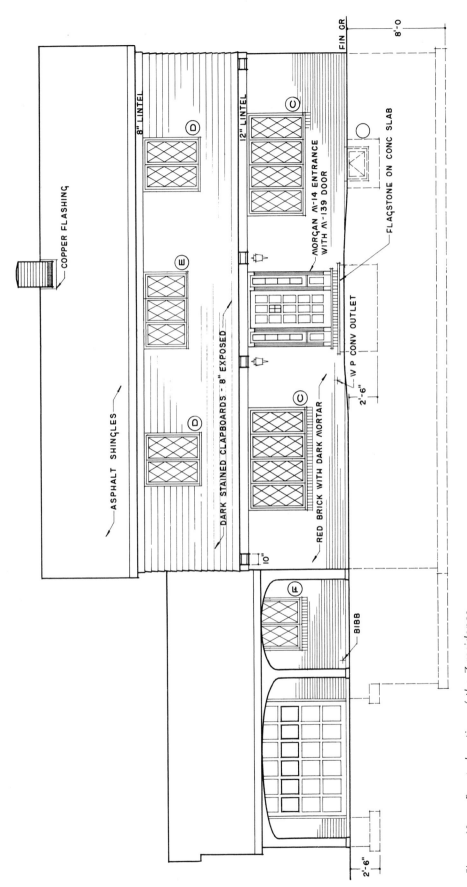

Figure 16   Front elevation of the Z residence.

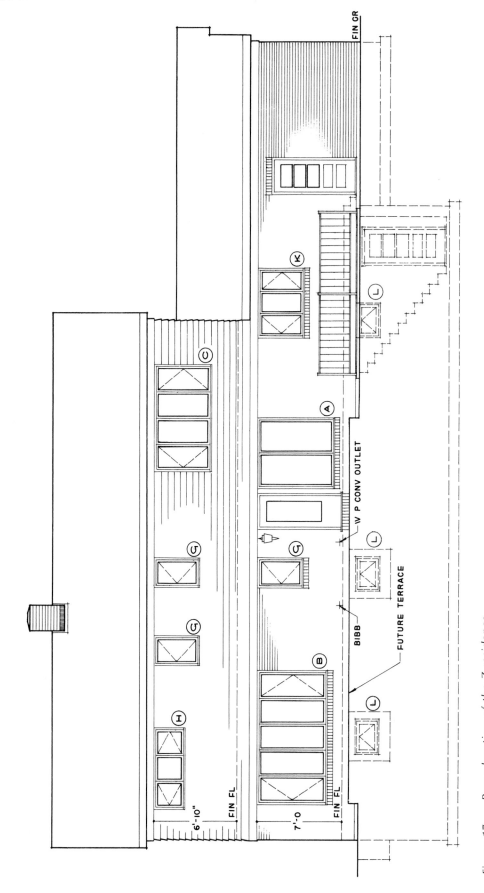

Figure 17   Rear elevation of the Z residence.

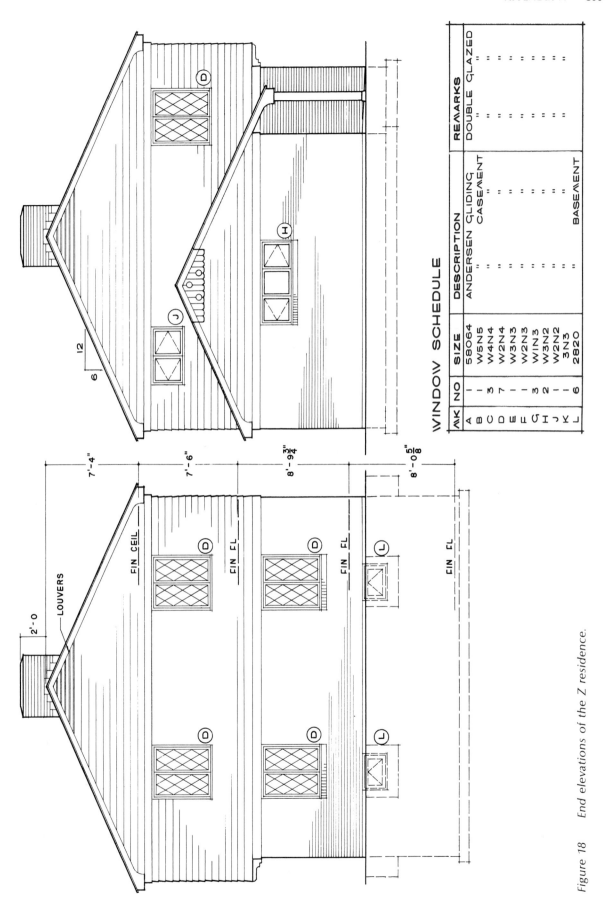

WINDOW SCHEDULE

MK	NO	SIZE	DESCRIPTION	REMARKS
A	1	58064	ANDERSEN GLIDING	DOUBLE GLAZED
B		W5N5	CASEMENT	" "
C	3	W4N4	"	" "
D	7	W2N4	"	" "
E		W3N3	"	" "
F	3	W2N3	"	" "
G		WIN3	"	" "
H	2	W3N2	"	" "
I		W2N2	"	" "
J	1	3N3	"	" "
K				
L	6	2820	BASEMENT	" "

Figure 18   End elevations of the Z residence.

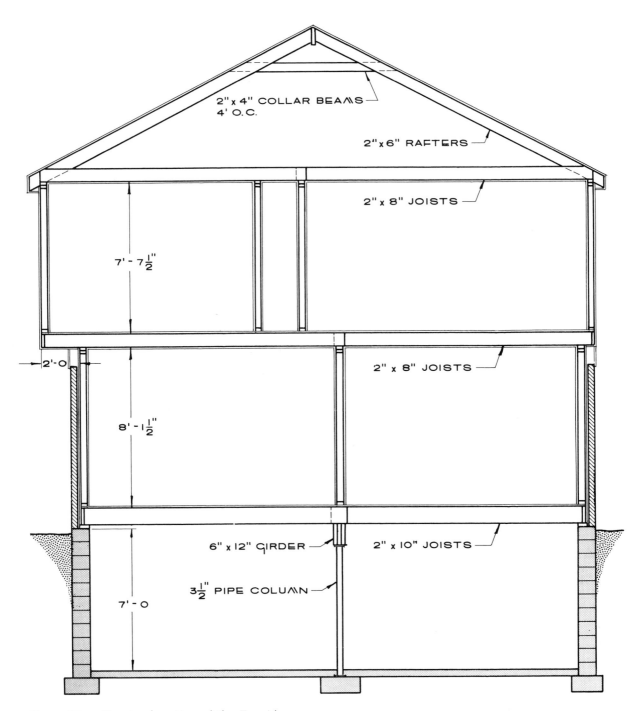

Figure 19   Structural section of the Z residence.

401

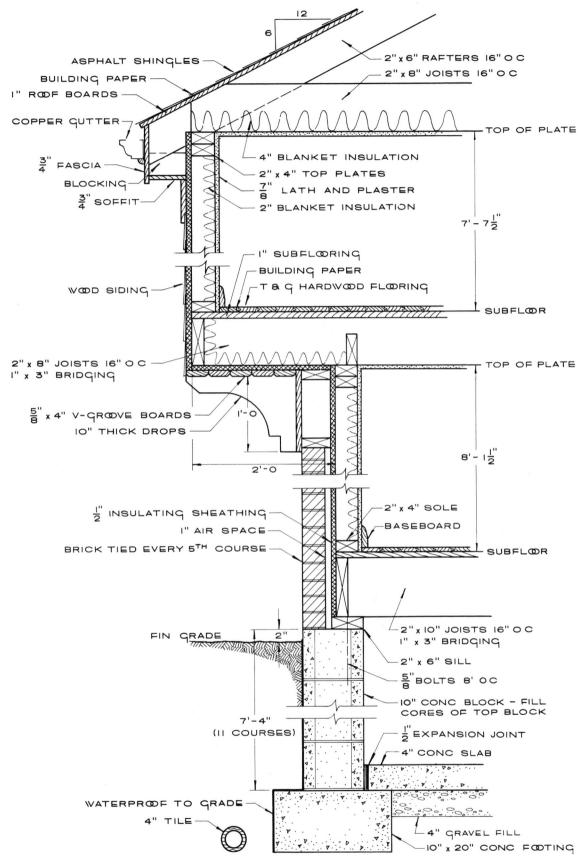

Figure 20   Typical section of the Z residence.

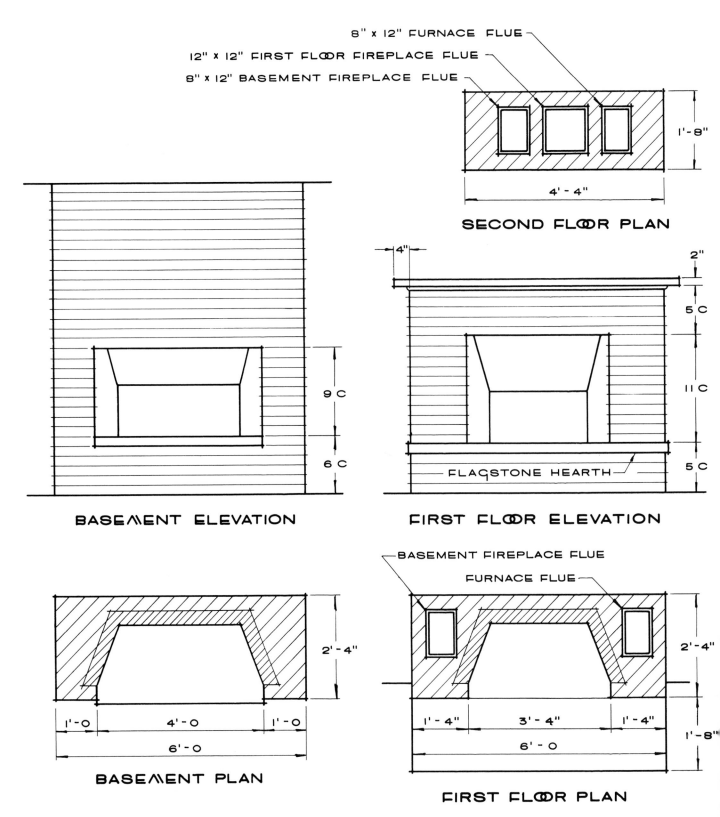

8" x 12" FURNACE FLUE

12" x 12" FIRST FLOOR FIREPLACE FLUE

8" x 12" BASEMENT FIREPLACE FLUE

1'-8"

4'-4"

SECOND FLOOR PLAN

4"

2"

5 C

11 C

9 C

6 C

FLAGSTONE HEARTH

5 C

BASEMENT ELEVATION

FIRST FLOOR ELEVATION

BASEMENT FIREPLACE FLUE

FURNACE FLUE

2'-4"

2'-4"

1'-0   4'-0   1'-0

6'-0

1'-4"   3'-4"   1'-4"

6'-0

1'-8"

BASEMENT PLAN

FIRST FLOOR PLAN

Figure 21   Fireplace details of the Z residence.

403

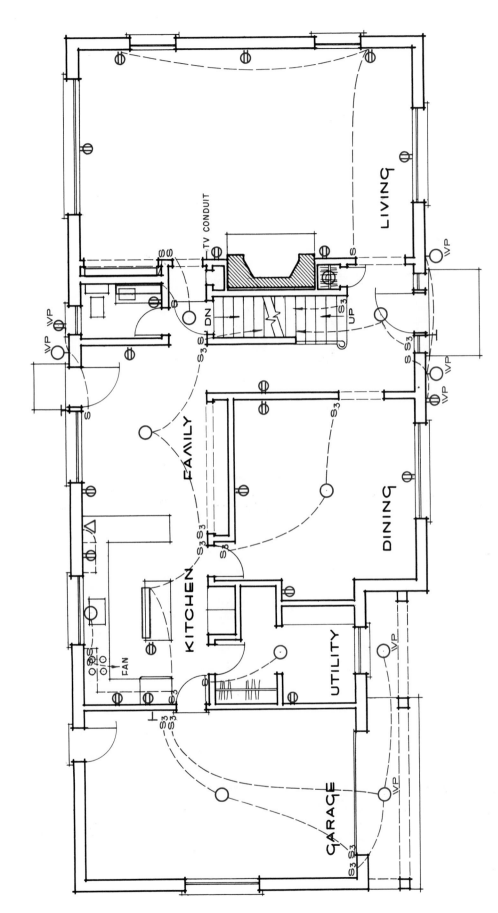

Figure 22   Electrical plan of the Z residence.

Figure 23   Rendering of the Z residence.

appendix b   windows

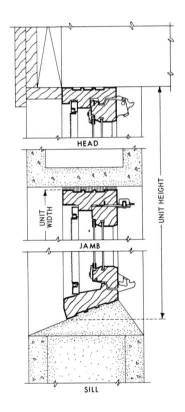

HEAD

UNIT WIDTH

JAMB

UNIT HEIGHT

SILL

BASEMENT WINDOW IN
CONCRETE BLOCK WALL

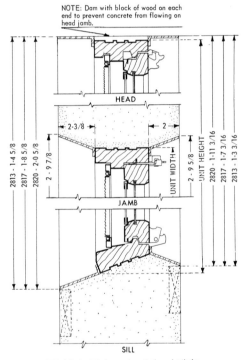

NOTE: Dam with block of wood on each
end to prevent concrete from flowing on
head jamb.

HEAD

2-3/8   2

2 - 9 7/8   UNIT WIDTH   2 - 9 5/8

JAMB

2813 - 1-4 5/8
2817 - 1-8 5/8
2820 - 2-0 5/8

UNIT HEIGHT
2820 - 1-11 3/16
2817 - 1-7 3/16
2813 - 1-3 3/16

SILL

NOTE: Split Steel Bucks are shown in these details for
the purpose of positioning window in wall form. Sash and
screen must be removed from frame when using split bucks
in order to bolt assembly together and to drive nails into
wall form. Temporary cleats shown in sill sections are
for resting assembled buck in position while securing
to wall form. Only one cleat needed depending on whether
inner or outer wall form is erected first. Cleat must be
removed after split buck assembly is nailed to form.

BASEMENT WINDOW IN
POURED CONCRETE WALL

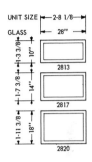

UNIT SIZE 2-8 1/8
GLASS   28"

1-3 3/8   10"   2813

1-7 3/8   14"   2817

1-11 3/8 18"   2820

MODULAR SIZES: Fit typical 8 x 16 inch
block walls for masonry openings 2 blocks
wide by 2, 2-1/2, or 3 blocks high. All three
sizes glazed one light only.

ANDERSEN BASEMENT
WINDOW - TABLE OF SIZES

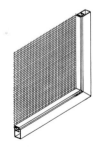

Corner section of aluminum
framed screen.

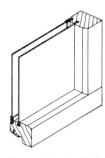

Corner section of sash with
Removable Double Glazing
panel applied.

Figure 1   *Andersen basement window.*

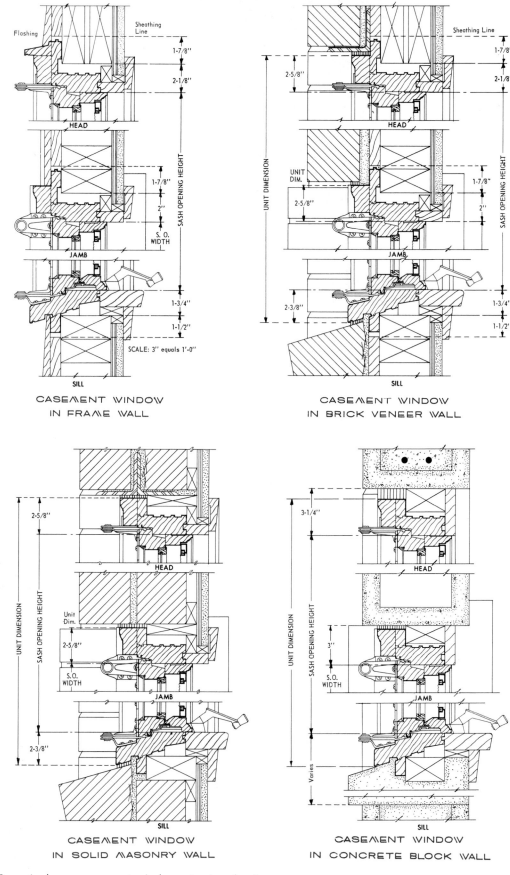

Figure 2 Andersen casement window—tracing details.

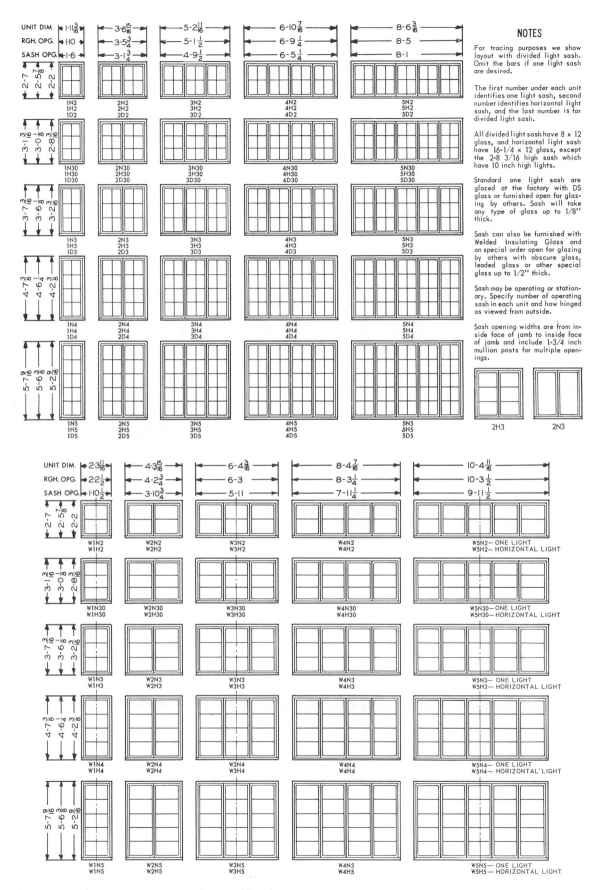

Figure 3   *Andersen casement window—table of sizes.*

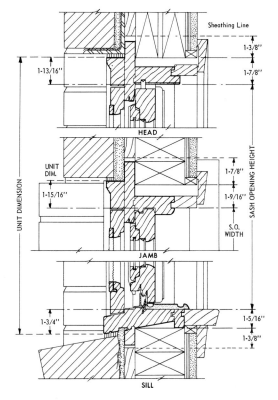

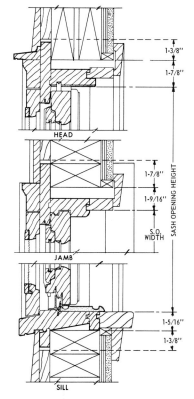

SLIDING WINDOW IN BRICK VENEER WALL

SLIDING WINDOW IN FRAME WALL

Figure 4   *Andersen sliding window —tracing details.*

STOCK SIZES AND LAYOUTS

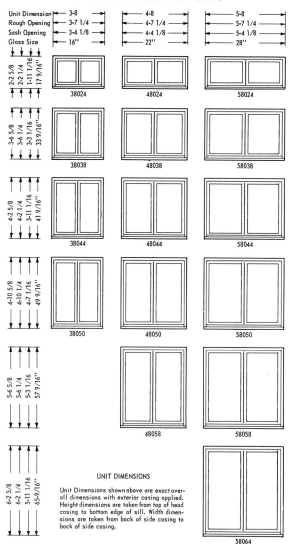

UNIT DIMENSIONS

Unit Dimensions shown above are exact over-all dimensions with exterior casing applied. Height dimensions are taken from top of head casing to bottom edge of sill. Width dimensions are taken from back of side casing to back of side casing.

All openings shown are single units having two sash that slide past each other and are in the same plane when closed. All sash furnished one light.

MULTIPLE OPENINGS

Multiple openings are formed by joining single units with side casings back to back and sill horns butt jointed to form 4-inch modular mullions, or jambs can be placed back to back to form a 2-inch narrow mullion. In either case lugs on back of jambs must be cut off.

The overall unit dimension width for a multiple unit using the 4-inch mullion is the sum of the single unit dimension widths. For the overall rough stud opening width, deduct 3/4-inch from the overall unit dimension.

Figure 5   *Andersen sliding window— table of sizes.*

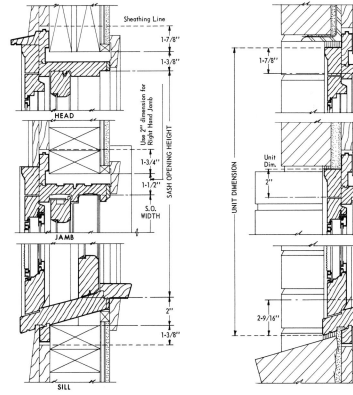

DOUBLE HUNG WINDOW IN FRAME WALL

DOUBLE HUNG WINDOW
IN BRICK VENEER WALL

Figure 6   Andersen double hung window—tracing details.

STOCK SIZES AND LAYOUTS

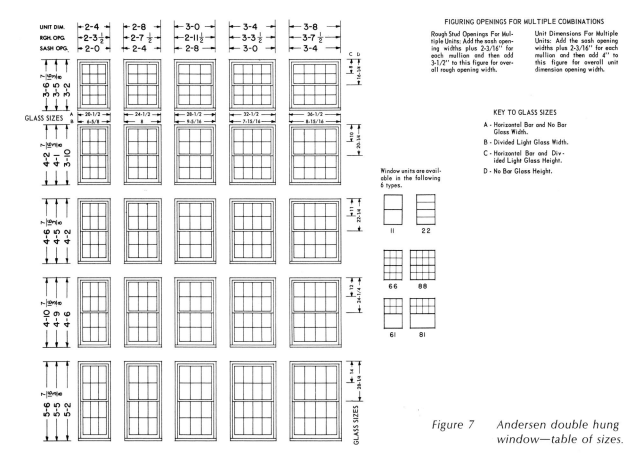

FIGURING OPENINGS FOR MULTIPLE COMBINATIONS

Rough Stud Openings For Multiple Units: Add the sash opening widths plus 2-3/16'' for each mullion and then add 3-1/2'' to this figure for overall rough opening width.

Unit Dimensions For Multiple Units: Add the sash opening widths plus 2-3/16'' for each mullion and then add 4'' to this figure for overall unit dimension opening width.

KEY TO GLASS SIZES

A - Horizontal Bar and No Bar Glass Width.

B - Divided Light Glass Width.

C - Horizontal Bar and Divided Light Glass Height.

D - No Bar Glass Height.

Window units are available in the following 6 types.

Figure 7   Andersen double hung window—table of sizes.

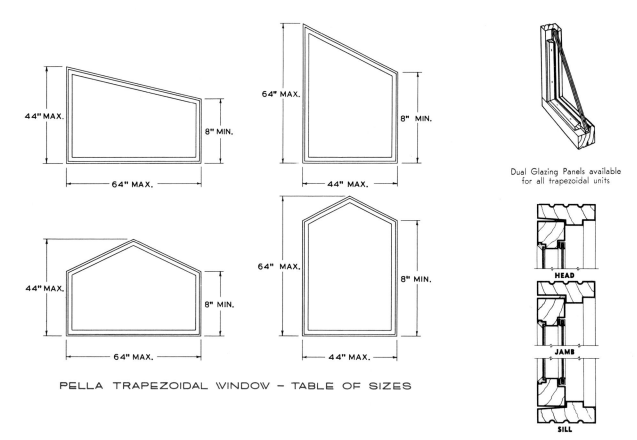

PELLA TRAPEZOIDAL WINDOW – TABLE OF SIZES

Dual Glazing Panels available
for all trapezoidal units

HEAD

JAMB

SILL

PELLA TRACING DETAIL

Figure 8   Trapezoidal fixed windows.

appendix c   doors

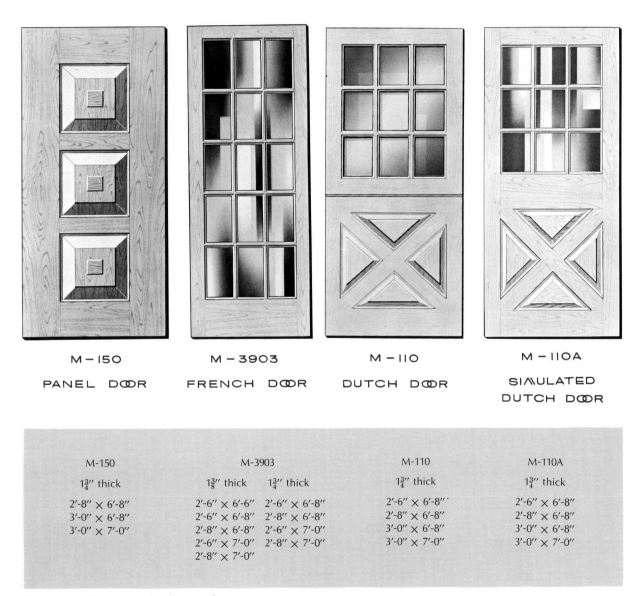

M – 150	M – 3903	M – 110	M – 110A
PANEL DOOR	FRENCH DOOR	DUTCH DOOR	SIMULATED DUTCH DOOR

M-150	M-3903		M-110	M-110A
$1\frac{3}{4}''$ thick	$1\frac{3}{8}''$ thick	$1\frac{3}{4}''$ thick	$1\frac{3}{4}''$ thick	$1\frac{3}{4}''$ thick
2'-8'' × 6'-8''	2'-6'' × 6'-6''	2'-6'' × 6'-8''	2'-6'' × 6'-8''	2'-6'' × 6'-8''
3'-0'' × 6'-8''	2'-6'' × 6'-8''	2'-8'' × 6'-8''	2'-8'' × 6'-8''	2'-8'' × 6'-8''
3'-0'' × 7'-0''	2'-8'' × 6'-8''	2'-6'' × 7'-0''	3'-0'' × 6'-8''	3'-0'' × 6'-8''
	2'-6'' × 7'-0''	2'-8'' × 7'-0''	3'-0'' × 7'-0''	3'-0'' × 7'-0''
	2'-8'' × 7'-0''			

Figure 1   Some exterior door styles.

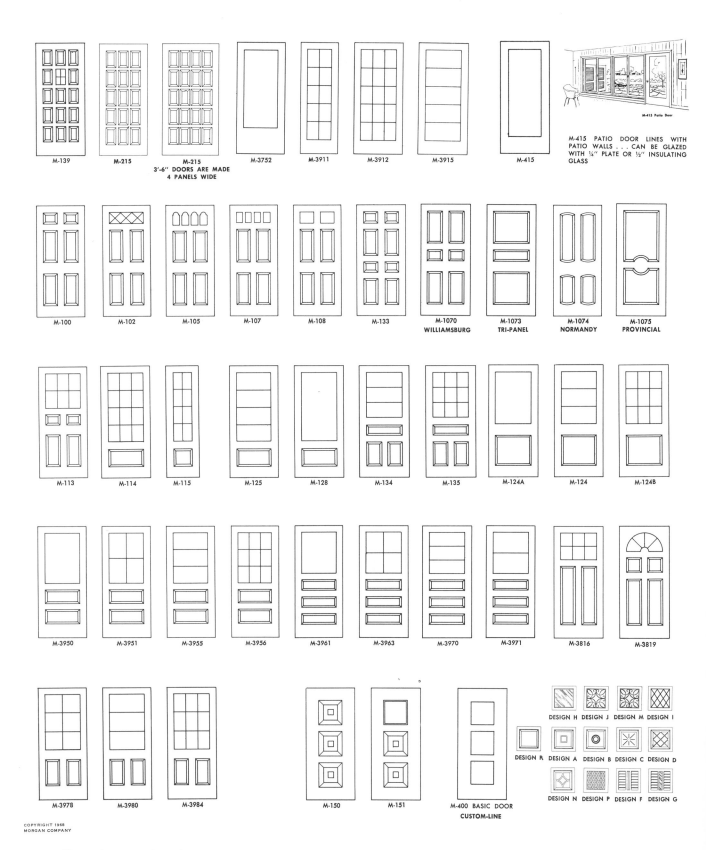

M-139
M-215
M-215
3'-6" DOORS ARE MADE
4 PANELS WIDE
M-3752
M-3911
M-3912
M-3915
M-415

M-415 PATIO DOOR LINES WITH
PATIO WALLS . . . CAN BE GLAZED
WITH ¼" PLATE OR ½" INSULATING
GLASS

M-100
M-102
M-105
M-107
M-108
M-133
M-1070
WILLIAMSBURG
M-1073
TRI-PANEL
M-1074
NORMANDY
M-1075
PROVINCIAL

M-113
M-114
M-115
M-125
M-128
M-134
M-135
M-124A
M-124
M-124B

M-3950
M-3951
M-3955
M-3956
M-3961
M-3963
M-3970
M-3971
M-3816
M-3819

M-3978
M-3980
M-3984
M-150
M-151
M-400 BASIC DOOR
CUSTOM-LINE

DESIGN H   DESIGN J   DESIGN M   DESIGN I

DESIGN R   DESIGN A   DESIGN B   DESIGN C   DESIGN D

DESIGN N   DESIGN P   DESIGN F   DESIGN G

Figure 1   *continued*

Units Made in the Following Sizes

2-Door units (M-2FD)		4-Door Units (M-4FD)	
Width of Doors	Jamb Opening Width	Width of Doors	Jamb Opening Width
$11\frac{11}{16}''$	2'-0	$8\frac{11}{16}''$	3'-0
$1'-1\frac{11}{16}$	2'-4''	$11\frac{11}{16}''$	4'-0
$1'-2\frac{11}{16}$	2'-6''	$1'-2\frac{11}{16}''$	5'-0
$1'-3\frac{11}{16}$	2'-8''	$1'-5\frac{11}{16}''$	6'-0
$1'-5\frac{11}{16}$	3'-0		

Units are made with doors 6'-6'', 6'-8'', and 8'-0 in height. Units are made only in the standard sizes and specifications listed.

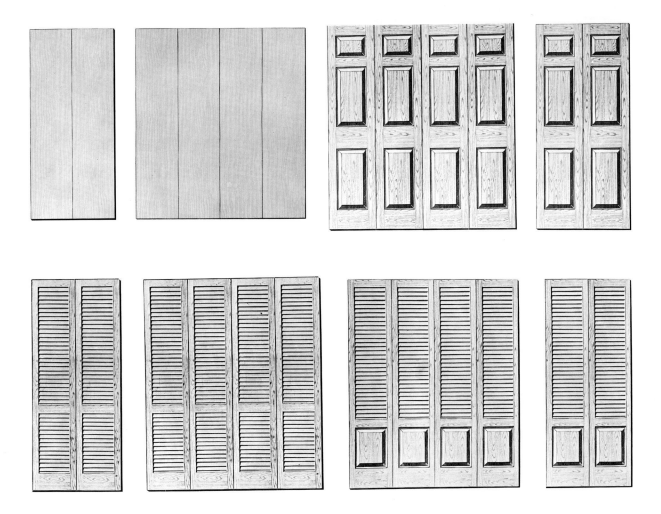

Figure 2   Some folding interior door styles.

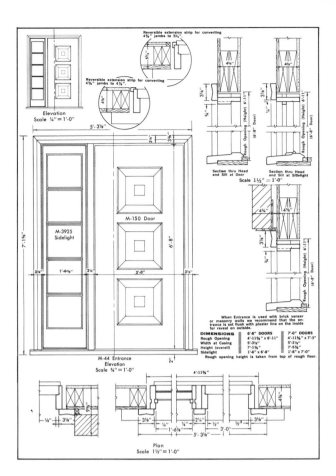

Figure 3   Morgan entrances—details and sizes.

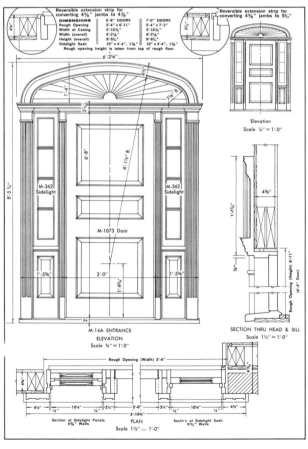

Figure 4   Morgan entrances—details and sizes.

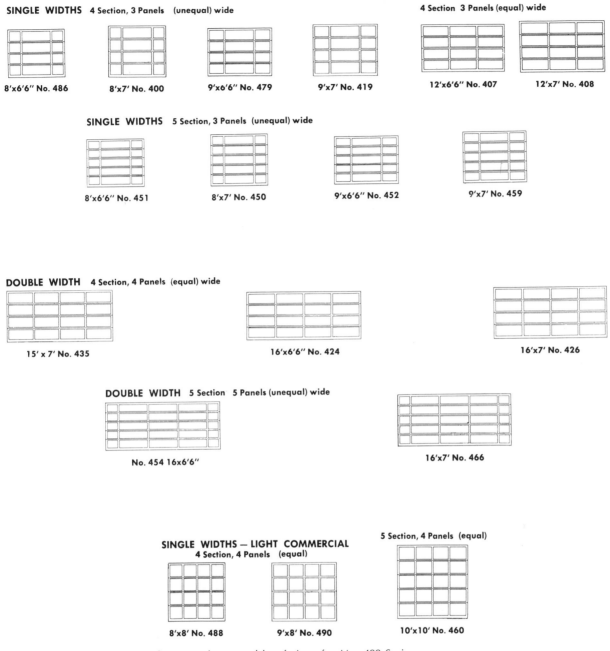

SINGLE WIDTHS   4 Section, 3 Panels   (unequal) wide

8'x6'6" No. 486   8'x7' No. 400   9'x6'6" No. 479   9'x7' No. 419

4 Section 3 Panels (equal) wide

12'x6'6" No. 407   12'x7' No. 408

SINGLE WIDTHS   5 Section, 3 Panels (unequal) wide

8'x6'6" No. 451   8'x7' No. 450   9'x6'6" No. 452   9'x7' No. 459

DOUBLE WIDTH   4 Section, 4 Panels (equal) wide

15' x 7' No. 435   16'x6'6" No. 424   16'x7' No. 426

DOUBLE WIDTH   5 Section 5 Panels (unequal) wide

No. 454 16x6'6"   16'x7' No. 466

SINGLE WIDTHS — LIGHT COMMERCIAL
4 Section, 4 Panels (equal)

5 Section, 4 Panels (equal)

8'x8' No. 488   9'x8' No. 490   10'x10' No. 460

Figure 5   Frantz sectional garage doors—table of sizes for No. 400 Series.

appendix d   bibliography

There are numerous publications on the various phases of architectural drafting and design. Those listed here were selected as being the most helpful and because they are commonly found in architectural libraries or drafting rooms. In addition to these references, you will probably find in the drafting room a file of available building materials and specifications. This file will be useful to you in determining materials.

REFERENCE BOOKS

Callendar, J. H., *Time-Saver Standards, 4th Ed.* New York: McGraw-Hill Book Co.
Similar to *Architectural Graphic Standards* in its graphic approach, but with emphasis on planning and design rather than on details. Thoroughly cross-referenced. This book is found in nearly every architectural drafting room.

Ramsey, C. G., and Sleeper, H. R., *Architectural Graphic Standards, 6th Ed.* New York: John Wiley and Sons, Inc. This book is at the elbow of nearly every practicing architect, and you should become familiar with its contents. It attempts to confine in only one volume all the factual information required by the architect. You will notice immediately the absence of written material. This is to be expected, because those trained in the graphic language will find more information more quickly from a graphic presentation. Since the book's usefulness is dependent on the index, extensive cross-indexing is provided.

Sweet's Architectural Catalog File. New York: F. W. Dodge Corp.
Any company manufacturing a consumer product usually publishes a pamphlet describing it. *Sweet's Catalog* is a file of those pamphlets which the architect might find occasion to use. There are twelve volumes, each indexed at the front by firms, products, and trade names. In addition to the architectural file, *Sweet's* has a four-volume *Industrial Construction Catalog File,* a two-volume *Plant Engineering Catalog File,* a two-volume *Product Design Catalog File,* and a one-volume *Metal Working Equipment Catalog File.* Before specifying any item, check with *Sweet's* catalog to see that it is the best available.

HISTORY OF ARCHITECTURE

Fletcher, Sir Banister, *A History of Architecture.* New York: Charles Scribner's Sons.
A well-known text on architecture from the Egyptians to the present.

Hamlin, Talbot, *Architecture Through the Ages.* New York: G. P. Putnam's Sons.
Western architecture from primitive to modern.

Joedicke, Jurgen, *A History of Modern Architecture.* New York: Frederick A. Praeger, Publisher.
The origins of modern architecture in the nineteenth and twentieth centuries.

Pevsner, Nikolaus, *European Architecture.* Baltimore: Penguin Books, Inc.
European architecture from the sixth to the twentieth century.

Safdie, Moshe, *Beyond Habitat*. Cambridge, Massachusetts: The M.I.T. Press.
A young architect's statement of ideals.

Whiffen, Marcus, *American Architecture Since 1780: A Guide to the Styles*. Cambridge, Massachusetts: The M.I.T. Press.
A study of the exteriors of American buildings from 1780 to present.

Withey & Withey, *Biographical Dictionary of American Architects (Deceased)*. Los Angeles: Hennessey & Ingalls, Inc.
Biographies of 2000 American architects, arranged alphabetically.

ARCHITECTURAL DRAWING

Bellis, H. F., and Schmidt, W. A., *Architectural Drafting*. New York: McGraw-Hill Book Co.
A condensed paperback text on architectural drawing.

Buss, Truman C., *Simplified Architectural Drawing*. Chicago: American Technical Society. A fairly complete text on architectural history, drawing, and rendering.

Goodban, W. T., and Hayslett. J. J., *Architectural Drawing and Planning*. New York: McGraw-Hill Book Co.
Volume five of McGraw-Hill's Technical Education Series.
Contains good pencil illustrations.

Hepler, D., and Wallach, P., *Architecture—Drafting and Design*. New York: McGraw-Hill Book Co.
A very well done and complete high school text.

Hornung, William J., *Architectural Drafting*. Englewood Cliffs, N.J.: Prentice-Hall, Inc.
A popular technical institute textbook on architectural drawing.

Muller, Edward J., *Architectural Drawing and Light Construction*. Englewood Cliffs, N.J.: Prentice-Hall, Inc.
A popular technical institute textbook with fine pencil illustrations.

Patten, L. M., and Rogness, M. L., *Architectural Drafting*. Dubuque, Iowa: Wm. C. Brown Co.
An extremely condensed text with excellent contemporary illustrations on drawing and rendering.

Stegman, G. K., and Stegman, H. J., *Architectural Drafting*. Chicago: American Technical Society.
A complete work by a father-son team, with two-color illustrations.

COMPUTER GRAPHICS

Clark, W. E., *The Computer in Building Design and Construction: Graphical Input and Output Forms*. Building Research, March/April 1966.
Computer applications in building design.

Computer Drafting Speeds Motel Design. Progressive Architecture, Sept. 1968.
Computer use by the world's largest motel designer.

Computer Graphics: Viewing the Future Plantscape. Landscape Architecture, Oct. 1967.
Computer use in landscape design.

Davis, M. R., and Ellis, T. O., *The RAND Tablet: A Man-Machine Graphical Communication Device*. Information Display, July/August 1967.
Use of the RAND pen and tablet.

Fetter, W. A., *Computer Graphics in Communication*. New York: McGraw-Hill Book Co.
One paperback volume of the Engineering Graphics Monograph Series.

French, T. E., and Vierck, C. J., *A Manual of Engineering Drawing for Students and Draftsmen, 8th Ed*. New York: McGraw-Hill Book Co.
See chapters 16 and 17.

Harper, G. N., *Computer Application in Architecture and Engineering*. New York: McGraw-Hill Book Co.
Practical uses of the computer in architecture.

Mann, R. W., and Coons, S. A., *Computer-Aided Design*. New York: McGraw-Hill Book Co.
A section of the McGraw-Hill Yearbook of Science and Technology written by two computer graphics pioneers.

Michael, G., *A Survey of Graphic Data Processing Equipment for Computers*. Englewood Cliffs, N.J.: Prentice-Hall, Inc.
A section of *Computers and the Policy Making Community*, Bobrow and Schwartz, editors.

Miline, M., *Computer Graphics in Architecture and Design*. Yale School of Art and Architecture, 1969.

Negroponte, N., *The Architecture Machine*. Cambridge, Mass.: The M.I.T. Press.
A look to the future where genuine man-machine dialogue is achieved.

Siders, R. A., *et al.*, *Computer Graphics, A Revolution in Design*. New York: American Management Association.

Sutherland, I., *Computer Graphics*. Datamation, May 1966.
Written by a pioneer in the design of light pen systems.

3-D Plotting Systems. Goleta, California: Spatial Data Systems, Inc.

Wood, R. C., and Hendren, P., *A Flexible Computer Graphic System for Architectural Design*. Information Display, pp. 35–40, March/April 1968.

PERSPECTIVES AND RENDERING

Halse, Albert O., *Architectural Rendering*. New York: F. W. Dodge Corp.
An excellent text on rendering, with color illustrations.

Martin, C. Leslie, *Architectural Graphics*. New York: The Macmillan Company.
Paperback text on multiviews, pictorials, and shadows.

Martin, C. Leslie, *Design Graphics*. New York: The Macmillan Company.
Well done hardback text on multiviews, pictorials, shadows, and rendering.

McCartney, T. O., *Precision Perspective Drawing*. New York: McGraw-Hill Book Co.
Written for the professional illustrator.

Thomas, T. A., *Technical Illustration*. New York: McGraw-Hill Book Co.
A practical book with several chapters on special mechanical equipment.

Wilson, Grace, *et al.*, *Geometry for Architects*. Champaign, Ill.: Stipes Publishing Company.
Paperback text on multiviews, pictorials, and shadows.

ARCHITECTURAL MODELING

Hohauser, Sanford, *Architectural and Interior Models*. New York: Van Nostrand Reinhold Company.

An excellent treatment of the design and construction of models. Beautifully illustrated.

Taylor, J. R., *Model Building for Architects and Engineers.* New York: McGraw-Hill Book Co.
Complete explanations of professional modeling techniques.

HOUSE PLANNING

Dunning, W. J., and Robin, L. P., *Home Planning and Architectural Drawing.* New York: John Wiley & Sons, Inc.
A brief, easily read text.

Hodgell, M. R., *Contemporary Farmhouses.* Urbana, Ill.: University of Illinois Press.
Contains numerous single-floor house plans and an abbreviated text.

Simon, Maron J. (ed.), *Your Solar House.* New York: Simon and Schuster, Inc.
Contains 49 solar house plans, each by a different architect.

Townsend, Gilbert, *et al., How To Plan a House, 3rd Ed.* Chicago: American Technical Society.
A fine textbook on home planning.

HOUSE CONSTRUCTION

Hornung, William J., *Blueprint Reading.* Englewood Cliffs, N.J.: Prentice-Hall.
A practical guide for rapid mastery of blueprint reading.

McGuinness, William J., *et al., Mechanical and Electrical Equipment for Buildings.* New York: John Wiley & Sons, Inc.
A complete college text for architectural engineering students.

Minimum Property Standards for One and Two Living Units. Washington, D.C.: Federal Housing Authority.
Gives the minimum level of construction quality acceptable to the FHA.

Morris, Howard H. *How To Build a Better Home.* Westport, Conn.: The Westport Publishing Co.
An excellent reference which is unfortunately out of print. However, copies are in most architectural libraries.

Parker, Harry, *et al., Materials and Methods of Architectural Construction, 3rd Ed.* New York: John Wiley & Sons, Inc.
Another complete college text for architectural engineering students.

Standard Construction Details for Home Builders. Washington, D.C. (2524 L St., N.W.): Standard Home Company.
Dimensioned pictorials of construction practices with estimating charts and tables.

LUMBER

Fine Hardwoods Selectorama. Chicago, Ill. (666 N. Lake Shore Drive): Fine Hardwoods Association.
A guide to the selection and use of foreign and domestic hardwoods. Shows veneer matching to achieve various patterns.

Hardwood Plywood Manual. Arlington, Va. (2310 S. Walter Reed Drive): Hardwood Plywood Institute.
A college manual.

What You Should Know About Lumber. Washington, D.C. (1619 Massachusetts Ave., N.W.): National Lumber Manufacturers Association.

How to identify the main hardwood and softwood species. How to classify wood by trees, manufacture, uses, sizes, and grades.

Wood Handbook. Washington, D.C.: U.S. Department of Agriculture.
Detailed information on wood, its properties and uses.

WOOD CONSTRUCTION

Douglas Fir Use Book. Portland, Ore. (1410 S.W. Morrison St.): West Coast Lumberman's Association.
Tables for the design of sawn and glued laminated Douglas Fir structures.

Heavy Timber Construction Details. Washington, D.C.: National Lumber Manufacturers Association.
Framing and fastening details of heavy timber construction.

Light Frame House Construction. Washington, D.C.: U.S. Department of Health, Education, and Welfare.
Vocational text designed for carpenters.

Maximum Spans for Joists and Rafters. Washington, D.C.: National Lumber Manufacturers Association.
Tables for joists and rafters used in residential construction.

Modern Timber Engineering. New Orleans, La. (National Bank of Commerce Bldg.): Southern Pine Association.
College text and guide for architectural engineers on fundamentals of timber engineering, with examples of truss design, timber joints, and bridge floor systems.

Southern Pine Manual of Standard Wood Construction. New Orleans, La.: Southern Pine Association.
Tables, formulas, and information on standard lumber construction.

Typical Designs of Timber Structures. Rockville, Md. (487 S. Stonstreet Ave.): Timber Engineering Company.
Dimensioned drawings of standard trusses.

Unicom Method of House Construction. Washington, D.C.: National Lumber Manufacturers Association.
Two illustrated reference manuals on the Unicom system.

Wood Structural Design Data. Washington, D.C.: National Lumber Manufacturers Association.
Data and tables include mechanical and physical properties of lumber, terminology, costs, symbols, design formulas, and load tables for beams, columns, stud walls, floors, and truss members.

MASONRY CONSTRUCTION

Besser Concrete Masonry. Alpena, Mich: Besser Company.
Gives shapes and sizes of various concrete blocks.

Concrete Masonry Handbook. Chicago, Ill. (33 Grand Ave.): Portland Cement Association.
Sixty page manual including masonry tracing details.

Principles of Clay Masonry Construction. Washington, D.C.: Structural Clay Products Institute.
A well done 110-page student's manual.

STEEL CONSTRUCTION

Ketchum, Milo S., *Handbook of Standard Structural Details for Buildings.* Englewood Cliffs, N.J.: Prentice-Hall, Inc.

Structural plans of six buildings, each designed for a different type of construction.

Steel Construction Manual. New York: American Institute of Steel Construction.
A complete manual of available sizes of steel shapes.

FIRE PROTECTION

Brannigan, Francis L., *Building Construction for the Fire Service.* National Fire Protection Association, 1971.
A fire officer's guide.

Fire Protection Handbook, 13th Ed. National Fire Protection Association, 1969.
A single-volume encyclopedia on fire and fire control.

Fire-resistant Construction in Modern Steel-framed Buildings. American Institute of Steel Construction, 1959.
A description of common methods of protecting steel members from fire.

Guide to OSHA Fire Protection Regulations. National Fire Protection Association, 1972.
A single-volume guide to the national Occupational Safety and Health Act of 1970.

International Conference on Firesafety in High-rise Buildings. U.S. General Services Administration, 1971.
Proceedings of a conference on fire protection for highrise buildings.

National Fire Codes. National Fire Protection Association, 1973.
A ten-volume encyclopedia of advisory codes widely used as a basis for local codes.

PLASTICS

Dietz, Albert G. H., *Plastics for Architects and Builders.* Cambridge, Massachusetts: The M.I.T. Press.
A polymer primer.

Skeist, Irving, *Plastics in Building.* New York: Reinhold Publishing Corp.
An authoritative work on plastics in construction.

COST ESTIMATING

Means, Robert Snow, *Means' Building Construction Cost Data.* Duxbury, Mass. (P.O. Box 36): R. S. Means.
A standard catalog for cost estimating, providing average prices for a wide variety of building construction items.

National Construction Estimator. Craftsman Book Company, 124 S. La Brea Ave., Los Angeles, California 90036.
A standard catalog for cost estimating, revised annually in February.

SPECIFICATIONS

Abbett, Robert W., *Engineering Contracts and Specifications.* New York: John Wiley & Sons, Inc.
An admirable reference on the business and legal aspects of architecture.

CSI Manual of Practice. Washington, D.C. (1150 Seventeenth St., N.W.): The Construction Specifications Institute, Inc.
The accepted standard of specifications practice. Chapters are published as separate booklets and are continually updated.

Watson, Donald A., *Specifications Writing for Architects and Engineers.* New York: McGraw-Hill Book Co.
A comprehensive guide and reference for "specs" writers.

CAREER GUIDANCE

Opportunities Unlimited for Careers of Prestige and Profit in the Forest Products Industries. Washington, D.C.: National Lumber Manufacturers Association.
Describes educational programs and lists colleges and universities providing those programs.

PERIODICALS

The Architectural Forum. New York (111 W. 57th St.): Urban America.
An excellent professional publication concerned with contemporary design.

Architectural Record. New York: McGraw-Hill Book Co.
Also deals with contemporary design.

Better Homes and Gardens. 1770 W. Hubbard St., Chicago, Ill.
A housekeeping magazine partially devoted to the subject of residential planning.

Design & Environment. 19 W. 44th St., New York, N.Y. 10036.
An interprofessional magazine for architects, city planners, landscape architects, and designers.

Good Housekeeping. 57th St. and 8th Ave., New York, N.Y.
Also partially concerned with residential planning.

House and Home. New York: McGraw-Hill Book Co.
A management publication of the housing industry.

Interiors. New York (18 E. 50th St.): Whitney Publications.
A publication for interior designers of retail stores.

Landscape Architecture. Louisville, Ky. (1500 Bardstown Rd.): ASLA.
Official publication of the American Society of Landscape Architects.

Progressive Architecture. 430 Park Ave., New York, N.Y.
An excellent professional publication on completed and proposed projects.

appendix e   abbreviations

Abbreviations must often be used by architectural draftsmen to fit notes into the available space. However, a list of the abbreviations used should be included on each set of drawings so that the meanings of the abbreviations are perfectly clear to all reading the drawings. The abbreviations shown in this section have been approved by architectural and engineering societies. They are based upon the following rules:

1. Capitals are used almost universally
2. Periods are used only when necessary to avoid a misunderstanding (like the use of *IN.* in place of *IN*)
3. Spaces between letters are used only when necessary to clarify the abbreviation (such as *CU FT* in place of *CUFT*)
4. The same abbreviation may be used for the singular and plural

Abbreviation	ABBREV
Acoustic	ACST
Acoustical plaster	ACST PLAS
Actual	ACT.
Addition	ADD.
Adhesive	ADH
Aggregate	AGGR
Air conditioning	AIR COND
Alternating Current	AC
Aluminum	AL or ALUM
American Institute of Architects	AIA
American Institute of Steel Construction	AISC
American Society for Testing Materials	ASTM
American Society of Heating, Refrigerating, and Air Conditioning Engineers	ASHRAE
American Standards Association	ASA
American wire gauge	AWG
Amount	AMT
Ampere	A or AMP
Anchor Bolt	AB
Angle	L
Apartment	APT
Approved	APP
Approximate	APPROX
Architect, architectural	ARCH
Architectural terra cotta	ATC
Area	A
Asbestos	ASB
Asphalt	ASPH
Assemble	ASSEM
Assembly	ASSY
Associate, association	ASSOC
At	@
Atmospheric pressure	ATM PRESS
Automatic	AUTO
Avenue	AVE
Average	AVG
Balcony	BALC
Barrel, barrels	BBL
Basement	BASMT
Bathroom	B
Beaded one side	B 1S
Beam	BM
Bedroom	BR

Bench mark	BM	Concrete masonry unit	CMU
Better	BTR	Construction	CONST
Between	BET.	Construction Specifications	
Beveled	BEV	Institute	CSI
Blocking	BLKG	Contractor	CONTR
Blower	BLO	Copper	COP or CU
Board	BD	Counter	CTR
Board feet	BD FT or FBM	Countersink	CSK
Board measure	BM	Courses	C
Book shelves	BK SH	Cover	COV
Bottom	BOT	Cross section	X-SECT
Boulevard	BLVD	Cubic	CU
Bracket	BRKT	Cubic feet per minute	CFM
Brass	BR	Cubic foot, feet	CU FT
British thermal unit	BTU	Cubic inch, inches	CU IN
Bronze	BRZ	Cubic yard, yards	CU YD
Broom closet	BC	Cylinder	CYL
Brown & Sharpe gauge	B&S GA		
Building	BLDG	Damper	DMPR
Built-in	BLT-IN	Decibel	DB
Bulletin board	BB	Deep, depth	DP
Button	BUT.	Degree	° or DEG
Buzzer	BUZ	Detail	DET
By	× (as 2′ × 4′)	Diagram	DIAG
		Diameter	ϕ or DIA
Cabinet	CAB.	Dimension	DIM
Candela	cd	Dining room	DR
Candlepower	CP	Direct current	DC
Carpenter	CARP.	Dishwasher	DW
Casing	CSG	Distance	DIST
Cast iron	CI	Ditto	″ or DO
Catch basin	CB	Division	DIV
Caulking	CLKG	Door	DR
Ceiling	CLG	Dozen	DOZ
Cement	CEM	Double hung	DH
Cement floor	CEM FL	Dowel	DWL
Centigrade	C	Down	DN
Center	CTR	Downspout	DS
Center line	CL or ₵	Drain	D or DR
Center matched	CM	Drawing	DWG
Center to center	OC	Drawn	DR
Centimeter, centimeters	cm	Dressed and matched	D&M
Ceramic	CER	Drinking fountain	DF
Cess pool	CP	Dryer	D
Chamfer	CHAM	Dry well	DW
Change	CHG	Duplicate	DUP
Channel	C or [(old designation)		
Check	CHK	Each	EA
Cinder Block	CIN BL	East	E
Circle	CIR	Edge grain	EG
Circuit	CKT	Elbow	ELL
Circuit breaker	CIR BKR	Electric	ELEC
Class	CL	Elevation	EL, ELEV
Cleanout	CO	Elevator	ELEV
Clear	CLR	Emergency	EMER
Closet	C or CL or CLO	Enclosure	ENCL
Coefficient	COEF	Engineer	ENGR
Cold water	CW	Entrance	ENT
Column	COL	Equipment	EQUIP
Combination	COMB.	Equivalent direct radiation	EDR
Common	COM	Estimate	EST
Company	CO	Excavate	EXC
Concrete	CONC	Extension	EXT
Concrete block	CONC B	Exterior	EXT
Concrete floor	CONC FL	Extra heavy	XH or XHVY

Fabricate	FAB	Information	INFO
Face to face	F to F	Inside diameter	ID
Family room	FAM R	Insulation	INSUL
Fahrenheit	F	Interior	INT
Feet	' or FT		
Feet board measure	FBM	Joint	JT
Feet per minute	FPM	Junior beam	M or JR (old designation)
Feet per second	FPS		
Figure	FIG.	Kalamein	KAL
Finish	FIN	Kelvin	K
Finish all over	FAO	Kilogram	kg
Finished floor	FIN FL	Kilowatt	KW
Fire brick	FBRK	Kitchen	K
Fire extinguisher	F EXT	Kitchen cabinet	KC
Fire hose	FH	Kitchen sink	KS
Fireproof	FP		
Fireproof self-closing	FPSC	Laboratory	LAB
Fitting	FTG	Ladder	LAD
Fixture	FIX.	Landing	LDG
Flange	FLG	Latitude	LAT
Flashing	FL	Laundry	LAU
Floor	FL	Laundry chute	LC
Floor drain	FD	Lavatory	LAV
Flooring	FLG	Leader	LDR
Fluorescent	FLUOR	Leader drain	LD
Foot	' or FT	Left	L
Footing	FTG	Left hand	LH
Foundation	FDN	Length	LGTH
Free-on-board	FOB	Level	LEV
Front	FR	Library	LIB
Fuel oil	FO	Light	LT
Full size	FS	Limestone	LS
Furnace	FURN	Linear feet	LIN FT
		Linen closet	L CL
Gallon, gallons	GAL	Lining	LNG
Galvanized	GALV	Linoleum	LINO
Galvanized iron	GI	Living room	LR
Gauge	GA	Long	LG
Glass	GL	Lumber	LBR
Glass block	GL BL		
Glue-laminated	GLUELAM	M shape steel beam	M or JR (old designation)
Government	GOVT	Machine	MACH
Grade	GR	Manufacture, manufacturer	MFR
Grating	GRTG	Manufactured	MFD
Gypsum	GYP	Manufacturing	MFG
		Mark	MK
		Masonry opening	MO
Hall	H	Material	MATL
Hardware	HDW	Maximum	MAX
Hardwood	HDWD	Mechanical	MECH
Head	HD	Medicine cabinet	MC
Heater	HTR	Medium	MED
Height	HT or HGT	Metal	MET
Hexagonal	HEX	Meter, meters	m
Hollow metal	HM	Millimeter, millimeters	mm
Horizon, horizontal	HOR or HORIZ	Minimum	MIN
Horsepower	H̶P̶ or HP	Miscellaneous	MISC
Hose bibb	HB	Model	MOD
Hot water	HW	Moderate weather (a common	
Hour	HR	brick grade)	MW
House	HSE	Molding	MLDG
Hundred	C	Mole	mol
I beam	S or I (old designation)	National	NATL
Inch, inches	'' or IN.	National Electrical Code	NEC

National Lumber Manufacturers Association	NLMA	Reinforce, reinforcing	REINF
		Reinforcing bar	REBAR
No weather (a common brick grade)	NW	Required	REQD
		Return	RET
Nominal	NOM	Revision	REV
North	N	Revolutions per minute	RPM
Not in contract	NIC	Right	R
Number	# or NO.	Right hand	RH
		Riser	R
Oak	O	Road	RD
Octagon	OCT	Roof	RF
Office	OFF	Roof drain	RD
On center	OC	Roofing	RFG
Opening	OPG	Room	RM
Opposite	OPP	Rough	RGH
Ornament	ORN	Round	Φ or RD
Ounce, ounces	OZ		
Outside diameter	OD	S shape steel beam	S or I (old designation)
Over head	OVHD	Schedule	SCH
		Screw	SCR
Page	P	Second, seconds	s
Painted	PTD	Section	SECT
Pair	PR	Self-closing	SC
Panel	PNL	Service	SERV
Paragraph	PAR	Severe weather (a common brick grade)	SW
Parallel	‖ or PAR		
Partition	PTN	Sewer	SEW.
Passage	PASS.	Sheathing	SHTHG
Pedestal	PED	Shower	SH
Penny (nail)	d	Siding	SDG
Per	/	Sill cock	SC
Percent	%	Sink	S or SK
Perforate	PERF	Slop sink	SS
Perpendicular	⊥ or PERP	Socket	SOC
Pi (ratio of circumference to diameter of circle)	π	Soil pipe	SP
		South	S
Piece	PC	Specifications	SPEC
Plaster	PLAS	Square	□ or SQ
Plate	℞ or PL	Square foot, square feet	SQ FT
Plate glass	PL GL	Stairs	ST
Platform	PLAT	Standard	STD
Plumbing	PLMB	Standpipe	ST P
Point	PT	Station	STA
Polish	POL	Station point	SP
Position	POS	Steel	STL
Pound, pounds	LB or #	Stirrup	STIR.
Pounds per square inch	PSI	Stock	STK
Poured concrete	P/C	Street	ST
Prefabricated	PREFAB	Structural	STR
Property	PROP.	Structural clay research	SCR
Push button	PB	Substitute	SUB
		Supersede	SUPSD
Quantity	QTY	Supplement	SUPP
Quart, quarts	QT	Supply	SUP
		Surface	SUR
Radiator	RAD	Surface 1 side	S1S
Radiator enclosure	RAD ENCL	Surface 2 sides	S2S
Radius	RA	Surface 4 sides	S4S
Random length and width	RL&W	Surface all sides	S4S
Range	R	Surface 1 edge	S1E
Receptacle	RECP	Surface 2 edges	S2E
Rectangle	RECT	Surface 1 side 1 edge	S1S1E
Redwood	RDWD	Surfaced and matched	S&M
Reference	REF	Suspended ceiling	SUSP CLG
Refrigerator	REF	Switch	S or SW
Register	REG		

Symbol	SYM	Volume	VOL
System	SYS		
		W shape steel beam	W, WF or WF (old designations)
Tar and gravel	T&G	Wall cabinet	W CAB
Technical	TECH	Wall vent	WV
Tee	T	Water	W
Telephone	TEL	Water closet	WC
Television	TV	Waterproof	WP or WP
Temperature	TEMP	Watt, watts	W
Terra cotta	TC	Weatherproof	WP or WP
Thermostat	THERMO	Weight	WT
Thick, thickness	T or THK	Weep hole	WH
Thousand	M	West	W
Thousand board feet	MBM	White Pine	WP
Thread	THD	Wide flange	W, WF or WF (old designations)
Tongue and groove	T&G		
Tread	TR	Width	WTH
Typical	TYP	Window	WDW
		Wire glass	W GL
Ultimate	ULT	With	W/
Unfinished	UNFIN	Without	W/O
U.S.A. Standards		Wood	WD
Institute	USASI	Wrought iron	WI
U.S. standard gauge	USG		
Vanishing point	V	Yard, yards	YD
Vent or ventilator	V	Year	YR
Ventilate, ventilation	VENT.	Yellow Pine	YP
Vertical	VERT		
Vestibule	VEST.		
Volt, volts	V	Zinc	Z or ZN

appendix f architectural spelling

These words are commonly used in architectural drafting and are often misspelled. Anyone seriously interested in drafting should know the proper spelling of the words of his trade.

Acoustical
Acre
Aisle (*isle* is an island)
Alcove
Aluminum
Appliance
Asbestos
Asphalt

Barbecue
Bathroom (one word)
Batten
Batter board (two words)
Bedroom (one word)
Bevel, beveled
Bracing
Brickwork
Bridging
Built-up roof

Cabinet
Canopy, canopies
Cant strip
Cantilever
Carport (one word)
Casement
Caulk, caulking
Center (*centre* is British spelling)
Centimeter (*centimetre* is British spelling)

Channel
Chromium
Cleanout door
Clerestory
Colonnade
Coping
Cornice
Corridor
Corrugated
Creosote
Cupola

Dampproof (one word)
Dining room (two words)
Dishwasher (one word)
Disposal unit
Double hung
Dovetail
Downspout
Downstairs (one word)
Draft, drafting, draftsman (*draught* is obsolete)
Dry wall (two words)

Eave (*eve* is evening)
Enclose, enclosure (*inclose* is used by land surveyors)

Fascia, facia
Fiberboard
Fiber glass (*Fiberglas* is trade name)
Fieldstone (one word)
Fire brick (two words)
Fireplace (one word)

Flagstone (one word)
Flue (*flu* is a disease)
Fluorescent
Formica
Freezer
Furring

Gable
Galvanized
Game room (two words)
Grill (a grid for broiling)
Grille or grill (a grating for protection)
Gypsum

Handrail (one word)
Hangar (for airplanes)
Hanger (for hanging)
Horizontal

Jalousie (*jealousy* is resentment)

Kiln

Lanai (a Hawaiian porch)
Lath (*lathe* is a machine tool)
Lavatory (a sink; *laboratory* for experiments)
Level, leveled, leveling
Linoleum
Lintel
Living room (two words)
Loggia (a roofed, open porch)
Louver (*Louvre* is an art museum in Paris)

Mantel (*mantle* is a cloak)
Masonry
Meter (*metre* is British spelling)
Millimeter (*millimetre* is British spelling)
Miter, mitered
Molding or moulding
Mortar
Mortgage
Movable
Mullion

Muntin

Nosing

Ordinance (*ordnance* are artillery)
Oriel (*oriole* is a bird)

Paneled, paneling
Parallel
Perpendicular
Playroom (one word)
Projector

Rabbet (*rabbit* is an animal)
Receptacle
Remove, removable

Sheathing
Sheetrock (one word)
Siding
Solder (*soldier* is a military man)
Stile (of a door)
story, storey
Style (of architecture)
Subfloor (one word)

Template
Terrazzo

Upstairs (one word)

Veneer
Vertical
Vinyl

Wainscot, wainscoting
Wallboard (one word)
Waterproof (one word)
Weatherstripping
Weep hole (two words)
Woodwork (one word)
Wrought iron (means "worked iron")

Zinc

appendix g   glossary of architectural terms

Aggregate: Material such as broken stone, gravel, cinders or slag used as one of the constituents of concrete, the other constituents being sand, cement, and water.

Alcove: A recessed space connected with or at the side of a larger room.

Anchor: A metal piece used to attach building members to masonry.

Anchor bolt: A threaded rod used to fasten the sill plate to the foundation.

Angle iron: A metal bar, L-shaped in section.

Apron: The finish board immediately below a window sill.

Arcade: A series of arches supported by a row of columns.

Arch: A curved structure which carries the weight over an opening.

Architect: A person who plans buildings and oversees their construction.

Architectural terra cotta: Terra cotta building blocks having a ceramic finish.

Areaway: A subsurface enclosure to admit light and air to a basement.

Asbestos: An incombustible material used in fireproofing.

Asbestos cement board: Sheet material of compressed asbestos fiber and portland cement.

Ashlar masonry: Masonry composed of squared units laid with horizontal bed joints.

Asphalt: An insoluble material used in waterproofing.

Backfill: Earth replaced around a foundation.

Balcony: A platform projecting from the wall of a building, above the ground.

Balloon frame: A type of building frame in which the studs extend from sill to eaves without interruption.

Balusters: The small, vertical members of a railing between the bottom and top rail.

Banister: A hand rail.

Baseboard: The finishing board covering a wall where it meets the floor.

Basement: The lowest story of a building, partially or entirely below ground.

Batten: A strip of board for use in fastening other boards together.

Batter: Sloping a masonry or concrete wall.

Batter board: A horizontal board nailed to posts and used to lay out the excavation and foundation.

Bay: Any division or compartment of an arcade, roof, building, space between floor joists, or other area.

Beam: A horizontal structural member that carries a load.

Bearing partition: A partition supporting any vertical load other than its own weight.

Bearing plate: A support member used to distribute weight over a larger area.

Bench mark: A reference point used by surveyors to establish lines and grades.

Bent: A rigid, transverse framework.

Bevel weld: A butt weld with one mitered member.

Bibb: A threaded faucet.

Blocking: Small wood framing members.

Bluestone: A hard, blue sandstone.

Board foot: The amount of wood contained in a piece of rough green lumber 1″ thick by 12″ wide by 1′ long.

Bond: Mortar bond between mortar and masonry units; structural bond between wythes; pattern bond for decorative effect.

Bond beam: A reinforced concrete beam used to strengthen masonry walls.

Book match: A veneer pattern of alternate sheets turned over as are the leaves of a book.

Box beam: A hollow, built-up structural unit.

Brick veneer: A brick facing laid in front of frame construction.

Bridging: Cross-bracing between floor joists to add stiffness to the floors.

Brownstone: A brown sandstone.

Btu: A unit used to measure heat (British Thermal Unit).

Building board (also Wall board): Boards made from repulped paper, shredded wood, or similar material.

Building line: An imaginary line on a plot beyond which the building may not extend.

Building paper: A heavy, waterproof paper used over sheathing and subfloors to prevent passage of air and water.

Built-up beam: A beam constructed of smaller members fastened together with the grains parallel.

Build-up roof: A roofing composed of several layers of felt and asphalt, pitch, or coal tar.

Butt: (See door butt.)

Butt weld: A weld of members butting against each other.

Canopy: A sheltering roof.

Cant strip: A form of triangular molding.

Cantilever: A beam or girder fixed at one extremity and free at the other. To "cantilever" is to employ the principle of the lever to carry a load.

Carbon steel: A basic structural steel containing carbon and manganese as main alloys.

Carport: A garage not fully enclosed.

Casement: A window whose frame is hinged at the side.

Casing: The framing around a door or window.

Catch basin: An underground structure for surface drainage in which sediment may settle.

Catenary: The shape of a chain hanging freely between two supports.

Caulking: A waterproof material used to seal cracks.

Cavity wall: A masonry wall having an airspace of about 2″.

Cement: A masonry material purchased in the form of a highly pulverized powder usually medium gray in color. The approximate proportions for portland cement are as follows:

Lime (CaO)	60–67%
Silica (SiO$_2$)	20–25%
Iron Oxide and Alumina	7–12%

Centering: Form work for poured concrete floor and roof slabs; temporary form work for the support of masonry arches or lintels during construction.

Center to center: Measurement from the center of one member to the center of another (noted oc).

Ceramic veneer: Architectural terra cotta having large face dimensions and thin sections.

Channel: A standard form of structural rolled steel, consisting of three sides at right angles in channel form.

Check: A lumber defect caused by radial separation during seasoning. Also see door check.

Circuit: The path for an electric current.

Clapboard: A narrow board, thicker at one edge, for weather-boarding frame buildings; siding.

Clerestory: A window between roof planes.

Client: A person who employs an architect.

Collar beam: A horizontal member tying two opposite rafters together at more or less a center point on the rafters.

Column: A vertical supporting member.

Common brick: $3\frac{3}{4}″ \times 2\frac{1}{2}″ \times 8″$ brick used for general construction.

Composite wall: A masonry wall of at least two adjacent wythes of different materials.

Concrete: A masonry mixture of portland cement, sand and aggregate, and water in proper proportions.

Condensation: Water formed by warm, moist air contacting a cold surface.

Conductor: A vertical drain pipe or material permitting passage of electric current.

Conduit: A pipe or trough that carries water, electrical wiring, cables, and so forth.

Conifer: see softwood.

Contractor: A builder.

Control joint: An expansion joint in a masonry wall formed by raking mortar from a continuous vertical joint.

Convector: A heat transfer surface which uses convection currents to transmit heat.

Coping: A masonry cap on top of a wall to protect it from water penetration.

Corbel: A bracket formed in a wall by building out successive courses of masonry.

Corner bead: A metal molding, built into the plaster corners to prevent the accidental breaking off of the plaster.

Cornice: That part of a roof which extends or projects beyond the wall; the architectural treatment thereof, as a "box cornice."

Counterflashing: A flashing used under the regular flashing.

Course: A horizontal row of bricks, tile, stone, building blocks, or similar material.

Court: An open space surrounded partly or entirely by a building.

Crawl space: The space between the floor joists and the surface below when there is no basement. This is used in making repairs on plumbing and other utilities.

Cricket: A roof device used at intersections to divert water.

Cupola: A small structure built on top of a roof.

Curtain wall: An exterior wall which provides no structural support.

Cut stone: Stone cut to given sizes or shapes.

Damper: A movable plate to regulate the draft in a chimney.

Dap: A circular groove (used for split rings and shear plates).

Decay: Disintegration of wood through the action of fungi.

Decibel: A unit of measuring the relative loudness of sound.

Deciduous: (See hardwood.)

Door buck: A door frame (usually metal).

Door butt: A hinge.

Door check: A device to slow a door when closing.

Door stop: A device to prevent a door from hitting the wall when opening.

Dormer: A structure projecting from, or cut into, a sloping roof, usually to accommodate a window or windows.

Double hung: Term used for a window having top and bottom sashes each capable of movement up and down in its own grooves.

Downspout: A vertical drain pipe for carrying rain water from the gutters.

Drain: A pipe for carrying waste water.

Dressed size: The dimensions of lumber after planing; usually

$\frac{1}{2}''$ less than nominal (rough) size. For example: a 2" × 4" stud actually measures $1\frac{1}{2}'' \times 3\frac{1}{2}''$.

Drip: A molding designed to prevent rain water from running down the face of a wall, or to protect the bottom of a door or window from leakage.

Dry rot: A dry, crumbly wood rot.

Dry wall: A wall finished with wallboard in place of plaster; stone wall built without mortar.

Dry well: A shallow well used for the disposal of rain water.

Ducts: Sheet metal conductors for air distribution.

Eave: The lower portion of a roof which extends beyond the wall.

Efflorescence: An undesirable white crystallization which may form on masonry walls.

Elbow: An L-shaped pipe fitting.

Electric arc process: A welding process which uses an electric arc to fuse both members.

Elevation: An orthographic projection of the vertical side of a building.

Escalator: A moving stairway.

Excavation: A hole formed by removing earth.

Expansion joint: A separation in a masonry or concrete wall to permit wall expansion due to temperature and moisture changes.

Facade: The front or face of a building.

Face brick: A special brick used for facing a wall. Face bricks are more uniform in size than common bricks and are made in a variety of colors and textures.

Faced wall: (See composite wall.)

Facing: Any material, forming a part of a wall, used as a finished surface.

Fascia (Facia, Fascia board): A flat banded projection on the face of the cornice; the flat vertical member of the cornice; the flat surface running above a shop window on which the name of the shop may be displayed.

Fenestration: The arrangement of windows in a wall.

Fiberboard: Sheet material of refined wood fibers.

Fieldstone: Building stone found loose on the ground (field) regardless of its exact variety. Don't confuse with *flag-stone*.

Filigree: Fine, decorative openwork.

Fillet weld: A butt weld with the weld metal filling an inside corner.

Finish lumber: Dressed wood used for building trim.

Finished size: The *nominal size* is the size of rough lumber. After planing, the actual *finished size* is about $\frac{1}{2}''$ smaller than nominal. The difference between nominal and finished size will vary depending upon the size of the lumber, ranging from $\frac{3}{4}''$ for lumber over 6" to only $\frac{1}{4}''$ for 1" lumber. The variations between nominal and finished size of American Standard Lumber are:

Nominal Size	Finished Size
1"	$\frac{3}{4}''$
2"	$1\frac{1}{2}''$
4"	$3\frac{1}{2}''$
6"	$5\frac{1}{2}''$
8"	$7\frac{1}{4}''$
10"	$9\frac{1}{4}''$
12"	$11\frac{1}{4}''$

Fire brick: A brick made of a refractory material (fire clay) that withstands great heat; used to line furnaces, fireplaces, and so on.

Fire cut: An angular cut at the end of a joist framing into a masonry wall.

Fireproofing: Any material protecting structural members to increase their fire resistance.

Fire stopping: Obstructions across air passages in buildings to prevent the spread of hot gases and flames; horizontal blocking between wall studs.

Fire wall: A wall extending from foundation through the roof to subdivide a building in order to restrict the spread of fire.

Fixture: A piece of electric or plumbing equipment.

Flagstone: Flat stone used for floors, steps, and walks.

Flashing: The sheet metal work used to prevent leakage over windows and doors, around chimneys, and at the intersections of different wall surfaces and roof planes.

Floor plan: An orthographic projection of the floor of a building.

Flue: A passage in the chimney to convey smoke to the outer air.

Flue lining: Terra cotta pipe used for the inner lining of chimneys.

Footing: The bases upon which the foundation and posts rest.

Formica: A plastic veneer trade name.

Foundation: The supporting wall of a building below the first-floor level.

Framing: Lumber used for the structural framing of a building.

Frost line: The depth of frost penetration in soil.

Furring: Wood strips fastened to a wall or ceiling for the purpose of attaching wallboards or ceiling tile.

Gable: The triangular portion of an end wall formed by a sloping roof.

Gambrel: A gable roof, each slope of which is broken into two planes.

Geodesic dome: A double faced dome formed of members of nearly equal length.

Girder: A large horizontal structural member, usually heavier than a beam, used to support the ends of joists and beams or to carry walls over openings.

Glazed brick: Brick finished with ceramic, clay-coated, or salt glaze.

Grade or grade line: The level of the ground around a building.

Granite: A durable and hard igneous rock.

Green efflorescence: An undesirable green stain which may form on masonry walls.

Ground cover: Usually roll roofing laid on the ground in crawl spaces to reduce moisture.

Grounds: Wood strips attached to the walls before plastering, serving as a plaster stop and nailing base for trim.

Grout: Mortar of pouring consistency.

Gutter: A trough or depression for carrying off water.

Gypsum board: Board made of plaster with a covering of paper. Also Plaster board.

Half timbering: A frame construction in which the spaces are filled in with masonry.

Hanger: An iron strap used to support a joist or beam.

Hardboard: Sheet material of compressed wood fibers.

Hardwood: Wood from trees having broad leaves in contrast to needles. The term does not necessarily refer to the hardness of the wood.

Header: A beam perpendicular to joists, into which they are framed; a masonry unit laid horizontally with the end exposed.

Head room: The vertical clearance in a room or on a stairway.

Hearth: The masonry portion of a floor in front of a fireplace.

Heartwood: The dead, inner layer of a tree formed from former sapwood.

Heat-treated steel: A high-strength steel which has been quenched and tempered.

High-strength bolt: A medium-carbon or heat-treated alloy steel bolt.

High-strength steel: A high-strength, low-alloy steel.

Hip roof: A roof with four sloping sides.

House drain: Horizontal sewer piping within a building which receives waste from the soil stacks.

House sewer: Horizontal sewer piping 5' outside the foundation wall to the public sewer.

Humidifier: A device to increase relative humidity in a building.

I-beam: A steel beam with an I-shaped cross section.

Insulation: Material for obstructing the passage of sound, heat, or cold from one surface to another.

Interference-body bolt: A high-strength bolt with raised ribs on the shank.

Jack rafter: A short rafter placed between the ridge and the hip rafter or valley rafter.

Jalousie: A type of window consisting of a number of long, thin, hinged panels.

Jamb: The inside vertical face of a door or window frame.

J-groove weld: A butt weld with one gouged member.

Joist: A member directly supporting floor and ceiling loads and in turn supported by bearing walls, beams, or girders.

Kalamein door: A fireproofed door covered with metal.

Keystone: The last wedge-shaped stone placed in the crown of an arch.

Kiln: A heating chamber for drying lumber (pronounced "kill").

Kip: 1000 pounds.

Knot: A lumber defect caused by an embedded limb.

Kraft paper: A strong, brown paper made from sulphate pulp.

Laitance: An undesirable watery layer found in the upper surface of curing concrete.

Lally column: A steel column.

Lamella roof: A roof formed of short members assembled in diamond-shaped patterns.

Laminate: To bond together several layers of material.

Landing: A stair platform.

Lath (metal): Sheet metal screening used as a base for plastering.

Lath (wood): Thin wood used to level a surface in prepara-

tion for plastering or composition tiles. Also called Furring.

Lattice: Openwork made by crossed or interlaced strips of material.

Lavatory: A wash basin or room equipped with a wash basin.

Ledger: A wood strip nailed to the lower side of a girder to provide a bearing surface for joists.

Lift-slab: A precast concrete construction method of casting all slabs on the ground and lifting them into final position.

Limestone: A sedimentary rock of calcium carbonate.

Lintel: The horizontal member supporting the wall over an opening.

Lobby: An entrance hall or reception room; vestibule.

Lookout: A short timber for supporting a projecting cornice.

Lot line: The limit of a lot.

Louver: A ventilating window covered by sloping slats to exclude rain.

Lumber: Wood which has been sawed, resawed, planed, crosscut, or matched.

Boards: Lumber less than 2" thick and more than 1" wide.

Dimension: Lumber from 2" to 5" thick and more than 2" wide.

Dressed size: See Finished size.

Finished size: The size of lumber after shrinking and planing; about $\frac{1}{2}$" less than the nominal or rough size.

Nominal size: The "name" size by which lumber is identified and sold.

Rough lumber: Lumber which has been sawed but not planed.

Structural lumber: Lumber over 2" thick and 4" wide, used for structural support.

Timber: Lumber over 5" in least dimension.

Yard lumber: Lumber of all sizes intended for general building purposes.

M shape: A lightweight structural steel I-beam.

Manhole: A sewer opening to allow access for a man.

Mansard: A hip roof, each slope of which is broken into two planes.

Mantel: The shelf over a fireplace.

Marble: A metamorphic rock used for building.

Masonite: A hardboard trade name.

Masonry: Material such as stone, brick, and block used by a mason.

Mastic: A waterproof material used to seal cracks.

Meeting rail: The horizontal rails of double hung sash that fit together when the window is closed.

Member: A part of a building unit.

Millwork: Woodwork which has been finished ("milled") in a milling plant.

Miter: A beveled cut.

Modular brick: 4" × $2\frac{2}{3}$" × 8" brick.

Module: A standardized unit of measurement.

Molding: Strips used for ornamentation.

Mortar: A mixture of cement, sand, and water used as a bonding agent by the mason.

Motif: The basic idea or theme of a design.

Mullion: The large vertical or horizontal division of a window opening.

Muntin: The small members that divide the glass in a window frame.

Newel or newel post: The post where the handrail of a stair starts or changes direction.

Niche: A small recess in a wall.

Nominal size: (See Lumber.)

Norman brick: 4″ × 2⅔″ × 12″ brick.

Nosing: The rounded edge of a stair tread.

On center: Measurement from the center of one member to the center of another (noted oc).

Outlet: An electric socket.

Overhang: The horizontal distance that a roof projects beyond a wall.

Panel: A flat surface framed by thicker material.

Panelboard: The center for controlling electrical circuits.

Parapet: The portion of a wall extended above the roof.

Parging (pargeting): Cement mortar applied to a masonry wall.

Parquetry: An inlaid floor in a geometrical pattern.

Particle board: Wood fiberboard.

Partition: An interior wall. (Wall: An exterior wall.)

Penny: A term for the length of a nail, abbreviated ''d.'' Originally, it meant the price per hundred nails (i.e., 8 penny = 8¢ per hundred nails).

Penthouse: A housing above the roof for elevator machinery.

Pier: A rectangular masonry support either freestanding or built into a wall.

Pilaster: Specifically, an attached pier used to strengthen a wall.

Pitch: A term applied to the amount of roof slope. It is found by dividing the height by the span. Also a liquid material used in roofing. Also the center-to-center distance between bolts.

Plank: Lumber 2″ and over in thickness.

Plate: A horizontal member in a wall framework which rafters, joists, studs, and so forth, rest on or are secured to, as in ''sole plate,'' ''sill plate,'' ''top plate.''

Plumb: Vertical.

Ply: The number of layers of roofing felt, plywood veneer, or other materials.

Plywood: Wood made up of three or more layers of veneer bonded with glue.

Poché: To darken in a wall section with freehand shading.

Pointing: Filling of joints in a masonry wall.

Post and beam: A type of building frame in which cross beams rest directly upon vertical posts.

Precasting: A casting in a mold which is not located at its final position in the structure.

Prestressing: A method of compressing concrete members so that they will not deflect when in position.

Priming: The first coat of paint, mixed and applied so as to fill the pores of the surface preparatory to receiving the subsequent coats.

Purlin: A horizontal roof framing member, laid perpendicular to main trusses and supporting the roof.

Radiant heating: Heating by radiating rays without air movement.

Rafter: A member in a roof framework running from the eave to the ridge. There are hip rafters, jack rafters, and valley rafters.

Random match: A veneer pattern of sheets randomly placed.

Rebar: Reinforcing bar.

Reflective insulation: Sheet material with a surface of low heat emissivity used to reduce heat loss.

Reinforced concrete: Concrete containing more than 0.2 percent of reinforcing steel.

Relative humidity: Ratio of the amount of water vapor in air to the maximum possible amount at the same temperature.

Retaining wall: A wall designed to resist lateral pressure of earth.

Retemper: To replace water evaporated from wet mortar.

Return: A molding turned back to the wall on which it is located.

Reveal: The depth of masonry between its outer face and a window or door set in an opening.

Ribbon: A wood strip let into the studding to provide a bearing surface for joists.

Ridge: The top edge of the roof where two slopes meet.

Ridge cap: A wood or metal cap used over roofing at the ridge.

Ridgepole: The highest horizontal member in a roof. It supports the heads of the jack rafters.

Riprap: Stone placed on a slope to prevent erosion.

Riser: The verical board of a step. It forms the front of the stair step.

Rocklath: A flat sheet of gypsum used as a plaster base.

Roll roofing: Roofing material of fiber and asphalt.

Roman brick: 4″ × 2″ × 12″ brick.

Roof boards (roofers): The rough boarding over the roof framework on which is laid the roof covering.

Rubble: Irregularly shaped building stone, partly trimmed.

S shape: A structural steel I-beam.

Saddle: A small, double sloping roof to carry the water away from the back of chimneys. Sometimes called *cricket*.

Salvaged brick: Used brick.

Sandstone: A sedimentary rock of cemented quartz.

Sandwich wall: A wall of at least two adjacent and connected panels, usually reinforced concrete panels protecting an insulating panel.

Sapwood: The living layer of a tree surrounding the heartwood.

Sash: A framing for window panes. A sash window is generally understood to be a double hung, vertically sliding window.

Scab: A small member used to join other members, fastened on the outside face.

Scarf joint: A joint made by tapering the ends of each piece.

Schedule: A list of parts (as a window schedule).

SCR brick: a 6″ × 2½″ × 12″ brick developed by Structural Steel Products Research for use in 6″ solid, load-bearing walls.

Scratch coat: The first coat of plaster. It is scratched to provide a good bond for the next coat.

Seasoning: Removing moisture from green wood.

Section: An orthographic projection which has been cut apart to show interior features.

Septic tank: A sewage-settling tank.

Shake: A hand-split shingle; a lumber defect caused by a natural separation of the annual rings.

Shear plate: A metal connector for timber-to-timber and timber-to-steel construction which distributes the load over a greater area.

Sheathing: The rough boarding on the outside of a wall or roof over which is laid the finished siding or the shingles.

Shim: A piece of material used to true up or fill in the space between two surfaces.

Shingles: Roof covering made of wood cut to stock lengths and thicknesses and to random widths. Also tile shingles, slate shingles, asbestos-cement shingles, asphalt shingles.

Siding: The outside layer of boards on a frame wall.

Sill: The stone or wood member across the bottom of a door or window opening. Also the bottom member on which a building frame rests (sill plate).

Slate: A metamorphic rock used for roofing and flagstone.

Sleeper: A wood member placed over a concrete slab to provide a nailing base for a wood floor.

Slip match: A veneer pattern of sheets joined side-by-side.

Slump block: A concrete block resembling stone.

Smoke chamber: The portion of a chimney flue located directly over the fireplace.

Snap header: A half brick header.

Soffit: The undersurface of a cornice, molding, or beam.

Softwood: Wood from trees having needles rather than broad leaves. The term does not necessarily refer to the softness of the wood.

Soil stack: A vertical pipe in a plumbing system which carries the discharge from a toilet.

Soldier: A masonry unit laid vertically with the narrow side exposed.

Sole: The horizontal framing member directly under the studs.

Sovent: A single-stack, self-venting sewage disposal system.

Space frame: A three-dimensional truss system.

Spackle: To cover wallboard joints with plaster.

Span: The distance between structural supports (i.e., the length of a joist, rafter, or other member).

Spandrel: The area between the top of a window and sill of the above window.

Spandrel wall: An exterior wall which provides no structural support.

Specifications: The written description accompanying the working drawings.

Split block: A fractured solid concrete block laid with the split face exposed.

Split lintels: Two lintels placed side by side in a wall.

Square: 100 sq. ft. of roofing.

Stack: A vertical pipe.

Stile: A vertical member of a door, window, or panel.

Stirrup: A metal U-shaped strap used to support framing members.

Stool: The wood shelf across the bottom and inside of a window. Also a watercloset.

Stop: (See door stop.)

Story (storey): The space between two floors, or between a floor and the ceiling above.

Stressed-skin panel: A hollow, built-up panel used for floors, roofs, and walls.

Stretcher: A masonry unit laid horizontally with the long face exposed.

Stringer: The sides of a flight of stairs; the supporting member cut to receive the treads and risers.

Stucco: A face plaster or cement applied to walls or partitions.

Studs: Vertical members which form the framework of a partition or wall.

Stud welding: An electric arc welding process used to weld threaded studs to structural steel.

Subfloor: The rough flooring under the finish floor.

Tail beam: Framing members supported by headers or trimmers.

Tee: A structural steel member in a shape of a T.

Tempered hardboard: Water-resistant hardboard.

Tensile bond strength: Ability of mortar to adhere to masonry unit.

Termite shield: Sheet metal used to block the passage of termites.

Terra cotta: Hard-baked clay and sand often used for chimney flues.

Terrace: A raised flat space.

Terrazzo: Floor covering of marble chips and cement ground to a smooth finish. Metal strips are used to separate different colors and create designs.

Thermostat: An instrument automatically controlling the heating plant.

Threshold: The stone, wood, or metal piece directly under a door.

Tie beam: A framing member between rafters.

Tilt-up construction: A method of precasting members horizontally on the site and lifting into their final vertical position.

Toe nail: To drive nails at an angle.

Tongue: A projection on the edge of a board that fits into a groove on an adjacent board.

Translucent: Having the ability to transmit light without a clear image.

Transom: A small window over a door.

Transparent: Having the ability to clearly transmit images.

Trap: A device providing a liquid seal to prevent passage of air and odor.

Tread: The horizontal part of a step.

Treillage: An ornamental screen.

Trim: The finish frame around an opening.

Trimmer: A joist or rafter around an opening in a floor or roof.

Truss: A braced framework capable of spanning greater distances than the individual components.

Trussed rafter: A truss spaced close enough to adjacent trusses that purlins are unnecessary.

U-groove weld: A weld with one gouged member.

Unfinished bolt: A low-carbon steel bolt.

Valley: The trough formed by the intersection of two roof slopes.

Valve: A device which regulates the flow in a pipe.

Vapor barrier: A thin sheet used to prevent the passage of water vapor.

Vault: A curved surface supporting a roof.

Vee weld: A butt weld with both members mitered.

Veneer: A facing material not load-bearing.

Vent pipes: Small ventilating pipes extending from each fixture of a plumbing system to the vent stack.

Vent stack: A vertical pipe in a plumbing system for ventilation and pressure relief.

Vestibule: A small lobby or entrance room.

W shape: A structural steel wide flanged beam.

Wainscott: An ornamental covering of walls often consisting of wood panels, usually running only part way up the wall.

Wall: An exterior wall (Partition: An interior wall.).

Wallboard: A large, flat sheet of gypsum or wood pulp used for interior walls.

Wall tie: A metal piece connecting wythes of masonry to each other or to other materials.

Warp: A lumber defect of a twist.

Waste stack: A vertical pipe in a plumbing system which carries the discharge from any fixture.

Waterproof: Material or construction which prevents the passage of water.

Weathering steel: A high-strength steel which is protected from further corrosion by its own corrosion.

Weatherstrip: A strip of metal or fabric fastened along the edges of windows and doors to reduce drafts and heat loss.

Weep hole: An opening at the bottom of a wall to allow the drainage of moisture.

Well opening: A floor opening for a stairway.

Wind bracing: Bracing designed to resist horizontal and inclined forces.

Winder: A tapering step in a stairway.

Working drawing: A drawing containing information for the workmen.

Wythe (withe): A masonry partition, such as separating flues.

index